D1569724

OF POWER AND RIGHT

Of Power and Right

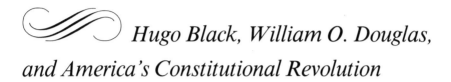 *Hugo Black, William O. Douglas, and America's Constitutional Revolution*

HOWARD BALL

PHILLIP J. COOPER

New York   Oxford

OXFORD UNIVERSITY PRESS

1992

Oxford University Press

Oxford   New York   Toronto
Delhi   Bombay   Calcutta   Madras   Karachi
Petaling Jaya   Singapore   Hong Kong   Tokyo
Nairobi   Dar es Salaam   Cape Town
Melbourne   Auckland

and associated companies in
Berlin   Ibadan

Library of Congress Cataloging-in-Publication Data
Ball, Howard, 1937–
Of power and right : Hugo Black, William O. Douglas, and America's
constitutional revolution / Howard Ball, Phillip J. Cooper.
p. cm.
Includes bibliographical references and index.
ISBN 0-19-504612-9
1. Black, Hugo LaFayette, 1886–1971.   2. Douglas, William O.
(William Orville), 1898–   .   3. Judges—United States—Biography.
4. United States—Constitutional history.   5. Political questions
and judicial power—United States—History.   I. Cooper, Phillip J.
II. Title.
KF8744.B275   1991
347.73'2634—dc20   [B]
[347.3073534]   [B]   91-4147   CIP

Photographs reprinted with permission of the collection
of the Supreme Court of the United States.

9 8 7 6 5 4 3 2 1

Printed in the United States of America
on acid-free paper

To Professor Paula Eldot.
At least once in a scholar's life, there must have been
one teacher like you who opened the door.

and
To Carol, Sue, Sheryl, and Melissa.

Preface

I<small>T WAS IN</small> many ways the most unlikely pair anyone could imagine. William O. Douglas and Hugo L. Black were enigmatic as individuals and absolutely strange as a pair. Douglas considered himself a man of the people, unaffected by social expectations and the drive for political power, which was so important to those around him. But this Ivy League–trained, Wall Street–hardened lawyer was anything but common, and he very much enjoyed running in Washington's inner circles. Hugo Black, a puritan moralist, was a tough Alabama politician who came to the bench with a puzzling background. A harsh inquisitor during his years in the Senate, Black had been simultaneously a vigorous defender of blacks in the courtroom and a member of the Ku Klux Klan.

These seeming contradictions notwithstanding, each of these men carved out a long career on the Supreme Court during some of the nation's most turbulent years. Each has been alternately celebrated and condemned. There are few neutral commentators on Justices Black and Douglas. Beyond their individual careers, however, the two shared both a partnership and a contest. They stood together in defense of freedom during some of our meanest political years and were vilified for their pains. Yet they were profoundly different men: one adamant in his resistance to judicial demands for influence and insistent on the written Constitution as well as the representative democracy it created, and the other passionately committed to liberty and suspicious of "the establishment" whether that establishment was the majority of Americans who expressed their demands for orthodoxy at the ballot box or those who claimed a right to leadership by virtue of economic privilege. This book is the story of these two men, their relationship, and their important differences. Their struggle with democratic power and individual right not only teaches us about a fundamental tension in American political life, but also tells us a great deal about the United States Supreme Court as an institution and as a force in our lives.

Like any project of this complexity, we have incurred many debts. We are particularly grateful to members of the Court and Court family who have helped us. They include Justices William J. Brennan, Jr., Louis F. Powell, Warren E. Burger, and Harry A. Blackmun; Cathleen Douglas-Stone; and the late Elizabeth Black. We could never have completed this volume without the assistance of the staff of the manuscript division of the Library of Congress, and particularly the generous assistance of David Wigdor.

Many of our colleagues provided assistance in a host of ways, from reactions to draft chapters to simple conversations about emerging themes. We particularly wish to acknowledge William Richardson, Stephen Wasby, Christopher McMahon, and Thomas Church. As always, a project such as this affects and is affected by the authors' families. We happily acknowledge their encouragement.

Naturally, none of those to whom we owe debts of gratitude are responsible for errors of omission or commission. Indeed, they tried to save us from both.

Burlington, Vt.   H. B.
Albany, N.Y.   P. J. C.
January 1991

Contents

1. Justices Black and Douglas on the Supreme Court   3

2. Hugo L. Black: From Alabama's Backwoods to Washington's Marble Temple   12

3. William O. Douglas: From Walla Walla to Washington, D.C.   33

4. Black and Douglas as "New Dealers"   54

5. The Brethren   76

6. The War Years   107

7. Red Scare in America   136

8. The Struggle for Racial Justice   158

9. Due Process: In Search of Fundamental Fairness   193

10. Maintaining Religious Freedom   229

11. Between State and Nation: Emergent Issues of Federalism   255

12. The Demand for New Constitutional Rights   277

13. Douglas Without Black   297

14. Standing the Test of Time: The Enduring Legacy of Justices Hugo L. Black and William O. Douglas   318

   Notes   323

   Bibliography   369

   Index of Cases   377

   Index   383

   Illustrations follow page 106

OF POWER AND RIGHT

 # 1

Justices Black and Douglas
on the Supreme Court

THE CORNER OF First and A streets in Washington, D.C., has been the site of a host of interesting and unusual events since the nation's capital was established in 1791. It was the location of the temporary Capitol after the British destroyed the permanent structure during the War of 1812, home for the Circuit Court for the District of Columbia, a boarding house that was once home to John C. Calhoun, a jail, a set of town houses (one of which was occupied by Justice Stephen J. Field), and the headquarters of the National Woman's party. But few events that took place at that particular spot on Capitol Hill were as significant as the day in 1937 when the first justice moved his chambers into what is now the home of the United States Supreme Court.[1]

That first judicial resident of what many have come to call the Marble Temple was Hugo Lafayette Black, the third Alabama native to serve on the High Court.[2] The first appointee sent by Franklin D. Roosevelt to the Court he had fought for so long, Hugo Black had been a solid New Deal senator before his call to the bench. Black was joined in 1939 by William O. Douglas, an active New Deal administrator, most recently chairman of the Securities and Exchange Commission. Together, these men would participate in more than three decades of critically important decision making, and their judgments would shape every facet of American life, from the limits of presidential power to the right of married couples to use birth-control devices.

Black and Douglas formed a fascinating personal and professional relationship that endured for more than three stormy decades. While many observers of the Supreme Court have regarded them as having a uniquely close alliance at the core of the Warren Court, they were very different jurists. Black, ever the Alabaman, was an ardent advocate of the maximum employment of the powers of the government to redress society's problems. Douglas, on the contrary, just as fervently sought to maintain and, indeed, enhance the rights and liberties of persons against what he saw as the unconstitutuional actions of state agents. For Black, the use of the legitimate power of the people to govern was the overarching value in a democratic soci-

3

ety, and its written Constitution was the foundation of self-governance. His friend Douglas, however, argued that the rights and liberties of the individual were the paramount value in a constitutional democracy. Both defended constitutional rights and liberties—the one because he thought the people through the Constitution had commanded it, and the other because he thought freedom to be prior to government.

Black and Douglas debated and argued their respective positions within the institution, the Supreme Court, they called home for almost thirty-five years. But their entanglement over these values involved more than these two men. Black and Douglas were two of a number of justices and chief justices who battled over the meaning and the scope of the Constitution as well as the proper role of the federal judiciary, especially the justices of the Supreme Court, in resolving many of the major problems that confronted the nation during the time they sat.

An examination of the lives and careers of Hugo Black and William Douglas offers an unusually interesting window on the Supreme Court and the society it serves. The complex social, political, and economic forces that shaped American society during their years on the bench were reflected within the Court. The Court was and is far from the kind of monastery that Felix Frankfurter insisted the Court must be if it was to survive.[3] It is a political body staffed, by and large, by politically experienced justices. That is not a criticism but a fact of American political life. Any body that decides the kind of questions the Supreme Court faces is engaged in what has been described as "the authoritative allocation of values,"[4] or a determination of "who gets what, when, how."[5] These phrases are the most commonly used definitions of politics. The Court's deliberations are calm and orderly, but, as Justice Holmes observed, it is "the quiet of a storm centre."[6]

It was indeed a stormy society during the years in which Black and Douglas sat. The justices were protected from the full force of the winds by their life tenure on the Court and their political independence, but they felt the effects. They rode out some turbulent seas inside the Court as well.

The members of the Court do enjoy a degree of insulation from the most immediate pressures of the political environment, but they are not wholly aloof. They are extremely aware of the political significance of their role and their decisions. They are sensitive to the forces around them, and there were many such pressures as Black and Douglas came to the Court.

Initially, the New Deal justices joined with a few of their predecessors to overturn previous Supreme Court rulings that had stifled efforts to fight the Great Depression. Almost immediately they were plunged, along with the rest of the nation, into a world war and, following that, into the volatility of life in a nuclear age. The 1950s and 1960s brought demands to reexamine definitions of equality and liberty in virtually every area of American life. Free-speech and free-association issues, demands for privacy protections, insistence on the inclusion of groups that had been excluded from full political participation, and critical assessments of the performance of the criminal justice system all came to the Supreme Court.

The legal issues were part of a much larger process of social change that raised economic as well as political questions, bringing about new definitions of morality and the rejection of traditional social structures. The demand for racial justice and protest against U.S. involvement in Vietnam became focal points for this intense set of conflicts. It was in this environment that Black, Douglas, and their colleagues attempted to fashion answers to the fundamental legal and political problems of their day.

The Court itself was not a calm eye in the midst of the social hurricane. While the conflicts within the Court were generally (though not always) handled with a relative degree of civility and decorum, according to institutional norms developed over the Court's history, they were serious and significant.

There is a tendency, particularly in popular work on the Court but even in some serious scholarship, to conjure up an image of the Warren Court when thinking of Black and Douglas. It is an image of a fairly cohesive group of judicial liberals who set out to reshape America. The reality was much different. Douglas and Black served with five chief justices and two dozen associate justices whose views ranged across the political spectrum from very conservative to extremely liberal (at least as those terms are used in contemporary political parlance). There were justices of extraordinary intellect with strong personalities and those whom their colleagues viewed as weak and limited contributors to the work of the Court. While there were warm personal relationships across ideological and partisan lines, there were also great tensions.

This book seeks a better understanding of the Court and the society it serves by focusing on the lives of two of its most interesting members. In particular, it seeks to learn from the differences between the two as much as or more than from their similarities and their colleagueship.

Hugo Black and William Douglas are such a well-known team that the mention of one of their names almost always produces comment on the other. They saw their relationship that way. In refusing an invitation to write an introduction to a twentieth-anniversary journal issue about Douglas, Black said: "You know without my stating it that I have the very highest regard for Justice Douglas as a friend and as a member of this Court. In fact, our views are so nearly the same that it would be almost like self praise for me to write what I feel about his judicial career."[7] Black finally did prepare such an introduction for a 1964 *Yale Law Journal* tribute to Douglas. He observed:

> In this situation I find myself following a habit of years and using his language to tell why I take this position. In a foreword to the February 1956 Journal, dedicated to me, he said:
>
>> And when one has been in such frequent agreement with a Brother as I have with Justice Black, it is impossible to write about him without seeming to write about one's self, or being so neutral as to appear to condemn by faint praise, or being so vague as to be stilted, or seeming to take advantage of the Brother's anniversary to perpetuate one's own favorite dissents.[8]

And it was a close professional relationship. Cathleen Douglas-Stone, Justice Douglas's widow, explains that the two men had a well-developed working relationship.

> The relationship that I saw was sort of an unconscious teamwork that existed. Bill once mentioned to me that when something came up at the Court, whether it was a petition for "cert." [a writ of certiorari bringing a case up to the Supreme Court for review] or a vote going around the table, he and Hugo would sort of look at each other and pass back and forth who would respond and who would do the drafting on this or that particular issue. . . . There was a comfortable almost automatic, quite seasoned well-travelled road between them.

There was a personal affection as well, but it was never as close as the professional association. The first term after Black's death was especially difficult for Douglas. According to his wife, "he hadn't realized the degree to which they had this unspoken communication between the two of them in terms of assigning areas in which they agreed." But "they were quite different men, in spite of shared views."[9]

The similarities in their views were striking. Both saw the Court as a coequal actor under the constitutional system, subordinate to neither the legislature nor the executive. Both saw the Bill of Rights as a set of essential and absolute protections against violations of individual freedom. Both were ready to risk criticism and abuse to maintain the Court's role as defender of liberty. Their friendship helped the two weather more than one storm of public criticism. Both understood deeply and from personal experience the political character of the society they served. Both Black and Douglas loved to play the "plain old country boy," but no one with a modicum of political savvy and a sense of recent Washington lore would buy it. Both were New Dealers committed to many of the principles shared by those reformers, and both had fought more than one battle in defense of Franklin Delano Roosevelt's programs.

But they were indeed "quite different men," not only in their personalities and professional styles, but in many more substantive ways as well. Hugo Black was a much admired, congenial member of the Court. Yet the gentle and gracious Southerner on the outside could be as hard and immovable as granite. He sometimes took years to reach a firm view on a point of law, but once he found his ground, he was unshakable. The man of enormous tolerance in matters of speech and press was a puritan who had difficulty accepting behavior and ideas outside the boundaries of his strict moral code.

He was a man who seemed to some of his critics to believe that the Court and the Constitution were as important as, if not more than, the society they were intended to protect. His unwillingness to have the Court grant the requests for a right to privacy, for example, led his detractors to that position. His deference to presidential war powers was another result of his rock-solid conviction that the Constitution prohibited judicial interference with proper political process, leading him to uphold the presidential order that established internment camps for Japanese Americans on the West Coast during World War II.

Black understood completely just how significant a political role the Court played, but determined that the Court could be protected only if its public image was apolitical. The Court had to be seen to be interpreting the law, not rewriting it according to the personal predilections of the justices. The words of the written Constitution were the touchstone. At the same time, Black the literalist was perfectly prepared to depart from literal interpretation when it was necessary in his view, though he denied doing so at every turn. The man who found an absolute requirement under the Sixth Amendment that indigent criminal defendants be represented by counsel at public expense rarely supported a claim that police had made an illegal search and seizure, even if the circumstances were, for most reviewers, obvious abuses of police authority. The justice who rejected the discovery of a right to privacy under the Constitution because no such liberty was defined in the document had no difficulty finding that the Fourteenth Amendment due process clause applied the entire Bill of Rights to the states, even though the amendment said no such thing. The jurist who was mightily offended by judicial creation of rights also had no difficulty supporting the creation of a right to freedom of association through interpretation of the First Amendment, despite the absence of such language in the document. Still, Black thought he could explain each of these decisions by reference to his theory of the Constitution and its proper, historical interpretation.

The object of great respect and affection, Black was frustratingly stubborn and unyielding even in the most unlikely cases. Although he had the political skills of an experienced senator, Hugo could move from negotiation to conflict very quickly.

He was a New Dealer, but from a principally populist, rather than progressive, foundation. He was ever the man from the rural South who represented the agrarian demands for reform, but reform from a rather special perspective. It was a reaction against the wealth and perceived corruption of northeastern urban power centers and in favor of economic change that could save farmers from ever deepening cycles of poverty and dependence. Yet it was a conservative movement in many respects, with strong nativist reactions against blacks, immigrants, and Catholics. Hugo was not a captive of these forces, but his life and career were clearly affected by them. Black moved away from some of his early views, first modifying his positions and opinions seemingly because of his efforts at self-education and his experiences on the Court. He later seemed to some of his colleagues (and even to his wife) to become more conservative and to return to the values he had developed in his Clay County, Alabama, years. He, however, categorically rejected their view of his judicial behavior and insisted, to the end of his tenure, that he had not changed his position on constitutional issues.

Black was an ardent defender of liberty and an advocate of democracy but a staunch defender of property rights. Douglas, by contrast, thought that property rights had been accorded too much importance in America relative to the rights of liberty and equality.

Douglas was every bit as complex as Black. The tough and even petulant individualist on the surface, Douglas was sensitive enough to pen poetic descriptions of tiny flowers in an alpine meadow. He could wield a pen like a weapon and was ready to cross intellectual swords on any topic, from the environment to international diplomacy. Yet he was fully capable of publicly admitting error when he felt he had been wrong. Douglas changed his views in a variety of areas of law during his years on the Court. Indeed, his willingness to change his position sometimes infuriated his colleagues when they thought his position was firm.

A man who was apparently willing to plunge the Court into the midst of the society's most divisive debates, Douglas was very much committed to the Court and the role it served. He argued, however, that the legitimacy of the Court was best protected not by hiding its political character but by openly admitting its central role in the political life of the nation and properly using its power to serve society. Proper use meant to him the use of the Court's power to obtain justice for all, particularly those least able to defend themselves.

Seemingly aloof and disdainful of the pace and character of life among the brethren, Douglas was in some ways extremely shy and intense, according to his widow, precisely because of his commitment to the importance of his task and his respect for his colleagues. Although he frustrated many of his colleagues who concluded that he must have been bored with his work on the bench, Douglas was regarded by virtually everyone as brilliant, and by many as a genius. Chastised for making sweeping generalizations and throwing off one-liners about complex questions, he was the Court's expert in some of its most complex fields, such as corporate law and securities regulations. Although he had mastered technical legal skills early in his career, Douglas's passion for justice was so great that he rankled when narrow technical debate seemed to block the resolution of an otherwise meritorious case. And he could not abide the idea that technical issues were sometimes interpreted in a way that prevented the Court from doing justice in a case when it was within the Court's power to do otherwise.

He was not always as ideological as he was publicly portrayed and therefore was able to work with a number of his colleagues on important cases despite his principal credo that he had "but one soul to save, his own."[10] Eliot Janeway captured Douglas's own view of himself when he referred to Douglas as a "pragmatic idealist."[11] That he could be accommodating and cooperative when he wanted to be but so often stood alone in sharply worded separate opinions that blasted his brethren for arguing erroneously or inadequately protecting fundamental liberties was another of the characteristics that his colleagues found maddening. That he sometimes did it to his allies as well as his adversaries only added to their frustration.

Douglas was a New Dealer. He retained his views as the Court changed around him, concluding his career as the pendulum swung to the other end of the political spectrum. He had come from the West to the Ivy League, and the effects of his early years and education were obvious. While sharing some of the populist traits common to a Westerner in the early part of this century, he was predominantly in the progressive mold (about which more will be said later). Unlike Black, Douglas had less confidence in the electorate and a stronger reformist instinct. Like urban progressives, Douglas was elitist enough to think he knew what reforms were needed. And, like them, his reformist tendencies were distinctly more liberal than Hugo Black's more populist inclinations.

Douglas increasingly became an internationalist who was often prescient in his assessments of the world situation. He was simultaneously denounced by the Russians as a spy as he traveled in the Middle East and accused of subversion in this country. He warned more than two decades before it hapened that oil politics in Iran and the Middle East would have a profound impact at home, and he was roundly condemned for insisting publicly that the United States recognize the Peoples' Republic of China. He warned President Truman that it would be a mistake to cross the thirty-eighth parallel in Korea and cautioned against involving American troops and risking U.S. prestige in Southeast Asia to prop up unpopular and corrupt regimes. His travels and the publicity they brought provoked criticism, but he could not tolerate what he saw as his nation's refusal to understand its relation to the rest of the world, particularly the developing societies emerging from colonial rule that faced critical decisions about the balance between the powers to be exercised by the regime and the rights and liberties to be enjoyed by the citizens.

Black shared little of Douglas's concern, for despite his political knowledge and experience, Senator Black had been first and foremost a representative of his constituents. Although he continued to educate himself before and after he came to the Court, Hugo focused on America's problems rather than the developing world community's. Douglas, however, who could see so much so clearly around the world, seemed almost intentionally to close his eyes to political realities at home and within the Court, so much so that Black expended considerable energy trying to act as a buffer between Douglas and his colleagues.

It is accurate to speak of them as a team in many ways, but it was not a collaboration. They supported each other in purusit of many common goals, but they often shared a goal for different reasons, chose different means to achieve it, and acted quite independently once the task was clear. The two were at the core very different men. The fact that they joined so many of the same opinions and stood together alone so many times was a measure of the importance of the principles they defended.

This set of similarities and differences, the duration and timing of their service on the Court, and their involvement in so many of the internal and external conflicts as members of the Court make Black and Douglas excellent subjects to consider for anyone interested in the times or the Court. The picture that emerges is of a Court more human, more politically aware, more diverse internally, and more reflective of its social and political environments than we have known.

And through these two men one can see the effort to play out the fundamental conflict of American constitutional life, the continuing tension between political power and constitutional rights. On one end of a continuum is democracy, the ability of the majority to establish governmental institutions and processes, determine public policy, and choose who is to lead. At the other is liberty, the protection of the individual to pursue the basic choices of life, to resist social pressure for conformity, and to be free from discrimination that prevents a citizen from participating in the democratic process or from enjoying the freedoms it is designed to protect. Choosing between the competing demands from both ends of the spectrum is the task that justices of the Supreme Court are called on to perform almost daily. There are other tasks, too, like resolving battles among governmental agencies over power and jurisdiction. And there are contests on the liberty end, with clashes between demands for equality and claims to liberty. But the enduring struggles have been of the first type, the tension between power and right.

The ironies in that tension fill the pages of political analysis and history. The most fundamental of these is the interdependence of the two concepts. What legitimate purpose is there for democracy if it is not the protection of liberty? How can there be liberty if citizens cannot freely come together to decide how they should govern themselves, recognizing that to be governed is to accept limitations on freedom?

This power–right paradox was certainly the challenge that Black and Douglas faced. The contrasts were drawn sharply during the years in which they served. The two men appreciated the competing values but often found themselves representing different places on the continuum. Where they thought the Constitution was clear, as in matters of freedom of speech, there was no difficulty. In close cases, however, Hugo Black saw the need for the judge to look to democracy and the positive law it produced. For Douglas, liberty was to prevail.

To Hugo Black, the issue was the power of the people to govern—first through their Constitution, and then, in less sweeping and fundamental ways, through their elected officials. Make no mistake, the Constitution was not for Black like other acts of government. Unless and until it was properly amended, the legislatures and executives could not violate its provisions, including the liberties protected by the Bill of Rights. When the First Amendment said that "Congress shall make no law . . . abridging the freedom of speech" it meant precisely that. No legislative majority, no emergency condition, and no judicial balancing process were adequate to contradict those words.

Yet where the Constitution was not, in Black's view, clear, the Court should not substitute its judgment for that of the peoples' representatives. As a senator, Black had seen judges use consitutional interpretation to block policy making by both the federal government and the states in the name of laissez-faire economics and conservative political ideology. Hugo had played an important role in the New Deal Court-packing fight launched to counter the judicial barriers to good government. Those judges had, of course, argued that their decisions were judgments in defense of liberty, but they had thwarted democratic efforts to deal with the nation's most serious problems. That kind of judicial behavior Black, who had grown up on the stump speeches of southern populists, could not abide. If the Constitution was inadequate, then the people could amend it by the proper means, not by judicial fiat.

Even for the literalist Justice Black, though, there were problems. Constitutional words like "unreasonable search and seizure" and "cruel and unusual punishment" were to be interpreted, but the difficulty was in how to do it without permitting the judge to substitute personal values for those norms inherent in the Constitution and reflected in the actions of the people's elected representatives. Black revered the words of the Framers and other key historical figures almost as much as he loved the Constitution. In these areas, Hugo tended to defer to elected officials, differing sharply from his colleague Bill Douglas.

For Douglas, the premise was liberty, discussed in law in terms of rights, and all subsequent debate concerned the limitations the state imposed on that natural freedom. Doubts must be weighed in favor of freedom. Liberty was prior to political authority, for it came from God, not man. This principle we had enshrined in the Declaration of Independence. We had justified our revolution to the world as a rejection of an illegitimate political power, illegitimate because it violated fundamental rights. For Douglas, it was in that spirit that the Bill of Rights was framed.

The most important job for the Court, according to Douglas, was to keep the government off the backs of the people. But Douglas was not a libertarian, and he did not agree with the tradition of judicial abuses that had bothered Black. Douglas, too, was a New-Dealer—appointed rather than elected—who had been frustrated by the rejection of Roosevelt's programs. He was also a pragmatist, an experienced administrator who knew how to get things done and understood the need for power and discretion in the hands of government officials. Beyond that, he was a democrat (small and large *d*) who thought that liberty included the freedom of the people to govern their community. His concern for the primacy of liberty notwithstanding. Douglas wrote a variety of important opinions in fields like zoning that supported the local community's authority against claims by individual property owners.

For Douglas, it was the exercise of power that was to be justified, not the claim to freedom. Since liberty—and it was liberty broadly understood—was prior to government authority, it made no sense to assume that government was authorized to act unless a right was specified in the Bill of Rights. The task of defining and protecting liberty, Douglas felt, was becoming more difficult in the modern world. He saw growing forces of conformity that made it difficult to carve out an individual life style or advocate new ideas. It was a time in which technology, such as computers and bugging devices, made the preservation of liberty all the more difficult.

Douglas found the challenge to liberty the greatest when the poor, the weak, and the traditional victims of discrimination were involved. It was in this that justice and liberty were for Douglas closely aligned. The courts were the only place where the individual and the minority could expect protection from the majority, so a coequal, potent, courageous, and fiercely independent judiciary was absolutely essential. Although he understood the tensions at play, Douglas believed that the failure by the judiciary to carry out its obligations meant a decision to surrender liberty.

The view of the Court through the perspectives of Black and Douglas requires an understanding first of the men. Chapters 2, 3, and 4 reveal something of their lives during the early years and the New Deal era before their appointment to the bench. The formative influences of these years are clear throughout the remainder of their careers. We then follow the two men's efforts to work out the tension between power and right in the wide range of critical social, political and economic issues brought to the Court during their years on the bench. Finally, we consider the situation confronting Douglas as he served his last years on the bench without his longtime friend Black, and we examine the legacy the two justices left.

Hugo L. Black:
From Alabama's Backwoods to
Washington's Marble Temple

THERE WAS A good deal of surprise and chagrin when, on August 13, 1937, President Franklin D. Roosevelt selected Senator Hugo L. Black, Democrat of Alabama, to be his initial nominee to the United States Supreme Court. Across the nation, people who had not known of him wondered who Hugo Black was and why the president would tap him for such an important position. People who knew Black by reputation from his Senate activities were amazed at the choice because he did not seem to have the judicial temperament for a position on the Court. And his colleagues in the Senate, who knew him best, were shocked that the president nominated someone as "common" as Hugo Black of Clay County, Alabama.

Yet it was not long before doubts turned to respect. Supreme Court watchers soon came to appreciate Hugo Black as a unique and important justice. He was a tough, courageous man of principle, always ready to defend his values, who had an almost religious commitment to the text of the Constitution. Black regularly carried a copy of it with him, and when queried about some portion of it, he would often slowly and carefully remove his well-worn copy from his pocket, turning to the appropriate passage as though he were preparing to present the Scripture reading for the morning service. The message was clear. The Constitution created a democratic republic in which the people should rule. Except where the Bill of Rights, our secular decalogue of thou shalt nots, limited democratically exercised power, the judiciary should not interfere. But where the document prescribed a right, the Court's duty was absolutely clear.

Much of what made Black unique is to be found in his Alabama background. For he began as and, in many important respects, remained the man from Clay Country.

Hugo Lafayette Black was born on February 27, 1886, on his parents' farm in Harlan, a small town in rural Clay County, Alabama. In 1889, the family moved to

Ashland, the county seat, with a population of about 300 where Hugo's father, William Lafayette Black, soon became the most successful merchant in town.[1] A common myth was that Hugo Black had grown up poor. Indeed, Black himself encouraged that view, but as George Freeman, one of Black's law clerks, observed, "this 'humble origins in Alabama' was grossly overdone. . . . If his father owned the farm and the store, he was probably the richest man in Clay County."[2]

The Blacks were certainly one of the wealthiest families in Ashland, and Hugo was raised in "modestly privileged circumstances."[3] When William Black died in 1900, he left an estate and $25,000 in cash that was divided among his surviving children.[4] Black's father had "earned a substantial part of his income from advancing to area farmers credit secured by crop liens."[5] In Alabama in 1886, the crop-lien system, as Mark Silverstein describes it, "defined the world for black and white farmers." A local merchant would provide farmers with credit for their supplies during the year at greatly inflated prices and receive a lien note on the fall crops in return. If the market value of the crop declined or if the crop failed, the farmer became more indebted to the merchant. After a few bad years, the lien notes would be foreclosed and the merchant would take over the property. When that occurred, the farmer became a "landless tenant."[6]

By 1890, when Hugo was barely four years old, the combination of the "lien system, hard money, and deflated prices [had] . . . proved ruinous to the Clay Country farmer."[7] Given these conditions, it was not surprising that Clay County became the center of Populist agrarian radicalism in Alabama. Black's father, having prospered under these market and monetary conditions, was politically unsympathetic to Populism.[8] As Hugo wrote later, "my father was not a Populist, in fact he was always much against that Party. He boasted that he was a Grover Cleveland Democrat."[9] One southern historian concluded that because Populism was a movement in Alabama "for those who lived on the economic margin," the Black family was "too prosperous to be Populists."[10]

Black's mother, Martha Toland Black, was an educated woman who raised her eight children (Hugo was the youngest) "strictly but with care and love and ambition."[11] Hugo's life-long love of reading and dedication to learning began when he was quite young, and Martha introduced him to Victor Hugo, Sir Walter Scott, and, of course, the Bible. As he recalled: "I read everything that was both readable and available. Along with Nick Carter detective stories, Fred Fearnots, young and old King Bradys, I remember reading many histories, Walter Scott's poems and novels, Dickens' novels, *Pilgrim's Progress,* and many other books generally thought of as too advanced for children. I read many of these books before I was ten years old."[12] When Hugo campaigned for the United States Senate in 1925, he would open speeches by praising his father but reserved his lushest praise for his mother, "whose worn and wrinkled hand pointed my way to the truth and light and faith."[13]

At an early age, Hugo knew that his mother did not love his father and that she was unhappy.[14] William Black's bad temper and "secret drinking" were the causes of the marital discord. Hugo's life-long aversion to liquor undoubtedly grew out of his strict Baptist upbringing and childhood memories of his father's condition.[15]

Hugo grew up surrounded by grim poverty and the language of Populism but was not himself part of the Populist movement. Although his boyhood coincided with the "decade of Populist turmoil" in Alabama, and although he attended every rally, parade, and stump speech of the agrarian radicals in Ashland, Hugo was a Democrat partisan.[16] Black recalled that by the time he was six years old, his political attitudes had begun to form: "Before I could articulate my syllables distinctly I recall how angry people could make me by saying: 'You are a Populist, a third party-ite.' My reply in those early days, . . . was: 'I am *not* a "third-party-ite." I am a Democrat.'"[17]

"I am my father's son," Hugo wrote shortly before his death in 1971.[18] Although he extolled the virtues of his family's southern roots, noting proudly that "my relatives, my ancestors were all, without exception, on the Southern side in the Civil War,"[19] there were tensions at home. Hugo could not respect his father "as a human being" and treated him with "cold indifference" because of his drinking and his involvement in the "hated" crop-lien system.[20] His ears rang "with the heady prescriptions of Populist orators as to what needed to be done,"[21] and he espoused economic views that led one of his in-laws to call him "a young Bolshevik."[22] While Hugo was never the Populist partisan, he was in fact a populist in his actions as senator and as justice of the Court.

He was a populist in the Senate who never forgot that he was from Clay County and represented the needs and aspirations of the citizens of Alabama. He was a populist on the Court in the sense that he kept in mind the importance of the little man, was fearful of centralized power (particularly in the hands of unelected judges), and resolved what he perceived as ambiguities in the law in favor of the democratic process rather than the dictates of his own conscience.

From his earliest days, Hugo was familiar with irony, as a bright, alert member of a family, whose prosperity was due in no small part to the poor luck and misfortunes of others. The Black children became doctors, lawyers, and merchants. A firm Democratic loyalist from his boyhood, Hugo Black was surrounded by the economic misery, the radical agrarian Populist movement, and racism. He was steeped in the politics, religion, law, and culture of his community. In a sense, Hugo Black's Clay County experiences mirrored the paradox of the South.[23] While the South was the richest part of the nation in natural resources, it was the poorest in venture capital. It had the most blight and poverty in the nation. And its people, in their miseries, still revered Jeffersonian ideals and devoutly believed in the primacy of the Bible

The impact of these economic and political events on Black has to be understood in the context of his commitment to Jeffersonian ideals, which were "political orthodoxy in Alabama," especially Jefferson's concept of fundamental rights for all, with special privileges to none.[24] Black was, as he proclaimed many times in later years, a Jeffersonian democrat.

The other key influence was the religious values of the Old Testament, with their emphasis on one's duty to others. Jefferson and the Bible gave Hugo Black his basic political and moral code, according to which he dedicated himself throughout his public life to improving the economic, political, and social status of the less privileged.

In the South of Black's youth, intellectual life centered on religion and law. When he noted, much later in his life, that the Constitution was his "legal bible," he was stating a profound truth about his cultural and religious heritage.[25] He attended Sunday school at the Baptist church in the morning and at the Methodist church in the afternoon. As to law, "the Courthouse was the secular temple of every [southern] county."[26] And while he played checkers and dominoes, fished, rode horses, and played baseball with other children, from the age of six Hugo was also to be found in the Ashland courthouse watching the proceedings and listening to the legal arguments. "It is hard for me to remember when I did not want to be a lawyer," Black wrote in his autobiography.[27]

When he was six years old, Black began attending the local school, Ashland College, which taught primary grades through college classes, with students from across the state. He also developed his ear for music while growing up in Ashland. After he had taught himself to play the family organ at four, a local music teacher convinced his parents to let her give him music lessons. In this relatively affluent, cultivated, religious orthodox environment, Hugo Black grew to early manhood.

When he was seventeen, in part because of his great affection for his brother Orlando, who had become a doctor, Hugo went to medical school in Birmingham. However, after Hugo's first year of medical training and a summer stint working in Orlando's medical offices, his brother encouraged him to go to law school. "My brother advised me that he thought I would make a good doctor but doubted if I could ever be happy in that profession. His doubt was based on his knowledge that I had always had an ambition to be a lawyer."[28] Hugo immediately left for Tuscaloosa and, in September 1904, enrolled in the University of Alabama Law School.

In 1904, the law school at the University of Alabama was weak. "It did not have—and was not entitled to have—a very high rating," Black commented in later years, "in comparison with the modern law school."[29] Students were admitted without a college degree and were taught by just two venerated law professors. They left a lasting impression on Hugo Black, who wrote that "my two law school professors taught us . . . that legislators, not judges, should make the law."[30] He did very well in law school, receiving at least 90 as a final grade in every course he took during his two years in Tuscaloosa. He also managed to sneak across to the College of Arts and Sciences and attend political science lectures. On the basis of his excellent law school grades, Black was admitted to Phi Beta Kappa when he received his law degree in 1906.

After graduation, Black, a boyish-looking 120-pound lawyer, returned to Ashland with what he described as "grandiose plans for my future": legal practice in Ashland, a seat in the state legislature, legal practice in Birmingham for about five years, "go to Congress and from there go to New York to practice law." Why New York? It was "the nation's largest city," wrote Black. And that was the place for an attorney to practice law. Black stayed in Ashland for just over a year, trying to compete for legal business with the five established lawyers in that small town. He eked out a living by collecting old accounts and defending indigent blacks. As Black recounted, "[m]y reputation as a lawyer was not greatly enhanced, but my reputation as a collector was."[31]

While developing a legal business, Black was absorbed in his (life-long) task of self-education. He walked in the woods to practice his speaking technique. He studied books on rhetoric, grammar, English, and history, when not practicing law.

Sadly, his law office, stocked with a fine law library purchased with his share of the inheritance funds from his father's estate, had burned down. He left Ashland for Birmingham in September 1907. By then, Black had developed his lawyering skills and felt confident about "talking on his feet."[32]

Birmingham Lawyer (1907–1926)

"Raw, still new industrializing," Birmingham was a city that had grown up in the Alabama piney woods at the end of the Civil War.[33] Twenty-one-year-old Hugo Black had moved from a country town of 300 to a city of 50,000, with more refugees from farm disasters moving in daily. They came to find work in the coal mines, blast furnaces, iron foundries, cotton mills, and lumber yards. In 1907, United States Steel moved to Birmingham, immediately taking over a great deal of the town and becoming a dominant presence in the city.

Birmingham was also nicknamed the "Murder Capital of the World" by some of its detractors. Its slums were populated by many of the white workers and by all of the city's blacks (who at that time made up 40 percent of its population). Gambling, prostitution, drunkenness, and an occasional murder were commonplace. In Birmingham, which had acquired "the reputation of the nation's most crime-filled city,"[34] Hugo Black saw "the drama of helpless people confronting the power of the big, absentee corporations that dominated their lives."[35] For Black, from his sheltered, somewhat affluent town, these impressions were indelible.

Black knew few people when he arrived in Birmingham. He began to earn a living as a personal-injury lawyer representing workers and labor unions. As an outsider, it was essential that he meet people if his career and personal life were to improve.[36] In the South, much more than elsewhere in the United States, "communal bonding [was] felt more intensely," and organizations such as the Elks, Moose, Civitans, and Ku Klux Klan were "organized grandly."[37] As these groups "were a fact of life in the South," Silverstein observes, "they became a fact of life for Hugo Black."[38] He gravitated to them in order to meet people and develop connections with more established members of the Birmingham community.

As he recounted later: "The only ethical way [to build the practice] was to meet as many people and make as many friends as possible. This I proceeded to do immediately after arriving in Birmingham," joining organizations such as the Masons, Odd Fellows, and Knights of Pythias. "Some of the closest friendships in my life," Black wrote, "were formed among the brethren in these . . . fraternities." He regularly attended the First Baptist Church. He became a Sunday school teacher and remained one until he left Birmingham in 1927.[39]

For the next few years, Hugo and his boyhood friend Barney Whatley were partners in the law firm of Black and Whatley. His new partner had a valuable asset in addition to a fine legal mind: "Barney was one of the best mixers I have ever known."[40] Both of them were joiners who met a great many people in Birmingham who, in turn, brought more and more clients to the firm. Whatley, however, contracted tuberculosis and had to leave the area in 1908. He sold his share of the firm to another friend of Hugo's, David J. Davis, and the firm then became known as Black and Davis.

Black appeared in many trial courts in the area. Because of a case brought by the young attorney, he soon came to the attention of Circuit Judge A. O. Lane, a fellow member of the Knights of Pythias. The case involved the infamous convict-lease system, which offended Black very much. A black convict, Willie Morton, had been leased by a large steel company and held beyond his term of imprisonment. Black's complaint was false imprisonment, and, in his first case before a jury, he won a verdict in his client's favor for $137.50 plus costs.

The case helped his career in two ways. When he ran for prosecutor of Jefferson County (Birmingham) in 1914, his opposing counsel in the Morton case, then a highly regarded federal judge, endorsed Black for the position. The endorsement was a counterweight to the charge that Black was too young and inexperienced to be the county prosecutor. More immediately, Lane, the sitting judge in the case, offered Black the position of city recorder (police court judge). Black took the job with the stipulation that the work would be finished by 9:30 each morning so that he could continue with his law practice. In April 1911, at the age of twenty-five, Hugo Black became a police court judge, at an annual salary of $1,500, a job he kept until October 1912, when he resigned to return to full-time law practice.

His work as a police court judge was an immensely important experience, for it brought Black in daily contact with poor people, many of them black, who faced fines and imprisonment for crimes ranging from vagrancy and drunkenness to gambling and other vices, including prostitution, dope peddling, and murder. Black was noted for clearing the docket rapidly; there were no delays in his courtroom. His commitment to action and fairness made him a figure about whom local journalists loved to write. In no time at all, "Hugo-to-Hell" Black's name was well known in Birmingham. When he stepped down in 1912, he said: "It has been a valuable experience and afforded me a broad insight into human nature."[41] In 1971, a more mature Black said of his police judge experience: "I learned much about life in that position."[42]

Because of the publicity from his work as police court judge, and as a result of his visibility as a member of numerous fraternal and civic organizations, Black's law firm prospered. Davis handled all the office work, and Black made all the court appearances. The partnership dissolved in 1912 because Davis felt he could not be in a firm "where he brought in less income than any other member."[43] Black moved into new offices and, within a few years, faced another important career decision. Although he was earning over $7,500 a year, Black began to think about reentering public life in Jefferson County, Alabama.

In 1914, Black sought the office of Jefferson County solicitor (prosecutor). Crucial to the outcome of the four-man race for the position was the major and difficult issue raised by Black, of whether the fee system and convict labor would continue in the county. In, the fee system, an integral part of local justice systems in the South, the salaries of officers of the court, including the police, were generated form fines paid by those arrested and convicted.[44]

The twenty-eight-year-old lawyer developed a successful campaign strategy, one that Black would use again when he ran for the Senate in 1926. Simply put, the campaign plan was for Black to travel across the county by car, meeting as many voters as possible face to face at "lodges, picnics, basket suppers, stores, basketball games."[45] Black talked with them about issues that concerned them that he as prosecutor could change. Attacking the fee system as immoral, for example, Black stumped the backwoods like a preacher, stating that "the people were tired of having hundreds of Negroes arrested for shooting craps on pay day and crowding the jails with these petty offenses."[46]

On primary day, in the spring of 1914, Black outpolled his three Democratic opponents, and, in late November 1914, he became the prosecutor of Jefferson County. On taking office, Black immediately confronted the fee-system and convict-labor issues, which he had addressed during the campaign. The resolution of those problems, however, was complicated by an additional burden.

Moving to the courthouse with his small staff, Black found a clogged docket. There were over 3,000 criminal cases awaiting trial, nearly 100 of which were murder cases. He also found that incarceration fees, which went to pay the officers of the Jefferson County criminal justice system, were charged for everything: entering and leaving jail, being arrested, posting bond, and even sleeping and eating. Because he had pledged to dismiss all cases "against honest-to-goodness working payday crapshooters," Black released 500 prisoners who had been mishandled under the fee system.[47] To quickly dispose of the murder cases awaiting trial, Black had judges from other parts of the state assigned to Jefferson County. Within a year, all the capital cases had been tried, including one that was ten years old.

In 1915, prosecutor Black uncovered the brutal third-degree measures used by the police in Bessemer (a suburb of Birmingham but outside county jurisdiction) to obtain confessions from black suspects. Although the Bessemer district was outside his jurisdiction, Black brought charges before the grand jury. That body adopted his report and ended the horrors that had been occurring in Bessemer.[48]

While Hugo Black had run as an anti-establishment candidate [in Birmingham], "nothing he ever did was very far away from the mainstream," as one scholar has pointed out. Black, who had been in the city for barely seven years when he became solicitor, was still an outsider who "accomplished what the legal establishment and the general public wanted him to accomplish."[49] By the summer of 1917, though, because of his vigorous prosecutorial efforts, Black had run afoul of some special interests in the state, especially the liquor and brewery industries. For many months, he had to fend off his opponents' efforts to curtail the power of the prosecutor's office. Finally, Black resigned in August 1917. Clearly, both the police court stint and the prosecutor's job were searing experiences for the young lawyer. As William O. Douglas observed, both he and Black early in their careers "were exposed to raw-boned experiences" which left their marks on their personal and professional lives.[50]

By the time Hugo left office, America had formally entered World War I. Although he was over age, Black enlisted in the army. Assigned to the field artillery, he taught himself trigonometry from a high-school text and spent three very hard months at officers' training school. He was commissioned a captain in the field artillery and stationed near Chattanooga, Tennessee. He remained stateside while his regiment, the Eighty-first Field Artillery, traveled to France. The day they arrived in the trenches, November 11, 1918, the armistice was signed.

After the armistice, Black returned to his Birmingham law practice. "Clients began to hire me immediately," Black recalled. He joined a firm that was thereafter known as Allen and Black. Black also hired one of his old army officers, Colonel Crampton Harris, whom he later took on as a partner.[51] In the 1920s, Harris was the leader (cyclops) of the Birmingham Ku Klux Klan Klavern; his role in the KKK and affiliation with Black's law firm were to be important issues later in Hugo's political career. Within a few years, the Allen and Black law firm was doing very well, with Hugo earning nearly $40,000 a year.

Black was an extremely eligible bachelor in Birmingham. Although he had planned to marry a young woman he had fallen in love with before going into the army, her parents, who were Orthodox Jews, forbade her to see him again when they learned of their plans to marry. After his return to Birmingham, he met and fell in love with the beautiful Josephine Foster, daughter of Dr. Sterling J. Foster, a prominent member of the Birmingham "landed aristocracy."[52] Although he was somewhat older, Hugo was smitten "by her beauty and charm."[53] He pursued her doggedly for a few years until she consented to be his wife.

Hugo and Josephine were married for thirty years, from February 23, 1921, until Josephine's death in 1951. They had three children: Hugo, Jr., born in 1922, followed by Sterling Foster in 1924, and Hugo's only daughter, Martha Josephine, in 1933. Hugo was a totally dedicated and loving husband for as long as Josephine lived.

Six years after her death, Hugo Black married Elizabeth Seay, another regal Alabaman, who had worked as his office secretary. Elizabeth had been a deputy clerk in the clerk's office in the United States District Court, Northern District, in Birmingham for fifteen years, when Hugo, Jr., arrived in the city in 1956 looking for an Alabaman secretary for his father. Hugo, Jr., prevailed on her to visit Washington, D.C., to meet the justice. Black initially demurred, telling his son that he did not "want a woman with middle-aged problems on my hands." (She was in the process of divorcing her husband of many years, Alabaman Fred DeMerritte. The divorce was finalized in November 1956.) The son responded quickly to the father: "But *Daddy,* she's so good-looking!" Elizabeth recalled her first meeting with Hugo. He whipped out a little black notebook and told her that her father "never was for me. . . . I was a strong prohibitionist and he was an anti. However, I liked your father." She became his secretary in 1956, and Black immediately began her on a reading program in a successful effort to broaden her knowledge. Her initial assignments were John Dewey and Bertrand Russell. Less than two years later, in September 1957, Hugo Black, twenty-two years Elizabeth's senior, proposed to her. And he did so in a most unusual manner. As Elizabeth tells it,

> Hugo said, I have had a prior love affair for almost twenty years now with an institution. It is the Supreme Court. I have a tremendous respect for the prestige of the Court. . . . Therefore, in my personal life I have to be like Caesar's wife: above reproach. I have to know that the woman I marry is a one-man woman. . . . I am sev-

enty-one years old. You are twenty-two years younger than I. In another five or ten years you may not find me as attractive as you do now. If that were to happen and you wanted a divorce, I would give you one. But I think it would finish me and hurt the prestige of the Court.

Elizabeth assured him that he had nothing to worry about and that she respected the Supreme Court as much as he did. With that, they kissed and set the date. After he left, she received a call. It was Hugo, who said: "I forgot something. I forgot to tell you I love you, darling—and good night." They were married on September 11, 1957, and were loving companions until his death fourteen years later, in September 1971.[54]

While there was speculation that the Foster family had not taken kindly to Hugo marrying Josephine, Josephine's sister, Virginia Foster, wrote in a letter to Hugo years later, "this is simply not true. . . . you were regarded as quite a 'catch' as the expression went then, from the standpoint of looks, money, attractiveness and intelligence. I am sure neither Daddy or Mommy objected to the marriage in the slightest, and if they did it would have done no good as Sister was determined to marry you."[55]

Virginia Foster, or Jinksie, as Hugo and Josephine called her, was a most unusual person—a southern, white, female liberal. Jinksie married Clifford Durr, a Montgomery, Alabama, lawyer who was a "second echelon brain truster of the New Deal" and a close friend of Lyndon Baines Johnson. He was a commissioner at the Federal Communications Commission (FCC) throughout Roosevelt's administration and left government service in 1947 in order to defend some of the government officials who had been dismissed because of President Harry S Truman's loyalty program which Durr vehemently opposed.[56]

Jinksie and Josephine had always been very close, and she and her husband became Hugo's life-long friends. In the 1950s, Clifford was an attorney for Martin Luther King, Jr., and the Southern Christian Leadership Conference, and in 1957, Jinksie was hauled before the Senate's Internal Security Subcommittee, which was investigating Communist infiltration in the South, and accused of "plotting with the Reds." Hugo Black continued his close, warm association with the Durrs during this tense period, but from a distance; after 1954, Black could not safely return to Alabama—nor did he feel it was safe for his children to live there, or even to visit. Jinksie and Cliff, however, refused to leave Montgomery, even though life was very hard for them throughout the years of the civil rights struggle.[57]

After his marriage to Josephine, Hugo continued to join organizations to be visible in the community, to find new clients, and to partake of the fellowship of such groups. After his return from the army, Black joined the American Legion, the Pretorians, the Fraternal Order of Moose, and the Odd Fellows. And in 1923, Hugo Black became a member of the Birmingham Ku Klux Klan Klavern, in which his law partner, Crampton Harris, was an officer.

The Ku Klux Klan of the 1920s, sometimes called the second Klan, was built on, as Bertram Wyatt-Brown describes it, a "fund of folk memory and reverence for the 'Lost Cause,' a set of emotions and passions more intense than those that inspired allegiance to the Elks or Moose."[58] The "Lost Cause" referred, of course, to what most Southerners called the War of Northern Aggression. Hugo Black, born of the South, whose father and other relatives fought for the South in the war, must have been touched by the Klan's bridge to the past. The Klan also, however, reflected more contemporary southern frustration with liberal immigration laws, alarm at the growth of Catholicism and Judaism in Protestant America, and, always, the nativistic conviction of blacks' inferiority.

In Birmingham in the early 1920s, the Klan and the Anti-Saloon League were powerful political groups. "In Alabama," wrote a newspaper editor in 1929, "it is hard to tell where the League ends and the Klan begins."[59] A person running for political office in Alabama could not offend either group without risking a loss at the polls. It was said that the Klan in Birmingham, the center of Klan power in the state, controlled 18,000 of the city's 32,000 votes.[60] Support from the Klan meant near certain victory for an Alabama politician in the years following World War I.

Hugo Black's decision to join the Klan in 1923, at a time when it was doing a "booming" business in the state, was nothing but "an act of purest expediency."[61] As a lawyer, Black felt he needed to belong to that organization to enter a legal culture populated by Klan prosecutors, jurors, and judges. When he joined in 1923, the Grand Dragon of the Alabama Klan was the assistant attorney general of the state of Alabama.[62] As Hugo later put the matter to his second wife, Elizabeth, he had joined "so that we would have an equal chance in trying cases before jurors who were largely Klan members in Alabama at that time and because most of the defendants as well as most of the lawyers who represented corporations and who opposed Hugo were also members."[63] Black told a *New York Times* reporter that "he was trying a lot of cases against corporations, jury cases, and I found out that all the corporation lawyers were in the Klan. A lot of jurors were too, so I figured I'd better be even up. . . . I wanted that even chance with the juries."[64] Black's liberal colleague on the Court, William O. Douglas, commented that, "like all trial lawyers, Hugo Black depended heavily upon the favor of local people who made up juries. The Klan was the biggest, most powerful club in the South and Hugo Black joined it."[65]

As a potential public candidate for office, Black concluded that he would need the Klan's help in a campaign. James Esdale, the Grand Dragon of the Alabama Klan, actually managed Black's senatorial campaign in 1926 and was one of his major advisers. Through Esdale's backing, Black received the full voting support of the Klan in that senatorial election. In addition to his law partner, Crampton Harris, two close friends who worked with him, Ben Ray and Hugh Locke, were publicists for the Klan. In 1921, Black had successfully defended an itinerant Protestant minister, Edwin R. Stephenson, who had been charged with the murder of a Catholic priest, Father James E. Coyle. In that sensational case, Black used all his courtroom skills to assist his client; it helped that Klansmen were on the jury and were on both the prosecution and defense staffs.[66]

However, again as a matter of expediency, a month after he decided, in June 1925, to run for the Senate, Black formally resigned from the Klan. While Black realized the Klan's strength, he knew that his membership would alienate all the Catholics, Jews, and blacks in Alabama. So, "in a deliberate act of political strategy, he resigned as secretly as he had joined almost two years before"; he continued to work with Esdale for over six months, however, speaking at Klavern meetings and making political speeches in the local courthouse square as Klan members in the crowd passed the word that Black was "their candidate."[67] If, toward the end of his life, Hugo Black admitted that joining the Klan was the biggest error in his life, in 1923, a much younger Hugo Black felt it was the appropriate thing to do to get ahead in Alabama. For Hugo Black the joiner, it was primarily an action of pure political and legal expediency.

In 1925, at thirty-nine, Black was a successful trial attorney, married to a lovely member of the Birmingham social register, with two young sons, a beautiful home on the fashionable south side of Birmingham, and an annual income of $40,000. As a member of a large number of fraternal and veterans' organizations, and a faithful Sunday school teacher at the First Baptist Church, Black was a highly regarded citizen of Birmingham.

Black's reputation was enhanced when, in April 1924, U.S. Attorney General (later Chief Justice of the United States) Harlan Fiske Stone appointed him to serve as special assistant U.S. attorney to handle the government's case against 117 prominent Mobile residents charged with bootlegging. These "booze trials" were front-page news for months, and Hugo Black became "known in all corners of Alabama."[68] In January 1925, fresh from his successful federal prosecution, Black successfully argued his first case before the United States Supreme Court. He won a unanimous ruling from the Court in *Lewis* v. *Roberts*, a tort suit.[69]

It was a few months later that Black told his former law partner David J. Davis of his plans to run for the Senate. The incumbent, Oscar W. Underwood, was extremely vulnerable because of his economic conservatism and "open defiance of the Klan," and Black seized the opportunity. Underwood announced his retirement from the Senate in early July 1925. On July 9, 1925, Hugo wrote his letter of resignation to J. W. Hamilton, secretary of the Robert E. Lee Klan No. 1 in Birmingham: "Dear Sir Klansman: Beg to tender you herewith my resignation as a member of the Ku Klux Klan, effective from this date on. Yours, I.T.S.U.B. [In the Sacred, Unfailing Bond], Hugo L. Black."[70]

Black soon announced a campaign for the Senate seat that would be waged "along the line of merit and principle alone."[71] With his announcement and his resignation from the Klan out of the way, Black had to plan a strategy for a statewide race in which he would be competing with four other Democrats. Black's senatorial campaign strategy was very similar to that of his 1914 campaign for prosecutor of Jefferson County. Purchasing two cars, Black traveled across the state, to the smallest towns and hamlets, with a "common man" theme.

He may have run as a Democrat, but his platform was vintage Populist. Hugo Black traveled back to Clay County, in the heat of August 1926, to formally open his campaign. His speech to his former friends and neighbors reflected the approach he used throughout the campaign: "I am," he said, "happy to be home again." Black pointed out that the "times cry aloud for men in public office who have not lost the common touch." He talked of power concentrations and of "blocs and cliques and rings" wielding power in Washington. And he spoke of the people electing public officials who would not be in control of these powerful forces. Those interests, he said, "have never shaped my ideals, fashioned my political creed, nor helped me in my aspirations for public office. They have not been a part of my environment. I am not a millionaire. . . . My father was a farmer. I have no hereditary claim to office, but is there any clause in our Constitution which says the son of a Senator shall be Senator, but the son of a farmer must always be a farmer?" Of course, he chose not to explain that his father was a "farmer" only because he used the crop-lien system to take property that his tenants later farmed for him.

Black then talked about the major planks of his campaign. It was political rhetoric to be sure, but it expressed Black's deep-seated beliefs, rooted in his religious faith and his commitment to both the Bible and the Constitution as the revered word and text. Black, who was not, like so many others, "politically dry and personally wet," declared, "I am now and have always been a prohibitionist in theory and in practice." On the question of tariffs and taxes, he noted that "the Democratic party has always opposed high tariffs. . . . Tariff and taxes alike, when imposed, should not unduly burden the toiling many for the idle few." He also supported the improvement of roads, rivers, and harbors, "fully realizing the[ir] absolute necessity." Black spoke strongly on behalf of cheap fertilizer, for its availability would mean "profit and prosperity to the farmer." He supported the federal government's Muscle Shoals power project. He regarded it as an inexpensive fertilizer project and opposed the proposal to sell it to the Alabama Power Company.

Hugo's nativistic sympathies—common to Populists, the KKK, and other rural groups—were revealed in his speech when he spoke of the immigration problem. "The greater proportion [of immigrants] however, are ignorant, illiterate and wholly incapable of appreciating during a lifetime, the ideals and duties of American citizenship," said Black. "The melting pot idea is dangerous to our national inheritance," he concluded. "I oppose further immigration, and always believe our nation would be greatly benefitted by closing the gates until such time as we can Americanize and educate those already here. This nation has cost too much in sacrifice, toil, and blood to jeopardize its safety in order to swell the profits of Millionaire Coal Operators, Millionaire Mill-Owners and the Millionaire Steel-Makers." The practice of maintaining low wages by importing impoverished foreign immigrants was no way to build an economy.

Turning to the veterans' issues, Black recognized the "debt of gratitude to the boys who left their homes to serve in the World War." Concerned about their economic well-being after their sacrifice, Black bitterly lashed out against the growing pauperism of the veterans. "If I am your United States Senator, and it is in my power to do so, no Honorably Discharged soldier shall die a *pauper's death*. It is a tragic generosity that extends the debts of Italy for 62 years at 1½%, and lets loyal American soldiers die neglected paupers."[72]

Black closed with a reminder about his limited campaign finances, painting himself as a man of the people rather than a professional politician. In his speech, he explained that the law limited him to an expenditure of $10,000, a fundamental constraint on his campaign that he would not circumvent: "What I cannot do directly, I shall not do indirectly. You will, therefore, receive no multitudinous literature and advertisements in my behalf, from imaginary clubs." He could not and would not compete with millionaire opponents; he would be bought by no one, he concluded in another speech: "If you want a United States Senator who is willing to buy the help of political parasites and machine politicians, you do not want me."[73]

As the speech suggested, he strategically eschewed support from the Alabama press and did not buy expensive newspaper advertisements. Running as the "poor man's candidate," Black's primary campaign slogan, used in that first Clay County speech, was "I am not now, and have never been a railroad, power company, or a corporation lawyer."[74] In a letter dated June 13, 1926, to a supporter named D. C. Arthur, Black wrote, "I know the needs of the people and if elected to the . . . Senate I can work in behalf of the whole people without having any strings tied to me by any selfish corporate interests. Since beginning my practice of law in Birmingham I have had the opportunity of representing practically every big utility corporation, . . . but have always fought on the other side, preferring to be always on the side of the people."[75] Black also enclosed "some advertising matter consisting of stickers for automobile windshields, placards, and some small cards. I would appreciate it if you will get the people in your community to place the stickers on their cars; also if you will display the placards where they can be seen best, and hand out the small cards."[76]

At rallies in courthouse squares across the state, with Klansmen whispering their support, Black continued to argue in favor of veterans' benefits, prohibition, better roads, cheap fertilizer, and limits on immigration into the United States. And it worked. The underdog candidate won forty-two of the sixty-seven counties in the Democratic primary, and his total of 84,877 votes (32% of the votes cast in a field of five Democratic party candidates) "came uncannily close," as one of his biographers observed, "to the estimated total of Klan membership in Alabama in 1926."[77] Addressing a public Klan rally after the primary, Black began by saying to the gathering: "I thank you, friends, from the bottom of my heart."[78] He was elected in November 1926 by a margin of 70,000 votes. The big winner in Alabama's elections in 1926, however, was the Ku Klux Klan. Its candidates for senator and governor, Black and Bibb Graves, won handily. The new senator-elect was to join another official long supported by the Alabama Klan, Senator Tom Heflin. One political observer noted that Alabama was "the most completely Klan-controlled state in the union."[79] Within a year, however, in a backlash against that violent group, membership would drop from 94,000 to 10,400.

Senator Hugo Black (1926–1937)

Hugo Black prepared for a reduction in salary (from $40,000 to $10,000, the salary of a U.S. senator) and readied himself for the Seventieth Congress by trying to master the rules of the Senate. He also continued his self-education program. In the thirteen months between the election and the convening of the new Congress, Black read the political theories of Montesquieu, Rousseau, Locke, Spencer, Veblen, and the ancient Greeks and studied the records of the 1787 Constitutional Convention.[80] Black's reading of these works, which continued for decades (long after he arrived on the Court), gave him a profound philosophical appreciation of democracy and the electoral process. He came to office with a practical, pragmatic appreciation of the relationship between the common people and their elected representatives; he grew to understand the enduring importance of the principles associated with electoral politics in a democracy. In a way, he had been preparing for his political career all his life. As a local judge and a county attorney, Black quickly grasped the nature of public power—its illegal, unconstitutional, excessive uses as well as the proper use of the authority to act granted him by the "people"—and its relation to the source of all power, the Constitution. By the time Black went to Washington, D.C., unlike Hollywood's Mr. Smith, he knew what political power was, that it should properly be used to reflect the will and needs of the people, and that, at its source, were the words of the Constitution.

On December 5, 1927, Hugo L. Black was sworn into office by Vice President Charles G. Dawes. He was one of forty-seven Democrats in the Senate, joined by forty-eight Republicans and one Farmer-Labor senator. Little noticed in Washington, the Blacks settled into a small house in the District of Columbia. During his first years in the Senate, Black was an enigma. Some of his colleagues regarded him as a "pariah" because he had Klan support and had taken the seat of an admired southern Solon.[81] His colleagues, associated him with his boisterous, racist, anti-Catholic Alabama colleague, Senator "Tom-Tom" Heflin. As the 1928 Democratic presidential contest grew closer, Black and other southern senators had to grapple with the prospect of having to support a northern, wet, pro-immigration, Catholic candidate Governor Al Smith of New York, at the top of the national ticket. Heflin began to speak as though he would bolt the party and support the Republican candidate, exclaiming at one Birmingham rally: "So help me God, I will vote against Al Smith if they read me out of the Democratic Party and drive me from every Senate committee!"[82]

Black was more restrained. Although he was personally dry and was reluctant to act contrary to the Klan and the Anti-Saloon League, he was also a life-long Democratic loyalist. He tried to walk a careful line between past supporters (who were rapidly losing support in the state) and the Democratic machine, both in Alabama and in Washington, D.C. "Hugo," said the former chairman of the Alabama Democratic Executive Committee, Ben Ray, "was really in the middle."[83]

Before the 1928 Democratic National Convention, Black was highly critical of Smith in letters to constituents. Hubert Baughn, the Washington correspondent for the Montgomery based *Alabama Journal,* wrote to Black on March 20, 1928, to ask one question: Did he favor the nomination of Governor Smith? Black responded:

> I am opposed to the nomination of Governor Smith for President by the Democratic Party. . . . [H]e is the exponent of views directly in conflict with the settled opinions of the majority of people of this Nation, and particularly of the Democratic South. . . . His views on law enforcement, immigration, and [action] permitting the sale of beer and wine in his state, contrary to the Constitution, . . . do not appeal to the patriotic and law-abiding citizens of this Nation. . . . I am convinced that Governor Smith's nomination would destroy party solidarity.[84]

Writing to Ed Nixon of Ozark, Alabama, a month earlier, Black had expressed fears that if Smith were elected, the Volstead Act implementing Prohibition would be repealed. He also wrote about Smith's Catholicism, "[w]hether Governor Smith would be able to rise above such natural human sympathies, no person can say," and observed, "It is . . . well known that most of the Catholics favor foreign immigration." Black concluded the letter by stating:

> I consider [Al Smith] to be the most over-estimated man in America, as to ability. I think him to be the living exponent of the predominating sentiment of the foreign element in the City of New York, and that the ideals of that element are totally at variance with the traditions and sentiments of the people of the South. In fact, I believe him to be the selected and chosen instrument of groups, all hostile to old-fashioned Jeffersonian Democracy. . . . The Democratic Party would be almost committing suicide to select him as the standard bearer of the followers of Jefferson and Jackson.[85]

While distressed that the Democrats nominated Smith, Black finally decided to support the national ticket and did not bolt the Party. In another letter to an angry constituent, Black wrote that it was his duty "either to support the Party, or to resign my position." Given the nature of work in the Senate, "a man without a party . . . is a man without influence." Therefore, he said, "I am absolutely convinced that by following the course which I have adopted, I can do more to carry out the principles in which you and I believe.[86]

To William G. McAdoo, Black wrote, "I was a Democrat, elected by the Democrats of Alabama and would, of course, adhere to the Democratic Party. . . . My staunch friends advise me, however, that the less I can say, the better it will be. . . . The situation is bad." Writing to another Alabama friend, John McCain, in November 1928, Black described the national Democratic party's situation as "chaotic."[87]

Black's public silence and lack of support for the Democratic ticket left him open to criticism from the Alabama press. The Montgomery *Advertiser* chided him for his "total indifference and neglect" during the election (won, narrowly, by Smith over Hoover in Alabama).[88] But as his letters revealed, Senator Black did what he felt had to be done: he provided nominal support for the ticket to maintain his bona fides as a Senate Democrat. While he felt that Smith was wrong for the nation, he respected the electoral process too much to follow Heflin in frontal attacks on the national party.

Justice Hugo Black (1937–1971)

Black was to develop a reputation as a spokesman for populist measures and as a tough legislative investigator. After Franklin D. Roosevelt became president in 1933, Black became a strong supporter of many, but not all, of the Democratic president's "New Deal" programs.

A major political crisis in 1937 was Roosevelt's controversial plan to restructure the United States Supreme Court. Angry with the Court and with no opportunity to appoint any new judges, Roosevelt had the proposal introduced a year after his reelection. It met, as will be seen, with overwhelming criticism. While the Court-packing bill was moving to its final defeat, Justice Willis Van Devanter announced his retirement, in May 1937 and on July 14, 1937, Senator Joseph T. Robinson (D-Ark.), Roosevelt's first choice for the Supreme Court and the legislator who was leading the fight for the Court-reform plan in the Senate, suffered a heart attack and died. The appointment went to Hugo L. Black.

The defeat of the court-packing plan in late July left the president "sore and vengeful," according to a contemporary account of Black's appointment. With Senator Robinson dead, Roosevelt had no candidate ready to submit to the Senate. Consequently, Roosevelt turned to his attorney general, Homer Cummings, for a list of possible nominees to replace Van Devanter. Sixty names were produced. At a White House meeting, Roosevelt and Cummings agreed on four criteria: the nominee had to be reasonably young, have solid New Deal credentials, be confirm-able by the Senate, and represent the West or the South. Using these criteria, by August 1, 1937, the two men had cut the list to seven names. The seven included four federal judges (quickly dropped because they were not liberal enough), Solic-itor General Stanley Reed (Kentucky), Senator Sherman Minton (Indiana), and Senator Hugo Black. Minton became the leading candidate "because he was closest to Cummings, the President's sole advisor in the matter" and because Reed "had no fire." Minton, however, did not want the job at that time, having just "attacked the justices of the high bench with an intemperate fury" in defense of Roosevelt's Court-packing plan. On August 9, after his name was removed, Minton raised the question of Court membership with Black.[89]

According to Harold Ickes, Franklin Roosevelt liked Hugo Black a great deal. The president thought that while he was perhaps not as well trained as others, Black would make a good justice because of his support for the New Deal.[90] Douglas claimed that Roosevelt favored Black for three reasons: Black's use of the Senate's investigative role to shape public opinion about needed reforms, his strong voting record in the Senate, and his early support for Roosevelt in 1933.[91] In the final anal-ysis, Douglas insisted, the president chose Hugo because he wanted "to throw a 'tiger,' as he put it, into the Court—an outstanding opponent of all that the old Court had done. Happily," concluded Douglas, "Black had greatness as well, but Roosevelt could hardly be expected to know that."[92]

Black initially rejected the idea. He had no real desire to leave the Senate because he really "preferred the rough and tumble and the opportunity for real pol-icy-making."[93] His wife, however, hated the cacophony of politics, and his younger son, Sterling, was not well. Hugo had been thinking of how he could spend more time with his family. Largely for that reason, he said that he would think the pro-posal over and get back to Minton the following day.

That evening, Josephine persuaded him to take the opportunity, and the next day he informed his friend Shay Minton that he would accept the appointment if it were offered to him. Word finally got to Cummings, who informed Roosevelt, and on August 11, 1937, Roosevelt summoned the senator to the White House. "Hugo," he said, showing him the presidential commission that is sent to the Senate for its confirmation, "I'd like to write your name here."[94] After seeing Roosevelt write his name, the senator quickly left the White House. On Friday, August 13, 1937, President Roosevelt formally sent the name of Hugo Black to the Senate.

The only people who knew of this transaction before the Friday announcement were the president, Cummings, Minton, the senator, and his family. At no time did Black's former membership in the Klan come up. James Farley, Roosevelt's close adviser and then postmaster general, had visited the White House on Thursday evening, and the president had not mentioned the appointment even to him.[95] When the nomination was read to the Senate by Vice President John Nance Garner, "it produced the effect of an explosive shell"; incredulity and then "a dark and fruitless irritation" spread in the Senate.[96] A week later, *Time* reported that "the nomination fell as a bombshell to the press" as well. To a person, the report continued, the Senate's anti–New Deal clique "saw the appointment as a Roosevelt trick to ram the furthest Left-winger available down the Senate's throat."[97]

Henry Ashurst, Black's Senate colleague, broke the tension (for many senators still considered Black an uncultured redneck supported by the hated Klan) when he asked for immediate confirmation (consistent with the practice of senatorial courtesy). Objections were immediately heard, and the Senate scheduled hearings before the Judiciary Committee on his nomination. Evidently, the president took delight in the "open discomfiture of his senatorial enemies" for the next five days.[98] On August 17, 1937, after a debate during which the Senate carefully but marginally touched on Black's association with the Klan, Hugo's colleagues confirmed his nomination to the Court, by a vote of 63 to 16.

After taking the oath of office on August 19, Black sailed with his wife for Europe. Black later told his second wife, Elizabeth, why he had quickly taken the oath: "I wasn't taking any chances. I knew that my enemies in big business and the press would inflame the public against me so much that they might get a judge to enjoin me from taking the oath. After I had taken the oath, my enemies would have to impeach me for something I had done *since* taking the oath of office."[99]

While Black was in Europe, the Pittsburgh *Post Gazette* ran a piece by Ray Sprigle in August 1937 charging that Hugo Black was a member of the Ku Klux Klan. The story exploded across the nation. The *American Mercury* called him a "vulgar dog." *Time* wrote that "Hugo won't have to buy a robe, he can dye his white one black."[100] These vicious attacks took place, wrote Douglas, not because of Black's "technical and brief membership in the Klan. That was only the facade." Black was attacked, he said, because of his support for New Deal policies, his investigations that had led, for example, to the Public Utility Holding Company Act, and his support of the Fair Labor Standards Act.[101]

Black agreed with that assessment. In late October, shortly after the Court's 1937 term began, Black wrote to his former Senate secretary, Hugh G. Grant:

> There was nothing strange about the fight against me. It was waged by the same old crowd. They brought out no new facts that have not been thoroughly brought out in campaigns in Alabama. . . . On Sunday, however, the Gallup poll showed that they had accomplished nothing. A previous poll indicated that immediately after the news broke, the public was 59% against me and Sunday's poll indicated that the public was 56% with me. Whether there is anything to these polls or not, I do not know, but I am sure that the campaign against me proved to be a dud.[102]

Roosevelt's reaction to the news of Black's Klan membership seemed, to some, most peculiar. He suggested, through his aides, that Black had deceived him. On

September 14, 1937, he told a press conference that when he appointed Black to the Court, he had been ignorant of any Klan link: "I only know what I have read in the newspaper.[103]

Interestingly, the Federal Bureau of Investigation and its director, J. Edgar Hoover, came in for criticism at this time for not having uncovered Black's connection with the KKK. In September 1937, Hoover wrote to his deputy, Clyde Tolson, that the *Washington Star* and the *Washington Times* "were contemplating publishing certain criticisms of the Attorney General and the Director for failure to ascertain former Senator Black's connection with the Ku Klux Klan before he was appointed to the Supreme Court."[104] When the criticisms of the FBI surfaced in late September, Attorney General Cummings issued a public statement exonerating the agency. Evidently, the attorney general said, the FBI had not been requested to do the background check on Senator Black. A radio announcer, and friend of Hoover's, reported that information over the air, and Hoover wrote him a note, thanking him for "squelch[ing] . . . that criticism."[105]

Roosevelt, who left for a trip out west as the new justice and his wife were returning from their European vacation, left it to Black to deal with the public's reaction. Constantly harassed by the press after his return, Black sought refuge in his sister-in-law's home in Alexandria. Douglas has suggested that this unhappy run-in with the angry public and press colored Hugo's views on the limits of the right of assembly and petition. Black's "house was picketed en masse," Douglas wrote, "an experience that I think colored his decisions in all subsequent cases involving picketing, mass demonstrations, protest marches. . . . [He] was seared by the experience."[106]

Finally, on the evening of October 1, 1937, Black spoke on national radio for about eleven minutes from Jinksie Durr's living room. He condemned the "concerted campaign" of those who sought to revive prejudice and religious intolerance by trying to show citizens that he was an intolerant person. He reaffirmed his belief in the primacy of the First Amendment's religious guarantees. He conceded that he had joined the Klan but said that he had resigned and "never rejoined." Claiming that he had many Catholic and Jewish friends, the new justice ended the brief broadcast by stating "my discussion of this question is closed."[107] Even this difficult moment had a humorous side for Black. In his radio address, according to his wife Elizabeth, he "started to disclose his secret membership in the CMA [Coming Men of America]," an organization he had joined after clipping an ad from a pulp magazine when he was eleven years old, "showing that, along with the Knights of Pythias, Eagles, Masons, Doakies, and so forth, he had joined all sorts of secret societies."[108]

Although Black never publicly challenged Roosevelt's assertion that the president had not known about Black's Klan membership, he did leave a statement in his file. In the document, written in May 1968, he said:

President Roosevelt, when I went up to lunch with him, told me that there was no reasons for my worrying about my having been a member of the Ku Klux Klan. He said that some of his best friends and supporters he had in the state of Georgia were strong members of that organization. He never in any way, by word or attitude, indicated any doubt about my having been in the Klan nor did he indicate any criticism of me for having been a member of that organization. The rumors and statements to the contrary are wrong. . . .[109]

Representative Claude Pepper, then in the Senate, also commented decades later that Roosevelt "might even have known at one point [that] Hugo Black had played footsie" with the Klan, but he "put his faith in that man."[110]

October 4, the first Monday in October, marked the beginning of the Supreme Court's October 1937 term. Justice Hugo Black took his seat with the brethren. He did not repeat the judicial oath in open court, as was the custom, because, Black had written, "Chief Justice Hughes said it was completely unnecessary. I would have repeated the oath in the courtroom had the Chief Justice not decided to the contrary. Fear of 'a sensational challenge' had nothing whatever to do with the Chief Justice's decision."[111] A lawsuit was introduced in an effort to bar Black from serving as a justice of the Supreme Court because, as a senator, he had voted on judicial salaries and thus raised a possible constitutional issue. Obviously, it did not succeed in preventing the Alabama jurist from taking his seat on the high bench.

Groups continued to criticize the appointment. The Independent Young Democrats, for example, ran an ad, complete with a black mourning border, referring to the opening of the Court as a black day, a day that will "be so mourned each year as the **Blackest Day** in the history of American Justice," and expressing outrage that a member of the Ku Klux Klan, "which organization is dedicated to racial and religious intolerance, bigotry and class hatred" should have taken a seat on the Supreme Court of the United States, "highest Tribunal of our Democracy and safeguard of equity, justice and liberty."[112] Within a short time, certainly by his 1940 opinion in *Chambers* v. *Florida*,[113] a criminal case involving four young black men convicted of raping a white woman, in which the Court set aside their convictions, the criticism of Black as a Klansman died down. However, as his friend Justice Douglas has said, the public attack was a searing experience for Black, one that bothered him for the rest of his life.

What sort of person was Hugo Black? His actions on the Supreme Court were manifestations of a strong-willed person who "combined the wisdom and breadth of vision of a learned student of history with the disingenuous certitude of a backwoods politician."[114] He was, throughout his life, a combination of the "steel hard and the soft."[115] Although gracious and unpretentious, Black was, as his wife Elizabeth described him, "an intense man [who] concentrated all his powers on whatever he was doing at the particular moment." She wrote that the "raw, naked force of Hugo's intellect and will [was] usually concealed beneath that kind, gentle exterior," but recalled the few occasions when they had a clash of wills: "I have seen the County Prosecutor, the Securities Investigator, the attorney Cross-Examiner and the Justice's analytical powers all rolled up into one."[116]

A former law clerk remembers that "at times the Judge was obstinate and unwilling to explore contradictory viewpoints." Another clerk recalled Black's "courtesy, his patience and his determination. More than anyone I have ever known he had the ability to remain steadfast in purpose, clear and sharp in thought, yet gentle and soft in personal manner of expression." Yet, as if to underscore his complexity, while some have maintained that Black was not "a 'court politician,' and did not seek to impose or push his views in any face-to-face kind of way," others, notably his colleagues on the bench, including Owen Roberts, Felix Frankfurter, William O. Douglas, Harry A. Blackmun, and William J. Brennan, found him a masterful, cunning politician in judicial robes. Perpetually engaged in constitutional explorations with his colleagues, Black was "willing to discuss points but did not seek to impose them."[117]

Black was "concerned only with his work," wrote another law clerk. "Indeed, there is no Justice more committed to the business of the Court than he."[118] He was extremely proud of the Court as a venerated institution of American government and was always careful to act in a manner that reflected well on the institution he grew to love.

Black was somewhat of a stern disciplinarian with his children. "Many times I was hurt by his harsh criticism," wrote Hugo Black, Jr.[119] Black was forever telling his sons, and his grandchildren, what to read and why each book was so important. In 1953, he wrote to Hugo, Jr., about the pleasures he found in reading "Milton's Areopagitica; Sidney Smith's Fallacies of Anti-Reformers; Mill's Essay on liberty and his autobiography. . . . There are countless other things in those volumes that have given me much pleasure and I am sure that they will give you pleasure as the years go on. Offhand I think of Pliny's letters, Cicero's letters, Meditations of Aurelius, and some of Seneca's writings."[120] And in a March 11, 1954, letter to Hugo, Jr., Justice Black noted his delight that the son "liked the edition of Plutarch." He closed that letter with a line typical of his humor: "Everything here goes on well, that is, provided being in the minority most of the time is well."[121]

He also gave fatherly advice when his children confronted professional dilemmas. When Hugo, Jr., lost a particularly hard case in the Supreme Court of North Carolina, Black wrote to him: "You had a hard case, one in which the court was not likely to feel much sympathy for your client. . . . It's all in the year's work. . . . It is time to go into Court but I just wanted you to know that you are not the only lawyer who has ever been disappointed at the dumbness of judges."[122]

Hugo Black was a compassionate, driven man who wanted to achieve the Jeffersonian–Jacksonian ideal of equal rights for all persons. As senator and as justice, Black worked tirelessly (in part, he claimed, because he suffered from an overactive thyroid) to achieve this economic and political goal. This meant a great many sleepless nights. As if fearful of running out of time in his quest to achieve his goals, he "didn't often sleep nights through. . . . He would get up at two in the morning and go sit at his desk and begin to write on a yellow pad," Elizabeth recalled. Frequently, he would wake her and softly talk to her about his dreams or perhaps read a passage from the Old Testament and discuss how it related to a constitutional or statutory or societal issue he had to confront in a case before him.[123] Committed to the dream of an ongoing and vigorous democracy from the time he was six and peered into the county courtroom or heard the raucous oratory of the agricultural Populists who flooded Clay County, Black's entire life, as lawyer, prosecutor, senator, and justice of the United States Supreme Court, was a sharply focused effort to realize that goal.

As a justice, Black's populist background informed his many judgments that were intended to protect the people's power. His experience as lawyer, police court judge, prosecutor, and senator confirmed his definition of democratic governance: the people must have the opportunity to achieve happiness, and government is a powerful vehicle through which that general goal can be realized. From his early years in Clay County to his last years on the bench, Black sought answers to the continuing problems of politics and life by turning to the U.S. Constitution and the Bible. For Black, these documents were all that was necessary to resolve the perennial dilemmas that men and women confronted.

William O. Douglas, however, coming to the Court with different experiences and a different background, had a different view of the role of the Constitution and a much sharper sensitivity than did Black to the rights of individuals in the democratic community. For Douglas, the Constitution was not enough; judges had to play a major role in the creation and defense of individual rights. What led him to travel this road is the subject of the next chapter.

 3

William O. Douglas: From Walla Walla to Washington, D.C.

From today's perspective, it is hard to believe that the most troublesome question raised about Douglas's appointment to the Supreme Court was whether he was really a Westerner. It is difficult to imagine anyone more western in attitude, image, and behavior. He was a tall, thin, horseback-riding, mountain-climbing, independent, tough-minded (others would say stubborn) character who thrived on being all those things. He was, as one of his colleagues later described him, "a tough guy" in the Gary Cooper mold. He hated cities, loved mountains, enjoyed a good joke (and told his fair share of the off-color variety) or a tall tale, and would as soon sit around a campfire as attend a White House dinner (though he also loved being a political insider).

Douglas was a complex man who was unlike his longtime friend Hugo Black in many ways. If opposites attract, then it is no wonder that these two men came together. They did share experience as New Dealers, though in very different circumstances. Douglas was in an independent regulatory agency and was later a confidant of FDR, while Black remained the senator from Alabama (never a White House insider, he was a New Deal stalwart nonetheless).

Douglas's background could not have been much more different from his friend Hugo's. To understand Douglas, one must consider the path that brought him from the Northwest to Washington, D.C.

By birth, Douglas was a Midwesterner, born in Maine, Minnesota, in 1898. It was the year in which his father, William Douglas, had been ordained a Presbyterian minister and taken up his first assignment in the small Minnesota community. William, who had originally come to Minnesota from Nova Scotia, had married Julia Fisk Bickford, a Minnesota native, two years earlier.

The future justice would later take great pride in the Douglas family history, from his great-great-grandfather's journey in 1787 from Scotland to Nova Scotia, where he was one of a group of voyage commanders who founded Pictou and the neighboring village of Alma, to his own rise to the Supreme Court. He was, after all, one of the few members of the Supreme Court whose life was a model Horatio Alger success story.[1]

Douglas was gifted with a near photographic memory, although he told different versions of a story when the mood struck him, and he wrote about his early experiences often, in autobiographies and even in opinions. He identified four factors in his early years, two negative and two positive, that he felt had shaped the rest of his life: illness, poverty, family trials, and a western boyhood.[2]

At age three, he contracted infantile paralysis, and then spent much of the next several years recovering. The family physician predicted that he would not regain the use of his legs and would probably not survive beyond his fortieth birthday. His mother administered the only treatment the physician could recommend in those days, massaging his legs with salt water every two hours for weeks. Eventually, he regained his ability to stand and then relearned how to walk. But his underdeveloped legs and residual weakness left him vulnerable to the taunts of his schoolmates. Determined to build his strength, William began taking long hikes into the foothills around Yakima and, later, to the Cascades. He eventually became known as one of the most prominent hikers and outdoorsmen of his generation, but he never forgot his physical pain and the abuse he took from those who perceived a weak person as an easy mark.[3]

As traumatic as his bout with polio was, it was but one of a number of serious challenges to the Douglas family. In 1901, they moved west to a new pastorate in Estrella, California, where the second son, Arthur, was born the following year. The family was on the move again in two years, this time north to a new pastorate in Cleveland, Washington, just north of the Columbia River. Revered Douglas rode circuit for three small communities in the area. The family had not been there long before tragedy struck.

William's father died from complications following abdominal surgery in Portland, Oregon. His death caught the family completely by surprise. William (or Orville, as he was then called) was only six, but he remembered the day of the funeral for the rest of his life. It was memorable not only for its sadness, but also for Douglas's consoling sense of a bond with the mountains, which lasted. He wrote:

> Then I happened to see Mount Adams towering over us on the west. It was dark purple and white in the August day and its shoulders of basalt were heavy with glacial snow. It was a giant whose head touched the sky.
> As I looked, I stopped sobbing. My eyes dried. Adams stood cool and calm, unperturbed by the event that had stirred us so deeply. Suddenly the mountain seemed to be a friend, a force for me to tie to, a symbol of stability and strength.[4]

Julia Douglas purchased a house in Yakima with part of the Reverend Douglas's estate and entrusted the remaining $1,900 to an attorney, James O. Cull, who lost the money after investing it in an irrigation project he was promoting.[5] That loss meant that the future justice experienced firsthand what it meant to be poor. Years later, when he returned to Yakima briefly to practice law, Douglas wrote to his friend A. Howard Meneely, "The old town got to me. I never felt more depressed in my life. All the old memories of days of privation [and] hard toil came back to me in ever increasing waves."[6]

During those years, William and his brother and sister worked at various odd jobs to make ends meet. Among other things, they did annual stints as farm workers, harvesting fruit. Bill Douglas delivered papers, distributed ice, swept stores, and, of all things, worked as an informant for a local churchman, who was conducting his own moral crusade against bootlegging and prostitution. He developed an abiding distrust of "the establishment" from his early work experiences and a sensitivity for those who were considered socially untouchable and were spurned because they were poor. He felt the sting of wealth and class discrimination, a fact that was evident in so many of his later opinions.

Douglas's autobiography reflects mixed feelings about the effects of his poverty and the impact of his illness. He claimed to be grateful that, unable to compete socially or athletically, he had concentrated on academic performance, which yielded rewards for the rest of his life. Douglas was happy that he never felt the need to belong so strongly that he would compromise his principles. He recognized the important lessons he had learned from working hard and from associating with people of the fields and the streets. He gained a healthy suspicion about upper-class morality and the hypocrisy that too often accompanies it.

At the same time, he wrote of suffering abuse from his classmates. Describing one such occasion, Douglas wrote: "The words were a lash across my face. The laughter burned like an iron on my neck."[7] He doubted his own worth because of the physical weakness that lasted long after the worst phase of his polio had passed. His words are bitter as he spoke of never having received an invitation to a birthday party in Yakima. He treasured recognition his brother and his few friends gave to his developing skill and endurance outdoors. He saw himself turning inward and becoming more rebellious. He viewed these as the forces that made him the loner he would be for the rest of his life.[8] There would always be the countervailing impulses of the loner and the man with a need to belong, to be recognized. Without doubt, both needs were fundamental forces in his life.

Later, Hugo Black would write, "I suspect that [Douglas] must have come into this world with a rush and that his first cry must have been a protest against something he saw at a glance was wrong or unjust."[9] He may not have been born an adamant defender of the weak, the handicapped, the despised, or the poor, but he was well on the way to that commitment by the time he left the West Coast for law school.

Douglas missed his father deeply, and greatly admired his mother for her courage after Reverend Douglas died. He later wrote of his gratitude for her determination during his recovery from polio and her concern for him during his difficult early years. He especially appreciated her insistence on self-discipline, particularly in his education.

His brother, Arthur, was one of his few close friends. Although he was not quite four years older than Art, Bill admired his brother's strength and gregariousness. He was the intelligent, athletic extrovert who became every bit as socially engaged during his high-school and college years as Bill was isolated. He later climbed the corporate ladder to become president of the Statler Hotel chain. While William was at the Securities and Exchange Commission, he regularly sought his brother's advice as a corporate attorney on technical issues central to SEC inquiries.[10] Unfortunately, Arthur died at a relatively young fifty-eight, not long after the takeover of the Statler firm by the Hilton organization.

His sister, Martha, who was a year older than Bill, remained at home to care for their mother as her health failed. Although she envied William's success while she felt trapped in Yakima during the early Depression years, Martha went on to become head of the personnel department of the Carson Pirie Scott department stores in Chicago. There were difficult times as well between William and Martha, but only once was there serious tension. When Martha told him she intended to marry a man who had been married several times before and whose most recent divorce was in some question, Douglas replied with some stinging letters, eventually telling her to "wake up!"[11]

In their early years, the Douglases were a strong family that provided just the sort of mutual support that William needed to deal with the challenges he faced. It was partly for that reason that he felt so bad about his own marital difficulties and his tensions with his son later in life. He wrote: "If someone had told me then that I would be divorced, not once, but three times, I would have been horrified. Divorce was, in my Presbyterian heritage, a sin, and I looked down on those who had gone that way. It is, it seems to me, the worst ordeal a man can suffer and it has for me a strong sense of shame—shame because of great failure."[12] But he was not a man to be controlled by convention, whether religious, social, or political. Still, his domestic life was extremely troubled, particularly during the 1950s and until his last marriage to Cathleen.

Given Douglas's personal struggles, physical and psychological, the West was the perfect place for him to grow up. The mountains gave him a sense of both freedom and stability. They were challenging, but they were also serene and familiar. The rivers and streams were close, and they cost nothing to enjoy.

The West was more than natural wonders, however. It was home to Native Americans, farmers, townsfolk, and Wobblies (members of the group known as the International Workers of the World); there were progressive reformers, big timber and cattle owners, conservationists, migrant workers, and itinerant sheepherders. It was big, open, complex, and fascinating. Douglas was taken by the mix, and his exposure to this diverse group of people and interests shaped his opinions.

He never liked the cities of the East, and, when he was able to do so later in his life, he returned as often as possible to his summer home in Goose Prairie, not far from the area he had grown to love as a boy. In fact, his dislike for New York was so great that he dissented from a Supreme Court opinion denying a business-expense deduction for the winner of a sales award who had been brought to the city for a round of meetings and sightseeing. He disagreed with the Court's view that the weekend in New York was a valuable form of compensation on grounds that no sensible person would willingly spend a weekend there if he or she could spend it elsewhere.[13] The New York *Herald Tribune* replied:

> Now, these are hot days, not to mention trying times, in New York, and when a Supreme Court Justice begins picking on us, it requires all our sang-froid and philosophic outlook to shrug it off. After all, we could mention that New York does have a pretty good farm (in the zoo), several sets of woods (Central or Prospect Parks), and

seashore galore (from Coney to City Island). . . . Anyhow, Judge, why don't we conclude that. . . . there are times when even a Supreme Court Justice wishes he could go climb a mountain, or a tree, or something. As a matter of fact, we were just going to suggest it.[14]

Among the many ironies in Douglas's life, however, was the fact that although he made much of his contempt for the city and his love of the West, he needed the stimulation of Washington and other northeastern urban centers. He was eventually able to have it both ways; his position on the Court allowed him to travel west for extended vacations and yet gave him a base in Washington from which to observe and shape critical events of his day.

Douglas was anything but a simple country boy. He was intellectually gifted, disciplined, and far more sophisticated than he was generally willing to admit. He was an excellent student, graduating as valedictorian of his high-school class. His accomplishments at Yakima High earned him a scholarship to Whitman College, 165 miles away in Walla Walla.

He was a strong student at Whitman, though he had to maintain three jobs most of the way through college to earn his living expenses and enough extra money to send home to his mother. His job at Falkenburg's Jewelry Store netted him more than income. He formed a long, lasting relationship with Kristian Falkenburg.[15] Even so, it was a grueling schedule and an experience that made Douglas vow that no child of his would have to face a similar challenge. Indeed, despite considerable tension between the two men, he made every effort to provide for his son William's education.

Although he returned to Yakima to teach Latin and speech for a time after graduating from Whitman, Douglas was clearly headed for some kind of postgraduate study. He had majored in English and unsuccessfully applied for a Rhodes Scholarship, which might have taken him into literature rather than law. As a result of his conversations with Yakima attorneys and his growing sense that there was a need for reformers armed with law degrees, he decided on law.

He was accepted by Harvard Law School, but, at the urging of James T. Donald, a recent Columbia graduate, he changed his mind at the last moment. Douglas set off for New York City, shepherding market-bound sheep as far as Minnesota and riding freight cars from there to Chicago. He arrived in New York with a total of six cents, ready to begin law school. As before, he was plagued by the need to finance his education at the very time when he felt the greatest pressure to focus on his studies. He skipped the first several weeks of classes and wrote a correspondence course in commercial law in order to earn the necessary funds but still performed well enough to make law review in the next year and to graduate second in his class in 1925. His financial difficulties were solved by a successful tutoring business, which brought in enough money to allow him to return to Yakima to marry Mildred Riddle, a colleague from his teaching days at Yakima High. His brother, Arthur, inherited William's business when he, too, went east to study law at Columbia. Douglas also received a loan from Walla Walla attorney Grant S. Bond, who had hoped that Douglas would return to Washington and join his practice.[16]

William's second-place standing in the class of 1925 was strong enough to land him a job with one of Wall Street's leading firms, but not to win the clerkship with Justice Harlan Fiske Stone that Douglas had so desired. Stone had been dean of Columbia Law School when Douglas arrived and had advised him on a variety of matters while he was a student there.

If the story of his education stopped here, it would seem Douglas was prepared to meet the challenge of his profession, but there was more. As Hugo Black's self-education exemplified, degrees are one thing; learning may be quite another. Like Black, Douglas was a seeker, filled with more questions than could be answered in the classroom. Like most who are taken by intellectual challenges, Douglas could point to a few classes and a number of special teachers who had fostered his development. He was most fond of his English, Latin, and history courses in what we would now call junior high and high school. He marveled at the use of language in literature and poetry, acquired enough Latin to give orations in the language, and was fascinated by his history teachers who studied history not so much to learn what had happened as to understand why.[17] Despite a kind of studied dismissal of craftsmanship on the bench, Douglas learned to write well and practiced it all his life.

At Whitman, Douglas found Professors Benjamin Brown and William Davis. He studied physics and geology with Brown, whom he credited with having instilled in him a sense of man's place in geologic time, the interconnected nature of the globe, and its place in the larger planetary system. Later in life, Douglas became very much a citizen of the world in both his attitude toward the environment and his view of politics. Davis was more than a teacher. "He was, indeed, a second father," Douglas wrote. His classes in literature addressed the political, economic, and historical issues of the period of the works under study, a linkage that Douglas saw and appreciated in his studies. It was because of Davis's influence that Douglas had difficulty deciding between literature and law as a career.[18]

At Columbia, Douglas met influential faculty members he would later get to know better as colleagues. Harlan Fiske Stone would serve with Douglas on the Supreme Court. When Douglas was appointed to the Court, Stone wrote: "I found one of my recent pupils sitting on the other end of the bench—then I knew it was time to reminisce."[19] While at Columbia, Stone was a trusted adviser. Douglas admired his ability to use the Socratic method to teach, questioning students and forcing them to learn how to learn the law themselves.

The other major figure during Douglas's law school years was Underhill Moore. Moore taught commercial law and hired Douglas as his graduate assistant to work on an antitrust treatise commissioned by the cement industry. He took Douglas on the road with him to visit the cement plants, as well as calling on him for library research. It was legal research tempered by on-site evaluations, a concern for economic realities, and management problems. He admired Moore's mind, but he was also taken with his approach to law, for Moore was one of a developing group of so-called legal realists at Columbia, of which Douglas was to become a member in later years.

Quite apart from teachers, he was shaped by critical changes in the society around him. The Populist and progressive movements were particularly important in his early years, as Populism was in Black's. While in high school, Douglas made a list of political heroes that included William Jennings Bryan, Hiram Johnson, William Borah, and Gifford Pinchot, important figures in the two movements. Although the progressive and Populist movements were contemporary and shared a number of political tenets, they were somewhat different in character.[20] The Populists were principally midwestern and southern farmers who feared the loss of the Jeffersonian ideal of a nation of yeoman farmers to the new reality of burgeoning industrial cities and the increasingly powerful economic institutions headquartered there. Economic power plays by railroads and banks in the last quarter of the nineteenth century sparked interest in the Grange, a farm advocacy pressure group, which, in turn, organized campaigns that resulted in Populist victories in several state legislatures. Populism was a radical democratic movement, local in orientation and majoritarian in character. The new breed of politicians spawned by the movement acted quickly to combat the apparent threats to established rural life.

Unfortunately, Populism had a dark side, as the discussions of life in Hugo Black's Alabama suggested. It was parochial and emotional, fearful of outsiders or those who differed from the majority. This is the side of democracy that the Framers of the Constitution had worried about so much during the summer of 1787.[21] Populist sentiment often was accompanied by a nativist fear of immigrants and racial minorities. Populists saw the city as the symbol of evil and corruption, but also shunned it as the home of the growing mass of primarily eastern and southern Europeans. The immigrants were threatening to many Populists. They often spoke languages other than English and practiced Catholicism or Judaism. Their labor made possible the growth of the industrial and financial giants that threatened life in rural America.

The Progressives, on the contrary, were largely urban and middle or upper class. They were reformers who considered themselves the keepers of America's new social conscience. They tried to take on the problems of health, sanitation, education, and settlement of the immigrants that the free market was not adequate to resolve. They challenged the laissez-faire attitude that government should assume no responsibility for social problems.

Progressives fought to reform the growing city political machines, which they saw as corrupt and interested in only their own power. They sought efficient, responsive government, free from partisan abuses. The tools of their trade included election reform. In some states, they succeeded in creating the initiative, referendum, and recall, which allowed citizens a direct vote on specific policy questions.

The progressives were not, like the Populists, radical democrats. Indeed, they were in many respects class conscious. Yes, they wanted to break up partisan domination of politics and permit greater participation, but they had very definite ideas about policy. At times, there policy judgments were quite elitist, betraying a lack of faith in the general electorate. These lawyers, doctors, scientists, and engineers may have tried to help the immigrants, but they did not necessarily view them as equals.[22] Many progressive activists were as certain that the city was the center of intellectual and political life as the Populists were convinced of its iniquity.

Douglas, like many other reform-minded people of the period, was sympathetic to both, but he was more of a progressive than a Populist. Like some of the leading midwestern and western progressives, he saw much that was good in grass-roots democracy, particularly outside the cities. Yet he was frustrated by the bigotry and parochialism of local politics and society. He would always be on guard against "the establishment" presuming to dictate what was best for everyone else, but he had very definite ideas about reform that he was reluctant to submit to the not so tender mercies of the local electorate. High on that list were questions of liberty, equality, and protection of the environment. He grew up wanting to protect the "little guy," but he was not one of them.

The Years in the Academy (1925–1934)

Douglas continued his reform efforts as a teacher and, later, as a political insider. He would continue to challenge "the establishment," but he quickly became a member of it—a status he enjoyed despite his protestations to the contrary.

After graduating from law school in 1925, Douglas joined the prestigious New York firm of Cravath, de Gersdorff, Swaine and Wood and at the same time began teaching bankruptcy, damages, and partnerships at Columbia. Given his background and his philosophy, it was ironic that William O. Douglas was not only teaching but practicing corporate and commerical law in New York City. Even so, fate seemed to move him toward national recognition as a leader in that field. One of his colleagues on the Supreme Court later observed that "he knew more corporate law than everyone else on the Court combined."[23] Douglas had taken a second major in economics at Whitman. He had written a correspondence course in business law to earn his tuition before he ever started law classes. He assisted a leading scholar of commerical law in a major antitrust study. While an associate at Cravath, Douglas worked on the corporate reorganization of the Chicago, Milwaukee & St. Paul railroad and on the bankruptcy of Kuhn, Loeb, & Co., both among the most important cases in those fields of law.[24] He later became one of the nation's leading experts on bankruptcy and corporate reorganization.

But life as one more associate in a large Wall Street firm was not Douglas's idea of a long-term career. He left New York the next year bound for Seattle, but ended up in Yakima, associated with James O. Cull, the attorney who, years before, had squandered his family's meager estate. That, too, was simply too limiting. As soon as he returned home, Douglas knew it was a mistake. Cull's practice was definitely a small-time operation. O. E. Bailey, an old friend, told Douglas, "Get the hell out of here. You'll go to seed, my boy."[25] He was right, of course. The idea of glad-handing in search of small-time business was more than Douglas could bear. Within a few weeks of his return to the West, Douglas received an offer from Columbia to become an assistant professor of law. He promptly accepted and once again headed east. He concluded: "So I am doomed to New York rattle and bang for another year. But I am so highly pleased the way things have turned out! I have seen the light. I know now what last spring I only dreamed. I know I would *never, never* be happy in Yakima."[26]

Columbia was the place to be in the late 1920s. It was the home of the legal realist movement, which Douglas became a part of almost immediately. Building on the earlier work of Oliver Wendell Holmes, John Chipman Gray, and Roscoe

Pound, the realists insisted that judges are important participants in the government and society.[27] The law is and must be influenced by economics, politics, and social reform; it is clearly more than the product of accurate fact finding and the analytically precise interpretation and application of rules.[28] Douglas carried this sense of the nature of law with him throughout his career.[29] While at Columbia, he worked with others active in developing this school of jurisprudence, including Karl Llewellyn, Herman Oliphant, Underhill Moore, Walter Wheeler Cook, Thomas Reed Powell, and Julius Goebel.

Douglas resigned from the Columbia faculty in the spring of 1928 because of what he called the "curse of the establishment." More specifically, his resignation was provoked by a fight over the appointment of a new dean, in which there were two issues, one having to do with procedure and the other with the qualifications and theoretical orientation of the candidate for the deanship, Young B. Smith. Douglas was convinced that Smith was not qualified as a teacher and that his scholarly orientation would stifle the legal realist development then so much alive among the faculty. But, as is often the case with such disputes, the argument was couched in terms of the administration's interference with faculty governance. The president had not paid attention to the faculty but had chosen a person the faculty would not support.

Douglas's story of his resignation has been disputed. James Simon charges that it is a prime example of Douglas's tendency to brag and to mold his story to fit his conceit.[30] Moreover, it is, according to Simon, evidence that Douglas was not quite the gutsy, anti-establishment individualist he is so often pictured to be. Simon argues that Douglas resigned on June 11, by which time he was assured of a job at Yale. Even so, the evidence suggests considerable independence and courage for someone so early in an academic career at a leading institution.

In the first place, it is clear that well before he had any prospect of another job, this virtually brand new young, untenured faculty member wrote President Nicholas Murray Butler, a man often described as an autocrat, a letter that few people in his situation would have the courage to dispatch. He lambasted the president's recent choice for the deanship and insisted that students had "no respect for him either as a person or a scholar," that "his lack of general culture and his uncouthness are patent," and that "his almost total lack of imagination and his decidedly deficient intellectual equipment make it not only unlikely but impossible that he can bind together and lead and direct that group of unusually promising" faculty members.[31]

Douglas also sent a copy of the letter to the Board of Trustees' Committee on Education. There was no likelihood at all that Butler would retract his nomination of Smith for the deanship. Therefore, there was every reason to believe that young Professor Douglas was going to be faced by a hostile dean, an angry president, and a Board of Trustees very much aware of his brashness. It was after these letters had been sent, and Douglas had at least implied his intention to depart, that he attended a party at which he met Robert M. Hutchins, dean of Yale Law School, who immediately obtained a position for Douglas at Yale. Even so, Douglas did not ultimately reach agreement on terms with Yale until the first week in June, by which time he had decided to move to New Haven.[32] He wrote to Howard Meneely in the midst of the Columbia battle, explaining what had happened. "The faculty was thunder-struck—and we have only from last Thurs. the 3rd till next Mon. the 7th to file our protests and make our plans.... Moore, Oliphant, and Llewellyn were out of town." He added that if the appointment went forward, he would resign. He correctly anticipated that the appointment would spark more resignations as well. "Every good man will leave. The school will disintegrate. All that in the face of the promising new project which would blaze the trail for legal education in the future."[33]

On May 8, President Butler made his reply, addressing it both to Douglas by name and as an open memorandum to the faculty, announcing his decision to move forward with the appointment. Douglas immediately made up his mind to leave. He wrote to Meneely on May 12:

> Well, the jig is up. Smith is Dean over the protest of a majority of the faculty. The morale is all shot. I'm leaving. And out of the blue comes an offer from Yale to go up there as a member of their law faculty. It's a peach of an offer.
>
> They have a wonderful dean—30 years old and a whiz. He was down yesterday and talked the situation over with me. Write me your notions. I am considerably perturbed for I had decided to go back into practice. I must admit New Haven offers a life more nearly that of your present environment and the life of the law school is marvelous.[34]

Douglas was but the first of a number of faculty members among the legal realists at Columbia to resign over the course of the next year. Yale then became the new home of the realist movement, and Douglas was in the thick of it. His years in New Haven were happy ones for Douglas, both personally and professionally.

With the move to Yale, the Douglases had the time and money to settle down and begin to enjoy themselves. When Robert Hutchins left Yale to become president of the University of Chicago in 1929, he obtained an extremely lucrative offer for Douglas to move with him, but Douglas preferred to remain at Yale. The competing job offer enabled him to leverage an offer of a named chair at Yale with one of the best salaries enjoyed by a law teacher anywhere in the nation at the time.

Although Douglas was extremely busy, he was still at home more during this period of his life than he would be at any other time during his thirty-year marriage to Mildred. There was time to have a social life and to start a family. It was in New Haven that their daughter, Mildred, and son, William, affectionately called Bumble, were born in 1929 and 1932, respectively.

Professionally, Yale was the perfect place for William O. Douglas. He was at the center of legal realist activity there not only in a rich scholarly community that included research but in teaching and curriculum design.[35] He joined Thurman Arnold, Charles E. Clark, Robert Hutchins, Wesley Sturgis, Carrol Shanks, and others who took an interdisciplinary approach to teaching, research, and practice. Before leaving for Chicago, Dean Hutchins acquired substantial funding for the Institute of Human Relations, which was to serve as an interdisciplinary research center, where Douglas worked with Dorothy Thomas and George Dession.

Yale also provided opportunities for innovative teaching. Douglas devised a new set of corporate law courses based on a functional description of the life cycle of a firm, beginning with incorporation and ending with bankruptcy and reorganization; he developed a number of casebooks based on this approach that were recognized as innovative contributions to instruction in that field.[36] Still, he was not satisfied that the real practice of law and business was adequately integrated into the law school curriculum, or into that of business schools for that matter.[37]

He and George E. Bates of the Harvard Business School spent several years building a joint law and business program, with students receiving their law degree from Yale and their business degree from Harvard. Both men invested a great deal of energy in the program, which lasted until 1938, by which time Douglas was a full-time resident of Washington, serving as chair of the Securities and Exchange Commission.

Douglas seemed to enjoy the innovation more than teaching itself. Apart from Robert Hutchins who claimed that William O. Douglas was the finest law teacher in the nation, few found him more than adequate in the classroom. Notwithstanding his brash exterior, Douglas was shy and unsure of himself. He wrote of his own nervousness in the classroom: "I was terribly nervous as I entered each classroom to give a course. . . . The students were the lions and the teacher was the tamer. Utter precision was demanded and sarcasm plus occasional humor was the technique. I got no calmer as the year progressed."[38] He was also not at all sure that his best professional contribution lay in training the sons of the rich who exploited the law in search of profits without concern for others. A number of excellent students did, however, find his brilliance and energy attractive. The most notable among them was Abe Fortas, who was to become one of Douglas's best friends and a colleague on the Supreme Court. Fortas's biographer, Bruce Allen Murphy, referred to him as "Douglas's Whiz Kid."[39]

It was, however, his scholarship that started Douglas on the road to the Supreme Court. He began his research into corporate receiverships and bankruptcy as a social scientist with an interest in law and business, but he soon became politically involved as a reformer seeking to remedy what he saw as the abuses of "predatory finance." Shortly after his arrival at Yale, Douglas launched the Business Failures Project. He commuted to Newark, where federal judge William Clark permitted him to interview parties in bankruptcy proceedings. From this study and other investigations of what happened when businesses failed came a number of widely recognized law review articles.[40]

An expert on business failures at the onset of the Depression was a person in demand. Douglas was called in by the Hoover administration as a consultant on bankruptcy to Secretary of Commerce Julius Klein, a recognized expert in corporate law and finance before FDR took office.

His studies in bankruptcy took Douglas beyond the consequences of corporate failure to the forces that brought it about. Douglas had "become a specialist in ruins."[41] He saw patterns of abuses that involved the managers of corporations, the banks that worked with them, and the lawyers who served their interests. As the New Deal attempted to address some of these problems, Douglas cast a critical eye on the reform proposals. He devoted considerable attention to the first of these, the Securities Act of 1933, and found it wanting.[42]

He was fast becoming impatient with playing the role of technical expert, dispassionately viewing developments in the marketplace from the sidelines. First, he was upset that his efforts to be detached and technical in criticizing legislation "might be taken as an advocacy of the cause of the goddam bankers, who have handled their own affairs so badly as to deserve no support." Moreover, he was concerned that his criticisms would be construed as a fundamental rejection of securities regulation, whereas his real position was that a much stronger regulatory program was required. He wrote to Felix Frankfurter:

> The Act is of secondary importance in a comprehensive program of social control over finance. Publicity of affairs, control over capital structures, control over directors, regulation of speculation, regulation of holding companies, protections of minorities are primary. Merely to tell the truth about securities is to give some protection (against fraud and excesses) but much of what has gone on can still go on with a Securities Act. . . . This is not to say that the Act should not be on the books. It should be. Its principles are sound.[43]

Indeed, the 1934 amendments to the act addressed some of his criticisms.

He was about to make the change from academic observer to policy player. In 1933 Max Lowenthal had prepared an article for the *Harvard Law Review* criticizing the role of investors' protective committees in corporate reorganizations.[44] Douglas challenged those arguments in a piece published in the *Harvard Law Review* the next year.[45] It was at that point that Congress, in the Securities and Exchange Act of 1934, called for a major study of protective committees to be completed by the fledgling SEC. Joseph Kennedy, first chair of the Securities and Exchange Commission, brought Douglas in to head the SEC study of corporate reorganization and the protective committees created during bankruptcy proceedings. It was in this capacity that Douglas went to Washington in the fall of 1934. He was there for life.

Washington for Life (1934–1980)

Soon after Douglas accepted the SEC assignment, he began the search for a number-two person, preferably someone in Washington. He found the perfect candidate in Abe Fortas, his prize student from Yale who was then working for Jerome Frank at the Agricultural Adjustment Administration (AAA). Fortas was ready to leave and was excited about the prospect of working with his mentor, but Frank promoted Fortas before Douglas was in a position to offer him a job with the SEC. There ensued a tug-of-war between Frank and Douglas over Fortas. Frank capitulated in November 1934. "I told Abe to prepare his trousseau but to stay with papa for a brief time until I can get a hired girl to take his place."[46]

Fortas became indipensable to Douglas. He was, for all intents and purposes, the project manager who carried out the day-to-day operations of the study, including staffing administrative details. Douglas was able to remain in New Haven much of the time and rely on Fortas to handle the rest. Fortas was enthusiastic about the study, but chafed under the administrative burden.

It was a huge project that involved a wide range of interviews, legal research, and survey analysis. The more Douglas delved into the practices of banks, law firms, and corporate officers, the more convinced he became that the financial community was more concerned with speculating to turn a quick dollar than with creating productive enterprises that provided goods and services for a profit. Moreover, the process was predatory, allowing virtually anything that produced money, regardless of the damage it did to the market, to small investors, or the productive capacity of the firms that the financial professionals claimed were their primary concern.

Douglas had been greatly impressed by the criticisms of the financial community made by Thorstein Veblen and Louis Brandeis. From Brandeis, Douglas took his belief in "the curse of bigness" and a sense of the danger of abuses by the banking and investment community. In particular, Douglas repeatedly cited Brandeis's *Other People's Money* as the foundation of his conception of the marketplace.[47] In fact, Douglas called Brandeis's work "a guiding star and inspiration" for himself and others at work on the SEC protective committee study.[48] It was Veblen who described the financial community as predatory, as well as making a critical distinction between finance and industry, which he considered more productive and less dangerous. Underhill Moore had introduced Douglas to Veblen's *Absentee Ownership* during his Columbia years.[49] Adolf A. Berle, Jr., political economist of the New Deal, agreed with Douglas during the early years, though his primary work was done after Douglas had already begun to propound his view of the financial community.[50]

These authors, coupled with the results of his own studies of the financial community, led Douglas to a set of principles that he repeated over and over again in his writings and speeches during the 1930s. They also guided his actions on the SEC. He began from the premise that the modern economy is tremendously powerful and interdependent. "The jungle psychology of everybody for himself will not work in an organized, delicately interdependent society," he said. Leaders of major financial institutions have fiduciary obligations essential to the operation of modern capitalism. Corporate officers have a variety of important responsibilities to stockholders. Investment bankers have a wider obligation because their institutions are clothed with a public interest. "In the final analysis they are the ones who control the lifeblood of the enterprise—its supply of capital." The purpose of the enterprise is to make a profit from investing capital to produce and sell goods or services. In the process, participants in the marketplace should not behave in ways that are ultimately destructive of the orderly operation of the economy. Douglas fully expected that in our business community a fool and his money would indeed soon be parted and that "markets go down as well as up." Businesses will fail as well as succeed. However, those normal market outcomes should not be manipulated by predatory practices. Douglas referred to opportunists who preyed on the marketplace as "financial termites." Instead of feeding on wood, they fed on other people's money, he concluded: "They destroy the legitimate function of finance and become a common enemy of investors and businesses."[51]

Douglas saw several factors creating hospitable conditions for the termites: the curse of bigness, the centralization of financial power, the separation of finance from commerce and industry, a primitive short-term, bottom-line mentality, and a private-club attitude that tolerated abuse and refused to enforce its own rules. Douglas agreed with Brandeis that the development of huge corporations and financial institutions had a variety of destructive consequences. First, "bigness taxes the ability to manage intelligently." Managers cannot possibly keep up with the critical details of manufacturing and sales. Instead, they spend their time managing the bureaucracy that manages the people who actually perform the functions of the business. Bankers lose touch with the farmer, homeowner, or small-business person and concentrate on grand strategies for making money without a sense that banks perform functions beyond simple profit making. He saw that bigness "concentrates tremendous economic and financial power in the hands of the few." Every decision by economic players of this order has profound consequences not merely for that enterprise but for the entire economy. This power discourages competition and forces conformity. It also destroys local and regional capital formation as financial institutions shift their funds to national and international markets.[52]

The growth of huge enterprises, Douglas felt, had "resulted in ruthless sacrifices of human values." Huge organizations drained the individuality from our communities and limited opportunities. "And when a nation of shopkeepers is transformed into a nation of clerks enormous spiritual sacrifices are made." Finally, Douglas was convinced that management of big business is impersonal. The ownership of the firm is distributed among so many stockholders that the managers come to behave as though they owned the organization, and they control it with little interaction with the real owners. "Values become translated. Service to human beings becomes subordinate to profits to manipulators."[53]

Douglas had no illusions that large enterprises were going to disappear. Nevertheless, he argued that it was important to try to maintain a free and fair marketplace and be prepared to take on the large firms if they were unwilling to control their own worst tendencies. Among other things, that meant that government had to be prepared to prevent market manipulation, to insist on honest and properly structured trading practices, and to take action when bankers, attorneys, and managers attempted to use technically complex and deceptive business practices to take advantage of stockholders. Even so, Douglas thought business could and should regulate itself in the interest of the marketplace. The job of the government regulator was to encourage businesses to behave responsibly and step in only if they did not do so.

Even some of his supporters thought him naive. Max Lerner, for example, thought that Douglas failed to understand some of the consequences of the ideas he professed.

> Douglas has been influenced, as I have said, by both Veblen and Brandeis, but I cannot see that he ever really understood Veblen. For Veblen's theory was not an ethical one, of seeing high finance as socially vicious only when it departed from a sound norm. To Veblen the norm itself was predatory, exploitative, and hollow; finance, as distinguished from industry, was "the art of getting something for nothing." And from this standpoint to ask high finance to be constructive and honest is to ask it to commit harakiri and rid itself of its own essence.[54]

Douglas disagreed. He simply saw himself, according to Lerner, as "a conservative from the old school."[55]

During 1934 and 1935, the team of Douglas and Fortas plunged into the protective committee study. The results of the study and the hearings conducted as a part of it were eight reports to Congress. From these reports came two pieces of legislation that Douglas had a hand in drafting. Chapter X of the Bankruptcy Act of 1938 and the Trust Indenture Act of 1939. A third piece of legislation, the Lea bill, died in Congress.

The protective committee study earned Douglas respect for its results, but also because it demonstrated his technical knowledge and his willingness to take on some of the toughest players in the financial community. Perhaps more important for Douglas was the fact that Joseph Kennedy valued his contribution and became his political mentor.

Kennedy and Douglas were an unlikely pair, but it was Kennedy who introduced Douglas to Roosevelt. When he left the SEC in 1936, it was Kennedy who managed Douglas's appointment to his seat. Later when Kennedy's successor as commission chair, James M. Landis, returned to Harvard Law School in September 1937, it was Kennedy who obtained the president's support to move Douglas into that seat as well. While Douglas quickly became a New Deal insider, Kennedy's role in the early years was crucial.

Douglas began his term as a commissioner in February 1936 and wasted no time in challenging the powers of Wall Street. He took to the hustings to explain securities laws, describe the role of the SEC, and proselytize on the proper values of the marketplace. He did not restrict his use of the rostrum to public relations. He used it as a pulpit and a means to serve legal and economic notice on financial predators. The first of these confrontations occurred in July 1936, when Douglas addressed the Institute of Public Affairs at the University of Virginia.[56] Charles R. Gay, president of the New York Stock Exchange, had preceded Douglas to Charlottesville, arguing vigorously in defense of market speculators. Douglas hit back hard, denouncing speculators as unnecessary and destructive to the interests of legitimate investors who were in the markets to earn a profit by supporting developing businesses and industries that actually produced jobs and provided services. Predators' practices of rapidly moving large amounts of money around the market exacerbated market fluctuations and destablized the flow of capital. Moreover, the lure of quick profits based on manipulation of the market encouraged abuses. The SEC, he said, intended to place limits on that sort of activity.

The University of Virginia performance was tame in comparison with Douglas's speech in October at the University of Chicago. This was the "financial termites" speech, in which he pressed his theme of the dangers of predatory finance and warned of its destructive consequences for the economy as a whole.

Politically, Douglas was able to get away with this kind of rhetoric because it was the year of the presidential campaign against the "economic royalists." The first New Deal had been a period of surprising cooperation between the public and private sectors. Much of the energy of the first Roosevelt administration was invested in restoring stable markets and supporting industrial and commercial recovery.

Once that recovery was under way, many business people became increasingly insistent that government leave the marketplace and resisted plans for major social-welfare programs.

Douglas did not moderate his tone after the election. In fact, he hit harder at a time when many observers saw him as a potential candidate to replace Landis in the chairmanship. In March 1937, Douglas addressed the Bond Club of New York. He was given a polite welcome, and his listeners paid close attention to this young man who might very soon head the SEC. *Time* reported that the audience of prominent New York investment bankers was "shocked into a state of profound grumpiness" as he accused them of conflict of interest, "economic royalism," abuse of financial power, and irresponsible behavior in the manipulation of the marketplace.[57] His rhetoric and behavior were those of a free-market capitalist. Indeed, he was lauded for his service by *Babson's 95% Republican Reports.* One of the few criticisms raised during his later confirmation proceedings in the Senate was that he was too conservative and his view of society was too close to that of corporate management. Even so, leaders of the financial community did not see him as a friend.

The question of who was to be appointed to the SEC chair after Landis was a matter of considerable interest and, in light of Douglas's public positions, concern. *Time* noted that "Wall Street hoped that anyone but Bill Douglas would replace him."[58] There was also pressure from reformers who insisted that James Landis had not been tough enough in his dealings with Wall Street.

Douglas had been offered the deanship at Yale Law School and was ready to return to New Haven when Joseph Kennedy once again intervened. Commissioner Douglas was convinced that Chairman Landis was attempting to block his appointment by refusing to leave until the last minute for his deanship at Harvard. The day Douglas was to leave Washington, Kennedy tracked him down at the Cosmos Club, where he was having breakfast, and told him to expect a call from FDR. The call came almost immediately. The president said, "Unpack your bag—you are the new chairman of the Securities and Exchange Commission."[59]

The new job was a challenge right from the start. First, there was the predictable reaction to his appointment from the financial community. He also received criticism from an unexpected source. The same Yakima *Republic* for which he had been a newspaper carrier as a boy, the paper that had greeted his appointment to the commission in 1936 with pride and praise, ran an editorial that was, in effect, a disclaimer, stating "Yakima Not at Fault."

> The Yakima school system should not be held responsible for the career of the infant prodigy who seems destined to become chairman of the securities and exchange commission. . . . Certainly when he sat at the feet of Prof. Davis and his faculty young Douglas was not subjected to any germ which could later have developed into a hate-the-rich attitude of mind; nor did he in his sojourn at Whitman College learn anything that would have inspired him to make the life of a man with a dollar as hectic as possible.[60]

In addition to the external criticism, Douglas faced a commission that was internally split. He was able to convince Roosevelt to appoint Jerome Frank, who had left the AAA and entered private practice, to fill the vacancy on the commission. When Douglas was later appointed to the Supreme Court, he successfully supported Frank for the chairmanship. Frank was not only an extremely capable and experienced attorney, but also the kind of ally Douglas needed on a commission that was frequently divided in its approach to the market.

Douglas's position as third chair of the SEC also made his new job a real test of his skill and political acumen. FDR had appointed Joseph Kennedy to be the first SEC leader, a move that surprised virtually everyone. Kennedy had been involved in stock pools and other market machinations that hardly marked him as a person likely to clean up Wall Street. What soon surprised everyone just as much was that he was an extremely effective chair.[61] He had essentially established a sense of the SEC's legitimacy in the financial community. Although the market was not ready to respond energetically to SEC leadership, it accepted a variety of trading rules and cooperated with some of the investigations launched under SEC auspices—including the protective committee study carried out by Douglas, Fortas, and company.

James M. Landis, referred to by the press as "one of Felix Frankfurter's Happy Hotdogs," was presumed to be a New Dealer activist who would move vigorously when he took over from Kennedy. While he fought a variety of political pressures against the SEC that were not highly visible, he did not move in any dramatic way against the financial community and was accused of breaking faith with his charge by other New Dealers.

Douglas was expected to move the commission forward. There was little doubt that he had the appetite for the task, but Wall Street was ready for him. His speeches as commissioner and his probing investigations during the protective committee study indicated that he was going to be a tough challenger. Among other things, he had become known as a tenacious inquisitor who had shown no respect for some of the leaders of the financial community during the study. His former mentor on Wall Street, Robert Swaine, said that Douglas "stood me on my head and shook all the fillings out of my teeth."[62]

The major problem, and the principal opportunity for action, came when the New York Stock Exchange virtually declared war on the SEC, only to capitulate in less than four months. There had been tension between exchange officials and the SEC during 1937, largely because the exchange had rebuffed the SEC's pressure for internal reforms, including a much more aggressive process for investigation and tougher sanctions for misconduct. Stock exchange president Charles Gay criticized the SEC and charged that excessive regulation was having an adverse impact on the market.

Douglas took office as SEC chair just as the market began a precipitous decline that lasted throughout the fall. Ironically, Gay immediately pressed Douglas to have the SEC suspend trading, but Douglas insisted that markets go down as well as up. Roosevelt called him on the point, but Douglas argued that the only problem with the economy was the president's attempt to trim spending sharply during that year.

In the midst of this downturn, the clash between the SEC and the New York Stock Exchange over the demand for reform came to a head. Douglas had entered into negotiations with the exchange in search of a public letter that would establish a working relationship between the exchange and the SEC, as well as explain the reform measures in progress in Wall Street. Fifteen such draft letters were sent to the SEC, but the commission saw no effort at real reform or any spirit of compromise. When the last draft was refused, a story was leaked to the New York *Herald Tribune* that ran on November 23, 1937, suggesting that the SEC had been attempting to clear itself of blame for the market downturn by trying to make the exchange take the heat publicly. While the exchange had negotiated in good faith to reach some kind of accommodation, the SEC had become recalcitrant and halted the discussions. Douglas and his colleagues countered with a public statement in which they warned that the SEC was not prepared to allow the exchange to continue to operate as a "private club."[63] While the SEC preferred to defer to self-regulation of the exchange, Wall Street had demonstrated little willingness to address a wide range of fundamental problems.[64]

The exchange formed the Conway Committee for further consideration of reforms, and it produced a number of proposals. However, the leaders of the exchange finally submitted to strong SEC direction when Charles Gay had to admit to Douglas that even while the exchange was insisting that there was no need to change its practices, Richard Whitney, a former exchange president and owner of an investment firm, was embezzling clients' securities and fraudulently obtaining large loans to cover losses incurred in market speculation. Two partners in the prestigious J. P. Morgan firm had known of Whitney's activities but said nothing. There was evidence that others had known as well. When the SEC reported to FDR on the Whitney affair in the fall of 1938, it found: "Investigation showed that the Whitney firm had been insolvent for 4 years prior to its failure. Investigation also showed that Richard Whitney, as far back as 1926, had misappropriated customers' securities, and that beginning in 1936 such misappropriations became his regular practice."[65] Whitney had been president of the exchange from 1930 to 1935.

On March 8, the day after Gay revealed his information about Whitney, Douglas called for an immediate investigation and announced that the SEC would become directly involved in reforming the exchange. When a lawyer for the stock exchange asked Douglas if there were any questions that he wanted to ask of the exchange officers, Douglas "leaned across the table" and said, "There's just one question I'd like to ask. . . . 'Where do you keep the paper and pencils.'"[66]

Throughout 1938 and 1939, until his appointment to the Court, Douglas continued his speaking crusade for an honest market as the SEC took on the broad problem of implementing the Public Utility Holding Company Act and more specific technical market practices under the Securities Acts of 1933 and 1934.

Justice William O. Douglas (1939–1975)

Douglas often told the story of how surprised he was when FDR had him summoned from a golf course one Sunday morning in March 1939 to offer him the seat on the Supreme Court that Louis Brandeis had occupied. He may not have known that he was going to be appointed, but he was extremely grateful to those who worked to obtain the appointment for him. Less than a month later, on April 17, 1939, Justice William O. Douglas joined the brethren. He would remain on the bench longer than any other justice in Supreme Court history.

Douglas had not heard of Justice Brandeis's February 13 resignation until he attended a cocktail party in Georgetown that evening. Arthur Krock of the *New York Times* proposed a toast to the next Supreme Court justice. Douglas professed surprise when he learned that the toast was in his honor. Krock explained that he and Justice Brandeis were promoting his candidacy and that the matter had been settled when Krock suggested Douglas to Attorney General Frank Murphy, who was then trying to think of an alternative to Senator Lewis Schwellenbach of Washington, whom Murphy disliked. As Justice Robert Jackson told the story, Thomas (Tommy the Cork) Corcoran promoted Douglas, and Murphy endorsed the idea. Murphy joined Douglas on the Court just a year later, and Jackson followed in 1941.[67]

The president wrote to Senator Schwellenbach, "For more than two weeks I have been confronted with the making of a choice between two old friends—you and Bill Douglas."[68] Schwellenbach had detractors in the executive branch and in the Senate. Douglas had no such liabilities, at least not among people who mattered to FDR in this regard. For Douglas, like Black, was a bona fide New Dealer.

The second, and more serious, issue was that Douglas was then technically a resident of Connecticut, though he was by character and by background a Westerner. It was essential to establish Douglas as a bona fide western representative, which Jerome Frank worked behind the scenes to do. He contacted Senators Borah of Idaho and Bone of Washington, obtaining their endorsements of Douglas as a Westerner in late February. He then wrote to Attorney General Frank Murphy:

> [Senator Borah] authorized me to say that he would be glad, at any time, if you should ask him to do so, to advise you or the President that he considers William O. Douglas a Westerner and is confident that, if Douglas were appointed to the Supreme Court, that appointment would generally be considered as in all respects satisfying the demand for the appointment of a Western man. He would also be glad to say that he considers Douglas eminently qualified to sit on the Supreme Court. He told me that sentiment in favor of Douglas on the Hill has grown to such a point that, in his opinion, his appointment would be exceedingly popular with most Western Senators.[69]

At forty, Douglas was one of the youngest nominees to be elevated to the nation's highest court. His youth was envied by at least one of his colleagues. Harlan Fiske Stone wrote, "You are fortunate in being able to begin at a good age, forty. How much I would have enjoyed the years between forty and fifty on the Court, and how much more it would have meant to the influence and success of my work." His former law school professor welcomed him. "I hardly know whether to congratulate one who had been picked to march in our chain gang, but I do know that I shall welcome you heartily as a colleague, and look forward to some years of association with you in what is really a great job, despite all its drudgery and confinement."[70] The Court was to be Justice William O. Douglas's home for nearly four decades. He brought to it a passion for justice, brilliance of mind, and technical legal skill honed during his fast-paced journey from one Washington to the other.

≈

Talented, and toughened by experience, Douglas burst onto the public stage in a way that few who knew of his early life would have anticipated. He was an individualist who revelled in his image as a loner and yet needed to be accepted in circles of power and influence. His nostaglia for the western life style did not displace his need for political and intellectual stimulation. Douglas tried early on to go home again but could not. He remained for many years a restless, energetic man who found it hard to settle down. He was a technical expert who was more interested in big questions than in the details.

He loved a studied informality. He liked to play with society and institutions, but he always wanted to be in control. For instance, it was common for Douglas to tell stories that dropped numerous important names one moment and promptly turn to tales of hard drinking and ribald humor the next. It was as though he was daring polite society and his critics to take him on. Still, he never was so accepted in the circles of power that he became complacent. There was always a tension, always a drive to do something new and different. And what was true of his public life was true for a period of his private life as well.

Politically and philosophically, he was an iconoclast. His legal realism was a serious commitment to challenge the law to meet the needs of society that it was created to serve. He insisted that capitalism was the right path, but only if mechanisms could be found to ameliorate its harsh consequences on the weak, needy, and powerless. It had to be made to operate so that the little guy playing by the rules had a fighting chance. His politics were liberal and progressive, but not predicated on a particularly optimistic assessment of human character. He was not a liberal who thought that people were in any sense perfectible. He had an immediate distrust of people with power, whether financial, political, or religious. Douglas took to heart Brandeis's warnings of the curse of bigness and fought it wherever he found it in American society. And he agreed, too, with Brandeis's assertion that one of the core American constitutional values was the right to be let alone.

He did not trust power in the hands of an unbridled majority any more than he did in the possession of corporate executives. The establishment was not just the elite: it was the society that enshrined values which placed excessive constraints on individual liberty, that punished nonconformity and celebrated mediocrity.

Douglas had important friendships, and he could be the life of the party. He could communicate with people from all walks of life, and yet he had difficulty being intimate. His ability to turn to ice was difficult for his family to understand or accept; it was painful for his children, much to his regret, and his marriages suffered.

Yet some of the qualities that made him such a tough and often difficult man equipped him well for the battles to come. They predisposed him to be the defender of liberty and champion of the weak. He did not come to the Court having thought much about many such issues, yet he came with a commitment to individualism and freedom as well as an abiding distrust of power.

But Black and Douglas are not to be understood without a careful look at their experiences during the New Deal era. It was an important formative part of both their lives. It brought them together, shaped the institution on which they were to serve for the rest of their lives, and set some of the critical terms of debate for years to come.

 4

Black and Douglas
as "New Dealers"

On one level, the New Deal was an extraordinarily pragmatic and, in some ways, surprisingly conservative attempt to solve a problem, the Great Depression. On another, it was a set of bold experiments in policy making, but even more it was a revolution in the way Americans thought about the role and responsibilities of government. Its arrival signaled the demise of an era in American economic, political, legal, and social life: the day of the Gospel of Wealth. Douglas and Black, who came from such different backgrounds to spend their professional lives in Washington, grew up in the age of laissez faire and saw the brutal consequences of a raw, uncontrolled, expanding industrialism that deprived the masses of workers of their dignity, economic security, and a decent living wage. Both Black and Douglas became central figures in the Roosevelt administration's New Deal, though they assumed very different roles. While both men played a part in shaping the New Deal, both were also, in part at least, shaped by it. To understand them as justices of the Supreme Court, one must understand them as New Dealers.

Black was among the elected New Dealers, a collection of legislators and a president who ran more than once on a set of assertions about government's role in addressing the problems of a troubled America. At the same time, these innovative New Dealers insisted that the federal government had to do a better job of enforcing existing laws. In particular, they reminded the executive branch that it was the duty of the federal government to protect the individual and the small-business person against financial abuses at the hands of powerful banks and corporations.

Douglas was one of the appointed New Dealers, the group of academics and professionals recruited by Tommy Corcoran, Ben Cohen, Jim Farley, and Felix Frankfurter to design and implement policies under the direction of the Roosevelt White House. It was in describing these people that the phrase "the best and the brightest" was coined (long before David Halberstam popularized it in the title of his book about the Kennedy and Johnson administrations). These two groups of

54

players were of two quite different political generations, those of the first and second New Deals.

Unlike present-day assumptions, the first New Deal was surprisingly conservative in a number of ways. The administration worried about stabilizing the markets, supporting financial institutions and businesses, and responding to the capital needs of the marketplace.[1] The FDR insiders in the first administration tended to be the more moderate Democrats, rather than the much more liberal circle of advisers closest to the president during and after the 1936 campaign.[2]

There was relatively limited action in the early years on public works and public relief. Even some of the programs with a strong human-service orientation, such as Social Security, tended to have a great deal to do with ensuring purchasing power and not solely with providing social welfare. As Secretary of Labor Frances Perkins put it: "If we are to maintain a healthy economy and thriving production, we need to maintain the standard of living of the lower income groups who constitute ninety per cent of our purchasing power."[3] Jobs programs were viewed as help for the victims of the crash, yes, but they were also seen as critical steps in restoring the marketplace and the economy it supported.

The government, in its efforts to regulate the financial community, was less the cop on the beat than the police officer directing traffic. Programs like the National Industrial Recovery Act (NIRA) regulated business practices, but the codes were written largely by the businesses themselves.

With the second New Deal, by contrast, government's relationship with business became more combative. The first change was an increasing willingness to take on private-sector critics. President Roosevelt ran in 1936 on the "economic royalist" theme attacking corporate abuse.[4] By late 1935, business spokesmen were increasingly strident in their criticism of the administration. In December, the president of the National Association of Manufacturers warned, "Industry, much against its will, has been forced, in sheer self-defense to enter the political arena or be destroyed as a private enterprise."[5]

Roosevelt fired back in his 1936 State of the Union Address, attacking what he termed the "resplendent economic aristocracy."[6] He pulled out all the stops in his acceptance speech at the Democratic Convention in Philadelphia in which an attack on the economic royalists was his central theme; he warned about the "privileged princes" who wanted to exercise the power of "economic dynasties."[7] By the end of the campaign, the battle had been fully joined. He cautioned about the need to block the economic royalists' efforts to take control of government, for "Government by organized money is just as dangerous as Government by organized mob."[8] In October, the president ended a speech in Madison Square Garden (an appropriate forum indeed) with the declaration,

> Never before in all our history have these forces been so united against one candidate as they stand today. They are unanimous in their hate for me—and I welcome their hatred....
>
> I should like to have it said of my first Administration that in it the forces of selfishness and of lust for power met their match.... I should like to have it said of my second Administration that in it these forces met their master.[9]

FDR rejected business's claims that the economy was recovering and the task of government was finished. Not so, argued Roosevelt. There was a lag between economic recovery for business and recovery in the day-to-day lives of the many Americans suffering the effects of the Depression. Moreover, he was unwilling to allow business to return to the same abuses that had helped bring about the crash in the first place.[10] From now on, it seemed, there would be a constable around the corner: a regulatory agency with the intention of staying out of the way of routine business but ready to take action if necessary against crime in the suites.

There was also growing tension between FDR and the holdovers from the Gilded Age who regarded the president as a traitor to his class. Many of these well-heeled families were Roosevelt's neighbors in the stately mansions overlooking the Hudson River in upstate New York. But FDR was a classic conservative in the British tradition, who saw duty associated with power. It was the duty of the powerful, including the leaders of government, to respond to the needs of the poor. To FDR, those who criticized efforts to meet that responsibility refused to accept the obligations that come with wealth, status, and power.[11] Since the social elite would not accept that responsibility, the New Deal administration would.

There was also conflict with the judiciary, as the Hughes Court, dominated by the so-called four horsemen—Justices Sutherland, Van Devanter, Butler, and McReynolds—led the assault on New Deal statutes like the Agricultural Adjustment Act, the McGuffy Coal Act, and portions of the NIRA.[12] In a bold tour de force, Roosevelt took on the Court in his famous attempt to get a Court-packing bill through Congress that would allow him to add new members, presumably New Deal supporters, to the high bench. While FDR ultimately prevailed in changing the Court through his appointments, the direct attack on the Court failed.

Senator Hugo Black was a vigorous supporter, "but participated little" in the Senate debate surrounding Franklin Roosevelt's plan to pack the Supreme Court, which he delivered to the Senate in February 1937.[13] The battle raged over the plan until mid-July and was finally defeated when Democrats deserted the president on the issue. Indeed, FDR suffered a rare political defeat through the surprisingly effective campaign against the plan by Chief Justice Charles E. Hughes.

The White House was also ready for conflict with Capital Hill, if necessary, though congressional elections in 1934 and 1936 meant that challenges to New Deal programs would not be principally partisan matters. Instead, the disputes were often disagreements within the Democratic party about whether New Deal policies were moving quickly enough in the direction of economic and social recovery. The conflict with the Supreme Court caused controversy in Congress, as FDR's unsuccessful battle to pass his Court-packing bill cost him legislative support on other matters.

During the second New Deal, the administration necessarily became more attentive than before to the international arena. The storm clouds in Europe and the Far East presaged World War II, with its profound effects on the place of the United States in world affairs. By that time, however, a number of key New Dealers, including Douglas and Black, had taken up new roles on the United States Supreme Court.

Black and the New Deal in Congress

The Depression continued in earnest in Alabama as Black announced his candidacy for a second term in 1932. He ran on the Democratic party ticket with presidential hopeful Franklin D. Roosevelt. In the campaign, Black vigorously campaigned for the New Deal as a means of overcoming the economic despair brought about by the inaction of the Hoover administration. In November, Black handily won reelection, and Roosevelt slaughtered Hoover. Roosevelt's New Deal had arrived.

While it is true that Hugo Black was a political ally of FDR's on a number of occasions, including the 1932 and 1936 campaigns, he was not really a White House insider. And like another member of the elected New Deal appointed to the Court by FDR, Senator James Byrnes (D-S.C.), he was not always in agreement with the president. Indeed, Black's power base and his legislative agenda were quite his own.

Black built his senatorial career on his advocacy of the legislative agenda born of the southern populism (with a small *p*) that had brought him to Washington in 1926 and that gathered momentum with the onset of the Great Depression. Given his Jeffersonian concern for rights and his Old Testament righteousness, he turned to crusading for the masses of Americans who were suffering from the evils of bigness and monopoly. Since his days of challenging the corporate landlords of Birmingham, Black had been critical of monopoly. Black used to tell his son that he would "bust 'em up into little firms."[14] He attacked monopoly from the Senate floor:

> Monopoly must be discouraged. . . . Chain groceries, chain dry good stores, chain drugstores, here today and merged tomorrow, grow in size and power. Railroad mergers, giant power monopolies, bank mergers, steel mergers, all kinds of mergers, concentrate more and more power in the hands of the few. In the name of efficiency, monopoly is the order of the day. . . . We are rapidly becoming a nation of a few business masters and many clerks and servants. The local business man and merchant is passing, and his community loses its contribution to local affairs as an independent thinker and executive.[15]

With the crash of 1929, the Seventy-first Congress had new economic concerns to deal with, and Black was involved in these debates. Farmers were suffering from low prices, huge farm surpluses, floods, and storms. But nothing much could be done under the Hoover administration. Foreign markets were poor, and, inexorably, the market indicators began to drop. Black fought the highly restrictive Smoot-Hawley tariff in 1930, pressed his committee investigations into abuses of public-utility holding companies, and exposed attempts by the power companies to use deception and inappropriate lobbying tactics to block reform.

In addition, Black saw that the secret to ending the economic disaster was to provide people with jobs. Amercia's financial problems were in large part due, he told his son, to "too little purchasing power of the needy consumer."[16] Black blasted President Hoover's claims that the ills of the nation could be solved by the private sector without the federal government. In response to a *New York Times* query about Hoover's moratorium on war-debt payments for European nations, Black retorted sharply, "Our crisis is not in Europe. It is in America."[17] But the vehicle that he used to gain wider popular support and power on Capitol Hill was his skill as the grand inquisitor of the New Deal Senate.

After the 1928 election, Black turned his attention to the congressional-investigation process. He had been a prosecutor in Jefferson County and had a recollection of the Teapot Dome hearings. In short order, Senator Black, the legislator with the "bulldog tenacity"[18] who always went for the "jugular,"[19] was investigating the U.S. Shipping Board. Hugo Black, wrote William O. Douglas, used the congressional investigation as it had never been used before, as an "instrument to achieve reform." Hugo Black used the committee investigation to mold public opinion on the need for reforms. To an executive who had written to Black complaining about the tactics of the investigating committee, Black wrote, in February 1936, "I consider their work to be most useful and most necessary, if graft, corruption and privilege are to be exposed and punished for the public welfare."[20]

Black wrote about his investigative work for *Harper's Magazine* in 1936. In his essay, entitled "Inside a Senate Investigation," he said that "there is no power on earth that can tear away the veil behind which powerful and audacious and unscrupulous groups operate save the sovereign legislative power armed with the right of subpoena and search." Investigations, Senator Black noted, had produced important legislation, saved the public millions of dollars, and led to the collection of millions of dollars of back taxes, "but most valuable of all, this power of the probe is one of the most powerful weapons *in the hands of the people* to restrain the activities of powerful groups who can defy every other power."[21] Black concluded that, with all the difficulties, "congressional investigations are among the most useful and fruitful functions of the national legislature."

By the summer of 1935, Hugo Black had been dubbed the Senate's "Chief Ferret" by one newspaper and, more ominously, "the Senate's No. 1 Inquisitor" by *Time*.[22] The labels resulted from a number of Senate committee investigations led by Black that produced nationwide publicity and important legislative action. Yet the titles carried a critical edge to them, suggesting questionable uses of congressional-investigation powers.

The first of Senator Black's investigations began as an inquiry into subsidies in the form of mail contracts to the marine-shipping industry and expanded into an even more careful examination of the administration of airmail contracts. The shipping probe had two key parts. The committee examined direct federal subsidies to the shipping firms through sales of vessels by the Shipping Board to the companies at bargain-basement prices, financed by loans at interest rates well below the prevailing capital market.[23] In one case, the investigators found, a company had been provided with "$27 of the taxpayers' money for every $1 of its own that it laid out to purchase ships"; the companies were permitted these opportunities despite the fact that some of them were simultaneously in arrears on existing debts to the government and had substantial debts to various banks.[24] Notwithstanding the companies' financial difficulties, several of the firms' leaders were paid high commissions and dividends on the ship transactions while the businesses reported losses. The committee investigators' other task was to assess operating subsidies in the form of mail contracts awarded to the same companies.

The Merchant Marine hearings got under way in the Senate in September 1933, and Black's name was soon on the front pages of newspapers across the nation. Here was the senator from Alabama bringing to the witness stand some of the biggest names in the shipping industry, including J. E. Dockendorff of American Diamond Lines, J. Stanley Dollar of Dollar Steamships, and Henry Herberman of the Export Steamship Corporation. These celebrity witnesses looked very bad under the bright light of national publicity. Testimony demonstrated that forty-seven of fifty-two ocean-mail contracts had been obtained without competitive bidding. The contracts went to firms whose ships were built or refurbished at the government's expense and sold to shipping firms at give-away prices under terms that made it possible to make large profits with little or no capital investment.

Newspapers carried stories filled with financial numbers that boggled the minds of Americans in the throes of the Depression. Black introduced evidence showing that the marine subsidies totaled more than $400 million, and there were strong indications that those dollars had been badly mismanaged. It appeared that it had cost the government as much as $66,000 a pound to send mail overseas.[25] The investigation recalled the Teapot Dome days and catapulted the Senate committee chairman into the limelight.[26] Publicity was widespread, even though part of the case against the shipping interests was that they had lobbied news organizations not to publish stories about any revelations that might come from the Senate investigation.[27] The hearings also found that the shipping interests' lobbying efforts had extended to Congress and the White House. Witnesses admitted having offered free ocean voyages to legislators and executive officials.

The Merchant Marine portion of the investigations did produce legislative action, the Merchant Marine Act of 1936, but it was Black's development of the airmail story that was really explosive.[28] The airmail hearings ultimately provided evidence of abuses that simply had to be dealt with, even if the consequences were severe—and they were.

According to Arthur Schlesinger's version of the story. Senator King (D-Utah), a member of the special committee, argued in favor of including the issue of airmail contracts in the inquiry. It was then that Black learned that a reporter for the Hearst papers had obtained information suggesting that Hoover's postmaster general had avoided competitive bidding procedures, deliberately using the mail contracts to close out small air carriers and support the development of those companies that were emerging as the leading airlines in the industry. It was information that the Hearts papers did not publish.[29]

The evidence indicated that former Postmaster General Walter F. Brown had convened meetings in Washington during May and June 1930 at which he proposed splitting the airmail business among the leaders of the growing airline industry. He had avoided competitive-bidding procedures and paid substantially more than was necessary in airmail contracts to such an extent that some of the executives involved openly said that practices would have been plainly illegal if they had not been sponsored by the federal government. James Farley, Brown's New Deal successor, claimed in a letter to Black's committee that the overpayments had totaled approximately $47 million since 1930. The letter explained that because the contracts were obtained through "conspiracy or collusion," Farley felt himself obliged under the law to cancel all of them immediately; the mail would be flown by the Army Air Corps. The cancellation meant that Air Corps pilots were required on a week's notice in the middle of February to undertake flight duties for which they were ill-equipped and untrained. Six Army fliers died in less than a week.[30]

No less a national figure than Charles A. Lindbergh attacked the decision to terminate the contracts, but Lindbergh had to defend himself against changes that he was on the payroll of the airlines that had the most to lose.[31] Lindbergh and other critics scored points in their testimony, though, not because there was widespread agreement with the challengers' broad claims against the Roosevelt administration's approach to the airmail revelations, but because the Air Corps alternative was a disaster. When the reformed contract airmail service was launched, the delivery was far more efficient than before and the savings over the cost of the Hoover administration's contract were substantial.

The Merchant Marine and airmail hearings demonstrated two facets of Black's investigative technique that were both widely praised and loudly criticized. The first was his skill as a questioner: "His technique was to persuade witnesses that he already had the facts and merely wanted confirmation for the record. Courteous, smiling, puffing gravely on his cigar, he undertook to 'refresh' their memories, leading them imperceptibly into admission which enabled him to conclude with incisive and damaging summations of their testimony."[32] His experience and skill as a prosecutor made him formidable, yet Black was a likable, gregarious man and he did not require a public image as mean-spirited or abusive. He had a flair for the dramatic. Black was more than willing to use the hearing room to present a show for the press and, ultimately, he hoped, the public.

Douglas was much less dramatic and, partly because of the nature of his position, less visible than Black. He was perfectly willing to foster an image in the press, but he was considerably less skillful than Black at doing so. Douglas had never run for office. He could do well at a party or in a speech, but he was no political campaigner. He could argue ideas and debate issues, but he was not in the business of mobilizing voters or building coalitions. He did not represent the views of a constituency. In political terms, he saw himself less as a delegate from a place or group than as a trustee put in a position of authority to stand above the fray and use his knowledge and best judgment.

Black's investigative behavior also drew attention for his use of wide-ranging subpoenas, seizures of evidence, and arrests by the Senate sergeant-at-arms. In the course of the airmail-investigation hearings, Black subpoenaed attorney William P. McCracken to surrender records on his airline clients and then had him arrested and tried for contempt when he refused to comply. The contempt finding was eventually upheld in the Supreme Court.[33] That is the story as it is often told, but there is more.

McCracken was no ordinary lawyer. He had served as assistant secretary of commerce for aeronautics until 1929. After leaving the government, McCracken went into practice in Washington, representing, among other clients, several aviation companies.[34] It was in his capacity as lobbyist that McCracken chaired the meetings of industry leaders convened at the post office by Postmaster Brown to carve up the airmail contracts and cut out smaller carriers. When subpoenaed by Black's committee, however, the lobbyiest turned lawyer and asserted that the subpoena was invalid on grounds of attorney–client privilege. McCracken refused to appear, leaving the senator to decide whether to press contempt charges. While the matter was under consideration, McCracken notified his airline clients of the subpoena, asked for instructions, and allowed them to review the files and remove whatever they chose. When word of McCracken's actions reached Black, he had the sergeant-at-arms arrest the wily McCracken and pressed his demand for a contempt citation. The committee's position was that McCraken was a party to the conspiracy to rig contracts and was acting as a lobbyist rather than an attorney.

When McCracken got word that Senate Sergeant-at-Arms Chesley Jurney was on his trial with an arrest warrant, the attorney tried an amusing but unsuccessful gambit. McCracken stayed out of sight, but left word with counsel that he would surrender to Jurney at the District of Columbia courthouse. The game was that he would then be within the jurisdiction of the court from which he would immediately seek a writ of habeas corpus. The litigation that would follow would keep Hugo Black and company at bay for some time. Jurney had seen that maneuver before and refused to be taken in by it. He informed Frank Hogan, McCracken's lawyer, that he would arrest Hogan's client when and where he chose. But McCracken still had a trick up his sleeve. The Jurney family was eating dinner at about 7:30 one Saturday evening when the doorbell rang. It was McCracken, who insisted that Jurney arrest him immediately. McCracken had an assistant in tow who was promptly dispatched for what turned out to be a writ of habeas corpus. The lawyer announced that he had no intention of leaving until the matter was resolved. Jurney replied that he had to have the warrant in his possession in order to arrest McCracken, and the warrant had been safely tucked away in the office safe in front of witnesses before Jurney had left for the day.

The following Monday, February 12, 1934, Judge O'Donoghue dissolved the writ that allowed Jurney to take McCracken away to his long-awaited date with Hugo Black. For good measure, the judge found McCracken in contempt of court and fined him $100 for his abuse of the writ. McCracken and others who attempted to evade the committee were "locked up" in a suite at the Willard Hotel. He eventually testified before the committee.

Jurney played a major role in another of Black's probes. The most spectacular of Black's investigations, known in press circles as "Chairman Black's Three Ring Circus," was the 1936 investigation of lobbying by public-utility interests.[35] It placed the southern gentleman Hugo Black at sword's point with some of the toughest political adversaries in the nation. The investigation into lobbying practices was prompted by reports that utility-company executives and their lobbyists had conspired to fabricate a grass-roots opposition movement to the Public Utility Holding Company Act of 1935. They hired people to send thousands of telegrams and letters from fictitious constituents opposing the utility-regulation proposal. In some cases, the constituents, whose names were chosen from telephone directories, existed but knew nothing of the bogus-telegram scheme.[36] One Pennsylvania congressman was alarmed when he saw hundreds of names he did not recognize from communities in which he was certain that he knew many of his constituents. Then he realized that all the names began with the first few letters of the alphabet.[37] News that company employees and Western Union officials had quickly moved to destroy their file copies of the telegrams heightened suspicion and strengthened Black's resolve to get to the bottom of the matter.

The chairman of the Committee of Public Utility Executives, and one of the leaders in the fight against the Holding Company Act, Philip Gadsden, became Black's special target once it was rumored that Gadsden had been behind the telegram scam. Gadsden was nabbed in his office by Senate authorities and immediately taken to testify on Capitol Hill before Black's committee. Senate investigators stayed behind in Gadsden's office to execute subpoenas, rounding up material from the utility lobbyist's files. Other witnesses were similarly "encouraged" to provide information and testimony.

Howard C. Hopson was a leading utility executive who arranged to have himself subpoenaed to appear before Representative John J. O'Connor's House Rules Committee in order to evade Black's lobbying investigation. The House committee was clearly a much friendlier forum than the Senate panel. Chesley Jurney was foiled on a number of occasions in his attempt to serve Hopson with the Black committee subpoena, first by House staff who protected Hopson and later when Hopson was hidden away at the Shoreham Hotel under an assumed name. Finally, the elusive Hopson was served with a Senate subpoena as he left the House committee hearing room. There ensued an exchange of threats between the Senate and House committee chairs, with Black threatening to have Hopson arrested for contempt and O'Connor promising to hold him in protective custody. Two days later, Hopson presented himself before Black's committee.[38] Black took Hopson apart verbally in the hearing room.

It was not so much his tactics in obtaining witnesses that generated the harshest criticism of Black the inquisitor, but his use of the subpoena power to obtain documents. During the utility-company battle, in one of his most controversial moves, Black demanded that Western Union surrender records on all telegrams that came to the nation's capital and enlisted the aid of the Federal Communications Commission (FCC) in enforcing the subpoena. The *New York Times* and a plethora of other leading newspapers rose in editorial protest.

Fortunately for Black, one of those who challenged him was the even more controversial publishing magnate, William Randolph Hearst. Hearst brought suit against Black and the FCC, seeking an injunction to block the FCC and the Senate committee from acquiring the telegraph records. He also asked for an order requiring that the documents already in the committee's possession be returned. His specific claim was that the committee had seized telegrams unrelated to the investigation that Hearst had sent to his Washington-based news staff. Black's response to the litigation was a speech on the floor of the Senate warning that if any court attempted to interfere with the Senate investigation, he would introduce a bill to strip the judiciary of its authority to issue injunctions.[39]

The district court refused to grant the injunction, and the case went on to appeal. In an opinion by Judge Groner, a court of appeals panel affirmed the lower court but chastised the FCC, and by implication the senator, for the "dragnet seizure of private telegraph messages." The court found that the FCC had violated a statutory prohibition against disclosing telegraphic records and that the Senate had not lawfully obtained the documents. However, it also found that the court was without authority to compel the legislature to return the records.[40]

The fact that Hearst was involved transformed the controversy from a legal matter to a clearly political one almost immediately. Moreover, it turned out that one of the telegrams in question revealed a plan by Hearst to launch a political attack on a member of the House. Once that gambit came to the attention of other congressmen, Hearst found himself on the defensive. Black then returned the Hearst telegrams, leaving the publisher politically wounded and with no effective way to counterattack.

Black defended his actions vigorously, charging that critics were attacking the investigative process to divert attention from their own culpability. He wrote to Warren Roberts of the *Mobile Times:* "You are probably sufficiently familiar with efforts to counteract committee exposures to understand that such efforts are frequently made. Charges are made against the investigators. A vigorous effort is now being made throughout the country not only to handicap the work of our Committee but to cripple the activities of Senatorial and Congressional Committees. We intend, however, to continue from time to time."[41]

He took his defense of vigorous committee efforts to the airwaves and into popular magazines. Among other things, Black argued, it was difficult to accept the telegraph company's claims of the importance of being able to maintain records but keep them in confidence, while evidence was presented that records were being destroyed by Western Union at the behest of the lobbyists and companies that were the target of the investigation. He had little patience for conspirators busily destroying evidence, hiding witnesses, planting news stories, and even generating whispering campaigns claiming that the president was suffering from mental illness. (The whispering campaign had been launched by a stockholder of the Electric Bond & Share Company, one of the nation's largest utility holding companies.) Black closed his counterattack against the utility lobby with the declaration that "contrary to tradition, against the public morals, and hostile to good Government, the lobby has reached such a position of power that it threatens Government itself. Its size, its power, its capacity for evil; its greed, trickery, deception, and fraud condemn it to the death it deserves. You, the people of the United States, will not permit it to destroy you. You will destroy it."[42]

Still, Walter Lippmann and other widely respected critics warned of the danger of Black's excesses. Lippmann observed that "When lawlessness is approved for surprisingly good ends, it will be used even more viciously for bad ones."[43] Later observers have charged that Senator Black was guilty of some of the same abuses that Justice Black condemned during the anti-Communist witch hunt of the 1950s. Schlesinger and others saw substantial differences between the two. Black's committee, he noted, subpoenaed only material related to its legislative purpose and conducted an investigation that was intended to produce lesislation, not merely to expose its targets to public derision. "His manner was tough, even brutal, but it was impersonal. He questioned the motives of few and the patriotism of none. He did not slander reputations, drag in innocent persons, or indulge in promiscuous character assassination. . . . Above all, the Black Committee inquired into people's action, not their opinions; into what they did, not what they thought."[44] Douglas, who had a national reputation as an investigator in his own right, agreed with that assessment. He adamantly rejected Black's critics' comparisons of his actions with those of Senator Joseph McCarthy or the House Un-American Activities Committee.[45]

Hugo Black was not just the Senate sleuth. He had an agenda of his own that was partly positive, imaginative, even radical in character and partly defensive, protective, and conservative. Probably nothing better typified Justice Black the populist than his call for a thirty-hour workweek. His opposition to the antilynching bill was also Black the southern populist at work.

Black was shortly to become, in some respects, the quintessential elected New Dealer. Indeed, he was soon seen as "one of the most liberal of the New Deal senators."[46] One of the very first actions he took, after Roosevelt became president, was to resubmit his radical thirty-hour bill, which was initially submitted during the December 1932 lame-duck session of Congress. The bill would have prohibited the movement in interstate commerce of any manufactured or mined products produced by workers who worked more than thirty hours a week or six hours a day.

He stayed with the effort to shorten the workweek until 1937, when the Fair Labor Standards Act was enacted. His reasons were essentially two, and both were drawn from the work of writers like Arthur Dahlberg, who championed the reduced workweek.[47] First, Black argued that the existing wage structure and working conditions were essentially unfair. The industrial revolution that was to have brought increased leisure and an improved standard of living for everyone had expanded wealth in the form of profits for industrial owners and operators, but it had not filtered down to most of those who labored for a wage or salary. Moreover, there was no reason to expect that that situation was going to change except by legislation, since labor had never been in sufficiently short supply to produce meaningful leverage of the sort that would generate increased wages.

Black's second point, and the one most immediately applicable to the Depression in which the nation found itself, was that the most effective way to stimulate the economy was to enhance demand, which would, in turn, increase production and hence create upward economic momentum. The only way to do that was to reduce the hours of labor and increase wages. The wage earners, unlike corporate owners and managers, would immediately spend the new increment to their income and stimulate demand. For Black, it was critically important to stimulate the economy. People without work cannot buy goods, he argued on the floor of the Senate. "We need to bring about a proper distribution of the income produced by all the people," wrote Black to a constituent. "Income is what counts in our economic system. . . . A work week, and work day, short enough to create an actual scarcity of labor, thereby causing employers once again to bid for labor, would be a wholesale economic tonic for America."[48]

His approach was not to establish a minimum wage, which Black and others thought would be found unconstitutional in the Supreme Court, but to exclude from the marketplace goods made by firms that exceeded the thirty-hour limit. To the surprise and consternation of many observers, the thirty-hour bill made it through the Senate. It was in the House that the White House began to mount its opposition to the proposal, headed by Secretary of Labor Frances Perkins. The administration succeeded in blocking the legislation, but it felt pressure from Black's bill and pending public-works bills to take some kind of bold action toward economic recovery.[49] It was then that FDR called in his advisers to produce what eventually became the National Industrial Recovery Act. As Black noted to another constituent: "[M]y thirty hour bill has been stopped. . . . [T]he President has indicated that he is going to send a message asking for some kind of substitute."[50] Black later claimed, in a letter to Irving Dilliard, that Franklin D. Roosevelt had not opposed his thirty-hour bill, but the evidence is clearly to the contrary.[51] It is for this reason that Senator Black is often credited with providing the impetus for the NIRA. Even so, Black's plan was popular with many Americans, and he continued to discuss the benefits of the thirty-hour workweek throughout the 1930s.

Black quickly became one of the NIRA's most vocal critics. Instead of stabilizing the economy by developing a stronger wage base and improving purchasing power, FDR's proposal moved to stabilize prices and limit competition by creating codes produced by the businesses themselves. Essential to any such program was the suspension of the antitrust statutes, and it was this provision of the NIRA bill that became the focal point of opposition by congressional populists like Black. The Alabama senator predicted that the legislation, if enacted, would be struck down on constitutional grounds by the Supreme Court.[52] It was passed over his vigorous opposition.

The Supreme Court, as Black predicted, declared critical elements of the president's plan unconstitutional when in 1935 it came before the Court.[53] While he did not favor the NIRA, Black "watched in horror as the Court employed due process and other devices to dismantle major portions of the Roosevelt New Deal and state economic legislation as well."[54] Incidents such as this one reaffirmed Black's view that judges must not impose their policy views in the guise of judicial interpretations of statutes.

Black's next big battle, the struggle for control over public-utility holding companies, found him allied with the president. FDR had long since decided that holding companies posed a real threat to the economy.[55] Unlike operating companies, the holding companies were merely financial entities that used the assets of their subsidiaries to underwrite the parent firm's investments. The companies were huge in every sense of the term. The House's National Power Policy Committee found that "in 1929 and 1930 twenty large holding-company systems controlled 98.5 percent of the transmission of electric energy across State lines."[56]

During his 1935 State of the Union Address, the president called for the "abolition of the evil of holding companies," though he later said that he had meant to say "the evil features of holding companies."[57] Few believed that the president had really misstated his position. Roosevelt removed any question as to his views when he issued a message to Congress to accompany the report of the National Power Policy Commission. He wrote, "If we could remake our financial history in light of experience, certainly we would have none of this holding-company business. It is a device which does not belong to our American tradition of law and business."[58]

Clearly, Hugo Black saw the holding companies as evil. When asked if he would be satisfied with the regulation as opposed to the prohibition of the huge firms, Black replied: "I have no more sympathy in the attempt to regulate them than to regulate a rattlesnake." The senator who had come to Congress proclaiming "I am not now, and never have been a railroad, power company, or corporation lawyer," and who had campaigned in 1926 against "power systems [that] spring up in one state and spread their wires over many states in a titanic web that entangles the destiny of our children and our children's children," was more than ready to support legislation aimed at the holding companies.[59]

The Wheeler-Rayburn bill, later known as the Public Utility Holding Company Act of 1935, was the focus of the fight. The companies saw it as a fight to the finish, particularly since the original bill contained what came to be known as the "death sentence," a provision that would have killed off virtually all the major holding companies. The firms left no check unsigned in their efforts to pressure legislators to kill the provision and the entire bill, if possible. It was these efforts that later led to Senator Black's investigation of lobbying practices.

The bill passed the Senate with the death-sentence provision intact but cleared the House only after the most controversial features had been modified. Most observers thought the death sentence had been jettisoned and that the remaining language was weak, but their assessment was premature. There remained a section of the statute that was also labeled the "death sentence," which allowed the Securities and Exchange Commission to move against holding companies that were not geographically integrated, where no overriding justification could be found for permitting their continued operation. It was none other than William O. Douglas who implemented this policy as SEC chair.

Black once again found himself at odds with the administration when he participated in the filibuster against the antilynching bill in the Senate. While he did not support the practice of lynching blacks for any real or imagined breach of law or custom, he considered the bill a threat to the powers of the states. It was the states' obligation to address criminal behavior and not the business of the federal government. It was another difficult and peculiar position in which the senator found himself. He was joined in this position by the phalanx of southern senators. The southern legislative community stood as one on this matter. Considering it a "states' rights" issue, they argued that the national government was powerless to intrude. That was plainly an inadequate reply, particularly since the states did not act to end this hideous practice after the bill's defeat. There is little information available about Black's thoughts on the matter; while it flies in the face of his actions as attorney, judge, and justice, it is clearly a troubling part of his life.

Soon, however, the liberal Senator Black was back, this time reintroducing his thirty-hour bill early in 1937. Once again his proposal failed, but, as before, his initiative resulted in an important piece of legislation, which was later entitled the Fair Labor Standards Act. It is that legislation that set minimum wage and hour restrictions for American workers. The importance of Black's role is indicated by the fact that the act came to be known as the Black-Connery Act, though the legislation was actually written by the White House.[60]

Douglas, Appointed New Dealer

As an appointed member of the New Deal, Douglas had a very different perspective and power base than Hugo Black. His authority came from his presidential appointment, which he did not receive until several years after his arrival in Washington, D.C. When he came to the capital, he was not well known, even within the legal community. He was a whiz kid with a fistful of highly technical publications who had been given a high salary and named chair at a ridiculously young age at Yale. In later years, Douglas was fond of quoting Mr. Dooley's criticism that historians spend their lives explaining what people "died iv" but that he, Douglas, was more interested in why they lived as they did. In those days, though, Douglas was a corporate coroner whose reputation was based on his studies of the pathologies that killed firms. It was his studies on bankruptcies that brought him to Washington, and later studies of the consequences of corporate reorganizations that kept him there until he was able to enter the New Deal inner circle.

Several characteristics contributed to Douglas's rising reputation, including his expertise, his penchant for hard work, an iconoclastic attitude that suited the times, an understanding of the corporate world, and an extraordinarily quick mind that permitted him to size up a situation and move quickly and decisively. But he needed more. He needed the patronage of key political figures who had the wherewithal to get him to more influential positions, and yet he needed sufficient favorable publicity to project the image that he was his own man. He also needed political clout to support his efforts to make important changes in the law and practice of corporate finance. He earned much of his success, but he needed help. He got it as a member of the appointed New Deal.

Yet precisely because he was an appointed New Dealer, Douglas had to be able to function in the shadow of the president and among FDR's many bright and able confidants. Moreover, he had to operate between two very different worlds, the executive branch of the federal government and the corporate and financial community. Unlike Black, Douglas represented no constituency. He worked, after all, in an independent regulatory commission. But he could not depend on any independent power base to support him. He had legal authority, but he was smart enough to know that the law alone was not enough. Indeed, he worked diligently to keep the legal power in reserve to be used only in extreme cases.

Moreover, Douglas knew that Roosevelt enjoyed manipulating his people, sometimes pitting one against another. That meant that one who wanted to be a part of the New Deal inner circle and have the support of the administration had to know how to play the game, frustrating though it often could be. Surprisingly, Douglas seemed to enjoy the sport and became reasonably good at it.

What he did not have to do was face reelection. In fact, the electorate, even the informed public, had very little idea of the kind of complex financial issues that Douglas worked with at the SEC. Quickness and enormous energy were his natural strengths, but he never had to acquire the skills of electioneering.

There is a certain irony in the fact that Hugo Black was in some respects a more liberal force in the Senate than Douglas was in the executive branch. While Black was concerned with reducing working hours and increasing wages, Douglas was worried about restoring capital markets and enhancing the stock exchange's performance. It is ironic in light of contemporary perspective on the two men, but it was not surprising at all in the 1930s.

Douglas was very much part of the machinery intended to restore the marketplace and to work with business to achieve that goal. The securities legislation that created the SEC and brought Douglas to Washington was not antibusiness. In fact, SEC historian Ralph DeBedts has pointed out that the business community considered the SEC practical and useful.[61] Indeed, in the early days it was debated whether the first securities statutes would be strong enough to help the market, let along significant enough to pose a threat.

The articles Douglas had published in 1933 and 1934 calling for a new agency to enforce the securities laws, and the criticisms he made in response to attacks on protective committees in corporate reorganizations were not attacks on the financial community. They recognized the need for reforms not as punitive measures, but as changes to be made in the interest of the marketplace.[62] But his critical remarks about other reform proposals were not intended to defend Wall Street against the political demand for reform. Douglas understood that his adamant reaction to Felix Frankfurter's defense of the Securities Act of 1933 and Max Lowenthal's critique of protective committees created political difficulties within the New Deal fraternity. He had been corresponding with Frankfurter and others and developing a number of relationships that grew out of his government consulting and his scholarship. Douglas's *Yale Law Journal* and *University of Chicago Law Review* articles of 1933 had severely criticized the Securities Act passed earlier that year, largely on grounds that it would have deleterious effects on the financial community. On December 6, 1933, Douglas wrote to the *Harvard Law Review* stating his intention to reply to Max Lowenthal's article on protective committees.[63] Two days later, he wrote to Felix Frankfurter, insisting that his articles should not be taken as support for the financiers or disagreement with New Deal progressivism.

> You know where my sympathy lies. I saw just enough of the horrors of Wall Street to know that an adequate control of those practices must be uncompromising. . . .
> The doing of these two articles has caused me great suffering. The first is that what I said might be taken as an advocacy of the cause of the goddam bankers, who have handled their own affairs so badly as to deserve no support. . . . The second is that some of the things that I said might be taken as an effrontery to you and the noble cause you serve. I have not been able to free myself from either of these fears. But I write to assure you that I have no cause except the public good and no client except the investor.[64]

Frankfurter had been very much involved in drafting the 1933 act and favored using tax penalties rather than direct federal regulation to punish abuse of corporate power. Notwithstanding the fact that he served the so-called alphabet-soup agencies as a talent scout and taught administrative law, Frankfurter was not sanguine about the ability of a regulatory agency to address the problems in the market. He replied to Douglas with a question: "Where do you men get your great confidence in the effectiveness of piling everything on the back of federal administration[?]" Frankfurter observed in a letter several weeks later that Douglas was "more tenderhearted toward" the worries of Wall Street lawyers and business interests than he and suggested that Douglas took Wall Street's warnings about the Securities Act more seriously than he should have. In fact, he wrote: "What's the big idea, Bill? First, you expose your bleeding heart to me, and now to Max Lowenthal. It is of course very generous of you, with everybody agin them at present, for you to champion the cause of 'the Street' and persecuted houses like J. P. Morgan and Kuhn, Loeb. But if you are going to do it, you ought to bring your head and heart into alignment."[65]

Douglas replied angrily. The thought that he "was aligned with the bankers on the current problems" was more than he could take. "My heart would indeed 'bleed' if I thought I was inadvertently championing the cause of 'the Street,'" he wrote. In an article in the *Yale Review* in 1934, Douglas tried to ensure that his values would not be mistaken. While he insisted that more needed to be done, he considered the 1933 act as a step in the right direction. "It is symbolic of a shift of political power. That shift is from the banker to the masses; from the promoter to the investor. It means that the government is taking the side of the helpless, the suckers, the underdogs. It signifies that the money-changers are being driven from the temples."[66]

He was frustrated with the banking community, but he thought the most effective road to reform was moderation. He decided that direct regulation from federal agencies was necessary, but thought those controls could be fashioned in a way that supported an effective market rather than battled it. He preferred decentralized controls, but his experience had taught him that only the power of the federal government was equal to that of the corporations. It was not enough to leave enforcement to civil suits after injuries had been suffered, or to threaten tax penalities that may or may not be levied. An effective federal regulatory agency was the only alternative.

The SEC was that agency, created in 1934 by the second Securities Act. While that legislation was pending in Congress, Douglas wrote to Representative Francis Maloney (D-Conn.); "I hope the bill as passed will give the Commission adequate administrative powers to cope with the situation. The lack of such powers respecting the Securities Act is the chief defect of that law. . . . I have had a lot to say about the Securities Act. But my criticism has largely been due to the fact that the Act is too conservative and too insistent upon reparation and compensation and sadly lacking in preventive measures."[67]

As he gained experience with Wall Street's recalcitrant reactions to attempts at modest and generally cooperative reform, Douglas gave up the measured approach in favor of direct confrontation by the SEC. If the "Street" did not get the message the easy way that things were changing, he was more than ready to make the point the hard way. First, there were the revelations of abuses during the protective committee study. Then, after his elevation to the commission, there was the utilities confrontational approach to the Holding Company Act, and, finally, after he became SEC chairman, there was the unwillingness of the New York Stock Exchange to reform itself, even in the face of overwhelming evidence of abuses by its own leaders and members.

The other thing that changed was the posture of the New Deal itself. With the second New Deal, conflict with significant private-sector players grew. Douglas's increasingly tough speeches fit the changing tenor of the administration. It was in the thick of one such fight that recently appointed Commissioner Douglas first encountered Hugo Black. Douglas charged across town to meet Black in the Senate cloakroom. One of the nation's largest utility holding companies, Associated Gas & Electric, had pushed a seemingly harmless bill through Congress that was actually designed to save the company from bankruptcy reorganization. Douglas told Black that he and other senators had just assisted the firm, one of Black's arch adversaries from the Holding Company Act battle, by voting for the legislation. Black managed to have the bill recalled and the trickery exposed.[68]

Douglas's true views were hard to discern from the confusing and seemingly contradictory messages he was sending in his early years in Washington. He clearly thought it necessary to approach financial change in a sophisticated way, recognizing that true reform could be achieved only if the participants in the marketplace accepted the appropriate norms that made capitalism work. Therefore, arguments based on a close technical discussion of the proper functioning of securities, bankruptcies, bond-market operations, holding companies, and corporate reorganizations were important. They conveyed a sense of credibility, a concern for the practical consequences of reform, and a desire for real reform rather than punitive sanctions. But Douglas was also very much a progressive of second New Deal stripe whose personal proclivities and Wall Street experience inclined him toward vigorous national regulation. At the same time, a young Douglas on the way up in Washington was acutely aware of his own limitations and political vulnerability. Once he became a member of Roosevelt's inner circle, he was less restrained and less vulnerable.

Douglas had all the right credentials, a prestigious law degree, experience in one of Wall Street's leading firms, and an Ivy League professorship, but he was just enough of an iconoclast to suit FDR, with a ready wit that he was always willing to exercise at the expense of proper ladies and gentlemen of the northeastern establishment. There was the two men's shared experience with polio. The president loved a rich mix of personalities, and Douglas was a great addition to his circle or advisers. He was enough of a loner to move vigorously on his own, but enough of a team player to stay in touch with the White House.

Douglas, unlike Black, was not running for public office. However, like Black, Douglas gained a reputation as a keen investigator. He took on the role of financial policy maker with the same relish with which Black challenged the holding companies and their lobbyists, and, like the senator, he was ready to defend the New Deal.

As SEC investigator, Douglas was in several substantive respects more restrained than the senator, even though he was personally less gracious and more aggressive than Black. Among other things, he tried to avoid putting witnesses into a position where they could or would take the Fifth Amendment. He also tried to avoid excessive use of subpoenas. His investigative efforts during the protective committee study and after were seen as vigorous, but he was rarely accused of abuse.

He was seen by many as a conservative out to restore the markets, rather than as a populist like Black who was more concerned with challenging contemporary capitalism. When it came to the marketplace, he claimed conservative credentials. In his first meeting with reporters after having been named chairman of the SEC, Douglas kicked back in his chair and pronounced himself "a pretty conservative sort of a fellow from the old school, perhaps too old to be remembered. . . . I'm the kind of conservative who can't get away from the idea that simple honesty ought to prevail in the financial world."[69] Douglas's speeches, his meetings with representatives of the financial community, and his discussions with stock exchange officials all began from the premise that the best course was for the participants in the marketplace to see their own interests in reforming financial practices and avoid the need for SEC involvement. Unlike Black, he rarely argued in legal terms, preferring to make his case in the language of sound business practice and profitability.

On the other hand, Douglas was regarded as a tough customer who was not afraid to take the shotgun out from behind the door. When he pointed the weapons of the SEC, they were loaded and the safety was off. His relationship with Roosevelt allowed him to move with the assurance of being given White House support—or at least a promise of no interference. Douglas related an exchange he had with Roosevelt before launching an SEC investigation of A. P. Giannini of Transamerica Corporation. Douglas asked the president if the front door to the White House would be closed when he moved in on Transamerica.

> "Absolutely," he replied.
> "Mr. President, how about the back door?"
> FDR roared with laughter and said, "The back door, too, is closed."[70]

In part because of his relationship with the president, Douglas was able to maintain his independence and simultaneously enjoy political support.

Douglas was also a New Deal advocate. He enjoyed the dynamism of the times and the people, particularly during the second New Deal. Recalling his relationships with Jerome Frank and his other New Deal colleagues, Douglas wrote, "These were the heady days of the New Deal when Washington, D.C., teemed with brave dreams and bold experiments."[71] Like other New Dealers, he was outraged by the Supreme Court's assault on FDR's programs.

The New Deal Versus the Supreme Court: The Court-Packing Battle

One of the most controversial of FDR's political initiatives was his effort to pack the Supreme Court. The president's plan would have permitted him to appoint one new justice for each sitting justice who reached age seventy, up to a maximum of fifteen justices. Publicly presented as a way to help the aging gentlemen of the Court deal with their challenging case load, the plan was the president's desperate attempt to take action against the Court, which had dogmatically damned New Deal programs for which he had fought so diligently. Once the fight had begun, FDR dropped the pretense and argued that we had "reached the point as a Nation where we must take action to save the Constitution from the Court and the Court from itself."[72]

Roosevelt miscalculated badly, however, when he announced his plan in February 1937 without thoroughly consulting New Deal stalwarts. As Douglas correctly observed, virtually no one other than Attorney General Homer Cummings was aware of the president's intentions. It was not at all clear that he could expect unified support from within his own New Deal ranks. Difficulty in Congress was assured, even within the Democratic party. His failure to consult not only wounded some egos, but also made it impossible for legislative allies to lay the groundwork essential to the passage of controversial legislation.

There were other reasons why the plan proved embarrassing for the administration. First, the Four Horsemen of the Court needed at least one additional vote for their majorities, which usually came from either Chief Justice Hughes or Justice Roberts, sometimes both. But Robert and Hughes had begun to shift their voting patterns in late 1936 in opinions that were announced just as the president began his assault on the Court. This is sometimes referred to as "the switch in time that saved nine," but the truth is that votes which had already been taken in a number of cases that upheld various New Deal programs and state regulatory efforts were announced during the debate over the Court-packing plan.[73]

Second, the chief justice proved to be a particularly able adversary who simply beat the president at his own political game. He made two forceful and successful arguments in his now famous letter to the Senate Judiciary Committee. In response to the president's ostensible justification for the legislation—that of the work load—the chief justice accurately observed that the Court was "fully abreast of its work. . . . There is no congestion of cases upon our calendar."[74] Critics of the plan wondered if the executive branch could say the same. The other case against the plan was made by shifting the argument to the need to protect the institutional integrity and independence of the Supreme Court. Here, the chief justice struck an extremely responsive chord, not merely in Congress but around the nation.

Among the several interesting ironies associated with the Court-packing battle was that Douglas and Black, who supported the plan, found themselves facing the same kind of criticism that was directed at the pre-1937 Court, though it came this time from conservatives rather than liberals. They were also to become the targets of Court-curbing efforts, and, in Douglas's case, impeachment attempts by opponents of the Court's rulings on First Amendment questions, civil rights, and criminal due process cases in the 1950s and 1960s. In fact, the Republican's desire to allow Richard Nixon to pack the Court played no small part in the effort to drive Douglas from the bench. Douglas, who had advocated a mandatory retirement age early in his career, found it difficult to step down at seventy-seven, and Hugo Black was not really ready to leave at eighty-five.

There was another irony at play, since Justices Van Devanter and Sutherland, two of the Four Horsemen, had wanted to retire but were discouraged by the fact that Congress's promise to allow for an adequate retirement at the time of Justice Holmes's resignation had not been honored. In effect, the New Deal Congress had assured the continuation of the old-line majority on the Court for some time. A new retirement bill was passed during the spring of 1937 and Justice Van Devanter promptly retired in May.

Hugo Black and William Douglas supported the president's plan, but in very different ways. Black had long been a critic of wide-ranging judicial power and an advocate of efforts by Congress to check the judiciary as it exercised checks on the executive branch. He was particularly outraged by the use of injunctions to block government action and the many decisions striking down both federal and state programs. Just days before FDR initiated his Court-packing plan, Black wrote to Roosevelt advocating a change in the structure of the Court, but in a slightly different form from what Roosevelt later proposed. Black argued that two justices should be added to the Court and that the larger Court could sit in two panels.[75] Having announced his Court-packing proposal, the president wrote back to Black, saying, "We seem to have been thinking along the same or else parallel lines."[76] Black endorsed the president's plan as soon as it was announced. To radio audiences and individual constituents alike, he argued that "the President's program is a wise one, both in the interest of expeditious and efficient administration of justice and in order to protect the people of this nation from judicial usurpation."[77]

Contrary to his later claims, Douglas also supported the plan, but by very different means. Although Douglas wrote in his autobiography, "I did not favor the Court-packing plan," in March 1937, in the midst of the fight, Douglas wrote to his friend A. Howard Meneely with a very different story.[78] "The President's court proposal has Wash DC (like the nation) stirred. Feelings run very high. I am for it. I am working behind the scenes long hours on it. It will pass—the only thing being 'when' and 'at what price.' I hope the price is not too heavy. I see Yale Law is for it 3 to 1; Harvard Law against it 9 to 1. I tell Jim Landis—Dean Elect—that that spells the difference between Yale and Harvard."[79] His time was spent writing law school faculty members to arrange expressions of support and to line up potential witnesses in favor of the plan.[80] He corresponded with the president of the American Association of Law Schools about the usefulness of a poll of law professors, but the two agreed to drop that idea when they sensed that the results of such a poll would be overwhelmingly against the plan.[81]

The bill was reported out of the Senate Judiciary Committee unfavorably, with several Democrats defecting. The efforts by Senate Majority Leader Joe Robinson to pull his partisans together in support of the plan in the summer of 1937 were failing when Robinson died unexpectedly. A few days later, the bill was recommitted to committee, effectively defeating the measure.

Black was one of the Democratic senators who stood with the president through the final vote tally. In letters to his constituents, Black insisted on the constitutional correctness of Roosevelt's Court-reform proposal. In one letter, he wrote, "I have thought for some years that there should be additional members of the Supreme Court, and that the Court should function in divisions as does our Supreme Court in Alabama." To Hugh Mallory, Black wrote that the Court-reform plan was a basic congressional "check on the Courts which would protect the people from judicial usurpation of powers." And he wrote to another constituent, "I am convinced that the majority of the judges have usurped so much power that they are actually threatening the existence of our Constitution and shackling the Government in exercising its ordinary function both in the states and throughout the Nation." For Senator Black, Congress was given, by the Framers of the Constitution, the power to check "judicial usurpation." And he favored congressional use of such powers to rein in the federal judiciary. A month after the plan went down in defeat, he became a member of the Supreme Court.[82]

≈

Black and Douglas as participants in the New Deal enjoyed an independence and freedom of action to be envied by others. Black was an elected official who did not owe his job to the president; furthermore, he had begun his relationship with the administration as an adversary, on the wages and hours legislation, for example, rather than as a person seeking support. Douglas was a presidential appointee, but he too enjoyed a rare degree of independence and an unusual amount of support for a member of a regulatory commission. It is true that his appointment came about because of Joseph Kennedy's support, but Kennedy chose Douglas principally for his virtually unmatched expertise in the fields over which the Securities and Exchange Commission was given jurisdiction. And despite the fact that he was ambitious, Douglas was always enough of an individualist to stay at arm's length from other New Deal insiders. He was the president's man, with unusual access and visibility, yet his position in an independent regulatory commission gave him insulation from the White House.

In the end, both Douglas and Black were rewarded for their New Deal service with seats on the Court they had so vigorously criticized. The question became what would they and their other New Deal colleagues appointed by FDR do with the judicial power they now possessed. The answer to that question rested in part on the individual qualifications, experience, and political positions of the new justices, but it also hinged on their relationships with one another and the changing society in which the Court found itself.

Black and Douglas came to the Court with a high regard for the powerful potential the federal government and its administrative agenices had to help overcome the country's social and economic problems. Wise and strong use of the constitutional powers of the national government by national leaders, thought Black, would eradicate the social and economic blight that had swept the nation. Having experienced, firsthand, the cruelty of uncontrolled economic development in Birmingham, Black was committed to the fullest constitutional use of national and state powers to end unfair economic practices and monopolies and to develop an economic and social system in which human qualities would flower. He undertook his work as a legislative investigator on behalf of the people of America, he wrote, to deal with defiant powerful economic groups.

Douglas, too, believed that the powers of the national and state governments had to be used to end the suffering brought on by the Depression. While not accused, as Black was, of being a national "inquisitor," Douglas used his SEC position to bring about needed reforms in the marketplace.

While both men brought a legacy of shared concerns from the New Deal, and however close Black and Douglas were on many key questions of principle, they were to take different approaches to fundamental issues of power and right.

Douglas, who, like Black, was largely interested in domestic issues, became very much a citizen of the world. His commitment to individual liberty was intensified by his increasing conviction that rights and liberties at home were related to human rights around the world. At the same time, Black grew as a leader of the Court and a national figure in his own right. Still, the two were pushed closer together by their willingness to take on their colleagues and outside critics in defense of constitutional liberties. Despite their differences, though, the two men developed a close working relationship that lasted longer than any other in the history of the Court. They saw many justices come and go over their three decades together. The changes mattered. To comprehend the road Black and Douglas traveled together and the issues they faced, it is necessary to see them among their brethren on the Court.

 5

The Brethren

WHEN HUGO BLACK joined the United States Supreme Court in 1937 for the start of its October term, it was, to Associate Justice Benjamin Cardozo's way of thinking, "no longer a Court."[1] By 1936, the majority of the justices of the court, in their zeal to curb the economic and social policies of the Roosevelt administration, had seemingly lost their "judicial temperament" and were, instead, "animated by aversion to the New Deal."[2]

The conservative justices known as the "Four Horsemen"—Willis Van Devanter, James McReynolds, George Sutherland, and Pierce Butler—dominated the Court. Van Devanter, appointed by President Taft in 1911, had been a federal appeals court judge from Wyoming. On the Supreme Court, he wrote fewer opinions than any of his colleagues, averaging three a term during his last decade on the Court.[3] A contemporary described Van Devanter as a very remote and reserved, tightly disciplined person afflicted by chronic "writer's block."[4] He was able, however, to coalesce the conservative bloc on the Court. Justice McReynolds, then attorney general, was appointed by President Wilson in 1914. Known as a trustbuster before his appointment, he became the most strident opponent of Roosevelt's New Deal programs.[5] An anti-Semite, McReynolds did not speak to Justice Louis D. Brandeis, the first Jewish justice, for three years after Brandeis was appointed in 1916.[6] Douglas, who served with McReynolds for a few terms, remembered him as a "lean and sour" jurist[7].

Sutherland had been a senator from Utah, and it was in the Senate that he had befriended then Senator Warren Harding. Sutherland later became one of President Harding's brain trusters. After his appointment to the Court, Sutherland held forth as "the lucid and articulate spokesman for the Court's solid Darwin–Spencer wing."[8] Douglas described him as reserved, while Herbert Wechsler wrote that Sutherland was a "very genial and twinkley kind of man."[9] Justice Butler was appointed by Harding in 1923. Called the "most doctrinaire" of this quartet of conservative justices, Butler grew up in Minnesota and was a millionaire railroad attorney at the time of his appointment to the Court.[10] Although he faced strong opposition from Senate progessives, Butler was finally confirmed.

The "Four Horsemen," who, as Abraham writes, were viewed as the "direct descendants of Darwin and Spencer," were "totally antagonistic to the New Deal."[11] Bitterly opposed to the policies created by New Deal legislators to end unemployment and encourage economic recovery, they caucused each day in the car that drove them home from the Court.[12] They were also a regular golf foursome. They probably continued their discussions on the links, for, as Justice Douglas recalled, "they were as slow as molasses, taking many shots and consuming what seemed like hours in putting."[13]

The Court liberals—Justices Benjamin Cardozo, Harlan F. Stone, and Louis D. Brandeis—met every Friday in Brandeis's apartment to plan a strategy for the Saturday conference session.[14] Chief Justice Charles Evans Hughes and Justice Owen Roberts, while generally conservative, occasionally voted with the liberal bloc to validate some New Deal legislation. By and large, though, the Court majority, by at least 5 to 4 votes, overturned over a dozen major New Deal statutes after 1934. Given the mix of jurists on the bench during these early years of the Roosevelt administration, "the fate of liberal reform legislation appeared precarious at best."[15]

Black was joined on the Court in 1938 by Roosevelt's former solicitor general, Kentucky-born Stanley Reed, "a tall, quiet person [who] never raised his voice or lost his temper." Douglas and Black grew to love Reed, though they seldom agreed with him on matters of constitutional law and took some pleasure in informing him, after his retirement, "whenever one of his reactionary opinions was overruled." Justice Cardozo retired shortly thereafter, and on January 5, 1939, Roosevelt sent Frankfurter's name to the Senate. "Brilliant and able, . . . effervescent, demanding, provocative and teasing," Frankfurter was "a towering advocate of a cause," wrote Douglas.[16]

On April 4, 1939, Douglas was confirmed by the Senate, by a vote of 62 to 4. For over thirty-two years, from April 1939 to September 1971, Hugo L. Black and William O. Douglas served together on the Supreme Court. In all, the two jurists were members of five successive Courts: the Hughes, Stone, Vinson, Warren, and Burger Courts. Black and Douglas, both together and separately, worked with thirty of the ninety-four justices who served on the Supreme Court from 1789 to 1975, some 31 percent of all the appointees ever to serve on the Court. Some of their working relationships with their brethren were extremely stressful, while others were friendly and productive, leading to major breakthroughs in constitutional law.

Black and Douglas

Douglas, who called Black "my closest friend on the Court and my companion in many hard judicial battles," had come to respect Black's judicial work even before they became colleagues on the bench.[17] In a letter he wrote to Black while still chairman of the SEC, Douglas said: "I have just read with great interest your dissenting opinion in the case of *Connecticut General Life Insurance Co. v. Johnson.* It is a perfectly swell job. An awful lot of people will agree with you. I congratulate you on your courageous stand."[18]

Black was, as Douglas described him, one of three "ardent proselytizers" on the Court (the others being Stone and Frankfurter) and "at heart, ... a Baptist preacher" always "seeking to convert any 'wayward' brother on the Court."[19] Much later, Justice Harry A. Blackmun had "kindly" memories of Black as a "canny, lovable manipulator. He was ever the politician, ever the U.S. Senator still."[20]

If Black was the "eloquent and unrelenting" evangelist, his friend Douglas was the "quintessential loner."[21] Bill Douglas was not, as Justice William J. Brennan said, a "consensus builder."[22] Blackmun has said that, to the best of his knowledge, "Bill Douglas never had a close friend" and observed that even Douglas and Black "didn't always get along. I think Hugo in his gentle way resented Bill sometimes but he never let it be too apparent."[23] Both Douglas's widow and Brennan recall Douglas's often repeated motto that "the only soul he had to save was his own."[24] And as Douglas often did not participate in the give-and-take of reformulating a majority opinion or in other Court activities, his colleagues saw him as cool and remote.[25]

Justice Brennan, a frequent ally of both justices, recalled these differences of style in an interview. Black, he said, was a "wily son-of-a-gun" who had "learned all the tricks in the Senate" and had no difficulty negotiating and bargaining as a justice of the Supreme Court.[26] Black's arch rival and enemy on the Court, Justice Robert H. Jackson, once said of Black, "you can't just disagree with him. You must go to war with him if you disagree."[27] Douglas, on the contrary, recalled Brennan, "was very different. He'd say, 'You don't like it? What do you want? Then, he'd change it."[28] Douglas would "rarely stoop to lobbying for his own position and seemed more interested in making his own stand public than in working to get it accepted."[29] But partly because he was a loner rather than a deal maker, Douglas felt free to change his mind during the opinion-writing process, exasperating justices who thought he was on board.

Black's son has suggested that the very close, almost symbiotic relationship between his father and Douglas led to an interesting role for Black. "For most of their service together, Hugo acted as liaison between Bill Douglas and the Court, and this function must be considered one of [Black's] important contributions to his country; talent like Bill Douglas's should not be allowed to go to waste." Bill Douglas was a brilliant "loner" with enormous energy. When working alone, such a person can accomplish an enormous amount; however, noted Hugo Black, Jr., "when required to work with others, he will be lost without a sympathetic person within his particular field of activity." Justice Black was that sympathetic person who clearly recognized the special character of his friend Douglas; his son remembers being told, "The fella is a genius, Son, and he's got right instincts on social and political issues." This was especially true, he felt, in the area of First Amendment freedoms. They shared the belief that courts had a responsibility to ensure that minorities had complete protection from majority oppression. In this area of constitutional law, said Brennan, "Douglas would say what Black had said."[30]

But Hugo Black also told his son, "with a wink," " Of course, nobody's perfect—but me."[31] Black did have a lasting, basic disagreement with Douglas—and with others on the Court. His son recalled his father's view that

> the Chief [Earl Warren], Brennan, Bill Douglas, Arthur [Goldberg], Thurgood [Marshall] are usually going to do the right thing. . . . While they're around, we'll generally get a just judgment. But when they're gone and we get a McReynolds type, he's free to let go with his bad sense of right and wrong. I believe we've got to tie the judges of this Court and the subordinate federal courts to something lasting, even if we've got to sacrifice doing some good through the federal courts. We don't want this Court to be like one of these agencies—one law when the Republicans are in and another when the Democrats are in. This Court's got to have some enduring principles."[32]

Black's jurisprudential commitment to the idea that judges must be bound to the words of the Constitution was basic to the Alabama jurist. "A judge untethered by a text is a dangerous instrument," he once wrote. He tried to get Douglas to accept his view, but he was unsuccessful at persuading the iconoclastic Douglas to constrain his policy-making instincts. Douglas simply did not agree that the Court could perform its job if it refused to engage the tough cases that inevitably involved political controversy. Justice Blackmun recalled Black, during his last year on the Court, telling him sadly that "things were fine between us until Bill Douglas left me." The parting, which was an important theoretical one, begin in the mid-1960s when the Court heard the "sit-in" and the right-of-privacy cases. Of course, Douglas did not see it that way. He argued that his views in the sit-in and privacy cases were grounded on constitutional principles but that he and Black disagreed on the controlling role of constitutional text in these and other controversial cases that came before the Court at that time.[33]

Brennan recalled that Black called to compliment him on his majority opinion in the 1965 *New York Times* v. *Sullivan* case, involving First Amendment issues and questions of libel and slander. Black told Brennan: "You know I can't join you. It's an excellent opinion and I congratulate you, but you know damn well I can't join you." Brennan speculated that Black was "always frightened to death that if he joined, he might end up with the same old business that led to the Nine Old Men." Black also could not join Douglas in some opinions; while the cause might have been just, the opinion was a judgment that was not, in Black's view, based on the enduring constitutional text.[34]

From their earliest days on the Court, Hugo Black and Bill Douglas shared political gossip and personal news about their wives and children, their parents' health, and their own health problems in letters and notes they wrote to each other throughout the year. When Douglas's mother was dying, for example, Black wrote to his colleague: "I hope your mother will improve, but anyhow it will be a great comfort to her that you can be with her." After her death a month later, Black wrote, "I am very happy that your mother lived long enough to see her son on the Court. The greatest joy and satisfaction that can come to any mother is to see her children move to high positions of trust by reason of innate ability and integrity. That is what your mother saw. If her life had not been rich before, your career would have made it so."[35]

In 1941, when Chief Justice Hughes retired, Douglas supported Black's elevation to the chief justiceship. Black wrote to him:

> I greatly appreciate the confidence and friendship which prompt you to hope that I
> shall be appointed CJ–It is a burden but at the same time an opportunity for whoever
> holds the position. I mean an opportunity for service, not merely for the individual. I
> do not feel that I should directly or indirectly make an effort of any kind to obtain the
> appointment. The importance of the duties makes the President's responsibility a
> heavy one, and I would not want to add to the difficulties in the matter. . . . I shall not,
> unless I am asked by [Roosevelt], express any views whatever on the subject.[36]

On June 12, 1941, one day after Black wrote the letter to Douglas, Roosevelt sent
Stone's name to the Senate for confirmation as chief justice.

In part because of conversations with Felix Frankfurter, Roosevelt chose Harlan F. Stone for the chief justiceship rather than his attorney general, Robert H.
Jackson. Roosevelt's "heart was clearly with Jackson,"[37] but Frankfurter and others
convinced him to go with the Republican Stone. Frankfurter said, in part:

> From the national interest I am bound to say that there is no reason for preferring Bob
> [Jackson] to Stone—quite the contrary. Stone is senior and qualified professionally to
> be C.J. But for me the decisive consideration, considering the fact that Stone is quali-
> fied, is that Bob is of your personal and political family, as it were, while Stone is a
> Republican. . . . [W]hen war does come, the country should feel you are a national,
> the Nation's President. Few things would contribute as much to confidence in you as
> a national and not a partisan President than for you to name a Republican, who has
> the profession's confidence, as Chief Justice.[38]

Jackson had little difficulty accepting Roosevelt's explanation of his decision,
noting, some years later, that Stone had been appointed because of the "desirability
for a symbol of stability as well as progress," as well as it being "in the interest of
the judiciary as an institution."[39] Jackson, not to the surprise of Court watchers, was
nominated by the president to fill the associate justice seat vacated by Stone.

Once the decision had been announced, Douglas wrote back to Black.

> We were motoring across Arkansas on our way to New Mexico when we heard on the
> radio that Stone had been made CJ. I said to Mildred, "Felix has done it again." There
> is no question in my mind that he was responsible. . . . I am sorry that it did not go to
> you. I thought you *deserved it.* And I knew it would strengthen the Court greatly if you
> were the Chief. The bar—being a conservative outfit—hails Stone's appointment. But
> unless the old boy changes, it will not be a particularly happy or congenial atmosphere
> in which to work—at least so far as I am concerned.[40]

Five years later, in April 1946, Chief Justice Harlan F. Stone suffered a fatal
heart attack while sitting on the high bench. It was strongly rumored that Roosevelt
had promised Jackson the next chief justiceship; clearly, Jackson was primed for
such an appointment and was bitterly disappointed when the coveted center seat
did not go to him. At the time, there were erroneous suggestions that Justices Douglas, Black, and Murphy had threatened to resign from the Court if President Truman appointed Jackson. After seeking advice from retired Chief Justice Hughes
and retired Justice Roberts, Truman had gone to someone off the high bench, Fred

Vinson, to fill the center seat with the hope of reducing strife within the Court. With the appointment of Fred Vinson as chief justice, Justice Jackson, then in Germany prosecuting German war criminals, let go with his public condemnation of Black.

In September 1953, Douglas again encouraged Black, for the third and last time, to think about the chief justiceship when Vinson died of a heart attack. On September 12, 1953, four days after Vinson's death, Douglas wrote to Black: "I wish Eisenhower would make you Chief Justice. It would be the smartest thing he could do *politically* and the best possible appointment on the merits. But I do not think he is smart enough to do it. I shudder when I think of Dulles or Vanderbilt in the job. And the reactionary forces would want one of them (or a recent ABA President) over Dewey or Warren. Dewey would, I think, be much better (i.e., liberal) than is suspected."[41] Eisenhower, grateful for Earl Warren's help at the Republican National Convention, offered the job to him.

Over the years, Black and Douglas often discussed politics and, during the war, political opportunities for Douglas that would have meant his leaving the Court. In the autumn of 1941, Douglas wrote to Black that Roosevelt had called him to offer him a job:

> he wants me to be the top guy in the defense work—to take it off his neck; to be his "alter ego." He apparently visualizes the present defense set-up continuing. Apparently, I am to be the top holding company, so to speak. I have not said yes nor have I said no. He's put it on a personal basis—that I was the only one who could swing it; that he needed me badly, etc, etc. I would have to resign from the Court. I have no enthusiasm for the project. . . . I can think of nothing less attractive—except practicing law in New York City. . . . Of course, there comes a time when all bets are off and every man has to shoulder a musket or do some chore for his country.

But Douglas was not too happy about the possibility of success at the defense job. "I think that as a member of the Court I can knock out a base hit once in a while. In the defense job, I would go to bat with 2½ strikes on me." After speculating about political payoffs in the future ("Some of the President's inner circle whisper that this is a big chance. That it will lead to the 1944 nomination. But that leaves me cold because I am not a bit interested in running for any office"), Douglas wrote: "I am quite sure that F.[elix] F.[rankfurter] has inspired this offer—at least that he has been influential. . . . If he could get me there and you back in the Senate I am sure he would be happier." Finally, he said that, though he recognized the wisdom of declining, he felt that Roosevelt was really pressuring him to accept. "It's hard to say no. . . . He is a hard one to get away from."[42]

Black, who was in Colorado at the time, wrote back and strongly encouraged his younger colleague to remain on the bench. "The prospect that you might leave the Court disturbs me greatly and I have been strongly tempted to cut my visit short, return home, and discuss the question with you personally. And I would do this," wrote the Alabaman, "were I satisfied that I could be of help to you in making your decision." While he agreed with Douglas that the times demanded that citizens respond fully to the needs of the country, the important question was where one could best serve the country: on the court or on the job as chief defense overseer.

For Black, the answer was easy. Work on the Court during the war was much more important than the new opportunity to serve the country. "You and I know that the Court has the last word on questions of law which are determinative of questions of public policy upon which the course of our republic depends." It would be very unwise, Black argued, to leave the Court. He went on to describe the difficulties Douglas would have working with and regulating the war industries. Battling them would not make the head of defense very popular with the press in 1944. Douglas, if he took the job, wrote Black, "would arouse antagonisms and bitterness of such depth and force, that you will be in the very center of a storm of abuse and vituperative criticism." Black concluded by saying that he had "grave doubts as to your success should you enter the defense picture at this stage."[43]

These tantalizing political queries continued throughout the war and into the immediate postwar period. Each one was rebuffed by Douglas—after discussing it with his friend Black. If Bill Douglas ever did harbor an ambition to be president of the United States, his chances were ruined by two events, one political and one personal. The first was Douglas's announcement of his view that the United States should recognize Red China. The second was his divorce from his wife of twenty-nine years, Mildred, to marry Mercedes Davidson. Said Tom Corcoran, "I told Bill, 'in politics you don't get a divorce. . . . Sure you have women. But you don't get a divorce. He could have been President if it hadn't been for this divorce business.'"[44] Douglas knew the consequences of his actions, however, and accepted them.

His divorces dismayed his friend from the Alabama Bible Belt, however. Black could not reconcile Douglas's marital problems with his own strict moral code. Furthermore, Douglas's behavior tarnished the reputation of the Court, and that troubled Black deeply. In fact, he and his wife, Josephine, had tried to effect a reconciliation between Douglas and Mildred before the first divorce, but Douglas went on to marry three more times. It was made worse by the fact that the marriages were to women many years his junior and that tremendous media coverage attended each of his three divorces.[45]

Of course, little was said in the media of the fact that his first marriage lasted for almost thirty years. The pundits who predicted a quick end to his relationship with his fourth wife, Cathleen Heffernan, were wrong as well. It was by all accounts a strong match and one that lasted for more than thirteen years, until Douglas's death in 1980. But Black would never see the success of Douglas's final marriage, and had to watch what was, to him, a troublesome personal area in the life of someone whom he had always deeply respected. Moreover, with each divorce, Black received many letters asking him to try to convince Douglas to leave the Court before his personal life damaged its reputation. Douglas's view was clear. His personal life was just that, personal. Black and his wife did accept Douglas's new wives, and the widows of both men, Elizabeth Black and Cathleen Douglas, became very good friends and remained close until Elizabeth Black's death.

Black and Douglas grew closer during Douglas's recovery from a particularly serious riding accident in 1949. His horse reared, threw him, and then rolled over on him, crushing him. Douglas wrote, simply, that he had been "rolled on by a horse and sent to Tucson, Arizona for a long convalescence." Hugo visited him for a week while Douglas was going through a very slow and painful recuperation.

Douglas later recalled, "I came to have a very close relationship with him as a result of that experience."[46]

In December, Douglas could report to his colleague that he was "coming along quite well, the doctor says. The rib pain is still considerable. The final count is 23 broken ones." He mentioned that he had "regained 10 of the 20 pounds I lost in the hospital," though, with the continuing pain he was experiencing, he concluded that he would be "no good if I were in Washington, DC—not good for more than a couple hours a day." Later on in the month, on December 23, 1949, Douglas wrote somberly to Black: "The bones are mending O.K. But it takes a long time to get the full reserve of strength back. . . . I had been thinking that . . . I should resign. I do not want to cripple the work of the Court by my absence." Black immediately replied that his resignation was out of the question. "Your letter," wrote Douglas, "is most reassuring and indicates that I will not cripple the Court if I stay away until March." Douglas returned to the Court in the spring of 1950.[47]

The two jurists also shared light moments. During oral arguments in the *Everson* case in 1947, Douglas sent a note to Black, a few chairs away: "Hugo / I think if the Catholics get public money to finance their religious schools, we better insist on getting some good prayers in public shools or we Protestants are out of business. WOD." And there were times when they conferred on sensitive Court political matters. In early August 1965, for example, Douglas wrote to Black: "Abe Fortas's wife is very upset over Abe's appointment. It is apparently a very serious crisis. I thought maybe you and Elizabeth could think of something to do." Elizabeth Black later recalled: "We have invited Carol and Abe Fortas for dinner in answer to an SOS by Bill Douglas, saying they were having a serious crisis about Abe's going on the Court. Carol told me . . . that they can't live on the small Court salary and may have to give up their new home. Later, Hugo talked to Carol in that dear, straightforward way of his. . . . It did have a great softening effect on Carol, I could tell. . . . I do believe Hugo's advice helped. They stayed until after midnight."[48]

Hugo Black and Bill Douglas grew together as colleagues and as friends. Although different in many ways, there was an affection and a professional similarity. Douglas certainly considered Black his "closest friend on the Court," and Black, for the most part, "reciprocated Douglas's affection and trust."[49] Gerald Dunne has speculated that "perhaps their sense of association sprang from their being exiles in the mode of the famous Joyce play. Certainly each was touched with a sense of alienation toward both the social order and the conventional wisdom into which they had been born." Whatever the reasons for these two independent men coming together, he wrote, "the overall consequence was a rapport, perhaps unique in judicial annals, that combined a disposition to let government efforts go to great length in the composition of economic problems—with a particular appreciation of the national dimension involved—and an instinct to cry alarm when the secular state placed its hand on political or intellectual processes."[50]

There was, however, a pair of justices on the Court, at least for an important decade in the Court's history, who mirrored Black and Douglas and were often at sword's point with them. To understand their battles, it is essential to consider the opposing team.

Frankfurter and Jackson

Justice Brandeis once labeled Felix Frankfurter "the most useful lawyer in America."[51] Douglas himself said, "Felix belonged on this Court. He knew constitutional history and he knew this Court."[52] Frankfurter was nominated in January 1939 by Roosevelt to fill the seat of a man Frankfurter greatly admired, Benjamin N. Cardozo. His appointment, like Cardozo's, met with near universal acclaim. Frankfurter was a New Deal insider, probably its leading talent scout. Having defended radicals during the Red Scare of the 1920s and Sacco and Vanzetti, he also had a reputation as a liberal. He was a founder of the liberal journal the *New Republic* and had fought for other liberal causes. He came to the Court after twenty-five years as a professor at the Harvard Law School.

Although Roosevelt wanted to delay naming Frankfurter until Brandeis left the Court, the pressure on the president to make the appointment was intense. Solicitor General Robert H. Jackson, soon to be Frankfurter's ally on the Court, wrote to Roosevelt that Frankfurter was needed because he was "someone who can interpret [the Constitution] with scholarship and with sufficient assurance to face Chief Justice Hughes in conference and hold his own in discussion."[53] The president acquiesced, and, twelve days later, the former professor was confirmed in the Senate by a unanimous voice vote. There was great celebration among the members of Roosevelt's administration when Frankfurter was nominated. Tom Corcoran "burst" into Harold Ickes' office at the Department of the Interior with two magnums of champagne for a party Ickes had organized to celebrate the occasion. Among the small group present were Ickes, Corcoran, Attorney General Frank Murphy, and William O. Douglas.[54] Ickes's diary recorded the moment: "We were all very happy. All of us regard this as the most significant and worthwhile thing that the President has done. He has solidified his Supreme Court victory, and regardless of who may be President during the next few years, there will be on the bench of the Supreme Court a group of liberals under aggressive, forthright and intelligent leadership."[55]

For twenty-three years, until his retirement in 1962, Frankfurter was a significant presence on the Court, but his judgments had little impact on society. He is remembered for his extreme judicial caution and for his judicial conservativism. Within three terms, he became a major antagonist of Justices Black and Douglas, in part because of his personality, but in greater part because of jurisprudential differences. Frankfurter's judicial philosophy reflected his passionate commitment to the notions of the supremacy of the popularly elected branches of government and the value of self-restraint of nonelected federal judges so as not to interfere in the democratic process. According to Henry Abraham, "Frankfurter became increasingly known as an articulate and persuasive advocate of judicial abnegation in favor of legislative action. 'When in doubt, don't,' became the Frankfurter maxim."[56] At the same time, Frankfurter was a common-law-oriented jurist in the British tradition. This well-stated public philosophy supported an unstated and significant political conservatism on a variety of issues that were to come to the Court in the 1940s and 1950s.

On social and economic issues, Frankfurter joined Black, Douglas, and the other New Dealers to validate national and state legislation. However, on issues of constitutional rights and liberties that came to the Supreme Court during and after World War II, Frankfurter fundamentally disagreed with the views of some of his New Deal brethren. In numerous and very lengthy memoranda to the conference, including a tome distributed at the beginning of each term, he argued vigorously (over and over and over again) that the cure for these civil and political wrongs was with the legislature, not the courts. He wrote, in 1962: "There is not under our Constitution, a judicial remedy for every political mischief. In a democratic society like ours, relief must come through an aroused popular conscience that sears the conscience of the people's representatives."[57] And if the people found no conscience, the Court was not capable of grafting one onto the body politic.

Frankfurter's affinity for British common law, however, made him comfortable with legal interpretations of a rather sweeping sort.[58] But when he thought it justified, Frankfurter was willing to draw on his broad understanding of the Anglo-American legal tradition as adequate grounds for judgment. He was willing, for example, to decide issues arising under the due process clause according to his understanding and love of English law and values associated with decency and fairness.

That was, in essence, the basis for the fundamental disagreement that Frankfurter had with Black and Douglas during his years on the Court. Both Black and Douglas insisted that "under our Constitutional system, courts," in Black's words, "stand against any winds that blow as havens of refuge for those who otherwise might suffer because they are helpless, weak, outnumbered, or because they are nonconforming victims of prejudice and public excitement."[59]

Beyond that, Black and Douglas, particulary Douglas, thought Frankfurter protested too much when he complained that he really wanted to rule in favor of more extensive protections for constitutional rights and liberties but felt that the need to protect the Court from political conflict precluded him from doing so. Felix somehow found a way to overcome his reticence in cases when he felt very strongly. Furthermore, they did not appreciate his tendency to fight his battles through surrogates, often his former clerks. Douglas was always ready to find Frankfurter's fine hand behind criticisms of either Black or him.

The fourth in the quartet of Roosevelt's brilliant New Deal Supreme Court appointees was Attorney General Robert H. Jackson. Jackson had been with Roosevelt since his tenure as governor of New York. Coming to Washington with Roosevelt, he became a vigorous defender of all New Deal programs, including Roosevelt's Court-packing plan of 1937. By the mid-1930s, Jackson was in the Department of Justice, as assistant attorney general (anti-trust), then as solicitor general of the United States, and, finally, as Roosevelt's attorney general. In June 1941, Jackson was nominated to take Harlan F. Stone's seat when he was moved to the center seat.

Jackson, like Frankfurter, wanted a more deferential judiciary. Before the year he spent in Germany (1945–1946) as chief United States prosecutor at the Nazi war-crimes trials in Nuremberg, Jackson had supported Black and Douglas's conception of courts as protectors of civil and political rights and had joined with them in cases involving civil and political freedoms and rights. In *West Virginia State*

Board of Education v. *Barnette,* writing for the Court majority in 1943, Jackson wrote:

> If there is any fixed star in our constitutional constellation, it is that no official, high or petty, can prescribe what shall be orthodox in politics, nationalism, religion, or other matters of opinion or force citizens to confess by word or act their faith therein. . . . The very purpose of a Bill of Rights was to withdraw certain subjects from the vicissitudes of political controversy, to place them beyond the reach of majorities and officials and to establish them as legal principles to be applied by the Courts. One's right to life, liberty, and property, to free speech, a free press, freedom of worship and assembly, and other fundamental rights may not be submitted to vote; they depend on the outcome of no election.[60]

As his friend Frankfurter noted, Jackson was "by long odds the most literally gifted member of the Court."[61]

However, when Jackson returned from Germany, he was a changed person. Whether it was a result of having been passed over for chief justice or of his public feud with Hugo Black, whether he was influenced by Frankfurter, who had been extremely supportive of him both before and during his absence, or by his experience as chief prosecutor at the Nazi war-crimes trials, Jackson "became a markedly conservative interpreter of the Bill of Rights [and] more often than not sided with the Frankfurter wing of the Court."[62]

A sympathetic Frankfurter became Jackson's confidant. William Rehnquist, Jackson's former law clerk, recalled that Frankfurter and Jackson "were in and out of each other's chambers often; they tended to agree on most legal issues, and enjoyed discussing them between themselves."[63] An entry in Frankfurter's diary records the following exchange between Frankfurter and Jackson:

> Jackson . . . again reverted to his own very great unhappiness on the Court. He said, . . . "It is an awful thing at this time of the Court's and country's history, with the very difficult and important questions coming before this Court, to have one man, Black, practically control three others, for I am afraid Rutledge will join the Axis [Douglas and Murphy]. But on the other hand, I say to myself it would be rather cowardly to leave the field to them. But I can tell you it is a very sad business for me and it isn't any fun to be writing opinions to show up some of their performances." I did the best I could to soothe him.[64]

Frankfurter's correspondence with Jackson comforted him while he was serving in Germany as chief prosecutor. Because he felt Jackson's task was of "profound importance," Felix did all he could to defend the absent justice and tried to counter the barbs Jackson had received from Stone and others. His critics charged that his prolonged absence would hurt the Court and that it was wrong to have a member of the Court involved in proceedings that several members of the Court considered illegal and immoral. Frankfurter wrote to Jackson, urging him to "dismiss all concern" about these criticisms because "neither in volume nor in quality [do they] really amount to a hill of beans." Jackson's absence from the Court, concluded Frankfurter, did "not [sacrifice] a single interest of importance."[65]

This episode further bonded Jackson and Frankfurter as friends and as justices who shared a jurisprudence. And there was, finally, a fatalistic good humor shared by the two. When Frankfurter missed a particularly rancorous conference session, Jackson wrote him the following: "Congratulations on your absence from today's session. Only if you had been caught playing the piano in a whore house can you appreciate today's level of my self-respect."[66]

Black Versus Frankfurter

Felix was an Austrian Jew who immigrated to the United States at an early age, went to public schools in New York City, and attended the City College of New York and Harvard Law School. Hugo was a rough-hewn, steely-tough, largely self-taught Alabaman who reflected in his Senate votes and speeches the fears and indignation of the poor, common men and women of the Depression.

Both men developed judicial philosophies that clashed dramatically. Their professional differences were magnified by their dramatically different personal styles. Black was forever the Senate politician, able to build coalitions or fight, while Frankfurter never ceased his professorial lecturing to his brethren. As he told Justice Charles Whittaker, "I have an incorrigibly academic mind."[67] Another colleague of Frankfurter's, Justice Potter Stewart, recollected that "Felix, if he was really interested in a case, would speak for fifty minutes, no more or less, because that was the length of the lecture at the Harvard Law School."[68] He often openly acknowledged his intention to continue to play professor in critical notes sent to his colleagues.

In conference sessions, Frankfurter would occasionally lecture his brethren "with his notes and records on a book rest, driving his colleagues, especially Bill Douglas, to distraction.[69] Felix, observed one scholar, related well to his mentors (intellectual giants such as Holmes, Stimpson, and Brandeis) and to his students and law clerks, but never to his peers. Benjamin Cohen described him in exasperation to a friend as "incapable of having adult relationships."[70] Black, however, was quite adept at developing close relationships and at building judicial coalitions among his colleagues on the Court. Not without cause (and not without deep bitterness and envy) did Frankfurter criticize Black for developing the "Axis," a bloc of justices including Douglas, Murphy, and Rutledge who shared a set of attitudes toward certain constitutional and jurisprudential issues.

For these reasons, Hugo Black's "constant adversary on the Supreme Court," as Baker characterized him, "was to be Felix Frankfurter," with whom he served for almost two dozen terms on the Court. There was no doubt in anyone's mind that there was a war taking place on the Court during the 1940s and 1950s. Black's nemesis, Felix Frankfurter, once told his law clerk, Elliot Richardson, who was preparing notes for the justice to use against Black and Douglas in conference, "This is a war we're fighting! Don't you understand? A war!"[71] Black's son underscored a major difference between the two when he wrote:

> With all his brilliance, charm and stratagems, however, FF could not really match [Hugo] in picking up converts. Even though their passionate conviction of the righteousness of their positions was equal, there was one important difference that gave Hugo the edge. FF had gained his reputation in an academic system, where he was mainly concerned with instructing, not persuading. But Hugo had gotten ahead by

convincing ordinary citizens . . . as well as congressmen and judges, that his view was right.[72]

Black's arrival on the high bench in 1937 had been less than auspicious. Called the "Alabama Hillbilly" by many and ridiculed by most (one of Frankfurter's law clerks referred to Black—and Douglas—as "clowns"),[73] Black began his career on the Supreme Court surrounded by doubts as to his training and intellect, the antithesis of Frankfurter's prestigious beginnings. Indeed, Justice Stone asked Professor Frankfurter to lecture Black on what a Supreme Court justice was expected to do! "Do you know Black well?" asked Stone of Frankfurter in 1938. "You might be able to render him great assistance. He needs guidance from someone who is more familiar with the workings of the judicial process than he is. With guidance, and a disposition to follow it until he is a little surer of himself, he might do great things." Frankfurter wrote to Black in February 1938, lecturing him on the role of the federal judiciary in our democracy. In so doing, he conveyed to Black his view of legislative supremacy: "Judges cannot decide things by invoking a new major premise out of whole cloth; they must make the law that they do make out of the existing materials with due deference to the presuppositions of the legal system of which they have been made a part."[74]

Justice Brandeis, too, encouraged Frankfurter to befriend Black in an effort to make the Alabaman a better jurist. In the spring of 1938, over tea, Frankfurter and his wife finally met the Blacks at Hugo's home in Alexandria, Virginia. Frankfurter was impressed with Black. As he wrote to Brandeis after this initial meeting: "I believe [Black] is uncorrupted and incorruptible—maybe a touch of the crusader—for there are not many Senators who acted on your wisdom and eschewed the rich and fashionable in Washington as a matter of principle because of its subtle corrupting influence."[75]

Black, at first anyway, appreciated this assistance. In a letter to his "professor," written on January 14, 1939, just after Frankfurter had been nominated by Roosevelt to serve on the Court, Black wrote: "You know, of course, how very happy I am that you will soon sit by me on the Court. . . . I am looking forward with unusual pleasure to our association in the important work—work which my experience here has convinced me more than ever is vital to the causes in which we believe."[76]

After joining the Court, Frankfurter continued to have a high regard for the southern jurist. "Black has a keen mind and he is a tremendously hard worker," he said to a friend in 1939.[77] After *Minersville School District* v. *Gobitis,* the first of the so-called flag salute cases, however, the relationship changed dramatically. By then, in 1941, Black had been joined by his close allies Douglas and Murphy on a number of key civil liberties battles in direct opposition to Frankfurter and Jackson. Black was such a battler on the Court that Jackson and Roberts had seriously thought of leaving the Court rather than continue to fight him. In his diary in 1943, Frankfurter wrote that he had to "really nail Bob Jackson to the wall to prevent him from resigning from the Court. He had all the steps taken to do just that."[78]

Black's developing jurisprudence, especially his understanding of the Court's task under the Bill of Rights, placed him in fundamental disagreement with Frankfurter. As early as December 1939, Frankfurter discerned some of the basic differ-ences. In a letter to Black, Frankfurter critiqued a Black opinion, "in the same spirit and for the same academic purpose as I would were I writing a piece as a professor in the Harvard Law Review." Black, said the professor, was a Benthamite who was gravely concerned about "judicial legislation." But, repeated Frankfurter, judges do make law. "The problem is not whether the judges make the law, but when and how and how much." And in the case under analysis, judges had to fill in holes left by the Congress when it passed the legislation. "Congress gave an exemption and impliedly left it to the courts" to reverse the potential problems. He closed with an admonition to Black: "By covering up the lawmaking function of judges, we mis-educate the people and fail to bring out into the open the real responsibility of judges for what they do, leaving it to the primary lawmaking agency, the legislature, to correct what judges do if they don't like it, or to give them more specific direc-tions that what they so often do is put on the statute books."[79]

That early 1939 lecture about the proper role of judges framed one very impor-tant set of differences, perhaps the key philosophic difference, between Black and Frankfurter, their view of the proper role of judges, especially justices of the United States Supreme Court. Black was forever concerned about judges "roaming at will" and finding new, natural-law meanings to man-made rights found in the Bill of Rights. Frankfurther, on the contrary, believed that the judge had the responsibility to find the essential meaning of the right in question by examining the standards and values of English and American law. Each thought the other an advocate of "natural law" but for different reasons.

Additionally, Black and Frankfurter disagreed about how much deference nonelected federal judges should show to the legislative branch. Frankfurter's posi-tion was one of utmost judicial deference to the judgments of the popularly elected branches of government, especially the legislative branch. While he yielded to no one in his respect for the legislature, Black could not have disagreed more with Frankfurter on this matter. "I think it is the business and the supreme responsibility of the Court to hold a law unconstitutional if it believes that the law is unconsti-tutional, without 'deference' to anybody or any institution. In short, . . . I believe it is the duty of the Court to show 'deference' to the Constitution only."[80] On this matter, Black considered Frankfurter's view "both an exercise in judicial hypocrisy as well as a refusal of judicial responsibility," while Frankfurter condemned Black's views as "constitutional heresy."[81] It was no wonder that these two men clashed continually throughout their tenure on the Court.

There were times when Frankfurter was downright disingenuous. In 1950, a news column revealed that Frankfurter had written to Jackson while he was serving in Germany as U.S. prosecutor and charged that Black and others had gone to Tru-man and threatened to resign if Jackson were appointed chief justice. Frankfurter wrote to Black denying the allegations

> [the story] is so unqualifiedly unfounded in fact that I am greatly tempted to sue both the publishers and the authors of the book for libel. . . . I want you to know that noth-ing is further from the truth than the quotation from the book in question to the effect

that I wrote to Jackson in Nuremberg about an alleged visit of yours to the President threatening to resign from the Court in case Jackson were named to be Chief Justice. Neither directly nor indirectly did I send any communication whatsoever to Jackson regarding the vacancy created by Stone's death.[82]

Black sent a "Dear Felix" letter on October 2, 1950, saying, in part, "I had neither seen nor read any part [of the book] until you sent me extracts from it. So far as I am concerned, it is the same as though it had never been written. For it too will pass away."[83] The truth is that Frankfurter did send Jackson a letter, *after* Vinson's nomination lamenting that "skullduggery" had not succeeded! Frankfurter's letter to Black was true only in the narrowest sense, for when he wrote to Jackson he was discussing not the "vacancy created by Stone's death," but Black's rumored, but never proven, action.

These battles, on the role of judges, on the scope and extent of the protections of the Bill of Rights and of the Fourteenth Amendment's equal protection and due process clauses, along with the inevitable clashes of strong-willed judicial personalities, began in 1939 and never ended for these two judges. There were bitter battles, but neither man ever gave ground. Black's firmly worded reactions to Frankfurter's pleas for reasonableness led to exasperated responses like that found in a 1954 letter to Stanley Reed, in which Frankfurter wrote: "[Black] has reached a conclusion and is not at all bothered about arguments which can be exposed. You might as well ask him to climb a greased telephone pole as to change his conclusion."[84] Frankfurter's ally Justice Sherman Minton wrote to Felix: "[Black] is a demagogue."[85] Black, like Douglas, lost his patience with Frankfurter during conference sessions or while on the bench and would enrage Frankfurter with his verbal assaults. Black's son, who recalled Hugo once laughingly saying after a conference, "I thought Felix was going to hit me today, he got so mad," observed that "although FF always resumed relations with [Hugo] immediately after one of their sharp encounters, the matter apparently did not leave his mind so soon. Frequently, he would retire to his office and . . . make an angry entry in his diary of his version of the encounter."[86]

Frankfurter and Black did develop a grudging admiration for each other, however, and their relationship was far less acrimonious than that between Douglas and Frankfurter.

Douglas Versus Frankfurter

Frankfurter once said of Douglas that he was one of "two completely evil men I have ever met." Douglas, alone among his brethren, did not attend Frankfurter's funeral in 1965.[87] Their mutual dislike was so bitter that for extended periods of time the two men did not speak to each other.[88] Douglas had no difficulty referring to Frankfurter as a "prevaricator" in the first volume of his autobiography, though he tried to downplay his war with Frankfurter in the second volume.[89] Frankfurter, in his diary, noted in 1943 that "Douglas is the most systematic exploiter of flattery I have ever encountered in my life."[90] That was a fascinating charge coming from the man most members of the Court believed to fit that description. But that was not the only such attack. He wrote to Learned Hand that Douglas was "the most cynical, shameless, immoral character I've ever known."[91]

Yet before their appointments to the Supreme Court, when both were toiling for their mutual friend Franklin D. Roosevelt, they formed a useful, if occasionally tense, relationship. For Douglas, Frankfurter was a major liberal defender of Sacco and Vanzetti and a spokesman for other important civil liberties causes. When Douglas was appointed to the Court, Frankfurter commented to a friend: "You do well to be glad over the appointment of Douglas. We shall have a man who is historic-minded about the law, but also knows that history is not a tale of dead things but part of a dynamic process."[92]

How, then, does one explain the enmity that existed between them? The initial break evidently occurred in 1939 when the justices were reviewing draft opinions in *Board of Commissioners* v. *United States.* By the time of the flag salute cases, *Minersville School District* v. *Gobitis* and *Barnette,* the divergence between Douglas and Frankfurter on jurisprudential issues was wide. Douglas had joined in Frankfurter's opinion for the majority but switched to Black's then-solitary dissent—without giving Frankfurter any reason other than that Black was out there alone. Frankfurter "was just furious" and, at that time, came to the conclusion, according to one of Frankfurter's clerks, Philip Elman, that Douglas was an "absolute cynic."[93]

Certainly, the fact that Douglas's view of the role of judges in civil liberties was far different from Frankfurter's was one reason for their tension. Douglas had no difficulty using the power of the federal judiciary to remedy a perceived violation of the Constitution. He usually did not hesitate to act when confronted with official, governmental violations of the guarantees of the Bill of Rights. For Douglas and Black, the First Amendment was written in absolute terms. "We thought," wrote Douglas, "that when the Constitution said in the First Amendment that there should be 'no law' abridging a specific right, it did not mean 'some law, provided it is reasonable,'" whereas Frankfurter's "school of thought" argued that the Constitution bans prohibitions on these and other freedoms only if the legislature "acts 'unreasonably'" and "either the state—or Congress—has freedom to regulate, the constitutional mandate being construed as only a constitutional admonition for moderation."[94]

To Douglas and Black, the responsibility of the Supreme Court was clear. Employ judicial review to invalidate acts of a legislature or other officials that invade the fundamental rights and liberties—as enumerated in the Bill of Rights— of the people. While Frankfurter and other jurists talked of the value of "balancing" the right of free speech with the state's interest in orderliness, Douglas maintained that "all the 'balancing' had been done by those who wrote the Constitution and the Bill of Rights. They had set aside certain domains where all government regulation was banned."[95]

But the origin of Douglas and Frankfurter's deep-seated animosity went beyond important jurisprudential differences. Temperamentally, they were opposites. From the beginning of their close association as justices, the two men simply grated on each other's nerves.[96] Abe Fortas described their differences simply: "Douglas was a Westerner. He either worked or played. Felix never played and he never understood Douglas, who did."[97] Douglas, who often played practical jokes on his brethren, was bound to clash with Frankfurter, who, according to Douglas, "didn't like to be kidded."[98]

Douglas, who had been a highly respected law professor at Yale, could not tolerate Frankfurter's professorial pontificating in front of the brethren at conference sessions and from the bench. "Frankfurter," Douglas wrote in his autobiography, "indulged in histrionics in Conference. He often came in with piles of books, and on his turn to talk, would pound the table, read from the books, throw them around and create a great disturbance. . . . At times, when another was talking, he would break in, make a derisive comment and shout down the speaker."[99] The purpose of these theatrics was to convert the undecided. As Douglas had little patience with such behavior, he did not appreciate the time that was taken by these lobbying efforts. And, as one of Frankfurter's law clerks, Edward F. Prichard, Jr., has noted, Frankfurter was not too successful in these activities. Never able to hold Black, Douglas, and Murphy, he succeeded only with Justices Jackson and Roberts.[100]

Douglas took every opportunity to "needle" Frankfurter, as Justice Potter Stewart recalled. After one of Frankfurter's fifty-minute performances, "Bill would say in a quiet voice: 'When I came into this conference, I agreed with the conclusion that Felix had just announced; but he's just talked me out of it'—which used to drive Felix Frankfurter crazy."[101] Douglas himself dismissed as "wholly aprocryphal" a news report that after one of Frankfurter's frequent questions from the bench during oral argument, Douglas commented, "Why doesn't the son of a bitch keep his mouth shut?"[102] Frankfurter would also write irritatingly professorial letters to Douglas critiquing his opinions. One such memo began, "I am bound to say that it is bad for both of us that we are no longer professors. Because if you were still a professor, you would have written a different elaboration and if I were still a professor, I would get several lectures out of what you have written."[103]

Frankfurter despised Douglas because he was such a "political figure." Although it was clear that Frankfurter was an equally major political figure in the Roosevelt administration, he did not think he was political because "he was not actually *in* politics."[104] Every time Douglas was mentioned as a possible candidate for some high office in the administration, or proposed as a vice-presidential or presidential candidate (as he was in 1940, 1944, 1946, 1948, and 1952), Frankfurter raged. As early as 1941, Frankfurter confided to his friend Harold Ickes that "Bill does not have a passion for the Court."[105] In 1943, Frankfurter asked Frank Murphy, "Doesn't [it] shock you to have this Court made a jumping off place for politics?"[106] Douglas felt sure when Roosevelt asked him to manage the national defense effort in 1941 that Frankfurter had suggested his name to Roosevelt to get him off the Court—and Black back in the Senate.

Beneath it all, there was a "real personal antagonism."[107] In Douglas's view, Frankfurter was a hypocrite and a coward. To Douglas, Frankfurter the Harvard law professor was a force for conservative education, while he had been among the leaders at Yale of the legal realist movement. Frankfurter represented everything that was wrong with establishment lawyers and law professors. Frankfurter wanted to have political power during the New Deal but always stayed in the shadows, not risking public accountability. He wanted to fight once he came to the Court, but would often use a surrogate. He frequently phrased his arguments in terms of judicial restraint amidst plaintive declarations of fealty to liberal principles. To Douglas, it was a smoke screen for a former fighting liberal who cared more for the adoration of the legal establishment than for liberty. He was one of the most arrogant men Douglas had ever met, and this after a career on Wall Street and dealing with corporate lawyers. Their memos to the conference clearly reflected this anger. In 1954, Douglas wrote to Frankfurter: "Today at Conference I asked you a question concerning [a memorandum opinion Frankfurter had written]. The question was not answered. An answer was refused, rather insolently. This was so far as I recall the first time one member of the Conference refused to answer another member on a matter of Court business. We all know what a great burden your long discourses are. So I am not complaining. But I do register a protest at your degradation of the Conference and its deliberations."[108] Frankfurter circulated Douglas's memo to the brethren, saying that "it seems appropriate that all the other members of the Court should see it."[109] In 1959, Frankfurter shot off another letter to Douglas, stating, "You have had, I am sure, ample proof by now of my predominantly academic-minded way of dealing with issues before this Court, by which I mean my interest in the intellectual process by which we reach decisions and not merely the results that we reach."[110]

In 1960, Douglas, in a real fit of anger at another of Frankfurter's outbursts at him, drafted a memo to the conference (which was not sent) in which he announced that he would no longer be attending the sessions because of

> the continuous violent outbursts against me ... by my Brother Frankfurter. [They] give me great concern. They do not bother me. For I have been on the hustings too long. But he's an ill man; and these violent outbursts create a fear in my heart that one of them may be his end. I do not consciously do anything to annoy him. But twenty-odd years have shown that I am a disturbing symbol in his life. His outbursts against me are increasing in intensity. In the interest of his health and long life I have reluctantly concluded to participate in no more conferences while he is on the Court.[111]

Frankfurter, Douglas concluded in the late 1970s, had always been "divisive": "At Harvard. On the Court. He liked to see people argue. He was Machiavellian."[112]

And thus it went. Although in 1974 Douglas claimed that there had been no "war" between him and Frankfurter, the evidence to the contrary is overwhelming. Frankfurter and Douglas, two important American jurists whose decades-long bitter debates (indeed, whose "wars") contributed a great deal to our understanding of constitutionalism in a modern democratic society, could not tolerate each other. Intentionally and unintentionally, they went out of their way to harass each other for over two decades.

Black Versus Jackson

Hugo Black and Robert H. Jackson, in Jackson's words written in 1949, "had little common background or experience." Black came from the "deep south" and Jackson was a "Yankee." Black had extensive political experience "in appealing to popular support," whereas Jackson, by his own admission, "had no legislative experience and was regarded as somewhat inept politically." Certainly, Jackson's self-assessment about political ineptness proved correct in his bloody, public tangle with Hugo Black in 1946. Jackson came to the Court from the Justice Department in 1941. When he met Black, he wrote, it was "doubtful if either of them recognized their latent antagonisms."[113] Douglas described Jackson as a "country lawyer of great versatility. . . . He had a sharp pen and an incisive mind. He was a lone wolf on the Court, having no close friend except Frankfurter. . . . His ambition to be Chief Justice truly poisoned his judicial career."[114]

By 1943, Black and Jackson, as Gerald Dunne has written, "typified the rival polarities" that were developing on the Supreme Court.[115] On the one side, there stood Black and Douglas, regularly joined by Murphy and Rutledge. On the other side stood Frankfurter, Jackson, and, on occasion, Roberts. The aging Chief Justice Stone fought a losing battle in his efforts to control these strong-willed factions. From the time of Jackson's appointment to his departure for Germany, in June 1945, he and Black were at odds over process and jurisprudence and feuded over a number of issues. After witnessing one such clash between Jackson and Black in 1943, Frankfurter wrote in his diary: "Black at his worst, violent, vehement, indifferent to the use he was making of cases."[116]

Perhaps the tense relationship with Black was one reason Jackson took the overseas assignment in 1945, even though it meant that the Court would function as an eight-person tribunal for almost a year, as well as generating criticism from Stone, Douglas, Murphy, and Black that a justice ought not to serve in an executive capacity unless he resigned his judicial post. Black's son wrote that Hugo showed "open hostility" to Jackson for taking the prosecutor's role and leaving the Court for a full term.[117] Douglas speculated that Jackson took the job because "he was planning to run for governor of New York and perhaps for President, so from a political viewpoint it was desirable for him to be our Nuremberg prosecutor, since the Jewish vote is important in many parts of our country."[118] Truman himself, in a conversation with Clark Clifford in the spring of 1946, "mentioned that there was one man—Associate Justice Robert H. Jackson—whose experience and talents seemed to make him presidential timber."[119] However, the long-simmering feud between Jackson and Black was soon to become a major public scandal that foreclosed any further mention of Jackson as a possible presidential candidate.

After Stone's death and the allegations in the press that Black and Douglas had gone to Truman and threatened to resign if the president appointed Jackson as chief justice, Fred M. Vinson, Truman's close friend and his secretary of the treasury, was appointed chief justice. The hope was that his political experience might help calm the Court. Black never commented on the matter; Douglas categorically rejected the news accounts: "Truman never broached the matter with us, and neither of us sent any message to Truman."[120] Black's son also categorically denied that Black had gone to Truman. "It was a plain lie. [Hugo] had said no such thing."[121] However, within four days of the announcement of Vinson's nomination, an angry Jackson shocked Washington—as well as the country—by publicly condemning Black in a telegram to the president. The White House counseled reconsideration, but it was too late. He had already sent copies to the chairmen of the House and Senate Judiciary Committees and to the media.

In the lengthy blast, Jackson cited feuds within the Court, including a major one that had been brewing with Black for some time. The issue was whether Black should have disqualified himself in the so-called portal-to-portal pay case of *Jewell Ridge Coal Corp.* v. *Local 6167, UMW.* It was a closely divided, 5 to 4, case in which Murphy, in May 1945, wrote for the majority (including Black) and Jackson wrote the dissenting opinion. Union miners had argued that they should be paid for their underground travel to and from work (portal to portal) and had brought suit under the provisions of the Fair Labor Standards Act. The case was argued on March 9, 1945. (The United States argued in support of the union miners' position.) In the conference session the following day, the justices voted 5 to 4 against portal-to-portal pay—with Jackson assigned to write the opinion for the majority. However, over the weekend, Justice Reed changed his mind, which changed the decision of the Court in favor of portal-to-portal pay.

As Black, not Jackson, was now the senior justice in the majority, he assigned the opinion to Murphy. Jackson's dissent infuriated Black because it included a 1937 quote in which Senator Black had taken a position on the scope of the Fair Labor Standards Act—the Black-Connery Act—contrary to Justice Black's position in 1945. Black wrote a memo to the conference, complaining that Jackson was misquoting him. "The very page from which the dissent quotes negatives the inference. . . . If the dissent does go down as now printed, it will not be a fair representation of the true facts."[122] Jackson did not modify the dissent. The draft opinions were circulated in early April 1945. The strike was settled before the opinion came down in May 1945. A petition for rehearing was filed at the end of May and was denied on June 18, 1945, the day the Court adjourned for the term and Jackson flew to Germany with his military administrative staff.

The flare-up that occurred over this labor case concerned Black's relation to his former Birmingham, Alabama, law partner (and a past Cyclops of Black's Ku Klux Klan chapter) Crampton Harris, who was the attorney for the United Mine Workers local. The partnership had ended twenty years earlier. The coal company petitioned the Court for a rehearing after the 5 to 4 ruling against its position on the grounds that Black should have disqualified himself because of his prior association with the miners' attorney. This set off a rancorous debate within the Court as to whether it should respond directly to this question raised by the company lawyers.

Frankfurter and Jackson were unwilling to give "blind and unqualified approval"[123] to Black's participation in the case and felt that some statement of the Court's concern should be appended to the denial of rehearing order. To simply deny the petition for rehearing without commenting on the fact that the Court had no power to pass judgment on the question of qualification, they felt, was not correct. The two jurists did not want to leave the impression that the Court condoned Black's action.

Jackson drafted a statement that Frankfurter supported. In that concurring opinion, Jackson had written, in part: "Because of this lack of authoritative standards [upon which a justice of this court may be disqualified in any case], it appears always to have been the responsibility of each justice to determine for himself the propriety of withdrawing in any particular circumstances. . . . There is no authority known to me under which the majority of this court has power under any circumstances to exclude one of its duly commissioned justices from sitting or voting in any case."[124] Frankfurter then wrote another classic "Dear Hugo" letter to try to explain his support of Jackson's statement.

> By silence I would impliedly be denying the truth of what he stated—that as to quali-fication I have no right to sit in judgment on my Brethren any more than they have a right to sit in judgment on my qualifications in a particular case. . . . I had no share in creating the situation whereby Bob felt it to be his duty to make clear the issue of qual-ification. But since he has done so, I could withhold joining him only by suppressing my belief in the truth. I do not propose to do that—and that is the sole reason why I join him. Needless to say I greatly regret the whole incident.[125]

The language of this statement, as well as of Stone's statement, was debated for weeks; finally, the Court issued a statement that met with the approval of the Mur-phy majority, including Black. Black had insisted on a simple denial of rehearing statement. If that was not forthcoming, Black allegedly threatened to issue a "dec-laration of war."[126] Jackson's statement, with Frankfurt concurring, was also printed. But Jackson continued to fume against what was to him gross misconduct by Black.

On May 16, 1946, just about one year after *Jewell Ridge* came to the Court and shortly after Stone's death, Doris Fleeson's column in the *Washington Star* appeared. Its catchy headline, "Supreme Court Feud: Inside Story of Jackson–Black Battle Laid Before a Harassed President," stunned most readers. The story illuminated the *Jewell Ridge* clash in detail and quoted at length Jackson's com-ments on the denial of a rehearing. Included in the story were quotes from Truman himself, who, it was claimed, confided to a southern senator that Black and Jackson had threatened to resign if the other was appointed chief justice.[127]

On June 7, 1946, Jackson sent his seven-page telegram to the president and to the legislators and distributed copies to the press. In it he proclaimed, "If war is declared on me, I propose to wage it with the weapons of the open warrior, not those of the stealthy assassin."[128] In his telegram, Jackson discussed the *Jewell Ridge* case because it reflected the clash of wills and values on the Court, going into detail about Black's relationship with Harris, the rehearing debate within the Court regarding disqualification, Black's "bullying" tactics in conference, Jackson's concurring opinion, and Black's threat of a "declaration of war" if Jackson published his con-curring opinion. Concluding, Jackson wrote: "Mr. Justice Black has apparently made good his threat of 'war'. He followed it by threatening the President if he dares to make a court appointment which is not to his liking. . . . Protection of my own name lies in disclosing the facts heretofore suppressed." He closed this telegram by indicating that he could not serve as justice unless the matter were cleared up in this way. "I cannot discharge my duties . . . if I allow the impression either that an Asso-ciate has 'something on me' which is disqualifying in your eyes, or that my opinion in the *Jewell Ridge* case was a 'gratuitous insult' to an Associate."[129]

While Black responded to this telegram with a "dignified silence," others were quite loudly reacting to the story. The press had a field day with this dirty linen. The *Washington Post* headline read: "Jackson's Charge Against Black Splits Supreme Court Wide Open." The *New York Times* ran the story under the following banner headline: "Jackson's Attack on Black Stirs Talk of Court Inquiry," "Jackson Attacks Black for Judging Ex-Partner's Case." Lewis Woods's story in the *Times,* dated June 10, 1945, began: "The national capital was stunned tonight to read of the bitter denunciation of Associate Justice Hugo Black delivered at Nuremberg by Associate Justice Robert H. Jackson." Drew Pearson's "Washington-Merry-Go-Round" column of June 13, 1946, focused on the feud, supporting Black's position in the dispute. Journals such as the *New Republic* and the *Progressive* featured stories on the clash. And members of Congress discussed the possibility of investigating the Supreme Court.

Black received a warm letter of support from Charles Grove Haines, a professor of political science at the University of California, Los Angeles.

> It is difficult for the general public to realize or understand, when an attack of this kind is made, the underlying forces and factors which are at work in the interpretation of the words and phrases of our fundamental law. My chief concern is that the publicity which has been aroused through this incident will in no way affect the constructive and extremely important work which you and the other liberal-minded Justices have been doing to restore something in the nature of democratic simplicity, fairness and balance in the process of Constitutional interpretation.

Black replied: "When I decided to enter public service, I did so with the belief that public servants who stand and fight for principles are likely to create powerful antagonism. Consequently, I have always viewed personal attacks as incident to my work. As a result, none of them have ever caused me to deviate from the fundamental purposes of my life. Nothing that has recently occurred has shaken this resolution."[130]

Jackson's telegram to the president and to the Judiciary Committee chairmen was unique in the annals of American jurisprudence. The justices who knew of the pressures and tensions that had motivated Jackson to write that virulent letter, were saddened by it. Frankfurter was concerned about his friend's inner turmoil. Douglas concluded: "The weapon Bob used against Black was forged in passion and intemperance."[131] And Justice Rutledge commented, "Too bad, but it's just like Bob. I'm not surprised."[132] Even Jackson, who in a personal memo written for his files said he had sought no advice on either the idea of sending it or the content, felt the telegram was intemperate: "This seems a capital blunder; for, accepting the policy of making a statement, some minds not so close to the events it dealt with could have clarified and strengthened the document. . . . There were deeper defects."[133]

According to one historian, Jackson believed that it was William O. Douglas, not Black, who "was responsible for Truman's choice of Vinson." The evidence he presents, however, is circumstantial and rests on the nonverifiable assertion that Jackson strongly believed that Douglas had encouraged Bob Hennegan, a former chairman of the Democratic National Committee and a confidant of Truman's, to speak to Truman against Jackson's candidacy a week after Chief Justice Stone died.[134]

The irony is that Truman saw Jackson as a possible running mate in 1948, not as chief justice. "Apparently," speculated Douglas, "[Truman] never knew of FDR's promise to Bob. There was no one on this side close to Truman who could plead his cause. Frankfurter tried, but was ineffective."[135] If Truman knew of Roosevelt's pledge, given Truman's estimation of Jackson as a potential vice-presidential candidate, he was not going to preclude the possibility by appointing him to the center seat on the Court.

Jackson resumed his duties on the Court in October 1946. He and Black, "after their passion had been spent," resumed a civil relationship.[136] They grew further apart on issues of constitutional interpretation, especially in the area of First Amendment freedoms and national security. As Jackson's memo for his files observed, "it always was naive to think that men of the type of Black or Jackson could be jollied out of their differences and convictions. Their disagreements are intellectual matters, fundamental to their respective characters. They are not likely ever to be reconciled to each other's viewpoint, however much each respects the other's ability."[137]

A close reading of another very revealing memo by Jackson, the "Black Controversy," written in 1949, suggests a portrait of a bright, lonely—indeed, ascetic— man who simply could not cope with or understand the natural ease and self-confidence of Hugo Black.

Murphy and Rutledge

Frank Murphy, who joined the Court in January 1940, after the death of Pierce Butler in November 1939, immediately found a friend in Hugo Black, who came to regard Murphy with "brotherly warmth."[138] He also found a soul mate of sorts in Douglas, whose liberalism and concern for fundamental issues of justice matched his own. He needed their friendship because Frankfurter and others (especially Reed, Stone, and Jackson) made it clear that they did not think that Murphy was suited for the job. When Roosevelt told Murphy that he wanted him to fill the seat left vacant by Butler's death, Murphy, who was Roosevelt's attorney general at the time, at first declined because he felt he was "utterly inadequate" for the position.[139]

Frankfurter, clearly, had an "ill-concealed contempt" for Murphy's intellect and his life style.[140] Frankfurter disdained Murphy's substitution of compassion for an overarching commitment to the disinterested rule of law. While Douglas was clearly a stronger intellect and tougher personality than Murphy, it is clear that Douglas was affected by Murphy's unabashed willingness to demand that the Court be humane and just. Like Murphy, Douglas was willing to accept the status of lone dissenter in defense of those causes.

Murphy was an ardent New Deal judge and one of the two most liberal men appointed by Roosevelt—as an examination of the Court's case law in the 1940s will illuminate. He was soon to be joined by another liberal, Wiley Blount Rutledge, a judge on the U.S. Court of Appeals for the District of Columbia Circuit. After many years as a law school professor and dean, and with a record as an ardent New Dealer and civil libertarian, Rutledge had been appointed by FDR to the federal appeals court in 1939.

The two men, Murphy and Rutledge, became the Court's "left wing," especially after their dissenting opinions in the 1945 case of *In re Yamashita,* involving the war crimes trial of a leading Japanese general.[141] In Rutledge, Black, too, "gained a coadjutor in his burgeoning libertarian views."[142] After 1945, these two men closed ranks with Black and Douglas on some major civil rights and civil liberties issues that the Court confronted; the relationship among the four men became one of "warm rapport."[143]

Warren and Brennan

After serving together for just three terms, Murphy and Rutledge died within months of each other in the summer of 1949. Their loss was hard on Black and Douglas, but they were succeeded on the Court by two replacements who proved to be profoundly important to the rest of Black's and Douglas's careers. What is more, they came from an unlikely source. Earl Warren and William J. Brennan were the judicial appointments of Dwight Eisenhower. As one of the "chiefs" with whom Black and Douglas served, more will be said of Warren later. After the resignation of Sherman Minton in October 1956, Eisenhower filled his seat with a nominee suggested by Arthur T. Vanderbilt, chief justice of the Supreme Court of New Jersey. The candidate was William J. Brennan, Jr., Vanderbilt's colleague on the New Jersey court. Intrigued by the idea of nominating a Catholic who was also a Democrat at the tail end of the 1956 presidential election, Eisenhower appointed Brennan to the Court during the congressional recess. The nomination came before the Senate in January 1957, and, after some harsh questioning by Senator Joseph McCarthy, of Wisconsin, Brennan was formally confirmed by the Senate in a voice vote in March 1957. President Eisenhower, asked later about mistakes he had committed while in the White House, replied that he had made two, "and they are both sitting on the Supreme Court."[144]

William Brennan quickly became, with Black, Douglas, and Warren, the fourth in the quartet of justices who would commence to act vigorously to incorporate the Bill of Rights into the due process and equal protection clauses of the Fourteenth Amendment. Brennan's vote was important in many critical cases that mattered mightily to Black and Douglas, but it was also his close relationship to Earl Warren that made him a critical liberal negotiator in many leading constitutional conflicts on the Warren Court. Brennan and Warren hit it off immediately, both personally and jurisprudentially. Brennan very quickly became the chief's "closest colleague."[145] The relationship between these two men became "a foil to that of . . . Warren and Frankfurter."[146]

Justice Brennan recalled in 1986 that it was the *In re Groban* case during the 1957 term of the Supreme Court, a few months after he had joined, that initially brought together the "BBD and W" (Black, Brennan, Douglas, and Warren) coalition. It joined the four for the constitutional battles over the scope and extent of the Bill of Rights that were to come in the next decade. At a conference session, Brennan had joined the Court majority in *Groban.* He almost immediately had second thoughts, which became full-blown doubts after he read Reed's draft opinion for the majority and Black's draft dissent. For the first time, the question Does a justice have to stay "joined"? arose in Brennan's mind. After rereading the opinions, Brennan was convinced that he had to change his vote. He then told Reed, "I am joining Black." When Reed responded angrily, "You *can't* do that!" Brennan asked, "Why not?", and received no answer from Reed. Brennan then informed Black that the dissenters (Black, Douglas, and Warren) had a fourth. With the addition of Arthur Goldberg, Abe Fortas, and Thurgood Marshall, they formed a cohesive alliance on many of the Court's civil rights and civil liberties cases over the next ten years.[147]

Warren and Brennan shared Douglas's commitment to the view that "anyone whose life, liberty or property was threatened or impaired by any branch of government—whether the President or one of his agencies, or the Congress, or the Courts (or any counterpart in a state regime)—had a justiciable controversy and could properly repair to a judicial tribunal for a vindication of his rights."[148] Ironically, in all his years on the high bench, Black had great difficulty with this attitude; for him, the critical element in any judicial action was the discovery and announcement of a timeless principle. Yet because he was moved to act on the basis of what he believed were timeless principles of liberty, Black worked closely with his liberal, policy-oriented friends on the Supreme Court.

The Chiefs

Hugo Black and Bill Douglas had the opportunity, given their long tenure on the High Court, to sit with five chief justices. They ranked two, Hughes and Warren, as major contributors to American legal jurisprudence. Douglas placed seven of his brethren on his list of "All-American" judges: two of the seven were Hughes and Warren.[149] (Both would have accepted colleague William Brennan's tagging of Earl Warren as "Super Chief.") The other three occupants of the center seat—Stone, Vinson, and Burger—were less respected.

Charles Evans Hughes

Charles Evans Hughes, though uncomfortable with Roosevelt's choice, greeted Hugo Black cordially when the Alabaman joined the Court in 1937, even though Black had voted against Hughes's confirmation in 1931. On the opening day of the 1937 term, Hughes welcomed Black "with all the courtesy and cordiality that could have been bestowed upon the most distinguished jurist in the land."[150] The chief justice, however, did give a speech to the American Law Institute in 1938, in which he said, speaking to Roosevelt, in effect, that, in the future, the president ought to appoint a Supreme Court justice who was "able and industrious . . . qualified by training and experience for his office."[151] Hughes, wrote Black, encouraged Black to dissent "whenever he wished."[152] The only thing, evidently, that irritated Hughes, unlike Chief Justice Stone, about Black was the squeaky chair Black used in the courtroom.[153]

Douglas, who also appreciated Hughes's sense of humor, thought his first chief justice "was brilliant. He knew how to conduct a judicial conference. He had perfect command of the cases."[154] Douglas also had great admiration for Hughes because he did not waste time in the conference session. The chief had first impressed Douglas in 1920, when Hughes protested the way socialists were being treated by New York legislators. Douglas saw his sensitivity to perceived injustices in *in forma pauperis* petitions (cases filed by people too poor to hire lawyers and pay court fees) as a very positive statement about Hughes's commitment to equal justice. Beyond being, to use Brandeis's words, a "very efficient Chief Justice," Hughes was, in Douglas's opinion, an eminently fair jurist who tried to respond to gross injustices in the state criminal justice system.[155] In fact, Douglas compared every successive chief with Hughes on these issues. Hughes retired during the summer of 1941, and Harlan F. Stone was elevated to the center seat by Roosevelt.

Harlan Fiske Stone

"Stone was a genial and affable man who," wrote Douglas, "for some reason did not like Black."[156] In 1938, it was widely speculated that Stone was the justice quoted in a *New York Daily News* column written by John M. O'Donnell and Doris Fleeson that reported that some of Black's distressed brethren "had hitched up their judicial robes and in dignified fashion were in the process of putting the slug on their colleague Associate Justice Hugo L. Black." The columnists wrote in a later column:

> A flat declaration that Black will not start a libel action or seek redress in any way came from an unimpeachable source late today. But before it became known that the Justice would take no action, the juicy morsel which rolled on legalistic tongues was the question of whether Black had been libeled professionally by the unknown "source close to the Supreme Court" who gave out the statement that legal opinions prepared by the Alabaman have had to "be rephrased by other members of the court" and that Black "has been unable to carry his share of the heavy work that falls on the court."[157]

Stone wrote continually to Black, trying to correct his errors. In the beginning, there were some basic errors. For example, on January 26, 1938, Stone wrote that "it is usually inadvisable to write a case reversing a state court on points involving state law which were not considered or decided by the court below."[158] And in a March 22, 1939, letter to "Black," Stone suggested some changes in an opinion Black was writing. As a postscript, Stone added: "I suggest you show what you have written to F.F. and invite his suggestions as to the way you have phrased the jurisdictional issues."[159] The stream of condescending criticisms and the knowledge that Stone was sharing his complaints about Black's work created serious tensions between the two men.

Douglas had been one of Stone's students at Columbia Law School and had remained in contact with his mentor and friend ever since. Losing the competition to be Stone's law clerk after graduation was one of his greatest disappointments in life. Yet Douglas did not consider Stone an effective Court leader. Douglas wrote in his autobiography that "[Stone] was not good as Chief Justice. We were always in conference. He couldn't move the cases along. When members of the Court disagreed with him, he would lean over to me and say, 'I can understand how the others might disagree, but not you. You, Bill, were my student at Columbia.' I'd lean back over to him and say, 'Mr. Chief Justice, I learned all the law I know from you.' He hit the table with his fist and said, 'By God, you did not learn that from me!'" Among the reasons for Stone's failure was the fact that he, unlike the punctual Hughes, was "first, last and always, a professor who wanted to search out every point and unravel every skein." It was as though each case had to be talked into submission.[160]

In 1944, Douglas and Stone had a series of exchanges regarding stories that had appeared in the press about Roosevelt's interest in Douglas as a running mate. Douglas wrote to Stone from Oregon in July 1944, repudiating the stories and claiming that he had instructed western state delegates that "no one was authorized to promote my nomination and that I would give no such authority; that if nominated, I would not accept. I hope this puts an end to the matter. But I wanted you to know the facts. I think a person who desires to put in a political campaign should resign from the Court. I think political ambitions are incompatible with performance of our judicial function. I do not think the Court should be used as a stepping stone to any public office."[161] In August 1944, he wrote Stone another letter, expressing his relief that the convention was over and saying, "I have always felt with you that one who has political ambitions should not go on the Court."[162]

The Stone Court was an acrimonious body, and the chief justice was never able to dampen the flames fanned by Black and Douglas on the one side and Jackson, Roberts, and Frankfurter on the other. Besides his penchant for running a lengthy disorganized conference, Stone, according to Baker, "lacked the political adroitness necessary to make a collegiate body run smoothly."[163]

Fred M. Vinson

President Truman was quite concerned about the outbreak of public feuding among the justices at the time of Stone's death. "The Supreme Court," he wrote on June 11, 1946, "has really made a mess of itself."[164] He turned to his friend Fred M. Vinson to resolve the conflicts on the Court. Truman thought Vinson's political background and negotiating skills would serve the Court well. Vinson was then secretary of the treasury and had served as a member of Congress from 1924 to 1938. He was also a former federal court of appeals judge and a member of Roosevelt's administration.

Vinson was warmly greeted by Hugo Black, who wrote: "I wish for you a long and happy career as Chief Justice. Should you need any information that I can give as to the administrative responsibilities which will devolve on you, I shall be happy to be of all assistance possible in this respect."[165] The Vinson Court was a transition Court, "still living in the aura of the New Deal, evading rather than confronting postwar issues."[166] As leader of the Court, Vinson was not any better than Stone at clearing the calendar. Indeed, he was responsible for preventing the Court from addressing some of the challenges it confronted between 1946 and 1953, especially the critical issue of segregation in public schools. Although the Vinson Court handed down decisions that ultimately led to the demise of the racially unfair and

restrictive separate but equal doctrine, Vinson, perhaps because of his own southern heritage, failed to provide leadership when the school segregation issue came
before the Court in 1950. It was left for Earl Warren to move the Court to unanimity in the *Brown* opinion announced in May 1954.

Evidently, Douglas liked Vinson's earthy humor and forgave him his weak-
nesses as a leader. He recalled that Vinson

> had a gentle voice and gentle manners, though underneath he had a resolution of steel.
> At Conference he seldom raised his voice, but he would filibuster for hours to have his
> way on a case. One day Frankfurter kept baiting Vinson. At last Vinson left his chair
> at the head of the Conference Table, raised his clenched fist and started round the room
> at Frankfurter, shouting, "No son of a bitch can ever say that to Fred Vinson!" Shay
> Minton and Tom Clark intercepted Vinson and held him until he had cooled off.
> Before the day was done, Vinson of course apologized.[167]

Frankfurter's initial assessment of the new chief was not very favorable. Felix
judged that the way Vinson dealt with argued cases was "further evidence that he
is likely to deal with complicated matters on a surface basis. He is confident and
easy-going and sure and shallow. . . . He seems to me to have the confident air of a
man who does not see the complexities of problems and blithely hits the obvious
points."[168] The other justices were no more impressed. To all of them, including
Stanley Reed (a jurist not known for his intellect), Vinson possessed "a second-class
mind."[169] Vinson left the Court as divided as it was when he became chief justice in
1946. As Bernard Schwartz has written, "By the time Warren was appointed, the
Court had become the most severely fractured Supreme Court in history."[170]

Earl Warren

President Eisenhower, like Truman before him, "was firmly convinced the prestige
of the Supreme Court had suffered severely in prior years," as he wrote in his diary
in 1953, and it could be restored only "by the appointment to it of men of nation-
wide reputation, of integrity, competence in the law, and in statesmanship."[171] For
Eisenhower, at that time, Earl Warren fit the bill. Warren was a well-known, experienced politician who was widely respected by both major political parties. While
no intellectual match for some of the justices, Warren was an affable, principled,
and politically skilled leader.

Black got along well with Warren, even though the new chief was initially
attracted to Frankfurter's positions on some key issues. Black said of the new chief
justice: "[He is] a very attractive, fine man. Just a short acquaintance with him
explains why it was possible for him to get votes in both parties in California. He is
a novice here, of course, but a man with his intelligence should be able to give good
service. I am by no means sure that an intelligent man with practical, hard common
sense and integrity like he has is not as good a type to select as could be found in
this country."[172] Much later, of course, Black told his son that Earl Warren was
much more "hard-headed and opinionated" than Black himself ever was.

According to Bill Douglas, "Warren was as nonchalant as Hughes was meticulous. . . . While Hughes had been fastidious when it came to dress, Warren was very casual. . . . Most of the time Warren was polite, considerate and friendly, handling the Conference with consummate skill. He had no monopoly on stubbornness. But when he felt strongly on an issue—obscenity or flag burning—he held forth at length."[173]

Douglas, however, while working with Warren to achieve certain mutually desired ends, did not really seem to like Warren very much. In a 1961 letter to Sherman Minton, Douglas wrote:

> You know how enthusiastic we were when Earl Warren came to the Court. But in retrospect it was a sad day. His attitude toward the Court is the attitude of a prosecutor to his staff. We all know how extravagant Felix often is in announcing his opinions. He often embellishes them, you know. Last Monday was the second time Warren spoke up after Felix had finished, denouncing Felix for "degrading" the Court. . . . I've never been a Felix fan, as you know. But I never dreamed I'd be here when a Chief Justice degraded the Court like Warren is doing. It's a nasty spectacle. Perhaps the old boy is off his rocker.[174]

In May, Douglas again wrote to Minton: "The CJ thinks the court is a bureau in Sacramento, and that he runs it. He's headed for tragedy. We all got here on our own. I don't know of a soul who respects him any more. I have defended him in public and in private. But no more. . . . The truth is, I think, that Earl Warren is a cheap politico with a Christ complex. It's sad, but true."[175] However, Douglas did speak well of Warren elsewhere and did work with the chief to achieve certain goals both men desired while on the high bench.

Warren E. Burger

After Warren's retirement in 1969, President Nixon tapped Warren Earl Burger, then sitting on the U.S. Court of Appeals for the District of Columbia Circuit, to serve as chief justice of the United States. Douglas considered Burger a very conservative jurist who espoused "law and order" themes during his tenure in Washington. He "thought of the Court as a symbol of an authority which had best not be exercised" Douglas wrote, and furthermore, "he loved the administrative aspects of the office. He loved being Chief."[176]

Hugo Black, according to Warren Burger, was an important asset in the new chief's first year on the Court. Beginning in the summer of 1969, and lasting throughout the next full term of the Court, Black, with his "wry sense of humor," often made it a point to drop in at Burger's office and chat at 4:00 P.M. on his way home. One day Black said to him: "Chief, you know you're not as bad as some people said you would be."[177] Douglas, too, would call up the new chief and ask if the tea was up. Burger recalled that his response was always: "The tea pot is on, Bill, come on up." And then Bill Douglas and Burger would talk about the operation of the Court—from assigning opinions, to hiring new clerks, to reviewing the prisoner petitions the Court received in the thousands.[178]

Burger's "love" of administrative control did lead to a serious clash with Douglas, however, when Burger tried to upset the Court tradition of the chief assigning opinions only if he had voted with the majority in the conference. In March 1972, Douglas wrote a letter to Burger chastising him for trying to assign an opinion to Byron White, even though Burger had voted in the minority. "With all due respect, I think Powell represents the consensus. I have not canvassed everybody, but I am sure that Byron . . . will not get a Court." Powell was one the five who voted in the majority—the others being Brennan, Stewart, Marshall, and Douglas—and he eventually did write the opinion in the watershed case of *United States* v. *United States District Court*.[179]

In another pointed letter to Burger on the same issue, written on May 1, 1972, Douglas tried, again, to educate the chief on the protocol of assigning opinions. Douglas had just found out that Burger, though in the minority, was writing the majority opinion in the free speech in shopping centers case, *Lloyd Corporation* v. *Tanner*. As the senior justice in the majority, Douglas had assigned it to Thurgood Marshall.[180] Douglas wrote to Burger in part:

> Historically, the Chief Justice has made the assignment if he is in the majority. Historically, the senior in the majority assigns the opinion if the Chief Justice is in the minority. You led the Conference battle against affirmance and that is your privilege. But it is also the privilege of the majority, absent the Chief Justice, to make the assignment. Hence *Lloyd* was assigned and is assigned. . . . If the Conference wants to authorize you to assign all opinions, that will be a new procedure. Though opposed to it, I will acquiesce. But unless we make a frank reversal in our policy, any group in the majority should and must make the assignment. . . . *Lloyd* stays assigned to Thurgood."[181]

There was no change in the Court practice of assigning opinions. Burger grudgingly backed off the issue. However, according to Burger, he did not respond to Douglas's "lashing out" at him in these letters.[182]

Burger was occasionally criticized for letting the Court's conference sessions run too long and for permitting too much discussion. His response was direct: "If one is going to err, it is better to err in the direction of too much discussion rather than too little."[183] Justice Powell characterized Burger's style as "discursive" and said that he simply "would let everybody talk as long as they want to talk."[184] (Throughout his tenure on the Court, he lobbied Congress and the executive for actions that would create another level of federal appellate review to ease the case burden on the Court. He was, in particular, concerned about the large number of cases being decided by the Court without the benefit of oral argument. Docket pressure, he said recently, has forced the Court to "increase the number of cases decided without oral argument.")[185]

"Under Burger," recollected Douglas, "there was pressure to join ranks."[186] For the iconoclast jurist who was anxious at term's end to be off to Goose Prairie, this was an intolerable situation, and Douglas always responded appropriately. The pressure from Burger was the effort "to align the Court with the political views expounded by the Nixon Administration."[187] It was doomed to failure from the beginning; the Burger Court revolution—overturning the great bulk of Warren

Court doctrines in civil liberties and civil rights—never occurred as Nixon and others had hoped it would.

In the years between 1937 and 1975, Black and Douglas worked with great jurists as well as judicial journeymen; they had decades-long intellectual battles with brethren such as Frankfurter, Jackson, Harlan, and White. Yet they had gentle, congenial relationships with weaker colleagues such as Sherman Minton and Charles Whittaker. And they joined forces, when possible, with natural allies, including Murphy, Rutledge, and, occasionally, Stone in the 1940s. In the 1950s and 1960s, there were Brennan, Warren, Goldberg, Fortas, and Marshall.

The issues they addressed and the contributions they were able to make were influenced not only by the personalities on the bench, but also by the political environment in which they worked and the peculiar problems presented by the kinds of questions about power and right that they were asked to resolve. Never were these factors clearer than during the war years.

Hugo Black, the young man from Clay
County, Alabama. *(Collection of the
Supreme Court of the United States)*

Black's first wife, Josephine.
*(Collection of the Supreme
Court of the United States)*

Josephine Black and daughter, Jo-Jo, early 1930s. *(Collection of the Supreme Court of the United States)*

Senator Hugo Black, arriving at the Capitol on the day he was nominated to the Supreme Court by President Franklin D. Roosevelt in August 1937. *(Collection of the Supreme Court of the United States)*

"Hugo-to-Hell" Black in the United States Senate. *(Collection of the Supreme Court of the United States)*

Black's second wife, Elizabeth. *(Collection of the Supreme Court of the United States)*

Justice Hugo Black in chambers. *(Collection of the Supreme Court of the United States)*

Bill Douglas, the young slugger as an undergraduate. *(Collection of the Supreme Court of the United States)*

William O. Douglas, SEC gunslinger. *(Collection of the Supreme Court of the United States)*

The Douglas family in the early years. *(Collection of the Supreme Court of the United States)*

The justice and his fourth wife, Cathleen. *(Collection of the Supreme Court of the United States)*

William O. Douglas at home. *(Collection of the Supreme Court of the United States)*

Justice William Douglas in chambers. *(Collection of the Supreme Court of the United States)*

Hugo L. Black, the justice. *(Collection of the Supreme Court of the United States)*

William O. Douglas, the justice. *(Collection of the Supreme Court of the United States)*

The new Court, 1939. *Front row:* Harlan F. Stone, James C. McReynolds, Charles Evans Hughes (chief justice), Pierce Butler, Owen Roberts. *Back row:* Felix Frankfurter, Hugo Black, Stanley Reed, William O. Douglas. *(Collection of the Supreme Court of the United States)*

The Court in wartime, 1940s. *Left to right:* U.S. Solicitor General Charles Fahy, Robert Jackson, William O. Douglas, Stanley Reed, Owen Roberts, Harlan F. Stone (chief justice), Wiley Rutledge, Hugo Black, Felix Frankfurter, Frank Murphy. *(Collection of the Supreme Court of the United States)*

The Warren Court off guard in the mid-1960s. *Front row:* Tom C. Clark, Hugo Black, Earl Warren (chief justice), William O. Douglas. *Back row:* Byron White, William J. Brennan, Potter Stewart, Arthur Goldberg (missing, John M. Harlan). *(Collection of the Supreme Court of the United States)*

The last time together, the 1970 term. *Front row:* John M. Harlan, Hugo Black, Warren E. Burger (chief justice), William O. Douglas, William J. Brennan. *Back row:* Thurgood Marshall, Potter Stewart, Byron White, Harry Blackmun. *(Collection of the Supreme Court of the United States)*

Justice Felix Frankfurter, "the Professor." *(Collection of the Supreme Court of the United States)*

Justice William J. Brennan. *(Collection of the Supreme Court of the United States)*

 **6**

The War Years

WORLD WAR II, according to Douglas, was an important period in constitutional litigation because war, "in the constitutional sense, is more than a state of hostilities."[1] War is a traumatic event that affects the entire nation. In the effort to wage war successfully, citizens' lives and liberty are curtailed by their government, and their property is controlled by government regulations in ways that aid the national effort. In that channeling of personal life, liberty, and private property in the national interest, fundamental clashes between right and power are inevitable. Given the existence of a "crisis government" in a military emergency, with a strong executive branch and Congress each claiming its constitutional war powers to wage the conflict successfully, challenges to these powers "rose for review" before Justices Hugo L. Black and William O. Douglas and their brethren on the Court during the war years.[2]

Black and Douglas had been on the Court only briefly when they were confronted with having to choose between the country's urgent needs in war, as defined by military authorities, Congress, and the executive branch, and the dangers these demands posed to constitutionally protected liberties. Black, who had served in World War I, but not in combat, "hated wars." He had joined the army because, as his son described it, not to have joined "would be a strike against him in postwar politics if he couldn't join the Veterans of Foreign Wars."[3]

Douglas, attending Whitman College when the United States entered World War I, also joined the army—although he had to fake a color blindness test to do it. He, too, did not go overseas, since the armistice was signed as he was about to be shipped to his training camp in Kentucky. Although he also had misgivings about war, Douglas wrote that he "never could have evaded military service. For I had a passionate love not only for the mountains, but for the nation and its institutions as well." Black and Douglas shared the view, a "disillusioned view," as Douglas put it, that war was a fine time for war-industry "barons" and others who profited from war, as well as for the officers, but that it was the common foot soldiers in the trenches who always made the supreme sacrifices.[4]

Both men, however, had seen the growth of fascism and other forms of totalitarianism during the interwar years, and both believed, unlike the American isolationists, that the national government had to respond forcefully to external threats to its sovereignty. War came to America just a few years after Black and Douglas had taken their seats and before their judicial philosophies on these issues had matured.

While the justices agreed with each other's conclusions in these wartime cases, they often disagreed about the legal rationale. On the Court, as well, there were also sharp differences of view regarding the wartime opinions. Through these very difficult cases, Black and Douglas were forced to decide fundamental questions of liberty, and the meaning and scope of due process of law. In some instances, they reluctantly gave a "different appraisal" of the protections of the Bill of Rights in wartime, though neither Black nor Douglas was pleased with the necessity to do so. While they were growing to understand, respect, and like each other, they also had to react to opposing forces within the Court as a whole.

It was during the war terms that Black and Douglas first clashed with two colleagues, Felix Frankfurter and Frank Murphy, but for completely different reasons. Frankfurter was a dominant figure on the Court in the early war terms. His prewar flag salute opinion, valuing the inculcation of loyalty over freedom of religion, commanded the votes of everyone but Stone. Extremely patriotic and deferential to the powers of the popularly elected agencies of government, the naturalized American justice spoke eloquently on behalf of national war powers.

During these years, Frankfurter, as J. Woodford Howard writes, had essentially "transformed a patriotism of passionate intensity into support of plenary congressional power to regulate immigration."[5] The total fight against America's enemies, he said in 1942, was "a war to save civilization itself from submergence."[6] In this battle, the justices of the Supreme Court were soldiers too. His powerful arguments convinced many of his brethren (including, until 1943, Black and Douglas) of the necessity of upholding actions taken in the effort to win the war and punish the enemy. For Frankfurter, there had to be total deference by the Court to policy makers. As he said to Frank Murphy, his opponent in many of these cases, "On this Court we are not sitting as Santa Clauses, or as the makers of policy."[7]

Murphy, though, was a Roosevelt soldier, until what was for him the watershed of his career, his authorship of the wartime denaturalization opinion and his dissents in the Japanese exclusion case, the Japanese war-crimes cases, and the domestic citizen treason trials. With these opinions, he broke with Frankfurter and took a more extreme liberal position on these issues than his other liberal brethren on the Court. Only Wiley Rutledge joined him on some of these arguments, especially in the war crimes litigation.

Murphy was no less patriotic than Frankfurter; indeed, at one point early in the war, he accepted a commission as a lieutenant colonel in the army reserve, wearing his uniform to the Court. He was, however, greatly moved by the denial of constitutionally guaranteed rights to some of the petitioners and wanted to rectify the injustices. In one such 1945 case, *Duncan* v. *Kahanimoku,* he wrote to Black to tell him that he was going to prepare a separate concurring opinion. "I will have to go a step further. I don't want to rest on the [statute] alone. Constitutional rights were flaunted without necessity and I feel obliged to comment on it."[8] Resisting the very considerable pressure from his brethren to keep silent if he was not going to join the Court in supporting wartime governance, he told Black on another occasion: "No man in public life, including yourself, has been flagellated more than I have been by the press and the people of wealth and power in the nation. All of this has been because of progressive measures I have fostered and battled for on behalf of poor inarticulate and minority groups. . . . I will do anything up to giving up life to defend others in their faith."[9]

Murphy evidenced that commitment in his dissenting opinions in the Japanese exclusion cases and other rulings involving minorities whose constitutional rights had been infringed by government. Before 1944, however, Murphy had written a powerful draft dissent in the curfew case, the first of the three major Japanese cases, that "stung" his brethren; Murphy, much more sharply than Douglas, questioned his brethren's "love of liberty."[10] He was persuaded by Frankfurter, however, on grounds of patriotism, to modify the draft into a concurring opinion. Yet Murphy's conscience bothered him until his exclusion-order dissent rectified his earlier surrender to Frankfurter. For "Saint Murphy," as Frankfurter disdainfully labeled him, the exclusionary action of the military went over the constitutional brink and fell "into the ugly abyss of racism."[11] Murphy would have no part in what he saw as the majority's "legalization of racism. . . . [Such racial discrimination] in any form and in any degree has no justifiable part whatsoever in our democratic way of life."[12]

All the justices perceived the threat to American values. Differences that developed among them were due to their differences of opinion about the extent to which fundamental constitutional rights of due process and of freedom of thought and religion could be abridged during the national emergency. These tensions, and Black and Douglas's role in resolving them, can best be seen in cases about loyalty and security, military-justice actions, draft questions, and disputes over governmental control of the economy.

Loyalty and National Security in Wartime

The critical questions of loyalty and security during the war arose primarily in cases that involved Japanese-American citizens and residents. Some of the cases argued not for incarceration but for denaturalization, stripping them of their citizenship. Other remedies suggested coercing loyalty to the state. All the cases that came to the Court forced the justices to evaluate their views of individual rights and powers of the government in time of extreme national danger.

The tragedy that hit American citizens of Japanese ancestry during World War II is, by now, familiar to most Americans. On February 19, 1942, seventy-four days after Japan's attack on Pearl Harbor, President Roosevelt signed Executive Order 9066. The order, ostensibly written to prevent espionage and sabotage, authorized

Secretary of War Henry L. Stimson to establish military zones from which Japanese Americans and Japanese aliens living in the United States would be excluded. One month later, Congress passed legislation that, in effect, sanctioned Roosevelt's executive order by authorizing criminal penalties for any violations of military orders issued under its authority. Also, in March 1942, General J. L. DeWitt began to issue the first of what would turn out to be hundreds of military orders establishing curfews for Japanese Americans, which ordered them to assembly centers and, finally, sent more than 112,000 people, including over 70,000 Japanese-American citizens, into relocation camps spread across the western United States and Arkansas.[13]

The constitutional controversy was clear: the "war powers" of the president and Congress versus the due process requirement in the Fifth Amendment. Thousands of men, women, and children were forcibly removed from their homes, businesses, and schools, and placed in barren, out-of-the-way, relocation centers—without benefit of any criminal charges, trials, or even hearings. The lack of due process "anguished" some of the justices as they struggled with the exclusion cases. A letter from Douglas to Stone raised the fundamental normative issue clearly. "Is it not necessary to provide an opportunity at some stage . . . for an individual member of the group to show that he has been improperly classified?" Wasn't it necessary that members of the group have the opportunity "to prove that they are as loyal to the United States as the members of this Court?"[14]

The first case to challenge the constitutionality of the curfew established by General DeWitt, *Hirabayashi* v. *United States,* came to the Court's conference in early May 1943.[15] By this time, American military actions in the Pacific had led to victories in the battles of the Coral Sea and Midway (1942), Guadalcanal (1943), and New Guinea and the Solomon Islands (1943). The defendant, then a senior at the University of Washington, had been convicted in federal court for "knowingly disregarding the curfew restrictions" and for failing to comply with the military orders that required all persons of Japanese ancestry to report to the assembly centers. Hirabayashi's appeal argued that the restriction of his freedom "unconstitutionally discriminated between citizens of Japanese ancestry and those of other ancestries in violation of the Fifth Amendment."[16] In the conference session, there was a clear desire on the part of the brethren to defer to military authorities.

The leading advocates of judicial deference were Justices Black and Frankfurter. While they had fundamental and life-long disagreements on other legal issues associated with the judiciary's role, when it came to the question of the scope of war powers, Black and Frankfurter agreed. In the Japanese exclusion cases, they worked hard to persuade two wavering colleagues, Douglas and Murphy, to join the majority.

Both Black and Frankfurter also worked with Stone, author of the *Hirabayashi* opinion, to get a jurisprudential statement that would essentially cede the decision to the other branches. In a memorandum to Stone, Black wrote: "Purely military orders . . . call for the exercise of a military, not judicial judgment. A curfew regulation in a zone of imminent danger is such a regulation. . . . Final authority to say what persons in the area were to be subjected to the curfew regulation was, I think, not in the courts, but in the military department charged with protecting the country against pressing danger."[17] Stone's response was a memo to the conference indicating that he was "willing" to change the majority opinion to capture Black's plea for restraint. Stone wrote, in part, that "it is not for any court to sit in review of the wisdom of [the military commanders'] action or substitute its judgment for theirs."[18]

Frankfurter picked up the second of two judicial deference arguments developed by the two justices. He urged Stone to modify the opinion so that it would be "eminently clear" to the nation that "we decide nothing that is not before us." The Court should focus solely on the curfew issue and not on the more controversial aspects of the military orders—the assembly centers and the relocation centers. "We decide the issue only as we have defined it—we decide that the curfew order as applied, and at the time it was applied, was within the boundaries of the war power." Stone immediately circulated a revision of his opinion containing Frankfurter's language—word for word.[19]

Douglas and Murphy were the two reticent holdouts. Both had prepared opinions (Douglas's was a concurring opinion, while Murphy's was a dissent) and had circulated them among their colleagues. Douglas was concerned about the issue of loyalty, which had been completely ignored; in the military's view, the Japanese were unassimilated and not to be trusted. Loyalty, he wrote, is "a matter of mind and of heart, not of race." Due process had to be provided to these persons, the vast majority of whom were as loyal as members of the Court.[20] Douglas pleaded with Chief Justice Stone: "Is it not necessary to provide an opportunity at some stage . . . for an individual member of the group to show that he has been improperly classified?"[21] For Douglas, the military orders were "justified only as a temporary expedient. And I would like to have it stated in substantially that way."[22] He had written to Stone in an effort to get the chief to craft the majority opinion from that perspective and with the following caveat: "that the individual must have an opportunity to be reclassified as a loyal citizen." If Stone added that modification to his opinion, Douglas would not write his own. But Douglas acknowledged that their differences might "be too great a gap for us to bridge."[23] He was right, and two days later Stone rejected Douglas's argument. "It seems to me that if I accepted your suggestion, very little of the structure of my opinion would be left, and that I should lose most of my adherents."[24]

Douglas's concurring opinion concerned Black and angered Frankfurter. In a strongly worded memo to the chief, Frankfurter asked Stone to "send for Brother Douglas and talk him out of his opinion by making him see the dangers that he is inviting." He was incensed at Douglas's due process/loyalty/review argument. That tack, exclaimed Frankfurter, quoting Black, was "an invitation to bring 'a thousand habeas corpus suits in federal district courts.'" The language of the concurring opinion clearly raised the possibility of "the institution of many such law suits. . . . It would be for me deplorable beyond words to hold out hopes [for the Japanese internees] by any language that we use. [We ought not to] encourage hopes, which, to put it very mildly, are not likely to be fulfilled." Douglas, concluded Frankfurter, "ought to act like a collaborator" but was instead behaving as though he were engaged "in a rival grocery business." But Frankfurter knew that trying to get Douglas to change his view was hopeless: Douglas, he said, would be "obdurate, largely because he will want to make the spread eagle speech."[25]

But if Frankfurter was determined and tugging in one direction, Murphy was anguished and pulling in quite another. Colonel Murphy wrote a draft dissent based on what he saw as undisguised racial discrimination in violation of the Fifth Amendment.

> The discrimination is so utterly inconsistent with our ideals and traditions, and in my judgment so contrary to constitutional requirements, that I cannot lend my assent. It is at variance with the principles for which we are fighting and may well have unfortunate repercussions among peoples of Asia and other parts of the East whose friendship and good will we seek. It [the relocation program] bears a melancholy resemblance to the treatment accorded to members of the Jewish race in Germany and other parts of Europe.[26]

Justice Reed pointed out, in rebuttal, that "you cannot wait for an invasion to see if loyalty triumphs."[27] Frankfurter was the major challenger, and Black was on board with the pro-government group arrayed against Murphy and Douglas.

Frankfurter did not relax the pressure on Murphy; as opinion day approached, he wrote Murphy note after note about the draft dissent. In part, he said:

> do you think it is conducive to the things you care about, including the great reputation of this court, to suggest that everybody is out of step except Johnny, and more particularly that the Chief Justice and seven other justices of this Court are behaving like the enemy and thereby playing into the hands of the enemy. Compassion is, I believe, a virtue enjoined by Christ. Well, tolerance is a long, long way from compassion—and can't you write your views with such expressed tolerance that you won't make people think that when eight others disagree with you, you think their view means that they want to destroy the liberties of the United States and "lose the war" at home?[28]

Frankfurter's remarks, according to one of Murphy's biographers, "had the desired effect."[29] After a week of reflection, Murphy decided to concur on the "narrow holding that there was a rational basis for a discriminatory curfew during the critical period of early 1942."[30] Frankfurter, his task accomplished, congratulated Murphy "on the wisdom of having been able to reach a concurrence."[31] In the concurring opinion, Murphy reflected on the racially discriminatory policy that was clearly present in the military order: "Today is the first time, so far as I am aware, that we have sustained a substantial restriction of the personal liberty of citizens of the United States based upon the accident of race or ancestry. . . . In my opinion this goes to the very brink of constitutional power."[32]

On June 21, 1943, the *Hirabayashi* opinion was announced. Six justices reaffirmed the power and authority of the president, Congress, and the military authorities to take whatever action was necessary to maintain national security in time of war. Justice Black, joined by Douglas, was one of them. "The war power of the national government is 'the power to wage war successfully.'. . . It extends to every matter and activity so related to war as substantially to affect its conduct and progress. The power is not restricted to the winning of victories in the field and the repulse of enemy forces. It embraces every phase of the national defense."[33] Given that judicial perspective, the Japanese who were affected by the military orders had not been treated in an unconstitutional manner. "In the time of war, residents having ethnic affiliations with an invading army may be a greater source of danger than those of a different ancestry."[34] Three justices concurred. In addition to Douglas and Murphy, Rutledge—who had written the "anguish" note to the chief justice—wrote a short concurring opinion. Taking exception to judicial abstention in this area of constitutional law, he stated that, while he accepted the curfew ruling, the military did not have unlimited power to act and that "the courts . . . have power to protect the civilian citizen."[35]

The Court, in *Hirabayashi,* focused on the narrow issue of the curfew order. In *Korematsu* v. *United States,* the issue was the constitutionality of the assembly and relocation centers across the western United States. Fred Korematsu had been charged with failing to report to a civil control station, or assembly center, for evacuation from the western military zone to a relocation camp. Korematsu claimed that the civilian exclusion order violated the Fifth Amendment in that it was racially discriminatory and citizens were being incarcerated without benefit of trial or other due process guarantees. In addition, he argued that the mass exodus of a racial class of citizens constituted cruel and unusual punishment, in violation of the Eighth Amendment.

In the October 16, 1944, conference session, there was a sharp 5 to 4 split on the fundamental issue of whether the military could forcibly detain, exclude, and then relocate a racial class of citizens who had not been formally charged with any crime. Five justices—Stone, Frankfurter, Black, Rutledge, and Reed—continued to defer to the judgments of the military leaders. Four—Roberts, Murphy, Jackson, and Douglas—maintained that the actions of the military exceeded the bounds of constitutionality and that the Court had to respond.

Hugo Black was assigned the task of writing the opinion for the Court. Reflecting in *Korematsu* the judicial deference shown to the possessors of the war powers in *Hirabayashi,* Black wrote that "pressing public necessity may sometimes justify the existence of some restrictions." In modern warfare, "the power to protect must be commensurate with the threatened danger."[36] Procedurally, Black and his colleagues in *Korematsu* were firmly committed to separating the exclusion order itself from the consequence of that order: relocation.

Black's opinion, therefore, had to divorce the issue of exclusion and assembly centers from what almost invariably resulted from being sent to an assembly center: forced relocation to a detention camp. Stone had made two telling points in conference. First, the exclusion order "was valid when made." Second, the requirement that Korematsu report to the assembly center did not "as a matter of law" mean that he "certainly would" be sent to a relocation center.[37] As it happened, Stone also thought that "detention at the assembly centers is within the authority of the orders, and has the same constitutional sanction as the curfew order in Hirabayashi."[38]

Black was encouraged by his Court allies to concentrate on this narrow question of exclusion. Stone, in early December 1944, wrote Black a critical note, saying that Korematsu's "principle contention before us was that his presence at the Assembly Center necessarily involved his being subject to a relocation order, and your opinion does not show why this is not true."[39] Stone also warned Black that "it is important for us to make it plain that we do not impose our judgment on the military unless we can say that they have no ground on which to go in formulating their orders."[40] Stone was so adamant on this point that he drafted a concurring opinion, never published, to emphasize that "this Court does not decide moot cases or give advisory opinions. It will be time enough to decide the serious constitutional issue which petitioner seeks to raise here when a relocation order is in fact applied or is certain to be applied to him, and we are advised of its terms."[41] Black took the message and incorporated, almost verbatim, those words in his opinion for the Court. Stone withdrew his concurrence.

Black's opinion linked the curfew validation *(Hirabayashi)* with the exclusion order. Although exclusion posed a greater deprivation of freedom than the curfew, argued Black, it had a close and definite relation to the prevention of sabotage and espionage. The Court accepted at face value the military claim that there cannot be a hasty separation of disloyal from loyal Japanese. The exclusion of a class of citizens, based on ancestry, was, Black said, a military imperative, not a group punishment based on racial prejudice. Finally, Black, who fervently defended the congressional and presidential war powers, justified the narrow scope of the majority opinion:

> It is sufficient here for us to pass upon the [exclusion] order which petitioner violated. To do more would be to go beyond the issues raised, and to decide momentous questions not contained within the framework of the pleadings or the evidence of this case. It will be time enough to decide the serious constitutional issues which petitioner seeks to raise when an assembly or a relocation order is applied or is certain to be applied to him, and we have its terms before us.[42]

William O. Douglas, once again, struggled with the constitutional issue. He was concerned with the denial of due process. He was also disturbed because of the significance of racial-discrimination claims in these cases. After the *Korematsu* conference, Douglas circulated a four-page dissenting opinion. For him, Korematsu's case was inextricably tied to the relocation orders. If you acknowledge that link, wrote Douglas, then "you come to the larger question," which was the legitimacy of these military plans that uprooted 120,000 persons, over 70,000 of them citizens of the United States, without trials or hearings. Douglas jotted down in his conference notes the important question: "Was confinement included in the authorization—no suggestion of enforcement in materials before Congress."[43] Douglas could not separate the exclusion from the detention in the military order that had led to Korematsu's conviction. "By May, 1942," wrote Douglas in his draft dissent, "evacuation, detention in an Assembly Center and detention in a Relocation Center, were but steps in a program which had acquired a unitary character. . . . Korematsu's choice was to go to jail or to submit to an indefinite detention in a Relocation Center. That detention was plainly more than temporary detention as an incident to exclusion. I therefore find no authority for it."[44]

His draft dissent met with criticism from Frankfurter, Black, and Stone because he had offered loyal Japanese citizens a choice: "stand on their own" or transfer to the relocation center "havens."[45] On December 6, 1944, Douglas wrote to Black that he had changed his mind and, "to lessen the confusion now existing from a multiplicity of opinions," would be "willing to waive my difficulties and join in the opinion of the Court provided one addition was made. As you know, I think evacuation and detention in an Assembly Center were inseparable. You do not think so. Therefore, I thought an accommodation could be made by adding a new paragraph to your opinion as follows: 'A minority are of the view that evacuation and detention in an Assembly Center were inseparable'. . . ."[46] Black incorporated it into the final version of the majority opinion. Douglas filed his dissent away. Yet Douglas, unlike his colleague Black, found that "the evacuation case . . . was ever on my conscience" and later wrote, "my vote to affirm was one of my mistakes."[47]

In the end, by a 6 to 3 vote, *Korematsu* validated the actions of the military authorities. Frankfurter wrote a short concurring opinion in which he focused on the nature of the war powers: "To find that the Constitution does not forbid the military measures now complained of does not carry with it approval of that which Congress and the Executive did. That is their business, not ours."[48] (Interestingly, throughout the war Frankfurter was receiving information, especially with respect to the Japanese exclusion cases involving the War Relocation Authority, on a weekly basis from John J. McCloy, one of the men in the War Department responsible for implementing the relocation program.)[49]

The three dissenters focused their dissents on the irrationality of the orders, the racially discriminatory character of the military actions, and the fundamental violation of due process by the government. Colonel Frank Murphy vented his moral outrage in dissent from the *Korematsu* majority. Jackson, like Murphy, a former U.S. attorney general, also dissented. It was clear to Jackson that the ruling violated a fundamental principle: "guilt is personal and not inheritable."[50] Moreover, to punish those never tried, yet alone convicted, was simply wrong. For the Court to validate the military orders was to validate "for all time the principle of racial discrimination in criminal procedure and of transplanting American citizens."[51] Owen Roberts was the third dissenter. He concluded that Korematsu was convicted "as a punishment for not submitting to punishment in a concentration camp, based on his ancestry, and solely because of his ancestry, without evidence or inquiry concerning his loyalty and good disposition towards the United States."[52]

Although he never really forgave himself for joining Black's *Korematsu* opinion, Douglas was able to rationalize his actions at the time in part at least because he was at that very moment writing the Court's unanimous opinion in *Ex parte Endo.* In *Endo,* which involved a woman seeking habeas corpus to free her from the relocation center in Topaz, Utah, the Court held that the incarceration of loyal Japanese Americans in internment camps without due process was unconstitutional. Mitsuye Endo had received a permit to leave the camp but had not been released due to "resettlement problems."[53] She then unsuccessfully petitioned the federal district court for a writ of habeas corpus. Endo, like Hirabayashi and Korematsu, argued that she had been denied due process. She asked for summary judgment that would allow her to leave Topaz without any kind of "conditional, revokable, indefinite leave."[54]

From Douglas's notes, it is clear that there was instant unanimity in the *Endo* case. The justices agreed that she was being illegally detained in the relocation center after her loyalty had been ascertained by the administrator, and that "once loyalty is shown, the basis for the military decision disappears—this woman is entitled to a summary release."[55]

Douglas's opinion was written quickly. Consistent with some of his earlier views on this issue, he concluded that Congress did not envision a civilian agency, the War Relocation Authority, developing and implementing relocation policies and processes for loyal citizens. Justice Reed, a day after he received Douglas's draft, reflected the Court's view when he replied: "I am quite satisfied with the opinion as a whole. . . . [Since sabotage and espionage] are not done by a loyal citizen, it is not possible to restrain the loyal citizen for the purpose of avoiding espionage and sabotage for a longer time than is necessary to determine loyalty."[56]

Hugo Black thought the Douglas opinion was as Douglas recalled, a "good job," and the problems were handled to his satisfaction. It seemed odd that that two men were writing such different opinions on such similar cases, but Black reassured Douglas. "The only feeling I have is one of admiration for the fine way you have done it."[57] Clearly, for Black, the issue raised by *Endo* was not that of the earlier Japanese exclusion cases, the constitutionality of the congressional war powers. *Endo*'s case, coming toward the end of the war, involved a series of procedural questions rather than the central issue of military powers in wartime.

Although the opinion was ready in early November 1944, Chief Justice Stone did not announce *Endo* until December 18. Douglas complained about the delay in a letter to Stone on November 28, 1944:

> The matter is at a standstill because officers of the government have indicated that some changes in detention plans are under consideration. Their motives are beyond criticism and their request is doubtless based on important administrative considerations. Mitsuye Endo, however, has not asked that action of this Court be stayed. She is a citizen, insisting on her right to be released—a right which we all agree she has. I feel strongly that we should act promptly and not lend our aid in compounding the wrong by keeping her in unlawful detention any longer than is necessary to reach a decision.[58]

The reason for the delay was that Stone was working behind the scenes with contacts in the War and Justice departments to coordinate the Court's announcement with a major policy change of the Roosevelt administration regarding the Japanese in the camps. After the presidential election of 1944, the president decided to rescind the exclusion order. On Sunday, December 17, 1944, the War Department issued statements announcing the change in policy. *Endo* came down the following day.[59] According to Peter Irons, Douglas never learned "that Stone had enlisted in the high-level campaign, directed by John McCloy, to protect President Roosevelt from the political consequences of the decision to end the internment program."[60]

These cases illuminate the Court's deferential posture during time of war—when the constitutional issue was entangled with that of national security. "The job of the Court is to resolve doubts [about military actions], not create them," Stone rebuked Murphy during the Court's deliberation of the Japanese exclusion case.[61] Noninterference with military judgments was the approach of the Court. In these cases involving military judgments, the chief considered the Court's views "irrelevant."[62] Black, too, insisted that these cases called for the "exercise of military, not judicial judgment."[63]

Years after these cases were decided, Douglas wrote that "preventive detention

. . . is inconsistent with the Fourth and Fifth Amendments of our Constitution."[64] But in 1943 and 1944, the majority of the justices supported a form of preventive detention. In a letter to Chief Justice Stone, written on May 29, 1943, during the *Hirabayashi* discussions among the brethren, he wrote: "War does not change the powers of Congress but it does provide occasion for a different appraisal of constitutional requirements."[65]

Military Actions in Wartime

There were a number of less complex cases that involved military actions against alien spies, the legality of military "war crimes" trials, accusations of atomic espionage, and the important concept of martial law. In a democratic system, courts, including the United States Supreme Court, invariably have to examine the constitutionality of aggressive actions, taken primarily by the executive branch, against "enemies" of the state. It has always been a painstaking examination for some of the brethren.

In these cases, Black and Douglas, while concerned about what process was due enemy saboteurs, alleged war criminals, and espionage agents, strongly supported the government's efforts to decisively respond to these enemy threats to national security in time of hot, and cold, war. While the two men, and most of their colleagues, affirmed the judgments of the government, they did raise some important questions about the limits of governmental powers and the corollary question of the vitality of individual rights in times of national crisis.

Ex parte Quirin has been described as "World War II's first major challenge to executive discretion."[66] Eight Germans, classified as "unlawful combatants" because they landed on American shores in mid-June 1942, without distinctive uniforms and for the purpose of sabotage and espionage against America, were arrested by the FBI. They were detained by military authorities for trial by a special military commission created by order of President Roosevelt on July 2, 1942. Claiming that the president was acting under the authority of congressionally written Articles of War, the defense attorneys insisted that the president could not unilaterally deviate from the letter or the spirit of the articles, as he had done by ordering a military commission to hear the case and issue judgment without appeal to the civilian courts.

They raised it, initially, in an extremely unusual setting: the Chester County, Pennsylvania, farm of Justice Owen Roberts. In attendance at this dramatic, informal meeting were Roberts, Justice Hugo Black, U.S. Attorney General Francis Biddle, the judge advocate general of the army, and two army colonels who were defense counsel for the eight Germans.[67] The defense attorneys argued that their clients should be tried in federal courts and not under the authority of a presidentially created military commission. After this informal meeting, the defense unsuccessfully petitioned in federal district court for a writ of habeas corpus. They immediately appealed to the court of appeals. During this time, the military commission was reviewing evidence and moving toward its judgment. The defense attorneys then asked the Supreme Court "to bring up to this court this case which is pending in the U.S. Court of Appeals for the District of Columbia, before judgment is given in that court."[68]

Black, Douglas, and Frankfurter were opposed to a Supreme Court hearing prior to judgment in the court of appeals, and there was a "sharp internal struggle" on the Court over this issue.[69] The Court decided to meet in a special session, July 29 to 30, to hear arguments on the matter. The defense petition had asked the Court to examine whether the president could detain petitioners for trial in a military compound, thereby not following the provisions outlined in the congressional Articles of War and, at the same time, by-passing the civilian federal courts and denying the defendants access to the federal courts. The attorney general argued the president had that power in time of war.

On Friday, July 31, 1942, the Court handed down its judgment in a short *per curiam* decision without an explanatory opinion. The Court, according to one historian, "reluctantly validated the power and jurisdiction of the Commission."[70] The petition for writs of certiorari before judgment was granted, and the Court held that the president was authorized to order the military commission to try the eight Germans, that the commission was lawfully constituted, and that no cause had been shown for the petitioners to be discharged by writ of habeas corpus. Therefore, concluded the short order, "the motions to file petitions for writs of habeas corpus are denied."[71] According to Douglas's account, Biddle had told the Court prior to judgment "that the claims of the saboteurs were so frivolous, the Army was going [to go] ahead and execute the men whatever the Court did; that the Executive would not tolerate any delay." To Douglas, "that was a blatant affront to the Court."[72] A few days after the July 31 *per curiam* order, six of the eight German saboteurs were secretly electrocuted by the government.

The new dilemma for the Court, after the *per curiam,* was the need to file an extended opinion justifying the short, unsigned order. The brethren, having handed down the ruling in July, now had to turn to explaining in detail the order that they had already made! That was to prove to be a difficult task. "While it was easy to agree on the original per curiam," Douglas wrote, "we almost fell apart when it came time to write out the views."[73] It was also macabre to be reading and discussing arguments of petitioners, six of whom were already dead and buried. In opening the discussion of the issue in late September 1942, Chief Justice Stone noted that the matter was "a question of some delicacy and difficulty."[74]

The chief justice wisely decided to file the extended opinion in *Ex parte Quirin* on October 29, 1942. In a thirty-page opinion, joined by eight of the brethren (Murphy did not participate in this discussion and decision), Stone concluded that the congressionally written Articles of War recognize, in addition to the court-martial, the "'military commission' appointed by military command as an appropriate tribunal for the trial and punishment of offenses against the law of war not ordinarily tried by court martial."[75] Congress also gave the president "the power to prescribe the procedure for military commissions," and other articles "authorize trial, either by court martial or military commission, of those charged with relieving, harboring, or corresponding with the enemy and those charged with spying."[76] Because the

Germans were charged with an offense against the law of war, the Constitution did not require they to be tried by jury in a civil court.[77]

By 1950, the United States and the Soviet Union had begun their protracted hot and cold war. Anti-Communist hysteria had spread in America, fueled by the Soviet's efforts to isolate West Berlin from the Western Allies in 1948 and 1949. It was in June 1950, that the "police action" in Korea began. Later that summer, Julius and Ethel Rosenberg, American citizens and avowed Communists, were arrested for espionage. Given the strong sense of Communism's imminent threat during the Korean conflict and early cold war, it was no surprise that the Rosenberg case was imbued with a sense of urgency rather like the case of the Nazi spies.

In the cold war spy trials, as in those of World War II, Black and Douglas, while violently opposed to the various totalitarian systems the spies represented, still insisted on raising, in conference and in their occasional dissents from denial of certiorari, essential due process questions. Regardless of the heinousness of the alleged violation, Black and Douglas always insisted on reaffirming the constitutional text regarding procedural due process. But they, like their colleagues in earlier epochs, were powerless in the face of an insistent War Department, which was not interested in the niceties of a due process argument.

The Rosenbergs were charged with having violated the 1917 Espionage Act, in that they were allegedly involved in transporting the secrets of the atomic bomb to the Russians between 1944 and 1950. With the information they supplied, it was claimed, the Russians developed the atomic bomb twenty years earlier than U.S. military leaders had predicted. In a tumultuous trial, with worldwide publicity, the Rosenbergs were found guilty and sentenced to death under Section 34 of the Espionage Act. The Rosenbergs appealed their convictions to the Supreme Court in 1952 and 1953.

As they had on the Japanese exclusion cases, Black and Frankfurter quickly aligned on one side of the issue and, from the first appeal to the Court to the very last appeals, voted to grant certiorari in the Rosenberg case. Douglas was indecisive, as he had been in the Japanese exclusion cases. However, once he became convinced of the need for a careful Supreme Court assessment of the case (after voting to deny cert in three critical votes when his vote would have brought the case to the Court on the merits), Douglas was prepared to face alone the loud, insistent political demands to execute the couple. Despite the dramatic difficulties created by Douglas's flip-flop on the case, Black stood by him against Chief Justice Vinson and the Court majority.

Between June 7, 1952, and June 18, 1953, the Court had an opportunity to review, on at least six occasions, on the merits, the Rosenberg convictions for conspiring to pass atomic secrets to the Russians in violation of the 1917 Espionage Act.[78] The justices rejected every opportunity.

The attorneys for the Rosenbergs, beginning with their June 7, 1952, petition to the Court, argued that the trial judge was prejudicial and that the death penalty contravened the Eighth Amendment and the general lack of due process for the alleged Russian conspirators. Black and Frankfurter voted to grant certiorari in this petition (denied, 3 to 6), again in November 1952 (denied, 3 to 6), and also in April 1953 (denied, 2 to 7). Both believed that there were important issues that should be heard by the Court.

In late May 1953, after the Court had again voted 2 to 7 to deny cert in another petition from the Rosenbergs, and after voting with the majority to deny cert three times, Douglas had a change of heart. Until then, Douglas explained, he had not considered the questions presented to the Court "cert worthy."[79]

He changed his mind, not because of any change in his views of the guilt of the Rosenbergs (they "were probably very guilty") but because the questions presented to the Court in May 1953 were related "to the indictment, statutes, and so called trial errors. . . . Even though an accused is clearly guilty," Douglas later wrote, "he deserves, under our regime, a fair trial. By the time No. 687 [the May 1953 petition] reached us I was doubtful if the Rosenbergs had had one."[80] To the surprise (and, for some, anger) of his brethren, Douglas, on May 22, 1953, sent a memorandum to the conference, informing them that he would join Black and Frankfurter in voting for certiorari. This changed the vote to 3 to 6, still one vote shy of granting certiorari. However, Douglas was prepared to publish a brief statement explaining his cert vote, which concerned members of the Court. The proposed statement was included in his May 22, 1953, memorandum, in which he wrote that, after having "done further work" and "given the problems more study,"

> I do not believe the conduct of the prosecutor can be as easily disposed of as the Court of Appeals thinks. I therefore have reluctantly concluded that certiorari should be granted. Accordingly, I will ask that the order of denial carry the following notation:
>
> > "Mr. Justice Douglas, agreeing with the Court of Appeals that some of the conduct of the United States Attorney was 'wholly reprehensible' but believing, in disagreement with the Court of Appeals, that it probably prejudiced the defendants seriously, votes to grant certiorari."[81]

Frankfurter immediately asked Vinson to reopen discussion on the certiorari petition, given Douglas's intention. Frankfurter's concern, and frustration, was that Douglas's statement would be published—if certiorari was not granted—and the world would be treated to the spectacle of a justice of the Supreme Court reaching substantive judgment on the behavior of the government in the Rosenberg case. Jackson was also angry. He had received a note from his law clerk, William Rehnquist, in which the future chief justice had written that to grant cert then "would be allowing one justice—WOD—to force the hand of the Court and get the result which he now so belatedly wants."[82] Jackson told Frankfurter that Douglas's memo was "the dirtiest, most shameful, most cynical performance that I have ever heard of in matters pertaining to law."[83]

Jackson, however, to avoid the embarrassment of Douglas's very substantive dissent from denial of certiorari, announced that he was reluctantly prepared to grant certiorari in the Rosenberg case because of Douglas's threat. Douglas then inexplicably told the brethren that he was withdrawing his memorandum—specifically, the reference to the behavior of the U.S. attorney. With this information, Jackson changed his cert vote—and Douglas did nothing. As Jackson told Frankfurter on May 25: "The SOB's bluff was called."[84] The Court, again, on May 25,

1953, denied certiorari, but this time Douglas joined Black and Frankfurter in voting to grant cert.

On June 13, 1953, the last conference session of the 1952 term of the Court, a deeply divided Court rejected another request from the Rosenbergs' attorneys. It was a request for a stay of execution, and it needed a majority vote (of five) of the justices to be granted. They had asked for oral argument before the Court to the question of a stay for the Rosenbergs (denied, 4 to 5) and had asked for a stay of the execution, scheduled for June 18, 1953 (denied, 4 to 5). Again, according to Frankfurter's notes, Douglas's actions were puzzling; they were also critically important.[85] He did not vote to hear oral argument on the defense lawyers' motions to stay the executions—and the defense lawyers lost that critical vote. Douglas then voted to stay the executions (without oral argument). Justice Harold Burton, "who had been willing to hear oral argument, was unwilling to grant a stay without it. . . . [A]gain the Rosenbergs lost."[86] On June 15, 1953, the last day of the 1952 term, the Court rejected the Rosenbergs' motion for a stay of execution.

The *Rosenberg* litigation drama then took an unusual twist. After the Court adjourned for the summer, two attorneys, who were not the Rosenbergs' attorneys of record, approached Douglas late on the night of June 15, 1953, with a petition requesting a stay of execution and a writ of habeas corpus. He took the papers with him and saw the attorneys the following day to hear their legal arguments. After listening to them for two hours, he spoke with Frankfurter, Black, and Vinson. Douglas's next move shocked the nation. Consistent with powers that all justices have, he issued an order that stayed the execution "on the penalty issue,"[87] pending further proceedings in the federal district court to determine the question of the applicability of the penal provisions of Section 10 of the Atomic Energy Act,[88] and pending a timely appeal to the court of appeals from the ruling of the district court.[89] Douglas then immediately left Washington on a vacation trip, assuming that the chief would not act after the order was issued.

However, contrary to precedent, Vinson had secretly talked with Attorney General Herbert Brownwell and Justice Jackson a day before Douglas granted the stay. In response to an appeal by Brownwell, Vinson immediately called the Court into special session to examine the stay. Black complained bitterly to the chief about the illegality of calling a special session and about the unwarranted judicial examination of an order issued by a justice of the Supreme Court. It had never been done, pointed out Black, futilely.

On June 18, 1953, the day before the execution was scheduled, the Court met in open court to hear arguments on two questions: Could the Court vacate the Douglas stay? Was the conflict between the Espionage Act and the Atomic Energy Act a "substantial" federal question? Douglas, in a letter to Fred Rodell some time later, pointed out that it was a closed issue by the time the brethren met in Court to hear arguments. "When the Court was convened, it was after the CJ had talked with six and got assurances from five to overrule me—in advance of argument—in advance of any exposure or explanation of the point."[90]

After poor oral arguments, since no one had time to prepare thorough presentations, the justices had two stormy conference sessions on June 18 and June 19, 1953. Four justices attacked the convening of the special session (Frankfurter,

Black, Douglas, and Burton) and voted to keep the stay in force; Vinson, Jackson, Clark, Reed, and Minton, however, voted to vacate the stay. Clark asserted starkly that "it was wrong to hold up the case any longer."[91] On June 19, 1953, the brethren met briefly in open Court to announce their judgment: the stay was vacated, and the legal question did not rise to the level of a substantial federal question. The Rosenbergs were executed later that afternoon. Years later, Douglas wrote of the conference sessions, "Probably a fifth vote could have been summoned. Vinson was in a towering rage at the suggestion and finally no one pressed the point."[92]

Grimly, as in the *Quirin* postmortem, the justices filed their full opinions after the Rosenbergs had been put to death in the electric chair. For Frankfurter, the exercise "had the appearance of pathetic futility," but, he said, "history also has its claims."[93] Five opinions were published on July 16, 1953. The chief justice delivered the opinion of the Court. Jackson wrote an opinion, in which Vinson, Reed, Clark, and Burton joined. Clark, also, wrote an opinion, in which the other five joined. Black, Frankfurter, and Douglas issued dissents.

Vinson's opinion summarized the process that had led to the special session and the unusual decision to set aside Douglas's stay order. "This Court has the responsibility to supervise the administration of criminal justice by the federal judiciary."[94] Vinson argued that this included seeing that punishments were enforced in a timely manner, whereas Douglas's stay would have delayed the Rosenbergs' punishment by many months. "We decided that a proper administration of the laws required the Court to consider that question forthwith."[95]

Jackson's concurring opinion criticized the irregularity of the attorney's actions in bringing the appeal to Douglas after adjournment: "Edelman is a stranger to the Rosenbergs and to their case. His intervention was unauthorized by them. . . . We discountenance this practice [of] disorderly intervention."[96] Clark's opinion argued that the 1946 Atomic Energy Act did not apply in the Rosenbergs' case because the violation of the Espionage Act of 1917 that they were charged with had occurred in 1944, before the Atomic Energy Act was passed. To apply the 1946 act would raise questions of "ex post facto criminality."[97]

The three dissenters sharply criticized their five brethren for their actions of June 18, 1953. Black's dissent maintained that the Court did not have the power to set aside the stay order issued by Douglas. He also reiterated the point he had made earlier to Douglas, that the Rosenbergs' death sentences were imposed "in violation of law."[98] Frankfurter's dissent focused on whether Douglas's order was frivolous or serious. Since even the Court majority, he said, agreed that Douglas's question was not a frivolous one, the judicial process should have run its course. Frankfurter concluded that "the claim had substance and that the opportunity for adequate exercise of the judicial judgment was wanting."[99] Douglas's dissent was his opportunity to state that he knew "deep in my heart that I am right on the law."[100] A death penalty, he wrote, cannot be imposed without the recommendation of a jury. Congress, in 1946, had adopted new penalties for crimes the Rosenbergs had been charged with committing. The stay should have been honored, and there should have been further proceedings in the federal courts, concluded Douglas.

The Court never heard any of the substantive issues raised by the Rosenbergs' case. The case was one of the opening salvos of the cold war, and the majority of the justices, as in World War II, were not very committed to hearing legal issues raised by enemies of the country. The judicial process and the federal judges were, again, as they always are in time of war and national emergency, "subjected to stress and strain," wrote Frankfurter.[101] Even Douglas was torn: he was, according to one scholar, "emotionally divided between his own self-image as judicial champion of the underdog and his equally powerful loathing for Communists—and those who betray their country."[102]

Some consider Douglas's switches in the case the "grandstanding" of someone who did not really want the Court to hear the case because of his hatred of Communism, yet who wanted to retain his "libertarian credentials." By withdrawing his threat to publish his sharply worded dissent from the denial of certiorari, he could effectively kill the grant of certiorari that Jackson's vote would have provided the Rosenbergs.[103] Defenders of Douglas, especially one of Douglas's former law clerks, argue that Douglas switched his cert vote in May 1953 because, as he said, the Rosenbergs' appeal at that time was "cert worthy." Douglas "took a fresh look at the briefs . . . and came to a different conclusion about the substantiality of the issue."[104] Recently, one of Black's law clerks, Charles Reich, recounted how, years after the Rosenbergs were executed, he and Douglas would take long walks along the C & O Canal, and their conversation inevitably would turn to the Rosenberg case.[105] Like the Japanese exclusion cases, the Rosenberg case seemed to be forever on Douglas's mind.

Among the other postwar issues the Court addressed was the question of how to answer the demand for war-crimes trials and punishments, as well as the insistent demands that the defendants be given the due process guarantees enumerated in the Constitution.

At the conclusion of the war in the Pacific, Tomoyuki Yamashita, commanding general of the Japanese Forces in the Philippines, called the "Tiger of Malaya," was put on trial by military authorities. He was charged by a specially created military commission of five generals with violating the laws of war by "unlawfully disregard[ing] and fail[ing] to discharge his duty as commander to control the operations of the members of his command, permitting them to commit brutal atrocities and other high crimes against people of the United States and of its allies and dependencies."[106] The general was found guilty and sentenced to death by hanging by the military commission on December 7, 1945—four years to the day after the Japanese attack on Pearl Harbor.

His defense attorneys were gravely concerned about the nature of the rules of evidence that had been specially developed for the trial of Yamashita. Many exceptions were made to normal safeguards, such as entirely eliminating the hearsay rule in the Yamashita rules.[107] Statements of unidentified or absent witnesses, inadmissible in a typical criminal trial, were admitted. The defense pointed out that there was not a single bit of evidence introduced by the prosecution that indicated that Yamashita ordered the commission of any of the atrocities committed by his troops.

His team of six defense attorneys, all U.S. Army officers assigned the task of defending Yamashita by the army's Judge Advocate's Office, petitioned for writs of habeas corpus and for a writ of prohibition to the Supreme court of the Philippines. After being rejected by the Philippines Court, they went to the Supreme Court. They argued that (1) the military commission was unlawfully created; (2) the indictment preferred against Yamashita failed to charge him with the violation of the law of war; and (3) the commission was without authority and jurisdiction because the procedures used under rules of evidence violated Articles 25 and 38 of the Articles of War and thereby deprived Yamashita of a fair trial in violation of the due process clause of the Fifth Amendment.[108] The Court received the appeal for a writ of habeas corpus during its 1945 term because federal courts have "jurisdiction to hear collateral attacks on the jurisdiction of military [tribunals]."[109]

For Stone, the issue was solely whether the military commission had jurisdiction to hear the case. It was a stormy issue for the brethren, so stressful that, within days after announcing the opinion of the Court and "having complained about the strain of *Yamashita*," Stone suffered a fatal heart attack in open Court.[110] For Stone and most of the justices, including Black and Douglas, the Yamashita prosecution was "utterly devoid of constitutional protection"; that is, his trial was covered only by the Articles of War.[111]

After the conference, Black raised serious questions about the legislative history of Article 25 of the congressional Articles of War. He was particularly interested in the role of military commissions, as developed by Congress in Article 15. Black also raised the question of precedent: Had the United States ever treated a vanquished foe in this manner? He sought information about the number of affidavits and items of hearsay evidence presented by some of the hundreds of witnesses for the government. From his review of the government's January 10, 1946, response to questions raised primarily by him, Black was seriously concerned about the validity of the actions taken against Yamashita. Black's judgment, however, as well as Chief Justice Stone's and that of four other justices (Douglas, Frankfurter, Roberts, and Reed), ultimately was to validate the death verdict handed down by the military commission.[112] Douglas was strangely silent on this case; there were few notes in his file, and his autobiography did not spend much time on it.

Speaking for the restless six-person majority, Stone wrote that the task of the civilian court was not to decide the guilt or innocence of the petitioner but to consider "only the lawful power of the commission to try the petitioner for the offense charged." Congress, he wrote, "conferred on the courts no power to review [the commission's] determinations save only as it has granted judicial power 'to grant writs of habeas corpus for the purpose of an inquiry into the cause of the restraint of liberty.'" If the military commission, Stone concluded, has "lawful authority to hear, decide and condemn, their action is not subject to judicial review merely because they have made a wrong decision on disputed facts. Correction of their errors of decision is not for the courts but for the military authorities which are alone authorized to review their decisions."[113]

After establishing this narrow framework for review, Stone's opinion concluded by deferring to military authority and denying the writs sought by Yamashita's attorneys. All the restraints on military tribunals in the Articles of War, Stone wrote, were for the benefit of personnel in the army and their dependents. "Enemy combatants are not included" in the articles; these congressional statutes were not applicable to the trial of Yamashita. Nor did they impose any "restrictions upon the procedure to be followed."[114] Yamashita's detention, trial, trial procedures, and conviction, "subject to the proscribed review by the military authorities were lawful."[115] The petitions to the Court were denied.

Murphy and Rutledge wrote eloquent, passionate dissents. Murphy's focused on "the charge with respect to the substance of the crime," while Rutledge's dissent examined the "commission's jurisdiction."[116] Murphy wrote that the military commission had "disregard[ed] the procedural rights of a person as guaranteed by the Constitution, especially by the Due Process clause of the Fifth Amendment"; what happened to Yamashita, concluded Murphy, "is clearly without precedent in international law or in the annals of recorded military history. This is not to say that enemy commanders may escape punishment for clear and unlawful failures to prevent atrocities. But that punishment should be based on charges fairly drawn in light of established rules of international law and recognized concepts of justice."[117] Their dissents led Murphy and Rutledge to be denounced as "Jap Coddlers" in the newspapers.[118] The two dissenters spoke eloquently and courageously in upholding the constitutional requirement of due process of law for all persons.

While *Yamashita* was another of those wartime cases in which Black and Douglas refused to seriously challenge the executive branch, they both were willing to stand against the use of martial law at home, despite their colleagues' strong demands that they defer to governmental authorities.

On December 7, 1941, immediately following the attack on Pearl Harbor, the governor of Hawaii issued a proclamation suspending the writ of habeas corpus and placing the American territory under "martial law." The Hawaiian Organic Act gave him the authority to take such action "in case of rebellion, invasion, or imminent danger thereof, when the public safety requires it."[119] The commanding general of the American forces became the military governor, responsible for defending the area and maintaining order. Military tribunals were created to take the place of civilian courts, including federal courts. As Black said later, in his opinion for the majority in *Duncan* v. *Kahanimoku,* "The military authorities took over the government of Hawaii."[120]

Duncan was a stockbroker who was arrested by military police and charged with stock embezzlement eight months after the attack on Pearl Harbor. Brought before a military tribunal, tried without a jury (which he requested), convicted, and sentenced to five years' imprisonment, Duncan (and another petitioner whose case was joined with his) challenged the authority of military tribunals to try cases without basic due process rights. The military authorities argued, in response to a show cause order of the territorial court, that Hawaii was still in the theater of war and the military had the obligation, under martial law, to try these types of offenses. In turn the petitioners argued that by the time they were arrested by the military authorities, there was no longer the need for martial law, that the civilian courts could function.

The federal district court found that no military necessity ever existed for closing the civilian courts, voided the trials, and ordered the release of Duncan and White. The circuit court of appeals, however, overturned that judgment. It ruled that the military orders and trial judgments were consistent with the declaration of martial law. Ironically, the case was argued before the Supreme Court on December 7, 1945, the fourth anniversary of the attack on Pearl Harbor and the same day that another tribunal sentenced General Yamashita to death.

Black's opinion for the Court carefully examined the statutory background of the Organic Act used by the military to justify the continuation of total martial law. As Black put it to Justice Stone, the situation was nothing less than a "totalitarian program."[121] The language of the act, he noted in his opinion, did not give the military commander the right to close all the civil courts. Indeed, "the language of the [act] fails to define adequately the scope of the power given to the military and to show whether the Organic Act provides that courts of law be supplanted by military tribunals." Black's argument went to the foundations of due process. Reviewing that history, Black noted that "our system of government is the antithesis of total military rule and the founders of this country are not likely to have contemplated complete military dominance within the limits of a Territory." Black concluded with a tip of the judicial hat to the constitutional value of civilian supremacy over the military. The military must always yield to the governance of law. While the military could be authorized by the declaration of martial law to maintain order and to protect the Hawaiian Islands against invasion, martial law "was not intended to authorize the supplanting of courts by military tribunals."[122]

Murphy was very concerned about Black's lack of a ruling based on the constitutional value of fairness. Murphy wrote, "Hugo: . . . I will join your opinion but I believe I will have to go a step further. I don't want to rest on the organic act alone. Constitutional rights were flaunted without necessity and I feel obliged to comment on it."[123] In his concurring opinion, Murphy discussed the value of the "open court" *Milligan* rule (*Ex parte Milligan,* 4 Wall 2 [1865]), developed in a case decided toward the end of the Civil War, in which the Court laid "down the rule that the military lacks any constitutional power in war or in peace to substitute its tribunals for civil courts that are open and operating in the proper and unobstructed exercise of their jurisdiction." The military actions in Hawaii "plainly lacked constitutional sanction," he concluded. The argument for unlimited, total control of the society after martial law was declared "is as untenable today as it was when cast in the language of the Plantagenets, the Tudors and the Stewarts. It is a rank appeal to abandon the fate of all our liberties to the reasonableness of the judgment of those who are trained primarily for war. . . . It deserves repudiation."[124]

What incensed Murphy was the racist aspect of the government's defense of the total control of Hawaii during most of the war. "Especially deplorable, however," he wrote in his opinion, "is this use of the iniquitous doctrine of racism to justify the imposition of military trials. Racism has no place whatever in our civilization. . . . It renders impotent the ideal of the dignity of the human personality, destroying something of what is noble in our way of life. We must therefore reject it completely whenever it arises in the course of a legal proceeding."[125]

Stone argued the opposite point, that Black's draft opinion improperly reached beyond the narrow statutory base and highlighted the value of civilian supremacy. The chief wrote in a letter to Black that he had

> no doubt that martial law could be constitutionally imposed in appropriate circumstances which would authorize the closing of the courts and the substitution of some kind of military justice adequate to the situation. For the disposition of these cases, however, I do not think we have to state what the constitutional limits of martial law are, or to define martial law, for all purposes, with precision. . . . I would suggest that before you circulate the opinion you get the five who voted with you together for a conference. This I think is important before some dissenter begins to mess things up.[126]

Black's response was sharp. It was appropriate to raise constitutional questions in this case: "The executive is without constitutional powers to suspend all legislative enactments in loyal, uninvaded states," nor does the executive have the power to establish a "complete military government in a loyal state whenever it is believed the 'public order and safety require it.' A Supreme Court invalidation of the convictions 'on limited grounds' that the circumstances did not justify it in this loyal territory . . . would be accepted as a declaration that other circumstances would." Firm in his conviction that these constitutional themes had to be part of the majority opinion, Black concluded, "If this prevents a court opinion, . . . I shall regret it."[127]

Stone replied with an earnest desire to maintain unanimity among the six brethren in the majority, asking Black to modify his draft opinion by taking out all references to the *Milligan* decision: "I think you will have great difficulty in supporting, by the *Milligan* case, the proposition that in no circumstances could the military, if authorized to administer martial law, set up any form of courts for trying offenses normally triable by civil courts, but which they were unable to try."[128] Black modified the opinion; however, Murphy then focused on the importance of the *Milligan* rule in the *Duncan* case.

Justices Burton and Frankfurter dissented. Their view was that the executive and the military had the responsibility to respond in the face of war and emergency and that the federal courts had no right to intervene after the fact. These two justices, who regarded war as largely an executive responsibility, dissented "to sound a note of warning against the dangers of over-expansion of judicial control into the fields allotted by the Constitution to agencies of legislative and executive action." For the Court to "intrude its judgment into spheres of constitutional discretion that are reserved either to the Congress or to the Chief Executive, is to invite disregard of that judgment by the Congress or by executive agencies under a claim of constitutional right to do so."[129] Stone dismissed their "objections that Hawaii was under lawful presidential authority in wartime," replying, "I don't think war was going on there any more than in Massachusetts."[130]

When the fighting had ended, the Black-led Court majority in *Duncan* spoke against an all-powerful military establishment. The ruling in the case, however, focused not on the power to declare martial law, but on the guidelines to be followed once martial law was declared. As *Duncan* illustrated, there were still sharp differences of opinion among the eight brethren who were reviewing these troublesome constitutional questions during the 1945 term. Unlike Frankfurter and some of the others, Douglas could not accept the idea that the Supreme Court should give the executive branch carte blanche, but drawing the line for the Westerner was still difficult.

Conscientious Objectors in Wartime

An army needs its troops, and military conscription is the bane of "everyman" in warfare. Black and Douglas, who knew that it was the GIs who suffered most in war, agreed that the government's draft policy had to be assessed constitutionally. The First Amendment's protection of religious freedom could be interpreted to excuse young men with religious objections from active service in the military. After the passage of the Selective Service Act in 1940, legal controversies pitted the religious beliefs and rights of an individual against the needs of the state in time of national emergency.

In the Court's first case involving the act, a Jehovah's Witness named Falbo was convicted of disobeying a local draft board's order to report for an assignment (as a conscientious objector) to work of national importance. When the court of appeals upheld the conviction, he appealed to the Supreme Court.

Black wrote for the majority.[131] Murphy dissented. Black and the brethren in the majority posed the basic question: At what point in the draft process was a person's administrative remedies exhausted and judicial review applicable? The answer: only *after* the person had been inducted into the armed services in some capacity—either to report for active duty or to report for national duty as a conscientious objector. The act did not have any provision for judicial review before a draftee had gone through all the administrative stages in the draft process and been inducted. Black took that position in the majority opinion because he was concerned about the disruption of the flow of manpower into the army if men were able to seek judicial recourse at any point before receiving their final induction notice from the local draft board. "Congress apparently regarded 'a prompt and unhesitating obedience to orders' issued in the process 'indispensible to the complete attainment of the object' of national defense," concluded Black for the Court.[132]

Whereas for the majority, the channeling of manpower into the war effort was critical, for Murphy the case presented yet another aspect "of the perplexing problem of reconciling basic principles of justice with military needs in wartime." The government had an obligation to provide Falbo, the Jehovah's Witness petitioner (sentenced to five years' imprisonment)— and others like him—with "the fullest hearing possible." Mobilization of the armed services, concluded Murphy, was neither "impeded nor augmented by the availability of judicial review of local board orders in criminal proceedings." The fact that Falbo was going to remain in prison for five years "without being provided the opportunity of proving that the prosecution was based upon arbitrary and illegal administrative action is not in keeping with the high standards of our judicial system."[133]

During its 1945 term, the Court had occasion again to examine the issue raised in *Falbo.* The majority opinion was written by Justice Douglas (who was to write a number of majority opinions in this area of conscientious objector litigation). In the case of *Estep* v. *United States,* the question for the justices was "whether there may be judicial review of his classification in a prosecution . . . where he reported for induction, was finally accepted but refused to submit to induction."[134] Estep and Smith were Jehovah's Witnesses who had claimed exemption due to their ministerial responsibilities. Both were indicted for willful failure to submit to induction. At their trials, they offered as defense the fact that they had been denied due process by the local draft board's irregular and unlawful proceeding. The federal courts refused to allow this defense.[135]

Douglas was assigned to write for the Court. Stone wrote to Douglas to assist him.

> We have here no case of suspension of the writ, and so it seems to me that one who is restrained of his liberty may resort to habeas corpus to test the question whether his detention is lawful. . . . Due process is satisfied so long as the draftee can secure prompt review before he suffers the loss of substantial rights. . . . In view of the clear constitutional provision preserving the writ [of habeas corpus] for its appropriate traditional use, I think you might well walk up to that question, decide it and make it the peg on which you really hang the rest of your opinion.[136]

The majority's intention seemed clear: provide the conscientious objector with the very minimum procedural protection. In a memo that shocked and angered some of his brethren, Douglas announced a few weeks after the conference that he had rethought the idea of habeas corpus and had come up with a somewhat different jurisprudential argument than that discussed and agreed on previously. He was concerned, as he had been in other wartime cases, about the availability of due process for individuals caught in the madness of war in a democratic society. Douglas wrote in his memo that he had come to the belief, "on further study," that the right of habeas corpus "should be available after conviction in these cases. If I am correct, the cases are put in quite a different posture, at least for me. For that reason I am circulating a [new opinion]."[137]

Douglas's revised majority draft opinion reasoned that, as congressional silence about judicial review was not necessarily a bar to federal judicial review, the Supreme Court could fashion a remedy that met with the spirit of the Selective Service Act but also reflected the constitutional text's protection of religious rights. And if a local draft board "acts so contrary to its granted authority as to exceed its jurisdiction," the Court may grant a petition for habeas corpus. Interpreting the intent of the Congress, Douglas concluded: "We cannot believe that Congress intended that criminal sanctions were to be applied to orders issued by local boards no matter how flagrantly they violated the rules and regulations which define their jurisdiction." Douglas's draft opinion was acceptable to the majority. When issued, the opinion reversed the convictions and ordered new trials for the two petitioners.[138]

Frankfurter, extremely angry with Douglas about his revised "egregious non-sequiter,"[139] wrote a separate concurring opinion (as did Murphy and Rutledge). Frankfurter wrote that Douglas's opinion, completely contrary to the "expressed will of Congress," ran "counter to the achievement of the great object avowed by Congress in enacting this statute." Understanding the 1940 act (and all the decisions of the forty federal judges in the federal circuit courts until *Estep*) to clearly and plainly state that the decisions of all the local boards were final, Frankfurter felt that to allow review "is not to respect the context of purpose into which a specific provision of the law is properly placed. To do so disregards that purpose."[140]

However, after a lengthy critique of the majority's faulty reasoning, Frankfurter explained his reason for concurring. Since, "in violation of the Board's duty under the Act and the Regulations," the local board had denied Estep the right to appeal its decision to the appeal board, "Estep should have been allowed to make proof of this claim [of religious discrimination] by appropriate motion to be disposed of by the court."[141] Justice Burton and Chief Justice Stone dissented.

Estep allowed the conscientious objector to raise, as a defense at a criminal trial for refusing induction into the military on religious grounds, the argument that the local draft board acted beyond its jurisdiction. Douglas's opinion did not allow pre-induction or preindictment judicial review. It did, however, support judicial review after conviction. But in wartime, that modest jurisdictional message was a very real check on the arbitrariness of the local draft boards.

Other draft cases came to the Supreme Court, for more than 6,000 men were convicted of violating the 1940 Selective Service Act, essentially for willfully failing to be inducted into the armed forces. Douglas wrote the majority opinions in the cases that followed *Estep*.[142] In cases heard by the Court under the leadership of Chief Justices Earl Warren and Warren Burger, the justices continued to accept the validity of the Court's *Falbo* principle that, by and large, the government's responsibility to raise an army, as exercised by the local selective service boards, should not easily be set aside by legal challenges. However, as the Court noted in *Estep,* the protestor did have the constitutional right to seek habeas corpus and other remedies consistent with due process of law.

For the most part, Justices Black and Douglas accepted the validity of this view. Certainly, during World War II, they, along with their colleagues, deferred to local draft boards and, except for the most egregious violations of due process, believed that the federal courts should be minimally involved with the executive's efforts to get men in uniform. More recently, although the Warren and Burger Courts expanded the scope of the "conscientious objector" exemption,[143] the Warren Court also validated the conviction of a petitioner who burned his draft card as an act of "symbolic speech" to protest the Vietnam War because the act blunted the government's interest in ensuring the continuing availability of such draft cards.[144]

As Douglas and Black knew so well, World War II was a much different war than the subsequent military engagements in which Americans fought and died. Black despised the consequences of war, but both he and Douglas felt that the World War II was a war of good versus evil that must be fought. The Vietnam War, however, was an illegitimate war. Douglas considered it the duty of the justices of the Court to review the critically important question that it raised about executive power waging war without constitutional authorization and to rule against the executive.

For Black, executive power had to be broadly based and, as long as it was bound by the constitutional text's commander-in-chief language, pervasive enough to deal with the national security dilemma. His *Falbo* opinion clearly states his understanding of executive power in wartime. Douglas, however, began building a bridge in these cases between the conscientious objector and the constitutional text's guarantee of religious freedom and due process rights. He was to continue to do so for the rest of his tenure on the Court.

Control of the Economy in Wartime

The power of Congress and the president to harness commerce and manufacturing is very broad. The civilian population must meet critical military and economic war needs. The Supreme Court, during and after World War II, accepted the assertion that in time of war (or other national emergency), Congress and the executive must spring into action to manage the economy.[145] Black and Douglas were upset by those who profited during wartime, and they supported the government's efforts to control wages and prices (and their profits).[146]

During the 1951 term, the Court heard a watershed case concerning the power of the president to control the economy using his "inherent" powers. While the United States was engaged in the Korean conflict, a war that was never formally declared, President Truman, Congress, and the federal courts clashed over the president's efforts to avert the dangerous shortage of ammunition on the battlefield that he feared if there was a strike of union steelworkers in 1952.[147]

Wage and price controls were in effect at the time, as the Wage Stabilization Board worked to control inflation. For political reasons, Truman refused to implement the provisions of the 1947 Taft-Hartley Act, which would have required a cooling-off period before a strike, when CIO steelworkers' contracts expired on December 31, 1951. The unions announced their intent to strike. Truman asked the Wage Stabilization Board to make recommendations on wages and steel prices and, at the same time, asked the steelworkers to remain on the job while the board tried to resolve the impasse. The board recommended an increase in wages, but management rejected the recommendation because of the board's refusal to allow price increases that the firms considered essential.

Truman, faced with a strike that, he deeply believed, would seriously threaten American armed forces fighting in Korea, had a limited number of options. He could invoke Taft-Hartley for an additional eighty-day cooling-off period, ask Congress for new legislation, or, consistent with a memo prepared by his former attorney general, Tom C. Clark, use the "inherent" powers of the president to seize the steel mills.

On April 8, 1952, a day before the strike was to begin, Truman issued Executive Order 10340, directing Secretary of Commerce Charles Sawyer to take possession of the nation's steel mills and run them for the government until the labor–management issues were resolved, or until Congress acted to end the dispute. As Robert J. Donovan writes in his study of the period, "Not the least remarkable [of these events] was private encouragement from his close friend Fred Vinson, Chief Justice of the United States. . . . [Vinson] privately advised the president to go ahead with the seizure, basing the recommendation on legal grounds."[148] Truman, like President Richard M. Nixon two decades later, thought his four appointees to the Court—especially Chief Justice Vinson and Justice Tom C. Clark, who wrote the memo on the president's inherent powers—would support him on the question of the constitutionality of the seizure.

The Supreme Court took the case from the court of appeals before it had rendered a decision. In response to the steel companies' request for an injunction, the federal district court judge had ruled that Truman's action was unconstitutional. The justices heard oral argument a little more than a month after the order was issued and announced their judgment promptly in June. By a 6 to 3 vote, the justices invalidated the presidential order.

After the Court adjourned and Douglas headed off for the summer, an outraged Truman drafted a letter to his friend Douglas:

> I appreciated very much your letter of July third and I am sorry that I didn't have a chance to talk with you before you left. In fact, I am sorry that I didn't have an opportunity to discuss precedents with you before you came to the conclusion you did on that crazy decision that has tied up this country.
>
> I am writing a monograph on just what makes justices of the U.S. Supreme Court tick. There was no decision by the majority although there were seven opinions against what was best for this country.
>
> I don't see how a Court made up of so-called "liberals" could do what that Court did to me. I am going to find out just why before I quit this office.[149]

Upon reflection, Truman decided not to send the letter.

The brethren met in conference on May 16, 1952, to examine "whether the President was acting within his constitutional power when he issued an order directing the Secretary of Commerce to take possession of and operate most of the nation's steel mills."[150] Douglas's law clerk had suggested to the justice that "to justify the President's exercise of power in a case where—as here—he has not exhausted those procedures prescribed by Congress could create a dangerous precedent . . . a dictator."[151] Douglas knew the significance of the case and took copious notes as the discussion proceeded around the conference table.

Vinson strongly defended Truman's actions. Seizures by presidents in the past had been carried out with and without an act of Congress, he argued. There was nothing unconstitutional about Truman's use of his "inherent" executive powers to continue to fight the Korean conflict. Black disagreed with the chief. Truman could act under the guidelines of Taft-Hartley or could use the Wage Stabilization Board to try to cool off the CIO. According to Douglas's notes, for Black, the question was whether Truman had "the power to seize without a statute. . . . Can the President make laws—here we have labor disputes and [a] law working concerning it." Black questioned if they should examine the constitutional issue of the president's inherent powers. "He thinks we must," since the damage to our constitutional system of government would be "irreparable" if Truman and other executives in the future could take over control of private management. Although Black knew that the Court did not have the capability to enforce a decision that went against presidential power, he strongly believed that the constitutional text had to be defended in the form of a definitive judicial opinion on the merits.[152]

Reed, who, along with Vinson and Minton, ultimately dissented, was more cautious: "Perhaps we should rest on the war power and say the president has the power to seize as Commander in Chief. Couldn't president seize a railroad to move troops? FDR closed the banks to protect economy" (during the first months of his administration). Frankfurter opened his comments by saying that "everyone should write in this case." On the substantive issue of inherent presidential powers, Douglas carefully noted Frankfurter's judicial caution. Frankfurter agreed with Black, but "he tries to avoid the constitutional issue—the less the Court pronounces constitutional doctrine the better—but he thinks here the constitutional question cannot be avoided." Douglas also agreed with Black that the president was bound by the Constitution and that the Court should examine the issue on the constitutional merits and reach judgment.[152]

Justice Robert Jackson did "not want the Court to pass on whether there is an emergency—the question is what [can] the President do in an emergency." Jackson said he would affirm the district court judgment. Justice Burton, one of Truman's appointees, was deeply troubled by the case. It called for a Supreme Court "decision that requires policy making and therefore it is for Congress to decide," but, he noted, the president has no power to seize apart from the congressional statutes. He, too, would affirm.

Justice Tom Clark, Truman's attorney general, whose memo had been used by Truman to justify the seizure order, concluded that the president had acted improperly. He, however, wanted "the decision limited to this case [for] he was unwilling to say President has no power—*here* the situation could have been averted by two methods not involving seizure."

Finally, Sherman Minton spoke. Minton, a former senatorial colleague of Truman's and another of Truman's appointees, joined Vinson and Reed in dissent. Truman, he urged his brethren, "did everything he could to avoid a strike. [T]here are no vacant spots in power when the security of the nation is at stake. Power is the power of defense. It rests in [the] president. There is an emergency now. Truman seized the plants because the defense of the country required it. The President had to act." Douglas also recorded in his notes, as Minton defended the president, *"Minton is very excited about this and pounds the table."* An agitated Minton concluded, saying that the president "gets his inherent power from the power to defend the nation in a day of peril" and that he would reverse.[154]

Immediately after the conference, Jackson told his clerks: "Well boys, the President got licked."[155] Black, the senior associate justice in the majority, assigned himself the task of writing for the majority. However, given that the Court wanted to announce the decision quickly, there was very little time to develop an institutional judgment. Every justice in the majority wrote an opinion. Frankfurter's request had been met. Justices Frankfurter, Jackson, Burton, Clark, and Douglas wrote separate opinions. Chief Justice Vinson, who had assured Truman that the seizure was legal, wrote a dissent, joined by Reed and Minton.

For the Court, Black concluded that "in the framework of our Constitution, the

President's power to see that the laws are faithfully executed refutes the idea that he is to be a lawmaker." Frankfurter's concurrence focused on the separation of powers and quoted Chief Justice Holmes: "The duty of the President to see that the laws be executed is a duty that does not go beyond the laws or require him to achieve more than Congress sees fit to leave within his power." While Douglas believed that there was an emergency, "the fact that it was necessary that measures be taken to keep steel in production does not mean that the President, rather than Congress, had the constitutional authority to act." Moreover, even if the president could seize the mills, he would be required to provide just compensation under the Fifth Amendment. That, in turn, required congressional authorization, since only Congress possessed appropriation authority.

Jackson concurred but took a very different approach. Black argued from the constitutional text, urging that even if the president had implied powers, he was obligated to show that the power claimed flowed from one of the powers specified in Article II. Jackson countered that the issue was not whether the chief executive could trace his claim to text, but the dynamic relationship between congressional and executive claims. The problem the president faced in this case was that Congress had opposed his position, having rejected seizure of the mills as an option during the Taft-Hartley debate, meaning that his actions were, at the least, suspect. In such a situation, the Court could not simply give the benefit of the doubt to Truman.

Chief Justice Vinson's dissent pointed to Congress's many actions in foreign policy, such as the Truman Doctrine, the Marshall Plan, the Mutual Security Act of 1951, defense funding, draft renewal, NATO, United Nations Charter support, and support for the war in Korea. "The President has the duty to execute [these] legislative programs. Their successful execution depends upon continued production of steel and stabilized prices for steel." Therefore, if continued production is threatened, he argued, the president may seize the steel mills. The inherent powers of the presidency had given Truman the power to so act. The majority of six rejected that view, however.

Rehnquist, Jackson's law clerk at the time, has speculated that the Court invalidated the president's action for three reasons: (1) public opinion's dramatic turn against the president's seizure policy, which "had a considerable influence on the Court," (2) public ambivalence about the Korean War, and (3) the low level of Truman's popularity at that time.[156] Truman wrote that Douglas voted against the presidential action because he was "afraid, apparently, that if the president is supported in this case, there would be a serious danger, that if the GOP were in power it could make a lot of seizures against labor unions."[157] According to Douglas, Truman was so upset with the opinion that "Hugo Black gave him a party. We all went and poured a lot of bourbon down Harry Truman. . . . He didn't change his mind, but he felt better, at least for a few hours."[158]

The Court's judgment in the steel seizure case did limit the power of the president. However, it was a time of less than national emergency, as the nation was fighting a limited war in Korea, with an unpopular president in the White House. It was also a case in which the facts clearly undermined the president's credibility. During other national emergencies, when the inherent power of the executive has been used to respond to the dangers, the Court has clearly deferred to the executive and his staff—especially the military authorities.

For Justice Black, what mattered when confronted with a military threat to the security of the state was the judgment of the military, not of the federal judges. Moreover, Black and Douglas agreed with Reed's observation that war had provided the Court with the occasion for a "different appraisal" of the requirements of the Constitution.

However, in cases that did not involve military judgment in wartime, the two jurists sided with the petitioner who claimed a deprivation of constitutional rights. At bottom, however, Black and Douglas's patriotism would not have allowed them to jeopardize the war effort, for instance in the manpower-needs cases. Their personal irritant, Felix Frankfurter, agreed with the two justices most of the time. The patriotic, naturalized citizen Frankfurter disagreed with Black and Douglas in the denaturalization cases and in the flag salute cases (after *Gobitis*).

Fundamental differences between their jurisprudence and that of Felix Frankfurter became apparent in these war term and national security cases. As Douglas said on reflection years later, "we had not fully divined" Frankfurter's view of due process. In these cases, and especially in the Red Scare–era cases involving freedom of speech, Frankfurter "was willing to allow the government to act only if its procedures were reasonable and fair," a view of due process that was fundamentally at odds with their own developing jurisprudential views.[159]

For the most part, as good soldiers, the justices of the Court made every attempt to resolve legal questions associated with the war effort rather than raise legal obstacles in the path of military victory and forthright action, after the war, against former enemy leaders. While many of the brethren admittedly felt anguish over these decisions of the Court in wartime, only Murphy and, to a lesser extent, Rutledge (in *Yamashita*) spoke out forcefully about the violence done to the constitutional guarantees of due process by the Court majority. The rest of the brethren, including Black and Douglas, felt it was appropriate to support the executive, military, and legislative agents as they acted to successfully wage war.

Most of the brethren regarded the new cold war against the Soviet Union as one that had to be waged as vigorously as America had waged war against the Axis powers. For Black and Douglas, however, it was a watershed in the development of their views on the meaning and scope of the First Amendment's freedom of speech. Their attitude toward the primacy of freedom of speech, press, association, and religion had roots in their earlier commitment—Black as a local judge and county prosecutor and Douglas as a dedicated legal realist—to the primacy of the constitutional text in a democracy.

The country's second Red Scare, beginning in the late 1940s, forced Black and Douglas, mostly jointly in dissent, to develop fully their conception of a constitutional absolute: freedom of speech.

 7

Red Scare in America

THE SOVIET UNION, America's wartime ally in its struggle against the Axis powers, very soon became the source of a witch hunt in the United States. A fear that Stalin was planning worldwide Communist revolution quickly gripped the nation's leaders and then the public. Many believed that failure to prevent the spread of Communism at home would endanger the nation, a concern that was heightened by the pace of events in Eastern and Western Europe; the Soviet Union's blockade of Berlin in 1948; the revelations of spy scandals that enabled the Russians to get the secrets of the atomic bomb; and, in 1950, the beginning of the Korean War.

In response to this new danger, the national government and many state governments instituted a number of programs to prevent an American *putsch* by the Communists.[1] Loyalty-security programs, developed by agencies to police their employees, "proliferated at all levels: the federal government imposed them, inter alia, on labor leaders, unclassified researchers, and licensed seamen; various states even applied them to social workers, veterinarians, boxers and wrestlers."[2] President Truman initiated the loyalty-security program for federal workers in 1947, laying the ground, Douglas said, "for the most intensive search for ideological strays that we have ever known."[3]

In addition to searches for membership in suspect groups or affiliation with "un-American" political agencies, loyalty oaths were given to many millions of Americans who worked for federal, state, and local government.[4] The vague oaths trapped unsuspecting citizens into perjury when they swore loyalty and only later found that their prior activities were considered subversive. In the late 1960s, Douglas claimed that the loyalty-security programs had, since 1947, processed 20 million men and women.[5] The attorney general's lists of subversive organizations, the vigorous enforcement of federal legislation such as the Smith Act of 1940, and the creation of antisubversive statutes and organizations (such as the Subversive Activities Control Board) to monitor and restrain the Communist party members and their "fellow travelers" were among the strategies employed to avoid Communist subversion. This period was an unfortunate example of what Baker has called "America's dark side."[6]

A sure way to prevent the spread of Communism in America, the argument ran, was to prevent these subversives, most of them American citizens, from speaking or writing about the virtues of Communism or criticizing the status quo. The problem, quickly subordinated by political leaders, of what to do about the protections afforded by the First Amendment was one that the federal courts in America had begun to address during the earlier Red Scare, which had seized the country from roughly 1919 to 1927.

Defending Free Speech in a Time of Peril

The 1917 Espionage Act and the 1918 Sedition Act were used during World War I to restrict the First Amendment rights of opponents of the war.[7] After the war, the legislation was used to convict Bolshevik sympathizers and Socialists.[8] State statutes prohibiting the advocacy of criminal anarchy and criminal syndicalist activities—most of them passed between 1917 and 1921 "in response to World War I and the fear of Bolshevism that developed in its wake"—were used to convict Bolsheviks or alleged supporters of radical causes.[9] These laws made the advocacy of ideas in speeches or by the distribution of handbills the basis for criminal convictions whether the speakers intended to incite illegal action or not. And advocacy was often defined in very broad terms. The federal courts upheld this use of legislation to repress the expression of deviant political and economic ideas.

Black and Douglas, then, came to the Court at a time when the judiciary generally took a cautious, narrow view of the meaning and scope of the First Amendment. Both of them considered the constitutional text absolute regarding the right to freedom of speech, press, religion, and assembly. In its entirety, the First Amendment states that "Congress shall make no law respecting an establishment of religion, or prohibiting the free exercise thereof; or abridging the freedom of speech, or of the press; or the right of the people peacefully to assemble, and to petition the Government for a redress of grievances." While Black strongly defended the broad use of constitutionally derived powers of the executive and the legislature, he was a near absolutist regarding constitutional restrictions on the censorship of free speech. Douglas, too, vigorously insisted that the constitutional right of free speech was so broad that the government was constitutionally powerless to intercede and curtail a person's rights under the First Amendment.

Black and Douglas were as oné in their defense of freedom of belief, association, and speech, but they had arrived at their positions by different routes. Moreover, their dramatically different understandings of the range of First Amendment protection proved to be one of the most divisive issues in their relationship. For Black, the constitutional text was both the starting point and the outer boundary, beyond which the people exercised their power to govern through their elected representatives. For Douglas, the Bill of Rights provided broad protection to freedom of expression in contemporary forms like symbolic speech (for example, burning a flag or draft card in protest) and extended to all forums where public opinion is molded, including such new "Main Streets" as modern shopping centers. Where they differed, very sharply, was over Douglas's view, expressed in his response to a fan mail letter, that the Bill of Rights protections "do not cover all of man's idiosyncracies" and, therefore, the Supreme Court has to read constitutional protections broadly.[10]

The First Amendment must never become a "tinkling cymbal," wrote Hugo Black to his good friend Edmond Cahn.[11] All judges, especially the justices of the Supreme Court, must act vigorously to ensure that the constitutional guarantee of freedom of speech remains a right of a free people. Black viewed the First Amendment as denying governments (national or local) "all power to act in certain areas—whatever the scope of those areas may be."[12] For the Alabaman, this clearly applied to the free speech guarantee: "Without deviation, without exception, without any ifs, buts, or whereases, that freedom of speech means that government shall not do anything to people or, in the words of the Magna Carta, move against people, either for the views they have or the views they express or the words they speak or write." Black, like Brandeis, believed "with Jefferson that it is time enough for government to step in and regulate people when they do something, not when they say something."[13]

In a letter to noted scholar Alexander Meiklejohn, Black wrote again of his acceptance of "the Jeffersonian idea that, in substance, it is time enough for government to step in when speech evolves into conduct or as some might say when speech evolves into 'other kinds of conduct than speech.'"[14] The First Amendment's guarantee of free speech was much more than "an admonition"; it was a categorical command to government to leave the people alone![15]

In Black's view, the right to freedom of speech and press was both an end in itself and the foundation of democracy's success. "The power to think, speak, and write freely without governmental censorship or interference is the most precious privilege of citizens vested with power to select public policies and public officials."[16] Black and Douglas respected the assumption behind the First Amendment that if the people heard all sides of an issue, such as Communism, they would choose "the better, wiser, more beneficial of alternative courses."[17] In a letter to journalist Irving Dilliard in 1953, Black wrote of the view that had "prevailed when Jefferson was elected," when "the United States was without power to pass laws that abridged discussion of public questions at all"; in a final comment, he added: "No group seems to be advocating such a view today."[18]

The First Amendment's protection was absolute. The Constitution's words in that amendment were categorical. And the words of the Constitution, not the much weaker, judicially devised tests, were the guides for the federal judges. Black found the "clear and present danger" standard, developed by two jurists he greatly respected. Supreme Court Justices Oliver W. Holmes and Louis D. Brandeis, deficient because it could "be used to justify the punishment of advocacy."[19] It was also too easily converted into a "balancing test," in which a citizen's rights were balanced against the majority's need for order, because someone had to determine when a danger from speech was so serious and imminent that it justified suppression. The balancing test, employed by the Supreme Court majorities during both Red Scares, was totally inconsistent with the command of the First Amendment; it was, Black said, "the most dangerous of the tests developed by the justices of the Court."[20] Black and Douglas were continually battling the views advocated by several colleagues on the Court, especially those held by Frankfurter and Harlan.

Douglas had a deep and abiding belief that absolutely unfettered freedom of speech and press was necessary for a democracy. The First Amendment, he wrote, enjoys a "preferred position" in the hierarchy of values because without freedom of speech and expression all other liberties are meaningless.[21] For Douglas, freedom of speech in the First Amendment "includes more than teaching in the abstract; it means all shades of advocacy from lukewarm endorsement to partisan promotion." Freedom of speech in the Bill of Rights, wrote Douglas, was "the right of advocacy for the purpose of incitement, as well as for education. . . . Free speech had traditionally included both."[22] In short, the Consitution, according to Douglas as well as to Black, protected all kinds of speech.

Douglas, like Black, did not accept a "clear and present danger" standard or a balancing test as the way to judge the extent of the liberty. In 1969, in *Brandenberg v. Ohio*, Douglas concurred in order to express himself on the matter: "I see no place in the regime of the First Amendment for any 'clear and present danger' test whether strict and tight as some would make it or free-wheeling as the Court in Dennis rephrased it. . . . The test was so twisted and perverted in Dennis as to make the trial of those teachers of Marxism an all-out political trial which was part and parcel of the cold war that has eroded substantial parts of the First Amendment."[23] Further, in a 1972 letter to a *New York Times* reporter, Douglas wrote that his use of clear and present danger in *Dennis* was to show that "it could not be satisfied. . . . But I have never thought clear and present danger has a place in our constitutional scheme."[24] His explanation was partly true, but it is also the case that he had changed since the 1951 case involving the conviction of Communist party leaders. As in other areas, a Douglas already predisposed to favor right over power had become an adamant First Amendment absolutist.

Like Justices Holmes and Brandeis before him, and with Hugo Black, Douglas saw the speech protected by the First Amendment as instrumental to maintaining the democratic republic. "The First Amendment," he said, "sets us apart from most other nations. It marks the end of all censorship, it allows the ability of the mind to roam at will over the entire spectrum of ideas, and the sanctity of one's beliefs."[25] Douglas incorporated into his free-speech discussions and opinions ideas that he had garnered while traveling around the globe. Uniformly, these were concepts that extolled the value of free expression as a generator of ideas and an uplifter of a community's values. While he considered Communism to be a brutal totalitarian system, his free-speech decisions were never anti-Communist diatribes. For Douglas, the essence of the free-speech right was the generation of ideas that would lead to a better society.

However, Douglas was realistic about the fate of political deviants in America. "The radical," he wrote in his autobiography, "has never fared well in American life, whether he was dubbed anarchist, socialist, Bolshevik or Communist. . . . The seeds of Communist thought . . . fell on inhospitable soil. America has long been and remains a very conservative nation. In the 1950s, when the Cold War flourished, the resulting climate of opinion made the dispensation of justice very unlikely when one was merely charged with being a Communist, let alone a person who was, in fact, a hard-core member."[26] It was for this reason that he wrote to Justice William J. Brennan during the 1956 term of the Court, saying that, while he liked Brennan's draft opinion, he was "greatly disturbed by the part on affiliation. . . . I think that the word 'affiliation' as used has an invidious connotation. The fact that a person may take identical positions over and over again on certain domestic issues does not mean that person should be condemned merely because those positions coincide with the Communist position. To condemn a man on that ground would, I think, raise serious questions under the First Amendment."[27] Clearly, Douglas's letter to Brennan reflected his concern that in a period of fear and hysteria, Americans would have little understanding or tolerance for those whose positions on public issues made them suspect as, at the least, Communist sympathizers.

Unlike his colleagues Felix Frankfurter and John M. Harlan, Douglas could not accept the idea that where state or local government was concerned, the Fourteenth Amendment due process clause provided a general protection for free speech but did not apply the specific requirements of the First Amendment. As Douglas wrote to Harlan: "If the right of free speech is watered down by the due process clause of the Fourteenth Amendment and made subject to state regulation, then the police power of the state has a pretty broad area for application."[28] Harlan and especially Frankfurter believed, according to Douglas, that the freedom of speech "as guaranteed against state abridgement by reason of the Fourteenth Amendment, was a watered-down version of the right guaranteed by the First Amendment, since those freedoms could "be modified or controlled by the states so long as they did not violate due process." Douglas wrote that in Frankfurter's mind, due process was "a concept of 'ordered liberty,' a regime of reasonable regulation. Thus, for example, freedom of the press could be abridged, as long as due process was observed," whereas "Black . . . and I thought that when the Constitution said in the First Amendment that there should be 'no law' abridging a specific right, it did not mean 'some law, provided it is reasonable'."[29] Frankfurter was exasperated by this "corkscrewery" behavior of Douglas, whom he occasionally called a "strange mommser," a Yiddish epithet meaning "bastard."[30]

Despite their agreement on most First Amendment issues, Black and Douglas locked horns over cases involving symbolic speech, or forms of communication, such as demonstrations, other than what might be called pure speech. While the two justices came to adamant opposing views on the implications of "speech brigaded with conduct," an issue that emerged in the Court's early-1940s picketing cases, they most assuredly could agree that so-called subversives were targeted not because of any conduct but only because of their beliefs and their speech.[31] These unfortunates were generally charged with violating the Smith Act's prohibition against advocating ideas that were potentially harmful to the government.

Black distinguished between speech rights—categorically protected by the First Amendment—and conduct, which could be regulated by the state under certain circumstances. "I have always been careful to draw a line between speech and conduct," he wrote. It is time enough, he claimed, for government to act when speech has been acted upon. Until and unless that conduct occurs—for example, picketing in violation of basic local ordinances that are not applied in a discriminatory manner—government cannot interfere with speech, no matter how inflammatory. A person picketing, however, was "not only communicating ideas . . . but pursuing a course of conduct in addition to constitutionally protected speech and press. [Such a person] has no constitutional right to appropriate someone else's property to do so."[32]

Black never accepted the argument that the First Amendment protects conduct. Protest, even hard political protest, need not, he thought, be carried out by breaking local ordinances. The decision to protest, he said in a 1968 television interview, does not automatically mean that

> the only way to protest anything is to go out and do it on the streets. That is not true. . . . I've never said that freedom of speech gives people the right to tramp up and down the streets by the thousands, either saying things that threaten others, with real literal language, or that threaten them because of the circumstances under which they do it. . . . Bill Douglas and I both expressed our view on that point about twenty-five years ago, in which we said that the First Amendment protects speech, and it protects writing. But it doesn't have anything that protects a man's right to walk around and around my house, if he wants to, fasten my people, my family up into the house, make them afraid to go out of doors, afraid that something will happen. It just doesn't do that. That's conduct.[33]

In *Gregory* v. *Chicago,* a case heard during the 1968 term of the Court, Black wound up writing a concurring opinion in which these values were reinforced: "Speech and press are, of course, to be free, so that public matters can be discussed with impunity. But picketing and demonstrating can be regulated like other conduct of men. I believe that the homes of men, sometimes the last citadel of the tired, the weary and the sick, can be protected by government from noisy, marching, tramping, threatening picketers and demonstrators bent on filling the minds of men, women, and children with fears of the unknown."[34]

Of course, this was the same Hugo Black who, in 1937, had been driven from his vacation suite in England and from his home in America by newsmen hungry for information about his KKK membership. This was the same Hugo Black who came to Washington with a strong commitment to the fundamental constitutional rights of property owners. Douglas, though none too happy with parts of *Gregory,* joined Black's concurring opinion.[35]

Douglas wrote, tersely and crisply, on the subject of speech plus conduct: "As to conduct, different considerations apply. . . . It is not beyond legislative power to treat only conduct."[36] Like Black, he differentiated between pure speech and speech plus conduct, such as picketing, but he differed with Black as to when speech and peaceful protest became illegal and subject to regulation by formal authorities.[37] Douglas considered picketing "'free speech plus,'. . . That means that it can be regulated when it comes to the 'plus' or 'action' side of the protest. It can be regulated as to the number of pickets and the place and hours, because traffic and other community problems would otherwise suffer."[38] As he wrote in his autobiography, "advocacy at some point can come so close to the line where action commences that the two become brigaded."[39] In the classic free-speech Communist party cases, however, Black's and Douglas's differences on this issue were imperceptible.

"Balancing" Away the First Amendment's Absolute Protections

Long after his lonely vigil with Black on behalf of free speech during the cold war, Justice Douglas wrote in his autobiography that the Court had had an opportunity to examine the constitutionality of the Smith Act during its October 1943 term in the case of *Dunne* v. *United States.* "We denied cert [with] Murphy, Rutledge and Black vot[ing] to grant. If I had done likewise, there would have been four to grant and the Court would have heard the case. It was clear that the majority of five— Stone, Roberts, Reed, Frankfurter, and Jackson—would have voted to affirm; and it seemed to me at that particular point in history unwise to put the Court's seal of approval on that doctrine. Better let the issue be presented at a more auspicious time! That is why I did not vote to grant the petition."[40] Consequently, the issue of the constitutionality of provisions of the 1940 Alien Registration Act, commonly called the Smith Act, which made the advocacy of ideas a criminal offense, did not come to the Court until the 1950 term.[41]

When *Dennis* v. *United States*[42] did reach the Court, presenting the justices with the question of the Smith Act's validity, Vinson was chief justice. Black's and Douglas's ideological allies, Justices Rutledge and Murphy, were no longer on the high bench, having been replaced after the Court's 1949 term by two conservatives, Tom C. Clark and Sherman (Shay) Minton, a conservative Democratic U.S. senator from Indiana. Given Frankfurter's clear predisposition on these controversial issues, as well as Jackson's shift in thinking after Nuremberg, it came as no surprise to Black and Douglas that the Court upheld the antisubversion program. It was clear that their views on the First Amendment were in the minority.

The Smith Act came to the brethren for review during the 1950 term. Eugene Dennis and ten other top Communist party members were convicted in a New York federal court for violation of Sections 2 and 3 of the Smith Act (conspiracy to organize the Communist party of the United States as a group to teach and advocate the overthrow of the government of the United States by force and violence). It was a long (nine-month), well-publicized, rancorous trial, which led to the summary conviction of the petitioners' lawyers for contempt of court—a contempt that was upheld over the dissents of Black and Douglas.[43]

Dennis was so well publicized and the notoriety was so great that Frankfurter wrote an unusual memo to his brethren. Dated February 27, 1951, it was a complaint about outside interference from two radically different groups: the Communist party and the American Bar Association! "If there are cases that call for undisturbed judicial determination, and therefore for abstention of outside interference, these surely are such cases [*Dennis* and *Sacher*]. . . . I wonder, therefore, whether the Court consults its self-respect in not taking notice of two occurrences as to these cases during the last few days." The Communist party had broadcast a radio statement calling for reversal and a special committee of the ABA had called for "disbarment of them and their like." Frankfurter's recommendation for the Court was quite dramatic. "As a single judge, I would not hesitate to issue an order to show cause why an attachment for contempt should not issue against the American Bar association—who certainly should know better—and the Communist Party."[44]

Oddly, according to Douglas's notes taken at the conference session of December 9, 1950, five days after oral argument, there was very little debate or discussion—or heat—among the brethren. "The amazing thing about the conference in this important case," wrote Douglas, "was the brief nature of the discussion. Those wanting to affirm had minds closed to argument or persuasion. The conference discussion was largely *pro forma*. It was the more amazing because of the drastic revision of the 'clear and present danger' test which affirmance requires."[45]

Vinson said that he would affirm the convictions, with "practically no discussion," according to Douglas. Reed, too, simply noted that he would affirm. Frankfurter spoke next and discussed "1) [the] status of clear and present danger since Gitlow— 2) how imminent must the substantive evils be? 3) should the clear and present danger be submitted to the jury? In Holmes and Brandeis' opinions it is a question of fact— 4) can we take judicial notice of the evil of the danger? He indicates he would affirm." Jackson's comments in conference reflected his later published views on the case: "The U.S.," he said, "can protect against activity—can stop some things because they are inherently dangerous without reference to clear and present danger—he has not made up his mind—he passes, but indicates he will affirm." Burton spoke of the need to change the test: "clear and probable rather than clear and present is the test—can take judicial knowledge of the danger [of the Communist menace]." And Shay Minton simply noted that he, too, would affirm. Clark did not participate.[46]

Clearly, except for Black and Douglas, the Court was ready to do all that was necessary to affirm the convictions, including taking "judicial notice" of the Communist peril and modifying, or, as Jackson was to recommend in his concurring opinion, even discarding the Holmes–Brandeis doctrine. In order to affirm the convictions of the eleven Communist party leaders, the majority had to somehow work around the Holmes–Brandeis doctrine. In the end, the task of finessing "clear and present danger" was attempted by the chief.

It was a poor effort, and the draft opinion was roundly critiqued by Black, in his characteristic marginal annotations. When Vinson wrote, "No one could conceive that it is not within the power of Congress to prohibit acts intended to overthrow the Government by force or violence," Black commented, "Of course—but these people [were] not convicted for *acts*." When Vinson referred to the "kind of activity" Dennis and the others were engaged in, Black noted, "What 'activity'?" And when Vinson misinterpreted, as he had to do in order to affirm the convictions, the "clear and present danger" doctrine, Black quoted from *Abrams* to try to show Vinson that Holmes and Brandeis were concerned about "imminent danger," not, as Vinson stated, "requisite danger." When Vinson, in a jab at Black and Douglas, wrote that "to those who would paralyze our government in the face of impending threat by encasing it in a semantic straitjacket we must reply that all concepts are relative," Black responded, "First Amendment and the Bill of Rights are words but not therefore a 'semantic straitjacket.'" After Vinson put together governmental power to limit speech with its power to protect the people from "armed internal attack," Black commented, "Now [he] puts 'speech' and 'armed internal attack' in [the] same category."[47]

As for Vinson's famous fear that Black would make the government delay action until the *putsch* had begun, Black noted acidly that it was a "ghost conspiracy." When Vinson said it was "impossible to measure the validity [of the damage the Communist party had done] in terms of the probability of success, or the immediacy of a successful attempt," Black countered that that was "precisely what clear and present [danger] meant." Clearly unwilling to accept the view put forward by the majority that the Communist party had to be stopped or America would be destroyed, Black commented whenever Vinson made such references: "The goblins'll get you!"[48]

Frankfurter's concurring opinion took judicial notice of the danger Communism posed to his beloved country and concluded that Congress had acted reasonably when it passed the Smith Act. Jackson discarded the Holmes–Brandeis test entirely and substituted, instead, the doctrine of conspiracy, which turned speech into seditious conduct. As Black accurately noted in his dissent, all the majority opinions in *Dennis* "show that the only way to affirm these convictions is to repudiate directly or indirectly the established 'clear and present danger' rule."

Black's criticism was fruitless. As Douglas had correctly observed, the Court majority was ready to modify *any* standard in order to affirm the convictions of the eleven Communists. "Five years ago," wrote Black, "few would have thought such convictions possible." But that was before the House Un-American Activities Committee and the beginning of the Red Scare. Now even the Supreme Court majority found these "miserable merchants of unwanted ideas" guilty of plotting the overthrow of the government by force and violence—without a shred of evidence ever presented by the government!

Black's dissent in *Dennis* was brief, for the two dissenters had agreed that Douglas would carry the primary burden of dissent this time. Black gladly joined what was clearly one of the best dissents Douglas would ever write. Yet Black had a word or two of his own to add. For him, the indictment for conspiracy to organize was a "virulent form of prior censorship of speech and press. . . . So long as this Court exercises the power of judicial review of legislation, I cannot agree that the First Amendment permits us to sustain laws suppressing freedom of speech and press on the basis of Congress' or our own notions of mere 'reasonableness.' Such a doctrine [developed by Frankfurter in his concurring opinion] waters down the First Amendment so that it amounts to little more than an admonition to Congress." Closing on a note of sadness, he wrote: "Public opinion being what it now is, few will protest the conviction of these Communist petitioners. There is hope, however, that in calmer times, when present pressures, passions and fears subside, this or some later Court will restore the First Amendment liberties to the high preferred place where they belong in a free society."[49]

Douglas's dissent was a powerful opinion, equally direct and poignant. For him, the Smith Act, as interpreted by all the federal courts, "requires the element of intent—that those who teach the creed believe in it. The crime depends not on what is taught but on who the teacher is. That is to make freedom of speech turn not on what is said, but on the intent with which it is said. Once we start down that road we enter territory dangerous to the liberties of every citizen." This case involved speech alone, not "speech plus acts of sabotage or unlawful conduct. Not a single seditious act is charged in the indictment," he wrote. Douglas took judicial notice of the fact that a Communist takeover was not imminent, that the Communists "on the world scene [are not] bogeymen," and that Communism has been so "thoroughly exposed in this country that it has been crippled as a political force. . . . [And] the fact that their ideas are abhorrent does not make them powerful." Closing, Douglas quoted Jefferson's thoughts on free speech: "The First Amendment reflects the philosophy of Jefferson 'that it is time enough for the rightful purposes of civil government, for its officers to interfere when principles break out into overt acts against peace and good order.'" The real danger, he said, lay in failing to hear and read the Communist arguments. Left in the light, their claims would crumble; but if driven underground, they could take on a life of their own.[50]

The clash of values was prominent in *Dennis*. Opposing Black and Douglas's view that the First Amendment had a high, preferred place in the hierarchy of constitutional values was that of Frankfurter, Jackson, and Vinson that a national emergency such as an international Communist conspiracy required the policy makers to make exceptions, disregarding the language of the First Amendment.

The Court in the postwar years had to wrestle with some very controversial First Amendment litigation involving persons accused of advocating subversive action against the government. It was a time that called for judicial decisiveness in determining the extent of freedom of expression in light of a widespread fear that Communism was an imminent evil.

Federal judges, especially the justices of the Court, had to aggressively employ the power of judicial review to ensure that other, more politically sensitive agencies of government did not infringe on the liberties protected by the First Amendment. Unfortunately, except for Black and Douglas, the Court was not sensitive to the preservation of freedoms for political deviants. Douglas felt that within a few years of the war's end, for the majority of the brethren, the "danger of Communist advocacy was magnified."[51] It seemed to Americans that the international Communist movement was a potent and monolithic force, devouring free nations around the world. And the postwar "subversives" were seen as part of the international Communist conspiracy. The existence of the Communist party in the United States was to many the harbinger of Communism in America. It had to be stopped at all costs, regardless of the language of the First Amendment.

Furthermore, in this postwar period of national hysteria, the justices were not immune from the xenophobia around them. The United States Supreme Court was touched by the new frenzy sweeping the country. Everywhere, it seemed to Jackson, people were being "destroyed by groups and smear."[52] Frankfurter, ever the cautious, anxious justice, asked Jackson to tone down a concurring opinion he had written in a 1949 contempt of Congress case. "Could [you] not say what you think you ought to say in *Dennis* without giving unavoidable reinforcement to the McCarthy's, the McCormick's and the other exploiters of the irrational in the land."[53] Hugo Black also reflected, in a note to Douglas, on the state of America during this terrible time. Commenting on the U.S. attorney general in 1953, he wrote: "[His action] shows how far some people think we are on the way toward some kind of government they appear to have in Russia, Spain, Argentina, and a number of other places in the world. Freedom is being whittled away in the name of freedom."[54]

The Smith Act and similar national and state statutes came to the attention of the Court. While Jackson could write in his notes that "Dennis has not had a fair trial," he, along with Frankfurter and the majority of the justices sitting on the Court during this period, chose judicial deference—which meant, as it had during the earlier Red Scare, that the Court neglected to pose substantive questions or acquiesced in criminal convictions or administrative rulings that led to the dismissal from government positions of alleged Communists and others who refused to discuss their past behavior or personal beliefs.[55]

As Douglas and Black often noted, the Court evaded some major constitutional issues. It was only Black and Douglas, joined later (but only in part) by Chief Justice Earl Warren and Associate Justice William J. Brennan, who defended the view that the First Amendment was an absolute bar to governmental action against spoken and printed ideas, no matter how radical or despised.

As "absolutists," Black and Douglas went beyond previously developed constitutional doctrines. Whereas their heroes, Holmes and Brandeis, had developed the concept of "clear and present danger," which would prohibit speech deemed a serious and imminent threat to the state, Black and Douglas pressed their view that the First Amendment barred all forms of governmental harassment of political speakers. For them, "there was no place in the regime of the First Amendment for any 'clear and present danger' test."[56] In so doing, they forced the entire Court into a prolonged examination of the meaning and the scope of the First Amendment. For Black and Douglas, the state had to allow a person, whether or not a citizen,[57] the full freedom to discuss ideas, spread propaganda, and use whatever means were available in a democracy to proselytize others. Most of their brethren did not share this view. Consequently, the debates in conference and in the opinions themselves were often robust.[58] Moreover, Douglas's view of his more conservative brethren's behavior during this period of time was not flattering: "*Dennis* [and other cases] show the Court running with the hounds and joining the hue and cry against unpopular people."[59]

Ominously, unknown to both Douglas and Black, the FBI, with the active participation of its director, J. Edgar Hoover, and the awareness of U.S. Attorney General Herbert Brownell, closely monitored the activities of these two justices—in part because of their liberal views of the First Amendment. When, for example, the Court was hearing the final arguments in the Rosenberg case, the FBI had agents in the courtroom who "kept abreast of the actions of the Supreme Court, the individual judges, and defense attorneys."[60]

Douglas, according to Justice Brennan, believed that his and other offices in the Supreme Court were bugged by the FBI. Brennan recalled occasions when Douglas asked him to walk with him in the halls to talk about a pending Court matter because of his fears about wiretaps. By the late 1950s, Black too probably suspected that the FBI was monitoring him. On June 5, 1957, his sister-in-law, Jinksie Durr, wrote to Black warning him not to have his daughter attend a wedding in Montgomery, Alabama, because an ugly scene might occur, which, "with the FBI watching you like a hawk and trying to link you to the 'communist conspiracy' and all the rest of that business," should be avoided.[61]

In the early 1950s, the FBI seriously entertained the idea that Douglas might have been a Communist dupe or even a spy, with a "ring" of left-wing law clerks who were undermining the American system.[62] Perhaps the most shocking examples of the FBI's suspicions were two wild claims made about Douglas, which Hoover and Brownell took seriously. In 1954, Hoover received a report alleging that Douglas and his friends and neighbors in Washington State, including the fishermen and the loggers in the area, were Communists and that, according to Chief James A. Pryor of the Washington State Patrol, Douglas's cabin in the woods was in a deserted area appropriate for the secret landing of foreign troops: "A large flat section of ground is in the vicinity near the ocean which would allow an estimated 100,000 soldiers to camp." They offered as proof nothing but rumors and the fact that Owen Lattimore had once stayed at the Douglas property. Hoover's response to this incredible communication? In a memo dated February 8, 1954, he directed his agent-in-charge in the Seattle office to "immediately institute security investigations on the following individuals."[63]

The other preposterous incident involving Douglas and the FBI director occurred later that year, when an informant told the New York FBI office that Douglas was a Communist who would "replace Alger Hiss in the Communist underground." The FBI recommendation: that Douglas be questioned by the FBI to ascertain whether he actually was approached to "engage in communist underground work."[64]

Clearly, during the Red Scare of the 1950s, Douglas was regarded by the FBI as a dangerous enemy of the state, who always took stands "favorable to Communist supported issues."[65] Indeed, J. Edgar Hoover called Justice Douglas "crazy" to boot.[66] Unquestionably, the Republican administration and J. Edgar Hoover, as well as many other Americans, took Black and Douglas's vigorous defense of the First Amendment to be an admission of Communist sympathies—or worse. The FBI's files on Black were replete with news clippings about his "pro-Communist" votes. As late as June 1970, Hoover and President Nixon discussed Douglas and Black's liberalism on First Amendment issues and the death penalty. Hoover also offered to help Nixon find material to support Gerald Ford's impeachment charges against Douglas.[67]

For most of the brethren, it was simple fact that the Communist "menace" had to be curtailed, and, during the first half of the 1950s, the Supreme Court majority of Vinson, Jackson, Frankfurter, Clark, Minton, Burton, and Reed managed to find for the governmental interest in subverting freedom of speech, press, and/or association. Black and Douglas were always in the minority.

Chief Justice Vinson, a deferential conservative, used what is generally known as a "bad tendency" test. This meant that the "clear and present danger" test had to be scuttled. It did not matter that there was no evidence of any immediate plan by the Communist party to foment a revolution. The Communists' views were so dangerous that it did not matter whether they were likely to take any particular action; the state must be able to prevent the *putsch* from taking place.[68]

Justice Jackson argued that it was one thing to apply "clear and present danger" and other vigorous standards for harmless protestors but quite another when confronting the "well-organized, nation-wide conspiracy," which was but a small part of the international Communist conspiracy. Jackson arued that the "clear and present danger" standard was created "before the era of World War II revealed the subtlety and efficacy of modernized revolutionary techniques used by totalitarian parties. . . . I would save [clear and present danger] as a 'rule of reason' in the kind of case for which it was devised: . . . hot headed speech on a street corner, or circulation of a few incendiary pamphlets, or parading by some zealots behind a red flag, or refusal of a handful of school children to salute our flag."[69]

Frankfurter, the great admirer of Holmes and Brandeis, totally rejected their doctrine in favor of a "balancing of interests" doctrine that enabled him to defer to the legislature in controversial First Amendment cases. He wrote, in an obvious reference to Black and Douglas, on the one hand, and those who had distorted the Holmes–Brandeis doctrine, on the other, that "the demands of free speech in a democratic society as well as the interest in national security are better served by candid and informed weighing of the competing interests, within the confines of the judicial process, than by announcing dogmas too inflexible for the non-euclidean problems to be solved." Frankfurter's view was that the Court should "set aside the judgment of those whose duty it is to legislate only if there is no reasonable basis for it." And Frankfurter took judicial notice of many reasons why the anti-Communist legislation was an appropriate response to those who would threaten the democratic republic he loved so much.[70]

After the death of Justice Robert H. Jackson, Frankfurter's ally on this controversial issue, his replacement on the Court in 1955, John M. Harlan, Jr., became an even closer ally of Frankfurter on key First Amendment and national security cases. Harlan wrote some of the Court's majority opinions during the 1950s that had, at their base, the notion of "balancing" congressional/national interests with the individual's interests in maintaining First Amendment freedoms. (Although Harlan and Black had clearly opposing views on the meaning and scope of the First Amendment, they came to respect and befriend each other, much more so than Black and Frankfurter ever did.)

After Vinson's death in 1953, Jackson's death in 1954, and Minton's retirement in 1956, the Court, according to Douglas, began to "swerve its course and act to protect the rights of the people by limiting the thrust of the anti-subversive program. The arrival of Earl Warren made part of the difference.[71] Nevertheless, the 1950s were, by and large, a time of intolerance and persecution for political deviants in America.

Interestingly, Black and Douglas took time in a number of their dissents to assert that had the Holmes–Brandeis test been properly employed—a test they did not believe was true to the spirit of the First Amendment—the petitioners would have been set free and the Smith Act declared unconstitutional. As Douglas said, years later: "It was sometimes said that Hugo Black and I initially went along with the 'clear and present danger' test but later repudiated it. What we did was to meet the arguments of the majority as in Dennis that the 'clear and present danger' test had been satisfied. We rejected that as a legitimate test at any time."[72]

When Earl Warren became chief justice in 1953, he had no well-developed First Amendment jurisprudence. On the substantive issues associated with freedom of speech for political deviants, especially Communist party members, Warren never accepted Black and Douglas's absolutism on the First Amendment. Typically, Warren would not join in a dissent by Black that amplified his categorical First Amendment beliefs. However, Warren's vote in many of these cases, along with the views and votes of Justice William J. Brennan, gave Black and Douglas support in their efforts to provide First Amendment protection to those whom most of the American public considered unworthy of it. Occasionally, the liberal quartet was able to make inroads and inhibit governmental restrictions on free speech and association. But the Court refused to go where Black and Douglas wanted to take it.

Black and Douglas's battle during the second Red Scare was fought in three kinds of disputes. There were the free-speech cases, litigation involving association with suspect groups, and challenges to investigations in which legislators sought to force disclosures from suspects about their personal beliefs and associations.

During the 1956 term, the brethren had further occasion to examine the Smith Act free-speech challenges in the case of *Yates* v. *United States.*[73] Yolanda Yates and thirteen other so-called second-string Communist party leaders were convicted under the Smith Act. It had taken almost two years for the case to arrive. Certiorari had been granted during the Court's 1955 term, and the case was argued on October 9 and 10, 1956. Like Dennis and the other Communist leaders convicted a half-decade earlier, the fourteen had been charged with violation of Section 2 of the Smith Act (conspiring to advocate and teach the overthrow of the government by force and violence). This time, however, with a new chief (Warren), a new associate justice (Harlan), and a somewhat changed atmosphere nationally, the disposition of the case was somewhat different—though not completely to Black and Douglas's liking.

Warren, unlike Vinson, was critical of the government's case against the Communists. "It has not been established," he said in the October 12, 1956, conference, "that the Communist Party is force and violence. The government has not made clear proof of the purpose of the Party."[74] He would reverse, as would Black, who said that the *Yates* prosecution "was a political trial—what the First Amendment was supposed to prevent."[75] There was not, Black continued, sufficient evidence to convict. In the *Yates* trial, he said contemptuously, "proof here is sufficient if Marx and Lenin [were] on trial." The government, he claimed, showed the presence of ideas, not actions.

Four brethren (Reed, Burton, Minton, and Clark) voted to affirm the convictions, and two (Frankfurter and Harlan) passed. Because of the "fragmented" Court,[76] Warren put the case over for a few weeks. By the time it was discussed again, Minton had retired and Frankfurter and Harlan voted to reverse on the narrow ground that the instructions given to the jury were muddy and inadequate. The vote was 5 to 3 to reverse, and Warren assigned the opinion to Harlan. By the time Harlan's opinion was announced, Reed had retired and Burton joined the majority.

Consequently, the Yates vote was 6 to 1, with Black and Douglas concurring in part and dissenting in part.

Black wrote the partial dissent opinion, with Douglas joining his colleague. Objecting to the technical basis for the reversal of five of the petitioners, Black felt obliged to protest that the First Amendment issue had not been the primary factor in a total reversal of all the convictions. "In essence, petitioners were tried upon the charge that they believe in and want to foist upon this country a different and to us a despicable form of authoritarian government in which voices criticizing the existing order are summarily silenced. I fear that the present type of prosecutions are more in line with the philosophy of authoritarian government than with that expressed by our First Amendment." He concluded with a repetition of their clarion call that the First Amendment is the bedrock of our democratic republic and must always be in its high preferred place. "The First Amendment provides the only kind of security system that can preserve a free government—one that leaves the way open for people to favor, discuss, advocate, or incite causes and doctrines however obnoxious and antagonistic such views may be to the rest of us."[77]

The Smith Act had a section providing that membership in the Communist party was a violation of the act, punishable by a term in federal prison. Junius Scales, an active party member who had grown up among the southern gentry in Greensboro, North Carolina, had been convicted under that section and his case had come to the Court. Given a new trial at the direction of the Court, he was again convicted and returned to the Court in October 1958. After an initial round of discussion that term, the Court set the case for reargument during its October 1959 term and then rescheduled the case for reargument during the 1960 term.

Justice Clark had dissented from the last order, setting the reargument for the 1960 term of the Court. No other appellate case in the Court's history, he said, had "been carried on the active docket so many consecutive terms."[78] Frankfurter wrote to him: "In any event, when I say, 'So what?' I do not mean to be flippant. . . . The kind of issues that we are concerned with demand, beyond anything else, due deliberation, which means casting wide the net of investigation followed by mature reflection. As is true of wine, wise judgment by this Court requires seasoning."[79] To which Clark responded, "When old wine becomes *too* old, it goes sour."[80]

The views expressed on October 14, 1960, after the *Scales* oral argument, were not too different from those expressed in *Yates*—with the exception of Justice Brennan's. Warren, supported by Black, Douglas, and Brennan, argued that reversal should occur on nonconstitutional grounds.[81] However, Frankfurter joined Clark, Whittaker, Harlan, and Stewart to form a majority. Harlan wrote the opinion for the Court, arguing that, since Scales was an "active" member of the party, he had full knowledge of its illegal purposes. Black, Douglas, and Brennan, joined by Warren, wrote dissents.

For Clark and Harlan, the evidence showed that "Scales advocated personally [the] overthrow of government."[82] Frankfurter was still of the opinion that "the Communist Party is not just another party—can't say that the threat of the Party is too remote."[83] For Black and Douglas, however, the First Amendment provided for all persons to freely associate, speak, and publish. Douglas wrote that "none of [Scales's] activity constitutes a crime. . . . Not one single illegal act is charged to petitioner. That is why the essence of the crime covered by the indictment is merely belief—belief in the proletarian revolution, belief in Communist creed."[84] Black was, as usual, to the point:

> Petitioner is being sent to jail for the express reason that he has associated with people who have entertained unlawful ideas and said unlawful things, and that of course is a *direct* abridgment of his freedoms of speech and assembly. . . . Nevertheless, [the brethren decided] that the government has power to abridge speech and assembly if its interest in doing so is sufficient to outweigh the interest in protecting these First Amendment freedoms. This, I think demonstrates the unlimited breadth and danger of the "balancing test" as it is currently being employed by a majority of this Court.[85]

Both men, Douglas later wrote, interpreted the First Amendment as giving Scales and all others "the right of advocacy for the purpose of incitement, as well as for education." Douglas continued: "Free speech had traditionally included both. . . . After Dennis and Scales, Congress may make some laws abridging freedom of speech."[86] Black and Douglas continued to argue for the high preferred place of the First Amendment in the hierarchy of constitutional values.

Black and Douglas were particularly angered by the loyalty-security program initiated by Truman in 1947 in his effort to uncover and convict Communists and "fellow travelers" in and out of government.[87] One need not have advocated unlawful action, or even been a member of the party, to be swept up in the loyalty net. It was enough to be accused of unsavory associations with groups or individuals who turned up on dreaded lists of subversives created by government bureaucrats.

During the 1950 term of the Court, the justices heard the case of *Joint Anti-Fascist Refugee Committee* v. *McGrath.*[88] The Joint Committee had been placed on the attorney general's "subversive list," compiled under the terms of Executive Order 9835. That order created the Loyalty Review Board, which the Department of Justice was to furnish with the names of organizations, associations, movements, and groups labeled by the attorney general as totalitarian, fascist, Communist, or subversive, or identified "as having adopted a policy of advocating or approving the commission of acts of force or violence to deny others their rights under the Constitution of the United States, or as seeking to alter the form of government of the United States by unconstitutional means."[89]

The Joint Anti-Fascist Refugee Committee, according to Douglas's law clerk, had been doing "charitable relief work to aid Spanish Republicans in exile and other anti-fascists who fought against Franco." Labeled a subversive organization, the group sued for relief in federal court. The "nub of the suit on the merits" was the question of the constitutionality of the actions of the attorney general and the constitutionality of the executive order itself. There were no provisions for the Joint Committee to defend itself. Douglas's law clerk argued that "what makes the power of the Attorney General (under the Executive Order) so frightening is the complete lack of any of the usual trappings of due process." There was no provision for a hearing, nor, the government argued, were the attorney general's actions reviewable by the federal courts. The government contended that the case was nonjusticiable and that there was no standing to sue.[90]

Black and Douglas disagreed with Vinson, who accepted the government's position at oral argument that there was no standing to sue. Furthermore, Black,
according to Jackson's notes, argued that "no official has the right to stigmatize
without [a] hearing, etc."[91] The Court, however, did not reach these merits and
instead reversed the lower federal courts' dismissal of the complaints. Black wrote
a separate concurring opinion that addressed the constitutional issue: "More fundamentally, however, in my judgment, the executive has no constitutional authority, with or without a hearing, officially to prepare and publish the lists challenged
by petitioners. . . . I cannot believe that the authors of the Constitution, who out-
lawed the Bill of Attainder, inadvertently endowed the executive with power to
engage in the same tyrannical practices that has made the bill such an odious institution."[92] Ultimately, the Court insisted on some form of due process before an
organization could be "listed."

Yet another piece of legislation, the omnibus 1950 Internal Security Act, was
strongly condemned by Black and Douglas for violating First Amendment freedoms. One aspect of that legislation was particularly onerous to the two jurists: the
Subversive Activities Control Board (SACB). Under the terms of the legislation, the
SACB's responsibility was to identify a group as a Communist-action organization,
thereby forcing it to register with the attorney general as a subversive organization.
The Communist party challenged the constitutionality of the Control Board during
the October 1955 term of the Court. However, the Court avoided the constitutional
question in 1955. Although Black, Douglas, and Burton had argued the constitutional issues, especially the First Amendment and the Fifth Amendment's requirement of due process, Reed, Clark, and Minton had voted to affirm the convictions
on constitutional grounds. Warren was torn; he supported the registration requirement but not the sanctions that followed identification by the SACB as a Communist-action organization.

Frankfurter and Harlan were concerned about a difficult split, and Frankfurter
suggested that the case be sent back to the SACB for additional evidence. Although
neither Frankfurter nor Black and Douglas had changed their views on the First
Amendment, evidently it was appropriate to forestall action on the constitutional
questions (in which case Black and Douglas would, again, lose), since it would produce a very closely divided Court on the constitutional issue, which Frankfurter
wanted to avoid. In a letter to Douglas, Frankfurter wrote, "How very deeply I feel
the inestimable moral consequences that would attend disposition of the case on
the legal ground on which, for me, it is necessary to dispose of the case. . . . [B]y
pooling our various views it ought to be easy enough to reach a consensus of view."[93]
And this was, evidently, what occurred. Clark wrote a bitter note to the conference
indicating that he "did not agree to a reversal of this case. It was my understanding
that the majority agreed to pass upon the constitutional issues."[94] With the exception of a dissenting opinion by Clark, which was joined by Reed and Minton, the
justices accepted Frankfurter's remedy, and the first SACB case was remanded to
the board for additional action.

However, like a phoenix, the issue of the Subversive Activities Control Board
rose up during the October 1960 term, and this time the Court decided the issue on
the merits. Most of the brethren who had participated in the 1955 judgment were

still on the Court; the one new, major actor was Potter Stewart, who had taken his seat on the Court in 1958, replacing Harold Burton. The line-up again, as in the *Scales* litigation, was 5 to 4. Frankfurter and Harlan, joined by Clark and the two new brethren, Whittaker and Stewart, voted to affirm the action of the SACB, but the others favored reversal on First and Fifth Amendment grounds.

In subsequent years, the Court invalidated other aspects of the Subversive Activities Control Act of 1950, Title (section) 1 of the Internal Security Act of 1950. Furthermore, the Court in its 1964 term invalidated the SACA provision denying passports to members of Communist organizations. During the 1965 term of the Court, the justices struck down the registration provisions on Fifth Amendment (self-incrimination) grounds. Finally, during the 1967 term of the Court, the brethren invalidated another section (5, a, 1, D) of the SACA that prohibited members of any Communist-action organization under orders to register with the Department of Justice from working in any defense facility.[95]

By 1974, the SACB had ceased to function, in part because Warren Court opinions had whittled away the essence of the board's business and because the legislature had ceased funding it. The Internal Security Act had been, as Douglas described it, "one of the most repressive measures enacted by Congress since the Alien and Sedition Act of 1798."[96]

Black and Douglas, in their response to restrictions on freedom of speech and association during the second Red Scare, ultimately had to confront the investigative powers of Congress and the state legislatures and their impact on freedom of speech and association. These cases, involving the House Un-American Activities Committee (HUAC) and other congressional investigating committees, like so many of the others that involved political deviants—especially Communists—"created a tempest."[97]

While some federal courts had defined the parameters of legislative investigative power, none of the cases had involved the use of the power to expose and uncover alleged subversive activities.[98] Chief Justice Warren wrote in the *Watkins* opinion that, following World War II, "there appeared a new kind of congressional inquiry unknown in prior periods of American history. . . . This new phase of legislative inquiry involved a broad-scale intrusion into the lives and affairs of private citizens. It brought before the courts novel questions of the appropriate limits of congressional inquiry. . . . The central theme was the application of the Bill of Rights as a restraint upon the assertion of [this type of] governmental power."[99] On June 17, 1957, a day referred to by critics of the Supreme Court as "Red Monday,"[100] the Court concluded its October 1956 term with decisions in two very important legislative investigation cases: *Watkins* v. *United States* and *Sweezy* v. *New Hampshire*.[101]

For Warren, there were two issues in *Watkins:* the pertinence of the questions directed to Watkins, a labor-union official, and the need for limits on Congress's investigatory power into the personal affairs of anyone hauled before an investigating committee. The investigatory power of Congress is a necessary part of its rule-making function. Ideally, the legislature investigates an issue before developing legislation. The reality, as Senator Black, the "inquisitor" knew so well, was that the investigatory function of a legislature was often used to ferret out wrongdoing and to expose for exposure's sake. In the Red Scare of the 1950s, unlike Black's days in the Senate when he was using the investigatory power to root out participants in economic scandals, the legislative investigations were public examinations of a person's personal beliefs and associations.

Except for Clark, the former attorney general, all the justices participating in *Watkins* were for reversal of the contempt of Congress citation. In this case, Watkins was willing to discuss his own activities, but not the activities of others who he had no reason to believe were active subversives. If Reed and Minton had still been on the Court, and if Burton's nephew had not been trial counsel, Clark would have had three additional votes. Bernard Schwartz has speculated, "Had the division gone that way, the four for affirmance might well have been able to persuade Frankfurter, who was dissatisfied with the broad scope of Warren's opinion for the Court, to join them."[102]

Black did not have much difficulty with Warren's draft because it focused on First and Fifth Amendment constitutional issues. Douglas joined Warren's opinion, however, only after commenting that the "discussions [should be] solely on separation of powers rather than First Amendment. I think the separation of powers aspect of the case is adequate to dispose of this controversy and we could save the First Amendment for other times."[103] Brennan and Harlan also fairly quickly joined Warren's opinion, Brennan stating that it was "splendid."[104]

While Warren's opinion for the Court reversed on the procedural point—that the questions Watkins had refused to answer were not pertinent—it went much beyond that, addressing fundamental questions concerning limits on the congressional investigating power. Congress, wrote Warren, does not have the "general authority to expose the private affairs of individuals without justification in terms of the functions of Congress. . . . Clearly, an investigation is subject to the command that the Congress shall make no law abridging freedom of speech or press or assembly. . . . We have no doubt that there is no congressional power to expose for the sake of exposure. . . . Fundamental fairness demands that no witness be compelled to [answer questions] with so little guidance [from the committee as to the pertinency of the questions]."[105]

The sister case heard in conference and announced the same day involved a University of New Hampshire professor, Paul M. Sweezy, who was convicted of contempt for having refused to answer questions put to him by the attorney general of New Hampshire, acting pursuant to legislative authority to investigate subversive activities because of Sweezy's classroom lectures and his knowledge of the Progressive party. He refused to answer questions about the content of his lectures (which included, among other subjects, socialism, Marxism's inevitability, and dialectical materialism).[106] The Supreme Court of New Hampshire upheld the conviction and Sweezy appealed to the United States Supreme Court. The Court, in an opinion written by Warren, ruled that the action of the state was an invasion of Sweezy's academic freedom and freedom of political expression, which were protected by the First Amendment (applied through the Fourteenth Amendment's due process clause).[107]

Once again, in that conference session, Frankfurter refused to accept the preferred position of the First Amendment. He referred instead to the "special position of educational institutions and teachers," adding, "I don't mean a 'preferred' position"; Brennan described the classroom as "a sanctuary. . . . In there is the first essential of preservation of purity."[108] For Harlan, *Sweezy* had to "squarely rest" on the First Amendment argument.[109]

Again, Frankfurter and Black and Douglas differed on fundamental First Amendment grounds. This time, Black and Douglas, with their new allies, Warren and Brennan, overcame Frankfurter's conservativism. However, it was to prove to be a temporary triumph. During the 1958 term of the Court, the brethren heard two cases, *Barenblatt* v. *United States* and *Uphaus* v. *Wyman,* that substantially and adversely modified the *Watkins* and *Sweezy* decisions.[110]

The Court was fairly split between the Black, Brennan, Douglas, and Warren foursome, who urged continued restraint on congressional investigative activities, and the five more conservative members of the Court, led by Frankfurter, who opted for a more deferential "balancing" test. Lloyd Barenblatt was a psychology professor at Vassar College who refused to answer questions about his possible membership in the Communist party. His contempt of Congress conviction was affirmed by a federal court, and he appealed to the Supreme Court, arguing that HUAC had not shown the relevance of the questions to a legitimate legislative purpose.

Frankfurter's group won the day.[111] Harlan wrote the opinion for the Court majority, arguing that, on balance, the government's interest in investigating Communist activities outweighed Barenblatt's First Amendment interest in protecting his associational rights: "Where First Amendment rights are asserted to bar governmental interrogation, resolution of the issue always involves a balancing by the courts of the competing private and public interests at stake in the particular circumstances shown." Harlan concluded that "the balance between the individual and the governmental interests here at stake must be struck in favor of the latter, and that therefore the provisions of the First Amendment have not been offended."[112]

Black took the opportunity to make his dissent a definitive essay on the dangers of balancing. Douglas joined Black and suggested in a letter that Black "cite *Barsky, Feiner* and other horribles" that used the balancing test to undermine the First Amendment.[113] Notwithstanding their differences on the "speech-plus" cases, when the question was whether to use a balancing test in the area of the First Amendment, the two were of one mind.

Black wrote that "the First Amendment says in no equivocal language that Congress shall pass no law abridging freedom of speech, press, assembly or petition. The activities of this Committee, authorized by Congress, do precisely that, through exposure, obloquy and public scorn." He appended material from the hearing records in which members bragged about exposing witnesses to abuse as suitable punishment for their subversive associations. Black turned to his second argument, the balancing standard itself: "I do not agree that laws directly abridging First Amendment freedoms can be justified by a congressional or judicial balancing process. . . . To apply the Court's balancing test . . . is to read the First Amendment to say 'Congress shall pass no law abridging freedom of speech, press, assembly and petition,' unless Congress and the Supreme Court reach the joint conclusion that on balance the interest of the Government in stifling these freedoms is greater than the interest of the people in having them exercised." Ultimately, Black concluded, "all the questions in this case boil down to one—whether we as people will try fearfully and futilely to preserve democracy by adopting totalitarian methods, or whether in accordance with our traditions and our Constitution we will have the confidence and courage to be free."[114]

Uphaus, the companion case, was equally frustrating for Black and Douglas. Willard Uphaus, the director of the World Fellowship, which ran a summer lecture program in New Hampshire, was convicted of contempt for having refused to turn over to Louis C. Wyman, the attorney general of New Hampshire, the names of the guests at the summer camp. At conference, Warren argued for reversal because the state did not show "an interest endangered or being subverted. [Such state action] would deter people from freely speaking." Black, Douglas, and Brennan "followed the Chief."[115] For Douglas, the state action violated the First Amendment: "There was no criminal here; they put a citizen [on the stand] and want to know with whom he associates."[116] However, Frankfurter, the First Amendment "balancer," argued in the conference that the state "can be jittery about having [possible subversive] organizations in the state and can ask threshold questions and find out who is there and get their correspondence."[117]

Clark wrote for the five-man majority upholding the contempt citation. Brennan wrote for the four dissenters, though Black and Douglas also prepared a brief joint dissent: "We would decide this case on the ground that the appellant is being deprived of rights under the First and Fourteenth Amendments. . . . But we join Mr. Justice Brennan's dissent because he makes it clear to us that New Hampshire's legislative program resulting in the incarceration of appellant for contempt violates Article I, Section 10 which provides that 'No state shall . . . pass any Bill of Attainder.'"[118]

Frankfurter, ironically, added the following postscript in a letter to Brennan on January 7, 1959: "Need I add another word, namely, that there isn't a man on the Court who personally disapproves more than I do of the activities of all the Un-American Committees, of all the Smith Act prosecutions, of the attorney general's list, etc., etc."[119] Black and Douglas had a much different angle on their colleague Felix Frankfurter. (After Frankfurter left the Court, *Uphaus*'s heavy-handedness on associational rights protected by the First Amendment was modified when the Court, in a decision written by Frankfurter's replacement, Arthur Goldberg, narrowed the scope of a legislative investigating committee's power.)[120]

≈

During their tenure on the Court, Hugo L. Black and William O. Douglas always gave their undivided attention to cases that involved alleged violations of First Amendment freedoms. For both jurists, this amendment was the bedrock of a functioning, vital democratic republic: governmental intrusion into lives of free men and women was characteristic of a totalitarian system. Indeed, this period of American history led Douglas to appraise the American political system harshly: "We kept a wider part of the spectrum open for discussion than does Russia, but where the clash of ideas is clear and vivid, we follow the Soviet pattern."[121]

If Douglas's observation is true, it is not because of his and Black's views or their decisions in First Amendment cases. Although they differed in some respects, Black and Douglas advocated the full and unfettered expression of ideas—no matter how heretical, subversive, or inflammatory these ideas seemed to others. They placed the First Amendment in the highest, preferred position in the hierarchy of constitutional values. For this, they were condemned—by some of their brethren and by the public outside the conference session.

Frankfurter and Harlan stand out in sharpest contrast to Black and Douglas. Although Frankfurter claimed, in his letter to Brennan, that he was more opposed to the Smith Acts and the HUACs than any other justice on the Court, the record is fairly clear. Frankfurter's love of his adopted country and his great respect for its (borrowed) traditions of due process and fairness, as well as his view that courts and judges must not interfere in the political affairs of the community unless there was a Draconian violation of the Constitution by a governmental body, led him to argue, again and again, in favor of the government in these free-speech and free-association cases.

Black and Douglas, however, were never deterred from what they considered to be their responsibility to the Constitution. Neither Frankfurter nor Harlan nor congressional threats to impeach Douglas after his *Rosenberg* stay kept them from asserting the fundamental character of the speech issue in most of the cases that came to the Court during a very difficult time. The schism that ensued was a painful one for the brethren.

It was painful for Black and Douglas to defend, time and again, the lonely minority view due to the Vinson majority's consensus regarding the threat of Communism. While they witnessed the vindication of their votes over time, Black and Douglas were never able to convince a majority of their brethren of the First Amendment's absolute nature.

They experienced more success in civil rights, in which they saw dramatic progress, at least in law if not always in social and political conditions. In that area, as in First Amendment issues, the two were often in agreement on the definitions of democratic power and individual rights. But not in all cases.

Indeed, it was in civil rights that some of their differences in background and experience began to manifest themselves in significant ways. Here Hugo Black's concern for the prerogatives of states and localities, his interest in preserving property rights, and his desire to avoid excessive intervention from Washington, along with his concern that judicial interference in the majoritarian political process be limited, sometimes put him at loggerheads with Douglas, who strove to vindicate the rights of the many kinds of people who were denied equality in American life whether because of race, gender, or class.

 *8*

The Struggle for Racial Justice

Shortly after the Civil War ended, former Union general and later reporter Carl Schurz traveled across the South to examine the condition of the recently freed black population. He wrote the following for presentation to the Senate:

> Wherever I go—the street, the shop, the house, the hotel or the steamboat—I hear people talk in such a way as to indicate that they are yet unable to conceive of the Negro as possessing any rights at all. Men who are honorable in their dealings with their white neighbors will cheat a Negro without feeling a single twinge of their honor. To kill a Negro, they do not deem murder; to debauch a Negro woman they do not consider fornication; to take property from a Negro, they do not consider robbery. The whites . . . still have an ingrained feeling that the blacks at large belong to the whites at large.[1]

Although the Fourteenth Amendment to the Constitution prohibited states from denying "to any person . . . the equal protection of the laws," the reality was as Schurz perceived it: stark, pervasive racial discrimination against the recently freed slaves. It was a discrimination that was present in all kinds of social and political interaction, from segregated hospitals to segregated cemeteries. The segregation laws that were developed in the decades after the Civil War formed the basis of the "Jim Crow" system.[2]

During the nineteenth century, the United States Supreme Court put the federal judiciary's imprimatur on the practice of race discrimination. In 1857, the Taney Court handed down *Dred Scott* v. *Sandford,* in which the Court held that the black man was not a "citizen" in the Constitution and therefore could not claim any of the rights, "Privileges and immunities," provided to American citizens.[3] In the 1883 case of *United States* v. *Harris,* a mob's lynching of a black prisoner was ruled to be no denial of the "equal protection" clause because the mob had committed the action, not the state or state officers.[4] The state had to bring the villains to justice; if it did not, then that simply "was unfortunate for black men."[5]

This idea that the Fourteenth Amendment covered only government action was fully developed in another important opinion handed down in 1883, the *Civil Rights Cases*.[6] The Court concluded that the Fourteenth Amendment's reach extended only to "state action" and that the provisions of the 1875 Civil Rights Act intended to end segregation in places of public accommodation were unconstitutional because they attempted to control private, not state, behavior. *Plessy* v. *Ferguson,* the watershed case on race in this period of American history, was heard in the next decade.[7] It was to remain the law of the land until the modern Court, led by Black, Douglas, and the newly appointed chief justice, Earl Warren, overturned it in *Brown* v. *Board of Education* in 1954.[8]

In *Plessy* v. *Ferguson,* the Supreme Court confronted—directly—the issue of separation of the races. In 1892, Homer Plessy, who lived in Louisiana and was one-eighth black, boarded an intrastate train in his home state. A group assembled to challenge segregated rail travel made sure the railroad knew of Plessy's heritage. Ordered into the car for blacks, he refused and was arrested, jailed, and convicted of violating the 1890 Louisiana Separate Car Act, a statute that called for separate accommodations for white and black passengers on trains in the state.

For the eight-man Court majority, Justice Henry B. Brown concluded that "equal but separate" requirements did not violate the Constitution. Blacks and whites, he said, had political equality, but not social equality. "In the nature of things, [the Fourteenth Amendment] could not have been intended to abolish distinctions based upon color, or to enforce social, as distinguished from political, equality, or a commingling of the two races upon terms unsatisfactory to either." Congress was "powerless to eradicate racial instincts or to abolish distinctions based upon physical differences. . . . If the civil and political rights of both races be equal one cannot be inferior to the other civilly or politically. If one race be inferior to the other socially, the Constitution of the United States cannot put them on the same plane."[9]

Justice John M. Harlan, grandfather of Black's and Douglas's colleague on the Court, was the sole dissenter. The former slaveholder from Kentucky wrote that "our Constitution is color blind, and neither knows nor tolerates classes among citizens. In respect of civil rights all are equal before the law. The humblest is the peer of the most powerful. The law regards man as man, and takes no account of his color when his civil rights as guaranteed by the supreme law of the land are involved. . . . [T]he arbitrary separation of citizens on the basis of color [was the same as pinning] a badge of servitude [on the blacks]."[10] The majority, however, judged that if the blacks chose to see "the enforced separation of the two races [as stamping them] with a badge of inferiority, . . . it is not by reason of anything found in the act, but solely because the colored race chooses to put that construction on it."[11]

Once decided, *Plessy* became the basis for the legalization of black codes across the South. It was to be the law of the land until 1954. Plessy ushered in the "era of genuine segregation—the era when 'equal but separate' was consciously applied to all possible areas of contact between the races, and when the code became a hard-and-fast dogma of the white race."[12] There were, across the South, waves of Jim Crow laws passed that ultimately led to an absurd separation of the two races. What started as equal but separate facilities on railroad cars in the 1890s "mushroomed" across the Deep South into hundreds of local ordinances; the local customs and usages that developed effectively separated the two races in *every* social, economic, and political sphere so that, for all practical purposes, a white person in the South had contact with only the black person who worked in his home as a domestic.[13]

For almost sixty years, the doctrine of "equal but separate" became the operative rule in federal courts and the legitimation of the absolute separation of the races. With *Plessy,* the era of reconstruction ended. It was followed by a pervasive institutional, legal, and cultural separatism that degraded blacks and by regional political discrimination aimed at ending blacks' political participation.[14] *Plessy* ushered in decades of violence, humiliation, and legal discrimination and, with them, the beginnings of formal, legal black resistance to Jim Crowism. It was the "symbol of the fundamental schizophrenia at the heart of American democracy."[15]

The Court that Black joined in 1937, followed in 1939 by Douglas, had, since *Plessy,* "seesawed" on the question of civil rights for blacks.[16] While the brethren generally upheld the arguments of black petitioners that the *Plessy* doctrine did not permit states to deprive blacks of legal and political rights, the Court continued to reinforce the "equal but separate" doctrine in litigation involving social relations between blacks and whites.

By the early 1930s, with "discontent in the air," as Douglas described it,[17] the NAACP began to develop a litigation strategy to challenge many of the restrictive southern racial policies, including controversial issues such as housing segregation, white primaries, unfair criminal procedures, police brutality against blacks, restrictive covenants, and the lack of truly "separate but equal" facilities in schools and other public services.[18] Under the leadership of Nathan R. Margold, the legal division of the NAACP began to develop a public-facilities strategy and a data base to show the federal courts that public facilities in the South were undeniably separate but not equal.[19] The results in the early and mid-1930s were mixed. In 1932, the Court ordered a new trial for the seven young black defendants in the Scottsboro case.[20] In other criminal cases during this same period, the Court invalidated convictions of blacks because the actions of the local police—in Alabama, Mississippi, and other states—violated their Fourth, Fifth, or Sixth Amendment rights.[21] However, the Court ruled in the 1935 *Grovey* v. *Townsend* case that the Texas Democratic party was a private club and, as such, could exclude blacks from participating in the primary elections; and in cases such as *School District No. 7, Muskogee County* v. *Hunnicut* (1931) and *Salvatierra* v. *Independent School District,* cert denied (1931), the Court revalidated *Plessy* in the area of public education.[22]

When Black and Douglas came to the Court, then, the *Plessy* "separate but equal" doctrine, while under legal attack by the NAACP, was still the operative doctrine, and the only effective strategy before the courts was to show both political or legal inequality and separateness. Clearly, the justices were not thinking of ways to weaken or set aside the 1896 *Plessy* decision.

Not surprisingly, Felix Frankfurter, before his elevation to the Court, alone among Roosevelt's first four appointees to the Court (Black, Reed, and Douglas being the other three), was the only active supporter of blacks' quest for justice.

Frankfurter was a member of the NAACP and had helped its legal and political leaders develop their litigation strategies. As early as 1929, Frankfurter, who had declined Executive Director Walter White's invitation to become one of the directors of the NAACP, served on the association's national legal committee. When he was appointed to the Court, however, Frankfurter "resigned from all outside activities, including the NAACP's legal committee."[23]

In the Senate at this time, Hugo Black of Alabama was doing all he could (successfully) to kill the antilynching legislation being debated. The senior senator, soon to be Roosevelt's initial Supreme Court appointee, objected to what he considered federal intervention into the affairs of the states. Senator Black's secretary maintained a file labeled "Negro Propaganda," which contained letters from the NAACP and other black organizations asking for Black's help in their struggle for racial justice. In one such letter, seeking Black's support of the antilynching federal law, its author, Dr. Charles McPherson, asked, "Can our government afford to permit lynching and mob violence to run rampant without any action on the part of you?" Enclosed was a dramatic photo of two black youths lynched in Columbus, Mississippi. Black's notation was brief: "Propaganda: File, No Reply."[24]

William Douglas, as Chairman of the Securities Exchange Commission, was heavily involved in the New Deal effort to restore confidence in the stock and bond markets and was not a major voice in the civil rights debates and policy making of the New Deal administration. His business travel in those years was largely limited to the nation's financial centers, none of which, at the time, were in the South. There is no evidence that he participated in any civil rights activity, or had any contact with the civil rights community, in the years before he served on the Court.

In fact, it appears that while Douglas had a natural inclination toward the claims of virtually any suffering minority group, his sensitivity to discrimination in this country came from his travels abroad, which had a major influence on his understanding of civil rights and his response to the claims of petitioners in cases before the Court. As Cathleen Douglas-Stone recalled, "Everywhere he went, he sought to discover how local minorities were treated. What kind of jobs did they perform? Were they allowed to vote? What laws were enacted that limited their horizons and burdened their paths? He studied the plight of the overseas Chinese in Thailand, the Muslims in India, the tribal people in Iran, the Jews in North Africa. The stark realities of the treatment of minorities abroad made more vivid for him, I think, the inequalities and injustices in his own country."[25] Douglas brought this developing concern for equality here and abroad, with a growing sense of anger at discriminatory behavior, to the civil rights cases, whereas Black brought his experiences and his commitment to the language of the Civil War Amendments.

Without a doubt, the public's perception of Hugo Black after his appointment to the Court was that the Alabaman was a pure, dyed-in-the-wool racist. All Southerners, living with Jim Crowism, were integral parts of the racist system.[26] While it seems clear, as Mark Silverstein has written, that Black "was hardly a racist in the worst tradition of southern politicians, he nevertheless did not rebel against the racism of the society in which he lived."[27] As a prosecutor, he played on the racial fears of jurors in Birmingham, and as a senator, he applauded the actions of Alabama jurors in the so-called Negro rapers case, better known as the Scottsboro case.[28] Although he had taken to the airwaves to respond to the charges that he had been a member of the Ku Klux Klan, his words rang hollow to those who knew of the KKK's role in his political career.

In a letter to Max Lowenthal, Walter White, executive director of the NAACP, recounted a revealing conversation that he and Black had on the evening of Black's nomination to the Court in August 1937. When White warned Black that he would be "on the spot" whenever an issue involving minority rights came to the Court, Black responded "frankly and soberly that he realized this and that he hoped that he would be able to measure up to what I and others of his friends expected of him."[29] Needless to say, many groups, especially black organizations, did not believe that Black would "measure up" as a justice of the Supreme Court. While White may not have been very concerned about Black, the rank and file were "greatly horrified, . . . sad, disappointed and sickened" at the news of Black's appointment.[30] Black's rejoinder to these cries from the heart, in the decades that followed the revelation of his Klan membership, was silence, after his October 1, 1937, speech, and action as a justice.

Chief Justice Hughes chose Black to write some early cases brought to the Court by black petitioners and by the NAACP in "a conscious effort to assign Black opinions that would rehabilitate him in the view of the liberal community."[31] Black was on the Court when it heard the Scottsboro case for the third time, but he did not participate after a southern senator read into the *Congressional Record* one of Black's senatorial speeches opposing antilynching legislation.[32] He did, however, join the majority in the 1938 case of *Missouri ex rel. Gaines* v. *Canada,* in which the Court ruled that a state had to admit a student into its white law school if there was no separate but equal law school for blacks.[33] Paying a black student, Lloyd Gaines, to go out of state to law school was a violation of the Fourteenth Amendment's "equal protection" clause, wrote Justice Owen Roberts for the Court. *Plessy* was retained, but Missouri had to either provide equal accommodations or integrate the University of Missouri Law School.

Black's participation in the majority opinion prompted an editorial in a black newspaper, the *Houston Informer:*

> To our great surprise and infinite relief, our good friend, Justice Hugo L. Black, was found with the majority, which upset a tradition of the South that is as old as the freedom of the Negro. Not a Negro in America would have been surprised if Justice Black had been found in the minority mumbling nothings with Justices Butler and McReynolds, two old men still actuated by the tenets of slavery days. Along with thousands of other Negroes, we fought confirmation of Justice Hugo Black, and were loud in our wailing after he was confirmed. . . . To say truth, the action of the justice is too good to believe, and we are still waiting for another occasion to see if our ears and eyes are deceiving us.[34]

The editorial staff did not have too long to wait, for during the 1939 and 1940 terms, the Court heard and decided *Pierre* v. *Louisiana* and *Chambers* v. *Florida.* Hughes asked Black to write for the Court in both cases.

In *Pierre,* the Court reversed a murder conviction because blacks had been systematically excluded from jury rolls in Louisiana. After reviewing the data in the disputed case, Black wrote that "equal protection to all is the basic principle upon which justice under law rests."[35]

The 1940 *Chambers* case was, for Black, a "difficult opinion" for two reasons: it raised questions about the role of federal courts intervening in the activities of the states, and it called for the overturn of the jury verdict.[36] But Black was also the man who cleaned up the abusive practices in Birmingham's criminal courts. The evidence of police wrongdoing against blacks in *Chambers* was so overwhelming that Black was able to develop, after some preliminary drafts that took him in different directions,[37] an opinion for the unanimous Court that was, for him and others, one of the finest statements of the importance of the federal judiciary and the Constitution in protecting the lives and procedural liberties of the powerless in American society. Black considered *Chambers,* of all his opinions, his "best writing," wrote Elizabeth in 1985. "Hugo," she wrote, "felt so strongly about the case that he could never read aloud from his opinion without tears streaming down his face."[38] In it, he wrote: "Under our constitutional system, Courts stand against any winds that blow as havens of refuge for those who might otherwise suffer because they are helpless, weak, outnumbered, or because they are non-conforming victims of prejudice and public excitement."[39] Hughes, with a certain flair, had Black announce the opinion on February 12, 1940, Lincoln's birthday. The response in the black community was electric. *Chambers* "was a resounding public success."[40]

Mary McLeod Bethune, a major figure in the black movement and then director of the Division of Negro Affairs of the National Youth Administration, wrote to say to Black: "God bless you. Our prayers are that you may live long to render such just decisions. The Negro race has been waiting for men like you on the bench for many year[s]. May He give you courage, vision and a growing spirit of justice. We need you in a day like this."[41] The president of the Fort Worth branch of the NAACP thanked Black for his "superb statesmanship" in the *Chambers* opinion. "If it were possible," he wrote, "Negroes all over the nation would recall every single word of derision heaped upon you and smother you with the glory of their praise."[42]

While there were still some critics of Black when *Chambers* came down,[43] for both Black and his brethren the case was a watershed. As one of his law clerks put it: *Chambers,* "after great internal struggles, was a turning point. . . .[It introduced] much of what was to become his mature philosophy."[44] Clearly, as one scholar has written, the 1940 opinion "established [Black's] credentials as a firm defender of civil liberties and helped to remove the doubts regarding his commitment to the Constitution his Klan membership had aroused."[45]

Unlike his friend and colleague Black, William O. Douglas grew up in a part of the country where the dominant minority group was the Native Americans who lived in the area, the Yakima Indians. While there was a feeling of white superiority and "an attitude of unfriendliness,"[46] "ugly actions against anyone," such as lynchings or beatings, and separate but equal accommodations were not part of his experience. Douglas recalled knowing only one black student, a star football player for Yakima High School, while growing up in Washington. In his chapter on minorities in the first volume of his autobiography, Douglas essentially wrote about the Yakima Indians and the Wobblies he first met while working in the summers with harvest crews in eastern Washington.[47] The issue for Douglas was always the matter of a persecuted minority, rather than the persecuted racial minority, which partly explains the critical differences between Black and Douglas on other group classifications and the appropriateness of the equal protection argument. Still, once he had seen racial discrimination in all its brutality and ugliness, at home and abroad, Douglas was eager to fight it vigorously.

In his book *The Anatomy of Liberty,* Douglas spelled out his feelings about racial discrimination and equality. For Douglas, such discrimination was the

> most pernicious of all and the easiest to detect. . . . The Constitution proclaims the principle of equality—equality for the man who disagrees with government, as well as for the party member; equality for a man no matter his religion; equality for a man no matter his race. . . . All men are of course not equal in talents or abilities. But once all men are treated equally by government and afforded equal opportunities for preferment and advancement, society undergoes a transformation. A new aristocracy emerges—not an aristocracy of family, wealth, race, or religion, but an aristocracy of talent. An aristocracy of talent that draws from all the roots of the community is indeed the distinguishing mark of democracy.[48]

To him, equality was the first premise of liberty.

Douglas came to the Court after serving as a "lawyer, teacher, administrator and reformer," as Abe Fortas described him, "whose career had been substantially confined to the narrow limits of the corporate domain." His views on the question of racial discrimination were still largely undeveloped. From his votes and written opinions, however, it became clear that he was a vigorous supporter of judicial actions that would eradicate the vestiges of racial and other forms of discrimination. While there had really been "no public manifestation" of his "commitment to individual freedom," Fortas's judgment that Douglas was "a man whose personal torment would yield a rich harvest of dedication to humanity" proved to be the case.[49] A review of Douglas's actions after he joined the Court makes it abundantly clear that his commitment to civil rights for all disadvantaged groups was absolute.

What Fortas's observations underestimated, however, was the extent of Douglas's commitment to try to end individual suffering at the hands of government. William Douglas as associate justice of the Supreme Court joined with Hugo Black in all the early votes against racial discrimination, stood side by side with him as they, unsuccessfuly, tried to decide the *Brown* segregation case during the Court's 1952 term, and, with him, took the legal path that ended segregation as a constitutional norm.

There were some crucial differences between Black and Douglas in their approach to race-discrimination cases, given their different views of the judiciary's role and of the tension between power and right. They disagreed quite dramatically about (1) the speech plus conduct cases involving blacks who marched and sang in civil rights protests; (2) black sit-ins in private establishments, which raised the question of "the extent to which private activity must possess a 'public' character before being deemed 'state action' within the meaning of the Constitution";[50] (3) the scope and the power of Congress to implement the "enforcement" provisions of the Fourteenth and Fifteenth Amendments; and (4) the breadth and scope of the equal protection clause itself.[51]

Their legal disagreements were based in part on their understanding of the role of equality in the constitutional system. Black had great difficulty in many important civil rights cases because of his predisposition to protect the right of property owners and his differentiation between speech and conduct. His commitment to property and to a pure speech, derived from his literalist, historical view of the constitutional text, created conflict for him when he confronted the black protesters' quest for their right to peacefully assemble and to petition for a redress of grievances. Douglas, on the contrary, felt no such legal and historical pressures. For him, the civil rights litigation issue came down to three core values: liberty, equality, and privacy. These norms were primary, and the Fourteenth Amendment's language had to be molded by the Court to protect them against intrusion by governmental and private powers.

During the mid-1960s, before the Vietnam protests gathered momentum, the "speech plus" debate was difficult to separate from the civil rights context in which it arose. There is a certain irony in the fact that at the core of this dispute was an argument between Black and Abe Fortas, Douglas's protégé and the man whom both Black and Douglas had convinced to join the Court.

The break between Black and Douglas began during the 1964 term, when Douglas and Black disagreed in an important civil rights case, *Cox* v. *Louisiana*,[52] and became permanent two years later in *Adderley* v. *Florida.* It was a difference that remained for as long as they served together on the Court, one based on philosophical and jurisprudential views that Black held and that Douglas could not accept as his own.

In *Adderley* v. *Florida,* black students were arrested for trespassing on the grounds of the Tallahassee county jail, where they were protesting the arrests of other students who had been demonstrating against racial segregation in Tallahassee movie theaters. Black wrote the opinion of the Court affirming the trespass convictions. According to Douglas's conference notes, Black thought the sheriff had acted correctly in arresting them for trespass, since the protesters were "on the grounds of the jail and tried to get in" and the sheriff was "custodian of the jail and the jail grounds under Florida law."[53] As Harlan wrote in a letter to Black, "Nothing in the Constitution of the United States prevents Florida from enforcing its general trespass statute against those refusing to obey the sheriff's order to remove themselves from what amounted to the curtilage of the jailhouse."[54] Black made it very clear that both private businesses and governments had the right to preserve their property for the conduct of normal business free from interference, regardless of the worthy purpose of the demonstration.

Douglas, joined by Brennan, Fortas, and Warren, wrote the dissent. Brennan worked closely with Douglas on the opinion, as he did on so many others. He pointed out in a letter to Douglas that Black's majority opinion would have "the most 'chilling effect' on legitimate protests on all forms of public property, parks, malls, etc. included" and complained that Black had misrepresented the facts. "Hugo's . . . whole treatment of the facts reflects a distorted picture of the actual situation. If Hugo prevails," Brennan warned, "he's certainly effectively overruled *Edwards*."[55]

Going to the heart of his disagreement with Douglas, however, Black pointed out that these "singing and clapping" demonstrators did not have "a constitutional right to stay on the property, over the jail custodian's objections" simply because the jail was an appropriate place for a reasonable protest. "Such an argument has as its major unarticulated premise the assumption that people who want to propagandize protests or views have a constitutional right to do so however and wherever they please."[56] To those who knew Black it was clear that he was speaking from the heart, having experienced the passionate force of the crowd, as well as as a constitutional scholar.

Douglas's response was a classic First Amendment dissent. He even quoted a close friend of Black's, Edmond Cahn, to the effect that demonstrations such as those in *Adderley* would overcome the enemies of liberty in our democracy. For Douglas, there was no difference between the jailhouse and other public buildings. It, "like an executive mansion, a legislative chamber, a courthouse or the statehouse itself, is one of the seats of governments whether it be the Tower of London, the Bastille, or a small county jail. And when it houses political prisoners or those who many think are unjustly held, it is an obvious center for protest. The right to petition for the redress of grievances has an ancient history and is not limited to writing a letter or sending a telegram to a congressman." Douglas felt that "violence" was done to the First Amendment when the trespass convictions were allowed to stand. The ordinance was used to "bludgeon those who peacefully exercise a First Amendment right to protest to government against one of the most grievous of all modern oppressions which some of our States are inflicting on our citizens."[57]

After *Adderley* was announced, Black received a letter from a New Yorker who was concerned by articles in the *New York Times* about Black's "clash" with Douglas, which he feared signaled the end of their work on behalf of civil rights and individual freedom. Black's response was brief: "Thanks for your nice letter. . . . Nothing whatsoever has occurred to break the long friendship between Justice Douglas and me—while many of our views have always been very similar some of them have always been different, as they probably always will be."[58] Yet if the two men differed over the marching-in-the-streets cases, the sit-in cases "marked Black's constitutional divide."[59]

As early as the *Civil Rights Cases* of 1883, the Supreme Court had concluded that the Fourteenth Amendment was a constraint on formal public actions taken by official agents of the state. In 1948, in the case of *Shelley* v. *Kraemer,* the Supreme Court determined that a state court's enforcement of a racially restrictive covenant that banned blacks from purchasing property and whites from selling to them was a form of "state action" prohibited by the Fourteenth Amendment's equal protection clause.[60] During the modern civil rights period, black protestors, in their effort to deal with the blight of Jim Crowism—whose segregation practices had become local custom and extended to public, yet privately owned, establishments such as hotels, motels, amusement centers, movie houses, and restaurants—devised a strategy that called for a very broad interpretation of "state action."

The "sit-in" strategy (or "sit-down," as Black referred to the litigation when the cases began coming to the Court), was a vigorous one developed by the Student Nonviolent Coordinating Committee (SNCC), an organization of college students that was much more militant than the NAACP.[61] Simply put, blacks, occasionally accompanied by white supporters, would enter a restaurant or another public accommodation that did not serve blacks and ask to be served. Typically, they would be arrested and convicted for trespass or for breach of the peace. Their defense, in the more than thirty cases that came to the Court between 1961 and 1965, was that state officers were "suppressing free speech and enforcing racial discrimination in violation of the First and Fourteenth Amendments."[62] The claim was that even though the restaurant did not violate the Constitution by its action, government did if it used the state statutes, local ordinances, local customs, police, and courts to aid the restaurant in its discrimination.

For the lawyers arguing the cases before the Supreme Court and for the brethren themselves, the critical question was whether "the state [or a local subdivision of government] could use its power to help a private owner to discriminate against blacks."[63] Strategically, the black petitioners had to show a connection between the racial discrimination of the private-property owner and "state action to entitle the demonstrators to [the Fourteenth Amendment's] 'equal protection of the laws.'"[64] If state action could be found in the local community's reactions to the peaceful sit-in protest, then the protests against segregation could continue with the imprimatur of the federal judiciary.

During the discussions of the 1962 term's sit-in cases, Black strongly defended the sanctity of property rights. In conference he argued: "We have a system of private ownership of property and . . . I see nothing in the Constitution which says [that an] owner can't tell people he doesn't want to get out. Therefore, he can call the police to help protect that right. If that right is in the owner, the law must enforce that right.[65] Warren noted that Black believed that "a store owner as a home owner has a right to say who can come on his premises and how long they can stay. If he has that right, he cannot be helpless to call the police.[66]

Douglas disagreed with Black. If his view were to prevail, Douglas asserted, the country would return to the days of *Plessy.* He exclaimed, "Retail stores can't discriminate and therefore state proceedings to help them are unconstitutional. . . . I would make the store owner a public utility and I'd overrule the Civil Rights cases."[67] Warren noted that Douglas would have decided all the sit-in cases "in a [constitutional] manner that would solve the whole problem."[68] However, the rest of the Court decided to follow Warren's and Goldberg's suggestion that the Court not reach the constitutional questions. Instead, the majority reversed the convictions on procedural grounds.[69] Douglas concurred, stating that public businesses such as restaurants cannot constitutionally "manage that business on the basis of apartheid."[70] The term ended with Black and Douglas's relationship of a quarter-century "under increasing strain" from the sit-in cases.[71]

During the 1963 term, the strain worsened when the Court heard *Bell* v. *Maryland.* It was a case involving a dozen or so blacks who had sat down at a lunch counter in Hooper's Department Store, in Baltimore, in 1960. Black held that the principle of property rights was inviolable. Regardless of the owner's racist or other motivation,[72] if he was not violating a statute or the Constitution and if the agents of the state were not involved in the discrimination, then there was nothing that federal judges could do. In his conference notes for October 23, 1963, after Goldberg's presentation in conference, Black wrote: "I deny that people have a constitutional right to trespass or stay on property over the owner's protest." In response to Goldberg's comments that such treatment amounts to an "indicia of slavery," Black wrote, "I think it is a indicia of slavery to make me associate with people I do not want to associate with."[73]

Douglas, however, insisted that federal courts, and especially the United States Supreme Court, had to intervene—on the constitutional merits—and set aside these convictions because they were manifestations of "state action" that violated the Fourteenth Amendment. The enforcement by the state—specifically, the state courts—of the trespass ordinances against the black protesters, at the request of the white store managers, was unconstitutional, discriminatory action. It was precisely the ground on which the Court had barred judicial enforcement of racially restrictive covenants in 1948. In a memo he circulated to the brethren a few days before the October 23, 1963, conference, Douglas wrote: "The question in the sit-in cases [is] whether States, acting through their courts, can constitutionally put a racial cordon around businesses serving the public." To affirm the convictions of the black protesters, Douglas concluded, handcuffs Congress and "fastens apartheid onto our society—a result incomprehensible in light of the purposes of the Fourteenth Amendment and the realities of our modern society."[74]

Ultimately, given the fluidity of judical choice in this controversial area, Black's five-person *Bell* majority turned into a minority.[75] Black had been afraid he would lose one of the "soldiers" who made up his five-man majority, which he called "scant and scared." In her memoir, his wife recalled that "Hugo [made] innumerable phone calls and [submitted] many rewrites, both to please his army and to answer the minority dissents." Although Black thought that Stewart would switch, it was Tom C. Clark who "deserted" in the spring of 1964 and ultimately joined in the opinion of the Court.[76]

The Brennan opinion for a narrow majority reversed and remanded the convictions of Bell and his friends on narrow, procedural grounds. Douglas, irate because the Court did not discuss the case fully on its merits, wrote a letter to Brennan to say that he had "suffered a real shock when I realized you were in dead earnest in vacating *Bell* and remanding it to the State Court and thus avoiding the basic constitutional question. I guess I underwent a real trauma when I realized that the spirit of Felix [Frankfurter] still was the dominant force here."[77] Brennan, at a later date, explained his decision to push for the procedural resolution: the Court was "aware that Congress under [President] Johnson's leadership was after the Civil Rights Act of 1964. I was so concerned that if we came down with *Bell* v. *Maryland* on constitutional grounds, it would kill the civil rights act. Hugo was just beside himself with me on that. He came storming in saying 'You can't do that!'"[78] And Brennan did not.

Both Black and Douglas, however, wrote substantive opinions, one dissenting and the other concurring, that flesh out their fundamental disagreement in the sit-in conflict. While they were in full agreement about the evil of race discrimination and both sought to eradicate all the formal manifestations of racism, they dramatically split on the question of the constitutionality of the sit-in protest. It was important to Black for the black protesters to know that they could not "continue to break the law in the belief that the Supreme Court will sustain the legality of their claims."[79] Douglas, however, asserted that it was imperative that the brethren reach the constitutional merits, expand the concept of "state action," and reverse the judgments, because the convictions were blatant Jim Crowism, which still existed in parts of the country.

Douglas could not accept Black's narrow view of equal protection as essentially a constitutional guarantee that should "not be allowed to extend beyond race."[80] They never reconciled their differences in this area of constitutional jurisprudence. Their estrangement over this important constitutional issue was not made any less painful by a note from Fortas (who disliked Black) to Douglas that stressed the split between the two venerable allies. "I think Felix, like a flea," wrote Fortas to Douglas as Hugo was reading his dissent in Court, "hopped over to occupy a corner of your friend's soul." (Harlan's note to Black after he read his dissent had just one word: "Amen!")[81]

Overturning *Plessy*

Despite their fierce disagreements about some of the constitutional issues raised by the civil rights cases, Black and Douglas, along with most of their brethren, advanced the civil rights of minorities throughout their tenure on the Court. During the late 1930s and the 1940s, the cases argued before the Court—by the NAACP and other civil rights groups on behalf of black petitioners—were based on the *Plessy* doctrine. A few breakthroughs were made, in the area of voting, for example, during the Stone and Vinson Courts, but *Plessy* remained as an anchor for segregation until 1954.

Nathan Margold, a Harvard-trained NAACP lawyer and close friend of Felix Frankfurter, reviewed the organization's strategy and, in the early 1930s, developed a plan to attack race segregation in the light of *Plessy.* It was, initially, a two-pronged attack: (1) have declared unconstitutional laws in seven states in the Deep South that had not, statutorily, followed the "separate but equal" mandate of *Plessy,* and (2) have declared unconstitutional, as being in violation of *Plessy,* the implementation practice in many other states of disproportionate expenditures for white educational facilities, which was in violation of equal protection. For Margold, the black attack on segregation had to occur "where the whites were most vulnerable and least likely to respond with anger . . . graduate and professional schools."[82]

By the 1940s, the NAACP's strategy for laying to rest the "separate but equal" doctrine was unfolding: have the federal judiciary address segregation in the professional and graduate schools, and then have the federal jurists face segregation in the high schools. After southern states' segregation practices had been invalidated under "separate but equal," then the NAACP would move to force an end to segregation in the elementary schools by overturning that standard. It was a blueprint that would soon force the Court into a fundamental reexamination of the 1986 *Plessy* doctrine.

The Court had heard *Gaines* in 1938, but the war interrupted the NAACP's efforts. However, the NAACP began again, under the leadership of Thurgood Marshall, with the case of *Sipuel* v. *Oklahoma,* heard by the Court during the 1947 term.[83] Ada Sipuel was a twenty-one-year old black woman who sought admission to the University of Oklahoma Law School on the grounds that no black law school existed in the state. Suit was brought by Marshall and the NAACP to have her admitted. Sipuel lost, as the Oklahoma court ruled that the state did not have to admit her and that it did not have to build a separate black law school until there was a much greater demand for such a segregated facility. Marshall's strategy before the Supreme Court was to show separateness and inequality and to urge a dismantling of *Plessy,* arguing "There can be no separate equality."[84]

The justices, however, were not yet ready to overturn *Plessy.* Their conference was relatively brief and uneventful, with the exception of an expression of concern by Murphy and an initial "pass" by Reed, who was "not in sympathy with what the Court has been doing in this field."[85] Most were for reversing the state court ruling in light of *Gaines.* Vinson asserted that "this girl" had a right to a legal education and "that talk of [black] demand is shadow boxing." Murphy insisted that an order be issued to admit her to the Oklahoma Law School and declared that he was "opposed to the equal but separate doctrine." Jackson suggested a short *per curiam* opinion because "every discussion of the race problem makes it worse."[86] His suggestion prevailed, and within four days of hearing oral argument, the Court issued a short *per curiam* stating that Oklahoma had to provide Sipuel with a legal education, in conformity with the Fourteenth Amendment's equal protection clause.

On remand, the Oklahoma Supreme Court ordered the university regents to admit her or to open a separate black law school; the white law school was to be closed until one was ready for black students. Overnight, in a roped-off area of the state capitol, the regents established a black law school with three professors from the white law school assigned to teach Sipuel and other blacks. Thurgood Marshall immediately appealed to the justices. The ad hoc law school could not comply with the definition of equality, even that expressed in *Plessy,* either physically or intellectually. He argued that since "exclusion of any one group on the basis of race automatically imputes a badge of inferiority to the excluded group," *Plessy* had to be invalidated and Sipuel had to be allowed to enter the University of Oklahoma Law School.[87]

However, with only Murphy and Rutledge dissenting, the Court avoided the constitutional question by ruling that the original litigation had not raised that issue and the Court was unwilling to resolve it at that time. For Marshall and the NAACP, as well as for Ada Sipuel, the decision was a setback in the effort to end Jim Crowism.[88]

Marshall, who lost in *Sipuel,* came back to the Court with just that question. In 1950, the justices examined two cases involving segregation in higher education: *Sweatt* v. *Painter* and *McLaurin* v. *Oklahoma State Regents.*[89] In a move that was quite similar to that of the Oklahoma regents in *Sipuel,* Texas had quickly established a black law school with three faculty members and a library of 10,000 books in three basement rooms in a state building in Austin to avoid having to admit blacks to the all-white University of Texas Law School. Sweatt, a black law student, sued the state of Texas because, he asserted, a law school established exclusively for blacks could not provide the students with an education equal to that offered to whites. *McLaurin* was a case brought by a sixty-eight-year-old man to be admitted to the all-white University of Oklahoma Graduate School of Education; facing the alternative of having to establish a black graduate school, the regents admitted him, but he was then cruelly segregated inside the university.[90]

Thurgood Marshall's strategy was to show the justices, through the testimony of expert witnesses such as scholars and deans of major law schools, that a good legal education required a mixture of students and faculty and that a segregated education was "scientifically unjustifiable and socially destructive."[91] He was asking, through an amicus brief prepared by Thomas I. Emerson of Yale Law School and signed by 187 leading constitutional scholars, the Supreme Court to invalidate *Plessy* v. *Ferguson.*[92] One of Frankfurter's former law clerks, Philip Elman, was in the Justice Department's Civil Rights Division helping to prepare a strong federal government statement against Jim Crowism and was in weekly communication with Frankfurter about it.[93] (Frankfurter regularly called his former law students and law clerks, wherever they happened to be employed at the moment, to chat with them about substantive issues, including pending cases or matters that posed a conflict of interest. Frankfurter, evidently, never gave this ethical matter much thought.)

But it was an appeal to a Court that had recently lost the two liberal and compassionate jurists who had dissented in the second *Sipuel* Court opinion: Frank Murphy and Wiley Rutledge. Tom C. Clark, Truman's attorney general and a Texas Democrat, had replaced Murphy, while Sherman Minton, a former Senate crony of Truman's, had replaced Rutledge. And the Court chose not to move on *Plessy.* Clark set the tone for the Court. In a printed memorandum to his new brethren, he "expressed some views" about the two cases, since, as he put it, "these cases arise in 'my' part of the country."[94] The "horribles" discussed by the southern states were "highly exaggerated," unless the Court were to "overrule" *Plessy.* Clark was "opposed to this course." He believed, however, that *Plessy* should not be extended to graduate and professional schools.

Along with the rest of the Court, Clark thought that a narrow ruling was necessary. "Limitation to graduate schools ignores, of course, the influence of segregation upon children's minds when they are four or five-years-old; but I see no reason why we should not concern ourselves here with the equality of education rather than social recognition." For Clark, elementary education was not the issue, for "it is entirely possible that Negroes in segregated grammar schools being taught arithmetic, spelling, geography, etc., would receive skills in these elementary subjects equivalent to those of segregated white students, assuming equality in texts, teachers and facilities." He did not believe that to be the case for all black law and graduate schools and concluded: "I join with those who would reverse these cases upon the ground that segregated graduate education denies equal protection of the laws. . . . If some say this undermines *Plessy* then let it fall, as have many Nineteenth Century oracles."[95]

Plessy was not to fall in these 1950 term cases. Vinson, writing for the Court in both *Sweatt* and *McLaurin,* followed *Gaines* carefully. Frankfurter, in a letter to the chief, wrote bluntly: "It seems to me desirable now not to go a jot or tittle beyond the Gaines test. The shorter the opinion, the more there is an appearance of unexcitement and inevitability about it, the better."[96] On the slip opinion he returned to the chief, Black wrote: "I sincerely hope it can obtain a unanimous approval—Certainly, I shall say nothing unless someone else writes. . . . Full Court acceptance of [these opinions] should add force to our holdings."[97] In *Sweatt,* Vinson wrote that the Court unanimously "found no substantial equality in the educational opportunities offered white and Negro law students by the state. . . . The University of Texas Law School is superior. . . . [It] possesses to a far greater degree those qualities which are incapable of objective measurement but which make for greatness in a law school."[98] Sweatt was ordered admitted to the University of Texas Law School by the justices. However, Vinson added that the Court did not feel the need to "reach [Sweatt's] contention that *Plessy* v. *Ferguson* should be reexamined in the light of contemporary knowledge respecting the purposes of the Fourteenth Amendment and the effects of racial segregation." In *McLaurin,* Vinson wrote, again for a unanimous Court, that the segregation experienced by McLaurin was unconstitutional because it restricted his "ability to study, to engage in discussions and exchange views with other students and, in general, to learn his profession."[99]

Thurgood Marshall and the NAACP were "gloomy" after the Court handed down these opinions on June 5, 1950,[100] having hoped that the Court would address the constitutionality of separate but equal facilities. However, as Clark reflected in his memorandum, the Court did not strike down *Plessy* because it was not the right time. But Clark had added that "perhaps at a later date our judicial discretion will lead us to hear such a case.[101] That time was soon to come, for, just as these higher education cases were being announced, the NAACP moved to challenge separate but equal facilities in public schools across the nation.

Brown v. Board of Education *(1953):*
Ending Segregation in Public Schools

In 1950, seventeen southern and border states and the District of Columbia had de jure segregated public-school facilities; four other states permitted separate but equal schooling. Thurgood Marshall and his staff of attorneys in the NAACP began to prepare their litigation strategy in four states—Kansas, South Carolina, Virginia, and Delaware—and the District of Columbia, challenging the constitutionality of *Plessy* by challenging the validity of the segregated dual school system. Mark Tushnet has observed that "the decision to attack segregation in elementary and secondary schools closed one era in the NAACP's attack on segregation. . . . But their decision opened another era of litigation, during which the problems the NAACP had earlier faced presented themselves in different forms."[102] The black plaintiffs in the five cases attempted to obtain admission to public schools on a nonsegregated basis. In every case, given *Plessy,* the black petitioners lost and the NAACP took the direct appeal from the federal district court to the Supreme Court. For Thurgood Marshall, the major question was whether "the Court [was] now ready to meet the [NAACP's] direct challenge of segregation per se as unconstitutional?"[103]

On June 7, 1952, the Court announced that it would hear arguments on December 9, 10, and 11 of that year. It consolidated the cases, with *Brown* as the lead case because it was from Kansas. As Justice Clark said, this was done "so that the whole question would not smack of being a purely Southern one."[104] Without a doubt, the justices were reluctantly preparing for the fundamental question. Marshall and the NAACP had developed, in the trial courts, the argument that segregated young black students were affected psychologically by segregation and that equality without integration would not resolve the problem of identity that had become a major one for blacks living in a segregated community.[105] But some of the justices were not exactly enthralled with the vision of the Court caught at the center of the segregation controversy. According to Frankfurter's former law clerk Philip Elman, who was in the solicitor general's office during this time (and who, in his words, "shmoozed" with Frankfurter every Sunday evening on the phone), "the Court was nowhere near ready to take on the issue. The justices (except for Black and Douglas) were deliberately pursuing a strategy of procrastination. The Court's strategy, and this was the Frankfurter–Jackson strategy, was to delay, delay, delay—putting off the issue as long as possible."[106]

Jackson's law clerk during the 1952 term was William H. Rehnquist. He prepared a draft for the troubled justice, entitled "A Few Expressed Prejudices on the Segregation Cases," in which he argued for retaining *Plessy*.

> As I see it, either you accept *Plessy* or overrule it. . . . To the argument made by Thurgood not John Marshall that a majority may not deprive a minority of its constitutional right, the answer must be that while this is sound in theory, in the long run it is the majority who will determine what the constitutional rights of the minority are. . . . I realize that [this] is an unpopular and unhumanitarian position, for which I have been excoriated by "liberal" colleagues, but I think *Plessy* v. *Ferguson* was right and should be reaffirmed. If the Fourteenth Amendment did not enact Spencer's Social Statics, it just as surely did not enact Myrdal's American Dilemma.[107]

The law clerk's frankness troubled Jackson.[108]

Jackson wrote to Charlie Fairman that the "cryptic words of the Fourteenth Amendment solve nothing." But the cases were coming to the Court, and he needed help. While not necessarily agreeing with Rehnquist, he was stumped and "perplexed" by some of the questions these race-relations cases raised: What was the Court's function in the matter? Would the Court's involvement in this matter stir up virulent anti-Communism in the country? "There is no doubt," he wrote, "that the present rather hysterical state of fear of communists, etc. is due in some large part to the identification of left-wingers with this movement to end segregation. . . . Nothing promotes fascism as surely as a real and widespread popular fear of communism and 'radicalism.'"[109]

If Jackson was perplexed, the chief was not. Chief Justice Fred M. Vinson, a conservative Democrat from Kentucky, was unwilling to accept the argument that *Plessy* was no longer a viable precedent for the nation. He considered the body of law to be very clear "on separate but equal. It was hard [for the Court to] get away from the long continued acceptance [of segregation] in the District of Columbia."[110] The Constitution should be left as it was, was his view of the issue. As Elman recalled it, separate but equal "had been the law of the land for over a half-century, and he was not ready to change it. . . . [He] was not going to overrule *Plessy*."[111] Sharing this view were fellow Southerners Justices Clark and Reed.

Felix Frankfurter, who had been so close to the NAACP, was also deeply concerned about the Court's growing involvement in the issue of racial segregation. "Issues legal in form but embroiled in explosive psychological and political attitudes require disposition by this Court," he wrote in September 1952, a few months before the Court heard arguments in the public-education cases. He reminded his brethren that

> it is not our duty to give a Constitutional stamp to our merely personal attitudes toward these issues, however deep individual convictions may be. The opposite is true. It is our duty not to act on our merely personal views. However passionately any of us may feel, however fiercely any one of us may believe that such a policy of segregation as undoubtedly expresses the tenacious conviction of Southern States is both unjust and shortsighted, he travels outside his judicial authority if on the basis of his private feelings he declares unconstitutional the policy of segregation.[112]

Alexander Bickel, Frankfurter's law clerk during the 1952 term, argued that what Frankfurter saw as "the main danger was a decision which would be disobeyed, which would be the beginning rather than the end of a controversy."[113] For Frankfurter, this dilemma was always a major concern. He did not wish to see the Court issue an opinion and then have it honored in the breach.

If Jackson was troubled, Vinson opposed to changing the precedent, and Frankfurter cautious about judicial involvement in the race-discrimination cases, most of the brethren "were uncertain" about the impact of the Court's overturning of *Plessy*.[114] While Black was certainly clear in his mind about the issue of racial segregation and *Plessy*, and concerned about the adverse impact of such a decision in the South, he was in fundamental disagreement with his fellow Southerners on the Court, whom he urged to overrule *Plessy*.[115] Elman, who heard Court gossip from Frankfurter, recalled that

> Hugo was telling the brethren that you cannot constitutionally defend *Plessy*, but if and when they overruled it, it would mean the end of Southern liberalism for the time being. The Bilbos and the Talmadges would come even more to the fore, overshadowing the John Sparkmans and the Lister Hills. The guys who talked nigger would be in charge, there would be riots, the Army might have to be called out—he was scaring the shit out of the Justices, especially Frankfurter and Jackson, who didn't know how the Court could enforce a ruling against *Plessy*. But Hugo was determined to overrule it on principle.[116]

Black's son recalled a conversation he had with his father in 1952. While living in Alabama, Hugo, Jr., had been approached by local Democratic party leaders and asked if he would be interested in running for Congress. He spoke to Hugo about the possibility and "was surprised and a little alarmed by his answer." Black asked his son to fly up to Washington for the conversation; when the young attorney arrived, Black told him about the public-education segregation cases on the docket that term, cases that were challenging *Plessy,* and said, "I agree with old Justice Harlan's dissent in *Plessy* v. *Ferguson.* I don't believe segregation is constitutional."[117] Black's son did not run for Congress; in fact,because of his father's role in overturning *Plessy,* he and his family left Alabama, and he took up law practice in Dade County, Florida.

Bill Douglas had absolutely no reservations about declaring *Plessy* unconstitutional. He did not have the ties to a region that Black had. He did not suffer from any of the "perplexities" that Jackson had expressed in letters to a historian, and he did not exhibit Frankfurter's extreme caution. He would have acted in 1952 to end *Plessy* if the Court, with Frankfurter leading the way, had not delayed the decision by scheduling reargument for the following term. In a letter a few years later to Judge Learned Hand, after the Court had announced its unanimous opinion in *Brown,* Frankfurter indirectly condemned Black and Douglas's impulsiveness on this issue: "If the 'great libertarians' had had their way we would have been in the soup."[118]

On December 13, 1952, one day after the oral arguments had concluded, the Supreme Court held its first of a number of conference sessions to discuss the school segregation cases. Clearly, the justices were deeply concerned—and divided— about the Court's response to the legal arguments presented by both sides in their briefs and in oral argument. Marshall and the NAACP refused, in the words of a lawyer working with Marshall, William T. Coleman, Jr. (who had been the first black law clerk at the Supreme Court, for Felix Frankfurter in 1948), to "concede equality without integration."[119] According to one scholar, this strategy, forcing the issue of *Plessy*'s continued vitality, "was perhaps the most militant position the NAACP had ever taken in its forty-two year history."[120]

The lawyers for the four states argued for keeping *Plessy* and pointed out that the states were making greater efforts to provide separate but equal school systems. Opposing Thurgood Marshall was a leading figure in American politics, former presidential candidate John W. Davis. His strategy was straightforward: attack the social-psychological arguments about black inferiority and draw on the precedents that accumulated in the decades after *Plessy* to validate the separate school systems. Importantly, and fortuitously, the federal government, through the efforts of Assistant Solicitor General Philip Elman, submitted a very helpful amicus curiae brief.

Given his conversations with Frankfurter, Elman knew that one major concern of the brethren was the potential disastrous impact of overturning *Plessy* and ordering an immediate end to the segregated school system. His brief suggested what Frankfurter was later to argue successfully in the Court—that implementing the order to end segregation be the responsibility of the federal district court judges and that it be accomplished with what the Court was to call "all deliberate speed." This strategy of the Justice Department placed Elman, in his own words, on the NAACP's "shitlist as a gradualist." Marshall and his legal staff "just didn't know how to count the votes on the Court" and "were lacking a sense of subtlety about the Justices' concerns. It had been a mistake to push for the overruling of segregation per se so long as Vinson was Chief Justice—it was too early. When Marshall and his staff felt I had betrayed them, they failed to grasp that our brief had been done the Frankurter way, bearing in mind the key problem [the impact of a judgment that overturned *Plessy*] and how it vexed the Court."[121]

The December 13, 1952, conference on these cases indeed suggested that Frankfurter's advice to Elman was correct. An ideologically divided Court, polarized around the Black (Douglas)–Frankfurter (Jackson) axis, met to discuss not only segregation but also the role and responsibilties of the federal judiciary in the policy-making process. And the four major figures on the Court at the time—Black, Douglas, Frankfurter, and Jackson—had little confidence in Vinson's competence to lead the fragmented Court in this and other controversial areas of jurisprudence. Indeed, both Black and Frankfurter, the putative leaders of the enemy camps on the Court, agreed that the justices had to carefully work with the chief to avoid the disastrous impact of a judicial order of the Court.

According to conference notes taken by Burton and Jackson, there were possibly five justices who leaned in favor of overturning *Plessey*: Black, Douglas, Burton, Minton, and Frankfurter. Four—Vinson, Jackson, Reed and Clark—were unwilling to rule that as a matter of law (as opposed to social or political policy), *Plessy* was unconstitutional. Frankfurter wrote to Reed, on May 20, 1954, that had they decided *Brown* in December 1952 it "would have been catastrophic."[122]

According to the conference notes, Vinson was unwilling to act in an area that Congress should legislate—if it desired. If the Court acted, its action would lead to the "complete abolition of public school systems in the South." Black felt that while there "would be some violence," he was "compelled for [him]self to say that segregation is [an] idea of inferiority. . . . [S]egregation itself violates [the Fourteenth] Amendment." He voted to end segregation. Reed argued in defense of *Plessy,* claiming there had been "great progress in the South." He could not say, at that time, that "17 states are denying equal protection or due process." He suggested that ten more years would make blacks "really equal" and argued that the Court should "uphold segregation as constitutional."

Frankfurter, concerned about the catastrophic effect of a Court opinion at that time, began to discuss the possibility of reargument in this conference session. He was the "grand strategist" of the Court in deciding what course to follow in its effort to decide the segregation cases. He was, "to use the Yiddish word that Frankfurter used all the time, the *Kochleffel.* It means cooking spoon, stirring things up; the man stirring everything up inside the Court was Frankfurter."[123] According to him, the Court had to hear rearguments because the brethren were deeply divided.

Douglas stated that the decision had been "very simple" for him. The Court "can't avoid [the] conclusion reached that [a state] cannot classify on [the basis of] color. It is not in [the] realm of argument." Burton would go "full length" to upset segregation, whereas Clark was concerned about the fact that the Court had "led the states on to believe [that] separate but equal [was] OK." Minton believed that there should be "no classification on [the] basis of race," while Jackson, according to Burton's notes, argued that a reading of the legislative and judicial history did not, until this point (1952), indicate that segregation was unconstitutional; while the Court could abolish *Plessy* for policy reasons, he could not see a legal basis for overturning the 1896 opinion.[124]

No formal vote was taken in December 1952.[125] At the May 29, 1953, conference, against the wishes of Black and Douglas, the Court set reargument in the cases for the following term and, with Frankfurter's guidance, developed five basic questions for the attorneys to address in reargument: (1) the congressional intent of the body that drafted the Civil War Amendments, (2) the understanding of the framers regarding public-school segregation, (3) whether the federal judiciary had the power to abolish public-school segregation, and (4) the kind of remedies the Court could devise should it conclude (5) that *Plessy* was not consistent with the Fourteenth Amendment.

On June 13, 1953, Black wrote a memorandum for the conference in which he argued against inviting the attorney general to participate in the rearguments.[126] Frankfurter and Jackson were able to defeat Black, however, and the invitation was extended through the order issued by the Court. (Elman, who was responsible for preparing the government's brief, asked Vinson for what turned out to be a critical time extension during the summer of 1953, which Vinson granted. The rearguments were postponed until December 7, 1953.) Fate then intervened.[127] On September 8, 1953, Vinson suffered a major heart attack and died. On hearing of the chief's passing, Frankfurter remarked to two of his former law clerks, "This is the first indication that I have ever had that there is a God."[128]

For scholars of the Court, there is no question that Warren's appointment as chief justice led to the dramatic change in the collective behavior of the brethren on the question of the fairness and constitutionality of school segregation. In less than a year, the Court went from 5 to 4 to 9 to 0 for overturn of *Plessy,* a change "attributable directly to Warren's leadership."[129] A glance at Warren's background would not have given one any reason to suspect that he would play a prominent role in the resolution of the school segregation cases. He was a member of a nativist, anti-Asian organization in California (the Native Sons of the Golden West) and, as California attorney general during World War II, worked with military authorities in the 1942 relocation of Japanese Americans.[130] He did, however, come to regret his actions, saying later, "now that society in general is so much more aware of civil rights, interning them seems like a terribly cruel thing to do, and it *was* a cruel thing, especially uprooting the children from their schools, their communities and friends, and having whole families transferred out to a strange environment and a less desirable environment."[131]

Yet during the 1953 term of the Court, moving skillfully among the brethren, discussing the litigation with each of them privately, and avoiding votes on the issue in conference, Warren was ultimately able to bring all of the Court around to his position on the merits. It was a position he discussed with the others at the conference held on December 12, 1953, one day after the reargument, stating unequivocally that segregation was wrong: "I don't see how in this day and age we can set any group apart from the rest and say that they are not entitled to exactly the same treatment as all others. [The Civil War Amendments] were intended to make the slaves equal with all others. Personally, I can't see how today we can justify segregation based solely on race."[132]

Warren's strategy was to argue that *Plessy* reflected the "concept of the inherent inferiority of the colored race" and that "if we are to sustain segregation, we . . . must do it upon that basis."[133] Any of his colleagues who wanted to defend *Plessy* would then also have to accept the concept of inherent racial inferiority. None did. After he finished, the others spoke informally, with the understanding that there would be no vote taken until they were ready to do so. There was no "polarization" of the brethren at that time; they spoke freely, and, in the end, Warren felt that there were six in support of ending *Plessy*. Two (Jackson and Clark) who had been opposed to overturning *Plessy* in 1952 were now wavering. Clark told his colleagues that he would go along with an overturn if it were written properly and "provided relief is carefully worked out . . . in such a way that will permit different handling in different places."[134] Jackson spoke much the same way. Only Reed still maintained that *Plessy* was viable law. At the end of this first session with the new "Super Chief," the message Warren had given to his colleagues was clear: *Plessy* was morally wrong, it violated fundamental standards of decency, and it deemed people inferior simply because of the color of their skin.

And that was how the Court moved in the spring of 1954. Warren continued to have informal conversations. In formal conference sessions on January 16, 1954 (which focused on the issue of remedies),[135] in February, and in March, they continued to talk. In March, the justices voted 8 to 1 to overturn *Plessy* and to have Warren write the opinion for the Court. Warren then discussed the value of a gracious, short, flexible, nonaccusatory, but unanimous, opinion and began writing after the March meeting. Warren, in the end, was able to convince Reed to join with the others so that the Court could speak with one voice on such an important issue.[136] Jackson, evidently, was planning to issue a concurring opinion, but after being incapacitated by a heart attack and having discussions with Warren in the hospital, he joined the rest of the brethren in standing behind Warren's opinion for the Court.

In April 1954, the chief was, in great secrecy, hard at work preparing two draft opinions, "short, readable by the public, non-rhetorical, unemotional and, above all, non-accusatory," for review and reaction from his brethren. On May 7, 1954, he sent a short memorandum to the others: "There should be two opinions [attached]—one for the state cases, and another for the District of Columbia case. Also, because of the divergent conditions calling for relief and because this subject was subordinated to a discussion of the substantive question in both the briefs and oral argument, the cases should be restored to the calendar for further argument on [the remedy questions] previously submitted by the Court for the reargument this year."[137]

The opinion was a short one, focusing on the importance of a contemporary interpretation for the equal protection clause. "In approaching this problem, we cannot turn the clock back to 1868 when the Amendment was adopted, or even to 1896 when *Plessy* v. *Ferguson* was written. We must consider public education in the light of its full development and its present place in American life throughout the Nation. Only in this way can it be determined if segregation in public schools deprives these plaintiffs of the equal protection of the laws."[138] It also addressed, very clearly, the harmful effects on black children of a segregated education. "To separate them from others of similar age and qualifications solely because of their race generates a feeling of inferiority as to their status in the community that may affect their hearts and minds in a way unlikely ever to be undone. . . . Whatever may have been the extent of psychological knowledge at the time of *Plessy,* this [Court's] finding is amply supported by modern authority."[139]

For Warren, *Brown* also reflected the significantly changed role of education in society. "Today, education is perhaps the most important function of state and local governments. . . . It is the very foundation of good citizenship. . . . In these days, it is doubtful that any child may reasonably be expected to succeed in life if he [or she] is denied the opportunity of an education. Such an opportunity, where the state has undertaken to provide it, is a right which must be made available to all on equal terms."[140] Therefore, Warren wrote, "we conclude[141] that in the field of public education the doctrine of 'separate but equal' has no place. Separate educational facilities are inherently unequal."[142]

Frankfurter responded to Warren's final drafts on May 14. Concerned about the "real danger of leakage," he suggested that Warren announce the opinion in the school segregation cases on Monday, May 17, 1954: "An opinion in a touchy and explosive litigation, once it has been agreed to by the Court, is like a soufflé—it should be served at once after it has reached completion."[143] Douglas wrote a note to Warren expressing his unreserved support. "I do not think I would change a single word. . . . The two draft opinions meet my idea exactly. You have done a beautiful job."[144]

Warren agreed with Frankfurter. On Monday, May 17, 1954, with an ailing Jackson out of the hospital and sitting with his brethren on the historic occasion, Warren announced the unanimous opinion of the Court in *Brown* v. *Board of Education of Topeka.* The era of *Plessy* had come to an end. The South was enraged, with the regional media calling the day "Black Monday." Thurgood Marshall and the NAACP legal staff's response was muted, as Richard Kluger has described it: "There was no dancing on the tables in Harlem."[145] They still faced the huge task of dismantling the evils of Jim Crowism. However, for most blacks, the May 17, 1954, opinion of the Court was an important watershed. A black reporter observed at the time that "'Black Monday' . . . was the day we won; the day we took the white man's law and won our case before an all-white Supreme Court with a Negro lawyer. . . . And we were proud."[146]

In the Court there was an ebullient reaction. Law clerks recalled that they "felt good—and clean. It was so good."[147] Some of the brethren wrote elated notes to congratulate Warren on his outstanding success in bringing the Court together. Frankfurter sent a handwritten letter, saying "*This* is a day that will live in glory. It is also a great day in the history of the Court and not in the least for the course of deliberation which brought about the result. I congratulate you."[148] And in another note, Burton wrote: "Today I believe has been a great day for America and the Court. . . . To you goes the credit for the character of the opinions which produced the all important unanimity. Congratulations."[149]

Brown *v.* Board of Education *II: The Remedial Decree*

In so very many ways, though, the work of the Court was just beginning. Warren, in *Brown,* had dealt with only the substantive question—the validity of *Plessy.* The remedial phase had not been addressed on the merits. Instead, Warren announced reargument on that issue during the 1954 term. "The parties are requested to present further argument on Questions 4 and 5 previously propounded by the Court. . . . [with] submission of briefs by October 1, 1954."[150] The *Brown* I phase was over; phase II would begin almost immediately.[151]

In July 1954, Frankfurter was hard at work trying to formulate the character of the remedial decree for Warren. In a letter he sent to the chief on July 5, 1954, he wrote that "the most important problem is to fashion appropriate provisions against evasion." Clearly, Frankfurter was concerned about the Court's fashioning a decree that "set forth with detailed particularity" how a segregated school system had to desegregate its facilities. In the letter, he presented two recommendations that would appear in the *Brown* II remedial decree that Warren wrote for a unanimous Court the following spring. The deadline would be flexible and the lower federal courts, rather than the Supreme Court, would deal with the school authorities. While the Court did not formally agree on the general outline of the decree until the April 16, 1955, conference session, almost nine months earlier Frankfurter had begun the task of convincing Warren that the Court should order desegregation of public schools with all deliberate speed.[152]

Oral arguments were held on how to implement *Brown* in April 1955. At the April 16, 1955, conference, Warren presented his conviction that the remedy should contain clear instructions for the federal district courts but be flexible too.[153] Most of the brethren, especially Frankfurter, supported Warren's views . Black, however, suggested something else. He recommended that the Court issue "a decree and quit. The less we say the better off we are. . . . Nothing could injure the Court more than to issue orders that cannot be enforced." Ominously, he warned that it was "futile to think that in these cases we can settle segregation in the South."[154]

During the conference it was agreed, with Black reluctantly joining in, that the chief should write for the unanimous Court. Frankfurter continued his *Kochleffel* work, writing letters and memos to Warren and to the conference, imploring the chief and his brethren to consider using an expression that Justice Holmes had used in earlier opinions. "I have only one further and minor remark to make. I still think that 'with all deliberate speed' is preferable to 'at the earliest practicable date.'"[155] By May 1955, Warren had drafted a short opinion that was discussed at the May 27, 1955, conference. After accepting the important change, introduced by Black and Douglas, that suits not be viewed as class actions and that lower courts issue remedial decrees to admit to desegregated public schools only "the parties to these cases," the Court unanimously agreed to go with the Warren opinion—including the phrase "with all deliberate speed." Frankfurter had succeeded in persuading Warren and his brethren.[156]

Confrontations Between State and Nation

In the years immediately following *Brown* II, the Court did not involve itself in public-school desegregation plans. However, the efforts of the Little Rock school board to develop a "good faith" desegregation plan led to a major clash between national and state agencies in 1957 and 1958. In May 1955, the local school board had developed a plan that called for the desegregation of Central High School beginning in the fall of 1957. The federal district court upheld the plan. Other state agencies intervened, however, including the legislature, which passed an amendment to the state constitution calling for opposition to *Brown*. On September 2, 1957, the day before black students were to integrate the high school, Governor Orval Faubus "dispatched units of the Arkansas National Guard to the Central High School grounds, and placed the school 'off-limits' to colored children."[157] Faubus acted on his own initiative; the school board and city officials had not sought such intervention. The school board, between a rock and a hard place, asked the black students not to attend until the matter could be clarified by the federal court. The federal district court judge ordered the school board to proceed with desegregation, and the next day, black children attempted to enter the high school.

For three weeks, the National Guard troops refused to allow the nine black students to enter the school. In a parallel proceeding, the federal court issued an injunction against the governor and the National Guard, enjoining them from any further attempt to thwart the lawful desegregation plan. When troops were withdrawn from the school, the black students entered but soon had to leave because of the large, menacing crowd that congregated in front of the high school. To quell this new lawlessness, President Eisenhower sent federal troops to Little Rock to protect the black students at the formerly all-white high school. These regular army troops, members of the 101st Airborne elite unit, were later replaced with state Guardsmen who were "federalized" by President Eisenhower in November 1957 and remained on duty at Central High School for the remainder of the school year.

The justices became involved in this dramatic clash between the state and the national government when the local school board requested a thirty-month delay in further desegregation efforts. The federal district judge, citing the "unfavorable community attitude," granted the delay but was overturned by the court of appeals. The case, *Cooper* v. *Aaron,* came to the Court on appeal during the summer of 1958, and in a special session, held on September 11, 1958, the Court met to examine what Justice Burton considered the "first real test of the power of the federal courts to implement the *Brown* decision."[158]

The justices were enraged by the behavior of the state officials, who were plainly disregarding the law of the land. Warren, at oral argument, pressed the attorney for the defendants to address the issue of the state's violence and evasion of the federal judiciary's legal orders. At the conference that immediately followed the oral arguments, the brethren took only a few minutes to uphold the court of appeals's decision and to issue a *per curiam* opinion that would, as Warren told the brethren, "reaffirm the duty of state officials to obey the law as laid down by the Supreme Court."[159] On the following day, September 12, the order affirming the court of appeals was issued; the full opinion was to follow shortly but, in any event, not later than early October 1958.

The Court's unanimity was threatened by Clark's wish to dissent, but after writing a longhand draft stating his concern that the concept of "all deliberate speed" was being rejected, he joined the opinion. The task of writing the full opinion for the Court had been assigned to Brennan, who had some difficulty with style and "verbal differences" introduced by Harlan when he circulated the draft in mid-September. He was helped, however, by a number of his colleagues, especially Hugo Black, who contributed an extremely powerful opening statement that Brennan grafted onto the body of the *Cooper* opinion without any changes:

> As this case reaches us it involves questions of the highest importance to the maintenance of our federal system of government. It squarely presents a claim that there is no duty on state officials to obey federal court orders resting on this Court's deliberate and considered interpretation of the United States Constitution. Specifically, it involves actions by the Governor, Legislature and other agencies of Arkansas, . . . that they are not bound by our holding in Brown . . . that the Fourteenth Amendment forbids states to use their governmental powers to bar children from attending schools which are helped to run by public management, funds or other public property. We are urged to permit continued suspension of the Little Rock School Board's plan to do away with segregated public schools until state laws and efforts to upset [*Brown*] have been further challenged and tested in the courts. We have concluded that these contentions call for clear answers here and now.[160]

The strong message, accepted by the brethren, was that all state officials were bound to obey the law of the land, including the orders of the Supreme Court.

Frankfurter suggested another change that the group quickly adopted. It was a significant one. According to Warren, Frankfurter "suggested that to show that we were all in favor of [*Brown*], we should also say so . . . by an opinion signed by the entire Court."[161] Only Douglas disagreed. It carried, however, by a vote of 8 to 1. With Frankfurter's suggestion accepted and with Black's modifications, the unanimous opinion was ready to be announced on September 29, 1958.

Frankfurter then shattered the tranquility of the group, dropping the "bombshell" at the last conference that he was publishing a concurring opinion.[162] "Warren, Black, [Douglas,] and Brennan were furious"[163] with the little professor. "We almost cut his throat," recalled Brennan.[164] However, none could persuade him not to write. "He blew up in conference saying it was none of the Court's business what he wrote," noted Douglas in his memo for the file.[165] His reason for writing, said Frankfurter, was that many of his former students were practicing law in the South, and his concurrence might persuade them to follow the orders of the federal courts.[166]

In *Cooper,* the Court firmly addressed the question of the constitutional responsibility of all officials: "No state legislator or executive or judicial officer can war against the Constitution without violating his undertaking to support it."[167] However, with increasing frequency and with great ingenuity, southern officials were warring against the Constitution—as interpreted by the Court. The pace of desegregation was, as Black had warned in 1954, "glacierlike." The operative language had given southern officials the wedge with which to keep open the segregated public-school system. For Black and for Douglas, it was important to bring the era of "all deliberate speed" to an end.

In the early 1960s, the justices responded firmly to southern barriers such as the development of transfer plans, threats to close the public-school systems, and "freedom of choice" plans to outflank *Brown*'s call for desegregation.[168] The movement toward an end to the dual school system in the South was, as Douglas wrote, "outrageously sluggish."[169] In *Green* v. *County School Board,* the Court, in the opinion written by Brennan, voiced its frustration at these local efforts to nullify the federal courts' orders to end the dual school system: "This deliberate perpetuation of the unconstitutional dual system can only have compounded the harm of such a system. Such delays are no longer tolerable. . . . The burden on a school board today is to come forward with a plan that promises realistically to work, and promises realistically to work *now.*"[170] This judicial concern led the Court, in the 1969 case of *Alexander* v. *Holmes County, Mississippi,* to formally end the era of "all deliberate speed."[171]

Justice Black was the first of the brethren to review the issues in the Mississippi case as he was the circuit justice of the Fifth Circuit when the appeal came in the summer of 1969. Justices of the Court still formally ride circuit when the United States Supreme Court is not sitting in Washington, D.C. Today's circuit riding, however, is done with telephone and computer, not by horse and buggy. On July 3, 1969, the Court of Appeals for the Fifth Circuit called for desegregation plans, to be put into effect in the fall of 1969, from thirty-three Mississippi school districts. At the request of the Justice Department under Nixon (for the first time in these school desegregation cases, the Justice Department sided with the defendants against the wishes of black petitioners), the circuit court, in late August, postponed, the date for the submission of plans until December 1, 1969.

Fourteen black plaintiffs immediately asked Black, as circuit justice, to vacate the suspension of the July order. For three days, Black and his law clerks debated the substance of the case as well as the propriety of the justice acting for the entire Court. Black "wrestled with the Government's and Mississippi's request for a three month delay in integration," wrote Elizabeth Black. "The boys [his law clerks] want Hugo to grant the Negro petitioners' request to force integration on September 1. Hugo denied this latter request but is writing an opinion stating his reasons and saying he will vote for immediate full integration when Court reconvenes."[172]

The plaintiffs immediately petitioned the full Court for a review of the Fifth Circuit action, and on September 29, the Court granted expedited certiorari. The Court discussed the case at its October 9, 1969, conference in a rancorous exchange. Chief Justice Warren Burger, recently appointed by Nixon, started off the discussion by arguing that since the school year had begun, the plan could not be put into effect until September 1970. Black then spoke eloquently about the need to abandon the "deliberate speed" approach. "There is no chance of getting the colored people into integrated schools unless we eliminate 'all deliberate speed.' . . . [T]he whites in the South will win the battle." Since, unfortunately, the issue had been "made a political football by Nixon and others will do the same, he would provide for instant integration."[173]

On October 24, 1969, the Court had its second conference on *Alexander.* Burger began by suggesting that the Court, speaking "as one voice," remand the case to the lower courts so that they could develop a plan and "terminate segregation" by December 31, 1969. For the chief, the task was to be accomplished, *not simply begun,* with "all deliberate speed." Black vigorously disagreed, feeling that to delay, even five weeks, was to give in again to the forces of racism. The Court should issue a short order that would mandate integration immediately.

Douglas agreed with his friend, and Brennan echoed these views in conference: "'Now' means 'now.'" Stewart said that "no more time is available." White would have told the court of appeals to implement the government's plan immediately. Burger wanted an interim order to come out of the conference for publication the following Monday. Black argued for a final order that "would do away with the dual system. He would not fool around with interim orders." Although Douglas suggested that a committee of three, Burger, Black, and Brennan, draft the opinion, the chief took it upon himself to write it—with the help of two conservative members of the Court, Harlan and Stewart.

His draft order, circulated on October 26, 1969, gave the Fifth Circuit the responsibility for determining the date for school desegregation. Brennan, Marshall, and Douglas expressed serious misgivings, and Brennan was asked to draft an alternative order calling for "integration NOW." Black responded sharply in a memo to the brethren, saying that if the chief's proposed order was issued, he would write a dissent. He closed the short note with the following observation: "The duty of this Court and of the others is too simple to require perpetual litigation and deliberation. That duty is to extirpate all racial discrimination from our system of public schools NOW."[174]

Black spent a good part of the evening writing his eight-page draft dissent. In it, he reviewed the history of the phrase "deliberate speed" and noted that, even for its originator, Justice Holmes, "the phrase connoted delay, not speed." Fifteen years of delay is "almost beyond belief," he wrote. He was dissenting because Burger's order "revitalizes the doctrine of 'all deliberate speed' under . . . euphemisms, in spite of the fact that we have already emphatically repudiated the 'deliberate speed' delay formula at least twice. . . . In my opinion there can be no more disastrous educational consequence than the continuance for one more day of an unconstitutional dual school system such as those in this case. . . . The time has passed for 'plans' and promises to desegregate."[175]

He closed his dissent with the order he would have issued, most of which was incorporated into the final order drafted by Brennan: "Desegregation of segregated dual school systems, according to the standard of 'all deliberate speed,' is no longer constitutionally permissible. The obligation of the federal courts is to achieve desegregation of such systems *now*." His draft order vacated the court of appeals order and remanded the case to that court "for it to issue a decree and order, to be effective immediately upon entry, declaring that each and all of the schools" were to desegregate immediately. Given the importance of the task, Black concluded his order with the request that the court of appeals "lay aside all other business . . . to carry out this mandate."[176]

Douglas noted on Black's draft, "I agree." So, too, did Brennan and Marshall. But Burger, Harlan, White, and Stewart did not. On Monday, October 27, 1969, therefore, Burger called a special conference to discuss *Alexander,* during which there was "a rather sharp interchange of views on the wording of the orders."[177] On Tuesday, October 28, after Brennan had incorporated Black's draft order into his own and had that circulated, Elizabeth Black noted in her diary: "Hugo is a winner in the Mississippi cases."[178] After some additional changes suggested by Black were made, Brennan's version was adopted by the Court. The four more conservative jurists gave in to Black's insistence that there had been enough writing but not enough action.

On Wednesday, October 29, 1969, the short *per curiam* order was issued. On the same day, Douglas wrote a short memo to his brethren recommending an article. He closed with the following observation: "I send this note merely to entertain you, not convince you, which of course makes this a most unusual memorandum."[179] If *Brown* was, in one symbolic respect, over, the practical problems of achieving an end to the dual, segregated school system were not. And these problems created new questions for the Court. For example, could the federal district courts decree the use of busing to achieve that goal?

The following year, a federal district court judge in North Carolina, James B. McMillan, decided that busing could be used to achieve the desegregation the Court had mandated in *Brown* and then in *Alexander*. He had ordered the schools (including the faculty) of Charlotte and surrounding Mecklenburg County to desegregate, using busing, among other methods, to accomplish that goal. (At about this time, President Nixon issued an extraordinary statement regarding such federal court–ordered busing decrees: "Unless affirmed by the Supreme Court, I will not consider them as precedents to guide administrative policy elsewhere.")[180] The Court of Appeals for the Fourth Circuit, in the spring of 1970, modified McMillan's order and remanded the case to the federal trial court. However, black petitioners took the case to the Supreme Court in March.

On March 16, 1970, the Court denied the motion to vacate the Fourth Circuit's order (though Black, Douglas, and Marshall were willing to hear the case at the time). On June 29, 1970, the Court did agree to hear the case in its October 1970 term. *Swann* v. *Charlotte-Mecklenberg Board of Education* was, for Black and Douglas, another philosophical battlefield. For Black, busing was not something that the federal judges could command. Douglas wrote that "Black vigorously opposed any 'busing' (Brennan said it was because the word 'bus' is not found in the Constitution)."[181] But Douglas denied cert because he believed that the federal district court judge had made the right, courageous decision in *Swann*. In a letter to Burger, Douglas had written, "I do not see how we could possibly do anything more than affirm when we reach the merits."[182]

The clash between Black and Douglas was to continue for almost a year, because the Court took until April 1971 to announce its judgment in *Swann*. It was the last unanimous decision of the Court in the area of race desegregation. Whereas Black considered judicial support of busing to achieve desegregation questionable at best, Douglas felt that the way to overcome the vestiges of Jim Crowism and to erode "the stigma—the stamp of inferiority . . . was through integration."[183] At the October 16, 1970, conference, when the brethren began to debate the question of busing, it appeared that Burger, Black, and Blackmun (who had replaced Fortas) supported narrowing the district court order, while Douglas, Brennan, and Marshall supported affirming McMillan's decree. The three other justices—White, Stewart, and Harlan—were undecided, though the latter two seemed to support portions of the district court order.

At the end of the session, Burger announced that he would draft an opinion, as the Court seemed to be fragmented on the question. This did not sit too well with Douglas, who had heard and recorded a much stronger show of support for retaining McMillan's decree. In mid-October, Burger began drafting the opinion of the Court in *Swann*. After the brethren received Burger's draft, in early December, the fur began to fly. It was an extremely critical draft, attacking the credibility of the federal judge who had used a number of devices, including busing, to try to eliminate a complex pattern of school segregation. Douglas responded immediately, focusing on Burger's (and President Nixon's) concern about busing. He wrote a sharp letter criticizing Burger's views on racial balance, residential discrimination, remedies that McMillan had used in addition to busing, and Burger's very narrow definition of "racial discrimination."[184]

In a memorandum to the conference, circulated on January 12, 1971, Marhsall wrote, "The time has come for the era of dual school systems to be ended. And when school boards fail to meet their obligations it is up to the courts to find remedies that effectively secure the rights of the Negro children. . . . Innovation and unrefined techniques are necessary when the work of 16 years has to be done in one." Finding "no abuse of discretion in this case" by Judge McMillan, Marshall would affirm the order. "The techniques used in the District Court's order were certainly within the Court's power to provide equitable relief."[185]

Potter Stewart carefully prepared a draft opinion for the Court in January that was not very much better, but it was one that Douglas, Brennan, and others could support. Douglas, in fact, wrote to Stewart, on February 19, 1971, that he would join Stewart's draft "at the appropriate time."[186] Modifications in the chief's opinion were made after Stewart met with Burger, but Douglas and Brennan voiced concerns, both telling Burger that they would have to write separately.[187] Burger called a conference on *Swann* on March 18, 1971. "At long last," wrote Douglas in his conference notes, "he will affirm the District Court." Black would "go along with the CJ though he prefers to reverse" and Harlan, Brennan, Stewart, and White would "go along with more editing." Burger said that he wanted the "opinion to be unanimous—Hugo Black goes along."[188]

In a note attached to a "work draft" the chief sent the brethren on March 22, 1971, he said he had made "substantial changes and now circulate what I trust is the final draft of the Swann opinion. I have adopted the express reservation . . . suggested by Justice Douglas and others . . . . I have adopted most of Justice Brennan's suggestions."[189] There were still complaints from Douglas,[190] and, on March 25, 1971, Black circulated a draft of a partial dissent he was then threatening to publish if the chief did not incorporate some of his suggested changes. In part, he wrote that he "gravely doubt[ed] this Court's constitutional power . . . to compel a state and its taxpayers to buy millions of dollars worth of busses to haul students miles away from their neighborhood schools and their homes. Such an order by this Court [was] bizarre."[191] If the chief could not make the changes, then Black would dissent, thereby denying Burger the unanimous Court he wanted. "I am of the opinion," Black concluded, "that it would be a mistake to give the appearance of a unanimity on the Court which does not actually exist."

Black's threat was not met with charity by his brethren, and he, too, began to reflect on the impact his dissent would have on efforts in the South to achieve an end to school segregation. In early April, he sent a short note to Burger: "Maybe it is safe to join now."[192] And on April 20, 1971, Burger announced the unanimous opinion of the Court in *Swann.* In order "to eliminate from the public schools all vestiges of state-imposed segregation" where local school authorities had defaulted on plans to desegregate schools, the requirement of a certain ratio of white to black students, as a starting point for a remedy, was within the equitable remedial discretion of the federal courts.[193] Pairing and court-ordered school busing were legitimate tools of school desegregation for federal district court judges, concluded Burger for the Court.

Douglas placed a note in the file the day *Swann* was handed down. It described the "slow turn-around" of the Burger opinion from a statement that incorporated "Nixon's view of 'freedom of choice'" to one that supported the district court judge. Changes had been made "haltingly and with great resistance." Although the Court tried to announce the opinion by December 1970, so that school boards would have appropriate criteria to "guide them," the April 20 announcement "defeated that purpose. . . . So the Nixon sabotage worked in part," Douglas concluded.[194] Douglas was angry that the Court had been divided for the first time on the question of race segregation, and he was apprehensive that in the future, when the Court faced dilemmas such as the de facto race segregation of multicounty school populations, there might not be the unanimity that had been pulled together in *Swann.* He was, of course, correct.

The Right to Vote

Black and Douglas, along with their brethren, heard and decided a number of important voting rights cases in addition to the Voting Rights Act cases and the poll-tax question. Some involved questions about the constitutionality of congressional legislation passed to enforce the protections of the Fifteenth Amendment right to vote. Others raised the question of the constitutionality of malapportioned legislatures.[195] When Black and Douglas had first come to the Court, a series of cases had challenged the segregated white primary in the South. In these controversial decisions, the justices dramatically abolished the practice of prohibiting blacks from participating in primary elections in the South.[196]

Even after the demise of the white primary in 1953, Black and Douglas and their colleagues saw other southern efforts to disenfranchise black voters. Literacy tests, poll taxes, and detailed, cumbersome registration procedures were used, along with economic and other forms of intimidation, to suppress black political participation. When the black voting strength appeared solid and potentially threatening to southern white local power, still another form of racial vote discrimination was used: the racial gerrymander. In 1960, in another Fifteenth Amendment case, *Gomillion* v. *Lightfoot,* the Supreme Court examined the constitutionality of the local redistricting process in Tuskegee, Alabama, which purged the small city of all its black voters by redrawing the city's boundaries.[197]

A gerrymander changed the shape of the city of Tuskegee from a square to a contorted twenty-eight-sided figure, excluding all but 4 of the 400 black voters to prevent them from having any influence on the city. *Gomillion* would not have been complicated but for the fact that the Court, in a judgment written by Frankfurter in 1946, concluded that malapportionment was a "political question" and therefore not a Fourteenth Amendment justiciable issue (denial of equal protection) for the Court.[198] Courts ought not get into the "political thicket" of reapportionment, warned Frankfurter in *Colegrove* v. *Green.*

Black was in fundamental disagreement with Frankfurter over *Colegrove.* The Alabaman, joined by his friend Douglas, believed that the urban population was being deprived of Fourteenth Amendment rights because the rural legislators refused to redistrict. Black's remedy called for holding at-large elections rather than maintaining the malapportioned legislature. *Gomillion* brought the question of standing and justiciability again to the Court, but these issues were quickly set aside so that the Court could focus on the question of racially motivated redistricting. In the Tuskegee case, because the malapportionment was done for discriminatory reasons, Frankfurter could see the issue in Fifteenth Amendment terms. In all the discussions, Frankfurter insisted that the *Gomillion* case was not an instance of the Court entering the "political thicket" but was another difficult Fifteenth Amendment case.

The brethren unanimously concluded that Tuskegee was racially malapportioned in violation of the Fifteenth Amendment. Warren asked Frankfurter to write the opinion for the Court. After discussing changes in his drafts with Black and Douglas, and deleting references to *Colegrove* in order to hold Black's vote, Frankfurter handed down his opinion on November 14, 1960.[199] The case was remanded for a trial on the merits. If the claims were shown to be valid, "the conclusion would be irresistible, tantamount for all practical purposes to a mathematical demonstration, that the legislation is solely concerned with segregating white and colored voters by fencing Negro citizens out of town so as to deprive them of their preexisting municipal vote."[200] Only Whittaker concurred, on Fourteenth Amendment grounds. (While Frankfurter insisted that *Gomillion* was not a reapportionment case, at base it was).

The Court was ready to reexamine *Colegrove* and did so the following year, in *Baker* v. *Carr.* It went on to announce, in an opinion by Brennan, that reapportionment was a justiciable issue and that federal courts could provide equitable relief, consistent with the Fourteenth Amendment, for petitioners who had been denied the equal protection of the laws.[201] Frankfurter dissented in the case, which was to be his last major dissent; shortly afterward, he left the court because of ill health.

At this time, the NAACP, the SCLC, CORE, and other black protest groups, aware of the need to go beyond the federal judiciary to achieve truly effective political participation, turned to their strategy of massive civil disobedience. It was their hope that Congress and the president would respond by developing a shield of civil rights laws that would effectively "enforce" the civil and voting rights guarantees in the Civil War Amendments. Their efforts led to a flood of legislation, especially the

1964 Civil Rights Act and the 1965 Voting Rights Act, as well as the exhumation, by the Court, of sections of the early Civil Rights Acts that had survived the initial attacks on their constitutionality in the 1870s.

Other Congressional Actions to Protect Civil Rights

Almost simultaneously with Congress's dramatic actions that culminated in the passage of the 1964 Civil Rights Act and the 1965 Voting Rights Act,[202] the Supreme Court had occasion to examine the constitutionality of sections of the Civil Rights Acts of the 1870s. The ruling in *Jones* v. *Alfred Mayer,*[203] a case heard by the Warren Court in 1967, typified that Court's response to a petitioner's use of nineteenth-century civil rights acts. Jones brought a civil suit in federal court against a real-estate company in Missouri that had discriminated in selling houses. The Court heard the case on appeal after lower federal courts had ruled against Jones.

Both Brennan's and Douglas's notes of the session indicate that there were dramatic goings-on in the conference. While Warren and a number of his colleagues spoke for reversal of the lower courts, Potter Stewart, surprisingly, "argued for a new and far-reaching theory that would greatly extend federal power to protect civil rights."[204] Crucial to Stewart's approach was that the Thirteenth Amendment was not addressed to ending discriminatory "state action"; rather, its central focus was to put an end to slavery. Therefore, an enforcement statute passed by Congress, such as the Civil Rights Act of 1866, could apply to private action that continued the prohibited practice. During the course of the Supreme Court's conference session, Justice Stewart focused on Section 1982 of the 1866 act as a possible remedy for Jones's request for damages and relief because it provided that all citizens "shall have the same right . . . as is enjoyed by white citizens thereof to inherit, purchase, lease, sell, hold and convey real and personal property."

Initially, with the exception of Douglas and Black, the Court did not move toward Stewart's argument. In a note for the file, Douglas wrote: "The Court was very eager at this conference to avoid any decision under Section 1982. Black, Stewart and myself were willing to proceed on that count. . . . Even Marshall was very anxious to avoid any important decision in this case fearing that the Congress would retaliate by perhaps repealing [Section] 1982. . . . In the midst of [the crisis brought on by the assassination of Martin Luther King, Jr.] the Court was timid and hesitant."[205]

For Stewart, Black, and Douglas, there was no need to go to the Fourteenth Amendment's concept of "state action" because of the existence of the 1866 statute. Stewart argued that Section 1982 "was a valid law operating against private people," which had been violated by Mayer's refusal to sell property to Jones because he was black.[206] Stewart persuaded all his brethren except Harlan and White that the 1866 statute was a valid use of the congressional enforcement power to reach and restrict private discriminatory action. On June 17, 1968, he announced the opinion for a seven-person majority.

If there were clashes on the Court over the scope of the 1866 Civil Rights Act, there was peace when the constitutionality of the 1964 Civil Rights Act came before the Court during the 1964 term. The justices heard two pivotal cases challenging the act's constitutionality: *Heart of Atlanta Motel* v. *United States* and *Katzenbach* v. *McClung*.[207] The brethren's hard, bruising battle over the scope of "state action," which had begun with the sit-in cases heard by the Court in 1962 and 1963, ended with the passage of the 1964 Civil Rights Act. In Title II of the act, Congress, using its Article I "commerce" powers, prohibited discrimination on the basis of race, color, religion, or national origin in motels, inns, hotels, rooming houses, restaurants, cafeterias, lunch counters, soda fountains, motion-picture houses, theaters, concert halls, sports arenas, stadiums, and gasoline stations.

On the day President Johnson signed the bill into law, the Heart of Atlanta Motel filed suit in federal court challenging its constitutionality. When the special federal court sustained the act, the owners appealed to the Supreme Court. The *McClung* case was brought by the owner of a barbeque restaurant in Birmingham, Alabama, who argued that since his customers were local the act did not apply. The government countered by pointing out that the act covered establishments which served food that came from out of state. The three-judge federal court granted injunctive relief, and the government appealed to the Supreme Court.

Some of the justices were puzzled by Congress's reliance on the "enforcement" section of the Fourteenth Amendment to desegregate public accommodations rather than on an expansive interpretation of the commerce clause. (The Johnson administration's drafts of the act had relied on the Fourteenth Amendment's "enforcement" provisions; they were deleted during the committee hearings on the act.) Douglas and Goldberg argued that the Fourteenth Amendment supported "even those sections of the Act which are phrased exclusively in commerce language."[208]

At the October 5, 1964, conference, Warren argued for affirmance and reversal of the respective appeals, adding, "we should not concern ourselves with the Fourteenth Amendment—Congress need make no findings [for their] Commerce power is adequate [and] their precedents are all in line." Black, according to the notes, agreed with Warren: "He'd prefer to go on the Fourteenth Amendment but he thinks Congress limited the Act to Commerce—otherwise he'd be for overruling the Civil Rights Cases." Douglas rested his affirmance and reversal on Fourteenth Amendment grounds, as did Arthur Goldberg, "who shared some of the troubles of WOD." But Harlan, Clark, White, Stewart, and Brennan agreed to go along with the chief's views, and Clark was assigned the task of writing for the Court.[209]

Douglas and Goldberg felt that the Clark opinion, because it focused on the constitutionality of the commerce clause as a device for desegregating facilities, "sound[ed] like hamburgers are more important than human rights."[210] Both wrote concurring opinions, arguing that the act should have rested on the Fourteenth Amendment, thereby, according to Douglas, "putting an end to all obstructionist strategies and allowing every person . . . to patronize all places of public accommodation without discrimination whether he travels interstate or intrastate."[211] Goldberg in his concurring opinion wrote that the "primary purpose" of the act "is the vindication of human dignity and not mere economics. . . . Discrimination is not simply dollars and cents, hamburgers and movies; it is the humiliation, frustration, and embarrassment that a person must surely feel when he is told he is unacceptable as a member of the public because of his race or color."[212]

Black, too, wrote a separate concurring opinion. His was written to underscore the "plenary" power of Congress, using the commerce clause in the company of the necessary and proper clause to eradicate discrimination in places of public accommodation. "There is no need," wrote the Alabaman to his friend Douglas, "to consider whether this Act is also constitutionally supportable under section 5 of the Fourteenth Amendment."[213]

Hugo Black and William O. Douglas, in over three decades of service on the Court, saw some extremely dramatic changes—both legal and social—in the status of blacks in the United States. Despite Black's racist background and Douglas's initial insulation from racism, the two justices were advocates of racial equality from the moment of their appointment to the high bench. They were instrumental in mobilizing the Court to make inroads on the racist doctrine of Jim Crowism, which tempered them for the struggle for racial justice that ensued after *Plessy* was overturned in 1954.

After the Court's *Brown* decision, as Black had warned, "the demagogues took over."[214] Without any strong support from the president and very little support from Congress (in the form of civil rights statutes), the Supreme Court justices and the federal district court judges responsible for implementing *Brown* II stood alone, uneasy in the glare of desegregation.[215] Black, for example, received among his hate mail some "Wanted For Impeachment: Earl Warren" posters from angry Southerners, which accused Warren and Black and, surprisingly, Frankfurter (but not Douglas) of defending Communists. They denounced Black for being a "rabid agitator for compulsory racial mongrelization" and for having a sister-in-law who was a "registered Communist."[216]

Justice Douglas, much like his friend Justice Black, kept all his hate mail in the appropriate case files. After *Brown,* Douglas and Black received hundreds of letters annually. Some were gently racist, reminding Douglas that the writer's maid or cook wanted the races separated "because God made us different." Others told Douglas that he knew only the educated blacks but not "the masses, with their primitive instincts and supersti[tions]." All the letter writers condemned the justice for interfering the the local customs and traditions of the South.

For Black, the Southerner who passionately loved his roots, the ostracism he felt after *Brown* was very painful. It was not until the twilight of his tenure as a justice that the University of Alabama Law School invited the justice back into the Alabama legal community. When a letter writer from Mississippi condemned Black for his desegregation activities and reminded the Alabaman that they had gone to Sunday school together in the old days, Black wrote back: "You worry about citizens being denied their 'freedom of choice.' Government is bound to deny citizens freedom of choice at some time, to some extent, and on certain subjects. That is one of the great objects of government; also that we have a country of law and order instead of one of anarchy and riot, and I believe in having the former kind of country as I always did back in the days when you were in my Sunday School class in Birmingham."[217]

Both men led the Court in the effort to successfully overcome the legacy of *Plessy*. They took aggressive positions in this area of constitutional jurisprudence, just as they led the Court in the deliberations on free speech, freedom of religion, and due process that enhanced the rights and liberties of all. As Justice Brennan has said, both men were at the very center of an "extraordinary revolution in constitutional law."[218]

 9

Due Process: In Search of
Fundamental Fairness

ONE OF THE difficulties Americans faced during the civil rights movement was a pervasive fear of crime and violence. Anxiety about fundamental social change was part of it, but there was more. There was a fear of apparent disorder and turbulence, of people taking to the streets, of threats to "law and order." Civil rights protest was seen in many American communities less as an assertion of constitutional claims than as a threatening spectacle of upheaval.

Of course, there were other unsettling and disruptive forces in the 1960s and into the 1970s. Protests against the Vietnam War, coupled with the general rejection of middle-class order and values that the hippies and "counterculture" represented, combined to produce a sense of social rootlessness and disorder. Women's groups and Native Americans also challenged the established order. Environmentalists and consumer advocates insisted on recognition of their causes. Given the nature of the growing bunker mentality in Middle America, encouraged by America's political leaders, it was often a bewildering chorus of strident voices that was heard, not the messages the groups tried to convey.

At the same time, there was a very real, well-founded fear at play, the fear of crime. There actually was a growing level of crime in the streets, attributable in part to the crisis conditions in the nation's cities, and perhaps in part to a general lack of respect for law and order. But a very large part of the problem was also the result of the simple demographic fact that the babies of the postwar boom were reaching the age range in which they were most likely to commit crimes—and did.

Not surprisingly, the Supreme Court was faced with more and more questions about the limitations imposed by the Constitution on the law-enforcement community. Its answers about the meaning and requirements of due process of law produced a storm of controversy outside the judiciary. These were not easy questions within the Court either, and the attempts to answer them posed difficulties among the brethren.

At the root of the disagreements among the justices were their varying understandings of the meaning, nature, and application of due process of law protected by the Fifth and Fourteenth Amendments. On one end of the spectrum, there was Felix Frankfurter's view that due process barred behavior that went beyond the normal boundaries of civilized conduct, prohibiting official actions that "shocked the conscience." At the other end was Hugo Black's contention that the due process clause of the Fourteenth Amendment incorporated all the protections of the Bill of Rights, but, in application, was limited to the guarantees specifically mentioned in the first eight amendments to the Constitution—neither more nor less. Whatever their individual predilections, the justices collectively incorporated most of the protections of the Bill of Rights into the due process clause of the Fourteenth Amendment, meaning that the states were now to provide more protections to those facing prosecution.

The society at large was split, too, but the majority overwhelmingly reacted against the decisions of the 1950s and 1960s that provided greater due process protections to those accused of crime. The charge that the Court had "handcuffed the police" became common. So vigorous were these protests that presidential candidate Richard Nixon was able to make the assault on the Warren Court a central part of the 1968 campaign that took him to the White House. The fact that the Court-against-the-cops image had little or nothing to do with the reality of the Court's actions did not seem to matter. Few knew or cared that successful prosecutions had increased, rather than decreased, or that some of the cases the Supreme Court sent back to the lower courts for proper trials resulted in convictions and lengthy sentences for defendants that politicians claimed had been "turned loose."

Black and Douglas were in the thick of the debates over due process within the Court. And though the two long-time constitutional allies often reached the same conclusions in criminal due process cases, they differed far more in this field than in most others. Even when they agreed on a case's outcome, they often arrived at their judgments by very different routes. They certainly disagreed on just how due process was to be defined and on precisely what process was due in any given situation.

Black the literalist demanded full enforcement of all the guarantees specifically presented in the Bill of Rights for those facing prosecution, but beyond that considered criminal justice an issue for the states. It was within the power of the people to determine crimes, try them, reach a verdict, and assess the penalty. But Black the constitutionalist thought that the Bill of Rights applied to the states as well as to the federal government.

Douglas started from a very different premise: that it should be hard for government to do anything to the liberty of the citizen. He proceeded from the foundation of liberty, not from the assumptions about the power of the state. When the language was unclear, the doubt was always to be weighed in favor of that liberty. The people acting democratically could make policy for everyone, but when government turned its force on an individual it was a very different situation.

From Hugo Black's perspective, the due process clause was one of the most dangerous provisions in the Constitution, not because of its language or its basic character but because of the way it has been used and abused over the years by judges, particularly members of the Supreme Court. Elizabeth Black recalled that Hugo often referred to due process as the "'shoot the works'" clause.[1] The due process clause was used by the Court in many of its rulings that struck down progressive reforms instituted by state and local governments ranging from regulating professions to setting fair labor standards. Indeed, the due process clause and the commerce clause were the two constitutional provisions that the Court had used for so many years to prevent Americans through their elected representatives from implementing a variety of economic and social policies that were widely recognized as essential to the resolution of festering problems.

The way to avoid the quagmire into which the Court seemed so willing to wade from time to time was, as was so often Black's answer, to pin the application of the due process clause to the rights specified in the Bill of Rights. The liberty protected by the due process clause of the Fourteenth Amendment, he said, meant the procedural protections listed in the first eight amendments. In particular, the Fourth, Fixth, Sixth, Seventh, and Eighth Amendments set forth the protections traditionally associated with the idea of due process of law. The bar against self-incrimination, the ban on double jeopardy, the right to counsel, and the right to a jury trial were all elements of due process that were the legacy of our British forebears, who had wrung from the Crown a respect for the concept of due process. The king had agreed on the fields of Runnymede that no person would be taken and punished except according to the "the law of the land."[2]

At heart, "the law of the land" required the rudiments of procedural fairness, due process. But, Black argued, it was not enough that the British had a fundamental commitment to due process. The issue was how the American Constitution defined the concept. It did so in what Black considered reasonably clear terms, not as clear as, say, the language of the First Amendment, but there were specifics. It was to those carefully written provisions of the Constitution that judges should look for the meaning of due process, not to their own consciences.[3] His feelings ran deep. There was a passion in his determination to protect the Constitution against the threat of an unleashed due process clause. As Justice Brennan recalled, "He used to get so steamed up about the due process questions. We'd often say: 'There goes Hugo again!'"[4]

Of course, his interpretation of due process presented Black with problems as well as answers. The broad question over which Hugo and some of his colleagues fought was just what grounds existed to support his claim that the due process clause of the Fourteenth Amendment incorporated the provisions of the first eight amendments. The language of the Constitution did not explain it. Black thought the history of the Fourteenth Amendment resolved it, but few were convinced that the historical approach could settle the disagreements.

There were more specific criticisms. For one thing, Black never explained why it was necessary to provide a Fifth Amendment due process clause if the Bill of Rights already specified the particular protections required by due process in the words of the Fourth, Sixth, Seventh, and Eighth Amendments as well as the other language of the Fifth. Certainly, Black never thought of the Constitution as containing unnecessary language. Well then, why all the extra verbiage? Then there was the problem of the kinds of words used in some of the provisions of the Bill of Rights. If the protections were to be specific and the judges were to be anchored to the language of the amendments rather than to their own consciences, then why was the wording left so loose? The government was prohibited by the Fourth Amendment from making unreasonable searches and seizures, yet just how to determine what was reasonable in any given situation was far from clear. Hugo Black had complained for years that judges had used concepts like reasonableness to read their personal philosophies into the Constitution. But since the Framers had used that terrible word, so be it. He would decide whether a search and seizure was "reasonable."[5] The Eighth Amendment prohibits excessive bails and fines as well as cruel and unusual punishment, but what do the words *excessive* and *cruel and unusual* mean? These ambiguities led to significant disagreements between Black and Douglas as well as among other members of the Court.

Some thought there was more involved in Black's treatment of criminal cases than his literalist theory of constitutional interpretation. More than one of Black's colleagues saw traces of the former prosecutor and police court judge in his interpretation, and that perception became stronger in his later years on the Court. Even Justice Black was aware that his own views were conditioned by his experience. He recognized that his understanding of the proper role of the judiciary and the meaning of the constitution grew "out of [his] experience as a citizen, a lawyer, a police court judge, a prosecuting attorney, a senator, and a Justice of the Supreme Court."[6] On more than one occasion, when they dismissed his fears that the Court was taking too many liberties, he reminded his brethren and the public that "to the people who have such faith in our nine justices, I say that I have known a different court from the one today. What has occurred may occur again."[7] It is nearly impossible to overestimate the impact of the pre-1937 Supreme Court on Hugo Black's assessment of the Court's role.

Black's willingness to defer to local police officials in matters of search and seizure, but adamant resistance to the possibility of police interrogation abuses raising self-incrimination issues, caused others on the Court to ask whether Hugo was quite as closely tied to the constitutional text as he claimed. And the fact that he rejected the application of the same notions of due process in administrative and civil matters that he allowed in criminal cases suggested a growing strain of conservatism in the later years in addition to his long-standing fear of judicial usurpation. He was angered by these challenges and made a defense of his own position on due process a central element in one of the few formal public lectures he made while on the Court, the 1968 Carpentier Lectures at Columbia University.

Chief Justice Burger explained that he and Black discussed this tension during his last years on the bench. Burger observed that Black insisted, "I haven't changed." Burger concluded, "I don't think he changed except as you have changed responses to new situations."[8] In an interview with Douglas toward the end of his life, Elizabeth Black raised the charge that Hugo had become more conservative. "I don't think that's true," Douglas replied. Elizabeth responded: "I don't think it is either. [Hugo] said 'I've been this way all the time. The times are swinging this way and this way but I've been going straight down the path.'"[9] On the other hand, Elizabeth Black saw in Hugo a tendency to become more southern in his later years. Justice Goldberg saw a pronounced "reversion to an earlier period in his life."[10] Justice Brennan sensed the change as well.[11]

All that having been said, Black could still point to greater consistency and more specificity than most of his brethren. He was more often than not able to pin his opinions more tightly to a constitutional commandment than his colleagues who chastised him for judicial activism and wrapped themselves in the mantle of self-restraint.

There was another element in the mix for Black, which was his populist sense of decentralization, his fear of federal encroachment into state matters. The criminal justice process was for Hugo largely a state and local matter; though the protections of the federal Constitution applied to state and local actions, he was prepared to grant state courts considerable latitude in applying those constitutional strictures.[12] It was one thing to demand that everyone be afforded due process but quite another for federal authorities to intervene unnecessarily in state courts on the assumption that they would not provide the proper protections.

Douglas had a much more positive view of the due process clause and saw no great problem in applying it without committing the judicial abuses of an earlier day. In fact, Douglas had written a number of the most important rulings overturning the decisions that had drawn the condemnation of the would-be Court-packers and Roosevelt appointees.[13] And given that the other liberties the Constitution protected against violation by the states depended on an application of those provisions through the vague language of the due process clause, it was not at all clear to Douglas how Black drew the distinction between his treatment of the Fourteenth and his literalist interpretation of the first eight amendments. Douglas plainly saw constitutional rights and liberties as resting on a higher law base and rejected the notion that the only reason courts sat to ensure due process was to check off procedural accomplishments and deficiencies. He wrote: "The basic premise on which the Declaration of Independence rests is that men are 'endowed by their creator with certain inalienable Rights.' This means that the source of these rights of man is God, not government. When the state adopts measures protective of civil liberties, it does not confer rights, it merely confirms rights that belong to man as the son of God."[14]

This sense of higher law became more important to Douglas over time as he increasingly became a citizen of the world and acquired a global perspective on issues of law and rights. For him, the Constitution and its Bill of Rights was a leading example of a basic charter of human rights. As he traveled the world, he compared American constitutional rights and liberties with those of other regions, cultures, and governments. It should come as no surprise that one of Douglas's most important statements of his understanding of due process came in his Tagore lectures, a series of talks given in Calcutta comparing the American and Indian constitutions.[15]

For Douglas, the means of governance and law enforcement were never independent of the ends of the Constitution but integral to them, and the ends were freedom, equal justice under law, and protection of individuality against the forces of conformity. Legal procedure mattered mightily. While he recognized that one of the interests that had led to the writing of the Constitution was the need to create a more effective and efficient government, he insisted that the Bill of Rights had a contrary purpose. The authors of those amendments "wanted to take government off the backs of the people" and to do so in part by making it "difficult for police, prosecutors, judges, legislatures, governors, and Presidents to do anything to the citizens."[16]

His view of due process was not based on any particular sympathy toward criminal suspects.[17] He joined more often than he led efforts by the Court to enhance protections for defendants. But he never forgot that criminal due process was necessary as a part of the larger panoply of protections for liberty. If officials could use illegal wiretaps against criminal suspects, they could apply the same techniques against political adversaries. There are no neat exceptions that allow violations of constitutional rights and liberties to get the bad guys but prohibit them from being applied to ordinary citizens. Too often, Douglas found, the threats of crime in the streets or dangers to national security were used to justify practices that had little to do with either.

Douglas was more concerned with equality before the law than whether any particular criminal defendant was acquitted. Due process was an assurance that everyone could insist on the full protections of the law even in the most highly charged trial for the most heinous criminal or political offenses, let alone far less visible legal disputes. Like Black, Douglas saw elements of the Bill of Rights as intended to limit the judiciary as well as the legislature and the executive. The due process clause was a way of ensuring equal justice under law through procedural rules. Due process was meaningful only as long as the same protections applied to everyone.

Beyond all that, Douglas, like a number of his brethren, saw law-enforcement authorities as historically dangerous. "If law enforcement were the chief value in our constitutional scheme, then due process would shrivel and become of little value in protecting the rights of the citizen. But those who fashioned the Constitution put certain rights out of the reach of the police and preferred other rights over law enforcement."[18] His conclusion was not simply the result of some legalistic study of criminal process. He had been a prosecutor of sorts himself while at the Securities and Exchange Commission and had seen crime in the suites. He and Thurman Arnold had prepared analyses for the Wickersham Commission appointed by President Hoover to examine police abuse.[19] The commission found that, if anything, critics underestimated the level of corruption and politicians' tendency to use police departments as arms of political machines. Long before that, though, as a young man, Douglas had seen Wobblies abused in the West and liquor and prostitution laws hypocritically enforced on the wrong side of the tracks in Yakima. He had also experienced abuse himself at the hands of "yard bulls" in the rail yards outside Chicago.

Like Black, Douglas knew that harassment by police and prosecutors had long been used to intimidate the nonconformist, the unpleasant person, the obnoxious character who was nevertheless an essential element in the social order. Arrests for vagrancy or on suspicion, street sweeps, detentions without charges or warrants, threats of possible arrest or prosecution had all been used to harass troublesome challengers to the establishment.[20] At various times in American history, that category has included immigrants, religious minorities, civil rights activists, antiwar protestors, and labor organizers.[21]

It was sometimes said that Douglas and others who participated in the interpretation of due process requirements during the Warren Court era worshipped technicalities over substance. He repeatedly and emphatically rejected that charge, arguing that "the greatest battles for liberty have indeed been fought over the procedure which the police and prosecutors may use."[22] The publicly proclaimed end of ridding the streets of crime never justified the use of means that violated due process of law. He insisted that "prosecutors may not use any means to the end of obtaining a conviction. They are officers of the court, guardians of liberty, and protectors of due process of law. They are employed to exercise a sound discretion to the end that the innocent are not convicted, the guilty are vigorously prosecuted, and only fair means are used to obtain convictions."[23]

Beyond the defense of particular trial rights, Douglas regarded due process as a constitutional requirement for fairness in any situation in which government rendered a decision that seriously affected an individual citizen. A person of considerable experience in public administration, he was every bit as concerned with the principle of due process in civil actions involving administrative agencies as in criminal prosecutions. He was not an advocate of weak government, but he was firmly committed to Lord Acton's admonition that "power corrupts," and he repeated it often.[24] Douglas may have been a liberal in many respects, but he saw human nature as essentially predatory and expected that natural tendency to show itself all the more once one was given authority over others. Given that view of human nature, Douglas depended mightily on due process as a safeguard of liberty.

Black and Douglas discussed and debated their respective positions in many areas, but not particularly in the arena of due process. While he was willing to accommodate Black's recommended changes in draft opinions, once Douglas reached a core issue, he was immovable. As he repeatedly told his colleagues, his friends, and even his wife, "I have but one soul to save, my own."[25] Black, whom Justice Brennan, a friend and frequent ally of both men, called a "tough son-of-a-gun,"[26] was even more rigid than Douglas when it came to the central tenets of his "constitutional faith."

On right to counsel and self-incrimination issues, they worked together to produce opinions and support each other's efforts. Not only did the constitutional language requiring counsel and prohibiting self-incrimination fit Black's literal approach exactly, but Black's own experiences reinforced his judicial philosophy. First as a private attorney and then as a prosecutor, Black had made the reform of Alabama's convict-lease system and the forced confessions in Birmingham's Bessemer Jail a priority.[27]

Both Black and Douglas tended to be sensitive to equal justice for the rich and the poor in their assessment of due process. Black incorporated a strong sense of equal protection into his due process calculus, particularly in the early opinions like his dissent in *Betts* v. *Brady* and the *Chambers* v. *Florida* opinion involving the interrogation of poor black suspects in a Florida murder case. Douglas was ready to go considerably further and wanted to say that due process stood as a bar to the use of the courts as collection agencies and other tools for the rich. He was also adamant not only about minimum due process protections, but also about the right to counsel, standing, and the rights of indigents on appeal. Black, while concerned about equality, parted company with Douglas in later years, unwilling to go as far as his colleague on poverty-related issues, as the earlier discussion of the poll tax indicated.[28]

On search and seizure cases, they were often at odds. Black was uncomfortable with the judge's obligation under the Fourth Amendment to determine the reasonableness of police actions. Douglas considered the only reasonable search to be one for which the authorities had a warrant. Moreover, Douglas, like Murphy and others, held that the Fourth Amendment provided a protection for privacy, though it was a much more limited idea of privacy than Douglas himself later developed for the Court in the 1960s. Black vigorously resisted the use of the term *privacy* in connection with Fourth Amendment cases whenever one of his colleagues happened to mention it in a search or seizure opinion.

Hugo read the word *seizure* literally as well. Just as he believed that an illegal search of a property meant a trespass, a seizure, by his definition, required physically taking evidence into possession. A wiretap that did not actually remove evidence from a location was not a seizure. The Framers knew what eavesdropping was, he said, and could have included words in the Fourth Amendment to prohibit it. They did not. Therefore, wiretapping, eavesdropping, and wiring witnesses with recording or transmitting devices were all permissible under the Fourth Amendment—a proposition that Douglas adamantly rejected.[29]

When Black did accept a search and seizure claim, it often also involved a question of self-incrimination. For example, when the police attempted to force a man to vomit morphine tablets, leading to the case of *Rochin* v. *California,* their conduct really raised not one but two constitutional issues: the search and seizure question, and the allegation that the authorities were attempting to physically force *Rochin* to provide incriminating evidence against himself.

Black and Douglas differed as well regarding the kind of jury required by the Sixth Amendment. Since Douglas thought the Bill of Rights was intended to make it difficult to take action against a citizen, any modification of the requirement of a unanimous verdict for guilt was simply unacceptable. Black did not agree. There was nothing in the Constitution specifying how many persons had to serve on a jury or requiring any kind of vote for conviction.

They agreed that the Fourteenth Amendment due process clause incorporated the protections of the first eight amendments. Under the Constitution, the states were no more able than the federal government to force confessions from criminal suspects. Douglas often deferred to Black's opinions as the best arguments in favor of the incorporation doctrine. His only objection was that Hugo tolerated a case-by-case "selective incorporation" of Bill of Rights protections if he could not get a blanket holding that incorporated all the first eight, which made him vulnerable to a charge of inconsistency.

Their major disagreement was over the question whether there were any rights beyond those specifically named in the first eight amendments, and, if so, whether the due process clause of the Fourteenth Amendment applied them to the states. Douglas plainly thought there were and played a part in developing some of them.

Black was opposed to the judicial creation of rights. Some of his harshest criticisms of his long-time friend came in cases presenting that kind of question.[30] In his Carpentier lectures, Black singled out two opinions to challenge as contemporary manifestations of the kind of due process abuses he had attacked as a senator in the 1930s and against which he had fought since coming to the bench. Both were majority opinions written by none other than William O. Douglas.

Douglas, adamant as he was in his convictions, never could quite accept the hard line Black demanded. He saw the interpretation of the Bill of Rights as more of a continuum than a dichotomy, he could not agree with Black's positivist idea of law, and he had a different way to resolve doubtful cases. He joined Black in rejecting what both saw as the wrong end of the spectrum, the point at which natural law was used to mean that judges were completely free to impose their economic views. The Court should not sit as a "super legislature," as Douglas so often said.

While he saw the dangers, he differed sharply with his friend Hugo on important features of due process. He rejected Black's view that due process was purely procedural. Douglas contended that "due process was both a substantive concept and a procedural concept. It meant that there were some things government could not do to man."[31] He also disagreed with Black's contention that due process did not require any general assessment of the fairness of government action. For Douglas, "it also meant that if government proceeded against a citizen, it had to proceed in a fair manner, avoiding certain indignities and certain unfair procedures."[32] It made no difference whether the government was engaged in a criminal prosecution or acting through administrative agencies; as long as its power was directed at an individual and carried serious consequences, its procedures had to be fair. Douglas agreed with Black that due process was intended to limit all branches and officers of government, including the courts. Therefore, the due process clause applied to anyone exercising quasi-judicial powers whether it was a court in a criminal trial or social-services administrators judging whether to terminate a welfare recipient's benefits. Black disagreed sharply (a discussion considered further in Chapter 12).[33]

It also made no difference to Douglas whether the person who was the focus of government action was an adult or a minor. He argued that the Constitution protected minors as well as adults in a wide range of cases from free-speech issues, to administrative procedures against schoolchildren, to juvenile-justice proceedings that were, to all intents and purposes, criminal prosecutions.[34] Again, his view differed from Black's, who was much more willing to leave the rights of juveniles in the hands of parents and the legislature.[35] Douglas joined opinions holding that juveniles were entitled to the full panoply of protections available to criminal defendants and had every reason to expect a fair proceeding.[36] In all this, Douglas could not accept the notion that the outer boundaries of due process were the words of the Bill of Rights.

Douglas saw the Constitution's principal purpose as the maintenance of liberty. When in doubt, the bias, according to Douglas, went to freedom. For Black, the bias went to democracy, and it was the Constitution that guaranteed both liberty and democracy. The way to preserve both was to maintain a working democracy free from unnecessary and inappropriate interference by the judiciary.

The Court Moves Toward Full Incorporation

If there were differences between Black and Douglas on the meaning and application of due process, there were even more dramatic disagreements within the Court as a whole. Virtually every argument made in the debates over due process outside the Court was made inside, and with similar levels of intensity. As Douglas put it, "The work of the Court always mirrors the worries and concerns of the people of a particular age."[37] Those conflicting viewpoints were reflected in the debates over the nationalization of the Bill of Rights, in disagreements over the meaning of due process, and in the justices' efforts to resolve the individual issues brought to the Court as due process questions.

While Black and Douglas may have agreed that the due process clause applied the Bill of Rights to the states, the Court as a whole certainly did not (and never would) accept that proposition. The popular notion that the Court, even during the Warren era, was unified in its approach to criminal due process is simply not true. But while debate continued well into the 1960s about the incorporation idea, the process, sometimes referred to as the nationalization of the Bill of Rights, inexorably but deliberately moved toward the application of all but a few of the provisions of the Bill of Rights to the states.

To most Americans today (and one might add to most contemporary members of the Supreme Court), it seems odd to imagine that there was a time not so long ago when we did not enjoy the same constitutional rights and liberties with respect to state and local authorities that protect us from abuses by the federal government. Few could accept a situation in which the Constitution would not prevent state and local governments from censoring the press or abridging the free exercise of religion, or conceive of a situation in which the United States Supreme Court would not stand ready to enforce those rights against any usurper at any level of government.

Yet by the time Hugo Black, and later William O. Douglas, came to the Court, only a few of those protections, mostly associated with freedom of speech and press, had been applied to the states. Both men were committed to the notion that when the Fourteenth Amendment provided that no state shall "deprive any person of life, liberty, or property, without due process of law," the word *liberty* had meaning and should be understood to include the rights protected by the Bill of Rights.

The Bill of Rights was originally added to the Constitution because of the fear that the new, powerful central government would abuse its citizens. At the time it was framed, most states had a bill of rights in their constitutions. But under the new Constitution of the United States, the central government was not required to deal with citizens through state governments. It could reach them directly. Therefore, states demanded the adoption of a bill of rights as a condition of ratification of the Constitution.

When the Bill of Rights was added, its First Amendment began with the words "Congress shall make no law." Even so, attempts were made to use its protections to block abuses by state governments. The most important of these, *Barron* v. *Baltimore,* concerned an allegation by a dock owner that a local government was taking his property without the just compensation required by the Fifth Amendment.

Chief Justice Marshall spoke for the Court, concluding that the amendments were for protection against the federal government "and not for the government of the individual states."[38] Thus things remained until the Civil War.

After the war, the Thirteenth, Fourteenth, and Fifteenth Amendments were adopted. While they were certainly meant to end slavery, provide full rights to former slaves, and ensure the freedmen's right to vote, the question was whether they did more, and, if so, how much more. In particular, the debate was about the meaning of the Fourteenth Amendment, which, unlike the other two, made no reference to race or previous condition of servitude. It provided a set of restraints on state government and indicated that there were certain actions the state could not take against any "person." In particular, it held that no state could deprive any person of life, liberty, or property without due process of law. While most people understood (or thought they did) what it meant to deny life or property, it was not at all clear what was meant by the word *liberty*. Few thought that it meant only protection against incarceration, but just how much more it meant has been a source of continuing debate since the adoption of the Fourteenth Amendment in 1868. The same is true of due process. What exactly did it mean? What kind of process, how much, when, and where? Did it mean only procedural constraints, or did it mean something more expansive, as it did in England?

The Supreme Court initially took the position that whatever it meant, the due process clause did not incorporate the particular provisions of the Bill of Rights into the Fourteenth Amendment's due process clause.[39] The Court's 1908 decision in *Twining* v. *New Jersey* was, for Hugo Black, the most important and dangerous of the early rulings.[40] According to Black, that "was the case where the Supreme Court took its longest step towards construing the Due Process Clause as a broad permission for courts to substitute their own notions of reasonableness for clear constitutional commands."[41] Specifically, the Court in *Twining* refused to apply to the states the Fifth Amendment prohibition against self-incrimination.

Two things bothered Black and Douglas about this precedent, already three decades old when they came to the Court. First, the Court was, in their view, simply wrong. By any reasonable standard, due process prohibits self-incrimination. Indeed, forced self-incrimination was one of the major abuses that led our British forebears to demand due process protections from the Crown. The prosecutor cannot use the defendants to prove the case against themselves.

In some respects, though, it was the rest of the opinion that most troubled Black.

> The most significant part of this opinion is where the Court states that "it is possible that some of the personal rights safeguarded by the first eight amendments against national action may also be safeguarded against state action, because a denial of them would be a denial of due process of law," but, and this is the critically important distinction, "[i]f this is so, it is not because those rights are enumerated in the first eight amendments, but because they are of such a nature that they are included in the conception of due process of law."[42]

Therefore, due process was in no sense tied to the freedoms presented in the Bill of Rights. Its meaning would be whatever the Court said it was. To Black, that was the root of the problem. It was open season on the Constitution.

The next major battle came as the Court tried to determine how due process should be defined after *Twining*. *Palko* v. *Connecticut*, a 1937 decision in which Black participated, presented a double-jeopardy claim and asserted that the Fifth Amendment provision should protect the defendant against the state as well as the federal government. The Court disagreed, and suggested further that few criminal due process guarantees mentioned in the Bill of Rights were important enough to warrant incorporation. However, the Court had to recognize the simple fact that it had already said in several cases that some provisions of the Bill of Rights were incorporated into the Fourteenth Amendment. Justice Cardozo met that contradiction by recognizing that some provisions had been "absorbed," or incorporated, because they were the "essence of a scheme of ordered liberty," because they were "so rooted in the traditions and conscience of our people as to be ranked as fundamental," or because the injury caused by their abuse would create a "hardship so acute and shocking that our polity will not endure it."[43]

Black joined the *Palko* opinion, but he later regretted it. What commended the decision was the fact that it recognized that the Fourteenth Amendment's due process clause does incorporate some of the provisions of the Bill of Rights. It allowed for selective incorporation, in the sense that each protection was to be considered individually to determine whether it should be incorporated against the states. The problem was that *Palko* left the judges as free as before by allowing them to determine whether a particular right was "essential to a scheme of ordered liberty." Why were First Amendment freedoms considered so fundamental and Fifth Amendment protections deemed unworthy? Black asked. By what standard would such judgments be made about other provisions of the Bill of Rights? While he did not raise these questions in *Palko*, Black's approach to due process became apparent soon thereafter and was fully developed by the late 1940s.

The first evidence of Black's movement toward total incorporation came in a footnote in his 1940 *Chambers* v. *Florida* opinion. Black observed that there had "been a current of opinion—which the court has declined to adopt in many previous cases—that the Fourteenth Amendment was intended to make secure against State invasion all the rights, privileges and immunities protected from Federal violation by the Bill of Rights (Amendments I to VIII)."[44] In 1962 he wrote to Irving Dilliard of the *St. Louis Post-Dispatch:* "I would still rank *Chambers v. Florida* very high among decisions expressing my constitutional views. This is not merely because of the emotional appeal evoked by the manner in which those young Negroes were treated, but because my views about due process later amplified in my *Adamson* dissent and many other cases were all pretty accurately foreshadowed by what I said in *Chambers*."[45]

His first direct statement on the incorporation issue came in a dissenting opinion in 1942. The case, *Betts* v. *Brady,* concerned a claim to right to counsel by an indigent defendant in a robbery case.[46] Black disagreed with the Court's refusal to require representation by an attorney at public expense because, in his mind, the Sixth Amendment included a right to counsel and the "fourteenth amendment made the sixth applicable to the states." In a footnote, he insisted: "Discussion of the fourteenth amendment by its sponsors in the Senate and House shows their purpose to make secure against invasion by the states the fundamental liberties and safeguards set out in the Bill of Rights."[47]

By this point, Black, Douglas, and Murphy supported the total incorporation idea, and Justice Rutledge became a fourth vote.[48] But there was opposition as well. While the *Chambers* case was pending, Justice Frankfurter had written to Black.

> Perhaps you will let me say quite simply and without ulterior thought what I mean to say, and *all* I mean to say, regarding your position on the "Fourteenth Amendment" as an entirety.
>
> (1) I *can* understand that the Bill of Rights—to wit Amendments 1–9 inclusive—applies to State action and not merely to U.S. action, and that *Barron v. Baltimore* was wrong. I think it was rightly decided.
>
> (2) What I am unable to appreciate is what are the criteria of selection as to the nine Amendments—which applies and which does not apply.
>
> This is not written to draw any comment from you—not that I should not have pleasure in anything you may say. But I have written the above merely to state as clearly as I am capable of, what is in my mind.[49]

He continued to press Black with similar arguments after the *Betts* ruling, but this time he added another claim. There was for Frankfurter a critical issue of federalism, a theme near and dear to Black's heart. He asserted that Black's position would usurp state control over criminal justice. It would limit the development of criminal due process by freezing in place the mandate of the eighteenth-century Framers of the Bill of Rights. Finally, Frankfurter asked, could Black imagine the states ratifying the Fourteenth Amendment if they had known that it would, in effect, federalize criminal justice? He concluded with a challenge: "I ask you quite humbly to lead me to the materials that show that the Fourteenth Amendment incorporated by reference the provisions—any or all—of the earlier nine Amendments."[50]

Black served notice to Frankfurter and the other justices that he intended to do just that. In March 1945, Black wrote a memorandum to the conference during discussion of *Malinski v. New York,* making his position vis-à-vis Frankfurter very clear.

> Mr. Justice Frankfurter has filed a concurring opinion which construes the Due Process Clause as authorizing this Court to invalidate state action on the ground of a belief that the state action fails to set "civilized standards." This seems to me to be a restoration of the natural law concept whereby the supreme constitutional law becomes this Court's views of "civilization" at a given moment. I disagree with that interpretation. Due Process, thus construed, seems to me to make the remainder of the Constitution mere surplusage. This Due Process interpretation permits the Court to reject all of those provisions of the Bill of Rights, and to substitute its own ideas of what legislatures can and cannot do. In the past, this broad judicial power has been used, as I see it, to preserve the economic status quo and to block legislative efforts to cure its existing evils. At the same time, the Court has only grudgingly read into "civilized standards" the safeguards to individual liberty set out in the Bill of Rights.[51]

Black warned that the debate had only begun. To the brethren who knew what Black was like in a battle, it was an ominous warning when Hugo announced,

"When the matter does hereafter arise in a proper case, I shall discuss it and shall also explain why I did not write about it here."[52]

The right time came in 1947. Black delivered his promised statement on incorporation as a dissent to a murder case, *Adamson* v. *California*.[53] Admiral Dewey Adamson was convicted of murder and sentenced to death under California law. In that state, it was lawful for the prosecutor, in his arguments to the jury, to make reference to the defendant's unwillingness to testify at the trial. Of course, if the defendant took the stand in his own defense, the prosecutor could introduce evidence of his prior criminal record and other incriminating information on cross-examination.

The *Adamson* case presented an opportunity for Black to confront the incorporation doctrine question directly. The majority admitted that it would assume that the prosecutor's comments "would infringe defendant's privilege against self-incrimination under the Fifth Amendment if this were a trial in a court of the United States under a similar law."[54] The only question, then, was why due process would be violated if this were a federal case but not a state action. Justice Reed for the majority relied on the *Twining* case for the proposition that the Fourteenth Amendment did not incorporate the Fifth Amendment ban on self-incrimination. In fact, he went further to assert emphatically that "the due process clause of the Fourteenth Amendment, however, does not draw all the rights of the federal Bill of Rights under its protection."[55]

Black issued a stirring dissent, joined by Douglas, in which he made the case for complete incorporation. He hit hard and quickly, drawing on the argument he had previously made to Frankfurter.[56] He recognized that at the time of their enactment the amendments did not apply to the states, but he insisted that the Fourteenth Amendment was intended to incorporate the Bill of Rights against the states. "My study of the historical events that culminated in the Fourteenth Amendment, and the expressions of those who sponsored and favored, as well as those who opposed its submission and passage, persuades me that one of the chief objects that the provisions of the Amendment's first section, separately, and as a whole, were intended to accomplish was to make the Bill of Rights applicable to the states."[57] He added a thirty-page historical appendix answering Frankfurter's charge that there was no such justification and explaining the basis for his historical argument.

Beyond that, Black argued that repeated references to *Twining* did not change the fact that the Court had indeed incorporated several Bill of Rights protections against the states through the due process clause, including a right to counsel in capital cases, cruel and unusual punishment limitations, notice requirements in criminal cases, just-compensation requirements, and virtually all the First Amendment guarantees. Indeed, the *Palko* ruling held that some but not all of the Bill of Rights protections applied. If any part of the Fifth Amendment protections apply to the states, Black insisted, there is no reason under *Palko* why the whole amendment should not.

Frankfurter issued a concurrence that was really a counter-opinion to Black's dissent.[58] He began by pointing out that Black had joined the Court in *Palko,* reaffirming *Twining.* Leaning on precedent, Frankfurter argued that "after enjoying unquestioned prestige for forty years, the Twining case should not now be diluted, even unwittingly, either in its judicial philosophy or in its particulars."[59] Beyond that, he charged that Black wanted to impose unreasonable technical constraints on prosecutors and jurors that showed disdain for their honor and intelligence.

Frankfurter's frustration with Black, Douglas, Murphy, and Rutledge had grown since they rejected his leadership and refused to accept his jurisprudence. His attack on Black was unusually sharp for a Supreme Court opinion, particularly a concurrence. He wrote that "the scope of that Amendment was passed upon by forty-three judges. Of all these judges, only one, who may respectfully be called an eccentric exception, ever indicated the belief that the Fourteenth Amendment was a shorthand summary of the first eight Amendments theretofore limiting only the Federal Government, and that due process incorporated those eight Amendments as restrictions upon the powers of the States."[60] The direct reference was to the late Justice John Marshall Harlan. Presumably, of course, Black's dissent had placed him in the category of eccentric exceptions. Finally, Frankfurter criticized Black on the grounds that he was willing to settle for selective rather than complete incorporation.[61]

Black saw that he was vulnerable to that attack, and so did Douglas, who urged him not to include language in the dissent that could be used as a target. But Black could not see disposing of the progress that had been made through selective incorporation in an all-or-nothing argument. In his first draft of the *Adamson* dissent, Black had closed with the following words: "I would therefore hold in this case, that the full protection of the Fifth Amendment proscription against compelled testimony must be applied by California. This I would do either because of reliance upon the original purpose of the Fourteenth Amendment or by use of the selective process discussed in *Palko v. Connecticut*."[62] Douglas saw the vulnerability and wrote back, indicating that he would prefer "elimination of the 'selective process' clause of the last sentence of the last paragraph."[63] Black dropped the clause, but he could not find a way around accepting the selective approach. But he wanted no misunderstanding about his primary position, so he added a longer qualifying paragraph to explain his two-part approach. Black's willingness to accept a selective process had given Frankfurter a target, and he used it.

Douglas joined Black but later changed his own position. In his autobiography, Douglas wrote: "[I]n those days we spent many long hours going through the dusty volumes of Civil War history and law trying to ascertain the meanings of the drafters of the Fourteenth Amendment."[64] He added, "Murphy and Rutledge, joining Black's opinion in the Adamson case, filed a separate opinion that said that they thought that the guarantees of due process were not necessarily limited to the provisions of the Bill of Rights but include other privileges and immunities—a decision with which I, in the years to come, was inclined to agree."[65]

Black's arguments drew sharp criticism, among the most noteworthy of which was an article by Charles Fairman charging that Black's historical arguments were badly flawed.[66] Frankfurter later wrote to Earl Warren, "If ever the history on which a judicial opinion was based has been exploded, it was the history in Black's dissent."[67] But his historical efforts drew praise from well-known scholars as well. Charles Grove Haines wrote, "Your dissent in the Adamson Case, with the historical appendix, in my opinion deals in a masterly way with an issue that has been one of the major controversies in constitutional interpretation since the Civil War."[68]

Years later, in his Tagore lecture, Douglas showed that the Court was proceeding on a case-by-case basis to incorporate provisions of the Bill of Rights.[69] Douglas was right, of course. While the justices were hotly debating the incorporation of particular criminal due process questions, they were simultaneously applying the establishment and free exercise of religion clauses of the First Amendment.[70] And while the disagreements over some of the criminal justice cases were intense in the 1940s, the Court quite easily incorporated the Sixth Amendment right to a public trial, the Eighth Amendment protection against cruel and unusual punishment, and the Fourth Amendment ban against unreasonable searches and seizures.[71] Black and Douglas were on the Court to witness the incorporation of the right to counsel in which Black had the pleasure of preparing the opinion reversing *Betts* v. *Brady*. They voted with the Court when it applied the Fifth Amendment right against self-incrimination ruling, finally overturning *Twining*.[72] Indeed, they wrote several of the Court's most important incorporation opinions.[73] Essentially all the remaining portions of the Fourth, Fifth, and Sixth Amendments were applied to the states as well.

The best known adversaries in this field, of course, were Felix Frankfurter and Hugo Black, but they were by no means the only contributors to the debate. While Frankfurter was extremely vocal and persistent in his attacks on Black, in their clash over incorporation, Hugo gave as good as he got, and with comparable enthusiasm. Frankfurter's view rarely prevailed after the 1940s. Although the Court never moved as far as Black wished toward a Bill of Rights interpretation of due process, he won more than he lost as the years passed.

Frankfurter persisted, but the argument had more to do with his view of the role of the judge and the legal heritage of due process than it did with the particular meaning of constitutional provisions. He wanted the judge to make the decisions and could not abide Black's positivist jurisprudence. There was an irony in his charge that Black was the activist precisely because it was, as Black charged, Frankfurter who used vague terms to define how due process was to be interpreted.[74] Frankfurter wanted it both ways. He wrote:

> The Amendment neither comprehends the specific provisions by which the founders deemed it appropriate to restrict the federal government nor is it confined to them. The Due Process Clause of the Fourteenth Amendment has an independent potency, precisely as does the Due Process Clause of the Fifth Amendment in relation to the federal Government. It ought not to require argument to reject the notion that due process of law meant one thing in the Fifth Amendment and another in the Fourteenth.[75]

His alternative was a wide-open judge-determined assessment on a case-by-case basis:

> Judicial review of that guaranty of the Fourteenth Amendment inescapably imposes upon this Court an exercise of judgment upon the whole course of the proceedings in order to ascertain whether they offend those canons of decency and fairness which express the notions of justice of English-speaking peoples even toward those charged with the most heinous offenses. These standards of justice are not authoritatively for-

mulated anywhere as though they were prescriptions in a pharmacopoeia. But neither does the application of the Due Process Clause imply that judges are wholly at large. The judicial judgment in applying the Due Process Clause must move within the limits of accepted notions of justice and is not to be based upon the idiosyncrasies of a merely personal judgment.[76]

There were difficulties, too, for Black and Douglas in Frankfurter's arguments based on questions of federalism. Federalism was no bar when Frankfurter thought that the states had exceeded his view of standards of civilized conduct or shocked his conscience. Moreover, he was not troubled by federalism on establishment of religion questions, for example, where he was quite willing to be an absolutist himself. That was a point that Black's friend Alexander Meiklejohn used in his critique of Frankfurter's attack on Black in the First Amendment area.[77]

As he approached the end of his years on the bench, Frankfurter was fast losing the battle of due process. Justice Harlan came to be the leading spokesman against incorporation, and he was nowhere near ready to concede defeat, even though he saw more and more provisions applied through the selective process. Harlan rejected incorporation, interpreting the due process clause as a constitutional guarantee completely independent of the Bill of Rights. As he wrote in *Pointer* v. *Texas,* "The incorporation doctrines, whether full blown or selective, are both historically and constitutionally unsound and incompatible with the maintenance of our federal system on an even course."[78]

Justice Clark was another incorporation critic, but he was not nearly as committed or as able as Harlan. In fact, Harlan and Frankfurter reacted sharply against Clark's majority opinion in *Mapp* v. *Ohio,* the case that applied to the states the exclusionary rule prohibiting the use of illegally obtained evidence at trial,[79] which Harlan saw as the beginning of the dramatic contemporary move toward incorporation.[80]

Still, Harlan's strongest statement on the subject was his dissent in *Duncan* v. *Louisiana,* in which the Court, in an opinion by Justice White, applied the Sixth Amendment right to a jury trial to the states through the due process clause.[81] It was a direct attack on Black. Harlan completely rejected Black's historical argument from *Adamson.* He was particularly pointed in his critique, mentioning the "overwhelming historical evidence marshalled by Professor Fairman," the man who had attacked Black's historical analysis in the wake of the *Adamson* opinion.[82] He then targeted the same weak point that Frankfurter had exploited earlier. While he could understand the argument for total incorporation of the Bill of Rights (though he disagreed with it), Harlan could not reconcile that approach with a willingness to join the Court's ongoing process of selective incorporation.[83] Finally, Harlan argued for a "fairness" standard of assessing criminal due process. The problem was to decide whether, in any given case, the defendant had received fundamentally fair procedures. It was precisely the use of the abstract notion of fairness that Black insisted had given judges free rein in an earlier day.

Black replied in a concurring opinion, joined by Douglas, that "thus due process, to my brother Harlan, is to be a phrase with no permanent meaning, but one which is found to shift from time to time in accordance with judges' predilections and understandings of what is best for the country. . . . It is impossible for me to believe that such unconfined power is given to judges in our Constitution that is a written one in order to limit governmental power."[84] He concluded that Harlan's approach would depend "entirely on the particular judge's idea of ethics and morals instead of requiring him to depend on the boundaries fixed by the written words of the Constitution. Nothing in the history of the phrase 'due process of law' suggests that constitutional controls are to depend on any particular judge's sense of values."[85]

Harlan's notion of due process was not particularly narrow; indeed, it was substantially wider than Frankfurter's. He agreed with the outcome of many of the cases decided during his tenure that recognized greater civil liberties protections, not merely in criminal matters but also in questions of privacy and voting rights. He would, however, have decided them strictly on his understanding of the due process clause and not through either incorporation or the discovery of substantive rights in the language of the Bill of Rights.[86]

While Frankfurter, Clark, and Harlan challenged Black from the right, Murphy and Rutledge raised questions from the left. Murphy and Rutledge clearly thought that the due process clause incorporated all the protections of the Bill of Rights and more. In his *Adamson* dissent (joined by Rutledge), Murphy added, "I agree that the specific guarantees of the Bill of Rights should be carried over intact into the first section of the Fourteenth Amendment. But I am not prepared to say that the latter is entirely and necessarily limited by the Bill of Rights."[87] Murphy did not like the selective incorporation process as an alternative to total incorporation, and he told Black so while *Adamson* was pending.[88] Murphy issued a brief dissenting opinion, which was joined by Justice Rutledge. In it, he took issue with Black only because he wanted it known that the language of the Bill of Rights was not the outer boundary of the freedoms protected by the due process clause.[89]

The Issues

There was more at issue in the Court than a broad philosophical debate about the meaning of the due process clause. There was the practical challenge for the justices of working their way through a string of specific issues presented to the Court, ranging from Fourth Amendment search and seizure questions through cruel and unusual punishment queries raised under the Eighth Amendment.

Search and Seizure

Different kinds of due process questions provoked varying reactions from each of the justices. Black disliked search and seizure debates because they pressed him to judge the reasonableness of police action. Frankfurter, on the contrary, was "'nuts about' searches and seizures."[90] He saw the privacy protected by the Fourth Amendment essential to the maintenance of liberty. Douglas agreed, which occasionally created an awkward situation in which he was allied with Frankfurter against Black. Earl Warren, the former California prosecutor, came to the Court with a relatively deferential attitude toward police practices, even though he had resisted law-enforcement excesses as district attorney. (D.A. Warren had refused to allow the Bakersfield, California, chief of police to bug a jail cell or introduce a wired undercover officer to extract incriminating evidence from a prisoner who was a suspect in the murder of his own father!)[91] Over time, however, Warren became less willing to defer as he saw the range of police abuses and the lack of effective remedies.[92]

Douglas was another justice whose views changed over time. The same justice who would later challenge anyone who complained that the debates over search and seizure issues honored technicalities more than substance, was the author of a 1946 majority opinion in which he concluded: "'A criminal prosecution is more than a game lost merely because its officers have not played according to rules.' To require reversal here would be to exalt a technicality to constitutional levels."[93] Federal officials who were lawfully inspecting the records of a defense contractor had found a fraudulent billing and had seized, without a warrant, an expense check at the heart of the dispute. Frankfurter dissented, joined by Douglas's two frequent allies, Murphy and Rutledge.

In 1971, Douglas would insist that " the concepts of privacy which the Founders enshrined in the Fourth Amendment vanish completely when we slavishly allow an all-powerful government, proclaiming law and order, efficiency, and other benign purposes, to penetrate all the walls and doors which men need to shield them from the pressures of a turbulent life around them and give them the health and strength to carry on."[94] Yet in 1942, along with Hugo Black, he had voted with the Court to uphold a conviction in which federal authorities used a "detectaphone" listening device to obtain incriminating evidence against the defendants.[95] Douglas's later opinions in this area read very much like the dissent drafted by Justice Murphy in that early case.[96]

Douglas changed his views relatively quickly. He had come to the Court with a less than charitable view of police practices. He saw a string of gross abuses during his early years on the bench. He also began to recognize the potential for the application of some of those abusive practices outside the normal criminal setting, most notably in the search for subversives. By the late 1940s, Douglas was a solid vote in favor of expanded protections of privacy under the Fourth Amendment. Murphy's potent dissents sound very like the rhetoric one finds in Douglas's opinions thereafter.

Douglas acknowledged Murphy's influence in one of the most important search and seizure controversies of the 1940s, *Wolf* v. *Colorado.*[97] Justice Frankfurter wrote for a 6 to 3 majority in this important case, which incorporated the Fourth Amendment protection against illegal search and seizure. However, Frankfurter stopped short of applying the federal exclusionary rule to the states. The Court had earlier ruled that illegally obtained evidence could not be introduced in a trial in federal court,[98] but Frankfurter thought the Court should allow alternatives in state courts to be explored before imposing the federal rule. Murphy and Rutledge disagreed, and so did Douglas. He wrote: "I agree with Mr. Justice Murphy that the evidence obtained in violation of it must be excluded in state prosecutions as well as in federal prosecutions, since in absence of that rule of evidence the Amendment would have no effective sanction. I also agree with him that under that test this evidence was improperly admitted and that the judgments of conviction must be reversed."[99] That was the principle on which *Wolf* was eventually overturned in *Mapp* v. *Ohio*.[100] Douglas lived to see his view become law. Murphy did not.

It was Clark who wrote for the Court in the 1961 *Mapp* v. *Ohio* decision, disposing of Frankfurter's *Wolf* ruling and applying the exclusionary rule to the states.[101] Police had come to Dolree Mapp's home with what they said was a search warrant seeking an alleged bomber. There is no evidence that there ever was a valid search warrant. They forcibly entered the premises over Mapp's objections and, once inside, searched the apartment and the basement storage area completely, finding no evidence of the person they sought. They did find some literature in the basement that they deemed obscene under Ohio's extremely broad obscenity statute, which allowed conviction for knowing possession of lewd materials. Mapp claimed that it belonged to a previous boarder and that she had stored it in case he returned to claim his belongings. She was nevertheless convicted of knowing possession of obscene materials and sentenced to one to seven years in prison.

The first conference took place on March 31, 1961. Warren voted to reverse because the obscenity statute was so vague.[102] Black also voted to reverse. Douglas argued two grounds for reversal. He agreed there was a First Amendment violation, but he also saw a Fourth Amendment problem and asserted that *Wolf* should be overturned. Clark joined the group for reversal on the First Amendment ground. Harlan voted to reverse as well, calling the Ohio obscenity law a "thought control statute." Brennan agreed with Harlan's comments on the vagueness of the statute but added, "this is candidate for overruling *Wolf*—officers have no warrant—They go through [the] cellar and find this stuff in box belonging to someone else—He will overrule *Wolf*." Warren agreed, and Clark joined them.[103]

Clark's majority opinion argued that the alternative means to protect the Fourth Amendment rights against unreasonable search and seizure advocated by Justice Frankfurter for the Court in *Wolf* had not been effective, and there was no reason to believe the situation would change. He wrote that the years in which other remedies had been tried had shown them to be "worthless and futile."[104]

Black saw this case as an opportunity to kill two birds with one case, and the more important target was not *Wolf* v. *Colorado* but *Twining* v. *New Jersey*. While Clark had relied principally on the Fourth Amendment prohibition against unreasonable searches and seizures, he had also made reference to the Fifth Amendment protection against self-incrimination. He suggested that the case presented "what is tantamount to coerced testimony by way of unconstitutional seizure of goods, papers, effects, documents, etc."[105] To Black, that sounded like a declaration that the Fifth Amendment provision was thereby applied to the states, which meant the end of *Twining!* In his first draft of the *Mapp* concurring opinion, Black wrote, "as I understand the Court's opinion in this case, we . . . now definitely hold that the Fifth Amendment's protection against unreasonable searches and seizures has been extended to the states through the Fourteenth Amendment."

After seeing Black's first draft, Clark wrote back to caution him about how far he thought the Court was moving: "[I]t was not my intention in drafting it to impliedly overrule *Twining v. New Jersey.* Actually, I do not believe it necessary for us to even consider the holding of that case in deciding this one."[106]

Black capitulated and removed the statement from his concurrence. However, his reply to Clark highlighted another problem with the majority opinion. Clark plainly said that the Fourth and Fourteenth Amendments protected a right of privacy, finding that "the Fourth Amendment's right of privacy has been declared enforceable against the States through the Due Process Clause of the Fourteenth."[107] Black attacked the notion that this case was not about the Fourth Amendment as written and interpreted, but rested on some right to privacy supposedly derived from the Fourth Amendment: "[M]y agreement to your opinion depends upon my understanding that you read *Wolf* as having held . . . that the Fourth Amendment as a whole is applicable to the States and not some imaginary and unknown fragment designated as the 'right of privacy.'"[108] Clark, who needed Black's vote to get a majority, accepted his interpretation, though he never changed the privacy language in his opinion.[109]

Harlan, joined by Frankfurter and Whittaker, objected that the Court unnecessarily reached out to take on the *Wolf* issue. While the search and seizure question had been raised, it had not been seriously argued by the attorneys. But since the majority was determined to take on the Fourth Amendment question, the dissenters were ready to defend *Wolf.*

Black's concurring opinion in *Mapp* marked a dramatic change in the way he evaluated search and seizure claims. He argued that while the Fourth Amendment standing alone might not require exclusion of illegally obtained evidence, the Fourth Amendment right against illegal search and seizure coupled with the Fifth Amendment protection against self-incrimination did. Black acknowledged that he had changed his mind since the days of *Wolf* and admitted that Rutledge had been correct in his dissent in that case: "It was upon this ground that Mr. Justice Rutledge largely relied in his dissenting opinion in the *Wolf* case. And, although I rejected the argument at that time, its force has, for me at least, become compelling with the more thorough understanding of the problem brought on by recent cases."[110]

After the *Mapp* opinions had been delivered, Black received a letter from Louis H. Pollak, then a professor of law at the University of Michigan, but Rutledge's law clerk at the time of the *Wolf* ruling. Pollak wrote, "It would have been, for him, a source of great gratification had he lived to learn that you ultimately came to share his view, and that your opinion and vote were decisive in jettisoning the holding announced in Wolf."[111] Black used the occasion of his reply to describe the continuing tension within the Court between himself and those he saw perpetuating a wrong-headed approach to due process: "There is a great difference between the Bradley–Rutledge approach to the Fourth Amendment based on what it was designed to accomplish and views expressed in other Court opinions, based upon the 'shabbiness' or 'dirtiness' of unreasonable searches and seizures. The first approach appears to me to rely on the Constitution itself, and the second approach on a question of policy, the propriety of which was determined by those who wrote the Amendment."[112]

For Black, one of the leading examples of the wrong approach was the attempt

214 • OF POWER AND RIGHT

to use the Fourth Amendment to block police use of wiretapping and other listening devices. It was a question on which Black and Douglas had once been in agreement and in the Court's majority, but their positions later diverged sharply, with Douglas, in fact, repeatedly quoting Justice Holmes's famous line that wiretapping was "dirty business." It is not overstating the point to say that Douglas, the one-time supporter of wiretapping, soon became its most passionate foe. Once again, his arguments were in no sense sympathetic to criminal defendants. They came from his growing recognition that this was another of those constitutional issues that had profound implications for all Americans as privacy began to disappear before evolving technology.

The Supreme Court had upheld wiretapping in the 1928 *Olmstead* v. *United States* ruling in a 5 to 4 decision by Chief Justice Taft, with Justices Holmes, Brandeis, Butler, and Stone dissenting.[113] Douglas, along with Black, had joined the *Goldman* v. *United States* "detectaphone" decision in 1942, upholding that precedent against a vigorous dissent by Justice Murphy. In a 1952 narcotics case involving the use of undercover agents "wired" for sound, however, Douglas repudiated his earlier position and attacked both *Goldman* and *Olmstead*.[114] He wrote: "I now more fully appreciate the vice of the practices spawned by *Olmstead* and *Goldman*. Reflection on them has brought new insight to me. I now feel that I was wrong in the *Goldman* case. Mr. Justice Brandeis in his dissent in *Olmstead* espoused the cause of privacy—the right to be let alone. What he wrote is an historic statement of that point of view. I cannot improve on it."[115]

The fact that Douglas had switched positions was critically important not only because his strong voice in the defense of liberty was heard outside the Court, but also because the brethren were sharply divided. The 1952 *On Lee* v. *United States* decision was a 5 to 4 ruling, as was the 1954 opinion upholding listening devices in *Irvine* v. *California*.[116] In fact, the fifth vote in *Irvine* came from none other than the newly appoined chief justice, Earl Warren. Even with his vote, the Court was unable to agree to more than a plurality opinion.

After Irvine had paid a federal gambling tax, the police bugged his house, entering it without a search warrant by using a key they had made. They drilled a hole in the roof to run the wire to a neighboring garage, where they listened to the conversations in the Irvine home. The investigators reentered the home twice to move the bug first into the bedroom and then into the bedroom closet. After the bug had been in place for more than a month, police again entered the house one night using their key and arrested the defendant for bookmaking. They thoroughly searched the premises and held the defendant's hand to ultraviolet light to see if there were traces of a powder the police had been using to mark betting slips in an effort to catch Irvine. He was convicted in a California court, and the conviction was upheld on appeal, though the appellate court concluded that the police behavior "would have been incredible if it had not been admitted in court."

There was general agreement that the police had been extraordinarily abusive, but the question was what could be done about it. Warren joined the unsuccessful effort to have the Justice Department take action against the police. Clark asserted that unless the Court was willing to overturn *Wolf* and apply the exclusionary rule to the states, nothing could be done. Black, who initially passed during conference, ultimately voted to reverse but not because of the police practices. He argued that the use of the federal gambling tax to force defendants to reveal their identities, after which state authorities would institute investigations and prosecutions, was federally mandated self-incrimination in violation of the Fifth Amendment. Any state action in the wake of such a disclosure would be barred by the Fourteenth Amendment due process clause.

Frankfurter dissented as well, joined by Justice Burton, on grounds that the police behavior was a patent violation of due process. Not only had the authorities violated the man's privacy, but they had illegally entered his house, not once but three times, and had in effect remained in his bedroom for over a month by planting the microphone. This was the same Felix Frankfurter who had written the *Wolf* v. *Colorado* opinion, which refused to apply the exclusionary rule to the states. He was caught on the horns of the dilemma Justice Clark had highlighted. Even so, Frankfurter insisted that he could have it both ways: "due process is not a mechanical yardstick, it does not afford mechanical answers. In applying the Due Process Clause judicial judgment is involved in an empiric process in the sense that results are not predetermined or mechanically ascertainable."[117] And in his judgment, this was simply a constitutional violation of a different order of magnitude than in other such cases.

Frankfurter was also mindful of his repeated arguments about the danger of interfering in local criminal prosecutions because of the anger that would be directed at the Supreme Court. Frankfurter nevertheless wrote: "Of course it is a loss to the community when a conviction is overturned because the indefensible means by which it was obtained cannot be squared with the commands of due process. A new trial is necessitated, and by reason of the exclusion of evidence derived from the unfair aspects of the prior prosecution a guilty defendant may escape. But the people can avoid such miscarriages of justice. A sturdy, self-respecting democratic community should not put up with lawless police and prosecutors."[118] Ironically, he went on to quote FBI director J. Edgar Hoover, of all people, for the proposition that the deliberate violation of a citizen's rights by law-enforcement officials was "no ordinary offense," which "if subtly encouraged by failure to condemn and punish, certainly leads down the road to totalitarianism."[119] While Hoover turned out to be guilty of many of the abusive practices in question, the FBI as an institution was considerably more advanced than most police forces, a fact that Douglas acknowledged on many occasions.[120]

For Douglas, *Irvine* was at one level a simple case of illegal search and seizure under the Fourth Amendment applied to the states through the due process clause of the Fourteenth; but it was, at·the same time, something more ominous, which he deplored: "The search and seizure in this case smack of the police state, not the free America the Bill of Rights envisaged."[121] Like Murphy in the earlier *Goldman* case, Douglas found what the police had done far worse than the abuses associated with the "writs of assistance" used by the British in colonial times.[122]

It was absurd, according to Douglas, to recognize in federal prosecutions that this sort of police behavior is patently unconstitutional and lawless, yet permit the states, which are subject to the Fourteenth Amendment due process clause, to do precisely the same thing. Anticipating the Court's *Mapp* decision, Douglas wrote:

"Exclusion of evidence is indeed the only effective sanction. If the evidence can be used, no matter how lawless the search, the protection of the Fourth Amendment, to use the words of the Court in the Weeks cases 'might as well be stricken from the Constitution.'"[123]

Douglas rejected out of hand the argument that the remedy for abuses was prosecution by the Justice Department for civil rights violations. He added an appendix to his dissent showing the caseload of the Civil Rights Division since it was created under Attorney General (later Justice) Frank Murphy, demonstrating its limited capacity even if it attempted to deal with police abuse.

For Douglas, the issue was part of a dangerous new chapter in the history of civil liberties, the fight to maintain that small precious space that citizens could call their own private lives against the intrusive forces of the state. He was not satisfied to wage the campaign solely within the Court, but took to the stump and the popular press. He wrote: "The truth is that wiretapping today is a plague on the nation. . . . Now all the intimacies of one's private life can be recorded. This is far worse than ransacking one's desk and closets. This is a practice that strikes as deep as an invasion of the confessional."[124] To those who argued for wiretapping on the basis of its effectiveness, Douglas replied: "The use of torture is also effective in getting confessions from suspects. But a civilized society does not sanction it."[125]

The battle continued within the Court in the 1960s. Threats to privacy had expanded beyond traditional searches and wiretapping to the use of remote listening devices that did not require a microphone to be physically placed within a room, closed-circuit-television cameras that were often set up in the most unlikely places, and polygraphs. Computerized data bases were being developed that were capable of handling hitherto unimaginable quantities of data about our personal and professional lives. In the final analysis, Douglas said, "[i]f a man's privacy can be invaded at will, who can say he is free?"[126]

Douglas was not alone in his crusade. Justice Brennan was a powerful voice for the cause, particularly in his dissent in *Lopez* v. *United States,* joined by Douglas and Goldberg, which called for reversal of *Olmstead* and *Goldman.*[127] In 1967, by a vote of 8 to 1 the Court disposed of the earlier approach. The lone dissenter was Hugo Black.

The best known wiretapping case during Black's and Douglas's tenure began because federal agents suspected a man named Katz of operating a gambling operation from public telephones.[128] They placed listening devices on the outside of the phone booth he favored, though they did not put anything inside the booth itself. That the authorities had probable cause to believe the bookmaking operation existed was not seriously disputed, but they made no effort to inform a magistrate or obtain a warrant.

Rejecting the idea that the amendment could be read so narrowly as to protect only invasions of one's home or so broadly as to convey a general right to privacy, the Court based its holding in this case on the determination that "the Fourth Amendment protects people, not places."[129] Therefore, the fact that it was a telephone booth was not as important as Katz's reasonable expectation of privacy there. The Court specifically disposed of the idea that there had been no search or seizure because there was no physical trespass: "[T]he Fourth Amendment governs not only the seizure of tangible items, but extends as well to the recording of oral statements, overheard without any 'technical trespass under . . . local property law.'"[130]

Harlan added in a separate opinion that *Goldman* had to go: "Its limitation on Fourth Amendment protection is, in the present day, bad physics as well as bad law, for reasonable expectations of privacy may be defeated by electronic as well as physical invasion."[131]

Douglas joined the Court but wrote separately to attack the concurring opinion issued by White, who argued that the warrant requirement for wiretaps should not apply in any national security matter. Douglas held that, apart from treason, the Constitution drew no distinction among types of crimes. After all, the most important point of the debate to him was wiretap's potential for the abuse of political adversaries, alleged subversives, and leaders of civil rights groups, not the fact that criminal defendants might suffer from its use. Some thought Douglas's fears overblown, but events like the bugging of the Reverend Martin Luther King's hotel rooms and the use of the tapes in an attempt to force him to refuse the Nobel Peace Prize or to commit suicide came as no surprise to the justice.

He was one of a number of justices who suspected that the Court itself had been bugged during the Nixon administration. The idea may sound far-fetched, but the concern was real, particularly after March 1969. At that time, a representative of the Justice Department went to Justice Brennan's chambers and warned him that unless the Court reconsidered its decision requiring disclosure to an espionage suspect of wiretap transcripts, there would be grave consequences.[132] Among other things, the transcripts would show that the department had bugged more than forty embassies in Washington. When, with that revelation, Chief Justice Warren inquired whether the Court had been bugged, he was assured that it had not. The representative from the Justice Department backed his plea with the not so subtle threat that resistance by the Court would prompt an effort by the administration to curtail its jurisdiction in wiretap cases. Warren politely threw the man out, with directions to file proper motions and briefs for rehearing, which the Court then promptly denied.

FBI files later revealed that members of the Court, including Douglas, had been under surveillance. Moreover, those documents showed that J. Edgar Hoover had used the Supreme Court police force and members of the clerk's staff to help him spy on the justices. It is very clear from these materials that Hoover had targeted Douglas as a person to get when the opportunity presented itself.[133]

Black issued a lone dissent in *Katz,* contending that the Framers intended a narrow meaning of search and seizure pertaining only to tangible places and objects. Finally, Black rejected what he saw as an abuse of precedents based on a desire to extend the Fourth Amendment to protect a broad right to privacy, a right mentioned nowhere in the Bill of Rights.

Douglas, however, contended that the Court had not begun to protect the broad right of privacy that he was absolutely sure was essential to constitutional liberty.[134] While it took a rigorous Fourth Amendment position on wiretaps, for example, it continued to allow the use of wired informants and other surreptitious means of acquiring evidence.[135]

Self-Incrimination

Other members of the Court accepted Rutledge's contention that Fourth Amendment search and seizure and Fifth Amendment self-incrimination questions overlapped. That was certainly true in the so-called bodily extraction cases, which involved blood, urine, or tissue samples that had been obtained voluntarily or involuntarily by the police. Douglas saw it as one more example of an ever increasing intrusion into privacy, whereas Black approached the cases as issues of self-incrimination, the kind of literal Bill of Rights–based due process claim that he could sink his teeth into. The first of these cases, *Rochin* v. *California*, decided in 1952, was something more; it was one of the most important stages for the debate between Black's and Frankfurter's theories of due process.

Antonio Rochin and his wife were in bed on the second floor of their home when three police officers burst into the room. They had no warrant. There were two cellophane-wrapped capsules on the nightstand which Rochin immediately swallowed. The police attempted to forcibly remove the capsules from his mouth and throat, and then took him to a hospital, where his stomach was pumped against his will. The remnants of the capsules were analyzed and found to contain morphine. He was convicted for possession of narcotics and sentenced to sixty days in jail. The California courts upheld the conviction, but indicated that the defendant had a strong case for breaking and entering as well as assault and battery.

The Supreme Court reversed the conviction in a now famous opinion by Justice Frankfurter.[136] Responding to Black's criticism, he argued:

> Due process of law thus conceived is not to be derided as resort to a revival of "natural law" . . . The faculties of the Due Process Clause may be indefinite and vague, but the mode of their ascertainment is not self-willed. In each case "due process of law" requires an evaluation based on a disinterested inquiry pursued in the spirit of science, on a balanced order of facts exactly and fairly stated, on the detached consideration of conflicting claims . . . , on a judgment not ad hoc and episodic but duly mindful of reconciling the needs both of continuity and of change in any progressive society.[137]

In this case, Frankfurter found "conduct that shocks the conscience. . . . They are methods too close to the rack and the screw to permit of constitutional differentiation."[138] Whatever the outer bounds of permissible police conduct might be, this exceeded them. Actually, Douglas's conference notes indicate that the discussion of the case was a bit more graphic, giving rise to an unfortunate choice of words. Douglas noted that Frankfurter, like Justice Reed, concluded by saying that the case "makes him puke." In response to Chief Justice Vinson's contention at conference that the critical question was the reliability of the evidence and not the manner in which it had been obtained, Frankfurter argued that coerced confessions are precluded not because they are unreliable (though they often are) but because they "offend the community's sense of fair play and decency."[139]

Black disagreed. Self-incrimination was barred because the Constitution said it was, period! On the merits, there was, however, no disagreement. Black wrote, "I think a person is compelled to be a witness against himself not only when he is compelled to testify, but also when as here, incriminating evidence is forcibly taken from him by a contrivance of modern science."[140] Then he went on to refute Frankfurter's "shock the conscience" theory of due process: "I regret my inability to accept their interpretation without protest. But I believe that faithful adherence to the specific guarantees in the Bill of Rights insures a more permanent protection of individual liberty than that which can be afforded by the nebulous standards stated by the majority."

Black later wrote that "the *Rochin* defense of the philosophy of due process which I oppose is the best one ever written to justify that philosophy." But that was his acknowledgment of a worthy opponent, not of the merits of the argument. He wrote, "The majority opinion in the Rochin case exemplifies in a concrete situation what I object to most in what I consider to be an unwarranted interpretation of the Due Process Clause." The idea that judges should make constitutional decisions on the basis of what "shocks the conscience" was precisely what Black thought most dangerous. What do they mean? Black asked. "[W]hat avenues of investigation are open to discover 'canons' of conduct so universally favored that this Court should write them into the Constitution? All we are told is that the discovery must be made by an 'evaluation based on a disinterested inquiry in the spirit of science on a balanced order of facts.'" Frankfurter's attempt to defend against the charge that there were no standards was unsuccessful.

Black went on to argue that "the accordion-like qualities of this philosophy must inevitably imperil all the individual liberty safeguards specifically enumerated in the Bill of Rights. Reflection and recent decisions of this Court sanctioning abridgement of the freedom of speech and press have strengthened this conclusion."[141] Here Black was making specific references to cases in which the same sort of loose reading of the Constitution had diminished freedom in an area the Bill of Rights insisted was to be absolutely protected from abridgement.

Douglas concurred as well. He asked why, if all agreed that these practices violated the community's sense of decency and were contrary to the values of an English-speaking people, only four states would bar the evidence used in this case. The plain fact was that the Bill of Rights was needed because the majority would not provide protections for minorities or those who were accused of crimes. The guarantee against self-incrimination exists, he insisted, not because the Court or society thought it decent or just but because the "Framers made it a standard of due process. . . . I think that words taken from his lips, capsules taken from his stomach, blood taken from his veins are all inadmissible provided they are taken from him without his permission. They are inadmissible because of the command of the Fifth Amendment."[142]

As Black and Douglas feared, once they moved beyond the extreme facts of the *Rochin* case, the apparent agreement within the Court melted. In two cases concerning automobile accidents allegedly caused by drivers under the influence of alcohol, the Court upheld the taking of the defendants' blood for testing. In the 1957 case of *Breithaupt* v. *Abram*,[143] blood was drawn from an unconscious patient; in the 1966 *Schmerber* v. *California* litigation,[144] blood was drawn over the objection of the driver, who was fully conscious at the time. In both instances, the blood was taken by a doctor in a hospital on the instructions of the police. Justice Clark argued for the Court that, unlike the abuses of *Rochin, Breithaupt* involved a routine, clinical blood test. Beyond that, the importance of responding to drunk-driving cases outweighed whatever intrusiveness was involved. Warren countered that according to that logic, the effort to deal with narcotics in the *Rochin* case should have been an even greater counterweight to constitutional protection. In *Schmerber,* Brennan, writing for the Court, drew the line somewhat differently. He argued that the self-incrimination provision provided protection against the forced delivery of "testimonial or communicative" evidence, but not independent forms of analysis. Moreover, the conduct of the test was reasonable and controlled, based on probable cause, and it was necessary to deal with the natural but immediate destruction of evidence as the body processed the alcohol.

Black and Douglas considered these plain cases of coerced self-incrimination of the worst kind. Douglas wrote in *Breithaupt:* "I would not draw a line between the use of force on the one hand and trickery, subterfuge, or any police technique which takes advantage of the inability of the prisoner to resist on the other. Nor would I draw a line between involuntary extraction of words from his lips, the involuntary extraction of the contents of his stomach, and the involuntary extraction of fluids of his body when the evidence obtained is used to convict him."[145] As Douglas tells the story, Black had taken the position in the conference discussion that it was "not as bad as pulling finger nails but it's in that category. Same as extracting of a confession at point of a gun."[146]

One of the problems Black and Douglas pointed out was that the facts of *Breithaupt* and *Rochin* were different, but not the law. Black insisted that if Breithaupt's conviction for manslaughter was upheld, *Rochin* should be reversed. Douglas noted that in conference Frankfurter "talked for 40 minutes trying to distinguish this case from *Rochin.*"[147]

The conference on *Schmerber* produced many of the same arguments. Black was committed to reverse on straight self-incrimination grounds, while Douglas argued for reversal on the basis of his *Breithaupt* dissent. Harlan was the new player, and he argued for affirmance, but not on the same grounds as Frankfurter had before him. Arguing that the state could justify the use of force involved to protect its highways, he rejected the idea of self-incrimination in these cases. Warren was still concerned that the facts were clouding the legal implications. Anticipating cases that would later reach the Court, he asked, "Wouldn't [the] same principle apply to testing blood for narcotics?" to which Harlan answered, "Yes."[148]

The use of illegally obtained confessions, like the question of bodily extraction, was an issue on which Black and Douglas agreed within a sharply divided Court. Hugo Black, from his 1940 opinion in *Chambers* v. *Florida* to the end of his career,[149] consistently attacked abuses in cases involving suspects held in police custody. In a Tennessee case in which a suspect had been questioned for thirty-six hours by rotating teams of interrogators, Black's rhetoric showed his impatience with the unwillingness of authorities to get the constitutional message. With the nation in the midst of World War II, Black wrote: "There have been, and are now, certain foreign governments dedicated to an opposite policy—governments which convict individuals with testimony obtained by police organizations possessed of an unrestrained power to seize persons and wring from them confessions by physical and mental torture. So long as the Constitution remains the basic law of our Republic, America will not have that kind of government."[150] Justice Stone saw the obvious comparison and asked Black to consider moderating his language.[151]

A number of the confession cases were frankly not very difficult, simply because the facts were often so extreme.[152] The greater difficulty came from the broader disagreements among the justices as to how to interpret due process, including the continuing discussion of incorporation. There was also occasionally a backwash from disagreements in other cases as well. The story of Brennan's attempt to get a majority in *Malloy* v. *Hogan* is illustrative.

Brennan thought he had a solid 5 to 4 majority when he circulated his May 13, 1964, draft opinion. It was not until early June that he received a curt memo from Douglas withdrawing from the opinion. Brennan scrambled to get Douglas back on board: "I have your note withdrawing your concurrence in my *Malloy.* Are there any changes you have to suggest which might meet your views? I purposely organized it to follow Hugo's model in *Gideon,* which you joined with a separate statement adhering to your views that the Fourteenth Amendment incorporated the entire Bill of Rights. I'd be very hopeful that we could arrive at some kind of agreement in *Malloy* because otherwise I'll not have a court for the opinion."[153]

Douglas responded with an angry memorandum saying that it was not just *Malloy* but other recent opinions that had caused him to be somewhat more careful in accepting his friend's opinions. He had "suffered a real shock" when he carefully examined Brennan's opinion in the civil rights sit-in cases and "underwent a real trauma when I realized that the spirit of Felix still was the dominant force here."[154] After reading one of Brennan's rulings on free press and libel, he wrote, he began "to realize I had been reading your opinions with my heart as well as my mind in view of my deep affection for you. . . . At that point I decided perhaps I better look again at *Malloy* to see if I had agreed to anything that might embarrass me in the future."[155] There followed a discussion in which Douglas's most serious problem, the failure to specifically repudiate *Twining,* was the subject of negotiation. "This has nothing to do with good intentions or anything else except my basic convictions that I forged rightly or wrongly in the long, bitter years here with Felix. And as I reread *Malloy,* I began to appreciate that you had not even overruled *Twining*—that it was still there to be used on other occasions and that Felix's highly subjective, personalized interpretation of the Bill of Rights was being perpetuated."[156] Brennan's later draft took on *Twining* more directly and dropped langauge that in the earlier draft attempted to cast this ruling in such a way as to reconcile the departure from the long-standing precedent. Douglas joined. Thus it was that Douglas played a key role in finally eliminating the *Twining* ruling that his friend Hugo and he had fought for so long.

Self-Incrimination and the Right to Counsel

Just as there were areas of overlap between the Fourth and Fifth Amendments, so were Fifth Amendment self-incrimination prohibitions and Sixth Amendment right to counsel questions related. And Douglas and Black were as uncompromising on the latter as they were on the former. The right to counsel was another of those specific requirements of the Bill of Rights that Hugo Black felt good about enforcing. There was more to it than that, though. Black had seen firsthand what happens to the poor and the weak who faced prosecution without a lawyer. Like Douglas, he knew from his own experience all the incentives for attorneys to concentrate their efforts on the prosecution side or in the defense of the well-heeled. But unlike some of the other issues before the Court in the 1960s, there was a great deal of agreement within the Court on the need to provide assistance of counsel, partly because of the continuing incorporation process.

Hugo Black had the privilege of writing for the Court in *Gideon v. Wainwright,* the now famous case of Clarence Earl Gideon, who was arrested for breaking into a Florida pool room and stealing coins from vending machines.[157] Gideon's penciled petition to the Supreme Court met a receptive audience, several of whose members had been on the lookout for just such a case. Warren had gone so far as to instruct his clerks, as one clerk put it, "to keep your eyes peeled for a right to counsel case."[158]

Black's opportunity to write in *Gideon* was a happy occasion for a number of reasons. For one thing, it allowed him to add another notch to his belt on the incorporation doctrine, since the decision applied to the states the Sixth Amendment provision of the right to counsel. For another, it permitted him to settle an old score, to overturn the 1942 decision in *Betts* v. *Brady* rejecting the call for right to counsel in all serious criminal cases.[159] Ten years before *Betts,* the Court had ruled that defendants in capital cases were entitled to representation,[160] but the majority would not go further. Black's stinging dissent in *Betts,* the case of an unemployed farm worker arrested for robbery in Maryland, had blistered the Court not only because it refused to incorporate the Sixth Amendment provision, but also because it was simply inconsistent with the reasoning of the earlier decision in *Powell* v. *Alabama.* Clearly, he said, "a practice cannot be reconciled with 'common and fundamental ideas of fairness and right,' which subjects innocent men to increased dangers of conviction merely because of their poverty."[161] His evidence of the acceptance of that proposition was that thirty-five states mandated the right to counsel and that state laws had recognized the essential importance of representation by counsel as early as the mid-nineteenth century. The *Gideon* decision ended that discussion once and for all.

Douglas enjoyed the *Gideon* ruling as well. He had joined Black's *Betts* dissent and was naturally happy to see it become law. Moreover, he had the distinct pleasure of seeing his old friend Abe Fortas argue the case for Gideon in what Douglas described as "in my time probably the best single legal argument."[162] While Douglas was glad the Court did the right thing, though, he later suggested that some members of the Court acted from less than lofty motivations: "A unanimous Court reversed that decision. . . not so much because it had changed its mind on constitutional theory, but because the failure of defendants to have counsel at their criminal trials resulted in a host of habeas corpus petitions which years later raised constitutional questions that would have been brought up at the trial had the accused been allowed a lawyer."[163]

Actually, Douglas thought the Court should go considerably further than requiring counsel at the time of trial in felony cases. In his mind, a lawyer was needed in any case in which jail was a possibility. The Court had considered extending the ruling that far in *Gideon,* but Warren advised against it.[164] Douglas ultimately wrote for the Court in a case mandating just that.[165]

It was also important to him that counsel be available earlier in the process. Douglas argued in 1958 that defendants needed lawyers before they were formally charged, while they were under questioning by police.[166] The Court ultimately agreed, producing some of the most controversial decisions to come from the Court during Black's and Douglas's careers on the bench.[167]

Danny Escobedo was arrested at 2:30 A.M. one January day in 1960. Police questioned him in connection with the murder of his brother-in-law until 5:00 P.M., when his attorney secured his release. Two weeks later, another man who was a suspect in the killing told police interrogators that Escobedo was actually the trigger man. They promptly took Escobedo into custody once again that evening. Although his lawyer appeared at police headquarters shortly thereafter, uncontradicted testimony showed that the police refused the attorney's repeated requests to confer with his client. Escobedo was continuously questioned into the early morning hours of the next day, despite his constant requests to see his lawyer before responding to questions. He ultimately provided police with a statement that was used at trial to convict him.

Justice Goldberg wrote for the 5 to 4 majority, which included Black and Douglas. Quoting Justice Douglas's concurring opinion in an earlier case,[168] the Court overturned the conviction, warning that to deprive a suspect in police custody of the right to counsel undermined "effective representation by counsel at the only state when 'legal aid and advice would help him.'"[169] The point of the questioning was "to get him," and the refusal to allow him to leave or to see his attorney underscored the fact that this was part of an effort to convict, not merely to gain information about a crime. Therefore, the Court held, the right to counsel begins at the point where "the interrogation is no longer a general inquiry into an unsolved crime but has begun to focus on a particular suspect."[170]

Harlan warned that this ruling "seriously and unjustifiably fetters perfectly legitimate methods of criminal law enforcement."[171] White, joined by Stewart and Clark, insisted that law enforcement would "be crippled and its task made a great deal more difficult."[172] The state had argued that the number of confessions would decline dramatically if the Court required a right to counsel. But Goldberg answered, "We have also learned the companion lesson of history that no system of criminal justice can, or should, survive if it comes to depend for its continued effectiveness on the citizens' abdication through unawareness of their constitutional rights."[173]

By the time *Escobedo* was announced in 1964, the criminal due process decisions issued by the Court were fast becoming a focus of national criticism. President Kennedy had been assassinated the previous November. It was the first of a number of long, hot summers in the nation's cities in which racial tensions spilled into violent episodes. It was also an election year.

The *Miranda* v. *Arizona* ruling was really the lead case of a group of appeals

brought on grounds similar to those of *Escobedo*. They involved custodial inter-
rogations in which the suspects did not have assistance of counsel and had not been
informed of their constitutional rights. After two years of experience under *Escobedo*, it was time for clarification. Writing for the same 5 to 4 majority that had
governed *Escobedo*, Chief Justice Warren observed: "This case has been the subject
of judicial interpretation and spirited legal debate since it was decided two years
ago. Both state and federal courts, in assessing its implications, have arrived at varying conclusions. A wealth of scholarly material has been written tracing its ramifi-
cations and underpinnings. Police and prosecutor have speculated on its range and
desirability."

Warren's opinion plainly challenged historical police practices from the evidence provided by the Wickersham Commission (for which Douglas provided staff
studies), through the "third-degree" confession opinions written by Black, to the
discussion of interrogation methods in Goldberg's *Escobedo* opinion. In the end,
the Court held that once a person is taken into custody and becomes the focus of
the investigation, whether formal charges have been lodged or not, the police must
inform the suspect of the right to remain silent, that anything said will be used
against the suspect, and that the suspect has a right to have an attorney present
before questioning and to have an attorney appointed if necessary.

Obviously, the Court's attempt to clarify the requirements of custodial interrogation did nothing to quell debate over its opinions. Indeed, it sparked further
controversy. Douglas wrote in his autobiography that "it is indeed difficult to see
how a civilized society could demand less. The Miranda decision, written by Earl
Warren, came in for a lot of abuse and was said to be responsible for increased crime
rates. But those knowledgeable in the field know that crime springs from poverty,
insufferable living conditions and from involvement in drugs. The presumption of
innocence is proclaimed not only for the rich and prestigious members of the community but also for the lowliest members."[174]

By 1968, it was clear that crime in the streets would be not merely an issue, but
one of the central issues, of the presidential campaign. President Johnson made the
war on crime a principal theme in his legislative agenda, pressing for enactment of
what came to be the Omnibus Crime Control and Safe Streets Act of 1968. Richard
Nixon came out swinging in the spring, charging the Johnson administration and,
by implication, the Democratic party with being soft on crime and promising to
move toward legislative reversal of Supreme Court rulings that had interfered with
law enforcement.[175] The Omnibus Crime Control and Safe Streets Act was hung up
in Congress precisely because of debates over provisions that sought to circumvent
or overturn Supreme Court decisions, but it was almost literally blown through the
legislative process after the assassinations of Martin Luther King, Jr., and Robert
Kennedy. It was politically impossible to block the bill after a violent spring in the
nation's cities and what promised to be an even worse summer. It was the kind of
environment Nixon could handle far better than the milder Hubert Humphrey.

Then there was the Fortas affair. Warren resigned to allow Johnson the opportunity to name his successor. He chose Associate Justice Abe Fortas, which gave the
Court's critics an opportunity to hold the appointee accountable for the decisions
of the Warren era. Strom Thurmond, chairman of the Senate Judiciary Committee,

was more than happy to lead the charge.[176] The nomination was, of course, ulti-mately unsuccessful.

The irony in all of this is that no group of people thought or worried more about the nature and implications of their decisions than the nine occupants of the build-ing across the street from the Capitol. Several had been battle-tested in years of experience as prosecutors. Others, like Black, had been elected officials who knew precisely how the public responds and can be manipulated in this area. The inten-sity of their disagreements and the efforts to achieve consensus where it was possible attest not to their isolation, but to their awareness. Even so, their rulings played a role in changing the very Court on which they sat because they helped to elect the man who would appoint nominees to the next four vacancies.

There were two other pieces to the puzzle. In 1967, the Court extended the right to counsel requirement to "police line-ups" as well as direct interrogation.[177] Then, in 1970, came a case that emphasized the requirement for counsel in pretrial hear-ings, which provided an opportunity for both Black and Douglas to say a last word on the subject.[178] Black was adamant in this Alabama case both because of his com-mitment to the right to counsel and because of his knowledge of Alabama criminal process. At conference, he insisted that "prelim is a very vital part of criminal pro-cess in Alabama. Use[d] to get the evidence and it's a real knock down fight."[179] He made that point again in his concurring opinion.

Burger stridently disagreed. On January 9, 1970, Burger wrote the first of two memoranda to the conference targeting Black as his foil and stating his intention to add an opinion: "A preliminary hearing, which is confined to the narrow ques-tion whether a person is to be held for further inquiry, simply is not 'a criminal prosecution' under the Constitution." Then, to add insult to injury, Burger added: "Thus, accepting the 'literal language' as a guide, I find it does not lead me where it leads Justice Black. I think legislatures should provide for counsel at the prelim-inary hearing but I cannot find that the Constitution commanded it, and, of course, no one thought so until quite recently."[180] Burger wrote the other memorandum to the conference insisting that he had "been unable to find anything in the Consti-tution calling for counsel at a preliminary hearing. (Hugo, please note and tell me what Article or Amendment covers this!)"[181] For Black, pretrial was in reality part of the trial, and it was formally part of that process according to Alabama law.

Douglas charged in his autobiography that Burger announced in conference his view that the Court should overturn *Miranda* and *Gideon,* among other cases.[182] Burger denies having taken any such position.[183]

Trial by Jury

Once past the right to counsel cases, however, due process discussions once again became more complex for Black, Douglas, and the rest of the Court. Both men had a strong sense of equal protection of the law in their understanding of the Consti-tution's due process requirements, but they differed sharply on whether there was a general obligation to provide a process that was fundamentally fair.

Black could work with the fact that the Sixth Amendment required a trial by an impartial jury, but the word *impartial,* like the term *reasonable* in the Fourth

Amendment, gave him pause. Those terms left judges too much room to impose their own personal preferences and provided too little guidance. Douglas had no such difficulty, largely becuase he read due process as requiring a procedure that was fundamentally fair. Fairness was not a standard Black considered adequate or, for that matter, justified by the language of the Bill of Rights. The Court was divided on this issue as well, though for varying reasons.

Both Black and Douglas joined opinions rejecting racially biased juries[184] and the use of blue-ribbon juries, specially selected for certain characteristics.[185] They joined decisions upholding juries of fewer than twelve members.[186] However, they split on whether a state could eliminate potential jurors from a murder trial because they were opposed to the death penalty, Douglas agreeing with a decision to reject the Illinois jury rule and Black dissenting.[187] In another murder case, they divided over whether a state could have a capital murder trial in which both guilt and punishment were determined in a single proceeding.[188] Douglas dissented from the Court's ruling in favor of the state on grounds that the defense could enter no evidence in favor of mitigation of the possible penalty without exposing the defendant to self-incrimination or other problems that would undermine its claims. He wrote:

> The Court is not concerned with the wisdom of state policies, only with the constitutional barriers to state action. Procedural due process is one of those barriers, as revealed over and again in our decisions. Some of its requirements are explicit in the Bill of Rights. . . .
>
> Other requirements of procedural due process are only implied, not expressed; their inclusion or exclusion turns on the basic question of fairness.[189]

Black replied, "This Court's task is not to determine whether the petitioners' trials were 'fairly conducted.' . . . The Constitution grants this Court no power to reverse convictions because of our personal beliefs that state criminal procedures are 'unfair,' 'arbitrary,' 'capricious,' 'unreasonable,' or 'shocking to our conscience.'"[190]

The cases posing conflicts between freedom of the press and the due process protections of criminal trials pressed Black to explore the outer boundaries of his barrier against "fairness as a standard." The Supreme Court overturned a conviction for prejudicial pretrial publicity for the first time in 1961. The case involved a defendant tried in a rural Indiana community as part of a multiple-murder investigation amid continuing intense publicity, which reported, among other things, that the defendant had confessed. Three hundred and seventy prospective jurors were disqualified for prejudice or because of their opposition to the death penalty. Of the twelve jurors who ultimately sat, eight admitted at the outset that they had some knowledge of the facts and thought the defendant was guilty.[191] The more complex litigation came later, first in the Billie Sol Estes case[192] concerning the use of television cameras in the courtroom, and then in the infamous Sam Sheppard murder case,[193] in which the trial was described by the Ohio Supreme Court as "a Roman holiday for the news media." In the first case, Black had no difficulty finding that there had not been an impartial jury, but in the second two it was plain that there was more at issue than just the jury. In *Estes,* there was the question of whether the whole proceeding was so affected by the presence of television that it was unfair. In *Sheppard,* not only was there the publicity at the coroner's inquest to consider, but also the fact that the judge and prosecutor were running for judge-ships at the time of trial. The issues were too broad to be limited by the specific language of the Sixth Amendment.

The differences in approach became clear at the *Estes* conference when Douglas said: "The Constitutional standard is a fair trial. Trial in a mob scene is not a fair trial." Black was troubled: "I have to say it deprives a man of a 'constitutional fair trial.' For me the test is what is in the constitution which I can grasp as a handle."[194] He joined the dissenters. It was a 5 to 4 decision, but Harlan's concurring vote was narrower than the Court's opinion, which declared a prohibition on televised trials. Black was the sole dissenter (with no opinion) in the *Sheppard* case, in which the Court reversed the conviction for violation of the right to fair trial.

The Court's rulings on criminal due process matters were bound to provoke criti-cism, and Douglas and Black were right in the middle of it. The reaction against those rulings was particularly harsh during the hunt for Communists in the 1950s, since the procedural requirements of due process stood in the way of the rush to judgment of those labeled subversive or worse. The turbulence and apparent lack of respect for law and order in the 1960s coincided with the Court's delivery of some of its most controversial rulings, which led many decent but frightened Americans to believe that the Court must be one of the causes. There was irony in the images presented in the popular media of a group of liberal social reformers, detached from the real world, who were abandoning law and order and coddling criminals. But by 1969, the reaction against the Court had played a significant role in changing it.

William O. Douglas saw the Communist witch hunt in just those terms and began his own crusade against it. He was not concerned with First Amendment issues alone, though they were important to him, as they were to Hugo Black; Doug-las was as worried about due process questions. In a speech to the American Law Institute, he admonished lawyers to take up the challenge with an educational pro-gram that would reaffirm the importance of due process. He knew it would be dif-ficult.

> History shows that government bent on a crusade, or officials filled with ambitions, have usually been inclined to take short-cuts. The cause being a noble one (for it always is), the people being filled with alarm (for they usually are), the Government being motivated by worthy aims (as it always possesses), the demands for quick and easy justice mounts. These shortcuts are not as flagrant perhaps as a lynching. But the ends they produce are cumulative; and if they continue unabated, they can silently rewrite even the fundamental law of the Nation.[195]

He cared little about criminals, but he cared mightily about the maintenance of constitutional rights, since what could be done to an accused criminal could just as easily be done to an apparent subversive or anyone else whose politics or life style did not suit the establishment.

The goal of protecting fundamental rights required a victory in the argument about the incorporation doctrine. After all, for Douglas, the often abusive "estab-lishment" was not in Washington but in one's hometown, where local majorities exercised control and had the ability to use the police and sometimes the local courts to enforce their will. Nothing short of a full incorporation of the Bill of Rights against the states would do. And having been incorporated, all the protections should be applied vigorously and with changing conditions in mind. Douglas, like Brandeis before him, saw protection from illegal search and seizure as the *sine qua non* for liberty. The right to counsel, the assurance of an impartial jury, and the general guarantee of fundamental fairness were essential each time government turned its force on the individual.

Black, the former prosecutor and New Deal senator, knew the dangers of a criminal justice system unfettered by due process, and yet had seen the dangers of a judiciary that had wreaked havoc on democratic policy making in the name of due process. The task was to pin both the criminal justice system and the judges to the Constitution, which necessitated a much closer and more limited reading of due process protections under the Constitution than that given by his friend Douglas. He was no less adamant in areas where the Constitution gave clear guidance, but was more wary where it gave none. To Black, the interpretation of due process was the delicate and difficult procedure of drawing the limits of legitimate power.

When the cases at issue were no longer due process questions, but problems of religious freedom, the tables were turned. Then it was Douglas who had great difficulty and Black who more quickly came to a settled understanding of the boundaries of power and right.

# 10

Maintaining Religious Freedom

FEW AMERICANS think of criminal due process as something that affects them, except, perhaps, as victims of crimes. But when the Court insisted on changing the popular understanding of freedom of religion in a series of rulings from the 1940s through the 1960s, the consequences of its decisions seemed threatening in a much more personal way. Judicial discussions about prayer in the classroom and support for parochial schools were not conversations about what to do with social deviants; they were about children, schools, and community.

There is no small irony in the fact that it is the cases concerning establishment of religion that have provoked the most resistance to Supreme Court decisions. To many, these rulings suggested a Court against God and country. Many law-and-order advocates put up the most intense resistance to judicial interpretations of freedom of religion.

The range of disagreement over religious freedom among the member of the court during much of the time Black and Douglas served was not as wide as it was over criminal justice. Indeed, for some years, the justices' differences were over the question of whether the brethren had adequately protected the separation of church and state. Black and Douglas were major players in the freedom of religion cases, between them writing most of the important opinions for the Court from the 1940s through the 1960s.[1]

Despite Black and Douglas's belief in the primacy of the First Amendment's guarantees of liberty, they differed, at times significantly, on how the constitutional text should be interpreted. Black, who had grown up in the Bible Belt's heartland, was a strong advocate of religious freedom, yet was reluctant to accept Bible-toting protesters marching in the streets or praying in public buildings. More than that, Black was very concerned with defining the legitimate boundaries of state power in matters of religion. His primary effort, therefore, was to develop a definition of "establishment," that part of the First Amendment prohibiting governmental establishment of religion. Douglas, however, was troubled by freedom of religion questions and the difficulty of working out the clash between free-exercise protections and the ban against establishment. It was another of those areas in which the two friends had fundamental disagreements.

Although called "Hugo-to-Hell" Black by some of his adversaries, the Alabaman always saw himself as a God-fearing man. Raised in both the Baptist and Methodist churches, Black taught Sunday school even after he went to the Senate. His attack on liquor was not merely good Prohibition-era politics, practiced on the stump by so many and at home by so few. For the most part, he abstained from spirits. So often described as a puritan by friends and associates, Black protected pornography because he thought the First Amendment required it. Even so, he had a fundamentalist's disdain for the public display of sexual material and disapproved of sexual permissiveness. Visitors to the Black home were treated to Hugo's renditions of spirituals like"Abide with Me" and "At the Cross" while waiting for the steaks to finish on the barbecue. He considered himself accomplished on both the songs and the steaks, but his friends were only polite about both claims. As Elizabeth Black said, he loved to sing the old church songs even when they were alone.[2]

But Black was also a constitutional fundamentalist. The debates over the constitutional boundaries of religious freedom meant discussions of the First Amendment. Black was no more willing to equivocate here than on other First Amendment issues. When the Bill of Rights said that "Congress shall make no law respecting an establishment of religion or prohibiting the free exercise thereof," his duty was clear. Although it took Hugo a few years on the Court to fully develop his understanding of what that language meant, he soon advocated his definition with all the force he could muster.[3]

Douglas was raised by his mother, a Presbyterian minister's widow, in a God-fearing tradition of strict obedience and responsibility. Although his upbringing was not what would be called fundamentalist, religion was important to the day-to-day life of the Douglas household. During his youth, Douglas hated the hypocrisy he saw in most of the churchmen he encountered, and as an adult, his antipathy turned to contempt for most religious leaders and organized churches. His travels around the world convinced him that the churches were in the business of placating the poor, blessing the rich, and protecting privileges enjoyed by the clergy. He wrote, in his autobiography, "I realized that heaven and hell were instruments whereby the clergy maintained the security of a static society" and quoted a Maryknoll priest with experience in Latin America: "The peasants are in the field, the destitute in the slums, the students in the classroom, the rich in their castles, and God is in his heaven." To Douglas, the darkest side of the religious establishment was revealed by another minister, who insisted: "Only the state which succeeds in making the poor appreciate the spiritual treasures of poverty can solve its social problems."[4]

For Douglas, virtually all the Western churches were corrupt institutions for the rich: "Heaven became in my mind a lovely pink cloud occupied by those who had made the greatest contributions to the church. I began to think how dreadful it would be to sit on that pink cloud with all those people, who were not only a thieving lot, but hypocrites, and above all else, dull, pious, and boring."[5] He also enjoyed his ability to shock and disturb the faithful. Douglas was proud to be a prodigious drinker. He was always on the lookout for a good off-color joke and supplied a number of his colleagues on the Court with a constant supply.

Even though he had great sport with organized religion, it would be a mistake to underestimate his own belief in the fundamental importance of faith. He had great interest in the cultures and religions of other lands, particularly those in the Far East. Douglas's own love of nature convinced him of the existence of God. He believed that nothing short of a "divine power" could explain the mountains, the great forests, and the magnificent birds and beasts he enjoyed from Katmandu to Mount Katahdin.[6]

Douglas had a more difficult time with religious issues before the Court than did his friend Hugo. While Black saw the problem of defining free exercise and non-establishment of religion, he did not concentrate on the inevitable tension between the two. Douglas did. At some point, a believer's desire to fulfill a religious duty to make the world over in the image of his or her faith meant establishing that faith by political authority. Yet if the state attempted too strenuously to avoid any association with religion, it would prevent the faithful from performing what they perceived to be their full range of essential religious practices.

Over the years, Douglas found himself unable to get the kind of clarity on the boundaries of religious freedom that Black insisted existed. Ironically, though Douglas joined Black's early opinions for the Court on religious issues, he later repudiated those votes, particularly on questions of establishment of religion. He became more absolute in his insistence on the separation of church and state than did his old friend, the Court's leading absolutist. His definition of free exercise, too, went further than Black's. For Douglas insisted that the free exercise of religion included freedom of conscience, which went well beyond the practices associated with organized religion.[7] As in most things, Douglas cared about the individual's liberty, not the protection of churches.

Free Exercise Versus Establishment

Like most Americans, the members of the Court during those years, whose decisions shaped our contemporary understanding of freedom of religion, felt strongly about the issues and brought their own religious backgrounds to the cases. There was Justice Frankfurter, who insisted on an absolutism with respect to freedom of religion that he rejected where freedom of speech was concerned. While pressing his claim, Frankfurter worried that the fact that he was a Jew would somehow produce a backlash by anti-Semites against the very freedoms he sought to protect. Then there was Justice Murphy, occupying what some have called "the Catholic seat." The former Michigan politician knew how politically volatile religious issues were, but he was adamant in defense of First Amendment protections. He was always conscious that he would be seen as a representative of the Catholic position on critical questions before the Court. Rutledge, who joined Black, Douglas, and Murphy in so many battles for civil liberty, was another justice who was even more insistent than Black on the need for an absolute separation of church and state. Defining the rights, setting the boundaries for freedom that everyone acknowledged, was the challenge for these jurists.

The Limits of Free Exercise

As is true of so many cases, the litigation that produced Supreme Court pronouncements on freedom of religion was brought by a fringe group, in this case the Jehovah's Witnesses. For that reason, Chief Justice Stone simultaneously pronounced the Witnesses "pests" and suggested that they "ought to have an endowment in view of the aid which they give in solving the legal problems of civil liberties."[8] One of the interesting facets of the Supreme Court's religion debates was that the free-exercise cases often concerned groups outside the historic mainstream of American churches, while the establishment litigation often involved the larger Christian denominations and some Jewish organizations.

What made the Jehovah's Witnesses troublesome was not that they insisted on advocating their faith, but that they spent so much effort insisting that all other faiths were false. They also were perfectly happy to use nonviolent confrontation in the streets to make their point. Beyond that, they regarded patriotism as a kind of secular religion, interpreting the biblical injunction against the worship of graven images as a prohibition against saluting the flag and participating in patriotic ceremonies. As the nation was drawn into World War II, there was little sympathy for the Witnesses or anyone else whose commitment to the flag was in doubt.

One of the difficulties for the Court was to understand the character of the cases brought by the Witnesses. Were they about the free exercise of religion, or were they free-speech disputes in which a local government had attempted to muzzle the caustic Witnesses or to punish them for their presumed disloyalty? The truth was that both kinds of issues were at stake. Yet a third argument was made by city officials who insisted that insofar as the Witnesses were engaged in the business of selling their religious tracts on the street, the disputes were merely indefensible efforts by the Witnesses to circumvent perfectly valid commercial regulations that should apply to anyone soliciting funds. The members of the Supreme Court disagreed about these claims.

The first two major cases, both decided in 1940, set the stage for several years of debate among the justices. The conviction of Jesse Cantwell and other Witnesses in New Haven, Connecticut, brought the first statement by the Court that the free-exercise clause of the First Amendment was incorporated against the states by the Fourteenth Amendment.[9] It also presented the basic problem for all courts of determining just how far free exercise could go. The Court warned that religious freedom consists of the freedom to believe, which is absolute, and the freedom to act, which is not. But even though the community had the authority to protect itself from serious threats of disorder and violence, that legitimate interest could not be used to disguise an attempt to dispose of an unwanted religious minority.

The case involved the convictions of a group of Witnesses who had played recordings and distributed publications in a Catholic neighborhood. The record advertised a publication called *Enemies,* which was an attack on all religions, but particularly Catholicism. When Jesse Cantwell had approached two men on the sidewalk and asked their permission to play his record, they agreed; but once the record began, they warned him that he had better move on or be prepared for the consequences. He left but was later arrested.

There were two major parts to this case. First, there was a conviction for violating a Connecticut statute that prohibited solicitation for religious (or other) purposes without first obtaining a certificate from the secretary of the local public-welfare council. Among other things, the official had to determine that the applicant represented a legitimate religion. The Court held that the statute was so vague as to constitute a censorship of religion. It was no mere time, place, or manner regulation because it left it to the administrator's discretion to prevent solicitation for religious purposes. The second part of the case concerned Cantwell's conviction for common law breach of the peace (there was no statute). But the Court rejected the application of such a vague authority in a situation in which free exercise of religion was implicated.

The second major case was in the long run much more explosive than *Cantwell v. Connecticut.* As Jehovah's Witnesses who believed the literal command of the Bible that they should not worship graven images, the Gobitis children had refused to participate in the Pledge of Allegiance and salute to the flag required by the school board of Minersville, Pennsylvania. The children were expelled, and, under the state's compusory attendance law, the family then had to shoulder the financial burden of sending them to private school. Gobitis sued to gain his children's readmission to the public classroom.

Justice Frankfurter wrote for the Court, upholding the compulsory flag salute against the Jehovah's Witness challenge.[10] He said in part, "The mere possession of religious convictions which contradict the relevant concerns of a political society does not relieve the citizen from the discharge of political responsibilities." Only Stone dissented.

Several members of the Court had no desire to take the case in the first place. Hughes began the conference on the matter by saying, "I come up to this case like a skittish horse to a brass band."[11] For him, there was no issue of religious freedom presented in the case. It was a simple matter of the unquestioned power of the state to inculcate loyalty. The Court had already disposed of three cases of this type by *per curiam* opinions denying that a substantial federal question had been raised. Frankfurter, like Hughes, was dismayed when he learned that some of his colleagues insisted on taking *Minersville School District v. Gobitis.*[12]

When Stone announced his intention to dissent, Frankfurter sent him a five-page letter with three forcefully stated themes. First, he insisted on his own personal concern for liberty but sought to differentiate it from the case. Second, he supported the authority of school officials to compel patriotic behavior in general and argued that the burden on religious minorities was not intolerable. Finally, and at greatest length, he argued why it was that he wanted to leave the whole matter to the legislature. He summarized the point in the middle of the letter: "For my intention . . . was to use this opinion as a vehicle for preaching the true democratic faith of not relying on the Court for the impossible task of assuring a vigorous, mature, self-protecting and tolerant democracy by bringing the responsibility for a combination of firmness and toleration directly home where it belongs—to the people and their representatives themselves."[13]

When the opinions were announced, Stone was as animated as anyone had ever seen him, reading his dissent in a tone that displayed the passion he felt. Douglas was convinced that Stone's service on the secretary of war's review board for conscientious-objector claims during World War I greatly influenced him and made him "particularly sensitive to the claims of Jehovah's Witnesses in the flag-salute case."[14] Stone's warning about the dangers of the *Gobitis* ruling were sadly prophetic. As Alpheus Mason described the aftermath, "In the wake of the Court's stamp of approval of the compulsory flag salute, religious bigotry and fanatical, unthinking patriotism became rampant. . . . Vigilante committees took it upon themselves to enforce respect for the flag by violent means. . . . The Department of Justice traced this wave of violence directly to the Court's decision in the first Flag Salute case."[15]

In the 1941 term, the Court upheld local ordinances requiring a license for street solicitation, which included distributing pamphlets for money, however small the amount.[16] Justice Reed contended that it was not a question of religion at all but simply of the authority of local governments to apply business taxes to commercial activities. Even so, the Court was on its way toward changing its position on matters of conscience. It was in the 1942 *Jones* v. *Opelika* case that Justices Black, Murphy, and Douglas filed their now famous dissent admitting a mistake and reversing their position in the flag salute cases. Justice Byrnes left the Court in 1942, to be replaced by Justice Rutledge, creating with Justice Stone's vote, a new majority on the Jehovah's Witnesses cases and the free-exercise issues they highlighted.

The response in the press to the wartime cases favored the protection of free exercise against Frankfurter's first flag salute case and the first *Jones* v. *Opelika* ruling. The *St. Louis Post-Dispatch* lauded the dissenters who repudiated their first flag salute decision and assured readers that the dissenters' position was "certain to become the prevailing view in time, just as the great dissents of Holmes and Brandeis have become law on many issues." The *Washington Post* applauded the "singular humility and intellectual honesty" demonstrated by Black, Douglas, and Murphy and warned of the dangers in the Court's *Opelika* decision.[17]

Opelika was reargued in the next term, along with eight new similar cases from Jeannette, Pennsylvania. The Court vacated its earlier *Opelika* ruling and reversed its position, setting forth its new reasoning in its opinion in *Murdoch* v. *Pennsylvania*, written by Justice Douglas. The *Murdoch* case actually was a composite of several cases that had followed the enforcement of Jeannette, Pennsylvania, ordinances against the Witnesses. Douglas wrote that this was a relatively simple case of speech essential to the exercise of religion. The fact that funds were solicited for the books and pamphlets did not convert the activity from religious speech into ordinary commerce, subject to standard business taxes.[18]

Jackson led the opposition, charging the Court with acting like men in Plato's cave who ignored the true dangers posed by the Jehovah's Witnesses, particularly the dangers to the mayor and citizens of Jeannette, Pennsylvania, when some 100 Witnesses arrived in the city on Palm Sunday. Jackson regarded the Witnesses' choice of an important religious holiday to confront residents at their own doors with a message they did not want to hear as a form of deliberate assault on the community. It was a message intended to provoke and challenge delivered in the wrong setting and under the wrong conditions. Frankfurter and Owen Roberts, who joined in his opinion, were particularly pleased by Jackson's lengthy and forceful reading of his opinion in the courtroom.[19]

Hugo Black was very much involved in the transformation of the Court's general approach to freedom of religion that was in progress. While Douglas was writing the *Murdoch* opinion, Black was drafting the Court's ruling in another Witness case, *Martin* v. *Struthers.* His opinion overturned the conviction of Thelma Martin for violation of a Struthers, Ohio, ordinance against door-to-door distribution of commercial literature. The ordinance was reportedly enacted to protect industrial shift workers. Black avoided her claim that the ordinance violated her religious freedom and simply found that "the ordinance before us is invalid because in conflict with the freedom of speech and press."[20]

But Hugo Black was wrestling with his own views in the *Struthers* case, trying to find a solid foundation for what would be his life-long understanding of freedom of religion. Originally, Black had written an opinion for the Court supporting the ordinance, to which Stone and Murphy promptly filed dissents. Black switched positions, changing the vote to 5 to 4 to strike down the ordinance.

Among other things, the first draft contained a preliminary statement of "familiary general principles" on the meaning of freedom of religion, which Black would refine over time until he produced his definitive statement on the subject in *Everson.* In the first draft he wrote:

> The First and Fourteenth Amendments are the Constitution's guarantee to the American people that the freedom of speech, press, and religion shall not be abridged. They assure to the citizen that for his religious beliefs he shall be responsible only to his own conscience and the God he worships. The appellant cannot be punished for her beliefs. Her freedoms may not be subordinated to a State religion, and she may not be harassed because the views she holds are not those of most of her fellow Americans. The cruelty of Stuart England or of our own colonies or of contemporary Germany will never under our Constitution, be practiced against the defendant. This Court has repeatedly protected the very sect of which appellant is a member from unconstitutional abuses.[21]

It is also interesting that in his first draft of *Struthers,* Black employed precisely the kind of balancing test that he would later so vigorously reject. He insisted that the problem was one of weighing the conflict between Martin's civil rights and the interests of the community in shielding its citizens. In later rulings, Black not only rejected the idea of balancing civil liberties claims but particularly attacked setting the rights of one citizen against the claims of the majority, on the grounds that civil liberties would always lose in such a balance.[22] At another point in the same draft opinion, he also suggested a sort of clear and present danger test, which he also later repudiated. "Approaching this legislation in the spirit of careful criticism, since it involves asserted conflict with a basic civil right, we conclude that the ordinance before us is valid. We base our conclusion on the fact that an ordinance of this sort can control conduct leading to substantial social evils which a city may find it necessary to restrain."[23] The other ironic twist is that Black rejected in *Struthers* the same distinction between expression and action that he later insisted on in cases concerning sit-ins and other kinds of demonstrations.

Stone argued very persuasively that the same arguments Black used to support this ordinance in his first draft opinion would sustain sweeping constraints on the dissemination of political ideas, the very essence of free speech. He emphasized the importance of protecting the right of the residents to receive information that the pamphleteers wished to distribute. Black's agitated response was to threaten Stone that he was wrong on the record and that if he did not change his statement Black would take him on directly. "I realize that it would be unfortunate to have the Court's opinion point out specific statements in the dissent as unsupportable by the record. This, I shall feel impelled to do, unless you correct them."[24] The influence of Stone's dissent on Black's revision and reversal is clear, particularly on page 2, where he virtually stole Stone's arguments from precedent. He cut his summary statement on the sweep of freedom of religion under the First and Fourteenth Amendments, but it would reemerge in much modified form four years later.

Black and Douglas were often asked what had caused them to join Frankfurter's first flag salute opinion and then make such a dramatic switch in so short a time. Douglas offered several explanations, writing of the *Gobitis* decision: "In those days, Felix Frankfurter was our hero. He was indeed learned in constitutional law and we were inclined to take him at face value."[25] Douglas believed that Black and he "were probably naive in not catching the nuances of his position from the opinion he had been circulating for some time." Douglas also claimed that things might have been different had Stone's powerful dissent been presented earlier, rather than the day before the last conference before the *Gobitis* opinion was released, after which Stone had made no effort to "campaign for it." At that late date, he and Black felt constrained, as junior justices, to maintain the position they had taken in support of Frankfurter's opinion, though in later years neither would have hesitated to change his vote even at the last minute. However, Douglas wrote, "as the months passed and new cases were filed involving the same or a related problem, Black and I began to realize that we had erred."[26] In truth, Douglas later admitted, "Hugo and I could never understand why we agreed to [Frankfurter's *Gobitis* opinion] to begin with."[27] For his part, Frankfurter never could accept his colleagues' defection. The last straw came when his new brother, Robert Jackson, who was so often his ally, wrote the opinion that reversed *Gobitis*.

A number of Jehovah's Witnesses saw the dissent in *Jones* v. *Opelika* as a signal that the Court was changing; more cases were brought, among which was an invitation for the Court to overturn the first flag salute case. It was an invitation the justices accepted. Justice Jackson's opinion for the Court in *West Virginia Board of Education* v. *Barnette* drew hearty praise from around the nation. The *Christian Science Monitor* observed how appropriate it was for the Court to deliver such an eloquent statement of liberty on Flag Day. (It was delivered on June 14, 1943.)[28] It is seemingly ironic that the decision was so well received in the midst of a world war, and yet it was apparently an awareness of the dangers to freedom from coercive forces that compelled support for the ruling. And the support came, with Rutledge, Douglas, Black, Stone, and Murphy joining Jackson even though the majority opinion relied primarily on freedom of expression rather than free exercise of religion. For Frankfurter, however, it was a bitter day indeed, and his dissent reflected his frustration with a Court unwilling to follow him, leaving him hanging in an exposed political position as a fairweather friend of religious liberty. His protestations against any such interpretation hardly countered the force of an honest admission of error by three members of the Court, as well as Jackson's powerful and eloquent defense of freedom.

Black's concurring opinion in *Barnette* was in part a reaffirmation of his switch in *Opelika*. He went beyond the free-speech argument advanced by Jackson for the majority to make his case on the ground that "the statute before us fails to accord full scope to the freedom of religion secured to the appellees by the First and Fourteenth Amendments." But he also added, very much in the same vein as the Jackson opinion, "Love of country must spring from willing hearts and free minds, inspired by a fair administration of wise laws enacted by the people's elected representatives within the bounds of express constitutional prohibitions."[29] Rutledge wrote Black a note of agreement but did not concur in his opinion, since Black's was obviously intended to be a solo exposition of his personal position.[30]

Stone, the author of the original *Gobitis* dissent, was obviously pleased with Black's transformation. He wrote: "I wish to express my personal appreciation for what you have said. . . . The sincerity and the good sense of what you have said will, I believe, make a very deep impression on the public conscience."[31] It is rare that a lone member of a court enjoys the kind of vindication Stone experienced in the flag salute cases, and he knew it. Although Stone had been one of Black's harshest critics, he understood how important Hugo's role was in the Court's dramatic change on the issue. By this time, Black had become, through the force of his personality, intellect, and determined commitment to the constitutional text, the leader of the Court liberals.

While these cases were exceptionally visible and dramatic, given the times, they really answered only some of the more obvious issues of religious freedom. Many issues remained unresolved. It was clear, given the Court's *Cantwell* ruling, that freedom of belief is absolute, but action must at some point have limits. The question, of course, was where to draw the line. Thus in another Jehovah's Witness case, the Court upheld the conviction of Elizabeth Prince for permitting her niece and ward to sell Witness publications in Brockton, Massachusetts, in violation of a Massachusetts statute barring minors from street solicitation.[32] Although he recognized the rights of parents and children under earlier cases, Justice Jackson found: "The state . . . , acting to guard the general interest in youths' well being, may restrict the parent's control by requiring school attendance; regulating or prohibiting the child's labor, and in many other ways. Its authority is not nullified merely because the parent grounds his claim to control the child's course of conduct on religion or conscience."[33] Black and Douglas joined the Court. They also joined a ruling upholding the conviction for breach of the peace of a Jehovah's Witness who verbally assaulted a town marshal, calling him "a God-damned racketeer."[34] And while virtually everyone agreed that crimes like fraud would not be permitted in the name of religion, the challenge was to decide where the boundary between belief and action was to be found. Douglas wrote for the Court that whatever the boundary might be, the truthfulness of a person's religious beliefs could not be made the subject of adjudication.[35]

Still, Douglas's own view of free exercise was a long way from settled as the Court entered a lengthy period during which it turned its attention to questions about establishment of religion. He harbored a fear of the tension between the two religion clauses of the First Amendment. As in most cases, when in doubt, Douglas leaned toward the protection of individual liberty, and so it was in free exercise of religion cases. But he was vexed by the problem of establishment. How much could the state protect the rights of the individual to pursue his or her faith without supporting religion? He was most concerned about minority faiths and beliefs with doctrines and practices other than those of the mainstream churches.

Thus he supported the claim of an unemployed South Carolina mill worker who had been disqualified by the state for unemployment compensation. As a Seventh-Day Adventist, she could not accept work on Saturday, which resulted in her disqualification on grounds that she was not willing to accept gainful employment. Douglas concurred in the finding that this law would force her to disobey her religion's commandment to receive a government benefit. He challenged the tendency to dismiss minority religious faiths in America, warning that "many people hold beliefs alien to the majority of our society—beliefs that are protected by the First Amendment but which could easily be trod upon under the guise of 'police' or 'health' regulations reflecting the majority's views. It was not about churches, denominations, or doctrines, for Douglas. It was about the individual's freedom of conscience: "The harm is the interference with the individuals' scruples or conscience—an important area which the First Amendment fences off from government. The interference here is as plain as it is in Soviet Russia, where a churchgoer is given a second-class citizenship, resulting in harm though perhaps not in measurable damages."[36] The individual could not demand a special program to support her faith, but neither could she be denied participation in a program available to everyone because of the dictates of her religion.

His concern with free exercise as freedom of conscience was central to Douglas's opinions in conscientious-objector cases during the Vietnam War. Yes, clearly one foundation for a claim to exemption from the draft was a church commandment against military service, but surely that was not the only ground. To say that it was, meant a discrimination in favor of established churches with relatively "orthodox" doctrines. No, for Douglas what mattered was the essence, the very core of free exercise, protection of the individual's freedom of conscience.

Another of the Court's important statements on free exercise was made in a case involving the Amish, *Wisconsin* v. *Yoder*.[37] The Court upheld Amish parents' refusal to honor the state's mandatory school-attendance law for high-school students on the grounds that the special character of the Amish faith and life style justified an exemption in the name of protecting free exercise. While he agreed that an important free-exercise problem was posed by the Amish parents, Douglas the individualist warned that something more was involved—the clash of interests between parents and children. Douglas's opinion in the *Yoder* case recognized a conflict that the Court would confront more directly some years later in a case involving a Missouri statute that required parental consent for a minor to have an abortion.[38] When minors are nearing adulthood and the most serious issues are at stake, what will the state sanction?

Initially, the participants in the conference on the Amish case were unanimous. Douglas indicated that he would affirm on the authority of *Pierce* v. *Society of Sisters*, a 1925 case that had first protected the right of parents to send their children to private and religious schools, though it specifically recognized the state's authority to regulate those schools for safety and minimum educational standards. He later changed his mind because of his concern about the importance of recognizing that at some point the children's constitutionally protected interests may be so different from those of the parents that the Court must stand as a protection. Moreover, he could not accept the proposition that the Amish were automatically exempt from claims to religious independence by their children merely because their way of life was unique. A person has a right to choose whether to be Amish, and, at some point, the state is obliged to protect that right, including ensuring that children can acquire sufficient education to realistically choose for themselves. He wrote: "If the parents are allowed a religious exemption, the inevitable effect is to impose the parents' notions of religious duty upon their children. Where the child is mature enough to express potentially conflicting desires, it would be an invasion of the child's rights to permit such an imposition without canvassing his views."[39]

What Does Establishment of Religion Really Mean?

The effort by state and local governments to work out competing parental demands in matters of curriculum and school policy have been at the core of the Court's debates over the establishment clause as well as disputes about free exercise. And the public's reactions to the Court's rulings about religious exercises in schools or government support for church-affiliated schools have been among the most intense ever seen at the Marble Temple.

Apart from the general tension surrounding rulings on church and state issues, the legal problems before the Court were two. First, it was necessary to develop a clear statement of what the First Amendment meant when it provided that "Congress shall make no law respecting an establishment of religion." Then the justices had to determine whether any given governmental action crossed that line. The seminal case that defined the terms of debate, *Everson* v. *Board of Education,* was followed by litigation challenging religious programs conducted in cooperation with public schools; questions about Bible reading, prayer, and the use of religious doctrine; and, finally, suits questioning direct and indirect efforts to support religious education.

The case that was the foundation stone in the Court's effort to build Jefferson's wall between church and state had nothing to with Bible reading or prayer; it did not concern the teaching of morality or the fears of fundamentalists about the exposure of their children to the theory of evolution. It was about transportation. Nevertheless, it was a profoundly important ruling because it applied the establishment clause to the states (allowing Black to add another notch to his belt on incorporation), provided a critical opportunity for Black to solidify his own constitutional position, developed the definition of freedom of religion that we still employ, and it sharply divided the Court with tensions that remained to affect later rulings.

Everson was a challenge to a New Jersey statute that allowed local school districts to pay for transporting students to public and private schools, but not to private for-profit institutions.[40] The Ewing Township board adopted a reimbursement program in which funds were not provided to the schools but were given to parents for their children's transportation expenses. Since a portion of that money went to parochial-school students, a suit was brought claiming establishment of religion in violation of the First and Fourteenth Amendments. Taxpayers also charged that they were illegally taxed to support a program with a private rather than a "public purpose," in violation of the due process clause. The dissenters in *Everson* later pointed out that the program was not as neutral as that presentation of the facts made it sound. While the state statute said nothing about parochial schools, the Ewing board's motion concerned "the transportation of pupils of Ewing to the Trenton and Pennington High Schools and Catholic Schools by way of public carrier."[41]

The New Jersey case required members of the Court to commit to a definition of establishment of religion, a challenge they had not faced before. Frankfurter and Rutledge were adamant in their opposition to any breach of separation of church and state and said so forcefully at the conference. Rutledge warned: "Every religious institution in [the] country will be reaching into [the] hopper for help if you sustain this. We ought to stop this thing right at [the] threshold of [the] public school."[42] Indeed, Rutledge took the point in challenging Black's opinion for the bare majority, which upheld the New Jersey program. The thrust and parry of opinions and revised opinions between the two altered Black's position substantially.

Rutledge emerged from the conference with a strong sense of mission, to defend the historic separation of church and state under the First Amendment. It was unclear whether he could prevail, but it was important for him to fight the matter vigorously if for no other reason than to develop a potent dissenting opinion. Jackson indicated that he would sustain the New Jersey program, but he admitted ambivalence on several points and noted that he might very well change his position. He eventually switched and prepared his own dissent. Burton joined the dissenters as well. The other key vote belonged to Murphy, who might also be turned. While Rutledge moved to persuade him by his dissenting opinion, Frankfurter tried the personal approach, attempting to play on Murphy's Catholic sensibilities.

> You have some false freinds—those who flatter you and play on you for *their* purposes, not for your good. What follows is written by one who cares for your place in history, not in tomorrow's columns, as lasting as yesterday's snow. . . .
>
> The short of it is that you, above all men, should write along the lines . . . of Bob's opinion in Everson. I know what you think of the great American doctrine of Church and State—I also know what the wisest men of the Church, like Cardinal Gibbons thought about it. You have a chance to do for your country and your Church such as [has] never come to you before—and may never again. The things we most regret— at least, such is my experience—are the opportunities missed. For the sake of history, for the sake of your inner peace, don't miss. No one knows better than you what Everson is about. Tell the world—and shame the devil.[43]

But Murphy held his ground and joined Black, providing the critical fifth vote to make up the majority.

Black's first draft was extremely brief and concentrated on rejecting the claim that the tax was the taking of private money for the benefit of a private purpose, the advancement of Catholic education. When he first penned the draft, Black made no attempt to define freedom of religion, let alone the boundaries of the establishment clause. He simply claimed that although the transportation program provided some support to the Catholic schools, it was indirect, insubstantial, and justified by the state's interest in protecting the safety of students on their way to school. In any case, the kind of assistance was no different than the provision of police crossing guards near a church or of city fire protection to church-owned property.

Rutledge fired back a strong salvo. Immediately after the conference, Rutledge had prepared a lengthy memorandum for the file that he built on as he constructed his potent draft dissent. When he received the first draft Black circulated on December 6, 1946, Rutledge marked the vulnerable passages and set to work. He made a number of telling points with his first circulation. Rutledge rejected the claim that the purpose of the program was to ensure the safety of school children. If that was so, why did the refund program not apply to all schools?[44] He saw a tremendous weakness in Black's admission that there was some support, indirect though it was, for the parochial schools. Rutledge pressed a historical argument based on Madison's famous essay "Memorial and Remonstrance Against Religious Assessments" and Jefferson's Virginia Statute for Religious Freedom. It mattered not how much money was involved, for, as Madison had said, "three pence" would have been too much under the First Amendment. Moreover, the idea that indirect support was acceptable meant to Rutledge that Black had fundamentally misunderstood the true scope of the establishment clause. It was not a narrow prohibition but a broad rejection of mixing church and state in public affairs. In his early drafts, Rutledge was content to quote passages of "Memorial and Remonstrance" and the Virginia Statute in footnotes, but in the end he appended the entire text of both documents to the dissent, openly challenging the reader to compare the majority and dissenting interpretations. Rutledge issued his draft dissent on December 31, 1946, and was quickly joined by Frankfurter and Burton.

Rutledge issued his second draft with these colleageus on board on January 10. Jackson joined as well. Rutledge's drafts continued to hammer away at his concern that Madison sought to prohibit establishment both in the general and in the particular. The notion of a general separation of religion and government was based, among other things, on Rutledge's view that Madison very deliberately did not employ the word *church,* but prohibited establishment of religion, in either the general or the particular.

Black studied Rutledge's drafts carefully. He was perfectly ready to cross swords with Murphy on history. In his effort to reply to the claim that he had misunderstood the history of the establishment clause, he virtually doubled the length of his opinion. He dropped the reference to "indirect" support, though he maintained that there was inevitably some admixture of state and church in education. In his margin notes on the copy of Rutledge's dissent, after Rutledge's observation that it was impossible to separate the secular and the sectarian in parochial schools, he noted that there was "also a mixture where Bible read in schools."[45] Of course, Black later joined the Court's opinion striking down Bible reading in public classrooms.

In many ways, the most important pressure Rutledge exerted on Black was to spur him to draft his basic definition of establishment under the First Amendment. After he had prepared his second draft, but before it went to the printer, Black took another stab at defining the idea. He had tried to articulate his definition once before, in his first draft of the *Struthers* opinion, but it was never published. In his first *Everson* draft, issued on December 6, 1946, he wrote: "Neither a state nor the Federal Government can set up a state church. *Neither can pass laws which prefer one religion over another.* Neither can force a person to go to or to remain away from a church against his will or force him to profess a belief or disbelief in any religion" (emphasis added).[46]

Rutledge drove home the fact that Black was still not comprehending the proper scope of the establishment clause. In his January draft, Rutledge made the point directly. "Now as then, not simply aid to a single sect, but *aid to any or all* is forbidden" (emphasis added).[47] Black marked the point in the margin. A week later, Black's much expanded and significantly modified third draft appeared. At the heart of it was a new statement of fundamental principles. The January 17, 1947, draft moved away from the no-preference-among-religions language to the language we now know: "Neither a state nor the Federal Government can set up a church. Neither can pass laws which aid one religion, aid all religions, or prefer one religion over another."

The Court has consistently used Black's definition over the years. That string of precedents made it difficult for Reagan-era supporters of religion in the schools to justify their positions constitutionally. The tenor of the debate in recent years would certainly have been different had Black's opinion defined establishment only in terms of governmental preference for one religion over another.

There is no question that Black ultimately issued a more important opinion because of the changes he made in reaction to Rutledge's challenge.[48] His strong historical defense of the separation of church and state was praised by his colleagues. The definition of freedom of religion that Black developed in *Everson* has been quoted repeatedly on and off the bench, and ranks as one of his most memorable contributions to constitutional rights and liberties.

The problem with Black's presentation, however, was pointed out first by Justice Jackson's dissent. "[T]he undertones of the opinion, advocating complete and uncompromising separation of Church from State, seem utterly discordant with its conclusion. . . . The case which irresistibly comes to mind as the most fitting precedent is that of Julia who, according to Byron's reports, 'whispering "I will ne'er consent."—consented.'"[49] Madison's biographer Irving Brant wrote to Rutledge that he was reading the opinion and appreciating the discussion of the history of separation of church and state when he came on the majority's conclusion and thought he must have missed something. The argument made a very strong case against permitting any form of aid to religious education, but the conclusion went the other way.[50]

Max Lerner, the well-known liberal author and columnist for the *New York Post,* entered what he called "an emphatic statement of dissent" to Black's *Everson* ruling. In fact, hoping to short-circuit any adverse reaction, he felt it necessary to write to Black to assure him of his continued regard for Black's work.[51] Signing his letter "Sincerely Your Friend," Black answered that of course Lerner was right to take him on if he felt the need, even lauding Lerner for pointing out what a good job Rutledge had done in his dissent.

From the *Everson* opinion on, the church–state cases aroused more public reaction than any other type, with the possible exception of abortion cases. Rather than perceiving the decision as favorable or unfavorable to churches or religious schools, the public seemed to divide along pro- and anti-Catholic lines.[52] Protestant leaders and parishioners from around the nation wrote to Black, attacking him for allowing the Catholics to get away with a political coup. Catholics praised his good sense and understanding. But the nature of the discussion was about to change.

After the immediate reaction had subsided, when lawyers and laymen began to read the opinion, they began to see the importance of its definition of separation, its insistence on vigorous resistance to support for any religion, and the narrowness of its holding. They began to worry that many forms of church–state cooperation were in jeopardy. They were right.

While Black's *Everson* opinion signaled trouble for programs of financial assistance to parochial education, it also threatened the other major element of the church–state debate: government participation in religious practices. Many school districts around the nation required prayer or Bible reading in the classroom. Still others worked with churches in what came to be called released-time programs. The next two major religion cases to reach the Court concerned such programs. They were the subject of a sharp disagreement between Black and Douglas and an opportunity for the *Everson* dissenters to continue the fight.

Illinois ex rel. McCollum v. *Board of Education* concerned a challenge to an on-site released-time program in Illinois, developed by the Champaign Council on Religious Education in cooperation with the local school board, in which ministers and religious teachers were permitted to conduct classes on school property during regular school hours.[53] Children were required by state mandatory attendance laws to be in school during that period. Only those students whose parents consented were given relgious instruction. Students who did not receive the instruction were removed from their classrooms during the released-time periods. Those whose parents agreed to the instruction were required by school regulations to attend, and attendance reports were maintained by the school.

It was clear that the only way the school board could save the program would be for the Court to repudiate its *Everson* ruling and, more specifically, reject Black's definition of establishment in that opinion. Given the fact that the dissenters' only complaint was that Black had not been severe enough in separating church from state, the defenders never had a chance.

Black, who wrote for the Court again in *McCollum,* repeated the *Everson* standard, including the clause that refused to permit government to "pass laws which aid one religion, aid all religions, or prefer one religion over another."[54] Black firmly rejected the request to reexamine and repudiate that definition from *Everson:*

> They argue that historically the First Amendment was intended to forbid only govern-
> ment preference of one religion over another, not an impartial governmental assis-
> tance of all religions. In addition they ask that we distinguish or overrule our holding
> in the Everson case that the Fourteenth Amendment made the "establishment of reli-
> gion" clause of the First Amendment applicable as a prohibition against the states.
> After giving full consideration to the arguments presented we are unable to accept
> either of these contentions.[55]

The "anti-*Everson* lads" in the Court, led by Frankfurter, decided to use the opportunity for a concurring opinion in *McCollum* to attack the earlier opinion. They caucused on the matter beginning on January 6, 1948, and worked together on revisions of the draft concurrence among themselves.[56] Frankfurter harbored hopes of turning the concurrence into a majority if he could only convince Murphy not to join Black. Murphy had agonized over *Everson* and in the end gave Black the needed margin of victory. But he remained uncomfortable about the opinion. Murphy had written to Judge J. F. T. O'Connor: "Today my religion is powerful and I am afraid too rich in this country. I know of the day in American history when convents were burned and churches leveled to the ground, not alone because of Romanism but because the bigots believed and still do that many of the beliefs of the church are frauds. It's a very delicate subject and for my own part I will struggle to be right. If I err I want to err on the side of freedom of religion."[57] He passed on the first vote on *McCollum* in conference and in a note to Frankfurter told him he had drafted a separate opinion, but "when I showed it to Hugo he just blew up and objected violently to my filing it."[58] He ultimately joined the Court's opinion.

Black's problem was getting five votes despite Frankfurter's campaign to deny him a majority. Harold Burton knew he intended to vote with Black, but he was not sure that he would join the opinion. He wrote to Black, "In this case I am merely awaiting an opportunity to consider any concurring opinions that may be submitted."[59] Black immediately replied: "I would be glad to have any suggestions regard-
ing the opinion I circulated. Having been assigned the job of writing for the Court, I shall do what I can to reconcile the views of those who agree that the case should be reversed. In this delicate field it would seem wise to have a Court opinion if possible, although some views expressed at the conference indicated that accomplish-
ment of such an objective might be difficult. Of course it cannot be done if the parochial school issue is injected into the different issue here."[60]

Frankfurter and the anti-*Everson* group submitted a concurrence. Burton, using his leverage as the critical vote, tried to avoid another badly divided Court. He sent a memorandum to "Hugo and Felix" on February 7, 1948, suggesting a formula for a possible opinion with seven votes. He suggested changes in Black's opinion that would essentially remove references to *Everson* and in Frankfurter's concurrence that would narrow it to this particular program, as opposed to a more global commentary and critique of Black's opinion. His concurrence would still recognize the group's disagreement with *Everson,* but the critical paragraph from the *Everson* opinion defining freedom of religion was one Black just could not remove. Frankfurter made some, but not all, of the changes.

The irresistible force had met the immovable object. Black wrote to the conference on February 11.

> I have just been handed a memorandum from Justice Frankfurter to the effect that he will not agree to any opinion in the *McCollum* case which makes reference to our decision in the *Everson* case. I will not agree to any opinion in the *McCollum* case which does not make reference to the *Everson* case. Time has confirmed my conviction that the decision in *Everson* was right, and since I attach great importance to the constitutional question involved, I desire to supplement the record made by Justice Frankfurter by stating this fact. Of course, there is nothing unusual about one who entertains the belief that the views opposite to his are "mischief breeding."[61]

He wrote an additional memorandum to Rutledge and Burton in which he said that "it is unthinkable that there should be a public declaration of agreement and a secret statement of disagreement." That would be true of any patched-together opinion that aimed at only five votes. Black was not ready to repudiate his views in *Everson* "expressly or by failure to refer to them." Rutledge and Burton concurred in both opinions.

The reaction was extremely complex. Interestingly, Edward S. Corwin immediately attacked the Court, and by implication the author of its opinion, Justice Black, charging that the decision made it a "National School Board," which, of course, is the last thing Hugo Black would have wanted to happen.[62] Committed to federalism and to a populist democrat's insistence on local control of schools, he was not interested in making local decisions about education. Ironically, Black had taken it on the chin from the public because he upheld what was perceived to be support for religion (Catholic, that is) in *Everson.* Now he was criticized again for attempting to block support for religion (Protestant, this time). But Black, unlike his colleague Douglas, did not feel free to defend himself or the Court. He would only send copies of his opinion to people who appeared to be thoughtful commentators.

Douglas, who had gone along with Black on *Everson,* stayed with him in *McCollum,* though his position was about to change. It was really the first of two major shifts in his understanding of the outer boundaries of the establishment clause. The split came over the second released-time case to reach the Court. The critical difference between the Illinois plan and the New York City program, challenged in 1952 in *Zorach* v. *Clauson,* was that New York did not allow the religious instruction on school grounds.[63] Instead, students were permitted to leave early to attend classes at their place of worship. The churches contacted the parents and even printed the applications. For Douglas, and five other members of the Court, those factors clearly made this program different from that challenged in *McCollum.*

There was more to it than that for Douglas, however. For him, the problem was once again that the Court had to do more than define the establishment clause. It had to address the relationship between free exercise and establishment, which

Douglas felt had been neglected. It was that concern that prompted Douglas to place provisions in his majority opinion that the dissenters saw as potentially disastrous to any effort to maintain the separation of church and state.

Although he recognized that the First Amendment mandated a separation of church and state, he added: "The First Amendment, however, does not say that in every and all respects there shall be a separation of Church and State. Rather, it studiously defines the manner, the specific ways, in which there shall be no concert or union or dependency one on the other. That is the common sense of the matter. Otherwise the state and religion would be aliens to each other—hostile, suspicious, and even unfriendly."[64] To read the prohibition as absolute would be to create a hostility to religion and to ban everything from the celebration of Thanksgiving Day to the words "God save the United States and this Honorable Court," with which the Court's sessions began each day.[65] The irony of the Court's use of an invocation had occurred to him early in the deliberations on the case and remained with him while he worked on the opinion, and, for that matter, for a considerable time in the future. The collision with free-exercise rights that was sure to come if there was no accommodation between competing First Amendment values would be tragic. What difference would there be, he said, between allowing this released-time program and permitting a Catholic child to be released from a day of school to attend a holy day of obligation at the parents' request? How could a Jewish student be excused for Yom Kippur? But Douglas went even further than that. "We are a religious people," he insisted, "whose institutions presuppose a Supreme Being. . . . When the state encourages religious instruction or cooperates with religious authorities by adjusting the schedule of public events to sectarian needs, it follows the best of our traditions."[66]

Black was upset that his colleague who had joined his opinion in *Everson* and *McCollum* could now repudiate the foundation on which his definition of establishment rested, the refusal to accept the notion that the clause meant merely no preference for one faith over another. Black's *Zorach* dissent proclaimed that while he recognized that his opinions on establishment had "been subjected to a most searching examination throughout the country," *Everson* had correctly stated the meaning of the religion provision of the First Amendment, and *McCollum* had resolved the question about the so-called no-preference argument.

Jackson was devastated. He protested to Frankfurter that "the Battle for separation of Church and School is lost. From here on it is only a question of how far the intermixture will go."[67] He saw the opening for the assault on the First Amendment in *Everson*. *McCollum* may have gone the right way, but it signaled the direction the debate would take. It was an approach that was, as he saw it, destined to fail. *Zorach*, a virtual rejection of any limitations imposed by the earlier decisions, foreshadowed the end. His dissent charged that Douglas's opinion had "warped and twisted" the supposed wall of separation. It was a ruling, he said sardonically, that "will be more interesting to students of psychology and of the judicial processes than to students of constitutional law."[68]

Jackson was crushed by the *Washington Post*'s coverage of the *Zorach* ruling. He wrote to Frankfurter:

Any lingering hope I had that Monday's deviation was a temporary one is shattered by the strong encouragement given in this morning's *Washington Post* to those who went with the Court's opinion and the rebuff of the dissenters. As probably the best-informed paper in the land on this subject, its complete failure to grasp the importance of not wavering and the significance of picking up each little distinction as a constitutional problem means, to me, that the cause not only is lost in this Court but with and for the public. I think we may charge it off as a lost cause.[69]

It was distressing to the *Zorach* dissenters that the newspapers could have supported the Court in the Illinois released-time case and yet support it just as fervently in the New York case, which went the other way, praising Douglas for his "common-sense approach to this question."[70]

Jackson was wrong in his assumption that the battle for separation of church and state had been lost. Indeed, *Zorach* turned out to be a mere skirmish that did not alter the basic definition of the establishment clause. Even Douglas later changed direction. The cases concerning Bible reading and prayer in the classroom reaffirmed the *Everson* definition and confirmed the Court's willingness to try to maintain the wall of separation, battered though it may be.

The challenge to prayer in the classroom came in a case involving the New York Regents' Prayer, led each morning at the beginning of school without additional comment by public-school teachers throughout the state. Black wrote the 6 to 1 majority opinion in *Engel* v. *Vitale* (1962), striking it as an establishment of religion (neither the ailing Frankfurter nor the recently appointed Justice Byron White was formally in the case).[71] Only Potter Stewart dissented.

The parents and students challenging the prayer had originally lost in the New York state courts on grounds that there was no establishment unless there was compulsion to say the prayer. Since children were not required to repeat the prayer and none of the plaintiffs were teachers who objected to leading it, there was no coercion. Black pointed out, though, that the lower courts had confused the limitations of the different freedom of religion clauses: "The Establishment Clause, unlike the Free Exercise Clause, does not depend upon any showing of direct governmental compulsion and is violated by the enactment of laws which establish an official religion whether those laws operate directly to coerce nonobserving individuals or not."[72]

Black's opinion was primarily based on a historical logic that asserted that the establishment and free-exercise clauses were indeed fundamentally different, that the establishment clause had to do with more than the creation of an official religion, and that the sponsorship of prayer by government was so fundamentally religious in character that its actions plainly violated the establishment prohibition. Black traced the establishment debate back to the conflict surrounding the *Book of Common Prayer* and the Act of Uniformity. Given the evidence of history, he said, there was no way to separate the ability of government to be involved in religion from its inherent tendency to favor one faith over another at different times in a people's history.

His first draft had summarized the previous case law and reaffirmed the *Everson* definition, but he had done that just the previous term in his opinion for the Court in a case striking down a Maryland requirement that a public servant attest to a belief in God.[73] As he had in *McCollum,* Black had reaffirmed *Everson.* He had rejected the arguments encouraged by the language in Douglas's *Zorach* opinion that *Everson* should be reexamined.

Black took pains to defend himself against a charge of hostility to religion: "It has been argued that to apply the Constitution in such a way as to prohibit state laws respecting an establishment of religious services in public schools is to indicate a hostility toward religion or toward prayer. Nothing, of course, could be more wrong. The history of man is inseparable from the history of religion."[74]

Black accepted the fact that the actions taken by New York were limited and not nearly as significant as some of the practices at the time the First Amendment was framed, but he maintained with Madison that no establishment is permissible. He quoted from Madison's essay "Memorial and Remonstrance": "[I]t is proper to take alarm at the first experiment on our liberties. . . . Who does not see that the same authority which can establish Christianity, in exclusion of all other Religions, may establish with the same ease any particular sect of Christians, in exclusion of all other Sects? That the same authority which can force a citizen to contribute three pence only of his property for the support of any one establishment, may force him to conform to any other establishment in all cases whatsoever."[75]

The irony is that this decision, so easy for most members of the Court, proved extremely difficult for Douglas. He voted to reverse at the April 1962 conference, but the difficulties he had experienced in the earlier cases were becoming more, not less, intense. Douglas ultimately concurred, though he was clearly troubled. On the one hand, he was the author of the *Zorach* opinion who insisted that we are a religious people. On the other, he was the skeptic whose experience with churches around the world had been almost invariably bad. He had found it impossible to draw sharp lines between acceptable and unacceptable support for religious exercise.

In late May, Douglas scribbled a quick note to Black in response to his draft opinion.

> I went over the opinion in the N.Y. prayer case rather hurriedly; and I still do not see how most of the opinion is relevant to the problem. As I see it, there is no penalty for not praying, no coercion; there is, as I read the record, no more compulsion than there is when our Marshal says "God save the United States and this honorable court." The question seems to me to be whether the state or the federal government can finance a religious service or exercise. Can they pay ministers to pray for them? Can they constitutionally start off each session with a prayer? . . . Is it not like the case where by regulation each school day is begun by singing God Bless America?
>
> I do not see how I can join the opinion as is, for I would be signing up to an essay— with which I do not disagree—but which seems irrelevant to our problem.[76]

Two weeks later, Douglas sent Black another letter, this time accompanied by a formal memorandum that appeared to be a dissent but could just as easily have been a concurrence. Noting that he was merely trying to work out his difficulties on paper, Douglas observed that he "was inclined to reverse if we are prepared to disallow public property and public funds to be used to finance a religious exercise."[77] He added, "If, however, we would strike down a New York requirement that public school teachers open each day with prayer, I think we could not consistently open each of our sessions with prayer. That's the kernel of my problem."[78] Ultimately, Douglas concurred. Because he wanted to focus on state financial support for religious exercises as the basis for striking down the New York Regents' Prayer, Douglas found himself facing another dilemma in the form of the *Everson* decision.[79] Where was the line between permissible and impermissible support for religion? How does one decide that paying parents to transport their children to parochial schools is acceptable but paying teachers to lead prayers is not? He was troubled by the inability to set a usable standard, and his *Engel* concurrence said so.

Later, in *Walz* v. *Tax Commission,* a case concerning tax exemptions for religious property, he openly retracted his vote in *Everson,* agreeing with Rutledge's earlier position that it was not possible to draw any kind of sensible line that would stand up over time. He concluded that "the *Everson* decision was five to four and, though one of the five, I have since had grave doubts about it, because I have become convinced that grants to institutions teaching a sectarian creed violate the Establishment Clause."[80] As if to underscore his realignment, Douglas appended a copy of Madison's "Memorial and Remonstrance" to his *Walz* dissent. Justice Rutledge had done the same in his *Everson* dissent. No support could be allowed, for any exception led to a piecemeal and ultimately impossible effort to defend the general separation of church and state.

Among the criticisms of Black's *Engel* opinion was that he had decided to avoid an argument based on precedent and to concentrate on history. When the Court took on Bible reading in public schools the next year, by contrast, Justice Clark's opinion was a veritable catalog of the principles and most often repeated quotations from the Court's free-exercise and establishment cases.[81] Indeed, it set out to synthesize those rulings into some kind of standard that could be used in the future. Based on Black's *Everson* opinion and the later opinions interpreting it, Clark concluded in *Abington School District* v. *Schempp:* "The test may be stated as follows: what are the purpose and primary effect of the enactment? If it is the advancement or inhibition of religion then the enactment exceeds the scope of legislative power as circumscribed by the Constitution. That is to say that to withstand the strictures of the Establishment Clause there must be a secular legislative purpose and a primary effect that neither advances nor inhibits religion."[82]

The Bible case differed from the prayer case in another way—on its facts. Whereas the New York case involved a "nondenominational" prayer that was extremely vague in its terms, Bible reading by definition could not be nondenominational, given the various doctrines in different faiths concerning the use or misuse of biblical material. The very choice of the King James Version of the *Bible* was a choice not merely in favor of religion, but in favor of some religions as opposed to others. *Schempp* was therefore in some respects an easier case than *Engel,* though neither the legal nor the factual issues would prevent the politically and emotionally charged reaction that erupted after the ruling was announced.

Erwin Griswold, dean of the Harvard Law School, launched a widely publicized campaign against Black's opinion in *Engel* while the *Schempp* case was pending before the Court.[83] Griswold both criticized Black's interpretation of the establishment clause and tried to influence the justices' decisions in *Schempp* and later cases.

It was not easy for the justices to respond with equanimity to some of the criticisms they read in the newspapers or their mail, particularly concerning the New York school-prayer case. While major newspapers greeted the decision as an important defense of freedom because it would keep government out of religion, church leaders and the lay public loudly objected.[84] The *New York Times* quickly captured the general distribution of opinion in its early coverage of the prayer case, reporting that Catholic leaders were among the most ardent opponents of the ruling, Jewish leaders its most vocal defenders, and Protestants badly split on the question.[85] Letters poured into the Court by the boxful. Indeed, Black's *Engel* decision netted him forty-six file folders of mail. They ranged from thoughtful, concerned expressions of dismay to anonymous, nearly illiterate penciled postcards containing the most vituperative comments. Unlike in most other cases, letters came while some of the religion cases were pending. In fact, one that reached the Court while the prayer case was pending was from none other than Vashti McCollum, plaintiff in the earlier New York released-time case. Not content with simply sending individual letters, some people sent petitions calling on the justices to uphold prayer and other religious practices.[86]

Public officials, both national and local, some of whom led the most virulent attacks on the Court's religion rulings, encouraged letter-writing campaigns. Politicians were outspoken in their reactions, which were much less positive than those that appeared in the leading editorial pages. Almost immediately after the *Engel* opinion was announced, politicians from every level of government were heard challenging the Court and suggesting countermeasures ranging from direct legislation that would support religious practices to constitutional amendments that would deprive the Court of jurisdiction in religion cases. Indeed, one of the earliest advocates of such measures was former president Hoover. Eisenhower said little, though he generally thought the Court should have recognized the nation's religious character.[87] President John F. Kennedy did not, however, join the critical chorus. He suggested that there was "a very easy remedy" in this matter. "I would think that it would be a welcome reminder to every American family that we can pray a good deal more at home and attend our churches with a good deal more fidelity, and we can make the true meaning of prayer much more important to the lives of our children."[88]

Congressional reaction was particularly strong among Southerners. Senators John Stennis of Mississippi and Robertson of Virginia denounced the decision and sponsored a constitutional amendment to allow "nondenominational prayer."[89] Representative Thomas Abernathy (D-Miss.) warned that the prayer ruling "would please no one but a 'few atheists' and world communism." Representative Roy Taylor of North Carolina introduced a constitutional amendment that read: "Notwithstanding the first or fourteenth articles of Amendment to the Constitution of the Untied States, prayers may be offered and the Bible may be read in connection with the program of any public school in the United States." Senator James Eastland of Mississippi, chair of the Senate Judiciary Committee, vowed to hold immediate hearings leading to a constitutional amendment overturning the *Engel* decision.[91] Mendel Rivers (D-S.C.) declared: "I know of nothing in my lifetime that could give more aid and comfort to Moscow than this bold, malicious, atheistic and sacrilegious [*sic*] twist of this unpredictable group of uncontrolled despots."[92] Senator Sam Ervin of North Carolina, who later gained such notoriety in the Watergate investigation, warned on the Senate floor: "I should like to ask whether we would be far wrong in saying that in this decision the Supreme Court has held that God is unconstitutional and for that reason the public schools must be segregated against him?"[93]

It was that kind of comment that led *New York Times* court watcher Anthony Lewis to speculate about the basis for some of the southern politicians' attacks on the Court's religion rulings. While he recognized that some of the outcry was an expression of the fundamentalist religious fervor of the region, he also found the criticism a none-too-subtle means of building sentiment against the Court, which had been pressuring the South to desegregate. As he put it, "they did their best to suggest that the prayer ruling only showed how equally wrong the court had been to outlaw segregation."[94] Of course, Lewis quickly added that among the critical voices in the nation's capital there were a number of "sympathetic critics" who had the Court's own best interests at heart and were concerned that it would perhaps have been wiser to avoid the conflict. Nevertheless, he charged that the worst of the attacks on the Court were political maneuvers not worthy of true statesmen.

At the state and local level, reactions varied. Virginia's attorney general openly instructed local school districts to continue as before, but open resistance was not as widespread as some had expected it would be. In many other state and local governments, officials said little or nothing, leaving the matter of compliance to the predilections of individual school superintendents, principals, or teachers. Consequently, compliance with the released-time, prayer, and Bible-reading rulings varied widely.[95] Criticism continues to this day.

It has not been easy for some of the justices to know how best to respond to external criticism of their efforts, or, for that matter, whether to reply at all. Some of the attacks were easy simply to ignore. Others hurt. It was hard to read broadsides like that in the *Alabama Journal:* "Demands continue that the President get rid of the crackpots surrounding him, but there is no way to get rid of Justice Black and the jurists who blindly follow him into the jungle of confusion into which his abuse of the Constitution has led him."[96]

The same Hugo Black who in the early religion cases refused to reply to criticism was willing to let fly in the later cases, such as *Engel* v. *Vitale.* The publicity and direct letter lobbying were so intense that Black and others even made specific reference to it in their opinions. But the attacks that hit the hardest were from friends. The widow of a dear friend of Black's wrote a cruel letter saying that she was pleased that her husband had not lived to see Black's *Engel* opinion, for "the shock of that decision would have hastened his demise."[97] In an unusual step, Hugo replied at length. He sent her a copy of the opinion and suggested that she read his other opinions in *Everson, McCollum,* and *Torcaso* v. *Watkins* (a case striking down a religious-oath requirement for public office). He recalled that his friend had been a Presbyterian and that the same mail that had brought the widow's letter had also brought statements of gratitude from Presbyterian leaders. He added, "Dave was a lawyer, and a good one, with a familiarity with constitutional problems needed in order to express the most informed views. He was, as I said, also a religious man. It was this kind of man that I recall in our old University days. I am not so sure, however, that Dave would ever have wanted political office-holders to write the prayers that I am sure came spontaneously from his heart during all the days that I knew him."[98]

Douglas was also ready to reply to his critics, but then he usually was. He was impatient with people who ignored the fact that constitutional rights and liberties are not left to simple legislative majorities to decide and that the Court was obliged to preserve them against the pressures of the moment. To one such critic complaining about the Bible-reading case, he wrote,

> The First Amendment was added to the Constitution years ago—and one of its purposes was to prevent public institutions from serving sectarian ends. The reason was the history of religious conflicts that tore society apart.
>
> The Court, in adhering to the First Amendment, promotes rather than retards the full spiritual development of the people. To hold as you think, we would have to rewrite the First Amendment. The people can do that, not the Court.[99]

Neither was he prepared to suffer critics who saw the world so narrowly as to believe that Christianity was the sole or dominant faith. He knew that were they to live in communities where their faith was in the minority, their attitudes would be quite different.

> I suppose you would be the first to object if the Moslims [sic], having obtained control of your school board should introduce the Moslim prayer to the classroom. But the Moslim prayer is as precious to them as your Catholic prayer is to you or my Presbyterian prayer is to me. You see the aim of the First Amendment was to keep government from using public institutions for sectarian ends. I think you would be interested in reading the history of New York from 1840 to 1842 to see what terrible tensions were created when the Protestants, over the objections of the Catholics, used the Protestant Bible in New York's public schools. I think that if you were aware of the history of the First Amendment, you would be writing not to condemn me but to send a word of praise.[100]

He never could understand how Court critics missed the essential lesson that what could be done to one person or minority today, could just as easily be done to them tomorrow.

Douglas attempted to establish his line between the facilitation of religious practices that he would allow and the expenditure of funds to support religion, which he would reject, regardless of the form of financial assistance or the amount of money involved. Other members of the Court had difficulty with that approach. All but Stewart tended to see government participation in religious practices as unacceptable, though a number of the justices equivocated on the appropriateness of financial dealings between the state and churches. Thus there was little disagreement about the decision to strike an Arkansas statute prohibiting the teaching of the theory of evolution in the classroom,[101] but there was less agreement when the Court upheld decisions to lend textbooks to students at parochial as well as public schools, to uphold property-tax exemptions for church property, to strike a program that provided partial salaries for faculty at parochial schools, and to uphold partial public funding for capital improvements at church-affiliated universities.[102]

Douglas was not impressed by arguments that the programs were loans of secular textbooks or grants of construction or operating funds for nonsectarian elements of religious schools. It was not possible in any realistic sense, he maintained, to separate the secular and sectarian elements of education in a religious school without producing the kind of excessive entanglement between church and state that would surely result in the hostility that the establishment clause was designed to prevent.[103] Further, government assistance freed dollars from one part of the church schools' budgets that could be spent elsewhere, so that the government would in effect be underwriting base-line financing of religious education quite apart from supporting any particular program or activity. It was for this reason that Douglas could not accept Chief Justice Burger's attempt to distinguish between acceptable and unacceptable forms of financial assistance in two 1971 cases.[104] Douglas observed that the United States had "gradually edged into a situation where vast amounts of public funds are supplied each year to sectarian schools."[105] By the late 1960s, Douglas had concluded that any financial assistance to parochial schools was too much.

Many of those who reacted to the Court's religion rulings neither knew nor cared that the justices had wrestled long and hard with the critical problems presented by the cases. To bitter church leaders and their flocks, it appeared that the Court wanted a Godless America. How could they produce such rulings when the Court itself had recognized that "we are a religious people whose existence presumes a supreme being"?

Actually, several factors contributed to the public's vehement responses, particularly to the rulings concerned with public schools and establishment of religion. For one thing, the early cases came at a time of religious revival. As historian Arthur Link points out, the "nation seemed to be undergoing a veritable 'surge of piety' at midcentury."[106] Church membership was up sharply for most major churches, with Catholics showing a particularly dramatic increase.

For another, the religion cases were coming before the Court at the same time as the subversive-activities rulings, when civil rights cases were increasing, and as the interpretation of due process requirements was changing. Ironically, Frankfurter was warning his colleagues about straying into the political thicket of reapportionment, while he had been in the middle of the political briar patch as one of the church–state activists for more than a decade.

Black and Douglas approached to freedom of religion cases with very different perspectives, though both brought a vigorous commitment to the protection of religious minorities and a respect for the importance of faith in American society. Both of their perspectives changed considerably as they strove to answer some of the nation's most difficult questions.

Hugo Black, with the help of criticisms from colleagues like Rutledge, developed his famous statement on the meaning of religious freedom in *Everson.* He applied it for the rest of his life. At the same time, he had difficulty holding the same kind of absolutist view in religious matters that he insisted on in questions of free speech. Still, he was able to define to his own satisfaction the outer boundary of legitimate authority, and that is what mattered.

Douglas, unable to resolve the clash between free exercise of religion and the ban against establishment, never was able to equal the clarity of Black's views on religion questions. He struggled to accommodate the tension, most notably in his *Zorach* opinion and in the *Engel* discussion, but could not. In the end, he found himself drawn to the absolutist position on establishment, at least in cases of financial support for religious practices. The decision to press for an absolute ban on establishment contained within it his characteristic bias toward individual liberty.

11

Between State and Nation: Emergent Issues of Federalism

UNLIKE SOME of the other substantive issues that Hugo Black and William Douglas explored over the decades, federalism was not, for the most part, a headline-grabbing one. Relationships among levels of government and between federal courts and state or local governments were and are controversial. They have created conflict within the Court as well as outside it. The important constitutional and political questions that the idea of federalism has generated since the early nineteenth century do not seem to touch people today as intensely as, for example, criminal justice, religious freedom, and war and peace litigation. Yet there is a federalist dimension to all these issues.[1]

Black and Douglas were appointed to a Court that had until recently enforced a rigid theory of dual federalism in which there were presumed to be strict boundaries between the powers of the state and federal governments. Since the turn of the century, the Court had busily constructed a democratic no-man's-land in which the federal government was denied the authority to make a wide range of social and economic reforms on grounds that they violated the prerogatives of the states. The states were similarly barred from acting, but on grounds that their policies violated due process of law.

While Black would not tolerate a judicial attempt to place barriers to the legitimate exercise of federal authority, he was second to none in his respect for the prerogatives of the states. They possessed reserve powers that they were free to exercise. Neither was Black prepared to allow the federal judiciary to displace the proper role of state courts in the resolution of important legal issues. The fact that the citizens of a state might choose an unwise policy was not grounds for interference by a federal court. It was an issue for the voters of the state.[2]

While he, too, recognized the danger of the Court's recent historical pattern, Douglas was not prepared to abandon the liberty of Americans to the vagaries of the local electorate. It was, after all, partly the history of jealousies and abuses among the states that had produced the need for the Constitution in the first place.

Among the concerns that troubled Doublas was the need to federally enforce constitutional rights and liberties in the face of recalcitrant states and localities. Beyond the rights proclaimed by the Civil War Amendments to the Constitution, a range of federal statutes faced stiff opposition in state capitals around the nation, and Douglas was prepared to support them.

Federalism and Judicial Review

In crafting the Constitution, the Framers separated (and, to some extent, overlapped) powers both vertically (between the national and state governments) and horizontally (within a government, through the separation of powers). In so doing, they created the dual citizenship that exists in America. One is a citizen of both the national and the state government and is bound to follow the law in both jurisdictions. Madison and others engrafted federalism onto the constitutional pattern in order to curb what was for them the very real possibility of tyranny: the more that power is fragmented, within a level of government and between governmental levels, the less chance there is for tyranny to emerge, Madison said.[3] The complex political and legal relationships between the national and state governments in the federal political system reflect the essentially pessimistic view of power held by the Framers.

Formally, the federal system is based on a constitutional allocation of powers and authority between the national government (Articles I, II, III, and IV) and the state governments (Article IV and the Tenth Amendment). The supremacy clause (Article VI) in the Constitution is the structural device that ultimately resolves conflict between national and state actions. It binds the states to recognize that the Constitution and the laws made pursuant to it are the supreme law of the land. From the beginning of our constitutional experiment, the national government has had the primary task of implementing the Constitution's general, enumerated powers. Under the terms of the Constitution, Congress has the task of raising and supporting the military—and of declaring war—and the president, as administrator, is commander in chief.[4]

However, there are also areas, such as taxing and commerce powers, where both the national and the state governments legislate and regulate the behavior of persons in their respective jurisdictions. Given the fear of tyranny and uncontrolled power held by most of the Framers and by some of those who had to ratify the Constitution in 1787 and 1788, a number of amendments have been added to the Constitution to clarify the limits of governmental authority—both national and state.[5] Ultimately, however, it has been the federal courts, using that other uniquely American concept, judicial review, that have had to determine both the scope of national and state powers and, as we have already seen, the limits on the powers of both national and state governments.

For example, Congress has been given the very broad power to regulate commerce between the states (Article I, Section 8, Clause 3). The Supreme Court, in *Heart of Atlanta Motel* v. *United States* and *Katzenbach* v. *McClung,* had to determine whether that power could be used to end discrimination in places of public accommodation. Could the Massachusetts legislators and governor, given their antipathy toward the Vietnam War in the late 1960s, block the national government's efforts to draft men from that state? During economic hard times, can a state prevent out-of-staters from moving into that state because of new job opportunities? Or set up a one-year residency requirement before new residents can receive family-care assistance? Finally, what was for Hugo Black and some of his colleagues a crucial question associated with federalism: Should federal judges "interfere"—by "taking" the case out of the state court—in pending litigation in state courts?

Throughout the Court's history, there have been a number of different responses to these kinds of questions about the division of powers between the national and state governments. When Black and Douglas joined the Court in the late 1930s, many of its members held extremely conservative views regarding the scope of the economic powers of both the federal and state legislatures. Most of the justices saw the actions of the national and state governments as intrusive "state" efforts to regulate a burgeoning free-market capitalist, industrial society and the Roosevelt administration's effort to guide the national economy as constitutionally impermissible.[6]

In one of his last opinions, Hugo L. Black expressed his life-long view of "our federalism." Federalism is, he wrote, "a system in which there is a sensitivity to the legitimate interests of both state and national governments, and in which the national government, anxious though it may be to vindicate and protect federal rights and federal interests, always endeavors to do so in ways that will not unduly interfere with the legitimate activities of the states."[7]

According to a former law clerk of Black's, he saw the Constitution giving Congress, "essentially plenary power in the area of commercial regulation. He believed that this power was supreme to any power possessed by the states, but that in the absence of federal action, the states also had essentially plenary power to act in matters of economic regulation."[8] Given this arrangement, the federal judges were to remain outside the policy-making arena.

Black's dissent from the majority opinion in *Southern Pacific Railroad* v. *Arizona,* during the 1945 term, was an indication of his view of federalism—and of the limited role of the Court. The Court had struck down an Arizona rail-safety law because of the undue burden the state had placed on the interstate movement of commerce. Black, who saw in the majority decision the actions of a judicial super-legislature, wrote that "the determination of whether it is in the interest of society for the length of trains to be governmentally regulated is a matter of public policy. Someone must fix that policy—either the Congress, or the state, or the Courts. A century and a half of constitutional history and government admonishes this Court to leave that choice to the elected representatives of the people themselves, where it properly belongs both on democratic principles and the requirements of efficient government."[9] If Congress was concerned about Arizona's legislation, then Congress could rectify the situation. As he was fond of reminding all who would listen: "My two law school professors taught us, as I recall, that legislators not judges should make the laws."[10]

Behind Black's dissenting comments about federalism were two seminal themes: (1) a profound concern about federal judges interfering with the legitimate activities of the national government and the states, and (2) a "profound respect for the democratic process." Black believed strongly "that federal courts should defer to elected legislatures—both federal and state—over a broad array of policy areas."[11] Short of a confrontation with the prohibitions in the Bill of Rights (or with the few restrictions on state and national legislative behavior that existed in the body of the Constitution itself), popularly elected legislators had a great deal of latitude to make policy for their constituents. "A state legislature," he used to say, quoting Justice Holmes, "can do whatever it sees fit to do unless it is restrained by some express prohibition in the Constitution of the United States or of the state," and federal courts, especially the Supreme Court, had to avoid the use of judicial review to interfere with such actions of the legislature—especially economic and social experimentation.[12] Throughout his tenure on the Court, Black fought a "generally solitary battle against judical review of state laws impinging upon interstate commerce."[13]

It is undeniably clear, as Timothy O'Rourke and Abigail Thernstrom have observed, that as an "orthodox new dealer," Black had "great respect for congressional judgment in the area of commercial activity," as well as a "similar approach to acts of state legislatures involving economic regulation."[14] As he noted in a 1946 concurring opinion, in *Morgan* v. *Virginia,* the commerce clause "means that Congress can regulate commerce and that the Courts cannot."[15] As one of his clerks said, Black had "a distrust of the infallibility of judges, coupled with a basic faith in the 'justice and wisdom' . . . of legislatures."[16]

This strongly held belief of Black's regarding the value of judicial deference (which was, ultimately, so unlike Douglas's view of the federal judiciary) "reinforced [his concept of] federalism," according to two scholars, "since it left the states relatively free from second-guessing courts on commerce, taxation, and other matters." His view of federalism was not an affirmative one, however; "it was a by-product of his . . . belief in restricting the power of courts that gave states the room to play."[17] Justice William J. Brennan recalled that Black was "frightened to death that if he [started interposing more,] he might end up with the same kind of business that led to the nine old men."[18] In a speech to a law school audience in 1968, Black summed up his fears of an unrestrained federal judiciary: "I deeply fear for our constitutional system when life appointed judges can strike down a law passed by Congress or a state legislature with no more justification than that the judges believe the law is 'unreasonable.'"[19]

With respect to the power and authority of the national government's Article I plenary powers in the area of economic and social engineering, Douglas, in 1939, had a view of federalism that was somewhat similar to the view held by Black and other dedicated New Dealers.[20] As a disciple of the legal realists, however, Douglas accepted the view that federal judges, especially the Supreme Court justices, were important participants in the governmental policy-making process and had the responsibility to respond when state or national government infringed on individual liberties.

Beyond that, Douglas was one of the nation's acknowledged experts in regulation, commercial law, and law and economics. Notwithstanding his personal preference for small decentralized financial decision making in the best Brandeis tradition, Douglas knew that the United States had a complex interdependent national economy. He saw a Constitution that recognized the dangers of individual states' narrow, self-serving decisions and the need for a national financial infrastructure. As cases came to the Court that raised these federalism issues, Douglas's positions began to differ from those of his friend Black.

Douglas's concurring opinions in *Heart of Atlanta Motel* and *Katzenbach* (1964) gave clear evidence of his strongly held view of the active role the national government—the Congress, the president, and the courts—had to take in the struggle to maintain civil rights and liberties. Douglas (along with Goldberg) maintained that the 1964 Civil Rights Act should be grounded on a (judicial) interpretation of the congressional "enforcement" power in the Fourteenth and Fifteenth Amendments. (Black concurred in these cases to argue that his friend Douglas had gone too far and that the commerce clause was sufficient grounds on which to base the authority for the Civil Rights Act.)

Douglas's view of federalism acknowledged that the Civil War and the postwar amendments had "fundamentally altered the nature of the federal system, giving the national government an important role in the safeguarding of federal rights against state interference."[21] But it would be wrong to suppose that Douglas was not concerned about local community decision making. He worried about protecting local decisions about such questions as zoning. He proclaimed that cities could make far-reaching decisions about property even on aesthetic grounds.[22] He was even willing to see local decisions about housing regulation place some limitation on what some litigants thought were privacy rights.[23] He was concerned that local governments should be able to retain their proper independence from federal domination.[24]

While Douglas was more of a progressive than a populist, he was also an independent Westerner with a strong Jeffersonian strain to his philosophy. He wrote some of the most often quoted opinions upholding state statutes and criticizing the *Lochner*-era abuses of due process.[25]

Fundamental Differences

Black and Douglas disagreed about a number of points in this area of constitutional interpretation. Some clashes, such as their disagreement on the reach of the national legislature regarding the actions of the states in the area of civil and voting rights, have already been discussed. Black was quite concerned, and occasionally "flaming mad," about the extent of Congress's reach, especially Section 5 of the 1965 Voting Rights Act.[26] He dissented in part from the Court in *South Carolina* v. *Katzenbach* (1965) and in *Allen* v. *State* (1969) in order to voice his anger about the unconstitutional intrusion of the national government into the affairs of the states. Black felt that the despicable "hat in hand" federal–state relationship that had been created in Section 5 of the Voting Rights Act and, unfortunately, validated by the Supreme Court had to be condemned.[27]

In addition, Black's position on the primacy of Congress and the almost absolute lack of power of the federal judiciary to determine whether the states had "burdened" interstate commerce clashed with Douglas's commitment to the federal judiciary's role in maintaining proper federal authority. (According to some scholars, Black tried, unsuccessfully, to convince the brethren, in a 1938 case written by Chief Justice Stone, that the Court should write into the opinion a minimalist judicial review role for the Court in cases involving state regulation of commerce.)[28]

Other disagreements, such as their never-resolved argument over the scope of the due process and equal protection clauses, have been mentioned in earlier chapters and will be examined in the next chapter. Black also never joined Douglas in his efforts to have the Court examine, as a major question of federalism and of the separation of powers, the constitutionality of the Vietnam War.[29]

Two other fundamental disagreements between the two colleagues were over judicial federalism and the police powers of the states. The issues were (1) whether federal judges should defer to the actions of their state colleagues until the state judicial process was exhausted by litigants, and (2) whether, given the Bill of Rights, states could nevertheless enact public policies that shaped public services in ways that were allegedly discriminatory.

Judicial Federalism

One manifestation of federalism that touched the brethren very closely, and sharply divided Black and Douglas, was the issue of federal judicial intervention in legal proceedings in state courts. Given the concept of abstention, throughout our history the federal courts have been wary of interfering while a case was pending in local tribunals. In a 1965 opinion of the Court, however (with Black not participating), the majority relaxed its position and ruled in *Dombrowski* v. *Pfister* that a federal district judge could enjoin state court proceedings that had commenced under a state statute that was vague or overboard and was being used to "harass a civil rights organization in the exercise of its First Amendment rights."[30] Only six of the brethren participated in the decision; Goldberg, Stewart, and Black did not.[31] Black was extremely unhappy about the ruling. When the issue arose again a few years later, in the 1971 case of *Younger* v. *Harris,* Black wrote that the "normal thing to do when federal courts are asked to enjoin pending proceedings in state courts is not to issue such injunctions."[32] He was able to command a Court majority to give *Dombrowski* "a very narrow reading and [to reaffirm] its traditional stance."[33] Douglas was his major opponent in these extended deliberations, though, ironically, Douglas did not participate in some of the early formal votes because he had not been present for the oral arguments. Douglas saw no reason to abstain if the principal legal issue was a federal constitutional question and as long as no new state issue required interpretation.[34]

In *Younger,* a three-judge federal court in California enjoined the prosecution of Harris under California's Criminal Syndicalism Act, pending a review of its constitutionality. Harris had argued that the statute prevented him from using his First Amendment free-speech rights, and the federal court invalidated the statute. When the case was debated in conference, five of the eight justices said that the three-judge federal court should be reversed. Warren, Brennan, and White were for affirmance.

Black, Harlan, and Stewart were for reversal with a dramatic narrowing of *Dombrowski*. Because Warren was in the minority, Black, given his passionate dislike of the *Dombrowski* precedent, took it upon himself to write the opinion for the five-person majority (Marshall and Fortas were the other two justices who had supported reversal, but on narrower grounds). However, Fortas did not go along with Black's strong draft, and Brennan then announced that he was writing an opinion that would maintain *Dombrowski's* viability while vacating the three-judge district court ruling in *Younger*.

Before the Court could coalesce around the polar views, Fortas resigned. Shortly thereafter, a flare-up occurred among the eight remaining justices because Douglas had, in a seeming contradiction, concurred with Black's opinion in one case but joined Brennan's quite different opinion in *Younger*. According to Bernard Schwartz, Douglas had promised Black that he would concur in Black's *Samuels* v. *Mackell* opinion. After reading Brennan's opinion, which stated that unless a state law had a "chilling effect" on free speech, federal courts would not intervene, via the injunctive relief remedy, in state court proceedings, Douglas told Brennan that he would concur in that opinion. That gave Brennan a five-person majority in *Younger*—Brennan, Warren, Marshall, White, and now Douglas—and meant that Black's view was a minority, dissenting view. During a contentious conference, in which it was pointed out that Douglas's actions were contradictory, Douglas stood up, turned toward Brennan, and said, "Take my name off your opinion." That deadlocked the brethren 4 to 4 on *Younger* and forced the arguments to be rescheduled for the following term.[35]

When these cases were heard again, Burger had replaced Warren, and Blackmun had replaced Fortas. The conference discussion was quite different during the 1970 term of the Court. Now all the justices except Douglas called for reversal of the three-judge federal district court action. Burger thought that there was "no actual case or controversy and the District Court should not have got into the matter." Even Brennan, according to Douglas's notes, spoke for reversal, rejecting Harris's argument "that they have exhausted their state remedies."[36] At the November 20, 1970, conference, the justices, including Blackmun, and again with the exception of Douglas, voted to reverse, and Black was given the task of writing the opinion for the Court.

Black's opinion was a classic. It was his "Our Federalism" statement, in which he stated that only "special circumstances" occurring in a state court proceeding would ever warrant injunctive or declaratory relief from a federal court. Black had worked hard to get the slim majority opinion restricting the reach of federal judges in state court proceedings, and when *Younger* was read, in February 1971, he felt "good and peppy . . ., having delivered himself of [*Younger*], which [has] been hanging fire three years."[37] Black's "Our Federalism" meant that the federal courts must continue to act in accordance with his conviction that "the national government will fare best if the states and their institutions are left free to perform their separate functions in their separate ways."[38]

Douglas alone dissented, arguing that the Civil War had dramatically changed the relationship between the federal government and the states. He was right, of course, but five justices, led by Black, nevertheless believed that the federal judges had to show more respect for the states. It is interesting but idle to speculate on what the Court's position on the question of judicial federalism would have been if, in 1968, Douglas had not pulled his vote from Brennan's column.

Police Powers of the States

Another basic disagreement between Black and Douglas concerned the scope of the power of the states and local governments to enact economic and social legislation. Black recognized only the constitutional constraints (basically those in the First Amendment as incorporated into the Fourteenth Amendment and thus applicable to states and local communities) on the power of the local government to enact legislation. As long as the legislation, on its face, was not discriminatory or otherwise in violation of a constitutional prohibition, it was a legitimate exercise of the state's police powers. Even though Black might think that a statute was stupid or otherwise unwise,[39] or his brethren argue that the rationale for the statute was a racially discrimnatory one, the statute had to stand unless clear and unambiguous *constitutional* infirmities were perceived. He eschewed all judicial efforts to understand the ulterior motivations of local and state officials.

Douglas, on the contrary, felt it was the Court's duty to carefully scrutinize cases in which states presented absolute barriers to adequate judicial consideration of legitimate claims for equal protection. In an era in which those who discriminated were no longer willing to admit their actions openly, the Court had an obligation to proceed carefully but effectively. These differences between the two colleagues were clearly revealed in two cases that came to the Court toward the end of Black's tenure: *Evans* v. *Abney* (1969) and *Palmer* v. *Thompson* (1970).

A segregated public park in Macon, Georgia, had been willed to the city by a segregationist, Senator Bacon, in 1911, with the stipulation that the park be used exclusively by whites. For fifty years, it had been a segregated facility run by the city. In 1964, to avoid "state action" litigation, the city turned over the management of the park to private trustees. During the 1966 term, the Court, in an opinion written by Douglas, stated that the park was local and entangled with a governmental character as to become subject to the constitutional limitations placed on state action.[40] Black vigorously dissented. On remand, the courts of Georgia determined that the park no longer had trustees and that the property must revert to the heirs of Senator Bacon.

The 1969 *Evans* case came to the Court because petitioners challenged the constitutionality of this state judicial action, claiming that the state court had violated the state laws.[41] The state argued that the terms of the trust could not be carried out by the state, and therefore, "state law operates to cause a reverter."[42] The justices voted 5 to 2 to validate the Georgia court decision. Brennan and Douglas were the dissenting justices. Thurgood Marshall, because he had been involved with the 1966 litigation as solicitor general, did not participate. Burger, Harlan, and Black maintained that the unfolding dilemma was, in Burger's words, "a state of Georgia problem," and, as Douglas recorded in his conference notes, "he does not see how it has violated the Constitution."[43]

Brennan argued that closing the park by voiding the trust was discriminatory action and that the validation of the Georgia court's action by the Supreme Court was wrong. He and Douglas regarded the state's action as a violation of the Fourteenth Amendment's equal protection clause. But although Chief Justice Burger very briefly flirted with the possibility of overturning the Georgia court decision, Brennan and Douglas could not find any additional supporters for their constitutional views.[44]

The opinion Black wrote for the five-person majority reflected his strong opposition to federal judicial intervention into the affairs of the states. When a park is "destroyed," he wrote, there is no question that all concerned, including the Court, are "disheartened." However, said Black, the Georgia court's action terminating the trust

> presents no violation of constitutionally protected rights, and any harshness that may have resulted from the state court's decision can be attributed solely to its intention to effectuate . . . the will. The language of the Senator's will shows that the racial restrictions were solely the product of the testator's own full-blown social philosophy. The loss of [such] charitable trusts is part of the price we pay for . . . freedom of testation. . . . The responsibility of this Court, however, is to construe and enforce the Constitution and laws of the land as they are and not to legislate social policy on the basis of our own personal inclinations.[45]

Brennan's dissent pointed out that the discriminatory closing of the park was "permeated" with "state action." Douglas's dissent argued that destroying the Bacon trust "does as much violence to Bacon's purpose as would conversion of an 'all-white' park into an 'all-negro' park. [The] purpose of the will was to dedicate the land for some municipal use. . . . Letting both races share the facility is closer to a realization of Bacon's desire than a complete destruction of the will."[46]

In Black's final term on the Court, the brethren heard the controversial "swimming pool closure" case from Jackson, Mississippi: *Palmer* v. *Thompson*.[47] After the city of Jackson, Mississippi, was ordered to integrate its public facilities, including its five public swimming pools (four had been used for whites only, and one had been used for blacks only), by the Court of Appeals for the Fifth Circuit in 1962, it decided, allegedly for safety and economic reasons, to close the pools rather than desegregate them. Black's wife noted in her diary that the city officials had closed the public swimming pools for "the *obvious* reason . . . that they did not want to integrate," but Black, writing the majority opinion that validated the actions of the Mississippi officials, "cited John Marshall's opinion in the Georgia lands case wherein he said the Court could not look into the motives behind the votes of legislators."[48]

After the city had surrendered its lease on one pool (to the local YMCA, which operated it as a whites-only private facility) and closed the other four, black petitioners brought a class action that sought to compel the city to reopen the pools and run them on a desegregated basis. The federal district court denied relief to them, and the court of appeals, while noting the racial basis for the closure, nevertheless affirmed the district court ruling. The case came to the Court during the 1970 term.

The conference was an argumentative one. Burger claimed that the closing was "racially motivated," that the city could not abolish public schools, and that "line drawing was difficult," but he was reluctant to talk about reversal. Black, supported by Harlan, argued that this matter "entailed" city policy making, and, in the absence of explicit conflict with the Fourteenth Amendment, he voted to affirm the court of appeals. Douglas, joined by Brennan, would have reversed, for he was in agreement with the dissenters in the court of appeals.[49]

Thurgood Marhsall argued that *Brown's* logic extended to swimming pools; the city could not "abolish" them. He was for reversal. Black immediately jumped in to disagree with Marshall, claiming that "nothing in *Brown* said [states] could not abolish public schools." Although Potter Stewart seemed concerned about the impact of earlier equal protection cases, he too joined Black in a vote to affirm. White strongly supported Douglas's position; he saw the Jackson officials' decision to close the pools not as economically driven, but as "racially motivated." Harry Blackmun, like Burger, his friend from Minnesota, struggled with this "difficult case," considering the economic issue as well as the equal protection issue. Douglas noted that "logically he would reverse. He was inclined both ways." Blackmun reserved his vote and passed. Burger, evidently, was the last to speak. He was "close to the line." Cities, he noted, "can be relieved of burdens for economic reasons." The final question was: Were the swimming pools a "mandatory public service"? Black's opponents' point was not that the government could not close schools, swimming pools, or parks, but that it could not do so with the deliberate and sole intention of discriminating against social minorities. Indeed, the Court, with Black writing the majority opinion, ruled against a Prince Edward County, Virginia, school board on precisely those grounds.[50]

Given the views presented in conference, Black, Harlan, Stewart, and Burger either had voiced "affirmance" positions or were leaning in that direction, while Douglas, Brennan, Marshall, and White held strong "reverse" views. Given the 4 to 4 deadlock, newly appointed Harry Blackmun was the key to the Court's final judgment. Black was assigned the task of writing for the affirmers and began a series of conversations with Blackmun. By February 1971, Blackmun was about ready to join Black's side. Blackmun wrote to him that the case was "one of the most troublesome ones of the 1970 Term," for he saw "persuasive arguments on each side." However, "for the moment," Blackmun was joining Black's proposed affirmance. His commitment was "tentative" because he wanted to read Marshall's dissent and give that and other dissents "due consideration before casting a final vote."[51]

After Blackmun again wrote to Black about a 1961 school integration decision, Black responded in a letter written on February 16, 1971: "If I had ever entertained an idea that any part of the decision in that case would stand for the principle that the United States Constittution compels a state to tax its citizens to run public schools, I would never have voted to affirm the judgment. I cannot believe . . . that you or I would hold that a majority of the lifetime judges of this Court could compel the state to operate public schools." Black said that the "same rule" would apply with even greater force "to a situation where for any reason, . . . good or bad, . . . a state through its legislature decided not to tax its people to operate swimming pools." For Black, it was intolerable to think that "a majority [of five] of our Court" could force a city to be "locked in" to providing public swimming pools when the city officials did not believe that the policy was a good one.[52]

Ultimately, Blackmun and Burger joined the Black opinion, but each wrote his own concurring opinion.[53] In all, there were five written opinions in *Palmer:* Black for the Court; Burger and Blackmun concurring; and Douglas, White, and Marshall each dissenting.

Black's opinion rejected the contention that closing the pools had deprived black petitioners of the Fourteenth Amendment's guarantee of equal protection. The amendment did not "purport to impose an affirmative duty on a State to begin to operate or to continue to operate swimming pools." Because the petitioners could not show that closing the pools to all "denied equal protection to Negroes, we must agree with the courts below and affirm." Black also rejected the argument that the Court should examine the motives of the legislators, and he concluded by stating, once again, that "cities [cannot] be forced by five lifetime judges to construct or refurbish swimming pools which they choose not to operate for any reason, sound or unsound."[54]

Douglas in his dissent asserted that the Ninth Amendment, which states that "the enumeration in the Constitution, of certain rights, shall not be construed to deny or disparage others retained by the people," had a bearing on the problem. He wrote that the "right of the people to education or to work or to recreation by swimming or otherwise . . . may well be rights 'retained by the people' under the Ninth Amendment." Believing strongly that the federal courts had to intrude and end Jackson, Mississippi's "perpetuating or installing *apartheid,*" Douglas would have extended the scope of the Ninth Amendment in conjunction with the Thirteenth, Fourteenth, and Fifteenth Amendments in order to invalidate the closing of the pools.[55] Justice Brennan's comment about Bill Douglas is appropriate here. While many legal scholars have written that Brennan is a constitutional expansionist, Brennan observed, correctly, that Douglas "was way beyond me."[56] Certainly, Douglas's dissent in *Palmer* went way beyond the boundaries of equal protection for all the sitting justices.

In addition to the questions of judicial federalism and of the police powers of the states, one of the major—and controversial—federalism issues that divided the justices for a number of terms (1962–1964) clearly was that of "state action" as it came to the Court in the guise of the classic sit-in cases during the Warren Court era.[57] The brethren, torn as they were and clearly affected by events taking place in Congress as well as on the streets and in the stores throughout the South, were finally relieved of the dilemma of extending state action when Congress passed and President Johnson signed the Civil Rights Act of 1964. Other important federalism issues that were addressed by the Court after Black and Douglas took their seats on the bench were the growth of national economic power and the commerce clause, the development of the preemption doctrine by the Court, the states' limited role in social legislation, and the concept of intergovernmental immunity.

The Growth of National Power and the Commerce Clause

The commerce clause in Article I, Section 8, of the Constitution is a plenary power of Congress. Certainly, it became such a potent power after 1937, when the Court turned away from dual federalism and a restrictive view of the commerce clause and adopted the contemporary view that enabled Congress to enact legislation that touched and regulated all forms of social and economic intercourse. Black and Douglas, along with the rest of their New Deal brethren, saw to it that judicial inter-position in order to invalidate national legislation based on the commerce clause ceased. Instead, these jurists and their colleagues supported acts of Congress that were based on a broad interpretation of the commerce clause. The high point of the newly constituted Roosevelt Court's support for the potency of the congressional powers inherent in the commerce clause were two cases that came to the Stone Court during the 1941 and 1942 terms, *United States* v. *Darby Lumber Company* and *Wickard* v. *Filburn.*[58]

Darby overruled *Hammer* v. *Dagenhart,* a 1918 opinion of the laissez-faire Court that had invalidated the 1916 Child Labor Act, a congressional effort to curb the evils of child labor based on the commerce clause.[59] Holmes dissented in *Dagenhart,* saying in part what Black would echo years later: "I had thought [the exercise of the commerce power] was for consideration of Congress alone and that this Court always had disavowed the right to intrude its judgment upon questions of policies or morals."[60] The Roosevelt administration, strongly supported by Senator Hugo Black of Alabama, introduced the Fair Labor Standards Act (FLSA) in 1937. It was a national effort to control the exploitation of workers and to eliminate sub-standard labor conditions by legislating a minimum wage and maximum working hours. The act's provisions prohibited goods from moving in interstate commerce if the employer did not pay the minimum wage or pay overtime.

The question for the Court was whether Congress had the power to prohibit the movement in interstate commerce of goods that were made in violation of the FLSA. The Court unanimously answered that Congress could reach into intrastate activities such as wages and hours of employment that had an impact on commerce. Writing for the Court, Stone said that "whatever their motive and purpose, regu-lations of commerce which do not infringe some constitutional prohibition are within the plenary power conferred upon Congress by the Constitution."[61]

Hugo Black, ever vigilant with respect to the possibility of federal judicial intru-sion, had objected to an early draft of Stone's opinion in which Stone had written that the Fifth Amendment objections to the FSLA in *Darby* were rejected because there had been no "contention" developed in the proceedings that the legislation was "unfair or oppressive." Black quickly wrote to Stone: "The inference is left that had we *found* the wage rate 'unfair or oppressive,' we would hold the law offended the due process clause. I would not agree to such a conclusion were it announced. In fact, so far as the due process clause of the Fifth Amendment is concerned, I am unable to see its application to an act properly coming within the commerce power."[62] The opinion handed down did not have that implication. As Douglas wrote, years after *Darby* was announced, "[In *Darby,*] the Court returned to the philosophy of [John Marshall and Oliver W. Holmes]. . . . Congress once more had the power to stand astride the stream of commerce and impose terms and condi-tions on those who were producing goods which after manufacture would enter that stream."[63]

This broad-based power of commerce became, if anything, even clearer the following term when the brethren decided *Wickard* v. *Filburn.* Again, the Court unanimously validated a broad use of the commerce clause by the national legislature. The Agriculture Adjustment Act gave a wheat acreage allotment to Filburn, a farmer in Ohio. He sowed and harvested more than his allotted amount and was hit with a monetary penalty of $117.11. He argued that the excess was for his own consumption and that the act was unconstitutional because the commerce clause cannot control the planting of goods that would not enter interstate commerce.

In a unanimous opinion, written by Jackson, the Court validated a congressional interpretation of the commerce clause that reached, in Douglas's words, "its outward limits."[64] Jackson noted that "home-grown wheat . . . competes with wheat in commerce. . . . Congress may properly have considered that wheat consumed on the farm where grown, if wholly outside the scheme of regulation, would have a substantial effect in defeating and obstructing its purpose to stimulate trade therein at increased prices."[65] If Congress determined that such home-grown wheat had an impact on the price and the other marketing conditions that affected the wheat that moved in commerce—and it had so determined—then it would come under the control of the acreage regulations of the Agriculture Adjustment Act.

Since these watershed cases, as already noted, the commerce clause has been used by Congress to end segregation in places of public accommodation,[66] to eradicate loan-sharking activities[67] or to try to control crime,[68] and to continue the effort, as will be seen later in the chapter, to ensure that a fair minimum wage exists throughout the federal system. The brethren have validated all congressional uses of the commerce clause since the Stone Court rulings.

The Preemption Doctrine

The justices of the Court have accepted that in a federal system national and state legislation can overlap. Unless an "undue burden"[69] is created by the state law on the federal system, state laws can coexist side-by-side with national legislation.[70] There is, however, some legislation that is exclusively national, and, given the supremacy clause of Article VI, these national laws have to supersede any state laws that attempt to establish public policy in the same arena.

The preemption doctrine identified with such congressional exclusivity has developed since Black's and Douglas's ascension to the Court. Typically, Congress does not go about labeling legislation as preemptive; it is found to be so by the Court as it reacts to cases and controversies. The concept is "one of the primary judicial vehicles for shaping federalism. . . . It serves to define spheres of governmental authority within the federal system."[71] When Congress legislates in an area, especially in foreign relations, and when there is litigation, it is then that the brethren determine whether the legislation is exclusively national. If it is such a statute, based on a judicial view of the legislators' intent or an understanding of the statute's legislative history, the Court will conclude that the national law supersedes, "occupies the field," or "pre-empts" all existing state laws. Two cases that illustrate the development of the doctrine after 1937 are *Hines* v. *Davidowitz* (1941) and *Pennsylvania* v. *Nelson.*[72]

In *Hines,* the Court considered a Pennsylvania statute that required the registration of all aliens when, at the same time, the congressionally passed Alien Registration Act of 1940 (the Smith Act) was the law of the land. Did the act of Congress preempt the field to the total exclusion of all state laws, such as Pennsylvania's? Justice Black concluded for the Court that because of the "full . . . superior . . . and exclusive responsibility . . . of the national power in the general field of foreign affairs, including power over immigration, naturalization, and deportation," the Smith Act preempted all state laws. The important consideration was Congress's intent. The Court concluded, looking at the history of the policy issue, that Congress wanted a "single, integrated and all-embracing system" for registering aliens; therefore, "the law of the state . . . cannot be enforced" and "must yield" to the national law.[73]

Steve Nelson was a leader of the American Communist party who was arrested in Pennsylvania for having violated the Pennsylvania Sedition Act. The Pennsylvania Supreme Court had reversed his conviction because it felt that the 1940 Smith Act had preempted the field. In *Pennsylvania* v. *Nelson,* the state petitioned the Supreme Court, posing the question of whether the Smith Act's prohibitions (and penalties) for advocating seditious action preempted the Pennsylvania statute. At the November 18, 1955, conference session, Warren raised the basic question, "Has the U.S. superseded this state act?" He believed that it had and voted to affirm, as did Black, Douglas, and Frankfurter. Although briefly stalemated at 4 to 4 because Clark decided that the two sets of laws could "live together," the Court finally voted 6 to 3 to affirm the judgment of the Pennsylvania Supreme Court.[74]

Chief Justice Earl Warren, speaking for the majority, concluded that the Smith Act preempted the field, and therefore the Pennsylvania Act was invalid. Nelson's conviction was set aside. Since "sedition against the United States is not a local offense [but] an offense against the Nation," and, given a "Congressional plan which makes it reasonable to determine that no room has been left for the states to supplement [the Smith Act]," Warren wrote, the national legislation "occupied the field to the exclusion of state legislation."

Given the judicial determination of a national law's preemption, as in *Hines* and *Pennsylvania,* the justices then had to decide whether the state statutes, while not necessarily in direct conflict with the national legislation, by their very existence might hinder the national policy.[75]

Interstate Travel

The right to travel from one state to another has generally been seen as one of the benefits of the federal system. Article IV of the Constitution was written expressly to illuminate the "full faith, credit, privileges and immunities" that citizens retained if they moved from one state to another. Many of the federal judges have seen it, in Douglas's words, as a "basic 'liberty' of which the citizen cannot be deprived without due process of law. . . . It is a privilege of national citizenship."[76] While the Supreme Court heard cases about this issue before 1937,[77] two post–Court-packing cases, *Edwards* v. *California* (1941) and *Shapiro* v. *Thompson* (1969), serve to illustrate how the Supreme Court has dealt with this issue of federalism.

In December 1939, Edwards left California and traveled to Spur, Texas, where he picked up his unemployed brother-in-law and drove with him back to California. Once in California, the brother-in-law received assistance from the Farm Security Administration. Edwards, however, had violated a California statute that made it a misdemeanor offense to bring an indigent nonresident into California. Convicted in state court, Edwards appealed his conviction on constitutional grounds. The Supreme Court heard the case during its 1940 term. The justices were concerned about the definition of indigent. It was undefined, noted Douglas, because the state's attorney general had not disputed the brother-in-law's indigency. "There was nothing to show he was unemployable or impaired in body or mind."[78] Although Chief Justice Stone argued that travel was one of the few "privileges and immunities" of national citizenship still protected by the Constitution, the Court rescheduled argument for the next term so that the state's attorney general could participate.

When the Court next discussed the issue, on October 25, 1941, Stone urged the conference to accept the view that "it is interstate commerce for a person to pass from state to state." "Arguably," he said, such travel "is a right of citizenship [and therefore the California statute] clearly is a violation of the commerce clause." While the state can regulate the behavior of persons within its jurisdiction, "not here," he concluded, calling for reversal of the statute. All the brethren but Roberts agreed with the chief; Roberts believed that the statute should stand "on the ground that the statute is regulating the conduct of its citizens," though, Douglas noted, "he would write it narrowly." However, the eight justices in the majority split over the rationale for reversal. Jackson would have accepted either Fourteenth Amendment "privileges and immunities" or "commerce grounds"; Frankfurter, Stone, and Reed were for overturning on commerce grounds, and Murphy, Byrnes, Douglas, and Black were for overturning on Fourteenth Amendment grounds.[79]

Given the breakdown of positions on the question, Byrnes was assigned the task of writing the opinion for the Court. Byrnes, however, soon had a change of heart and, in a memorandum to the conference, indicated that he had moved away from the constitutional justification and was adopting the commerce clause rationale for overturn. He believed that "as a practical advantage," it would be better to go the safer commerce route.[80]

As a new sitting justice, James Byrnes had been "helped" in his decision by Chief Justice Stone. Stone had written to him, on November 1, 1941, that the "Court had held over and over again" that the commerce clause allows a person to move from state to state. Furthermore, warned Stone, if Byrnes were to write on Fourteenth Amendment grounds, he would be involved in a "construction of that clause which has been repeatedly rejected for more than half a century and [which would] require an extension of the clause in a way which, in the future, and with a changed complexion of the Court, might well expose our constitutional system to dangers to which it has been exposed in the last fifty years through the over-expansion and refinement of the due process and equal protection clauses."[81]

Byrnes wrote the opinion for the Court on commerce grounds. He wrote, for the majority, that a single state cannot "isolate itself from difficulties common to all of them by restraining the transportation of persons and property across its borders."[82] Jackson wrote a separate concurring opinion. Douglas wrote to Byrnes on November 14, 1941, "[while I] would stand on my head to join with you, . . . I finally concluded . . . I cannot [for] there is a fundamental constitutional right here which we must meet."[83]

Joined by his friend Hugo Black and by Frank Murphy, Douglas concurred but developed a constitutional judgment for overturn: the seldom used privileges and immunities clause of the Fourteenth Amendment. The three justices were of the opinion that "the right of persons to move freely from state to state occupies a more protected position in our constitutional system than does the movement of cattle, fruit, steel and coal across state lines. [This right] is an incident of *national* citizenship protected by the privileges and immunities clause of the Fourteenth Amendment against state interference."[84]

This "right to travel" from state to state without restraint that Douglas and Black strongly defended in *Edwards* was to reappear in a number of guises (in civil rights and Communist party cases in particular) during Earl Warren's tenure as chief justice.[85] *Shapiro* v. *Thompson* and the accompanying cases heard during the 1967 and 1968 terms of the Court found the brethren split *initially* 6 to 3 on the question of whether a state could restrict the movement of persons into its jurisdiction by denying welfare payments to anyone who had resided in the jurisdiction for less than one year. Almost three decades after *Edwards*, Black (along with Warren) found himself in fundamental disagreement with Douglas and the majority of the Court.

Shapiro involved appeals from the decisions of three federal district courts in Connecticut, Pennsylvania, and the District of Columbia. All three courts had ruled that local statutes denying welfare assistance to residents who had lived in these areas for less than a year were unconstitutional. In each case, there were distinctions drawn between those who had resided for more than one year and those who had resided for less than one year. The petitioners, who had been denied welfare assistance because of their recent arrival in Connecticut, Pennsylvania, or the District of Columbia, claimed that they were being deprived of the equal protection of the laws guaranteed to all persons by the Fourteenth Amendment.

Vivian Marie Thompson, a nineteen-year-old unwed mother, was pregnant with a second child when she moved from Massachusetts to Connecticut to live with her mother in August 1966. In November 1966, she was denied welfare assistance solely on the ground that she had not lived in the state for a year before her application was filed. The lower federal court ruled that the Connecticut statute was unconstitutional because it violated the equal protection clause of the Fourteenth Amendment and because it had "a chilling effect on the right to travel."[86] Essentially, two basic constitutional issues were raised in all three federal courts: congressional use of the commerce clause, and the scope of the due process and equal protection clauses in the Constitution.

The cases first came to the Court during the 1967 term. Chief Justice Warren argued for the constitutionality of the local residency statutes. Contending that the congressional Social Security Act permitted the one-year residency requirement, he said he could not "see how I can say that the federal statute is unconstitutional."[87] Black, Harlan, Brennan, Stewart, and White joined with the chief in this initial cut at the issues. Douglas argued, in dissent, that there was the right to travel, which the states did not have the constitutional authority to block. He was joined by Fortas and Marshall. Given the 6 to 3 breakdown, Warren assigned the writing of *Shaprio* to himself and, as he argued in the conference session, relied entirely on an interpretation of the Social Security Act to overturn the lower federal courts.

While Warren was concerned about the poor and the destitute, his good intentions could not justify overriding a congressional statute. Congress's purpose in allowing the states to develop durational residence requirements was an appropriate one. Warren wrote in his draft, "We cannot ignore these legislative realities in assessing the validity of the congressional decision to authorize the duration residence requirements challenged in these cases." Further, given that Congress has plenary power in the area of commerce, it could delegate to the states the authority to regulate commerce in the form of these durational residence requirements. Indeed, the welfare recipients were not restricted from moving in interstate commerce. They were "still free to move from state to state and to establish residence wherever they please." Finally, Warren rejected the Fourteenth Amendment argument, for there was "nothing inherently suspect, arbitrary or invidious about the durational residence requirements." Given the presence of rational legislative purpose, Warren's draft opinion concluded with the order to overturn the federal court judgments in the three cases.[88]

Douglas wrote a short dissent. Fortas wrote a much longer one in which he argued that the petitioners were being denied the right to travel and that the residence requirements invidiously discriminated between wealthy and poor. Brennan, at this point, demonstrating again the fluidity of judicial choice, slipped away from the Warren camp and told Fortas that he could join him if the equal protection argument were dropped. (Ironically, in the 1968 term, it was Brennan who wrote the opinion for the majority upholding the lower federal court actions; the opinion was based on the equal protection clause!)[89] At the June 13, 1968, conference, the last scheduled conference of the 1967 term, Brennan formally broke away and Stewart refused to cast a vote. That left the Court deadlocked 4 to 4, and it was decided to set the cases for reargument during the 1968 term of the Court.

After the rearguments, Stewart told the brethren that he was now in favor of validating the federal court's judgments. At that conference session, on October 25, 1968, the split was 5 to 3, with White passing. The majority now consisted of Brennan, Douglas, Fortas, Marshall, and Stewart; the three dissenters were Warren, Black, and Harlan. Brennan wrote the opinion for the majority. Rejecting the rational basis test, he instead raised the question, for the majority, of whether there was a "compelling interest" for the state and Congress to act in such a manner (establishing durational residency requirements) that persons were deprived of "fundamental rights."

Justice Stewart felt somewhat uneasy about basing the opinion on the compelling interest standard. Brennan's view, however, as expressed in an unsent memo to Stewart, was that to overturn state statutes based on the "rational basis" test "might invite a flood of challenges to ordinary economic or social legislation having no relation to the right to travel or any other underlying constitutional right." In these residency-requirement cases before the Court, Brennan concluded for the slim majority that Congress did not have the authority to compel states to create those requirements.[90]

Black, in late October 1968, then surprised Brennan by announcing that he would join the majority opinion! The octogenarian justice, however, soon changed his mind and told Brennan that he would be filing a dissent. Schwartz writes: "When his law clerks had informed him of his prior agreement to join Brennan's opinion, he did not remember it. Brennan made no attempt to get Black to change his mind."[91] (He subsequently joined in Warren's dissent.) Although Brennan tried to rewrite the majority opinion so that the chief could concur, Warren, joined by Black and Harlan, dissented. His majority views had become a minority view of these colleagues.

Brennan (and Douglas) asserted that when persons move from state to state they are "exercising a constitutional right, and any classification which serves to penalize the exercise of that right, unless shown to be necessary to promote a *compelling* governmental interest, is unconstitutional."[92] Neither the state nor Congress could justify the limitation of the right to travel freely, argued the majority opinion; therefore, even though Congress has a plenary power to regulate commerce, the congressional statute permitting the states to have durational residency requirements was unconstitutional. "Congress," concluded Brennan, "may not authorize the states to violate the equal protection clause."[93]

Warren, drawing on his ideas that had been planted in the draft majority opinion, maintained that Congress had the plenary power to authorize the states to establish such requirements if they desired. For the dissenters, the issue was, "[May] Congress create minimal residence requirements, not whether the States, acting alone, may do so." Warren pointed to a host of restrictions placed on commerce by Congress and validated by the Court. Further, Congress need show only a "rational basis" for the Court to find "that a chosen regulatory scheme is necessary to the furtherance of interstate commerce." Warren wrote that the "era is long past when this Court under the rubric of due process has reviewed the wisdom of a congressional decision that interstate commerce will be fostered by the enactment of certain regulations."[94]

By the time the Court heard *Shapiro,* Hugo Black had moved far away from the "fundamental right of national citizenship" language of his 1941 *Edwards* opinion. With the assent of most of the brethren, however, the right to travel, like the right of privacy, though not a part of the written Constitution, became a judicially created constitutional right. In that development, the federal judiciary's impact on the federal system was clearly felt. "In terms of legal impact," wrote one scholar, "no decision rendered by the Warren Court was more far-reaching than that in *Shapiro* v. *Thompson.*"[95]

Intergovernmental Immunity

In *United States* v. *Darby Lumber Company,* the Court validated the broad use of the commerce clause by Congress and legitimized the minimum wage–maximum hours legislation. The Court also minimized the impact of the Tenth Amendment as it placed its imprimatur on the piece of national legislation that expanded the plenary powers of the national legislature.[96]

In the 1938 Fair Labor Standards Act, Congress, reflecting a respect for state governments and intergovernmental immunities, excluded the United States "or any state or political subdivision of a state" from the coverage of the minimum wage–maximum hours legislation. Congressional amendments to the FLSA in recent decades, however, along with judicial declarations in cases and controversies involving these changes in the national legislation, have raised questions in the minds of many about the continuing vitality of the states in the federal system. In 1961, the national legislature had amended the FLSA so as to reach any employee "in an enterprise engaged in commerce or in the production of goods for commerce." In 1966, Congress added to the list those employees "engaged in the operation of a hospital, . . . an elementary, a secondary, or an institution of higher learning," and the exemption that states and their local subdivisions had received in the 1938 legislation was removed.

Two years later, the justices heard *Maryland* v. *Wirtz,* a case involving Congress's extension of the FLSA's wage and hour provisions to employees in state-operated institutions, such as hospitals and public schools.[97] After a three-judge federal district court validated the 1966 amendments, Maryland and twenty-seven other states appealed to the Supreme Court, arguing that Congress had unconstitutionally applied its commerce powers when it amended the 1938 act. The creation of "enterprise zones" and the placement of hospitals and schools under the scope of the commerce clause were invalid in light of the Tenth Amendment, as well as the judicially defined parameters of the commerce clause. These institutions, they argued, did not "have the statutorily required relationship to interstate commerce."[98]

When the Court discussed the case in conference, most of the justices took the position voiced by Warren and Harlan. Warren saw it as a case in which Congress was regulating activities "affecting commerce." And while Harlan was concerned about the impact of the FLSA amendments on state government activities, he, too, acknowledged that Congress had a rational basis for passing the amendments. "Something should be said," he stated in conference, "which recognizes the difficulties of possible interference with the functions of state governments." After stating his concern, however, he concluded that there was a "rational basis" for the congressional amendment that extended the wage coverage to state and local employees.[99]

Stewart and Douglas were strongly opposed to the congressional amendments because of their adverse impact on federalism. (When the opinion came down, the two of them dissented, in a strong opinion written by Douglas, from the majority opinion written by Harlan.) Stewart said in conference that there was "no problem of the reach of the commerce clause to hospitals and schools. But, the thrust of the S[olicitor] G[eneral]'s argument bothers me—making them [states and local communities] pay time and one half."[100] Douglas saw the amendments to the FLSA interfering with the state's sovereignty in performing its governmental functions. It had an adverse impact on the "fiscal policy of the states and interfered with their traditional police powers in regulating health and education."[101]

Darby controlled the Court's decision. The FLSA was passed, wrote Harlan for the majority, in order to avoid workers' strife in the factories that sent goods into interstate commerce. If there was peace in these work places, then there would be no disruption of goods and services in interstate commerce. For Harlan, it was "clear that labor conditions in schools and hospitals can affect commerce," and, whether the hospital or school worker is an employee of the state or of a private health facility, both types of workers can legitimately be placed in an enterprise zone and their hours and wages can be regulated in order to ensure that the free flow of goods in interstate commerce continues.[102] At the end, the Court noted that while Congress's plenary power to regulate commerce was not without limits, those limits had not been reached when Congress passed the 1966 amendments to the FLSA.

Douglas, joined by Stewart, wrote in his dissent that "the utter destruction of the State as a sovereign political entity," was the hard issue the litigation raised. They concluded that because of the adverse impact on state sovereignty the amendments were invalid extensions of the FLSA. "What is done here," wrote Douglas, "is a serious invasion of state sovereignty protected by the Tenth Amendment that is in my view not consistent with our constitutional federalism."[103]

Douglas admitted that the states were not immune from federal regulation under the commerce clause and that, in the past, the national government had invaded some aspects of state sovereignty; "in none of these cases, however, did the federal regulation overwhelm state fiscal policy." Clearly, Douglas and Stewart were concerned about the national government passing legislation that would "devour the essentials of state sovereignty, though that sovereignty is attested by the Tenth Amendment." Their concluding sentence illustrated their deep fears about the future vitality of state government in the federal system: "In this case, the state as a sovereign power is being seriously tampered with, potentially crippled."[104]

Douglas's reasoning in his dissent was adopted by the Court in the 1976 case of *National League of Cities* v. *Usery. Usery* invalidated a set of 1974 amendments to the FLSA that would have extended coverage to almost all state and local employees. Rehnquist's opinion for the narrow 5 to 4 majority rested on the argument that the power of the commerce clause is constrained by the Tenth Amendment. The commerce power has to yield to the Tenth Amendment when it interferes with "traditional aspects of state sovereignty."[105]

Less than a decade later, however, in the 1985 case of *Garcia* v. *San Antonio Metropolitan Transit Authority,* the Court, in a 5 to 4 opinion, overturned *Usery.*[106] For the narrow majority, Blackmun wrote that "the attempt to draw the boundaries of state regulatory immunity in terms of 'traditional governmental function' is not only unworkable but is inconsistent with established principles of federalism." In the overturn, Blackmun specifically relied on *Maryland* v. *Wirtz* and *Darby.*[107] Powell wrote in the dissent for the minority of four that they were shocked at the way the Tenth Amendment had been reduced to "meaningless rhetoric when Congress acts pursuant to the commerce clause."

During the years that Black and Douglas sat on the Court, it granted far greater deference to legislators than it had previously, including policies adopted by the states. Yet it is also clear that it sanctioned assertions of commerce and taxing and spending powers, as well as the enforcement clauses of the Civil War Amendments, by the federal government that plainly shifted the focus of decision making toward Washington and away from the states. Virtually no aspect of state activity remained untouched by federal policy.[108]

State and local officials were frustrated by federal preemption and mandates imposed from Washington. The threat that their decisions might be deemed excessive burdens on interstate commerce caused some to doubt their ability to meet increasing economic challenges. Some even doubted whether the state had a future as a viable political entity.

A number of justices, too, were worried about the possible overextension of national power at the expense of the states' autonomy and diversity, and they sometimes drew back from where the contemporary momentum seemed to be taking them. Their concern extended to federal judicial intervention as well as congressional action. Certainly, the *Younger, Evans,* and *Palmer* cases illustrated this concern.

Hugo Black was one of those concerned justices. He perceived a very real threat to "Our Federalism," that of the diminution of the states' importance until they became little more than "conquered provinces" governed by Washington. There was also a danger that well-meaning contemporary judges would forget the abuses of the past. If these well-disposed modern justices could ignore the critical importance of federalism, how much worse would it be if the Court were populated at some future time by judges like those who had served in the days of dual federalism? As he put it in a 1970 opinion, "our Constitution was not written in the sands to be washed away by each wave of new judges blown in by each successive political wind that brings new political administrations into temporary power. Rather, our Constitution was fashioned to perpetuate liberty and justice by making clear, explicit and lasting constitutional boundaries.[109]

Douglas saw no such bright line between federal judicial intervention in the proper sphere of state government action and federal judicial responsibility. The Court had the role to play under the Constitution, according to Douglas, of maintaining the personal liberties of all Americans, regardless of which state they called home or visited on business. It was Douglas who said toward the end of his life that the Constitution's guarantees were "not self-executing." Federal judges, as well as the people, had to be vigilant for "as nightfall does not come all at once, neither does oppression. In both instances there is a twilight when everything remains seemingly unchanged. And it is in such twilight that we all must be most aware of change in the air—however slight—lest we become unwitting victims of the darkness."[110]

He could not, for example, abide the use of claims to local autonomy to insulate from federal action obvious racial discrimination. He would not accept the use and abuse of local statutes, police, and courts to violate liberty when the federal laws and courts were available to remedy the abuses. To refuse to answer the call was to him a form of judicial abdication.

Yet Douglas had an important strain of respect for local autonomy amid his commitment to national action and the protection of individual rights. His fear of the "curse of bigness" extended to big government as well as big business. He had written important opinions in support of decisions on local control of land use and control of local government operations.

Even so, he knew instinctively and by personal experience that Madison had been right in warning that the greatest dangers of abuse of power were to be expected from those political bodies closest to the people. When the choice was between a risk of curtailing state or local power and a threat to individual liberty, Douglas did not hesitate.

However, there were various areas developing in which the issues were not that stark. The Court began to be called on to consider demands for the recognition of new rights and for their enforcement against state and local officials. It was a process that was extraordinarily controversial at the time, but produced protections that most Americans now take for granted.

12

The Demand for
New Constitutional Rights

I<small>T WAS NOT</small> the first time Dr. C. Lee Buxton had been a party to a case before the United States Supreme Court. Four years before, in 1961, he had been involved in litigation as a result of his advice to a couple that they should use contraceptives to avoid pregnancy. Their babies from three various pregnancies had been born with severe physical abnormalities, and all three had soon died. Buxton had reported that the problems were genetic and recommended against any further attempts by the couple to have children. The state's attorney had warned family-planning advocates that he intended to enforce the Connecticut statute making the practice of using or advising the use of contraceptives a criminal offense, even though the provision had not been enforced before that time. The couple and the physician sought a judicial declaration that the Connecticut law was unconstitutional, but the Supreme Court, in an opinion by Justice Frankfurter, avoided a ruling on the merits of that case because the state had not yet actually prosecuted anyone under the statute. The controversy was therefore speculative and nonjusticiable.

Well, so be it. Following the first Supreme Court ruling, the Connecticut Planned Parenthood League opened a center in New Haven of which Buxton (also a faculty member at the Yale Medical School) was named medical director. Buxton and the staff provided contraceptive information to married couples. The authorities were made aware of the operation, and the state's attorney made good on the threat to prosecute. Buxton and Estelle Griswold, executive director of the Planned Parenthood League in Connecticut, were convicted as accessories because they had advised married couples to violate the contraceptive law, which stated, "Any person who uses any drug, medicinal article or instrument for the purpose of preventing conception shall be fined not less than fifty dollars or imprisoned not less than sixty days nor more than one year or be both fined and imprisoned."[1] This time it would not be so easy for the Supreme Court to duck the increasingly controversial birth-control debate.

William O. Douglas had no doubt about his position in the case as he listened to his former student Thomas I. Emerson argue on behalf of the Planned Parenthood officials in late March 1965. Douglas had dissented from the 1961 decision. He eventually wrote the Court's opinion in the second case, *Griswold* v. *Connect-icut*,[2] overturning the Connecticut statute and establishing for the first time a constitutional right to privacy.

In one sense, the Supreme Court had played a role in the development of new rights for a very long time. Each time the Court rendered an opinion interpreting constitutional rights and liberties, it in effect created or redefined rights. In some situations, the interpretations were of relatively specific constitutional provisions, such as the free-press protections of the First Amendment, while in others the Court was asked to speak to rights that were said to be implied by the language of the Bill of Rights, though they were mentioned nowhere in the Constitution.

During the time that Black and Douglas served on the Court, demands for new rights increased dramatically. Sometimes the demands were calmly stated in courtrooms. Other times they were shouted in the streets, resulting in prosecutions that brought cases to their docket. In some instances, the demands came from long-abused racial minorities who insisted on decisions from the Court recognizing the rights they had so long been denied, while at other times they came from advocates of controversial causes ranging from welfare rights to access to birth control and abortions.

Probably nothing divided Black and Douglas as much as their individual reactions to these demands for new rights. Black was ever the constitutional literalist on guard against the judiciary's intrusion into what was properly a legislative domain, while Douglas was willing to creatively extend constitutional safeguards to ensure greater personal protection against governmental intrusion. On the other hand, Black participated in the legal recognition of several new rights, and Douglas, who led some of these efforts, continued to chastise his pre–New Deal predecessors for reading their own social philosophies into the Constitution. The two saw no irony in any of that behavior. As they faced these challenges, they were very much aware that, as Douglas put it, "the crises that face a democratic country under the stresses and strains of modern society are shared by judges."[3]

Although neither bowed to anyone (including each other) in his commitment to liberty, Douglas and Black saw the priorities of the Constitution and the role of the Court very differently. Those differences affected not only the battles over which particular rights were to be recognized, but also how they thought and talked about constitutional rights and liberties more generally.

Well before he replaced Louis Brandeis on the Supreme Court, Douglas was a Brandeis admirer. He had taken Brandeis's themes and used them as critical watch-words for his own public career. While at the SEC, Douglas had lived by the "curse of bigness" slogan. Big government and big business were dangerous to liberty. The other recurring Brandeis theme in Douglas's work was that the people had a "right to be let alone."[4] But Douglas took it even further. To him, the Constitution was "designed to take government off the backs of the people and make it difficult to do anything to the individual."[5] "Government exists for man, not man for government. The aim of government is security for the individual and freedom for the development of his talents."[6] Since Douglas always began with a presumption of liberty, he really did not see himself so much as defining new rights as explaining the long-standing limits to government power. Freedom was always to be presumed and government limitations on it always in need of justification.

For Douglas, the critical questions in this larger debate were four. They concerned the nature of rights, the need for change in the law (and the role of the Court in that process), the effort to protect the rights of all, and the relationship of domestic rights and human rights.

The idea of legal rights was never a narrow conception for Douglas. He began from the premise that many of our rights are natural rights, which are prior to man-made law, including the Constitution. It was the height of conceit for temporary political majorities to assume that they could simultaneously claim a constitutional heritage that traced its foundations to the belief in the natural law "rights of Englishmen" and yet reject the implication of that background by assuming that citizens possessed only those liberties enumerated in the Bill of Rights or granted by legislature.[7] In that, Douglas was more Jeffersonian than Madisonian, more committed to the statement of the primacy of liberty in the Declaration of Independence than the tamer language of the constitutional debates.

There was something of the early-twentieth-century Westerner in his expression of faith in liberty. To the man who walked the Cascades, camped by the streams, and fished the high mountain lakes, that view of freedom was a simple recognition of creation, not a reaffirmation of a church creed. Liberty was natural; its limitation an unnatural manifestation of some people's ability to gain power over others.

Beyond that, and in part because of it, Douglas had never thought that rights were to be narrowly construed. He was comfortable with the New Deal approach to liberty embodied in Roosevelt's famous "Four Freedoms" speech. In his January 1941 address, FDR had insisted on a world founded on four freedoms. The first was freedom of speech and the second free exercise of religion, but it was the third and fourth freedoms that sparked the imagination: "The third is freedom from want—which, translated into world terms, means economic understandings which will secure to every nation a healthy peacetime life for its inhabitants—everywhere in the world. The fourth is freedom from fear—which, translated into world terms, means a world-wide reduction of armaments to such a point and in such a thorough fashion that no nation will be in a position to commit an act of physical aggression against any neighbor—anywhere in the world."[8]

Douglas did not see those assertions as global pie-in-the-sky. Above all, he could not accept the idea that rights were to be so narrowly compartmentalized that liberty meant the freedom that remained in the society after all government powers had been accounted for. He wrote: "My Almanac [of Liberty] ranks freedom to eat with freedom to speak, the right to work with freedom from racial discrimination. My Almanac is concerned with the Sermon on the Mount, the United Nations, workmen's compensation, social security, as well as habeas corpus and the Fifth Amendment."[9] These were words written for a lay audience, not for lawyers. It was an audience who remembered Roosevelt's speech and who grew up with Norman Rockwell's depiction of each of the four rights in now famous paintings. Douglas never argued in case law that the freedom to eat was a constitutional right per se.

He did, however, insist that when government threatened a poor person's continued receipt of government assistance, there were serious due process questions to be considered. He never claimed that government was constitutionally obligated to find everyone a job, but he did argue vigorously that when government threatened someone's employability, by labeling the person subversive or terminating a public employee for cause, there was at least a right to due process.[10]

In the end, Douglas saw the independent judiciary as the vehicle designed to protect rights against the tendency of the establishment, the temporary majority, to narrow and even eliminate liberty in the name of property or good order. He was fully aware that the need to take on the majority in defense of liberty was not going to be popular. That went without saying. He was also aware that some of his colleagues on the bench were troubled by his willingness, even eagerness, to take on the establishment. It was partly the breadth of his definition of constitutionally protected liberty that bothered them and partly his forthright willingness to define a broad role for the Court as a political institution that produced criticism. He answered the challenge directly.

> There has been a school of thought that the less the judiciary does, the better. It is often said that judicial intrusion should be infrequent, since it is "always attended with a serious evil, namely, that the correction of legislative mistakes comes from the outside, and the people thus lose the political experience, and the moral education and stimulus that come from fighting the question out in the ordinary way, and correcting their own errors; that the effect of a participation by the judiciary in these processes is to dwarf the political capacity of the people, and to deaden its sense of moral responsibility." J. Thayer, *John Marshall* 106, 107 (1901).
>
> The late Edmond Cahn, who opposed that view, stated my philosophy. He emphasized the importance of the role that the federal judiciary was designed to play in guarding basic rights against majoritarian control. He chided the view expressed by my brother Harlan: "We are entitled to reproach the majoritarian justices of the Supreme Court . . . with straining to be reasonable when they ought to be adamant."[11]

Douglas rejected the idea that the way to protect the Court as an institution was to pretend that it did not participate in the policy-making process. It would be hypocritical to deny what everyone knew the courts did all the time. He also refused to accept the contention that it was better to allow injustice than to risk being labeled a judicial activist. Finally, he thought it both dangerous and wrong for the Court to ignore its important obligation to facilitate change in the law.

For Douglas, there were two fundamental facts that made change inevitable. First, the Constitution and the Bill of Rights are not documents written to be read narrowly. Second, precedent in the area of constitutional rights and liberties should not be a barrier to a broader interpretation of constitutional liberty. "The Constitution is a compendium, not a code," Douglas wrote, "a declaration of articles of faith, not a compilation of laws."[12] And that set of articles of faith should be read from the assumption of liberty and a presumption against constraints on freedom. There was no reason, in his view, to limit the freedoms enjoyed by Americans to those specifically mentioned in the Bill of Rights and no reason to believe that the Framers intended such a narrow reading.

But what of the fact that there were opinions by the Court refusing to read the Bill of Rights as broadly as Douglas would read them? Did the rule of precedent, *stare decisis,* not matter? Douglas answered that "precedent has small place in constitutional law."[13] In the final analysis, "it is the Constitution which we have sworn to defend, not some predecessor's interpretation of it."[14]

It was not that Douglas wanted to dispose of precedent; he simply considered that precedents must be changed or reinterpreted in light of a changing nation, and that when there was a clash between a correct understanding of constitutional liberty and the previous interpretations of those liberties, the correct constitutional understanding should prevail. "This search for a static security—in law or elsewhere—is misguided." "So far as constitutional law is concerned stare decisis must give way before the dynamic component of history." The Court ought to reexamine its decisions, and when they are found to have been in error, it should reverse them.[15]

The other argument that was sometimes made when the Court departed from an earlier and narrower interpretation of constitutional liberty was that the Court should not be seen to be changing, even if it was. Douglas the legal realist could not abide that approach, a judicial game he thought hypocritical and insulting to the intelligence of the nation. He believed that "a judiciary that discloses what it is doing and why it does it will breed understanding. And confidence based on understanding is more enduring than confidence based on awe."[16]

There was no reason, then, in Douglas's mind for failing to address claims for new rights. Indeed, the Court was obliged to do so as a part of its responsibility for maintaining liberty under the Constitution.

Above all, according to Douglas, the Constitution provides liberty for all. There was no reason to exclude racial minorities, women, the poor, or students and other minors from its protections. The fact that the Court had not historically condemned some of the injustices visited on those groups was no reason to continue to ignore their claims.

Finally, through his travels and participation in international literacy programs, Douglas came to view the way his Court interpreted constitutional liberties more as international observers saw it and with a greater eye toward the increasingly important discussion of international human rights. As an ardent anti-Communist, Douglas was convinced that only by a vigorous defense of his country's best principles could developing nations be convinced that we, not the Russians, had the best model for modern life. At the same time, Americans were citizens of the world, and other nations' citizens were free to judge them on whether Americans indeed provided the human rights generally agreed on by civilized governments.

Black could accept Douglas's eccentricities in many respects, but not in the creation of new rights. His view of law and rights was simply so different from what Black could tolerate that there was not much ground for even limited agreement. The starting point for Black was, as always, the language of the Constitution.

Black remained a positivist who looked to what the Framers had written as the source of rights, rejecting in the most vigorous terms any effort to employ a natural law approach to the interpretation of constitutional rights and liberties. He

reminded his critics that the fundamental starting point for discussions of constitutional interpretation is the fact that "our country has a written constitution." He
returned again and again to the proposition that "it is language and history that are
the crucial factors which influence me in interpreting the Constitution—not reasonableness or desirability as determined by justices of the Supreme Court."[17]

That did not mean that Black rejected all constitutional change through
Supreme Court interpretation. Indeed, he agreed with Douglas that the justices'
oath was to support the Constitution, not their predecessors' views of its meaning.
His view of precedent was rather an interesting one. While he did not consider himself constrained by constitutional precedents, he did consider himself bound by his
own prior opinions. Hence, he had a long-standing practice of citing his own primary opinion in a given area in virtually all his opinions and refusing to join an
opinion that cited a precedent case in which he had dissented.[18]

Black's literalist view also did not stop him from participating in the development of a number of new rights. He joined the Court in *NAACP* v. *Alabama*,
upholding the freedom of association. As has been seen, he was a leading proponent
of the application of all Bill of Rights protections against interference by state and
local governments. He wrote vigorously in defense of the right to vote, nowhere
mentioned in the Bill of Rights, and he was prepared to create a right for the press
to be free of defamation suits. All these were certainly considered by the Court's
observers and critics to be new rights. Even so, Black saw fundamental differences
between the new rights he helped to create and those proposed in cases during the
Warren years that he rejected.

His votes were cast for new rights, yes, but only, according to Black, those drawn
from the language of the Constitution. They were not new rights predicated on the
judge's preference or abstract notions of justice. In his view, they were either
expressly or impliedly justified by the language of the Constitution. Thus while the
right to have an attorney provided at public expense in criminal prosecutions may
not have been specified in those terms, the Sixth Amendment maintained that "in
all criminal prosecutions, the accused shall . . . have the assistance of counsel for
his defense."[19] To Black the implication was clear and directly drawn from the language.

Another influence to be considered in Black's treatment of the demands for new
rights was that he remained a southern man raised in a Populist environment who
lived by relatively traditional values. Property, particularly real estate, mattered,
and property rights could not be pushed aside merely because changing social pressures called for new ways of thinking about property. He could not see government
benefit programs in the same context as property rights. He was the former prosecutor and police court judge for whom order was important. The accused had
rights, but the community also had the authority to take such action, short of violating those rights, as was necessary to protect itself. If that meant invading privacy,
and if no language in the Constitution prevented it, then so be it.

Just as Douglas's many opinions chastising earlier judges for reading their own
philosophies into the Constitution clashed with his view of the need to respond to
legitimate claims for new rights on the other, so Black had his own inconsistencies.
While to him the connections between constitutional language and the new rights

that he was willing to recognize were clear, to many of his critics they were not. It was in part that difference in perspective that earned Black the judicial activist label that he detested and never understood. But there was more.

From the beginning, when Black referred to the Bill of Rights he included only the first eight amendments, yet others always made reference to the first nine amendments. The question was whether Black could really have it both ways. Could he say that the Bill of Rights defined the rights protected by the due process clause and yet read out of the Bill of Rights the provision specifically placed there to prevent too narrow a view of the rights retained by the people?

In any case, Black concluded that Douglas "had left him" during the late 1960s, and one of the critical points of cleavage was the matter of new rights.[20] Still, the stresses were not between Black and Douglas alone, but were felt by other members of the Court as well. Those tensions were manifest in cases seeking a right to privacy, in those demanding a new equal protection, in calls for protections for what some people call the new property, and in disputes about new dimensions to freedom of expression.

The Right to Privacy

The history of the Court is filled with irony, and nowhere is that better illustrated than in the development of the right to privacy. First, what was perhaps Douglas's most important opinion is not even mentioned in either volume of his autobiography. Then there is the behavior of Felix Frankfurter, one of the Court's most ardent advocates of a broad reading of privacy under the Fourth Amendment, who ducked the sexual-privacy question in *Poe* v. *Ullman*. At the same time, the man who (to date at least) has been considered the modern Court's most distinguished conservative, John Marshall Harlan II, was one of the most committed advocates of the right to privacy and in such sweeping terms that his *Poe* dissent would have suited Frank Murphy, arguably the most liberal of modern justices, very nicely! The *Griswold* decision continues to be one of the more controversial pronouncements to come from the Court during the time that Black and Douglas served there, and yet even some of its severest critics are not ready to tell the public and the legal community that they would overturn that case. For example, former federal judge Robert Bork told Senate Judiciary Committee members considering his nomination to the Supreme Court in 1987 that he would uphold the right to privacy, notwithstanding his attacks on the *Griswold* ruling, because it was now "settled law."

It seems clear that much of the consternation over the decision came from the fact that it was at the heart of what came to be known as the sexual revolution. In truth, there was little new in the debate over whether there existed a constititional right to privacy, except the idea that the right, if it existed, would protect decisions regarding sexuality. At heart, the *Griswold* case was a battle by family-planning organizations to take advantage of developing medical technology that would make birth control an important part of American life. Even the open discussion of the subject was difficult, let alone the contemplation of the changes that might occur in American society if sexuality and its consequences were reevaluated. The "pill" was on its way and would soon be in wide use. Within three years, the controversial papal encyclical *Humanitae Vitae* would issue from Rome condemning artificial means of birth control. Communities debated the possibility of sex education in the public schools. This sexual revolution was almost as frightening for many Americans as the one they feared was brewing during the long hot summers in the nation's inner cities.

Before the birth-control cases, the Supreme Court had discussed privacy in its debates over constitutional criminal procedures and disputes about the constitutional status of the family. Considerations of constitutionally protected privacy had been common in cases challenging searches and seizures for years. Indeed, the Brandeis opinion from which Douglas drew his oft-repeated belief in the right to be let alone came from a case concerning wiretaps by federal agents seeking convictions of bootleggers during Prohibition. Brandeis did not, however, limit his criticism of invasions of privacy to criminal investigations in general or wiretaps in particular. He spoke broadly of the "right to be let alone" as "the most comprehensive of rights and the right most valued by civilized men." His definition of the scope of that right of privacy was substantial. He wrote, "To protect that right, every unjustifiable intrusion by the government upon the privacy of the individual, whatever the means employed, must be deemed a violation of the fourth Amendment." Such actions were not to be justified in the absence of a warrant. He was worried not merely that government would become a criminal because it broke the law to enforce it, but also by the more general problem that some day authorities might use various devices to "expose to a jury the most intimate occurrences of the home."[21]

Justice Murphy had taken the Court, including Black and Douglas, to task in his 1942 dissent in *Goldman* v. *United States,* challenging the conclusion that the use of a detectaphone was constitutionally permissible. Murphy insisted that there "is [a] right of personal privacy guaranteed by the Fourth Amendment."[22] While Douglas did not come to his views on search and seizure immediately on entering the Court, by 1952 he had made up his mind that there was a right to privacy protected by the Fourth and Fourteenth Amendments that protected citizens against a wide variety of government abuses. In so doing, he acknowledged that he had been wrong in his early position, that Murphy had been correct in *Goldman,* and that Brandeis had stated the principal properly in his *Olmstead* dissent.

Douglas quickly took privacy beyond the criminal context. It was also in 1952 that he issued an opinion that some observers thought one of this most important in a case concerning loudspeakers on public buses. The District of Columbia Public Utilities Commission refused to block a decision by the Capital Transit Company to place speakers in its buses that would broadcast a particular radio station's programming. A small number of passengers protested the decision, but the Supreme Court upheld the ruling. Douglas dissented on grounds that the unconsenting passengers were a captive audience. The constitutional ground for his argument was that "liberty in the constitutional sense must mean more than freedom from unlawful governmental restraint; it must include privacy as well, if it is to be a repository of freedom. The right to be let alone is the beginning of all freedom."[23]

At the heart of his discussion of privacy was the idea that government simply had no business in people's lives absent a very strong justification. He saw in the invasion of privacy an implied judgment about the capacity of the individual to make the right decisions. He wrote, "The strength of our system is in the dignity, the resourcefulness, and the independence of our people. Our confidence is in their ability as individuals to make the wisest choices. That system cannot flourish if regimentation takes hold. The right of privacy, today violated, is a powerful deterrent to any one who would control men's minds."[24]

The reactions to Douglas's opinion were enthusiastic. Black, who was adamantly opposed to any right to privacy, nevertheless wrote to Douglas, "I think that your dissent in this case is one of the best pieces of writing you have ever done—I regret that my own consitutional ideas prevent my agreeing with you."[25] He even received fan mail from Groucho Marx.[26]

Douglas continued to press the point that the right of privacy could not be limited to criminal proceedings. In a 1959 opinion by Felix Frankfurter, the Court refused to apply the Fourth Amendment to bar a city health inspector from entering a home without a warrant. Douglas dissented.[27] Naturally, he was not concerned with protecting a resident whose home may have been a breeding ground for rats. What did matter was the ability of the state to enter a home without any constraint. That, he thought, was the point of the Fourth Amendment. He argued that it was not designed for the purpose of preventing self-incrimination but to secure the right of privacy. In that, as in so many things, Douglas followed Brandeis. Brandeis had claimed that the search of a home was barred by the Fourth Amendment right of privacy, but the use of any evidence that might be found was prohibited by protections against self-incrimination in the Fifth Amendment.

Discussions about protecting family decisions from government intrusion had occurred long before these criminal justice–related discussions of privacy. In the 1920s, the Court had twice issued opinions stating that the liberty protected by the due process clause of the Fourteenth Amendment included protection for people in their decisions to marry and have children, and in their judgments about how their children were to be raised.[28] There was one contrary ruling, in which Justice Holmes wrote for the Court upholding a Virginia law permitting mental-health officials to order the sterilization of mental patients.[29] It was not a precedent that anyone cared to cite in postwar America, after German war criminals had cited that case in their defense at Nuremberg.

Douglas's first foray in this field came in an opinion for the Court in *Skinner* v. *Oklahoma,* a case concerning an Oklahoma law permitting sterilization for repeat offenders of crimes of moral turpitude. The Court held that the law was discriminatory in that it permitted sterilization as a penalty for larceny, including the theft of chickens involved in the *Skinner* case, but not for such crimes as embezzlement. In the opinion, though, Douglas spoke of the right to marry and have children as one of the most fundamental in the panoply of American freedoms. "Marriage and procreation," he wrote, "are fundamental to the very existence and survival of the race."[30]

Douglas spoke even more broadly about this freedom in his writings during the 1950s. He defined three broad classes of rights in *The Rights of the People,* those associated with freedom of expression, those concerned with protection against military and wartime abuses, and those that he thought fit a category best described by Brandeis's "right to be let alone." The first protection in the last category was the right to privacy, which Douglas described as "drawing substance from several provisions of the Constitution, including the First, Fourth, and Fifth Amendments." Speaking of the several rights that fit under the rubric of the right to be let alone, Douglas added: "Some are written explicitly into the Constitution. Others are to be implied. The penumbra of the Bill of Rights reflects human rights which, though not explicit, are implied from the very nature of man as a child of God."[31]

By the time the contraceptive cases came to the Court in the 1960s, then, Douglas and his brethren debated the claims against a considerable history of privacy discussions. But it was in those cases that the Court actually held that there was a constitutional right to privacy.

In the conference on the first Connecticut birth-control case, *Poe* v. *Ullman,* there was an interesting array of positions on whether to decide contraceptive cases at all, as well as on the core question of a right to privacy. Warren and Frankfurter led the argument for dismissal, which was ultimately the position the majority took. Black supported the state but observed that he did not "think [the state] could get doctor as aider and abetter even if the patient uses [contraceptives]. [The] first amendment would protect [him]." Black considered the attempt to punish a doctor for merely talking with a patient about birth control a bald violation of freedom of speech. Douglas rejected the idea that the case could be dismissed on grounds that the law had not been enforced. It had, he said, been used earlier to get rid of family-planning clinics. He preferred to strike the statute as unconstitutional. The most interesting arguments came from the Court's leading conservative, John Marshall Harlan, who insisted that they had "no business dismissing this case." "I think [this] statute is egregiously unconstitutional on its face. [The] argument submerged the real constitutional question. Due process has substantive content for me. . . . The 'right to be let alone' is embodied in due process despite broad powers to legislate in area of health. There are limits. This is more offensive to 'right to be let alone' than anything possible could be." Harlan's eventual dissent was a powerful statement on the need to recognize the right to privacy. But it was clear that a majority of the Court was unlikely to come around to his broad reading of due process with no connection to any particular provision of the Bill of Rights.[32]

When the *Griswold* case came back to the Court, there was no longer an opportunity to escape the ruling on privacy. While it was clear at the conference that there was a majority for striking the Connecticut law, there was considerable diversity among the justices on just how to do it. Warren could not accept the assertion that the doctors were protected by the First Amendment. He concluded that "this is [the] most confidential relationship in our society, has to be clear cut and it isn't." In sum, the statute was "not narrowly enough written." Black could accept the idea that vagueness in a criminal law was a due process violation, but he could find no evidence that the law was vague. Neither could he accept the claim that the case implicated the First Amendment–protected freedom of association, saying, "[The] right of association is for me [a] right of assembly and [the right] of husband and wife to assemble in bed is [a] new right of assembly to me."[33]

Douglas answered that the "right of association is more than a right of assembly.

It's a right to join with, to associate with. The right to send child to a religious school is on the periphery. . . . We've said right to travel is in radiation of First Amendment and so is the right of association. Nothing more personal than this relationship and if on the periphery it's within First Amendment protection."

Another of the Court's conservatives, Tom Clark, disagreed with Black and joined Douglas's argument. There is "a right to marry, maintain a home, have a family." Black countered that in his opinion, "a state can abolish marriage." Clark answered, in the Brandeis tradition, "This is an area where [we] have [a] right to be let alone." Douglas noted that Clark "prefers that ground for reversal."

Goldberg found "no compelling reason in that circumstance justifying the statute." He considered the earlier family decisions pertinent, finding all these matters "related to 1st amendment rights of association." Stewart countered that he could not "find anything in 1, 2, 4, 5, 9 or other amendments," and he would have to affirm.

Douglas, who was given the assignment to write for the Court, considered the conference discussion and concluded that the greatest agreement in the Court's position focused on First Amendment freedom of association claims. He wrote his first draft accordingly. It was from start to finish a First Amendment freedom of association argument, beginning from the proposition that the Court had held in 1958 that the First Amendment implies a right of freedom of association and privacy in those associations.[34] No association is more fundamental or more important to the society than the marital relationship.

When he completed the work, Douglas sent the draft on to Brennan for comment. Brennan responded with a lengthy letter encouraging Douglas to expand his approach and not pin the case to the First Amendment alone. Douglas took virtually all of Brennan's suggestions and dramatically expanded the opinion. In fact, he placed Brennan's letter almost verbatim just before the conclusion of his original opinion. The finished opinion was more in line with his own earlier arguments, contending that just as the First Amendment implied freedom of association, so there was a constitutionally protected right to privacy, the foundations for which were found in several sections of the Bill of Rights. Citing cases in several fields, the Douglas–Brennan opinion asserted that the specific amendments had been read by the Court to protect a wide variety of unstated but clearly implied freedoms. The "specific guarantees in the Bill of Rights have penumbras formed by emanations from those guarantees that help give them life and substance"; and, more specifically, "[v]arious guarantees create zones of privacy."[35] In particular, it found protection for privacy in the First Amendment freedom of association; the Third Amendment ban on quartering troops without permission of the home owner; the Fourth Amendment right "to be secure in their persons, houses, papers, and effects, against unreasonable searches and seizures"; the Fifth Amendment protection against self-incrimination; and the Ninth Amendment provision that "the enumeration in the Constitution, of certain rights, shall not be construed to deny or disparage others retained by the people." In the end, though, the opinion returns to the theme of the most important association: "We deal with a right of privacy older than the Bill of Rights—older than our political parties, older than our school system. Marriage is a coming together for better or for worse, hopefully enduring, and intimate to the degree of being sacred. It is an association that promotes a way of life, not causes; a harmony in living, not political faiths; a bilateral loyalty, not commercial or social projects. Yet it is for as noble a purpose as any involved in our prior decisions."[36]

There was another matter at play in the development of the *Griswold* opinion. As Justice Goldberg told the story, he had originally intended merely to join Douglas's majority opinion, but Earl Warren came to see him and changed his mind. It seems that Warren and Douglas had been at odds for some time, and Warren was reluctant to join the Douglas majority opinion. Since there were only four votes for the Court's opinion, though there was a clear majority to strike down the statute, if Warren joined White's concurrence, which was his original intention, then Douglas's opinion would be only a plurality, leaving serious doubt about the Court's support for the right to privacy. Goldberg offered to write a concurrence in which Warren could join that would stress the Ninth Amendment argument. Warren agreed. Since Goldberg began by announcing that he joined the opinion of the Court, it was possible to garner a majority supporting Douglas without Warren having to join him directly.

Douglas and Warren had indeed had some run-ins. In fact, Warren ultimately joined both the Douglas and Goldberg opinions. However, their relationship seemed to improve as the 1964 term ended. On the day *Griswold* was announced, Douglas even wrote to Warren and encouraged him to visit his cabin at Goose Prairie.

Goldberg's opinion emphasizing the Ninth Amendment prompted a strong reponse from Hugo Black, in addition to Black's reproach to Douglas. For good measure, Black also took on White and Harlan, whose separate concurrences raised the kind of broad application of the due process clause that triggered Hugo's worst fears of an abusive judiciary. In fact, Black was considerably rougher on the concurring justices than he was on the majority opinion.

For Black, like Stewart, the Connecticut statute was bad and even stupid, but that was not enough. "I like my privacy as well as the next one," Black wrote, "but I am nevertheless compelled to admit that government has a right to invade it unless prohibited by some specific constitutional provision."[37] There were only two such provisions referred to by the Court that Black took seriously. The first was the claim that privacy was protected by the First Amendment. While he would have agreed that the statute breached the First Amendment if all that had been involved was simply counseling by the physician, Black found that in the operation of the clinics and distribution of the contraceptives there was action, not merely speech. Therefore, the freedom of speech did not apply. As to the use of the Fourth Amendment, Black once again rejected what he saw as the ongoing attempt by members of the Court to transform what was a clear and specific prohibition against crime-related search and seizure abuses into a general right of privacy.

In the end, the critical point was that judges had no business departing from the clear language of the Constitution. It was that general lesson, Black concluded, that the concurring justices seemed particularly unwilling to comprehend. After all, at least Douglas had tried to pin the so-called right to privacy to specific provisions of the Bill of Rights, unconvincing though he may have been in that effort. "My disagreement with the Court's opinion holding that there is such a violation here is a narrow one, relating to the application of the First Amendment to the facts and circumstances of this particular case. But my disagreement with Brothers Harlan, White and Goldberg is more basic."[38]

White and Harlan were guilty of the worst sins of the past, he said, the effort to use the global language of the due process clause to strike down duly enacted legislation. "Indeed," Black said, "Brother White appears to have gone beyond past pronouncements of the natural law due process theory." As for Goldberg, Black rejected "the recent discovery that the Ninth Amendment as well as the Due Process Clause can be used by this Court as authority to strike down all state legislation which this Court thinks violates 'fundamental principles of liberty and justice,' or is contrary to the 'traditions and [collective] conscience of our people.'" Black would read the Ninth Amendment as adding nothing to the Bill of Rights.[39]

Black, however, was not done with his colleagues, for he had one more broad admonition. Once again, he rejected the calls for new rights, for the Court to "keep the Constitution in tune with the times." That was, he maintained, a pernicious doctrine that was bad for both the Court and the Constitution. No, he said, "the Constitution makers knew the need for change and provided for it. . . . That method of change was good enough for our Fathers, and being somewhat old-fashioned I must add it is good enough for me." To those who knew him, it was no surprise that Black was paraphrasing the concluding line from the refrain in the popular revival song "Give Me that Old Time Religion."

The plain truth, however, was that Black had lost. For though they differed on the best approach to the subject, the majority of the justices had concluded that there was a right to privacy. The Court faced growing pressure to address the widespread use of contraceptives and the even more controversial issue of abortion. The question of a state's ability to prohibit abortions came to the Court in the 1970 term, but Black, writing for a fragmented Court, avoided a ruling on the merits and concluded only that the District of Columbia law making abortions other than those needed to protect the life or health of the mother criminal offenses was not unconstitutionally vague. Douglas dissented. Although he did not take a firm position on how far government could go in the area, Douglas considered that such a law "touches intimate affairs of the family, of marriage, of sex, which in *Griswold* . . . we held to involve rights associated with several express constitutional rights and which are summed up in the 'right of privacy.'"[40] At a minimum, laws affecting such areas of life must be narrowly written to avoid unnecessary interference with protected liberties. The problem with the statute was that submitting to a jury a doctor's judgment about whether a particular abortion was "necessary for the preservation of the mother's life or health" would leave physicians far too vulnerable to "the jury's predilections or religious prejudices."[41]

The next year, in an opinion by Justice Brennan, the Court struck a Massachusetts law that made it a felony to distribute contraceptives to unmarried persons on grounds that it violated the equal protection clause of the Fourteenth Amendment. Recognizing that the *Griswold* ruling had been related to the significance of the marital relationship, Brennan nevertheless added: "Yet the married couple is not an independent entity with a mind and heart of its own, but an association of two individuals each with a separate intellectual and emotional makeup. If the right of privacy means anything, it is the right of the individual, married or single, to be free from unwarranted governmental intrusion into matters so fundamentally affecting a person as the decision whether to bear or beget a child."[42]

By this point, the Court was clearly in the midst of the sexual revolution and the clamor of demands for new applications of the equal protection clause.

The New Equal Protection

The brethren had long faced demands for protection against discrimination on the basis of race where states and localities had legislated segregation. As we have already seen, their task was made more difficult as the Court was called on to address race-discrimination claims in cases where no such segregation laws existed. Still, race was an inherently suspect classification, according to the Court, and when government treated people differently because of race it had the heavy burden of justifying such treatment. The problems were complex but all too familiar. That was about to change.

Victories by civil rights groups encouraged others who felt excluded from society to bring discimination claims. Ironically, the Court's rulings on birth control and abortion contributed to these social changes, as women who were freed from early or unwanted pregnancies began to insist on the opportunity to enter professions previously dominated by men. That meant a need for greater educational opportunity and elimination of employment barriers based on outmoded gender stereotypes. There were others who asked for equal treatment, including resident aliens who felt that since they were required to pay taxes and to be prepared to perform mandatory military service, they ought to enjoy the benefits of equal protection of the law, and illegitimate children who rejected the outmoded notion of the bar sinister, which deprived them of property and inheritance because of their parents' sexual conduct. Finally, there were the challenges by the poor who asserted that their poverty should not force them into a second-class citzenship with respect to government policies and programs.

For Douglas, the new equal protection cases and the so-called new property cases came close to the realization of his dream that one day the outcasts and the underdogs would get justice. He was more than ready to play an active role in the quest. Douglas was quick to argue that all these classifications—race, alienage, gender, religion, poverty, and "class or caste" (which covered such questions as legitimacy)—were inherently suspect.[43] If government employed them, it had better be prepared to demonstrate a compelling interest to justify its discrimination. In general, the Court was moving Douglas's way during the late 1960s and early 1970s, and, as in the privacy cases, conservatives like Harlan were involved as well as more liberal justices. But there was considerable disagreement within the Court, as well as outside it, about just how far the equal protection clause would reach. In Douglas's later years on the bench, the Court drew back from some of its expansive readings.

Douglas had written for the Court in 1966 striking down the poll tax because it disciminated on the basis of wealth.[44] Discrimination in a matter so fundamental as the right to vote required a solid justification. Black later used that opinion, however, along with the *Griswold* decision, as an example of judicial abuse. Black warned that "there is creeping into Court opinions a willingness to hold laws unconstitutional on the same 'shock the conscience' basis [as the earlier due process opinions] by invoking equal protection or some other clause."[45] Black's dissent was harder and stronger than his criticism of Douglas in the privacy case. He called the poll-tax ruling "an attack not only on the great value of our Constitution itself but also on the concept of a written constitution which is to survive through the years as originally written unless changed through the amendment process which the Framers wisely provided."[46]

For his part, Douglas saw nothing unusual about applying the "equal protection of the law" clause to preclude discrimination in legal affairs or the enjoyment of other rights where deprivations were based on no other reason than poverty. Thus he argued in a concurring opinion that Connecticut violated equal protection by requiring all applicants for divorce to pay filing fees regardless of their financial status.[47] To deny poor people the opportunity for a divorce simply because of their poverty was not equal protection of the law. Black dissented vigorously, not only to the majority opinion by Harlan but to the concurrences as well, insisting that the state had all but complete power over marriage and divorce. He recognized that the state could not bar interracial marriage, but saw that as different from other restrictions.[48]

Douglas dissented, in an opinion joined by Brennan, when a 5 to 4 Court later upheld a requirement that all persons applying for bankruptcy pay a filing fee.[49] For similar reasons, Douglas protested when another sharply divided Court upheld an Oregon filing-fee requirement for appellate review in a case involving a dispute with the state's Public Welfare Division. He asserted that the Court had supported "a scheme of judicial review whereby justice remains a luxury for the wealthy."[50]

Douglas found that discrimination in state laws based on legitimacy was also suspect, and he wrote for the Court in two Louisiana cases striking such statutes. The first involved a ruling that Louise Levy's five illegitimate children could not bring a wrongful-death suit to recover damages at her death, and the second was a suit by a mother seeking to recover damages after her son died in an automobile accident.[51] In both cases, Douglas concluded that the state was treating illegitimate children as "nonpersons," despite the fact that they were clearly not to blame for their status and even though they were clearly persons within the meaning of the equal protection clause. The real issue, he wrote, was that it was supposedly acceptable for the state to impose this different status because the "legislature is dealing with 'sin.'"[52] Justice Harlan, joined by Black and Stewart in dissent, replied that the nonpersons charge was "frankly preposterous" and that the state was merely requiring legal rights to be based on the kind of family that was legally recognized, not merely biological. He rejected the proposition that legitimacy was an inherently suspect classification and that the Court had any business second-guessing the state in its judgments on the matter.

Three years later, Black wrote for a 5 to 4 majority in *Labine* v. *Vincent,* upholding a Louisiana inheritance statute.[53] Although that decision did not openly reverse the earlier cases, it clearly rejected their reasoning. When Ezra Vincent died without a will, his daughter, Rita, who had been born out of wedlock, was not entitled to sue as her father's heir under Louisiana law, even though the natural parents had sworn a statement before a notary acknowledging themselves as the parents. Black, like Harlan in the earlier cases, recognized the authority of the state legislature to set laws defining the family and the relative rights of its members. It was most assuredly not the province of "the life-tenured judges of this Court to select from among possible laws."[54]

Brennan dissented for four justices, including Douglas, writing that the Court had "resort[ed] to the startling measure of simply excluding such illegitimate children from the protection of the [equal protection] Clause, in order to uphold the untenable and discredited moral prejudice of bygone centuries which vindictively punished not only the illegitimate parents, but also the hapless, and innocent, children. Based upon such a premise, today's decision cannot even pretend to be a principled decision."[55] For Douglas, Louisiana had added insult to injury. First, it began from the discriminatory assumption about illegitimate children. However, in crafting a way to legitimize offspring, the state had plainly created a process that favored those who could afford to hire a lawyer to meet the technical requirements of its law and penalized the poor who could not understand its requirements.

The New Property and the New Due Process

The discrimination problems involving poverty and caste were, to Douglas, related to a much larger body of cases in which the poor were treated less charitably than others by the Constitution, which should protect everyone equally. Some commentators referred to these issues as questions of "the new property" because they often involved the legal constraints on recipients of public benefit programs or jobs.[56] The legal bases for these cases ranged from due process issues concerning the procedures by which claimants were denied benefits or removed from programs for which they previously were qualified,[57] to equal protection claims, to charges of illegal search and seizure, and even to the right to travel from one state to another.[58] For Douglas, the root of the problem was the same. It was the assumption that because the people involved were poor, it was somehow acceptable for government to treat them in a punitive manner or to attempt to force them to trade away constitutional rights and liberties for benefits.

Douglas, and a majority of the Court, found what he considered the worst abuses in the Aid to Families with Dependent Children (AFDC) program—popularly known as welfare—which provides aid to children through their parents. He concurred with the Court in a decision striking down the so-called substitute-father rule in a case in which a state had ceased providing benefits to the children because their mother had been having sex with a man (who was not the father of any of the children) on weekends at her home. As in the legitimacy cases, Douglas found this treatment of the children on the grounds of the mother's allegedly immoral behavior, which had nothing to do with the children's eligibility or need for assistance, discriminatory.[59] He objected to the states' attempts to disqualify children or provide them with lower benefits when he concluded that the federal standards required the contrary.[60] But the "new property" case that caused Douglas more frustration than any of the others was one involving mandatory warrantless searches of homes of welfare recipients.

Barbara James and her son lived in New York City and received benefits from Aid to Families with Dependent Children. When in May 1969 the caseworker told James that she would be visiting her homes, James volunteered to provide any information that was reasonable to the caseworker but refused to permit a home visit. The caseworker informed James that such a refusal would result in the elimination of her payments. After a full hearing before a hearing examiner, her benefits were ordered terminated. Ultimately, the Supreme Court rejected the lower court's judgment that there had been a violation of the Fourth Amendment.

Douglas issued a ringing dissent in which he leveled his charge directly at the hypocrisy underlying the treatment of welfare recipients.

> We are living in a society where one of the most important forms of property is government largesse which some call the "new property." The payrolls of government are but one aspect of that "new property." Defense contracts, highway contracts, and other multifarious forms of contracts are another part. So are disbursements by government for scientific research. So are TV and radio licenses to use the air space which of course is part of the public domain. Our concern here is not with those subsidies but with grants that directly or indirectly implicate the home life of the recipients. . . .
>
> If the welfare recipient was not Barbara James but a prominent, affluent cotton or wheat farmer receiving benefit payments for not growing crops, would not the approach be different?[61]

Douglas had similar feelings, and for the same reasons, about the treatment of citizens in public housing.[62]

The Court was divided on many of these issues, but none of the justices seemed to be farther apart than Hugo Black and William Douglas. With few exceptions, Black was on the opposing side in these cases; moreover, his opinions were filled with hard statements.

In dissent from Douglas's majority opinion striking a Wisconsin wage-garnishment statute for lack of notice and opportunity to be heard before wages were taken, Black determined that the Court's opinion was "a plain, judicial usurpation of state legislative power to decide what the State's laws shall be. . . . The Court thus steps back into the due process philosophy which brought on President Roosevelt's Court fight."[63] In opinion after opinion, he challenged the Court on the same ground, that it was substituting its views of policy for that of the legislature. As in other new rights cases, Black was not content simply to take on the majority but had words for those who concurred as well. He added an "ADDENDUM" to his dissent specifically aimed at Harlan. The Court's leading conservative rankled at being lumped into the category of judges who defined due process from their own "predilections."[64] He had argued that what procedural due process required was in part derived from our "Anglo-American legal heritage," which Black said was

> no more definite than the "notions of justice of English-speaking peoples" or the shock-the-conscience test. All of these so-called tests represent nothing more or less

than an implicit adoption of a Natural Law concept which under our system leaves to judges alone the power to decide what the Natural Law means. These so-called standards do not bind judges within any boundaries that can be precisely marked or defined by words for holding laws unconstitutional. On the contrary, these tests leave them wholly free to decide what they are convinced is right and fair. If the judges in deciding whether laws are constitutional, are to be left only to the admonitions of their own consciences, why was it that the Founders gave us a written Constitution at all?

Black's frustration reached a high point with the Court's ruling in 1970 that due process was required before welfare benefits could be terminated. Following the conference, Douglas asked Brennan if he wanted the welfare cases. Brennan replied, "Yes, but I'd have to write it more narrowly than you and I might like—Maybe it would be best to let John [Harlan] do it and leave us free to join him and write more broadly."[65] But Brennan got the assignments in *Goldberg* v. *Kelly,* involving termination of welfare benefits, and *Wheeler* v. *Montgomery,* concerning Social Security survivor's payments. They were ready by late February 1970. Brennan urged at conference that the decisions come down the next week. His conference notes show that

> all present agreed, save Black, who indicated that the decisions might be announced, but if they were he would add a paragraph to his dissent stating the Court gravely erred in not dealing with all of the pending welfare decisions together, so that all Justices— and the country—could see that the results were dictated by the majority's view of what the law ought to be, rather than by the Law. Black was unmoved by the arguments of all others present that the Goldberg–Wheeler decisions had little in common with the other pending welfare cases. One of Black's clerks indicated . . . that the Justice has become increasingly concerned that various members of the Court have let their views of due process run wild. Thus, he's eager to take an unusually strict constructionist—The Words—approach to attempt to pull the Court back into line. A part of his eagerness stems from an awareness that each year may be his last as an active Justice.[66]

The cases did not come down for another month, and no such paragraph was ultimately appended to Black's opinion. Even so, his dissent was filled with language chiding the Court for using the due process clause to read its views into public policy.

Black sternly criticized Harlan relatively often in new rights cases, even though Harlan and Stewart were the members of the Court who most often joined Black in challenging the Court's majority on the creation of new rights. Harlan was willing to draw lines, but Black disapproved of that effort.

New Press Protections

In spite of his vehement opposition to what he regarded as judicial usurpation of legislative authority, Black advocated or joined rulings creating or expanding First Amendment claims into new areas that most commentators would recognize as, in effect, the creation of new rights themselves. Perhaps the best example was Black's claim that libel suits should be abolished in any matter touching on public affairs or discussion of public officials. He concurred in the Court's decision in *New York Times* v. *Sullivan,* striking down a libel judgment against the newspaper for having run a civil rights organization's advertisement that was found by an Alabama jury to have libeled Public Safety Commissioner Sullivan. He disagreed, however, with that part of the ruling which found that an official might collect damages for injury from false statements if the publication acted with "actual malice," which was defined as the knowledge that what was said was false or was a reckless disregard for truth or falsity.[67] To Black, that exception swallowed the rule. He thought that the "nation can live in peace without libel suits based upon discussion of public affairs and public officials. But I doubt that a country can live in freedom where its people can be made to suffer physically or financially for criticizing their government, its actions, or its officials."[68] Three years later, following other opinions in which the Court had attempted to refine its "actual malice standard,"[69] Black wrote, "I think it is time for this Court to abandon *New York Times* v. *Sullivan* and adopt the rule to the effect that the First Amendment was intended to leave the press free from the harassment of libel judgments."[70]

Black, though, joined the Court in a holding that reporters were required to reveal confidential source information to a grand jury without any showing of particular necessity or of the unavailability of that information from other sources.[71] Douglas considered that to be every bit as dangerous as libel or any other external force that would constrain the acquisition or dissemination of news. Black also joined an opinion for the Court in *Red Lion Broadcasting* v. *F.C.C.* upholding the fairness doctrine, which required broadcasters to permit a reply by anyone, including public officials, who was attacked in a broadcast. The opinion found that "although broadcasting is clearly a medium affected by a First Amendment interest . . . , differences in the characteristics of news media justify differences in the First Amendment standards applied to them."[72]

Finally, Hugo Black, author of the famous company street decision upholding the right of a speaker to distribute pamphlets in an Alabama company town wholly owned by the Gulf Shipbuilding Corporation, now roundly chastised the opinion in *Amalgamated Food Employees* v. *Logan Valley Plaza,* joined by Douglas, that held that modern shopping centers possess the same "Main Street" character and therefore are open to otherwise protected First Amendment speech.[73] To Black, the shopping center was not Main Street; it was private property. One sees in his shopping-center opinion less a concern with what is or is not Main Street and far more the growing anger he felt that the First Amendment had been stretched beyond acceptable limits to protect picketers and other demonstrators. The fact is, of course, that shopping malls soon had become much like the city. Even so, the Court ultimately reversed its shopping-center-access ruling when the Nixon appointees joined ranks with the *Logan Valley* dissenters (except for Black, who had by then left the Court).[74]

≈

The Court found itself in an interesting position in American society as it responded to the various demands for new rights. With respect to its most controversial decisions, those having to do with birth control, the court was clearly following rather than leading the society. In the months prior to the Court's *Griswold* ruling, the nation was alive with movements in many major cities to expand the availability of birth-control information and devices. Notwithstanding the controversial character of birth control as a subject of public discussion, the momentum was clear and, outside legal circles, the *Griswold* opinion was met as nothing particularly surprising.

By the later 1960s and early 1970s, when the "new property" cases began to emerge from the Court, attention was riveted elsewhere, on the problems in the cities, on social-protest movements, and on the Vietnam War.

The public's reaction to the public benefits cases was mixed. On the one hand, concerned people complained about being ground up in the bureaucracy and insisted on what they thought was simple fairness. Most Americans could identify with that. More and more people either worked for government or dealt with agencies in grants, contracts, or entitlement programs. On the other hand, there was a growing frustration with the idea of expanding welfare programs, a sentiment that a variety of political candidates exploited. The result for the agencies administering the congressionally created benefit programs was a squeeze between a demand for humane and generous assistance to the needy and a call for tight-fisted, efficient management of public programs that some considered necessary evils. That ambivalence was reflected in the debates among the justices.

It was a hard time for Black and Douglas. Black saw the Court moving in directions he thought entirely wrong. He feared judicial usurpation, and he knew that he would not be on the Court to fight it much longer. Douglas saw too many cases of the judiciary abandoning its critical responsibility to be fair to those in society who most needed assistance. And the gulf between the two long-time allies seemed to be widening. The next few years would be hard ones, bringing Hugo Black's death and the end of Douglas's career.

13

Douglas Without Black

ELIZABETH and Hugo Black had been playing tennis one Friday morning in July 1969. Hugo was down one game to two when he "kind of wobbled off the tennis court and sat down."[1] He was obviously in trouble, but it was not clear what was wrong. It was just after noon when Elizabeth got him to the Bethesda Naval Hospital. More than a week passed before they learned that Hugo had suffered a limited stroke, but the Blacks sensed immediately that the episode was serious. The anxiety grew as hours and then days went by with Hugo seemingly unable to rebound. Grudgingly, he began to talk about whether he should resign from the Court.

He was not ready to leave the Court just yet. So much was happening, and there were so many things he wanted to do before it was time to go. The new chief justice, Warren Burger, had just been appointed. Recently inaugurated President Richard Nixon was about to nominate Clement Haynesworth to fill the seat left vacant by the resignation of Abe Fortas. The Court had drawn the line in the sand on school desegregation and was now engaged in the legal equivalent of house-to-house fighting, responding to alternative desegregation plans proposed by school districts throughout the South. Battles over the Vietnam War and civil rights had presented a range of critical First Amendment issues of the sort Black was driven to address.

Although it would be more than two years after the stroke that Black would leave the Court, it was an important time and it virtually flew by. It was a complex period for Douglas as well, a difficult time in his life personally and professionally. He was about to lose his friend and ally and had to contemplate the years ahead without the assurance of Black on the bench, a fact of Douglas's life since he had come to the institution in 1939.

Indeed, it was to be an era of major change for the Court as a whole, very dramatic change from Douglas's point of view. For the first time in his long career, Douglas saw the gains in liberty achieved by the Court jeopardized by appointees brought to the bench by a president who had campaigned against it. While the new justices did not openly attack Warren Court precedents, they made important changes not only in what the law meant but in the availability of federal courts as a forum in which to challenge policy makers. Douglas would take pleasure in eventually playing a role in Nixon's undoing, but that was cold comfort to a judicial warrior who believed that the Court and its accomplishments were endangered.

Douglas's declining health and the criticism of his personal life added to the tension; yet his years with his last wife, Cathleen, were among his happiest, and she ultimately came to be admired by members of the Court and other Washington observers for her behavior during difficult times.

There was the heartbreak of the impeachment effort, which came hard on the heels of the downfall of his friend of three decades, Abe Fortas. And there was the rupture of his friendship with Lyndon Johnson.

Douglas had acted out of a long personal tradition dating back to the 1940s of providing Democratic administrations with information that he acquired on his trips around the world. Indeed, his correspondence with Harry Truman about U.S. actions in Asia led to a break between the two men. When Douglas returned from a trip to Asia in the summer of 1951, he discussed a number of topics, including commenting in a San Francisco interview that he thought the United States should recognize China.

Truman was livid. He wrote to Douglas: "As long as I am president, if I can prevent it, that cutthroat organization will never be recognized by us as the Government of China and I am sorry that a justice of the Supreme Court has been willing to champion the interest of a bunch of murderers by a public statement. . . . I am being very frank with you, Bill, because fundamentally I am very fond of you but you have missed the boat . . . if you really wanted to get into politics."[2]

Douglas answered with regret that his letter and his statement had created such tension. Among other things, he reminded the president that he really had no interest in politics: "I have no ambition except to stay on the Court. That has indeed been my consistent course: I called off my friends in 1944 and denied them the opportunity to get the Vice Presidential nomination for me; and I declined your most gracious invitation for me to be Secretary of the Interior in 1946 and your running mate in 1948." He reminded Truman of many of the things he had said in 1951, including the assertion that crossing the thirty-eighth parallel in Korea would have disastrous results. He had disagreed with Truman about policy toward China.

> Your view is an understandable one. It is today perhaps the popular view. But my travels in Asia during the last three summers have convinced me that there is only tragedy to our country if it is maintained. . . . These are times that try the souls of all of us. I have returned from Asia full of fear. The world you and I love is shrinking each year, Mr. President. I have been to Asia three summers now and each year I have found that the influence of the West has grown smaller and smaller. The trend against us is alarming. I have returned this time with fear in my heart for the country I love. The red tide rolls on and on in Asia; the bulk of the people of the world are slowly lining up against us; we rather than Russia are tragically coming to be the symbol of their enemy. The day may not be far distant when we are left in all our loneliness and our atomic bombs.[3]

Later, he communicated his foreign policy observations to Lyndon Johnson. It appeared he would have significant entrée with Kennedy in the White House, Johnson as vice president, and Abe Fortas as the developing key adviser to Johnson. However, it was not always clear just how far LBJ was willing to rely on Douglas's judgment in such matters. The two clashed over Douglas's accusation that Johnson had ignored his warnings about the rise of Ayub Khan in Pakistan. But their most important battle came over Vietnam.

Douglas attempted on four occasions to provide the Johnson administration with alternative private channels through which to pursue negotiations to end the escalating war in Vietnam. In 1965 and 1967, two Pacem in Terris convocations were held under the auspices of the Parvin Foundation and the Center for the Study of Democratic Institutions (about which more will be said shortly). Officers of the center had interviewed Ho Chi Minh and felt quite confident that he would accept an invitation to the conferences and be open to private talks at the same time. They issued a formal invitation letter that had been cleared by the State Department.

Douglas met with LBJ on June 8, 1966, and explained the plan for the conference to be held the next year and the desire to make it an opportunity for informal talks with North Vietnam. He recounted the meeting in a letter to Robert Hutchins the next day: "I asked him if he had any objections to our getting together with Ho Chi Minh and others from Asia, including, hopefully, the Peking regime. He said without hesitation he had no objection, and that he hoped we could do it."[4] In May 1967, Douglas wrote to Senator Charles Percy (R-Ill.), "I might note, in confidence, that what appeared to be an effort in the State Department to undercut the convocation has now been reversed in the White House, and we are now proceeding with full (if still reluctant in some quarters) approval."[5]

According to Douglas, Johnson then moved to block the pending negotiations with Hanoi over North Vietnam's possible participation in the conference. Douglas claimed that administration representatives even attempted to disrupt the 1967 conference in Geneva and supported South Vietnamese efforts to grandstand at the meeting.[6] However, the invitation to the Saigon representatives had been made contingent on the participation of representatives from Hanoi, who had been dissuaded by various means from attending. To allow the South Vietnamese to attend under those conditions would have been to provide a platform for propaganda rather than an opportunity for serious discussions.

Douglas's next efforts were through the Indian ambassador to Moscow, P. K. Banerjee, an old friend, who attempted to use Douglas as a conduit through which to pass messages from Hanoi via Moscow to Washington. The first time, LBJ dismissed Douglas's communication on grounds that the message was a Soviet ploy to embarrass the administration. Then, in February 1968, Banerjee came to Douglas with a message for LBJ from Hanoi in response to a speech the president had given in the fall of 1967 concerning a possible cessation of the bombing of North Vietnam. Defense Secretary Clark Clifford had just explained in testimony before the Senate Armed Services Committee on January 25, 1968, the conditions under which that might occur. Douglas wrote to Clifford, who promised to pass on the message to Johnson. "The attached message from Hanoi has just reached me through the good offices of a noncommunist country. It has not apparently been presented as yet to the Department of State, the desire of the intermediary nation being to get the message directly to the President." The message read:

Q. If the bombing ceases, when will talks start?
A. 7 to 15 days.
Q. What will be the subject matter of the discussion?
A. Anything within the frame of reference of the Geneva Conference.
Q. Who will be parties to the talks?
A. North Viet Nam and the United States. Either can bring in another party.
Q. Will any advantage of the United States be taken in case of cessation of the bombing?
A. Hanoi accepts Clark Clifford's statement of January 25, 1968.[7]

Douglas later came to believe that Johnson ignored the opportunity.

It is said that in Johnson's final break with Douglas, the president remarked, "Liberty and Justice, that's all you apparently think of. And when you pass over the last hill, I suppose you will be shouting 'Liberty and Justice!'" Douglas replied, "You're goddamn right, Mr. President."[8]

Although there was still the challenge ahead for Douglas of battling the changes in the Court and its political environment, and of trying to rouse the conscience of the courts, the Congress, or the people, facing those challenges without Hugo Black was not a pleasant prospect.

Black Leaves the Court

It was a difficult time for Black as well as Douglas. Black knew that the time of his departure from the Court was coming soon, and he was not pleased by the idea. He was the quintessential Supreme Court justice.[9] By this point, his service on the Court was no longer his profession; it was his life. Black, too, feared that the Court was moving in a dangerous direction, though his anxiety was very different from that of his friend. In fact, Black had come to see Douglas as part of the problem rather than as an ally in its resolution. More and more often, Black cited Douglas's opinions for the Court as the worst kinds of judicial abuse. Black saw the Court moving in the direction of judicial usurpation in the new rights cases and knew he would not be there to fight the tendency.

While he sensed that the end was not far off after his stroke, Black was a long way from giving up. When the new term began in October, Hugo was ready. By the end of October, he had received a clean bill of health. As if to prove the point, Hugo was unwilling to accept his defeat by Elizabeth in two straight sets of tennis. He insisted on a best three out of five series and took the match.[10] The opportunity to fight what he considered the Court's wrong-headed approach to due process in the welfare cases during that term was more than enough to raise Black's spirits, even though it taxed his energies.[11]

By the end of the term, however, Black wondered whether it would be his last. Once again he met the challenge, even though his eyesight was fast deteriorating as the new term opened on Monday, October 5, 1970.[12] There were important voting rights cases, including the *Oregon* v. *Mitchell* litigation, which called for the vote for eighteen-year-olds.[13] Coming as it did during a war, when young men whose age prevented them from voting were asked to risk their lives for their country, it was a controversial case. Even so, it was precisely the kind of case in which Black wanted to reiterate his credo. If new rights were to be granted, it should be through the proper democratic process of constitutional amendment. This time the nation read his opinion for the Court and took his advice. On July 1, 1971, the Twenty-sixth Amendment was ratified, granting the franchise to eighteen-year-olds.

The news of its ratification came the day after Hugo Black issued his last major opinion, in a case that also had to do with the Vietnam War. The government was seeking to block publication by the *New York Times* and the *Washington Post* of the "History of U.S. Decision-Making Process on Viet Nam Policy," better known as the Pentagon Papers. It was somehow so fitting that in his last opinion, Black had the chance to beat back an effort at prior restraint of publication. Also satisfying was the fact that Bill Douglas was back with him, each man joining the concurring opinion issued by the other. It was the old Hugo, as adamant at eighty-five as he had been more than thirty years earlier, rejecting the government's argument "that the First Amendment does not mean what it says."[14]

Suddenly, Black's health took a serious turn downward. He was in and out of Bethesda Naval Hospital over the next several weeks with what was diagnosed as temporal arteritis, then bounced back briefly during early August, but by mid-month he was uncertain about his health and seriously considering resigning from the Court. Former clerk (and later federal district judge) Louis Oberdorfer spent much of the weekend of August 19 and 20 in conversations with the justice about leaving the Court. The discussion continued on Monday, and they decided to set September 1 as a tentative date. Later that week, Hugo signed an undated letter of resignation, though he instructed Elizabeth not to transmit it to the president until he gave the word.[15]

Far too soon, Black found himself back in the hospital in the room adjoining that of his colleague John Harlan. Both were deteriorating rapidly. On Wednesday, September 15, Hugo, Jr., talked to his father about the resignation, and on September 17, Elizabeth dated the resignation letter and had it delivered to the Court.[16] Less than a week later, Harlan, too, resigned. Two days after that, Black died, leaving so many people who had known him with a strong sense of loss. Other than Black's immediate family, probably no one felt that loss more than William O. Douglas.

The parting was all the more difficult because it came at the end of a period in which their relationship had been sorely tested. Each felt that the other had, in a sense, abandoned him some time earlier. At least since 1965, there had been less of a common enterprise and more of a need to reconcile all too frequent tensions. Their friendship did not end, but it was strained by their repeatedly finding themselves committed to opposite sides of critical cases.

The tension over the right-to-privacy cases, the speech-plus sit-in and picketing cases, and the due process disputes over the "new property" was obvious. In earlier years when the two had differed, the terms of the dispute were usually limited and the resulting opinions understated. But by the late 1960s, in cases such as *Sniadach* v. *Family Finance,* striking the Wisconsin wage-garnishment statute, the conflict

302 • OF POWER AND RIGHT

was more direct and fundamental.[17] Black more and more often lumped Douglas with the others he considered guilty of judicial usurpation, particularly in cases concerning issues of federalism and state action. It did not help that Black included Fortas, Douglas's protégé and lifelong friend, in some of the most vehement of these criticisms.[18]

The pressure on Douglas and public disapproval of his private life continued for years. Douglas's three divorces and marriages to very young women were not easy for a puritan like Hugo to bear, and the amount of news coverage that his private life attracted made them impossible to ignore. For one thing, the Blacks had received a heart-wrenching letter from Douglas's second wife, Mercedes, during that divorce and had seen some of the abuse Joan Douglas suffered from the press after the marriage. Later, they watched Cathleen adjust to life in a fishbowl. Elizabeth Black recounted a story Joan Douglas told them in 1965 about an encounter she had had with a cab driver: "The cabbie was knocking the Court and said, 'That Douglas is a real creep, married a twenty-five-year-old girl,' and she replied, 'Yes, I'm that twenty-five-year-old girl.'"[19] At which point, the cab nearly went out of control.

Douglas's congressional foes had a veritable field day with his marital problems. In fact, six House members co-wrote House Resolutions 918-922 and 928, seeking investigations of grounds that poor character should constitute impeachable behavior.[20] Congressman Findley (R-Ill.) addressed the House, saying, "In my view, Justice Douglas' personal life points up a weakness in our judicial system. A means should be established under which the justices can be removed from the bench without the necessity of finding them guilty of treason, bribery, or other high crimes and misdemeanors." It was a speech considered important enough to some Justice Department staffers to prompt an internal FBI memo to Director J. Edgar Hoover.[21] Douglas's last marriage, to twenty-three-year-old Cathleen Heffernan, played a role in the effort to drive him from the Court. (Of course, an article in the *Saturday Review* observed that few people were upset when Frank Sinatra married the twenty-one-year-old Mia Farrow in the same month, June 1966; apparently, one does not challenge the "Chairman of the Board.")[22]

Fighting Impeachment

Efforts to remove Douglas from the Court had been made on at least two previous occasions. The first attempt was in 1953, when Representative Wheeler introduced an impeachment resolution in the House following Douglas's decision to stay the Rosenberg execution pending an appeal. Wheeler argued that the stay of execution, Douglas's announcement in a 1951 interview that the United States should recognize the People's Republic of China, and Douglas's dissent from the Court's decision upholding the convictions of top Communist party officials in *Dennis* v. *United States*[23] were more than enough grounds for impeachment. The second attempt was made when Douglas married Joan Martin. The most serious effort, though, did not occur until 1970. It resulted, oddly enough, from the publication of some university lectures and the politics of the Nixon administration. It was a bitter experience for Douglas, though he was ultimately vindicated.

Justice Douglas delivered the Walter E. Edge Lectures at Princeton University in March 1960. The lectures were published as a book, *America Challenged,* later that year. Essentially, the lectures called on Americans to resist the forces attempting to impose conformity. Douglas was concerned that creativity and dissent would be stifled. He also called on Americans to critically reevaluate their role in the nation and the nation's role in the world, themes he had discussed from the rostrum and in print for nearly a decade. In July, a man named Albert Parvin wrote to Douglas from Los Angeles saying that he had been inspired by *America Challenged* and wished to establish a philanthropic foundation to further the purposes advanced by Douglas in the book. Parvin requested Douglas's assistance and his services as a director of the new foundation.

Douglas accepted the invitation to meet with Parvin to discuss the proposal and expressed his enthusiasm for such a project.[24] Thus began a series of discussions that culminated in the filing of articles of incorporation in October 1960. The Parvin Foundation came to its full operating strength in February 1962, when the foundation amended its charter to include two additional directors, Robert M. Hutchins and Robert F. Goheen.[25] Hutchins, aside from being an old friend of Douglas's, was the president of the Fund for the Republic, which operated the Center for the Study of Democratic Institutions. Goheen was the president of Princeton University. From that time until May 21, 1969, Justice Douglas was both the president and a director of the Parvin Foundation. During that period, he also served as a director of and in various other capacities for the Fund for the Republic and its Center for the Study of Democratic Institutions.[26]

The two institutions worked together on a number of projects, including sponsoring foreign students in programs at Princeton and, later, at U.C.L.A., as well as supporting literacy programs in developing countries, particularly in Central and South America. They also sponsored the Pacem in Terris convocations that Douglas had hoped might be the occasion for behind-the-scenes negotiations with Ho Chi Minh. Pope John had delivered an encyclical of the same title in 1963.

Things seemed to be going well until the Internal Revenue Service began investigating Albert Parvin in August 1964 about his personal finances and his connections with the Parvin-Dohrman Corporation, a firm connected with hotel and casino operations in Las Vegas. Justice Douglas was interviewed by IRS agents concerning the foundation in October 1964.[27] There were no charges of any kind, but the fact that the investigation was under way was leaked to the press in late October. The publicity meant that the foundation's tax-exempt status would be scrutinized. Justice Douglas spoke with Carolyn Aggers at the Washington firm of Arnold and Porter about representing the foundation in these tax matters. She agreed, but warned Douglas that she might not be the best person to handle the case because (as Douglas well knew) she was Justice Fortas's wife. Douglas waved off the warning and informed Harry S. Ashmore, the secretary of the Parvin Foundation, who wrote to Aggers, formally retaining her services.[28]

Ashmore requested opinions from Aggers on several specific questions, including whether the foundation should merge with the Fund for the Republic. At the time, Ashmore, Douglas, and Hutchins were serving as directors and officers of both institutions. Carolyn Aggers responded to Ashmore on November 10, 1966, and suggested in response to the specific points he had raised that Parvin should "disassociate himself entirely from the operation of the Foundation." In any event, Parvin should not have sole power over disbursement of funds and investments. Finally, she concluded that it might be frutiful to transfer "the Foundation's assets and activities to the Fund for the Republic."

Ashmore informed Parvin that Aggers had been retained and noted her suggestion that Parvin move out of the center of the foundation's operations. Parvin objected to Ashmore's letter, both because he saw no need to retain the lawyer and because he did not understand what good it would do for him to disassociate himself from the foundation's administration: "Honestly, Harry, what is wrong with me? And frankly, what does Miss Aggers think I am? I am certain that the financial investment program of the Foundation, if handled by anyone but me, would result in the loss of income to the Foundation of perhaps $50,000 to $100,000 per year."[29]

Ashmore, wary of Parvin's attitude and his possible business relationships with gambling interests, wrote to Douglas warning that he ought to be prepared for possible political attacks. "While there is no actual connection between the Parvin Foundation and gambling operations in Las Vegas, such connections do exist between the Parvin-Dohrman Company and hotels maintaining gambling casinos. Tenuous though they may be, it provides the basis for political attacks on you in Congress and in the press. These can be expected to resume as soon as Congress convenes in January."[30]

There was reason for Douglas to be concerned. In late October, he had written a letter to Chief Justice Warren and his colleagues explaining his connection with the Parvin Foundation.[31] One of the major problems was that Parvin had insisted on paying Douglas for his services as president. Although Douglas rejected the payment of a salary per se, he did consent to use the money as an open expense account, travelling extensively on behalf of the foundation. Unfortunately, it was an open account with no itemized listing of expenses. The money he received from the Parvin Foundation and his income from royalties and honoraria made a tempting target for his critics. His relationship to the foundation became known just at the time of his highly publicized wedding.

By 1967, then, Justice Douglas was under heavy attack. A number of people were concerned that he would be hurt by distortions and innuendo, and by Parvin, who was using the names of the officers and directors of the foundation quite freely in order to protect himself.[32] Parvin was not charged with any crime as the result of the tax investigation, but he was at one point named as a co-conspirator with Louis E. Wolfson in a stock-fraud case, a connection that proved to be important for Douglas.[33]

Some weeks before his appointment to the Supreme Court, Abe Fortas had been approached by Wolfson to handle some legal matters. Wolfson also asked his advice on some philanthropic work he had been doing through an institution known as the Wolfson Family Foundation.[34] When Justice Goldberg resigned and Fortas was named to fill the vacancy, Wolfson approached Fortas with the request that he serve as a consultant to the foundation. Fortas, who had taken a huge pay cut in accepting the Supreme Court assignment, settled on a contract with Wolfson calling for $20,000 per year for life. By the summer of 1966, Wolfson was in deep trouble with the SEC. Justice Fortas resigned from his post with the foundation on June 21, but he did not return the fee for the year until December. Wolfson was tried and convicted on one violation in the fall of 1967 and on another in June 1968.

At the same time, it was becoming clear that the Democrats were in trouble in the 1968 election. Chief Justice Warren chose to give Lyndon Johnson, a lame-duck president, the option of appointing his successor on the Court by providing LBJ with an undated letter of resignation. Johnson chose Fortas for the center chair, which would permit him another appointment to the Court, but Republicans, sensing victory in November, charged that there had been collusion between Warren and Johnson. The challenge to the Fortas nomination was really an attack on the Warren Court, but Fortas was the lightning rod.

Soon after Nixon's election, William Lambert of *Life* learned of Fortas's connection with Wolfson. It appeared to the president, whom the Justice Department informed about Lambert's story, that Fortas had done himself in and that the administration could stand back and appear nonpartisan as Fortas was brought down. At a meeting of Republican leaders, Nixon reportedly implied that his people should keep quiet. As Robert Shogan describes the events: "Gerald Ford missed the point. Like an earnest school boy who had diligently done his homework, Ford plunged into an enthusiastic discussion of impeachment lore. 'I'm amazed,' he said, 'how easy it is to start an impeachment proceedings and how broad the grounds are.'"[35] After the *Life* story broke on May 4, the pressure was intense. On May 14, 1969, Fortas resigned.

The resignation did not end the matter, however. Douglas's congressional opponents, led by Senator John Williams, worked to tie Douglas to Fortas through the Parvin–Wolfson relationship.[36] Douglas, who had been in Brazil when the Fortas story was published, wrote to Parvin en route from Brazil on May 12. "The manufactured case against you and the Foundation is a shocking thing that we must fight to the end and win. But as the issues are formed it may get nastier and nastier. . . . The strategy is to get me off the Court and I do not propose to bend to any such pressure."[37]

There is no doubt that a number of legislators sensed the possibility of making a quick change in the Court by forcing the exodus of other Warren Court justices. Only five days after Fortas stepped down, Representative Rarrick argued, "The confidence of the American people in the Federal judiciary cannot be restored until Abe Fortas's resignation is followed by a like departure of Earl Warren, William Douglas and William Brennan."[38]

Douglas resigned from the Parvin Foundation on May 21, but Parvin was still attempting to clear his public image. He permitted reporters full access to the foundation's files. Bernard Collier wrote a piece for the *Los Angeles Times* on May 25 that was reprinted in the *New York Times* the next day. In it he discussed the Parvin–Wolfson connection, Wolfson's fee to Fortas, and the foundation's fee to Douglas, revealing that Carolyn Aggers was Fortas's wife and that money from the sale of the Flamingo Hotel in Las Vegas had been used to fund the foundation. Again there were calls for impeachment.

Douglas stood firm. He had known his enemies were after him long before the serious impeachment effort was launched. He wrote to his attorney, former defense secretary Clark Clifford, in October 1969.

> Enclosed is a news item from yesterday's STAR. It is, I think a token that the campaign against me has started all over again. The grossly unfair and malicious character of this particular item is that it relates to episodes that happened before I ever met Mr. Parvin. He did, late in 1961 or early 1962, transfer a fractional interest in a mortgage on the hotel in question to the Parvin Foundation, an interest which the Foundation got rid of because it was on a Las Vegas property that had a gambling casino. But fractional interests in mortgages are always hard to liquidate. . . . There is nothing that this article pertains to with which I had any connection whatsoever.[39]

He had learned from a friend that "Clark Mollenhoff of the White House is planting a story that in 1963–64 I was in Santo Domingo trying to get out of Juan Bosch a gambling casino for certain Mafia interests. I was there at the time representing the Parvin Foundation, and preparing a TV adult literacy course." He closed the letter by asking Clifford, "Isn't it time I sued someone?"[40]

There were other pressures on Douglas at this time. He had written decisions in a number of cases that barred the activation of military reserve units and individual transfers to Vietnam.[41] F. Edward Hebert wrote to Chief Justice Warren, Chief Justice Burger, and, finally, Solicitor General Erwin N. Griswold insisting that Justice Douglas be disqualified from any case "involving Vietnam, the draft, or the military in general." Hebert went so far as to claim: "If he were a man of high character and probity, he would abstain on his own accord. But obviously he isn't, as evidenced by his conduct in other matters."[42] The recipients of the tirade ignored it.

It is true that Douglas was convinced that the war in Vietnam was a patently unconstitutional presidential conflict. However, he was guilty of nothing more sinister than attempting to force the Court to consider the constitutionality of the war. As for the draft cases, Douglas was convinced that the Selective Service Act was administered arbitrarily and capriciously and that the rights of conscientious objectors were regularly violated by both military and civilian authorities.

There was another political influence behind the move to impeach Douglas— the failure of Nixon's nominees to the Court to be confirmed. Nixon's selection of Clement Haynesworth in August 1969 went down in defeat. Nixon followed that with the nomination of G. Harold Carswell. Then House Minority Leader Gerald Ford made not-so-veiled threats about possible moves against members of the Court in a speech delivered in November concerning the federal judiciary and the appointment process.[43] The Carswell nomination was rejected in early April. Nixon immediately attacked the Senate Judiciary Committee.

On April 15, Ford launched an assault on Justice Douglas on the House floor, introducing House Resolution 290, which called for his impeachment.[44] Ford's speech indicted Douglas for the Parvin affair and accused him of practicing law for the foundation, failing to disqualify himself on several cases, publishing seditious material, allowing his work to be published in allegedly pornographic magazines, and practically anything else anyone could think of, although the actual bill of particulars was more narrowly drawn. The investigation was given to Emmanuel Celler's House Judiciary Committee, which was a stroke of good fortune for Douglas, who had a longstanding friendship with Celler.

At first, Douglas was tempted to ignore the proceeding, but his friends convinced him that he had better defend himself. Simon Rifkind, an old law school colleague, led the defense team, which included Ramsey Clark, David Ginsburg, Charles A. Miller, J. Roger Wollenberg, and Sidney M. Davis. Douglas opened all his files to the committee without any subpoena or other pressure. The Judiciary Committee eventually cleared Douglas of the charges, finding that "intensive investigation of the Special Subcommittee has not disclosed evidence that would warrant preparation of charges on any acceptable concept of an impeachable offense."[45]

While Douglas worked to keep up his steely exterior, "he was saddened by the impeachment effort."[46] He found a creative outlet for the pressure and frustration in writing a play, *The Couch,* under the pen name William Frazier, which he had "used in years past to write short stories for the pulp magazines."[47] The play was about a mythical first "Secretary of Mental Health," who immediately after his appointment began to criticize the cherished, unexamined values of the culture, starting with motherhood. The secretary eventually was impeached—not because of any wrongdoing, but because he had the temerity to attack the symbols of the establishment.

Douglas's friends knew he needed help and tried to provide it. A group of former clerks met on the West Coast and contemplated what they could do apart from indicating their support. Fred Rodell, a longtime friend, wrote to Hugo Black: "I do hope you're helping Bill keep his chin up. He does need loyal friends these days, despite the absurdity of what Ford is trying to do."[48] Black replied:

> You may rest assured that if there is anything I can do to help our friend Bill "to keep his chin up," I shall do it. In fact it seems to me that he is weathering the storm very well indeed. I cannot believe that it is possible that anyone would think that Bill Douglas has been guilty of a "high crime or misdemeanor." Unless I am mistaken, the present political hub-bub about him will get exactly no where. Only should he do something which is really bad (which he will not do) could he be in danger.[49]

Concerned that perhaps Black might have misunderstood, Rodell wrote, "Of course, I knew that you would do anything possible to help Bill Douglas against that damn-fool ex-student of mine, Gerald Ford. But I'm delighted to know you agree with me that the hoopla is a lot of nonsense." Black answered, "I still do not believe it is possible for anyone to succeed in stirring the Senate up to do anything serious about the suggested impeachment of Bill Douglas. There is nothing he has done to justify impeachment and I do not believe the Senate can be bamboozled into believing he has."[50]

It was not until after Black's death that Douglas learned the depth of Black's support, despite their difficulties during that period. Some months after his father's death, Hugo Black, Jr., told Douglas that some Southerners had tried to get the younger Black to convey a message to Hugo about their desire to be rid of Douglas.

The justice had replied: "I have known Bill Douglas for thirty years. He's never knowingly done any improper, unethical or corrupt thing. Tell his detractors that in spite of my age, I think I have one trial left in me. Tell them that if they move against Bill Douglas, I'll resign from the Court and represent him. It will be the biggest, most important case I ever tried."[51]

Defending the Legacy

Not only did Douglas weather the storm, but he stayed at work in spite of it. He was there for five more years, participating in some of the most difficult cases of his career. Douglas did not have Black to work with any longer, and he felt the loss very deeply. In several respects, Douglas saw himself as defending the legacy of his three-decade effort with Black to protect constitutional liberty. It was a period of transition in which the Burger Court made headway against some of Douglas's most ardently held constitutional understandings. There were changes in constitutional criminal procedure, in First Amendment interpretations, in the right to privacy, in the field of race discrimination, and in decisions concerning just how wide the courthouse doors should be opened to public law litigation.

Chief Justice Burger came to the Court in 1969. Blackmun was elevated to fill Fortas's seat in 1970. Rehnquist and Powell joined in 1972. In short, the Nixon appointees had enough votes to grant a hearing in any case they chose. Douglas, Brennan, and Marshall generally needed either Stewart or White, and, given the tendency of these two to vote on a variety of issues with the Nixon appointees, that was not all that easy to do. Moreover, on many questions the Burger Court justices needed only one vote to gain a majority when they stuck together, as they often did, particularly in the early years. Douglas concluded that the changes were of major importance and not for the better. "The contest within the Court in my early years," he wrote,

> was between the Frankfurter school, which thought that even specific constitutional guarantees could be watered down by "reasonable" regulations, and those of us, especially Black and myself, who read those specific guarantees more literally as part of the plan of the Framers to take government off the backs of the people when it came to specified civil rights. With the passage of time the Frankfurter school of thought came to be sponsored by Burger and Blackmun—though they were quite inappropriately called "strict constructionists"—and it will probably endure. Black's death gave this view great momentum.[52]

It was not simply a question of ideology or voting proclivities in any given policy area. Douglas was now the senior justice, and because he and Burger were often on opposing sides of a case, he had the responsibility of assigning opinions when the chief was not in the majority and he was. Douglas thought that Burger abused the assignment power, manipulating vote counts in order to control assignments. There were several open conflicts on this question. He also clashed with Burger over administrative issues, such as office space and clerk assignments. One of his colleagues in those later years remarked that it appeared as though Justice Brennan was called on to mediate some of these tensions, rather like Black had before him.[53]

One of the most dramatic of these clashes came over the abortion cases, *Roe* v. *Wade* and *Doe* v. *Bolton*.[54] Douglas took issue with Burger's discussion of an assignment in *Doe,* the Georgia case, on grounds that the alignment was Brennan, Stewart, Marshall, and Douglas to strike elements of the law and Burger, White, and Blackmun to uphold it.[55] Burger disagreed, claiming that "there were, literally, not enough columns [in the docket sheet] to mark up an accurate reflection of the voting in either the Georgia or the Texas cases."[56] The stakes were raised considerably when Harry Blackmun produced his memorandum calling for reargument in both abortion cases and issued his memorandum in *Roe* v. *Wade* suggesting that the Court avoid the direct constitutional question on abortion and strike the state bar on grounds of vagueness.[57] Douglas and Brennan tried to persuade Blackmun to take on the issue directly and disputed the need for reargument. When, on June 1, the recently appointed justices Powell and Rehnquist decided to vote for reargument in the case, Douglas was outraged. He warned Burger that he would "file a statement telling what is happening to us and the tragedy it entails" if the Court held the cases over to the next term, and he immediately set to work on a memorandum, which he had printed and sent to Brennan.[58]

Douglas's memorandum charged that Burger improperly assigned the cases in the face of Douglas's request that he not do so. Douglas insisted that "the matter of assignment is not merely a matter of protocol." He recalled the tradition of assignment by senior associate in cases where the chief was not in the majority and warned that "when a Chief Justice tries to bend the Court to his will by manipulating assignments, the integrity of the institution is imperiled." He speculated that "perhaps the purpose of the Chief Justice . . . was to try to keep control of the merits. If that was the aim, he was unsuccessful."[59]

Brennan told Douglas that he had "serious reservations" about his publishing the memorandum and requested a number of specific deletions if Douglas was determined to go ahead with it. Douglas decided not to publish it, but a copy found its way to the *Washington Post.* When Douglas, then at his summer home in Goose Prairie, Washington, learned of the leak, he wrote to Burger to assure him that he was not the source. "I am upset and appalled. I never breathed a word concerning the cases, or my memo, to anyone outside the Court." Burger decided to answer Douglas's memo "to keep the record straight, and to allow any future scholar who may peruse the current press accounts or papers of Justices to have the 'due process' benefit of all the facts in context, as I have tried to place them fairly." While Doulgas answered in a more conciliatory tone, he maintained his original position on the assignment question.[60]

But in the end, what mattered most to Douglas was what he saw as an erosion of the liberty that had been earned slowly and painfully over his years on the bench. He intended to speak out against it and did. From 1960 through 1970, Douglas published 171 dissents, or just over a 15 a year. From 1971 until his departure from the bench in 1975, he wrote 200 dissents, or an average of 40 a year, and that included his last year, when he produced fewer opinions because of illness.

Many observers saw the speech, press, and religion issues presented to the Court in these years as complex ones. Douglas did not. The First Amendment was, as Black had said so often, absolute. Thus Douglas had no patience with the argument that controversial speakers could be kept out of the country. He dissented vigorously when the Court upheld a State Department decision withholding a visa from a Marxist speaker who had been invited to address a number of university audiences in the United States.[61] He dissented sharply when the Court refused to require an opportunity for a hearing in a case in which a faculty member's contract was not renewed allegedly because of controversial positions he had taken on campus.[62]

His broad view of freedom of expression, association, and political action was not limited to the college campus. Douglas found Burger Court decisions upholding Hatch Act restrictions on public employees' expression and political association extremely troublesome. He and Black had first addressed the Hatch Act in 1947, dissenting from the Court's ruling that upheld the statute.[63] The cases that emerged in the 1970s challenged the federal restriction and state statutes modeled on the federal civil-service limitations. The requirements in these restrictions were so vague that employees could not be certain what they could or could not say or do, and the scope of the rules was much too broad even if there were some justification for limiting the political activity of civil servants.[64] Douglas saw a threat not just to the individuals who worked for the government, but to the bureaucracy itself: "A bureaucracy that is alert, vigilant, and alive is more efficient than one that is quiet and submissive. It is the First Amendment that makes it alert, vigilant, and alive. It is suppression of First Amendment rights that creates faceless, nameless bureaucrats who are inert in their localities and submissive to some master's voice."[65]

As in areas of free speech, Douglas found nothing particularly complicated in matters of freedom of the press. The absolute protections of the First Amendment freedoms covered the ability to acquire, edit, and disseminate news. Douglas dissented from the Court's decision requiring reporters to testify about their confidential sources before grand juries.[66] He objected to the Court's rulings that upheld the authority of state and federal officials to limit reporters' access to prisons and interviews with inmates.[67] Douglas saw no authority for any governmental restraint on the press, including punishment after the fact. He had joined Black's position in *New York Times* v. *Sullivan,* rejecting the idea of libel applied to public matters or public officials. He complained bitterly when the Court in 1974 differentiated between public and private figures, even in cases concerning public issues, and allowed private figures to collect defamation judgments with no protection at all for the press.[68]

During his time on the bench, Black saw only one major dispute concerning the changing status of broadcasters under the First Amendment—the battle over the fairness doctrine. In 1969, he and Douglas had joined the Court in upholding the fairness rule. Douglas later rejected the argument that broadcasters and print journalists are different under the First Amendment in a case concerning the networks' refusal to sell time to the Democratic National Committee. He argued that "TV and radio stand in the same protected position under the First Amendment as do newspapers and magazines."[69] In so doing, Douglas, at least, thought he was defending the principle of free speech and press in contemporary America. Much as he and Black had joined the Court in the 1950s to find that modern conditions required the association with others for the advancement of ideas, he now asserted that modern political free speech required access to the media.

One of the most difficult First Amendment problems for many of the justices during this period was obscenity. Douglas, like Black, had no difficulty with it at all. The Court faced a string of obscenity cases in 1973 and 1974 that became the forum in which Chief Justice Burger argued for a relaxed standard under which communities could be rid of this worthless stuff. Brennan, who had been the leading author of opinions on the obscenity doctrine for more than a decade, made clear his intention to switch positions and to oppose obscenity convictions except when the material had been thrust on unwilling recipients or had been made available to children.[70] Burger called for a "division of the house" between Brennan and himself on the general question of the obscenity stand. The standard was relaxed in 1973 in *Miller* v. *California*.

Douglas, much in the spirit of Hugo Black, rejected the Court's approach and insisted that it was impossible for authors to know whether their works would be protected by the First Amendment.[71] He found it utterly ridiculous that the Court would decide in 1969 that willing adults could have obscene literature in their own homes,[72] but that they could be prohibited from purchasing or transporting it.[73]

The final area of First Amendment debate in which Douglas found himself defending their legacy was the free exercise and establishment of religion. Douglas, like Black, was not impressed by arguments that the programs providing construction or operating funds for nonsectarian elements of religious schools did not advance religion. It was not possible to separate the secular and sectarian elements of education in a religious school without producing the kind of excessive entanglement of church and state that would surely result in the hostility that the establishment clause was intended to prevent.[74] Further, government assistance freed dollars from one part of the church schools' budgets that could be spent elsewhere. Since Black and Douglas could not accept a situation in which the government was underwriting base-line financing of religious education quite apart from any particular program or activity, they could not accept Chief Justice Burger's attempt to define a line between acceptable and unacceptable forms of financial assistance in the 1971 finance cases.[75] Any assistance was too much, and after Black's departure, Douglas joined Brennan and a few others within a badly divided Court to fight efforts to find means of providing financial aid.[76]

Despite his hard line on establishment issues, Douglas remained sensitive to the complexity of some of the more difficult free-exercise issues. Nowhere is this more evident than in his effort to resolve for himself the difficult questions presented by the 1972 Amish school-attendance case, in which Douglas dissented on grounds that the rights of the children as well as the parents had to be considered in determining whether mandatory school-attendance laws should be waived.[77]

For many Americans, issues of religious freedom and the question of privacy were joined in the hard-fought debate over whether the right to privacy supported a right to obtain an abortion. Just how far would the *Griswold* opinion reach?

Black was gone by the time the Court, in 1972, struck down a Massachusetts law making it a felony to provide contraceptive materials to unmarried persons.[78]

It is clear that Black would have resisted this and other privacy-related decisions just as vigorously as he had *Griswold*. Of course, it was the 1973 *Roe* v. *Wade* decision, recognizing the right of a woman in consultation with her physician to terminate a pregnancy, that produced the most intense controversy. But *Roe* was not the first abortion case to come to the Burger Court.

In 1971, Douglas had dissented from a decision that upheld the District of Columbia ban on abortions unless they were required for the life or health of the woman. Following that, Douglas, Brennan, and Marshall were ready to take the next step and establish the right to an abortion. As the story of *Roe* v. *Wade* recounted earlier indicated, Douglas was ready to go to war over the handling of the case, against both Burger's assignment of the opinion and Blackmun's handling of it unless the opinion actually confronted the core question of a women's right as a matter of privacy to terminate a pregnancy. In the end, that was the resolution.

Douglas saw a variety of decisions in the area of equal protection during his later years that were clearly wrong in his judgment, though, again, he and Black would often have disagreed. He joined the dissenters when the Court held in 1973 that property-tax-based school-funding systems did not discriminate on the basis of race and wealth.[79] Like the others, he could not understand how the Court could conclude that equal education is not a right either explicitly or implicitly protected by the Constitution, given *Brown* v. *Board of Education.* The *Brown* opinion, after all, had said that "education is a right which must be made available to all on equal terms."[80]

He disliked the developing distinction between de jure and de facto school segregation when cases challenging race discrimination in schools moved north, to areas where there had never been a statute specifically mandating segregation. His answer to the problem was to eliminate the distinction and simply determine whether there were racially segregated schools. If so, there was a violation of equal protection, and it ought to be corrected.[81] In this case and others, Douglas found it ironic and clearly unacceptable that segregation was treated as accidental when the government had been implicated in it for years. The government's participation had included the encouragement of racially restrictive covenants, discriminatory zoning decisions, administration of school districts, assignment of personnel on the basis of race, and administration of grant programs to perpetuate segregation within a community. Dissenting in *Milliken* v. *Bradley,* which overturned a multidistrict busing plan that included Detroit-area suburbs, Douglas warned:

> The issue is not whether there should be racial balance but whether the state's use of various devices that end up with black schools and white schools brought the Equal Protection Clause into effect. . . . It is conceivable that ghettos develop on their own without any hint of state action. But since Michigan by one device or another has over the years created black school districts and white school districts, the task of equity is to provide a unitary system for the affected area where, as here, the state washes its hands of its own creations.[82]

As for the other areas of equal protection that he had pressed so vigorously, Douglas saw the Court refuse to maintain that gender, legitimacy, alienage, or poverty were inherently suspect classifications.[83] Neither did his views with regard to the state action doctrine, in which private firms or individuals connected with government were discriminatory, fare well.[84] He found himself struggling to hold ground that he thought had already been won, and it was clear he was engaged in a losing battle.

One new question for Douglas in the 1970s was whether some kind of affirmative action was permissible in cases where racial minorities or women were treated differently to compensate for prior discrimination. Writing for the Court, Douglas upheld a Florida tax exemption for widows but not widowers.[85] Noting the historic discrimination against women in the work place, Douglas found the situation that often confronted widows forced back into the marketplace quite different from that of widowers.

In the other major case of affirmative action he faced, Douglas sought to be flexible in response to historic patterns of discrimination, but he was not willing to allow programs to rely solely on race as the criterion for government action in the absence of a proven case of prior discrimination.[86] Anticipating the position the Court would eventually take in *University of California Regents* v. *Bakke,* Douglas argued that race could be one factor among many that universities might take into consideration, but he rejected the idea of a minority-only admissions program.[87]

Of all the changes Douglas witnessed in his final years on the Supreme Court, none was more troubling than the set of rulings that began to push the doors of the federal courthouse closed. For Douglas, judicial power was also a judicial responsibility. The abdication of the judicial duty to decide cases and controversies arising under the Constitution and laws was just as dangerous as the abuse of judicial power.[88] It was critical, in his view, that the citizen could believe that a forum was available in which justice could be obtained.

Douglas's great fear was that the Burger Court was developing precisely the wrong image. He argued that it was using procedural devices to avoid important questions. It seemed unwilling to make the kind of substantive decisions needed to ensure checks on the abuse of power by other branches of government and to guarantee constitutional rights and liberties. Douglas produced a variety of opinions on standing to sue in which he advocated a flexible and open policy.[89] Particulary in Douglas's last two years on the bench, the Court's rulings suggested an intention to stop the expansion of the standing doctrine and, in fact, to read standing much more narrowly than it had been interpreted for some time.[90] Douglas responded angrily.[91]

Just as it was somehow appropriate for Black to have written his last major opinion in a free-press case, so it seems fitting that one of Douglas's last decisions was a plaintive cry against efforts to restrict access to the courts when those who complained of a serious injustice came in search of a hearing. The decision had denied standing to a wide variety of plaintiffs seeking to prosecute an open-housing case concerning a zoning decision in an upstate New York community. Douglas wrote in dissent,

> Standing has become a barrier to access to the federal courts, just as "the political question" was in earlier decades. The mounting caseload of federal courts is well known. But cases such as this one reflect festering sores in our society; and the American dream

teaches that if one reaches high enough and persists there is a forum where justice is dispensed. I would lower the technical barriers and let the courts serve that ancient need. They can in time be curbed by legislative or constitutional restraints if an emergency arises.[92]

Douglas saw the trend toward tighter access rules as well in the Court's rulings on abstention and mootness, and with respect to a more guarded approach to the use of class action suits.[93] He viewed these cases as "monuments to the present Court's abdication of its constitutional responsibility to decide cases properly within its jurisdiction."[94]

One of the reasons Douglas was so concerned about the possibility of access to the courts being limited was the trend he saw toward abuse of power, particularly in the executive branch. The principal presidential-power issues during the Burger Court years centered on Vietnam, national security policy, and Watergate. Given his view that Vietnam was a "presidential war," not authorized by Congress, Douglas found the draft cases particularly troublesome. They were more than First Amendment problems or due process cases; they raised issues of executive power.[95]

The draft challenges could be divided into several categories. First, there were the cases Douglas hoped would cause the Court to address the legitimacy of the Vietnam War directly. His opinions on this subject frequently appeared as dissents or dissents from denials of certiorari. Second, there were cases that dealt with the meaning and boundaries of conscientious-objector status. Third, there were cases that concerned the harrassment of conscientious objectors before induction or abuse in the service while the objectors attempted to process CO claims. Fourth, there were the claims of arbitrary and capricious administration of the draft laws by local draft boards and the selective service system. Finally, there were procedural questions associated with ensuring adequate legal oversight of the selective service operation.

The cases presenting challenges to the validity of the war in Vietnam came in many forms, and often in litigation concerning the draft. The draft cases ranged from classification questions, to preinduction resistance, to refusal to accept induction, to postinduction applications for conscientious-objector status, to refusal to accept shipment to Southeast Asia. They presented First Amendment issues of free exercise of religion, Thirteenth Amendment claims of illegal involuntary servitude, and Fifth Amendment allegations of due process violations; most also contained a foundation assertion that the legitimacy of the war itself was in question. Recalling this period, Douglas said: "I wrote numerous opinions stating why we should take these cases and decide them. Once or twice Potter Stewart and Bill Brennan joined me. But there was never a fourth vote. I thought then—and still do think—that treating the question as a 'political' one was an abdication of duty and a self-inflicted wound on the Court."[96] During the Vietnam War, Douglas argued for a broad interpretation of conscientious-objector status, in favor of checks on arbitrary behavior by draft boards, and in favor of protections against abuses by both military and civilian authorities.[97]

Douglas was also concerned about the Nixon administration's domestic activities, including the effort to block publication of the Pentagon Papers, though there was no statute preventing it. He was concerned that security classifications were being used to cover up misdeeds rather than to protect important national security interests. He rejected claims of inherent presidential powers in the area of national security, such as the domestic use of warrantless wiretaps,[98] and saw the domestic-surveillance cases as part of a much larger problem.

> As illustrated by a flood of cases before us this Term, . . . we are currently in the throes of another national seizure of paranoia, resembling the hysteria which surrounded the Alien and Sedition Acts, the Palmer Raids, and the McCarthy era. Those who register dissent or who petition the government for redress are subjected to scrutiny by grand juries, by the FBI, or even by the military. Their associates are investigated. Their homes are bugged and their telephones are wiretapped. They are befriended by secret government informers. Their patriotism and loyalty are questioned. . . . More than our privacy is implicated. Also at stake is the reach of the Government's power to intimidate its critics.[99]

The irony is that Douglas did not know that the FBI had been keeping a substantial file on him since the early 1950s, which included evaluations of his speeches and writings, with particular attention to those that might be considered subversive.[100]

The attempt to abuse power did not surprise Douglas, but he did have great difficulty accepting the Court's reluctance to meet the challenge to rights and liberties that he saw as so obvious and so serious. He dissented vigorously when the Court refused to review the military domestic-surveillance program in 1972 on standing grounds.[101] He argued that the program, which rested on "brute power" and nothing more, "must be repudiated as a usurpation dangerous to the civil liberties on which free men are dependent." He termed it "a cancer on the body politic . . . a measure of the disease which afflicts us," and, given that the "Constitution was designed to keep government off the backs of the people," he found it difficult to believe that the Court would stand by and do nothing.

Given his disdain for Richard Nixon, Douglas thought that Watergate or something like it was more or less to be expected. In fact, in his dissent to a 1972 case, Douglas suggested that the problems presented by the use of the secret stamp and of executive privilege to prevent congressional inquiry into the practices of the executive branch "looms large as one of separation of powers."[102] Douglas joined the Court's unanimous opinion in *United States* v. *Nixon*.[103] In fact, he had been waiting for Nixon to slip and considering just how to go after him if the opportunity presented itself. He was not pleased by the abuse of power, but he was happy to see Nixon brought down and glad that the Court performed its historic role.

Douglas Leaves the Court

Among the many ironies in Douglas's career was that in 1969 he had been making plans to retire from the Court just as the movement to impeach him began.[104] Once the criticisms began to be voiced publicly, Douglas started to have mixed emotions. On the one hand, he had had it! As his widow explains it, Douglas expressed the feeling more than once during this period that he had worked terribly hard throughout his whole professional life, laboring over opinions, books, and articles that it was likely no one would read, only to be labeled a subversive and worse. It just was not worth it. As late as February 1970, Douglas told Black that he planned to retire.[105] Yet Bill Douglas was not about to be frightened or hounded into resigning from the Court. Once serious talk of impeachment began, there was no way he was going to turn tail and run. He stayed for four years after Black's departure, and, like his colleague, it was health and not politics that made him leave the bench.

After the impeachment attempt had been disposed of, Douglas resumed his active schedule. On New Year's Eve 1974, he and Cathleen flew to Nassau, where he suffered a massive stroke at 7:30 that evening. Chief Justice Burger was immediately informed, and he, in turn, promptly telephoned President Ford in Colorado. Ford dispatched a military aircraft to take Douglas's doctor to Nassau and to return them to the United States. By 9:30 the next morning, Douglas was in Walter Reed Army Hospital. At first, his recovery proceeded reasonably well, though it was clear that a long and difficult period of therapy would be necessary to restore the full use of his left arm and leg.

As time passed, however, it became less certain that Douglas would be back on the bench any time soon. He began intensive therapy, which he hoped would have him ready to resume his duties at the beginning of the October term. Rumors of retirement spread, but Douglas dismissed them in an interview with the *New York Times* in July: "There's no chance I'll retire. . . . I'll be there in October, positively." When the term began, he tried to attend oral arguments, having his wheelchair moved to the bench, but the pain persisted. By mid-November 1975, it was clear that the strain was simply too much.[106]

Douglas called Chief Justice Burger and asked permission to join the justices who met in the upstairs dining room for lunch. It was an unusual request because he had usually avoided the luncheons. He was wheeled to the luncheon, where he asked Burger to read a letter to his colleagues that he had in his vest pocket. An associate justice is not required to involve the chief justice in any decision about retirement and many choose not to do so, but Douglas wanted to communicate a message to Burger and the brethren. Despite the disagreements they had had since Burger's arrival, Douglas appreciated the courtesy he had been shown over the past year and was thanking Burger symbolically, as well as indicating respect for the institution and the office of chief justice. On November 18, 1975, Justice Douglas retired from the bench.[107]

His wife, Cathleen; Clark Clifford, their attorney; and his longtime friend Abe Fortas had been at work drafting the formal resignation letter for the president. After he signed the letter and the messenger was dispatched to the White House, Cathleen and he waited together in his chambers until confirmation came from President Ford that his resignation had been received. As they left the chambers after hearing from the White House, Justice Douglas "lifted his good arm and said to the staff, which had assembled at the door, 'keep the faith.'" He wrote:

> Keep the faith in the rule of law not only for our own people but for the people of the world.
> Keep the faith in a unity of mankind irrespective of race, intellect, color, religion, or ideology.

Keep the faith in the informed citizenry who can govern wisely and justly.

Keep the faith in the system that allows a place for every man no matter how lowly or how great.

Keep the faith in a system which does not leave every issue of human rights to the ups and downs of the political campaigns.[108]

Tributes came from far and wide. Those who participated in Congress's recognition of his thirty-six and a half years of service on the bench took particular pleasure in recalling the attacks Douglas had withstood and the many contributions he had made.[109] Among the most touching of these came from his colleagues on the Court, and to them he replied:

I am reminded of many canoe trips I have taken in my lifetime. Those who start down a water course may be strangers at the beginning but almost invariably are close friends at the end. There were many strong headwinds to overcome and there were rainy as well as sun drenched days to travel. The portages were long and many and some were very strenuous. But there was always a pleasant camp in a stand of white bark birch and water concerts held at night to the music of the loons; and inevitably there came the last camp fire, the last breakfast cooked over last night's fire, and the parting was always sad.

And yet, in fact, there was no parting because each happy memory of the choice parts of the journey—and of the whole journey—was of a harmonious effort filled with fulfilling and beautiful hours as well as dull and dreary ones. The greatest such journey I've made with you, my Brethren, who were strangers at the start but warm and fast friends at the end.[110]

Some of those who joined the chorus of recognition recalled the poem written for the celebration of Douglas's twentieth anniversary on the Court by Stanley Young. It ended with the following lines:

Let us, then, honor the far traveler,
Let us honor him who makes
The world his walk and window,
And the long almanac of liberty
The calendar of his days.

This is the high, the final
Adventure of history.

Let us honor brave men, and the
road taken.

14

Standing the Test of Time: The Enduring Legacy of Justices Hugo L. Black and William O. Douglas

THERE IS NO question that Justices Hugo L. Black and William O. Douglas were, in the words of Justice Brennan, at the epicenter of an "extraordinary revolution in constitutional law."[1] It is equally clear that both of them were "elemental force[s] in American constitutional development."[2] For more than three decades, these two battle-hardened New Deal colleagues examined, discussed, debated, agreed, and often disagreed, with each other and with thirty others who debated, agreed, and warred with them on the parameters of the Constitution. Black and Douglas, especially on substantive questions of civil liberties and civil rights, were judicial leaders in the difficult and continuing effort to uphold and strengthen the Constitution's protections against the government's effort to restrict or deny personal liberty. However, while Black devoted himself to defining the extent of the powers of government, including the Supreme Court itself, under the Constitution, Douglas was ceaseless in his efforts to protect the rights of all Americans under the Constitution by using the interpretative power of the Court to expand the meaning of the Bill of Rights.

Douglas and Black differed in their views of the relation between democracy and liberty under the Constitution, and of how the Supreme Court could protect its legitimacy so as to play its critical role in defining power and protecting rights.

Hugo Black, with a "near religious fervor" for most of his tenure on the Court, fought and argued to base his and the Court's constitutional interpretation on the literal text itself. Black's preference was always for fixed legal norms. This deeply held judicial belief came about when, as a legislator, he had watched "in horror" as a reactionary Social Darwinist Supreme Court used its powers carelessly and without attention to the historic meaning of the phrases in the Constitution to eviscerate governmentally created social and economic policy.[3]

William Douglas, however, whose commitment was as strong and, indeed, as intense as Black's attachment to the constitutional text, wanted the Court to go beyond these fixed legal standards and to maintain the freedoms that, in his judgment were immune from governmental curtailment. As he wrote to Edmond Cahn, the Bill of Rights' protections "are negative and do not generate the forces of freedom. They are merely designed to see to it that opportunities for freedom are not destroyed by the government."[4] The Court had to extend the scope of the Bill of Rights to protect the rights of free persons in a highly technological society. To leave them defined as they were in an earlier day would permit a changing society to render them weak or even meaningless.

Hugo Black's judicial philosophy was centered around his love of democracy and reverence for the men of the "constitutional period." The instruments of government they created meshed well with the nation's capacity for democratic rule. Black considered democratic principles essential to a functioning, free society; without them, liberty could not exist. And liberty was limited in turn by democracy and its inherent policy-making processes. When in doubt, Black favored democracy. Unless there were patently offensive and fundamental violations of clearly defined constitutional rights by the majority, a person's privacy or liberty could be invaded by the state's agents to fulfill legitimate ends of government.

In Black's jurisprudential view, history and the constitutional text were important because they provided the Supreme Court judge with a fairly clear set of legal standards for adjudicating disputes. Always at war against judicial roaming in the murky "natural law" ether of substantive rights—whether economic or political or civil—Black tried to interpret constitutional phrases in accordance with the intent of the Framers and the history of the clause or amendment. This attitude disappointed many because it led to "conservative" judgments. Robert Mack Bell, the successful petitioner in the controverial 1963 case *Bell* v. *Maryland,* wrote: "I was totally disappointed in Black. . . . I was surprised that Black took the position he did. I would have assumed that Black would have gone the other way."[5]

However, as Black said in a 1966 Georgia election case (in which Douglas had dissented): "This Court, *this* Court, this *Court* is not allowed to write laws. We are here to interpret only" (Black's emphasis).[6] For Black, the Court had to be protected from itself by judicial self-restraint: Supreme Court judges must avoid the kind of natural law–based interference with the legitimate outcomes of the democratic process.

It is clear that Black's jurisprudence was irrevocably shaped by his antipathy and subsequent hostility, as an Alabama politician in the Congress, to the Supreme Court. He saw in that institution an inordinate level of judicial discretion. Giving the constitutional text a Social Darwinist gloss, Court majorities declared unconstitutional numerous legislative efforts by the national and state governments to respond to the economic ills that beset the nation in the 1920s and 1930s. Black vowed, after he became a justice, to be religiously consistent in his decisions and to fight vigorously against a judiciary that used its discretion freely.

This commitment to avoid judicial discretion (for example, by faithfully following the logic of his own actions in prior cases) was accompanied by his doctrine of First Amendment absolutism. Black exhibited a dual pattern of judicial behavior and doctrinal development that emerged fully during the late 1940s and early 1950s. For D. Grier Stephenson, Black's "consistency combined with absolutism . . . guard[ed] the First Amendment from 'balancers' (led chiefly by Frankfurter) who would not only weaken constitutional commands in deference to Congress and state legislatures but would leave the meaning of the First Amendment in the hands of those who found its restriction most convenient."[7] Black's attitude toward judicial discretion clashed sharply with those of many of his colleagues. They, however, generally respected him because of his unshakable attachment to his beliefs. As one scholar wrote, "No justice of the Court conscientiously and persistently endeavored, as much as Justice Black did, to establish consistent standards of objectivity for adjudicating constitutional questions."[8]

Douglas believed the Supreme Court had to be defended, but not as an end in itself. The end was the protection of the rights of persons to their liberty and the freedom to act consistent with their beliefs. The Court must exercise its independence forthrightly in the very purpose for which that protection was given: to defend rights and freedom against the incursions of temporary majorities whose whims and passions were translated into governmental policy by elected and appointed officials.

Because many citizens, Douglas thought, understood the Court's purpose dimly, the best way to defend the Court was for it to perform its duty proudly and openly. The hypocritical façade that the Court did not make policy would not, he believed, be accepted by citizens. It was not the foundation on which to build and maintain support for the institution. The true foundation was the belief by every person in the nation, regardless of class, religion, gender, or race, that there is a place where justice can be obtained.

While he believed that the Bill of Rights "guarantee[d] to us all the rights to personal and spiritual fulfillment,"[9] he also believed that the guarantee was viable only as long as the Court acted on that general promise of freedom. It was inevitable that Black and Douglas would clash over this basic tenet of Douglas's. During the height of the cold war, when free speech in its purest form was denied to certain persons and groups by legislation such as the Smith Act, Douglas and Black spoke with one voice. Once the "speech plus–symbol speech" dilemma arose, especially in the civil rights cases of the early 1960s, they began to diverge. Douglas believed the Court had to reach beyond the literal and historic concepts of judicial interpretation of the Constitution to defend the rights of persons to act freedly without government restrictions of liberties.

In their examinations of constitutional doctrine, one zeroed in on issues of power; the other was most concerned about the maintenance of liberty in a democracy. Elizabeth Black recalled that Hugo always tried to "talk" these differences out with her because he could not talk them out with Douglas and that it always bothered him when he and Douglas could not agree because they were "so close in their thinking."[10] The wonder was that they remained such close friends over the intervening decades; in Douglas's own words, Black "was my closest friend on the Court, and my companion in many hard judicial battles."

While they did go separate ways in the last decade of their joint tenure, they had, together, a dramatic impact on civil rights jurisprudence. Both Black and Douglas vigorously defended the rights of the people to absolute protection of the First Amendment's guarantees. Many of their opinions—majority, concurring, and dissenting—are landmarks in the nation's repository of political theories of freedom, responsibility, power, and rights in a democracy. They have been and will continue to be studied as much for their substantive philosophical content as for their doctrinal significance. Together, in the face of the terrible gale of invective and personal attacks (along with secret FBI investigations of their loyalty), the two spoke in defense of the rights of free people and spoke about the limits of government in a civilized society.

Felix Frankfurter, President Roosevelt's trusted adviser, had close associations with some of the giants on the Supreme Court: Holmes, Brandeis, Cardozo, Stone, Taft, and Hughes. Yet as a participant in a small group's development of constitutional doctrine for the society, Frankfurter's martinet-like character and academic style did not serve him well. Instead, ironically, it was Hugo Black, a self-described "backward country fellow," a plodding, self-taught, stay-up-till-4-A.M. Black, joined by brilliant Bill Douglas, who became the major jurisprudential actor in the Supreme Court's post-1937 constitutional revolution.

Although he came to the Court lacking Frankfurter's academic credentials and depth of understanding of the Constitution and the federal judicial process, Black was a much stronger leader than Frankfurter. Black had a much greater impact on constitutional development in large part because he knew how to work with his peers and because he was right on the substantive issues—and because, at last, there developed a national audience that accepted Black's and Douglas's views on the meaning and scope of First Amendment freedoms as more appropriate than Frankfurter's perspective.

Black was always, as Justice Harry Blackmun once respectfully said, the "canny, lovable manipulator" of men and ideas on the Court in order to defend his commitment to a functioning, self-educating democratic society. Black obeyed his conviction that the Court had to practice self-control. As his friend Douglas acknowledged, "Hugo Black was fiercely intent on every point of law he presented."[11] His judicial (and senatorial) opponents knew, and both Frankfurter and Jackson had written, that when they disagreed with Hugo Black, they had to prepare for a war of ideas with a worthy opponent.

If Hugo Black was the profound thinker, the craftsman who constructed the First Amendment absolutist jurisprudential arguments he and Douglas employed as they defended those freedoms, then Bill Douglas was the conscience of the Supreme Court. Although his intellect was greatly admired and some of his colleagues considered him a near genius, Douglas did not focus his energies on building majorities and fine-tuning doctrines, as Black did.

Douglas cared passionately for principles of liberty and justice. In contrast to Black, he saw the world as more complex and the role of the Court in it as multifaceted. That complexity forced him to reconsider issues over time, but always with an eye toward the rights of persons and liberty. Law, like life itself, he said, was change. He was prepared to be a loner if that was what a stand in defense of liberty required. "Douglas was just as happy signing a one-man dissent as picking up four more votes," said one of his law clerks.[12] Certainly, his pleas for a review of the constitutionality of presidential power to conduct the Vietnam War and his arguments on behalf of conscientious objectors during that war were evidence of that noble attribute.

Bernard Schwartz commented that "great men do make a difference, even in the law."[13] Hugo Black and Bill Douglas, two New Dealers from very different cultural and political tracks, are classic examples of the truth of that aphorism. Both had a profound impact on the constitutional development, and on national policy, that occurred during and after their tenure on the Court. Through their long journey as justices of the Court, one gets a clear sense of the major struggles and dilemmas the justices and American society confronted: wars, both declared and undeclared; the Communist "Red Scare" xenophobia; a major revolution in race relations; growing national fear of crime; the threat to privacy of a highly technical, bureaucratized society; and new tensions in the modern federal political system.

Black and Douglas, in the almost revolutionary judicial effort to resolve these and other constitutional issues, had the zeal and the commitment of those dedicated to the hope that their actions might ultimately lead to "a world in which men everywhere shall be entitled to walk upright, to enjoy full individual freedom, and to live in peace."[14]

Black never let Americans forget that there are limits to the uses of governmental power, as described in the Bill of Rights, but that, short of these limits being reached, powerful governmental actors, reflecting the will of a literate, civil, and orderly electorate, can act to move the community toward the better life. Bill Douglas never let Americans forget that there are certain rights of free men and women that must never be abridged by government. In so reminding the nation of the nature of power and right, these two jurists continue to have a profound impact on American constitutional and political life.

Notes

Abbreviations

DDEP	Dwight D. Eisenhower Papers, Dwight D. Eisenhower Presidential Library, Abilene, Kansas
EWP	Earl Warren Papers, Library of Congress, Washington, D.C.
FDRP	Franklin Delano Roosevelt Papers, Franklin Delano Roosevelt Presidential Library, Hyde Park, New York
FFP	Felix Frankfurter Papers, Harvard Law School, Cambridge, Massachusetts
FFP/LC	Felix Frankfurther Papers, Library of Congress, Washington, D.C.
HFSP	Harlan Fiske Stone Papers, Library of Congress, Washington, D.C.
HHBP	Harold H. Burton Papers, Library of Congress, Washington, D.C.
HLBP*	Hugo L. Black Papers, Library of Congress, Washington, D.C.
HSTP	Harry S. Truman Papers, Harry S. Truman Presidential Library, Independence, Missouri
JMHP	John M. Harlan Papers, Mudd Library, Princeton University, Princeton, New Jersey
RHJP*	Robert H. Jackson Papers, Library of Congress, Washington, D.C.
WBRP	Wiley B. Rutledge Papers, Library of Congress, Washington, D.C.
WJBP*	William J. Brennan Papers, Library of Congress, Washington, D.C.
WODP	William O. Douglas Papers, Library of Congress, Washington, D.C.

Chapter 1

1. Harold R. Burton, "The Story of the Place: Where First and A Streets Formerly Met at What Is Now the Site of the Supreme Court Building" (Speech prepared for the dedication of a plaque presented by the Columbia Historical Society, May 1952). WODP, Box 313. Although the building was completed in 1935 and Court sessions were held there after it opened, the other justices refused to break the tradition of maintaining their chambers in their homes to move into the new building (David M. O'Brien, *Storm Center* [New York: Norton, 1986], p. 115).
2. Richard L. Williams, "The Supreme Court of the United States: The Staff that Keeps It Operating," *Smithsonian,* February 1977, p. 42.

*Some restrictions placed on use of files.

3. Joseph P. Lash, ed., *From the Diaries of Felix Frankfurter* (New York: Norton, 1974), p. 155.
4. David Easton, *The Political System* (New York: Knopf, 1953), p. 129.
5. Harold Lasswell, *Who Gets What, When, How* (New York: Meridian Books, 1958).
6. O'Brien, *Storm Center,* p. 13.
7. Hugo L. Black to Alan V. Washburn, 17 December 1958, HLBP, Box 59.
8. Hugo L. Black, "William Orville Douglas," 73 *Yale Law Journal* 915, 916 (1964).
9. Interview with Cathleen Douglas-Stone, 14 November 1986, Boston.
10. Ibid.
11. Eliot Janeway, "Bill Douglas, Fighter," *The Nation,* 11 January 1941, p. 49.

Chapter 2

1. Mark Silverstein, *Constitutional Faiths: Felix Frankfurter, Hugo Black and the Process of Judicial Decision Making* (Ithaca, N.Y.: Cornell University Press, 1984), p. 93 n. 6.
2. "My father was a farmer," said Hugo Black in his first campaign speech for the United States Senate in 1926. He described their struggle "with a rocky soil and high priced fertilizers, in an effort to grow enough cheap cotton to purchase the very necessities of life" (HLBP, Box 90). George C. Freeman, Jr., quoted in "Justice Hugo Black," *Richmond Times-Dispatch,* 12 December 1971, p. D1.
3. Sheldon Hackney, "The Clay County Origins of Mr. Justice Black: The Populist as Insider," 36 *Alabama Law Review* 835, 839 (1985).
4. Virginia Van der Veer Hamilton, *Hugo Black: The Alabama Years* (University: University of Alabama Press, 1982), p. 22.
5. J. Mills Thornton III, "Hugo Black and the Golden Age," 36 *Alabama Law Review* 899, 900 (1985).
6. Silverstein, *Constitutional Faiths,* p. 93.
7. Ibid., p. 94.
8. Thornton, "Hugo Black and the Golden Age," p. 899.
9. Hugo Black and Elizabeth Black, *Mr. Justice and Mrs. Black* (New York: Random House, 1986), p. 7.
10. Hackney, "Clay County Origins," p. 839.
11. James F. Simon, *The Antagonists: Hugo Black, Felix Frankfurter, and Civil Liberties in Modern America* (New York: Simon and Schuster, 1989), p. 69.
12. Black and Black, *Mr. Justice and Mrs. Black,* pp. 13–14.
13. Hugo Black, speech, 20 March 1925, HLBP, Box 82.
14. Simon, *Antagonists,* pp. 68–69.
15. Gerald T. Dunne, *Hugo Black and the Judicial Revolution* (New York: Simon and Schuster, 1977), p. 88. William Black's house had a strict moral code that he laid down—even if he chose to ignore it at times. "Coffee drinking, smoking and card playing were forbidden the young Blacks" (Hamilton, *Hugo Black,* p. 22).
16. Hamilton, *Hugo Black,* p. 15.
17. Black and Black, *Mr. Justice and Mrs. Black,* p. 8.
18. Ibid.
19. Hugo L. Black, "There Is a South of Union and Freedom," 2 *Georgia Law Review* 1, 15 (1967).
20. Hugo Black, Jr., *My Father: A Remembrance* (New York: Random House, 1975), pp. 4, 5; Silverstein, *Constitutional Faiths,* p. 95.
21. Daniel M. Berman, "Hugo L. Black: The Early Years," 8 *Catholic University Law Review* 103, 111 (1959).
22. Clifford J. Durr, "Hugo Black, Southerner," 10 *American University Law Review* 27, 28 (1967).
23. Daniel M. Berman, "The Racial Issue and Mr. Justice Black," 16 *American University Law Review* 386 (1967).

24. Hackney, "Clay County Origins," p. 839.
25. Hugo Black, Foreword to Lenore Cahn, ed., *Confronting Injustice: The Edmond Cahn Reader* (Boston: Little, Brown, 1966), p. xi.
26. Bertram Wyatt-Brown, "The Ethical Background of Hugo Black's Career," 36 *Alabama Law Review* 915, 917 (1985).
27. Black and Black, *Mr. Justice and Mrs. Black,* p. 15.
28. Ibid., p. 16.
29. Silverstein, *Constitutional Faiths,* p. 96, n. 13.
30. Hugo L. Black, "Reminiscences," 18 *Alabama Law Review* 1, 10 (1965).
31. Black and Black, *Mr. Justice and Mrs. Black,* pp. 17, 20, 25. As a young man, Black had two ambitions for the future, neither of which was realized. Black had "dreamed of occupying the White House. But [after he] was exposed to the nation as a former Klan member . . . the presidency became an unattainable goal" (Virginia Hamilton, "Lister Hill, Hugo Black, and the Albatross of Race," 36 *Alabama Law Review* 845, 859 [1985]). In 1969, Hugo told his wife that the biggest error he had ever made was joining the Klan. He felt sure that he would have been named vice president, instead of Harry Truman, to run with Franklin D. Roosevelt in 1944 (Black and Black, *Mr. Justice and Mrs. Black,* pp. 216, 228). His second unattained goal was to be chief justice of the United States. He rapidly emerged as a natural leader of the brethren, and there were two occasions, in 1940 and in 1946, when it was thought that Black might be elevated to that position, but due in part to conflicts among the brethren, he was never appointed.
32. Black and Black, *Mr. Justice and Mrs. Black,* p. 22. In the mid-1960s, Hugo Black and his wife rose early in the morning regularly to watch "Sunrise Semester" on television. He enjoyed the discussions about the ancient Greek philosophers but was not too happy with a "professor of political science [who] did not understand . . . 'Search and Seizure and the Fourth Amendment'" (p. 117).
33. Daniel J. Meador, "Mr. Justice Black: A Tribute," 57 *Virginia Law Review* 1109, 1111 (1971).
34. Hamilton, *Hugo Black,* p. 30.
35. Durr, "Hugo Black, Southerner" p. 30.
36. Hackney, "Clay County Origins," p. 835.
37. Wyatt-Brown, "Ethical Background," pp. 920–21.
38. Silverstein, *Constitutional Faiths,* p. 98.
39. Black and Black, *Mr. Justice and Mrs. Black,* pp. 31, 32.
40. Ibid., p. 34.
41. Hamilton, *Hugo Black,* pp. 45, 46.
42. Black and Black, *Mr. Justice and Mrs. Black,* p. 37.
43. Ibid., p. 53.
44. Hamilton, *Hugo Black,* p. 47.
45. Black and Black, *Mr. Justice and Mrs. Black,* p. 40.
46. Berman, "Early Years," p. 109.
47. Black and Black, *Mr. Justice and Mrs. Black,* p. 44.
48. Berman, "Early Years," p. 110.
49. Hackney, "Clay County Origins," p. 840.
50. William O. Douglas, *Go East Young Man: The Early Years* (New York: Random House, 1974), p. 447.
51. Black and Black, *Mr. Justice and Mrs. Black,* pp. 58, 59.
52. Hackney, "Clay County Origins," p. 840.
53. Black and Black, *Mr. Justice and Mrs. Black,* p. 62.
54. Ibid., pp. 75, 85, 86.
55. Virginia Foster Durr to Hugo Black, 5 March 1971, HLBP, Box 7. She did comment that there was "some objection to you from people like Dr. Wyman and Forney Johnson on the ground that you were a 'Bolshevik' and a labor union lawyer or as they said a 'Damage Suit Lawyer.'"

56. Taylor Branch, *Parting the Waters: America in the King Years, 1954–63* (New York: Simon and Schuster, 1988), pp. 121–22, 129–30.

57. "Kin of Justice Black Denies She's Communist," "Hugo Black's Sister-In-Law Is Accused," and "Ex-Red Accused of Being a Liar" were some of the March 1957 headline stories in Black's Durr file (HLBP, Box 7).

Jinksie described how Wellesley College changed her views on race in a May 10, 1954, letter to the *Alabama Journal:* "I came into contact with Negro girls who were just as well educated, just as smart (some a lot smarter) and just as well mannered as I was."

In June 1957, when Jo Jo, Black's daughter, was invited to a wedding in Montgomery. Jinksie wrote to Hugo, "I know all the Hounds of Hell are after you and you are the No. One enemy as far as they are concerned and I wonder if . . . JoJo's [being here] will cause any situation? I mean for you. . . . You have done a wonderful job and certainly become the Defender of the Faith, but by doing so you have become the enemy of all the evil forces that are trying to destroy the country and I don't want to do anything to embarrass you." On June 6, 1957, Hugo wrote back to Jinksie, agreeing "that under the circumstances I am sure that it would be most unwise for Josephine to go to Montgomery. Of course she has a mind of her own and all I can do is tell her what I think." Jo Jo did not go to the wedding. When Black's son Hugo, Jr., and his family had to leave Birmingham in 1962 because of his father's reputation, Jinksie wrote to Hugo on that occasion: "We do hate to see them move [but] I am glad he is leaving Birmingham as I not think he is made of the kind of iron that it takes to live in Birmingham."

Jinksie at times felt less inclined to stay in Alabama than did Cliff. In another letter to Hugo, June 18, 1958, she commented: "I cannot understand Cliff's almost desperate need to stay here in Montgomery, where we barely make a living, are practically isolated in the community and have to be constantly on our guard to even carry on a casual conversation. I think it comes down to the fact that in spite of their differences he loves the people here and I don't. In fact I don't even like them very much and besides they frighten me with their suppressed violence and complete irrationality. But he says they are no worse than other people and at least he knows them" (HLBP, Box 7).

58. Wyatt-Brown, "Ethical Background," p. 922.
59. Thornton, "Black and the Golden Age," p. 905.
60. Silverstein, *Constitutional Faiths,* p. 101.
61. Hamilton, *Hugo Black,* pp. 108, 305.
62. Berman, "Early Years," p. 112.
63. Black and Black, *Mr. Justice and Mrs. Black,* p. 70.
64. Hugo L. Black, quoted in *New York Times* obituary, 26 September 1971.
65. Douglas, *Go East Young Man,* p. 455.
66. Thornton, "Black and the Golden Age," p. 902; Hamilton, *Hugo Black,* pp. 80–81.
67. Hamilton, *Hugo Black,* pp. 119, 120.
68. Ibid., p. 108.
69. *Lewis* v. *Roberts,* 267 U.S. 467 (1925).
70. Hamilton, *Hugo Black,* pp. 117, 119.
71. HLBP, Box 90.
72. Hugo Black, speech, 1926 campaign, HLBP, Box 81.
73. Hugo Black, speech, 1926 campaign, HLBP, Box 90.
74. Black and Black, *Mr. Justice and Mrs. Black,* p. 68.
75. Hugo Black to D. C. Arthur, 13 June 1926, HLBP, Box 84.
76. HLBP, Box 85.
77. Hamilton, *Hugo Black,* p. 134.
78. Ibid., pp. 136–37.
79. Ibid., p. 143.
80. Ibid., pp. 142, 144.
81. Ibid., p. 151.
82. Ibid., p. 154.

83. Ibid., p. 156.
84. Hugo Black to Hubert Baughn, 23 March 1928, HLBP, Box 72.
85. Hugo Black to Ed Nixon, 23 February 1928, HLBP, Box 72.
86. HLBP, Box 72.
87. Hugo Black to William G. McAdoo; Hugo Black to John McCain, 20 November 1928, HLBP, Box 72.
88. Hamilton, *Hugo Black,* p. 157.
89. Joseph Alsop and Turner Catledge, *The 168 Days* (New York: Doubleday, Doran, 1938), pp. 295, 297, 302, 303.
90. Hamilton, *Hugo Black,* p. 273.
91. William O. Douglas, *The Court Years, 1939–1975* (New York: Random House, 1980).
92. Douglas, *Go East Young Man,* p. 494.
93. Alsop and Catledge, *168 Days,* p. 305.
94. Ibid., p. 307.
95. When Virginia Hamilton suggested that Postmaster General James A. Farley, a close political adviser to Franklin D. Roosevelt, would have warned the president about Black's Klan connection, Black wrote to her and said that "[Farley] congratulated me warmly . . . but said that he did not want to mislead me, that he had not known anything . . . until he heard it on the radio. . . . He followed this up with the statement that had he been consulted, however, he would have strongly recommended me and was very happy about my appointment" (Black to Hamilton, n.d., HLBP, Box 31).
96. Alsop and Catledge, *168 Days,* p. 308.
97. "Nominee No. 93," *Time,* 23 August 1937, pp. 13, 14.
98. Alsop and Catledge, *168 Days,* p. 309.
99. Black and Black, *Mr. Justice and Mrs. Black,* p. 69.
100. Berman, "Early Years," p. 103.
101. Douglas, *Court Years,* p. 19.
102. Hugo Black to Hugh G. Grant, 4 November 1937, HLBP, Box 31.
103. Berman, "Early Years," p. 104.
104. J. Edgar Hoover to Clyde Tolson, 16 September 1937, Hugo L. Black file, 62-90518, Federal Bureau of Investigation Files, Washington, D.C.
105. J. Edgar Hoover to Boake Carter, 24 September 1937, Hugo L. Black file, 62-90518, FBI Files.
106. Douglas, *Court Years,* pp. 19–20.
107. Hamilton, *Hugo Black,* p. 295. The reaction to the speech, by the press and public, was uniformly condemnatory (pp. 296–97).
108. Black and Black, *Mr. Justice and Mrs. Black,* p. 230.
109. HLBP, Box 31.
110. Claude Pepper, quoted in *Tuscaloosa News,* 13 April 1985, p. 3.
111. HLBP, Box 31.
112. HLBP, Box 240.
113. *Chambers* v. *Florida,* 309 U.S. 227 (1940).
114. Vincent Blasi, ed., *The Burger Court* (New Haven, Conn.: Yale University Press, 1982), p. 240.
115. Meador, "Mr. Justice Black," pp. 1109, 1113.
116. Black and Black, *Mr. Justice and Mrs. Black,* pp. 84, 99.
117. Law clerk, 1969 term, to Howard Ball, October 1972; law clerk, 1961 term, to Howard Ball, October 1972.
118. Daniel J. Meador, "Mr. Justice Black and His Law Clerks," 16 *Alabama Law Review* 57, 61 (1963).
119. Black, Jr., *My Father,* p. viii.
120. Hugo Black to Hugo Black, Jr., 1953, HLBP, Box 4.
121. Hugo Black to Hugo Black, Jr., 11 March 1954, HLBP, Box 4.
122. Hugo Black to Hugo Black, Jr., 5 March 1962, HLBP, Box 4.
123. Black and Black, *Mr. Justice and Mrs. Black,* pp. 90, 112.

328 • *Notes*

Chapter 3

1. On the backgrounds of the justices, see John R. Schmidhauser, *Judges and Justices* (Boston: Little, Brown, 1979), and David Danelski, *A Supreme Court Justice Is Appointed* (New York: Random House, 1964).
2. Douglas wrote three autobiographies, *Of Men and Mountains* (New York: Harper, 1950); *Go East Young Man;* and *The Court Years.* Like most autobiographies, Douglas's must be read with considerable care, particularly *The Court Years,* which he plainly wrote for posterity and not always from fact. His protestations about his generally good relationship with Felix Frankfurter provide an example.
3. Douglas, *Go East Young Man,* chap. 3.
4. Ibid., p. 13. *Of Men and Mountains,* the first of his many books, was Douglas's attempt to speak to the influence of the mountains in his life.
5. Douglas, *Go East Young Man,* p. 17.
6. William O. Douglas to A. Howard Meneely, 31 July 1927, WODP, Box 10.
7. Douglas, *Go East Young Man,* pp. 33–34.
8. Ibid., p. 34.
9. Black, "William Orville Douglas," p. 915.
10. See, for example, William O. Douglas to Arthur F. Douglas, 13 November 1933, WODP, Box 5.
11. See, generally, the correspondence between them (WODP, Box 238).
12. Douglas, *Go East Young Man,* p. 144.
13. *Rudolph* v. *United States,* 370 U.S. 269 (1962), Douglas, J., dissenting.
14. Douglas, *Go East Young Man,* p. 142.
15. See his continuing correspondence with Kristian Falkenburg (WODP, Box 325).
16. Grant S. Bond to William O. Douglas, 12 January 1931, WODP, Box 2.
17. Douglas, *Go East Young Man,* pp. 56–57.
18. Ibid., pp. 105, 106.
19. Quoted in Alpheus Thomas Mason, *Harlan Fiske Stone: Pillar of the Law* (New York: Viking Press, 1956), p. 550.
20. On the general tendencies of Populism and progressivism, see Richard Hofstadter, *The Age of Reform* (New York: Vintage Books, 1955); Eric F. Goldman, *Rendezvous with Destiny* (New York: Vintage Books, 1955); and William E. Leuchtenburg, *The Perils of Prosperity* (Chicago: University of Chicago Press, 1958).
21. James Madison, Alexander Hamilton, and John Jay, *The Federalist Papers* (New York: Mentor, 1961), No. 48, pp. 308–13.
22. Gordon A. Schwarz, *Liberal: Adolph A. Berle and the Vision of an American Era* (New York: Free Press, 1987), pp. 16–17.
23. Interview with Justice Lewis Powell, 18 November 1987, Washington, D.C.
24. Richard W. Jennings, "Mr. Justice Douglas: His Influence in Corporate and Securities Regulation," 73 *Yale Law Journal* 920, 922 (1964).
25. Douglas to Meneely, 31 July 1927, p. 6.
26. Ibid., p. 10.
27. Laura Kalman, *Legal Realism at Yale, 1927–1960* (Chapel Hill: University of North Carolina Press, 1986); Wilfred E. Rumble, Jr., *American Legal Realism* (Ithaca, N.Y.: Cornell University Press, 1968).
28. See, for example, Jerome Frank, *Courts on Trial* (New York: Atheneum, 1971).
29. John W. Hopkirk, "The Influence of Legal Realism on William O. Douglas," in *Essays on the American Constitution,* ed. Gottfried Dietze (Englewood Cliffs, N.J.: Prentice-Hall, 1964); Rumble, *American Legal Realism.*
30. James F. Simon, *Independent Journey: The Life of William O. Douglas* (New York: Harper & Row, 1980). Simon's skepticism is reflected in Melvin I. Urofsky's assessment in *The Douglas Letters* (Bethesda, Md.: Adler & Adler, 1987).
31. William O. Douglas to Nicholas Murray Butler, 5 May 1928, WODP, Box 1.
32. William O. Douglas to A. Howard Meneely, 8 June 1928, WODP, Box 10.

33. William O. Douglas to A. Howard Meneely, 5 May 1928, pp. 2, 3, WODP, Box 10.
34. William O. Douglas to A. Howard Meneely, 12 May 1928, pp. 1–2, WODP, Box 10.
35. Kalman, *Legal Realism at Yale,* p. 97.
36. See, generally, Jennings, "Mr. Justice Douglas." William O. Douglas and Carrol M. Shanks, *Cases on Business Units—Losses, Liabilities, and Assets* (Chicago: Callaghan, 1932); Douglas and Shanks, *Cases on Business Units—Management* (Chicago: Callaghan, 1931); Douglas and Shanks, *Cases and Materials on the Law of Finance of Business* (Chicago: Callaghan, 1931); Douglas and Shanks, *Cases and Materials on the Law of Corporate Reorganization* (St. Paul, Minn.: West, 1931).
37. William O. Douglas, "A Functional Approach to the Law of Business Associations," 23 *Illinois Law Review* 673 (1928).
38. Douglas, *Go East Young Man,* p. 150.
39. Bruce Allen Murphy, *Fortas: The Rise and Ruin of a Supreme Court Justice* (New York: Morrow, 1988), chap. 1.
40. See, for example, William O. Douglas and Dorothy S. Thomas, "The Business Failures Project: A Problem in Methodology," 39 *Yale Law Journal* 1013 (1930); Douglas and Thomas, "The Business Failures Project, II: An Analysis of Methods of Investigation," 40 *Yale Law Journal* 1034 (1931); William O. Douglas and Charles E. Clark, "Law and Legal Institutions," in "Report of the President's Research Committee on Social Trends," vol. 2, "Recent Social Trends in the United States"; and William O. Douglas, "Protecting the Investor," 23 *Yale Review* 521 (1934).
41. Max Lerner, "Wall Street's New Mentor," *The Nation,* 23 October 1937, p. 431.
42. William O. Douglas and George E. Bates, "The Federal Securities Act of 1933," 43 *Yale Law Journal* 171 (1933); Douglas and Bates, "Some Effects of the Securities Act upon Investment Banking," 1 *University of Chicago Law Review* 283 (1933); Douglas and Bates, "Protecting the Investor," 23 *Yale Law Journal* 52 (1934).
43. William O. Douglas to Felix Frankfurter, 8 December 1933, p. 1, WODP, Box 6.
44. Max Lowenthal, "The Railroad Reorganization Act," 47 *Harvard Law Review* 18 (1933).
45. William O. Douglas, "Protective Committees in Railroad Reorganization," 47 *Harvard Law Review* 565 (1934).
46. Jerome Frank to William O. Douglas, 3 November 1934, WODP, Box 6.
47. Louis D. Brandeis, *Other People's Money* (New York: Harper & Row, 1967).
48. William O. Douglas to Louis D. Brandeis, 6 May 1936, in Urofsky, *Douglas Letters,* p. 35.
49. Veblen's effects on Douglas are considered in some detail in Lerner, "Wall Street's New Mentor," pp. 429, 430.
50. See, for example, Adolf A. Berle, Jr., and Gardiner C. Means, *The Modern Corporation and Private Property* (New York: Macmillan, 1932); Adolf A. Berle, Jr., *Power Without Property* (New York: Harcourt, Brace & World, 1959); and Berle, *The Three Faces of Power* (New York: Harcourt, Brace & World, 1967).
51. William O. Douglas, *Democracy and Finance* (Port Washington, N.Y.: Kennikat Press, 1969), pp. 1, 44, 8.
52. Ibid., pp. 14–15.
53. Ibid., pp. 15–16.
54. Lerner, "Wall Street's New Mentor," p. 431.
55. Ibid., p. 431.
56. Douglas, *Democracy and Finance,* chap. 9.
57. Ibid., p. 32.
58. "Bill and Billy," *Time,* 11 October 1937, p. 61.
59. Douglas, *Go East Young Man,* p. 281.
60. WODP, Box 8.
61. Fred Rodell, "Douglas over the Stock Exchange," *Fortune,* February 1938, p. 16.
62. Ibid., p. 260.
63. Douglas, *Democracy and Finance,* p. 65.
64. "No Casino Allowed," *Time,* 6 December 1937, p. 75; Rodell, "Douglas over the Stock Exchange."

65. Memorandum, William O. Douglas to Stephen T. Early, 27 October 1938, p. 6, Whitney folder, FDRP.
66. Richard E. Neuberger, "Mr. Justice Douglas," *Harper's,* August 1942, p. 314.
67. Douglas, *Go East Young Man,* pp. 459, 190. See also RHJP, Box 188.
68. Franklin D. Roosevelt to Lewis Schwellenbach, 21 March 1939, FDR Papers, PSF1, 186.
69. Jerome N. Frank to Frank Murphy, 21 February 1939, RHJP, Box 13.
70. Harlan Fiske Stone to William O. Douglas, 21 March 1939, HFSP, Box 74.

Chapter 4

1. See, for example, James MacGregor Burns, *Roosevelt: The Lion and the Fox* (New York: Harcourt, Brace & World, 1956).
2. See Arthur M. Schlesinger, Jr., *The Politics of Upheaval* (New York: Houghton Mifflin, 1960), pp. 386–87, and Joseph P. Lash, *Dealers and Dreamers* (New York: Doubleday, 1988), chap. 20.
3. Frances Perkins, "The Principles of Social Security," in *New Deal Thought,* ed. Howard Zinn (Indianapolis: Bobbs-Merrill, 1966), p. 280.
4. Burns, *Roosevelt,* p. 274. It is true that different kinds of businesses had different relationships with the New Dealers. The private sector was, then as now, not a monolith (Thomas Ferguson, "Industrial Conflict and the Coming of the New Deal," in *The Rise and Fall of the New Deal Order, 1930–1980,* ed. Steve Fraser and Gary Gustle [Princeton, N.J.: Princeton University Press, 1989]).
5. Schlesinger, *Politics of Upheaval,* p. 501.
6. Ibid., p. 503.
7. Burns, *Roosevelt,* p. 274.
8. Ibid., pp. 282–83.
9. Ibid., pp. 283.
10. On those practices, see John Kenneth Galbraith, *The Great Crash of 1929* (Boston: Houghton Mifflin, 1961).
11. Burns, *Roosevelt,* pp. 235–38.
12. *United States* v. *Butler,* 297 U.S. 1 (1936); *Carter* v. *Carter Coal Co.,* 298 U.S. 238 (1936); *Schechter Poultry Co.* v. *United States,* 295 U.S. 495 (1935).
13. David A. Shannon, "Hugo Lafayette Black as U.S. Senator," 36 *Alabama Law Review* 789, 895 (1985).
14. Hugo Black, quoted in Howard Ball, "Hugo L. Black: Twentieth-Century Jeffersonian," 9 *Southwestern University Law Review* 1049, 1054 (1977).
15. Ibid., p. 1055.
16. Black, Jr., *My Father,* p. 82.
17. Hamilton, *Hugo Black,* p. 193.
18. William A. Gregory and Rennard Strickland, "Hugo Black's Congressional Investigation of Public Utilities," 29 *Oklahoma Law Review* 543, 544 (1976).
19. Bob Woodward and Scott Armstrong, *The Brethren: Inside the Supreme Court* (New York: Simon and Schuster, 1979), p. 38.
20. HLBP, Box 129.
21. Hugo L. Black, "Inside a Senate Investigation," *Harper's,* February 1936, pp. 276, 285–86.
22. Robert W. Horton, "Senator Black Dons Cloak of Chief 'Ferret,'" *Washington Post,* 31 July 1935; *Time,* 26 August 1935, p. 16.
23. Lyle C. Wilson, "Senate Opens Hoover Mail Subsidy Quiz," *Birmingham Post,* 27 September 1933, HLBP, Box 109.
24. "Probers Told Export Line Got Subsidies in Five Ways," *Baltimore Sun,* 30 September 1933, HLBP, Box 109.
25. "$66,000 a Pound," *St. Louis Post-Dispatch,* 1 October 1933, HLBP, Box 110.
26. "Dockendorff Testifies His Interests Were Pushed by O'Connor of Ship Board," *New York Times,* 5 October 1933, HLBP, Box 109.

27. Scottish Rite News Bureau, 4 December 1933, HLBP, Box 109.

28. Merchant Marine Act of 1936. See the discussion of this investigation in Dunne, *Hugo Black and the Judicial Revolution*, p. 153, and Nicholas Johnson, "Senator Black and the American Merchant Marine," 12 *University of Southern California Law Review* 399 (1967).

29. The story of these investigations is best told in Arthur M. Schlesinger, Jr., *The Coming of the New Deal* (Boston: Houghton Mifflin, 1958), chap. 4.

30. "Postal Chief Reveals Basis of Annulment," *Washington Herald*, 15 February 1934; "Sixth Army Aviator Dead as Plane Falls into Sea," *Washington Herald*, 24 February 1934, p. 1; "Aeronautics," *Time*, 26 February 1934, HLBP, Box 110.

31. "Senate Wrath May Fall on Lindbergh," *Washington Times*, 13 February 1934, HLBP, Box 110.

32. Schlesinger, *Politics of Upheaval*, p. 449.

33. *Jurney* v. *McCracken*, 294 U.S. 125 (1935).

34. "Air Mail Subsidies Under Fire," *Alexander City Outlook*, n.d., HLBP, Box 109.

35. Hamilton, *Hugo Black*, p. 247.

36. Lash, *Dealers and Dreamers*, p. 212.

37. Schlesinger, *Politics of Upheaval*, pp. 319–20.

38. "The Congress—Investigation by Headlines," *Time*, 26 August 1935, pp. 15–16, HLBP, Box 182.

39. Hamilton, *Hugo Black*, p. 253.

40. *Hearst* v. *Black*, 87 F.2d 70, 71 (D.C. Cir. 1938).

41. Hugo L. Black to Warren Roberts, 28 March 1936, HLBP, Box 181.

42. Hugo L. Black, *The Utilities Lobby, Radio Address and Speech* (Washington, D.C.: Government Printing Office, 1935), p. 9.

43. Schlesinger, *Politics of Upheaval*, p. 322.

44. Ibid., p. 323.

45. Douglas, *Go East Young Man*, pp. 363–64.

46. Daniel M. Berman, "Hugo Black and the Negro," 10 *American University Law Review* 35, 40 (1961).

47. Arthur Dahlberg, *Jobs, Machines, and Capitalism* (New York: Macmillan, 1932).

48. Hugo L. Black to William Yarby, 3 July 1937, HLBP, Box 73.

49. Schlesinger, *Coming of the New Deal*, pp. 95–96.

50. HLBP, Box 128.

51. Hugo Black to Irving Dilliard, 13 July 1962, HLBP, Box 25.

52. Ibid. See *Panama Refining Co.* v. *Ryan*, 293 U.S. 388 (1935).

53. *Schechter Poultry Co.* v. *United States*, 295 U.S. 495 (1935).

54. Tinsley E. Yarbrough, *Mr. Justice Black and His Critics* (Durham, N.C.: Duke University Press, 1988), p. 50.

55. Ralph DeBedts, *The New Deal's SEC: The Formative Years* (New York: Columbia University Press, 1964), pp. 30–31.

56. U.S. Congress, House of Representatives, National Power Policy Committee, *A Report of the National Power Policy Committee with Respect to the Treatment of Holding Companies*. 74th Cong., 1st sess., H. Doc. 137, 1935.

57. Schlesinger, *Politics of Upheaval*, p. 305.

58. Message from the president of the United States, transmitting *Report of the National Power Policy Committee*, p. 3.

59. Schlesinger, *Politics of Upheaval*, p. 313.

60. Schlesinger, *Coming of the New Deal*, pp. 91–92.

61. DeBedts, *New Deal's SEC*, pp. 106–7.

62. Douglas, "Protective Committees in Railroad Reorganization."

63. William O. Doulgas to chairman, *Harvard Law Review*, 6 December 1933, WODP, Box 9.

64. William O. Douglas to Felix Frankfurter, 8 December 1933, WODP, Box 6.

65. Felix Frankfurter to William O. Douglas, 16 January 1934, pp. 3–4, and 5 February 1934, WODP, Box 6.

66. William O. Douglas to Felix Frankfurter, 19 February 1934, p. 1, WODP, Box 6 (see also

Douglas to Frankfurter, 6 April 1934, FFP/LC, Box 6); Douglas, "Protecting the Investor," p. 522, WODP, Box 33b.

67. William O. Douglas to Francis T. Maloney, 9 May 1934, WODP, Box 9. See also William O. Douglas to Harold J. Laski, 15 May 1934, WODP, Box 9.
68. Douglas, *Go East Young Man,* p. 280.
69. Fred Rodell, "Bill Douglas, American," *American Mercury,* December 1945, p. 656.
70. Douglas, *Go East Young Man,* p. 298.
71. William O. Douglas, "Jerome N. Frank," 10 *Journal of Legal Education* 1, 4 (1957).
72. Quoted in Merlo J. Pusey, *Charles Evans Hughes* (New York: Macmillan, 1951), vol. 2, p. 754.
73. Ibid., p. 757. See also Charles A. Leonard, *A Search for a Judicial Philosophy: Mr. Justice Roberts and the Constitutional Revolution of 1937* (Port Washington, N.Y.: Kennikat Press, 1971). In an important state minimum wage case, *West Coast Hotel* v. *Parrish,* heard by the justices during the Court's 1936 term, Justice Owen Roberts, during the fall 1936 conference session, agreed to hear the case. The case was argued in December 1936, and during the conference session that followed, Roberts cast the decisive vote to affirm the minimum wage statute.
74. Pusey, *Charles Evans Hughes,* vol. 2, p. 756.
75. Hugo L. Black to Franklin D. Roosevelt, 28 January 1937, FDRP, cited in Hamilton, *Hugo Black,* p. 262. See also Dunne, *Hugo Black and the Judicial Revolution,* p. 168.
76. Franklin D. Roosevelt to Hugo Black, 6 February 1937, FDRP, cited in Hamilton, *Hugo Black,* p. 262.
77. Hugo Black to Hugh Mallory, 18 March 1937, HLBP, Box 134.
78. Douglas, *Go East Young Man,* p. 324.
79. William O. Douglas to A. Howard Meneely, 13 March 1937, WODP, Box 10.
80. See, for example, William O. Douglas to Scott Rowley, 1 March 1937, WODP, Box 23.
81. William O. Douglas to Lloyd K. Garrison, 1 March 1937, WODP, Box 23.
82. For Black's correspondence on the plan, see HLBP, Box 134.

Chapter 5

1. Quoted in Katie Louchheim, ed., *The Making of the New Deal: The Insiders Speak* (Cambridge, Mass.: Harvard University Press, 1983), p. 96.
2. Ibid.
3. Henry J. Abraham, *Justices and Presidents: A Political History of Appointments to the Supreme Court* (New York: Oxford University Press, 1974), p. 161.
4. Louchheim, *Making of the New Deal,* p. 53.
5. In his autobiography, Douglas recalled that McReynolds regularly raised the same questions with him about the president (after Douglas had joined the Court): "The man is really insane, isn't he?" "Do you think he will ever regain his sanity?" (*Court Years,* p. 13).
6. In 1922, McReynolds refused to visit Philadelphia with his brethren. He wrote to Chief Justice Taft: "As you know, I am not always to be found when there is a Hebrew abroad. Therefore, my 'inability' to attend must not surprise you" (Abraham, *Justices and Presidents,* p. 167).
7. Douglas, *Go East Young Man,* p. 440.
8. Abraham, *Justices and Presidents,* p. 176.
9. Douglas, *Go East Young Man,* p. 440; Herbert Wechsler, quoted in Louchheim, *Making of the New Deal,* p. 53.
10. Abraham, *Justices and Presidents,* p. 177.
11. Ibid., p. 196.
12. Louchheim, *Making of the New Deal,* p. 59.
13. Douglas, *Court Years,* p. 10.
14. Louchheim, *Making of the New Deal,* p. 59.
15. Silverstein, *Constitutional Faiths,* p. 49.

16. Douglas, *Go East Young Man,* pp. 445, 456.
17. Douglas, *Court Years,* p. 20.
18. Black had dissented in the case on the grounds that the state action was legitimate and because the majority had extended the protection of the Fourteenth Amendment's clause to include corporations as persons. He wrote, "Neither the history nor the language of the Amendment justifies the belief that corporations are included within its protection" (*Connecticut General Life Insurance Co.* v. *Johnson,* 303 U.S. 77, 85, 87 [1937]). William O. Douglas to Hugo L. Black, 4 February 1938, WODP, Box 308.
19. Quoted in Simon, *Independent Journey,* p. 11; Douglas, *Go East Young Man,* p. 450.
20. Interview with Justice Harry A. Blackmun, 19 November 1986, Washington, D.C.
21. Urofsky, *Douglas Letters,* p. 100; Bernard Schwartz, *Super Chief: Earl Warren and His Supreme Court* (New York: New York University Press, 1980), p. 50.
22. Interview with Justice William J. Brennan, Jr., 29 October 1986. Washington, D.C.
23. Blackmun interview.
24. Interview with Cathleen Douglas-Stone, 14 November 1986, Boston. Justice William J. Brennan, in an October 29, 1986, interview in the Supreme Court, recounted having heard Douglas make the same comment about soul-saving.
25. In a 1986 interview, Justice Byron White, a colleague of Douglas's, recalled that Douglas was "a more remote person" than Black and that he "wasn't the kind of person to come around and ask you for changes in opinions."
26. Brennan interview. Justice Felix Frankfurter, Black's major philosophical opponent, was always critical of Black's politicking on the Court (and Douglas's [alleged] politicking off the bench). Justice Stanley Reed, in a letter to Frankfurter, wrote of Black, "you can't change people. Black was always a politician and he didn't cease to be one by becoming a judge" (quoted in Lash, *From the Diaries of Felix Frankfurter,* p. 64).
27. Schwartz, *Super Chief,* p. 33.
28. Brennan interview.
29. Schwartz, *Super Chief,* p. 51.
30. Black, Jr., *My Father,* p. 240; Brennan interview. Justices Arthur Goldberg, Harry Blackmun, William J. Brennan, Warren Burger, Lewis Powell, and others all noted Douglas's uniqueness and idiosyncratic behavior; all the justices interviewed believed, however, that Black had a much more profound impact on constitutional jurisprudence than Douglas had.
31. Black, Jr., *My Father,* p. 240.
32. Ibid., p. 243.
33. Black, Foreword to Cahn, *Confronting Injustice,* p. xii; Blackmun interview. See, for example, the discussion of *Bell* v. *Maryland* (1964) and *Griswold* v. *Connecticut* (1965) for an analysis of this jurisprudential difference of opinion.
34. Brennan interview. See, for example, Black's dissent from a Douglas majority opinion in *Griswold* v. *Connecticut* (1965).
35. Hugo L. Black to William O. Douglas, 11 June 1941, and 24 June 1941, WODP, Box 308.
36. Black to Douglas, 11 June 1941.
37. Abraham, *Justices and Presidents,* p. 216.
38. Mason, *Harlan Fiske Stone,* pp. 566–67.
39. Abraham, *Justices and Presidents,* p. 217.
40. William O. Douglas to Hugo Black, 22 June 1941, WODP, Box 308.
41. William O. Douglas to Hugo L. Black, 12 September 1953, HLBP, Box 59.
42. William O. Douglas to Hugo L. Black, 8 September 1941, HLBP, Box 59. In his autobiography, Douglas remembered accepting the new job when Roosevelt offered it to him over the telephone. Douglas had asked if it were a real draft, and the president had assured him that it was. "Then I'll do it," recalled Douglas in his book. However, when Douglas returned to Washington, D.C., he did not receive a call from Roosevelt. Evidently the president had changed his mind (Douglas, *Court Years,* p. 268).
43. Hugo L. Black to William O. Douglas, 15 September 1941, WODP, Box 308.
44. Quoted in Simon, *Independent Journey,* p. 286.
45. Black and Black, *Mr. Justice and Mrs. Black,* p. 156. See, for example, "Justice Douglas Faces

Divorce," *New York Times,* 12 April 1963, p. 14; "Justice Douglas at 64 Marries Upstate New York Woman 23," *New York Times,* 6 August 1963, p. 33; "Justice Douglas's Wife, 25, Sues Him for Divorce," *New York Times,* 16 December 1965, p. 27; "Wife of Justice Douglas Granted Divorce on Coast," *New York Times,* 25 June 1966, p. 19.

46. Douglas, *Go East Young Man,* p. 448.
47. William O. Douglas to Hugo L. Black, 3 December 1949, and 23 December 1949, HLBP, Box 59.
48. William O. Douglas to Hugo L. Black, n.d., WODP, Box 308; William O. Douglas to Hugo L. Black, n.d., HLBP, Box 59; Black and Black, *Mr. Justice and Mrs. Black,* pp. 120–21.
49. Urofsky, *Douglas Letters,* p. 106.
50. Dunne, *Hugo Black and the Judicial Revolution,* pp. 193, 194.
51. Urofsky, *Douglas Letters,* p. 73.
52. Simon, *Independent Journey,* p. 8.
53. Ibid.
54. Lash, *From the Diaries of Felix Frankfurter,* p. 64.
55. Quoted in Simon, *Independent Journey,* p. 202.
56. Quoted in Abraham, *Justices and Presidents,* p. 207.
57. *Baker* v. *Carr,* 369 U.S. 186, 270 (1962), Frankfurter, J., dissenting.
58. See, for example, *Dennis* v. *United States,* 341 U.S. 494, 524 (1951), Frankfurter, J., concurring.
59. *Chambers* v. *Florida,* 309 U.S. 227, 241 (1939).
60. *West Virginia State Board of Education* v. *Barnette,* 319 U.S. 624, 638, 642 (1943). Frankfurter dissented in this case and, in a moving opinion, voiced his view of judicial self-restraint: "One who belongs to the most vilified and persecuted minority in history is not likely to be insensible to the freedoms guaranteed by our Constitution. . . . But as Judges we are neither Jew, nor Gentile, neither Catholic nor agnostic. . . . As a member of this Court I am not justified in writing my private notions of policy into the Constitution, no matter how deeply I may cherish them or how mischievous I may deem their disregard" (at 646).
61. Quoted in Schwartz, *Super Chief,* p. 36.
62. Abraham, *Justices and Presidents,* p. 219.
63. William H. Rehnquist, *The Supreme Court: How It Was, How It Is* (New York: Morrow, 1987), p. 76.
64. Lash, *From the Diaries of Felix Frankfurter,* p. 209.
65. Felix Frankfurter to Robert H. Jackson, 11 May 1946, and 6 February 1946, FFP, Box 170.
66. Robert H. Jackson to Felix Frankfurter, 20 September 1950, FFP/LC, Box 70.
67. Felix Frankfurter to Charles E. Whittaker, 9 April 1959, FFP/LC, Box 111.
68. Quoted in Schwartz, *Super Chief,* p. 39.
69. Leonard Baker, *Brandeis and Frankfurter: A Dual Biography* (New York: New York University Press, 1986), p. 418.
70. Bruce Allen Murphy, *The Brandeis/Frankfurter Connection* (New York: Oxford University Press, 1983), p. 191. See also Baker, *Brandeis and Frankfurter,* p. 380.
71. Baker, *Brandeis and Frankfurter,* pp. 335, 418.
72. Black, Jr., *My Father,* pp. 227–28.
73. Quoted in Baker, *Brandeis and Frankfurter,* p. 419.
74. Lash, *From the Diaries of Felix Frankfurter,* pp. 67–68.
75. Quoted in Baker, *Brandeis and Frankfurter,* p. 423.
76. Hugo L. Black to Felix Frankfurter, 14 January 1939, HLBP, Box 57.
77. Baker, *Brandeis and Frankfurter,* p. 424.
78. Lash, *From the Diaries of Felix Frankfurter,* p. 114.
79. Felix Frankfurter to Hugo L. Black, 15 December 1939, JMHP.
80. Hugo L. Black to Fred Rodell, 5 September 1962, HLBP, Box 47.
81. Schwartz, *Super Chief,* pp. 44, 42.
82. Felix Frankfurter to Hugo L. Black, 30 September 1950, HLBP, Box 60.
83. Hugo L. Black to Felix Frankfurter, 2 October 1950, HLBP, Box 60.
84. Felix Frankfurter to Stanley Reed, 21 December 1954, FFP/LC, Box 93.

85. Sherman Minton to Felix Frankfurter, n.d., 1948–1949 files, FFP/LC, Box 84. The note was passed to Frankfurter during a conference in which, according to Frankfurter's note, "Black made one of his inflammatory outbursts."
86. Black, Jr., *My Father,* p. 234.
87. Simon, *Independent Journey,* p. 217. In her diary, Elizabeth Black noted that "we arrived at 3:00. All the Court except Bill and Joanie Douglas were there" (Black and Black, *Mr. Justice and Mrs. Black,* p. 102).
88. Black and Black, *Mr. Justice and Mrs. Black,* p. 102.
89. Douglas, *Go East Young Man,* p. 324, but see, for example, *Court Years,* pp. 21–24.
90. Lash, *From the Diaries of Felix Frankfurter,* p. 175.
91. Schwartz, *Super Chief,* p. 53.
92. Quoted in Baker, *Brandeis and Frankfurter,* p. 420.
93. Quoted in Murphy, *Brandeis/Frankfurter Connection,* pp. 265–66.
94. Douglas, *Court Years,* p. 47.
95. Ibid., p. 48.
96. Baker, *Brandeis and Frankfurter,* p. 420.
97. Quoted in Simon, *Independent Journey,* p. 218.
98. Douglas, *Court Years,* p. 24. Douglas tells the story of looking for Nifty Rooms, a house of prostitution owned by the Mortensens, when he visited Grand Isle, Nebraska, shortly after the war. He was going to use a piece of their stationery to write Justice Murphy a "thank you" note for voting to invalidate the Mortensen conviction under the Mann Act. As the business was closed, Douglas went to the Chamber of Commerce and used its stationery instead. He sent the letter to Murphy, who was perplexed but suspected that his brother Douglas was somehow behind it (p. 25).
99. Ibid., p. 22.
100. Louchheim, *Making of the New Deal,* p. 72.
101. Schwartz, *Super Chief,* p. 53.
102. Ibid.
103. Felix Frankfurter to William O. Douglas, 2 December 1941, FFP/LC, Box 52.
104. Joseph L. Rauh, Jr., quoted in Louchheim, *Making of the New Deal,* pp. 63–64.
105. Baker, *Brandeis and Frankfurter,* p. 421.
106. Lash, *From the Diaries of Felix Frankfurter,* p. 155.
107. Schwartz, *Super Chief,* p. 53.
108. Memorandum, William O. Douglas to Felix Frankfurter, 29 May 1954, WODP, Box 329. Twenty years later, Douglas wrote: "Most of us thought the function of the Conference was to discover the consensus. His idea was different: he was there to proselytize and to gain converts. . . . One would err greatly to conclude that Frankfurter and I were at war. We clashed often at the idiological level but our personal relations were excellent and I always enjoyed being with him" (William O. Douglas to Michael E. Parrish, 16 December 1974, WODP, Box 362).
109. Felix Frankfurter, memorandum to the brethren, 1 June 1954, EWP, Box 353.
110. Felix Frankfurter to William O. Douglas, 2 November 1959, WJBP, Box 23.
111. William O. Douglas, memorandum to the brethren, 21 November 1960, WODP, Box 1232. A handwritten note by Douglas attached to the note indicates that it was not to be circulated pending his conversation with Chief Justice Earl Warren on the matter. Evidently, Warren convinced Douglas not to circulate the memo.
112. Quoted in Simon, *Independent Journey,* p. 9.
113. Memorandum, "The Black Controversy," pp. 4, 6, RHJP, Box 7.
114. In his memo "The Black Controversy," Jackson described himself as follows: "Jackson's life was a long defiance of the political sentiments of the majority of his neighbors, for whose votes or favors he never asked except in one place—when they sat on the jury. Otherwise, he lived a dissent and seems to have enjoyed standing alone [unlike Hugo Black]" (RHJP, Box 7); Douglas, *Court Years,* pp. 31–32.
115. Dunne, *Hugo Black and the Judicial Revolution,* p. 225.
116. Lash, *From the Diaries of Felix Frankfurter,* p. 97.

117. Black, Jr., *My Father,* p. 190.
118. Douglas, *Court Years,* p. 28.
119. Dunne, *Hugo Black and the Judicial Revolution,* p. 226.
120. Ibid., p. 29.
121. Black, Jr., *My Father,* p. 191.
122. Hugo L. Black, memorandum to the conference, 5 May 1945, WODP, Box 122.
123. Jackson, quoted in Rehnquist, *Supreme Court,* p. 66.
124. HLBP, Box 57.
125. Felix Frankfurter to Hugo L. Black, 9 June 1945, HLBP, Box 57.
126. Dunne, *Hugo Black and the Judicial Revolution,* p. 239.
127. Doris Fleeson, "Supreme Court Feud," *Washington Star,* 16 May 1946.
128. Robert H. Jackson to chairmen, House and Senate Judiciary Committees, 7 June 1946, p. 5, RHJP, Box 26 (copy to Harry S. Truman).
129. Ibid.
130. Charles Grove Haines to Hugo Black, 26 June 1946, HLBP, Box 32; Black to Haines, 2 July 1946, HLBP, Box 32.
131. Douglas, *Court Years,* p. 31.
132. Dunne, *Hugo Black and the Judicial Revolution,* p. 247.
133. RHJP, Box 8.
134. Dennis J. Hutchinson, "The Black–Jackson Feud," in *The Supreme Court Review, 1988,* ed. Philip Kurland and Gerhard Casper (Chicago: University of Chicago Press, 1989), pp. 206, 226, 227. Hutchinson also noted, trying to substantiate Jackson's perception, a comment made by a law clerk of Black's, Jerome A. "Buddy" Cooper. Cooper has written that Black told him that "another Justice, whom [Black] did not name, had played [the] role and [had] opposed and possibly prevented Jackson's appointment as Chief Justice" (*"Sincerely your friend"... Hugo L. Black* [University: University of Alabama Press, 1973], p. 4).
135. Douglas, *Court Years,* p. 31.
136. Baker, *Brandeis and Frankfurter,* p. 424.
137. RHJP, Box 8.
138. J. Woodford Howard, *Mr. Justice Murphy* (Princeton, N.J.: Princeton University Press, 1968), p. 270.
139. Abraham, *Justices and Presidents,* p. 212.
140. Howard, *Mr. Justice Murphy,* p. 270. Other justices on the Court who shared Frankfurter's view of Murphy included Chief Justice Stone and Jackson. Stone once wrote on the back of a slip opinion of Murphy's, "the English in this opinion is very bad in spots," telling him "it ought to be thoroughly canvassed with that in mind" (HFSP, Box 134).
141. *In re Yamashita,* 327 U.S. 1 (1946).
142. Dunne, *Hugo Black and the Judicial Revolution,* p. 217.
143. Howard, *Mr. Justice Murphy,* p. 425.
144. Quoted in Abraham, *Justices and Presidents,* p. 246.
145. According to Schwartz, "Warren was more comfortable with Brennan than with any of the other Justices, and an intimacy developed between them of a type that never took place between Warren and Black or Warren and Douglas, however close the latter's views may have been to his" (*Super Chief,* pp. 205–6).
146. G. Edward White, *Earl Warren: A Public Life* (New York: Oxford University Press, 1982), p. 185.
147. Conversation, Justice William J. Brennan, Jr., and Howard Ball, 17 March 1986, University of Alabama Law School, Tuscaloosa, Alabama (on the 100th anniversary of the birthday of the late Justice Hugo L. Black).
148. Douglas, *Court Years,* p. 55.
149. Ibid., p. 42.
150. Dunne, *Hugo Black and the Judicial Revolution,* p. 78.
151. Ibid., p. 187.
152. Black and Black, *Mr. Justice and Mrs. Black,* p. 71.

153. Dunne, *Hugo Black and the Judicial Revolution,* p. 187.
154. Quoted in Simon, *Independent Journey,* p. 11.
155. Douglas, *Court Years,* pp. 214, 219.
156. Ibid., p. 223.
157. John M. O'Donnell and Doris Fleeson, "Stone Denies Hand in Attack on Black," *New York Daily News,* 12 May 1938, p. 6.
158. Harlan F. Stone to Hugo Black, 26 January 1938, HLBP, Box 62.
159. Harlan F. Stone to Hugo Black, 22 March 1939, HLBP, Box 62.
160. Douglas, *Court Years,* pp. 222, 223.
161. William O. Douglas to Harlan F. Stone, 12 July 1944, HFSP, Box 74.
162. William O. Douglas to Harlan F. Stone, 21 August 1944, HFSP, Box 74.
163. Baker, *Brandeis and Frankfurter,* p. 419.
164. R. Ferrell, ed., *Off the Record: The Private Papers of Harry S Truman* (New York: Harper & Row, 1980), p. 78.
165. Hugo L. Black to Fred M. Vinson, 21 June 1946, HLBP, Box 62.
166. Ferrell, *Off the Record,* p. 90.
167. Douglas, *Court Years,* p. 226.
168. Lash, *From the Diaries of Felix Frankfurter,* p. 274.
169. Schwartz, *Super Chief,* p. 72. Reed once said to Frankfurter that Vinson was "just like me, except that he is less well-educated" (Lash, *From the Diaries of Felix Frankfurter,* p. 270).
170. Schwartz, *Super Chief,* p. 72.
171. Diary note, 8 October 1953, DDEP, Box 4.
172. Hugo L. Black to Hugo, Jr., and Sterling Black, 15 October 1953, HLBP, Box 6.
173. Douglas, *Court Years,* pp. 227–29.
174. William O. Douglas to Sherman Minton, 27 April 1961, WODP, Box 355.
175. William O. Douglas to Sherman Minton, 8 May 1961, WODP, Box 355. In a letter to newsman Irving Dilliard, Douglas wrote that "Earl Warren, in his personal relations, is a very petty man" (Douglas to Dilliard, 27 March 1961, WODP, Box 321).
176. Douglas, *Court Years,* pp. 231, 232.
177. Interview with Justice Warren E. Burger, 21 December 1987. Washington, D.C.
178. Ibid.
179. William O. Douglas to Warren E. Burger, 6 March 1972, WODP, Box 1570. Douglas wrote to Lewis Powell two days later, asking him "to put on paper the idea you expressed in Conference and I am sure you will get a majority" (Douglas to Powell, 8 March 1972, WODP, Box 1570). *United States* v. *United States District Court,* 407 U.S. 297 (1972), involved a ruling of the Court invalidating Nixon's efforts to place wiretaps without a search warrant. There were three concurring opinions: Douglas's, Burger's, and White's. Rehnquist did not participate.
180. *Lloyd Corporation* v. *Tanner,* 407 U.S. 551 (1972).
181. William O. Douglas to Warren E. Burger, 1 May 1972, WODP, Box 1570.
182. Burger interview.
183. Ibid.
184. Interview with Justice Lewis F. Powell, 18 November 1987, Washington, D.C.
185. Burger interview.
186. Quoted in Simon, *Independent Journey,* p. 14.
187. Urofsky, *Douglas Letters,* pp. 138–39.

Chapter 6

1. Douglas, *Court Years,* p. 278.
2. Howard, *Mr. Justice Murphy,* pp. 277, 278.
3. Black, Jr., *My Father,* p. 32.
4. Douglas, *Go East, Young Man,* pp. 89–93, passim.

5. Howard, *Mr. Justice Murphy,* p. 307.
6. Felix Frankfurter, speech delivered at inauguration of Dr. Harry N. Wright as president of City College, New York, 30 September 1942, FFP/LC, Box 198.
7. Notes, FFP/LC, Box 198.
8. Frank Murphy to Hugo L. Black, n.d., HLBP, Box 280.
9. Frank Murphy to Hugo L. Black, n.d., HLBP, Box 278.
10. Howard, *Mr. Justice Murphy,* p. 306.
11. *Korematsu* v. *United States,* 323 U.S. 214, 233 (1944), Murphy, J., dissenting.
12. Ibid., p. 242.
13. The relocation centers, or "concentration camps," as Justice Owen Roberts and others referred to them, were technically known as War Relocation Authority (WRA) camps and were located in California, Arizona, Wyoming, Utah, Idaho, Colorado, and Arkansas. There were ten WRA camps, which, from 1942 to 1946, housed a total population of 120,313 internees (including the 5,918 children born in the camps). For an interesting collection of essays on the issue, see Roger Daniels, Sandra Taylor, and Henry Kitano, eds., *Japanese Americans: From Relocation to Redress* (Salt Lake City: University of Utah Press, 1986).
14. William O. Douglas to Harlan F. Stone, 31 May 1943, WODP, Box 92.
15. In an interesting footnote to this litigation, the authors uncovered a letter written by Douglas to his friend Black before the United States entered the war, while Douglas was traveling in the West. Douglas wrote that "we had dinner with some admirers of yours—General and Mrs. DeWitt. They really are grand people. We enjoyed them immensely" (Douglas to Black, 21 June 1941, HLBP, Box 59).
16. *Hirabayashi* v. *United States,* 320 U.S. 81, 82 (1942).
17. Memorandum, Hugo L. Black to Harlan F. Stone, n.d., HFSP, Box 68.
18. Harlan F. Stone, memorandum to the conference, n.d., HFSP, Box 68.
19. Felix Frankfurter to Harlan F. Stone, n.d., HFSP, Box 68; Stone memo.
20. *Hirabayshi* v. *United States,* 320 U.S., at 107, Douglas J., concurring.
21. William O. Douglas to Harlan F. Stone, 31 May 1943, HFSP, Box 92.
22. William O. Douglas to Harlan F. Stone, 7 June 1943, HFSP, Box 92.
23. Ibid.
24. Harlan F. Stone to William O. Douglas, 9 June 1943, HFSP, Box 68.
25. Felix Frankfurter to Harlan F. Stone, 4 June 1943, HFSP, Box 68.
26. Frank Murphy, draft opinion, WODP, Box 92.
27. Memorandum, Stanley Reed to Frank Murphy, n.d., WODP, Box 92.
28. Felix Frankfurter to Frank Murphy, 10 June 1943, FFP/LC, Box 85. "Please, Frank," he wrote in another note, "with your eagerness for the austere functions of the Court and your desire to do all that is humanly possible to maintain and enhance the **corporate** reputation of the Court, why don't you take the initiative with the Chief in getting him to take out everything that . . . offends you." Murphy rejected these appeals, but he was nevertheless "filled with nagging insecurities about a lone dissent in the middle of a war" (Frankfurter to Murphy, 5 June 1943, FFP/LC, Box 85).
29. Howard, *Mr. Justice Murphy,* p. 308.
30. Ibid.
31. Quoted in Peter Irons, *Justice at War* (New York: Oxford University Press, 1982), p. 247.
32. *Hirabayashi* v. *United States,* 320 U.S., at 111, Murphy, J., concurring.
33. Ibid., p. 93.
34. Ibid., p. 101.
35. Ibid., p. 102.
36. *Korematsu* v. *United States,* 323 U.S., at 216, 220.
37. William O. Douglas, conference notes, 16 October 1944, WODP, Box 112.
38. Harlan F. Stone to Hugo Black, 9 December 1944, HLBP, Box 59.
39. Ibid.
40. Ibid.
41. Harlan F. Stone, draft concurring opinion, HFSP, Box 71.
42. *Korematsu* v. *United States,* 323 U.S., at 227.

43. Douglas, conference notes.

44. William O. Douglas, draft dissenting opinion, 1 December 1944, WODP, Box 112.

45. Ibid.

46. William O. Douglas to Hugo L. Black, 6 December 1944, HLBP, Box 59.

47. Douglas, *Court Years,* pp. 281, 39.

48. *Korematsu* v. *United States,* 323 U.S., at 225, Frankfurter, J., concurring.

49. For an examination of Frankfurter's relationship with McCloy, see, generally, Irons, *Justice at War.*

50. *Korematsu* v. *United States,* 323 U.S., at 243, Jackson, J., dissenting.

51. Ibid., p. 246.

52. *Korematsu* v. *United States,* 323 U.S., at 226, Roberts, J., dissenting.

53. *Ex parte Endo,* 323 U.S. 283, 297 (1944).

54. Memorandum, Eugene A. Beyer, Jr. (law clerk) to William O. Douglas, n.d., *Endo,* WODP, Box 115.

55. Douglas, conference notes, *Endo,* 16 October 1944, WODP, Box 115.

56. Stanley Reed to William O. Douglas, 9 November 1944, WODP, Box 115.

57. Douglas, *Court Years,* p. 35.

58. William O. Douglas to Harlan F. Stone, 28 November 1944, WODP, Box 115.

59. Irons, *Justice at War,* p. 344.

60. Ibid., p. 347.

61. Quoted in Mason, *Harlan Fiske Stone,* p. 793.

62. Harlan F. Stone, memorandum to the Court, *Hirabayashi,* 4 June 1943, HFSP, Box 68.

63. Hugo Black, note for the file, *Korematsu,* n.d., HLBP, Box 59.

64. William O. Douglas, *The Anatomy of Liberty* (New York: Trident Press, 1963), p. 69. On April 19, 1984, U.S. Federal District Court Judge Marilyn Hall Patel granted a writ of *coram nobis* (a writ used to correct errors that result in a miscarriage of justice) in the case of *Fred Korematsu* v. *United States,* CR-27635. Korematsu brought the petition in an effort to vacate his 1942 conviction on grounds of government misconduct. The government, concluded the judge, acknowledged prosecutorial impropriety in the original litigation. While it still is precedent, "it is now recognized as having very limited application. . . . It stands as a caution that in times of distress the shield of military necessity and national security must not be used to protect governmental actions from close scrutiny and accountability."

65. William O. Douglas to Harlan F. Stone, 29 May 1943, HFSP, Box 78.

66. *Ex parte Quirin,* 317 U.S. 1 (1942); Howard, *Mr. Justice Murphy,* p. 300.

67. For an examination of this unusual meeting, see Dunne, *Hugo Black and the Judicial Revolution,* pp. 209–10.

68. Petition for writ of certiorari to the Court of Appeals for the District of Columbia, *In re Quirin* et al., Special Term, 1942, WODP, Box 76.

69. Dunne, *Hugo Black and the Judicial Revolution,* pp. 209, 210.

70. Ibid., p. 210.

71. *Ex parte Quirin,* 317 U.S., at 19.

72. Douglas, *Court Years,* p. 139

73. Ibid.

74. Harlan F. Stone, memorandum to the members of the Court, 25 September 1942, p. 1, WODP, Box 76.

75. *Ex parte Quirin,* 317 U.S., at 27.

76. Ibid.

77. "It has never been suggested . . . that an alien spy, in time of war, could not be tried by military tribunal without a jury" (ibid., p. 41).

78. Section 32(a) of that act provides that when a person or persons, for the purpose of either injuring the United States or giving a foreign country an advantage, transmits documents, etc., that person shall be punished by imprisonment for not more than twenty years, except that, in time of war, the penalty is either thirty years or death. When two or more so act, it is a conspiracy.

The Rosenbergs were never charged with treason, although many persons, including the

340 • *Notes*

federal trial judge, accused them of having committed treason against America. Naturally, if they had been charged with acts of treason, the provisions of Article III, Section 3, would have applied.

. William O. Douglas to Michael E. Parrish, 13 December 1974, WODP, Box 1070.
80. Ibid., p. 2.
81. William O. Douglas, memorandum to the conference, 22 May 1953, WODP, Box 233.
82. William Rehnquist to Robert H. Jackson, n.d., RHJP, Box 6.
83. Simon, *Independent Journey,* p. 303. Also, FFP, Box 65.
84. Quoted in Simon, *Independent Journey,* p. 302.
85. In a memorandum to the conference, Douglas wrote that since the Court decided not to take the case, "there would be no end served by hearing oral argument on the motion for a stay" (WODP, Box 233).
86. Simon, *Independent Journey,* p. 305.
87. Douglas to Parrish, 13 December 1974, p. 2.
88. The lawyers argued that the Rosenbergs had been convicted under the wrong statute, the Espionage Act of 1917; they should have been tried under the provisions of the Atomic Energy Act of 1946—which had the death penalty for transmitting atomic secrets if done to injure the United States and if the death penalty was determined by a jury.
89. Order, *Rosenberg* v. *United States,* 17 June 1953, WODP, Box 233.
90. Quoted in Simon, *Independent Journey,* p. 307.
91. Ibid., p. 310.
92. Douglas, *Court Years,* p. 237.
93. *Rosenberg ex ux.* v. *United States,* 346 U.S. 273, 310 (1953).
94. Quoted in Simon, *Independent Journey,* p. 287.
95. Ibid.
96. *Rosenberg ex ux.* v. *United States,* 346 U.S., at 292.
97. Ibid., p. 296.
98. Ibid., p. 298.
99. Ibid., p. 310.
100. Ibid., pp. 313, 311.
101. Ibid., p. 310, Frankfurter, J., dissenting.
102. Michael E. Parrish, "Justice Douglas and the Rosenberg Case: A Rejoinder," 70 *Cornell Law Review* 1048, 1056 (1985).
103. Ibid., p. 1054.
104. William Cohen, "Justice Douglas and the Rosenberg Case: Setting the Record Straight," 70 *Cornell Law Review* 211, 217, 234, 238 (1985). See also Parrish, "Douglas and the Rosenberg Case."
105. Conversation with Charles Reich, William O. Douglas Commemorative Program, 16 April 1989, Seattle.
106. Charge against General Tomoyuki Yamashita, [s] Alva C. Carpenter, Colonel, JAGD, United States Army, 25 September 1945.
107. George F. Guy, "The Defense of General Yamashita," *Supreme Court Historical Society Yearbook, 1981* (Washington, D.C.: U.S. Supreme Court Historical Society, 1981), p. 57.
108. Ibid., p. 64.
109. Lawrence H. Tribe, *American Constitutional Law,* 2nd ed. (Mineola, N.Y.: Foundation Press, 1987), p. 45.
110. Mason, *Harlan Fiske Stone,* p. 67; Howard, *Mr. Justice Murphy,* p. 376, n. 1.
111. Dunne, *Hugo Black and the Judicial Revolution,* p. 214.
112. Justice Robert H. Jackson was not sitting on the Court during this term of the Court; he was in Nuremberg, serving as America's chief prosecutor in the German war-crimes trials.
113. *In re Yamashita,* 327 U.S. 1, 8 (1946).
114. Ibid., pp. 19, 20.
115. Ibid., p. 25. Military control of Yamashita left undisturbed, the attorneys appealed to President Truman and to General Douglas MacArthur for clemency. The appeal was rejected by both, and Yamashita was executed on February 23, 1946.

116. Ibid., p. 47, Rutledge, J., dissenting.

117. Ibid., pp. 26, 40, Murphy, J., dissenting.

118. Howard, *Mr. Justice Murphy,* p. 374.

119. Section 67, 31 Stat. 141, 48 U.S.C.A. Section 532.

120. *Duncan* v. *Kahanimoku,* 327 U.S. 304, 309 (1946).

121. Hugo L. Black to Harlan F. Stone, 18 January 1946, p. 2, HLBP, Box 280.

122. *Duncan* v. *Kahanimoku,* 327 U.S., at 316, 322, 324.

123. Frank Murphy to Hugo L. Black, n.d., HLBP, Box 280.

124. *Duncan* v. *Kahanimoku,* 327 U.S., at 326, 329.

125. Ibid., p. 334.

126. Harlan F. Stone to Hugo Black, 17 January 1946, HLBP, Box 280.

127. Black to Stone, 18 January 1946.

128. Harlan F. Stone to Hugo L. Black, 19 January 1946, HLBP, Box 280. Evidently, in the draft Black first showed to Stone, and in a letter to Stone dated January 18, 1946, he drew some important constitutional ideas from the 1865 *Milligan* opinion. It is also evident that Stone's advice influenced Black, for the final version of the *Duncan* opinion has no references to the *Milligan* rule.

129. *Duncan* v. *Kahanimoku,* 327 U.S., at 338, 343, Burton, J., dissenting.

130. Howard, *Mr. Justice Murphy,* p. 378.

131. *Falbo* v. *United States,* 320 U.S. 549 (1943).

132. "The Act was passed to mobilize national manpower with the speed which that necessity and understanding . . . integrating all the nation's people and forces for national defense . . . required" (at 551–52); ibid., p. 554.

133. Ibid., pp. 555–56, 560–61, Murphy, J., dissenting.

134. *Estep* v. *United States,* 327 U.S. 114, 116 (1945).

135. Cert notes, *Estep,* n.d., WODP, Box 129.

136. Harlan F. Stone to William O. Douglas, 24 November 1945, WODP, Box 129.

137. William O. Douglas, memorandum to the conference, *Estep,* 14 December 1945, WODP, Box 129.

138. Ibid., pp. 120, 121, 125.

139. Douglas, memorandum to the conference, 14 December 1945.

140. *Estep* v. *United States,* 327 U.S., at 134, 136, Frankfurter, J., concurring.

141. Ibid., pp. 144–45.

142. See, for example, his opinions for the majority—upholding convictions of petitioners who had claimed religious reasons for disagreeing with the local board's classification judgments—in *Eagles* v. *United States ex. rel Samuels,* 329 U.S. 304 (1946), and *Sunal* v. *Large, Alexander* v. *United States ex rel. Kulick,* 332 U.S. 174 (1947).

143. See, for example, *Sicurella* v. *United States,* 348 U.S. 385 (1954); *United States* v. *Seeger, et al.,* 380 U.S. 163 (1964); and *Welsh* v. *United States,* 398 U.S. 333 (1970).

144. *United States* v. *O'Brien,* 391 U.S. 367 (1967). Writing the opinion for the majority, Chief Justice Warren wrote: "Pursuant to this power [to conscript manpower for the military], Congress may establish a system of registration for individuals liable for training and service, and may require such individuals within reason to cooperate in the registration system. . . . The issuance of certificates . . . is a legitimate and substantial administrative aid in the functioning of this system. And legislation to insure the continuing availability of issued certificates serves a legitimate and substantial purpose in the system's administration" (at 377–78).

145. See, for example, *Case* v. *Bowles,* 327 U.S. 92 (1945); *Hulbert* v. *Twin Falls,* 327 U.S. 103 (1945); *Fleming* v. *Mohawk Wrecking and Lumber Co.,* 331 U.S. 111 (1946); *Testa* v. *Katt,* 330 U.S. 386 (1946); and *Woods* v. *Miller,* 333 U.S. 138 (1948).

146. His son wrote that Black believed that "earnings in any form—salary, wages, dividends, interest—should be limited to $25,000 per person during the war" (*My Father,* p. 145).

147. Robert J. Donovan, *The Tumultuous Years* (New York: Norton, 1982), p. 385.

148. Ibid., pp. 382, 386.

149. Harry S. Truman to William O. Douglas, 9 July 1952 (not sent), HSTP.

150. *Youngstown Sheet and Tube Co.* v. *Sawyer,* 343 U.S. 579, 582 (1952).

151. Cert notes, *Youngstown,* n.d., WODP, Box 220.
152. Ibid.
153. Ibid.
154. Ibid.
155. Rehnquist, *Supreme Court,* p. 92.
156. Ibid., p. 95. "Judges are influenced by [public opinion] and I think that such influence played an appreciable part in causing the steel seizure case to be decided the way it was" (p. 98).
157. Donovan, *Tumultuous Years,* p. 388.
158. Dunne, *Hugo Black and the Judicial Revolution,* p. 292.
159. Baker, *Brandeis and Frankfurter,* p. 455.

Chapter 7

1. The phrase was used by Chief Justice Vinson in the opinion for the Court in *Dennis* v. *United States,* 341 U.S. 494 (1951).
2. William B. Lockhart, Yale Kamisar, and Jesse Choper, *The American Constitution,* 5th ed. (St. Paul, Minn.: West, 1981), p. 449.
3. Douglas, *Court Years,* p. 57.
4. "More than one-sixth of the total civilian labor force [was] subject to some type of loyalty qualification" (Note, "The National Security Interest and Civil Liberties," 85 *Harvard Law Review* 1130, 1160 [1972]).
5. *Brandenberg* v. *Ohio,* 395 U.S. 444, 456 (1969), Douglas, J. concurring.
6. Baker, *Brandeis and Frankfurter,* p. 450.
7. See *Schenck* v. *United States,* 249 U.S. 47 (1919); *Frowerk* v. *United States,* 249 U.S. 204 (1919); and *Debs* v. *United States,* 249 U.S. 211 (1919).
8. See *Abrams* v. *United States,* 250 U.S. 616 (1920), and *Pierce* v. *United States,* 252 U.S. 239 (1920), respectively.
9. Lockhart, Kamisar, and Choper, *American Constitution,* p. 402. See *Gitlow* v. *New York,* 268 U.S. 652 (1925), and *Whitney* v. *California,* 274 U.S. 357 (1927).
10. William O. Douglas to Steve Smith, 6 October 1965, WODP, Box 986.
11. Hugo L. Black to Edmond Cahn, 19 October 1960, HLBP, Box 21.
12. Hugo Black, "The Bill of Rights," 35 *New York University Law Review* 865, 874 (1960).
13. Hugo L. Black, *A Constitutional Faith* (New York: Knopf, 1968), pp. 45, 48.
14. Hugo Black to Alexander Meiklejohn, 25 July 1962, HLBP, Box 42.
15. Hugo L. Black to Edmond Cahn, 24 October 1960, HLBP, Box 21.
16. Black, *Constitutional Faith,* p. 43.
17. Cahn, *Confronting Injustice,* p. 103.
18. Hugo L. Black to Irving Dilliard, 7 January 1953, HLBP, Box 317.
19. Black, *Constitutional Faith,* p. 52. Holmes and Brandeis expounded the "clear and present danger" test for use in cases involving the free speech and other First Amendment rights of persons charged with sedition or violation of espionage laws. The doctrine, created by Holmes in the 1919 case of *Schenck* v. *United States,* 249 U.S. 47, held that "the question in every case is whether the words used are used in circumstances and are of such a nature as to create a clear and present danger that they will bring about the substantive evils that Congress has a right to prevent." In *Abrams* v. *United States,* 250 U.S. 616 (1919), Holmes wrote that "it is only the present danger of immediate evil or intent to bring it about that warrants Congress in setting a limit to the expression of opinion where private rights are not concerned. . . . [T]he ultimate good desired is better reached by free trade in ideas—that the test of truth is the power of the thought to get itself accepted in the competition of the market, and that truth is the only ground upon which their wishes safely can be carried out. That at any rate is the theory of our Constitution. It is an experiment, as all life is an experiment."
20. Black, *Constitutional Faith,* p. 50.
21. Urofsky, *Douglas Letters,* p. 196.

22. Douglas, *Court Years*, pp. 93–94, 101.
23. *Brandenberg* v. *Ohio*, 395 U.S. 444, 467 (1969).
24. William O. Douglas to Alden Whitman, 24 January 1972, WODP, Box 1544.
25. Urofsky, *Douglas Letters*, p. 89.
26. Douglas, *Court Years*, p. 92.
27. William O. Douglas to William J. Brennan, 9 May 1957, WODP, Box 1188.
28. William O. Douglas to John M. Harlan, 22 April 1958, WODP, Box 1204.
29. Douglas, *Court Years*, pp. 44, 47. For Frankfurter, Communists or others who challenged the very core of their adopted land's set of fundamental principles were committing an intolerable act. While he could understand their actions, he could not approve of them, nor would he allow them to avoid the consequences of their seditious behavior. Frankfurter could never accept Black's talk of the categorical commands of the plain words of the First Amendment, or the position, which Frankfurter argued vigorously against, that the First Amendment's protections had a preferred position in the Constitution's hierarchy of values. In a letter to his colleague Justice Stanley Reed, he wrote, "Please tell me what kind of sense it makes that one provision of the Constitution is to be 'preferred' over another. . . . I do not think there is a second-class citizenship among the different clauses inhabiting the Constitution" (Frankfurter to Reed, n.d., FFP, Box 93).
30. Philip Elman, "The Solicitor General's Office, Justice Frankfurter and Civil Rights Litigation, 1946–1980: An Oral History," 100 *Harvard Law Review* 817, 839 (1987).
31. In *Thornhill* v. *Alabama*, 310 U.S. 88 (1940), the Court determined that peaceful picketing during a valid labor dispute was constitutionally protected free speech.
32. Black, *Constitutional Faith*, pp. 53, 54, 57.
33. Quoted in Elizabeth Black, "Hugo Black: A Memorial Portrait," in *Supreme Court Historical Society Yearbook, 1980* (Washington, D.C.: Supreme Court Historical Society, 1980), p. 77.
34. *Gregory* v. *Chicago*, 394 U.S. 111, 125–26 (1968).
35. During the conference session, Black saw the 1940 *Cantwell* doctrine governing the *Gregory* case. According to Douglas's notes, Black said that "there was no statute to prohibit a parade here—statute applied is too vague and broad to say what it means" (William O. Douglas, conference notes, 13 December 1968, WODP, Box 1433). According to Douglas's notes in the *Gregory* file, Black was assigned the task of writing the *Gregory* opinion for the Court "and wrote one that none could agree with. It was 'broad and sweeping' on the law and order side. After talking to Brennan and Fortas, I got him to take out four objectionable parts and to revise others partly. He did so gladly and I joined his opinion though it was not exactly as I wanted it. I was sure that the others would make other suggestions and that in time we would have a good opinion. But the rest did not do so. Brennan thought Black had rubbed off some of his opinions; and Fortas became more and more incensed as time went by. His relations with Black worsened and they became very cool to each other. . . . So, when the Chief wrote, the others quickly followed him. [Brennan told Black he and Thurgood Marshall were joining the chief's opinion on February 27, 1969.] I did so too. But, having joined Black, I hesitated to withdraw as he had met my basic suggestions. Fortas complained bitterly about my staying with Black as I was not too happy with the result. The Fortas–Black relation grew worse as Fortas realized it was Black who had got Senator Lister Hill (D-Ala) to come out against Fortas for confirmation as C.J. last year" (HLBP, Box 405).
36. Douglas, *Court Years*, pp. 104–5.
37. See, for example, *Tinker* v. *Des Moines School Board*, 393 U.S. 503 (1969). See also Black's dissenting opinions in *Street* v. *New York*, 394 U.S. 576 (1969), and *Cohen* v. *California*, 403 U.S. 15 (1971). In these cases, Black disagreed with his friend Douglas on the speech plus conduct issue, arguing that the expulsions in *Tinker* and the convictions of Street and Cohen should stand because the defendants had been arrested for their conduct, not for their speech.
38. *Brandenberg* v. *Ohio*, 395 U.S., at 455–56, Douglas, J., concurring.
39. Douglas, *Court Years*, p. 93.
40. *Dunne* v. *United States*, 320 U.S. 790 (1943), cert. denied; Douglas, *Court Years*, p. 94.
41. Sections 2 and 3 of the Smith Act made it unlawful for any person to "attempt to commit, or

to conspire to commit, . . . knowingly or willfully advocate, abet, advise or teach the duty, necessity, desirability, or propriety of overthrowing or destroying any government in the United States by force or violence, or by the assassination of any officer of any such government."

42. *Dennis* v. *United States,* 341 U.S. 494 (1951).
43. *Sacher* v. *United States,* 343 U.S. 1 (1951). Douglas, Black, and Frankfurter were the only justices to vote to grant certiorari. It was therefore denied on June 4, 1951. However, the petition for a rehearing was granted on October 22, 1951. There was only one question for the Court's review: Was the federal judge's action, at the conclusion of the *Dennis* trial (i.e., finding the lawyers to be in contempt of court and summarily sentencing them to brief prison terms) valid? Black, Douglas, and Frankfurter were of the opinion that the federal judge, Harold Medina, should not have ruled on the contempt citations. However, they were in the minority, and, in a decision for the majority written by Justice Jackson, the contempt citations were affirmed by the Court.
44. Felix Frankfurter, memorandum to the conference, 27 February 1951, WODP, Box 207.
45. William O. Douglas, conference notes, *Dennis,* 9 December 1950, WODP, Box 206.
46. Ibid.
47. Hugo Black, conference notes, n.d. [February 1951], pp. 6, 7, 9, 113, HLBP, Box 307. When Vinson misrepresented the important *Gitlow* and *Whitney* dissents and the concurrences of Holmes and Brandeis, Black objected and quoted from these cases to remind the majority of the precise words of the two jurists who developed the doctrine a generation earlier. See, for example, pp. 11, 13. On page 14, after Vinson remarked that the *Gitlow* threat was, in the minds of Holmes and Brandeis, a minor event, Black noted: "How does he know that? It is not true according to what they said."
48. Ibid., pp. 7–13, passim.
49. *Dennis* v. *United States,* 341 U.S., at 580, 581, Black, J., dissenting.
50. Ibid., pp. 583, 584, 588, 589, 590, Douglas, J., dissenting.
51. Douglas, *Court Years,* p. 94.
52. See, for example, *Feiner* v. *New York,* 340 U.S. 315 (1951). Robert H. Jackson, conference notes, *Dennis,* 1949 term, n.d., RHJP, Box 8.
53. Felix Frankfurter to Robert H. Jackson, 25 March 1950, RHJP, Box 8.
54. Hugo Black to William O. Douglas, 19 May 1953, WODP, Box 308.
55. Jackson, *Dennis* conference notes.
56. *Brandenberg* v. *Ohio,* 395 U.S., at 454, Douglas, J., concurring. Black joined in the opinion.
57. But recall Douglas's views on the powers of Congress to control the behavior of aliens who were Communists. See his views in *Schneidermann* v. *United States,* 320 U.S. 118 (1943).
58. However, see Douglas's notes from the *Dennis* conference session (WODP, Boxes 205, 206). He expressed disappointment about the lack of discussion of the important substantive questions raised by the defendants regarding their rights under the First Amendment.
59. Douglas, *Court Years,* p. 96.
60. Letter from J. Edgar Hoover to Supreme Court employees thanking them for cooperating with the FBI in the surveillance of the justices, Supreme Court file, 62-27585, pt. 1, Federal Bureau of Investigation Files, Washington, D.C. The employees who received the letter were Thomas Veggeman, marshal (20 May 1953); Harold Willey, clerk of the Court (23 June 1953); Philip H. Crook, chief of police; and T. Perry Lippitt, marshal.
61. Interview with Justice William J. Brennan, Jr., 29 October 1986, Washington, D.C. Virginia Durr to Hugo L. Black, 5 June 1957, HLBP, Box 7. In a September 26, 1957, letter to Clark Clifford, Douglas wrote that he hated "to talk personal matters on the telephone because I am sure it is tapped" (WODP, Box 315).
62. Memorandum, J. Edgar Hoover to Clyde Tolson, 23 May 1957, Supreme Court file, 62-27585, pt. 1, FBI Files.
63. James A. Pryor to Arthur B. Langlie, 4 January 1954; memorandum, J. Edgar Hoover to D. M. Ladd, 8 February 1954, file 101-2983, pt. 1, FBI Files.
64. Memorandum, A. H. Belmont to L. V. Boardman, 1 June 1954, file 101-2983, pt. 1, FBI Files.

65. Memorandum, D. M. Ladd to J. Edgar Hoover, 9 February 1954, file 101-2983, pt. 1, FBI Files.
66. Memorandum, J. Edgar Hoover to Clyde Tolson, DeLoche et al., 23 April 1969, describing a conversation he had with President Richard M. Nixon, file 101-2983, FBI Files.
67. Memorandum, J. Edgar Hoover to Tolson, DeLoche, Rosen, and Bishop, 5 June 1970, Hugo L. Black file, 62-90518, document 44, FBI Files.
68. "Obviously," wrote Vinson, "['the clear and present danger' test] cannot mean that before the Government may act, it must wait until the putsch is about to be executed, the plans have been laid and the signal is awaited" (*Dennis* v. *United States,* 341 U.S., at 509).
69. Ibid., p. 568, Jackson, J., concurring.
70. Ibid., pp. 524–25, Frankfurter, J., concurring.
71. Douglas, *Court Years,* p. 96.
72. Ibid., p. 103.
73. *Yates* v. *United States,* 354 U.S. 298 (1957).
74. William O. Douglas, conference notes, 12 October 1956, WODP, Box 1188.
75. Ibid.
76. Schwartz, *Super Chief,* p. 233.
77. *Yates* v. *United States,* 354 U.S., at 343, Black, J., concurring and dissenting.
78. Quoted in Felix Frankfurter to Tom C. Clark, 5 February 1960, JMHP.
79. Ibid.
80. Quoted in Schwartz, *Super Chief,* p. 363.
81. William O. Douglas, conference notes, 14 October 1960, WODP, Box 1238. In a similar fashion, Black, in his conversation in conference, relied on an interpretation of Section 4f that meant that "activities mean more than membership—it means 'overt' acts as in the Treason clause—prosecuting membership alone is precluded in the Constitution—can't proscribe political parties" (ibid.).
82. William O. Douglas, conference notes, 5 June 1959, WODP, Box 1288.
83. Ibid.
84. *Scales* v. *United States,* 367 U.S. 203, 269 (1961), Douglas, J., dissenting.
85. Ibid., p. 274, Black, J., dissenting.
86. Douglas, *Court Years,* p. 101.
87. Black and Douglas were equally critical of state loyalty programs that forced people out of jobs because they had been accused of being Communist sympathizers, had refused to sign loyalty oaths, or had used the "self-incrimination" protection of the Fifth Amendment. See, for example, their dissents in *Adler* v. *Board of Education,* 342 U.S. 485 (1952), *Barsky* v. *Board of Regents,* 347 U.S. 442 (1954), and *Slochower* v. *Board of Education,* 350 U.S. 551 (1956); their concurring opinions in the "bar association" case, *Konigsberg* v. *State Bar,* 366 U.S. 36 (1961); and their dissents in *In re Anastaplo,* 366 U.S. 82 (1961).
88. *Joint Anti-Fascist Refugee Committee* v. *McGrath,* 341 U.S. 123 (1950).
89. Executive Order 9835, Part III, Section 3, found in Douglas's notes on *Joint Anti-Fascist Refugee Committee,* WODP, Box 201.
90. Ibid.
91. Robert H. Jackson, docket sheet, *Joint Anti-Fascist Refugee Committee,* 14 October 1950, RHJP, Box 6.
92. *Joint Anti-Fascist Refugee Committee* v. *McGrath,* 341 U.S., at 143, Black, J., concurring.
93. Felix Frankfurter to William O. Douglas, 4 April 1956, WODP, Box 1173.
94. Tom C. Clark, memorandum to the conference, 4 April 1956, WODP, Box 1173.
95. *Aptheker* v. *Secretary of State,* 378 U.S. 500 (1964); *Albertson* v. *S.A.C.B.,* 382 U.S. 70 (1965); *United States* v. *Robel,* 389 U.S. 258 (1967).
96. Douglas, *Court Years,* p. 107.
97. Ibid., p. 99.
98. See, for example, *Kilbourn* v. *Thompson,* 103 U.S. 168 (1881); *McGrain* v. *Daugherty,* 273 U.S. 135 (1927); *Sinclair* v. *United States,* 279 U.S. 263 (1929); and *United States* v. *Rumely,* 345 U.S. 41 (1953).
99. *Watkins* v. *United States,* 354 U.S. 178, 195 (1956).

100. Schwartz, *Super Chief*, p. 231.
101. *Watkins* v. *United States*, 354 U.S. 178 (1956); *Sweezy* v. *New Hampshire*, 354 U.S. 234 (1956).
102. Schwartz, *Super Chief*, p. 236. A year later, in a letter to Harlan, Frankfurter was already regretting his decision to join the majority. He referred to the opinion as that "god-awful Watkins decision. . . . You know what I think of that opinion" (Felix Frankfurter to John M. Harlan, 23 April 1958, JMHP).
103. William O. Douglas to Earl Warren, 23 May 1957, WODP, Box 1178. On June 6, 1957, after changes were made, Douglas joined, stating, "I agree with your fine opinion . . ." (Douglas to Warren, 6 June 1957, WODP, Box 1178).
104. William J. Brennan to Earl Warren, 29 May 1957, WJBP, Box 401.
105. *Watkins* v. *United States*, 354 U.S., at 187, 197, 200, 214.
106. Douglas, *Court Years*, p. 99.
107. *Sweezy* v. *New Hampshire*, 354 U.S., at 250.
108. Conference notes, 8 March 1957, quoted in Schwartz, *Super Chief*, pp. 235–36.
109. John M. Harlan to Earl Warren, 31 May 1957, EWP, Box 634.
110. *Barenblatt* v. *United States*, 360 U.S. 109 (1958); *Uphaus* v. *Wyman*, 360 U.S. 72 (1958).
111. William J. Brennan, conference notes, n.d., WJBP, Box 405.
112. *Barenblatt*, v. *United States*, 360 U.S., at 126, 134.
113. *Barsky* v. *United States*, 347 U.S. 442 (1954), involved the suspension of a medical doctor from practice because he did not produce records for HUAC. According to Douglas, "this suspension order . . . was sustained, even though there was not a shred of evidence that he was not a competent doctor, nor that he used improper conduct toward his patients. It was obvious that he lost his right to be a doctor merely because of his political beliefs and his mistaken notion that his constitutional rights entitled him to defy the House committee" (*Court Years*, p. 96). William O. Douglas to Hugo L. Black, 28 May 1959, WODP, Box 1184.
114. *Barenblatt* v. *United States*, 360 U.S., at 140–41, 143, 146, 163, Black, J., dissenting.
115. William J. Brennan, conference notes, 21 November 1958, WJBP, Box 405. Douglas noted that Warren stated in conference that "to publish [the lists] would deter people to come to the lecture or listen—an invasion of their rights of free speech and association" (conference notes, WODP, Box 1204).
116. Douglas, conference notes.
117. Ibid.
118. Hugo L. Black and William O. Douglas, draft dissent, 12 January 1959, WODP, Box 1204.
119. Felix Frankfurter to William J. Brennan, 7 January 1959, FFP/LC, Box 30.
120. *Gibson* v. *Florida Legislative Investigating Committee*, 372 U.S. 539 (1963). Black and Douglas concurred in *Gibson* because Goldberg had separated the Communist party from all other associations (for purposes of special investigations by state committees). Black wrote that the "right of association includes [the right to associate] with people of all beliefs, popular or unpopular." Douglas, again interestingly, chose his words carefully: "Government is not only powerless to legislate with respect to membership in a lawful organization; it is also precluded from probing the intimacies of spiritual and intellectual relationships in the myriad of such groups that exist in this country."
121. Douglas, *Court Years*, p. 102.

Chapter 8

1. Quoted in Juan Williams, *Eyes on the Prize* (New York: Viking Press, 1987), p. 8.
2. See, generally, C. Vann Woodward, *The Strange Career of Jim Crow* (New York: Oxford University Press, 1957).
3. *Dred Scott* v. *Sandford*, 19 Howard 393 (1857).
4. *United States* v. *Harris*, 106 U.S. 629 (1883).
5. Richard Kluger, *Simple Justice* (New York: Vintage Books, 1975), p. 64.
6. *Civil Rights Cases*, 109 U.S. 3 (1883).

7. *Plessy* v. *Ferguson,* 163 U.S. 537 (1896).

8. *Brown et al.* v. *Board of Education of Topeka, Kansas,* 347 U.S. 483 (1954).

9. *Plessy* v. *Ferguson,* 163 U.S., at 543.

10. Ibid., p. 549.

11. Ibid., p. 539.

12. Woodward, *Strange Career of Jim Crow,* p. xvii.

13. Ibid., pp. 81–95, passim.

14. Charles A. Lofgren, *The Plessy Case: A Legal-Historical Interpretation* (New York: Oxford University Press, 1987), p. 204.

15. Clayborne Carson et al., eds., *Eyes on the Prize: A Reader and Guide* (New York: Penguin, 1987), p. 5.

16. Baker, *Brandeis and Frankfurter,* p. 472.

17. Douglas, *Court Years,* p. 111.

18. See, generally, Kluger, *Simple Justice,* chap. 5.

19. Ibid., pp. 133–35.

20. *Powell* v. *Alabama,* 287 U.S. 45 (1932).

21. See, for example, *Brown* v. *Mississippi,* 297 U.S. 278 (1936).

22. *Grovey* v. *Townsend,* 295 U.S. 45 (1935); *School District No. 7* v. *Hunnicut,* 283 U.S. 810 (1931); *Salvatierra* v. *Independent School District,* 284 U.S. 580 (1931).

23. Baker, *Brandeis and Frankfurter,* p. 474.

24. Charles A. J. McPherson to Senator Hugo L. Black, 16 June 1936, HLBP, Box 200.

25. Cathleen H. Douglas-Stone, "William O. Douglas: The Man," in *Supreme Court Historical Society Yearbook, 1981* (Washington, D.C.: Supreme Court Historical Society, 1981), p. 8.

26. Black's sister-in-law, Virginia Durr, put it sharply when she said, at the centennial celebration of Black's birth at the University of Alabama Law School, "We [Southerners] were all segregationists when we grew up. You can't say everybody else is a son-of-a-bitch or wrong if you were exactly the same way yourself" (quoted in *New York Times,* 14 April 1985).

27. Silverstein, *Constitutional Faiths,* p. 102.

28. Hugo L. Black to A. Hatley, 30 April 1932, HLBP, Box 158.

29. Walter White to Max Lowenthal, 20 August 1937, FFP/LC, Box 79.

30. George D. Flemings (president, Fort Worth, Texas, NAACP) to Hugo Black, 23 March 1940, HLBP, Box 258.

31. Silverstein, *Constitutional Faiths,* p. 136.

32. Dunne, *Hugo Black and the Judicial Revolution,* p. 300.

33. *Missouri ex rel. Gaines* v. *Canada,* 305 U.S. 337 (1938).

34. *Houston Informer,* 24 December 1938, HLBP, Box 255.

35. *Pierre* v. *Louisiana,* 306 U.S. 354 (1939).

36. Dunne, *Hugo Black and the Judicial Revolution,* p. 301.

37. In an earlier version of *Chambers,* Black argued for the fair-trial concept developed by the Court in *Palko* and in *Carolene Products,* opinions in which Black had not joined or about which he was unhappy because they were poor reflections of the judicial function and the meaning of due process. Black's final version concluded that the police violated the Fourteenth Amendment's due process requirement of "conforming to fundamental standards of procedure in criminal trials" (Silverstein, *Constitutional Faiths,* pp. 137–42).

38. Black and Black, *Mr. Justice and Mrs. Black,* p. 73.

39. *Chambers* v. *Florida,* 309 U.S. 227 (1940).

40. Silverstein, *Constitutional Faiths,* p. 142.

41. Mary McLeod Bethune to Hugo L. Black, 24 February 1940, HLBP, Box 258.

42. Flemmings to Black, 23 March 1940.

43. See, for example, David Lawrence, "Not Yet Time to 'Apologize' to Justice Black" ("Washington View" column), *New York Times,* 15 February 1940, HLBP, Box 258.

44. Robert Reich, "Mr. Justice Black and the Living Constitution," 76 *Harvard Law Review,* 673, 679 (1963).

45. Yarbrough, *Mr. Justice Black and His Critics,* p. 84.

46. Douglas, *Go East Young Man,* p. 67.

47. Ibid., pp. 67–84.
48. Douglas, *Anatomy of Liberty*, pp. 43, 50, 51.
49. Abe Fortas, "Mr. Justice Douglas," 73 *Yale Law Journal* 913, 917 (1964).
50. Tinsley E. Yarbrough, "Justices Black and Douglas: The Judicial Function and the Scope of Constitutional Liberties," 1973 *Duke Law Journal* 441, 472 (1973).
51. See Black's partial dissent in *South Carolina* v. *Katzenbach,* 383 U.S. 301 (1966), and Douglas's dissent in *Oregon* v. *Mitchell,* 400 U.S. 112 (1970); see, for example, their differences in *Harper* v. *Virginia State Board of Elections,* 383 U.S. 663 (1966).
52. *Cox* v. *Louisiana* (I), 379 U.S. 559; (II) 379 U.S. 574 (1964).
53. William O. Douglas, conference notes, 21 October 1966, WODP, Box 1385.
54. John M. Harlan to Hugo Black, 2 November 1966, HLBP, Box 60.
55. William J. Brennan to William O. Douglas, 8 November 1966, WJBP, Box 149.
56. *Adderley* v. *Florida,* 385 U.S. 48, 45, 47 (1966).
57. Ibid., pp. 49 n. 1, 50, 52, 56, Douglas, J., dissenting.
58. Hugo Black to Hugh G. Grant, n.d. [December 1966], HLBP, Box 31.
59. Schwartz, *Super Chief,* p. 630.
60. *Shelley* v. *Kraemer,* 334 U.S. 1 (1948).
61. Black refers to "sit-down" cases in Black and Black, *Mr. Justice and Mrs. Black,* p. 91. See also Mary King, *Freedom Song: A Personal Story of the 1960s Civil Rights Movement* (New York: Morrow, 1987).
62. Jack Greenberg, "The Supreme Court, Civil Rights and Civil Dissonance," 77 *Yale Law Journal* 1520 (1968).
63. Bernard Schwartz, ed., *The Unpublished Opinions of the Warren Court* (New York: Oxford University Press, 1985), p. 144.
64. Jack Greenberg, *Judicial Process and Social Change: Constitutional Litigation* (St. Paul, Minn.: West, 1977), p. 147.
65. William O. Douglas, conference notes, n.d., WODP, Box 1289.
66. Earl Warren, conference notes, n.d., EWP, Box 604. Warren indicated that Black drew differences between a store owner and a home owner, but "[the Court] cannot make a constitutional difference."
67. Ibid. See also WJBP, Box 410.
68. Warren, conference notes.
69. Schwartz, *Super Chief,* pp. 480, 481. See also Warren, conference notes.
70. *Peterson* v. *City of Greenville,* 373 U.S. 244 (1963), Douglas, J., concurring.
71. Schwartz, *Super Chief,* p. 487.
72. Douglas's concurring opinion in *Bell* had argued that the owner of the restaurant did not allow blacks to eat at the lunch counter because the corporation would lose profits, since whites would cease to do business with the store.
73. These notes evidently survived the destruction of Black's conference notes after his death (by his son Hugo, Jr., at his father's request) because they were transcribed by two of Black's law clerks, A. E. Dick Howard and John G. Kester, and included in a summary of the 1963 term sit-in cases entitled "The Deliberations of the Justices in Deciding the Sit-In Cases of June 22, 1964, from the Files of Justice Black" (pp. 4, 5, HLBP, Box 376). Schwartz noted that Black "delivered an emotional statement," in this conference, "declaring that he could not believe that his 'Pappy,' who operated a general store in Alabama, did not have the right to decide whom he would or would not serve" (*Unpublished Opinions,* p. 146).
74. William O. Douglas, memorandum, "In Re: Sit-In Cases," 21 October 1963, p. 3, WODP, Box 1299.
75. See, generally, J. Woodford Howard, "The Fluidity of Judicial Choice," *American Political Science Review* 62 (March 1968): 43–56.
76. Black and Black, *Mr. Justice and Mrs. Black,* pp. 92, 96. Douglas, in a handwritten note for the file dated May 19, 1964, said that Clark had seen him that day and had told him he was switching his vote. "His [switch] upset HLB very much as HLB had hoped the Court would act promptly. There was considerable speculation as to why TC [switched, but] it now appears that he has concluded that these cases all represent 'state action'" (WODP, Box 1311).

77. William O. Douglas to William J. Brennan, 3 June 1964, WODP, Box 1312.
78. Interview with Justice William J. Brennan, Jr., 29 October 1986, Washington, D.C.
79. Black and Black, *Mr. Justice and Mrs. Black,* p. 92.
80. Yarbrough, *Mr. Justice Black and His Critics,* p. 226.
81. Abe Fortas to William O. Douglas, 24 March 1966, WODP, Box 1363; John M. Harlan to Hugo L. Black, n.d., HLBP, Box 387.
82. Kluger, *Simple Justice,* pp. 136, 133–39, passim.
83. *Sipuel* v. *Oklahoma,* 332 U.S. 631 (1947).
84. Kluger, *Simple Justice,* p. 259.
85. Conference notes, 10 January 1948, WODP, Box 176.
86. Ibid.
87. Kluger, *Simple Justice,* p. 260.
88. Ibid.
89. *Sweatt* v. *Painter,* 339 U.S. 629 (1950); *McLaurin* v. *Oklahoma State Regents,* 339 U.S. 637 (1950).
90. "Reserved for Colored" signs were placed on chairs and desks, and "George McLaurin was made to sit at a desk by himself in an anteroom outside the regular classrooms where his course work was given. . . . In the cafeteria, he was required to eat in a dingy alcove by himself and at a different hour from the whites" (Kluger, *Simple Justice,* p. 268).
91. Ibid., p. 264
92. Ibid., pp. 275–76.
93. Elman, "Solicitor General's Office, Justice Frankfurter and Civil Rights Litigation," p. 817.
94. Tom C. Clark, memorandum to the conference, 7 April 1950, RHJP, Box 160.
95. Ibid., p. 4.
96. Felix Frankfurter to Fred M. Vinson, 19 May 1950, quoted in Kluger, *Simple Justice,* p. 281.
97. Hugo Black to Fred M. Vinson, slip opinion note, n.d., HLBP, Box 306.
98. *Sweatt* v. *Painter,* 339 U.S. 629 (1950).
99. *McLaurin* v. *Oklahoma State Regents,* 339 U.S. 637 (1950).
100. Kluger, *Simple Justice,* p. 284.
101. Clark, memorandum to the conference, 7 April 1950.
102. Mark V. Tushnet, *The NAACP Legal Strategy Against Segregated Education, 1925–1950* (Chapel Hill: University of North Carolina Press, 1987), p. 138.
103. Kluger, *Simple Justice,* p. 290.
104. Ibid., p. 540.
105. For an outstanding analysis of the strategies and the fears of the NAACP, see, generally, Kluger, *Simple Justice.* Kluger also provides a very clear analysis of the public-school integration litigation from these early strategies to the judgments of the Supreme Court.
106. Elman, "Solicitor General's Office, Justice Frankfurter and Civil Rights Litigation," pp. 817, 822.
107. Conference notes, *Brown,* n.d., RHJP, Box 7.
108. While Rehnquist, in later years, insisted that this memo "was prepared by me at Justice Jackson's request; it was intended as a rough draft of a statement of his views at the conference of the justices, rather than as a statement of my views," the facts in the record clearly suggest otherwise. A review of the draft concurring opinion of Justice Jackson, prepared but never delivered, clearly shows that Jackson believed that *Plessy* was wrong and had to be set aside (Bernard Schwartz, "Chief Justice Rehnquist, Justice Jackson and the Brown Case," in Kurland and Casper, *Supreme Court Review,* p. 251).
109. Robert H. Jackson to Charles Fairman, 13 March 1950, RHJP, Box 7.
110. Conference notes, *Brown,* 13 December 1952, RHJP, Box 7.
111. Elman, "Solicitor General's Office, Justice Frankfurter and Civil Rights Litigation," p. 829.
112. Felix Frankfurter, statement on discrimination, 26 September 1952, RHJP, Box 7.
113. Quoted in Baker, *Brandeis and Frankfurter,* p. 479.
114. Ibid.
115. Elman, "Solicitor General's Office, Justice Frankfurter and Civil Rights Litigation," p. 825.
116. Quoted in Kluger, *Simple Justice,* pp. 593–94.

117. Black, Jr., *My Father,* p. 208.
118. Felix Frankfurter to Learned Hand, 1954, FFP, Box 65.
119. Quoted in Kluger, *Simple Justice,* p. 293.
120. Ibid., p. 294.
121. Ibid., p. 560.
122. Felix Frankfurter to Stanley Reed, 20 May 1954, FFP, quoted in Schwartz, *Super Chief,* p. 78.
123. Elman, "Solicitor General's Office, Justice Frankfurter and Civil Rights Litigation," p. 832.
124. See conference notes, n.d., RHJP, Box 7. Jackson's comments, from Burton's notes, are quoted in Kluger, *Simple Justice,* pp. 608–9.
125. Burton, in his notes, wrote, "We discussed the segregation cases thus disclosing the trend but no even tentative vote was taken" (Schwartz, *Super Chief,* p. 78).
126. Hugo L. Black, memorandum to the conference, 13 June 1953, HLBP, Box 319.
127. Elman said it directly: "Without God, we never would have had Brown, a unanimous decision. . . . Without God, the Court would have remained bitterly divided, fragmented, unable to decide the issue forthrightly. . . . God won Brown, not Thurgood Marshall or any other lawyer or any other mortal. . . . God takes care of drunks, little children and the American people. He took care of the American people and the little children and Brown by taking Fred Vinson when he did" ("Solicitor General's Office, Justice Frankfurter and Civil Rights Litigation," p. 840).
128. Schwartz, *Unpublished Opinions,* p. 446. Elman recalled that Frankfurter told him: "Phil, this is the first solid piece of evidence I've ever had that there really is a God" ("Solicitor General's Office, Justice Frankfurter and Civil Rights Litigation," p. 840).
129. Schwartz, *Unpublished Opinions,* p. 446.
130. White, *Earl Warren,* p. 162.
131. Amelia Roberts Fry, "The Warren Tapes: Oral History and the Supreme Court," in *Supreme Court Historical Society Yearbook, 1982* (Washington, D.C.: Supreme Court Historical Society, 1982), p. 14.
132. Schwartz, *Unpublished Opinions,* p. 446.
133. Ibid.
134. Schwartz, *Super Chief,* p. 89.
135. All the justices, including Black, wanted the Court to stay out of the business of administering the decree. "Leave it to the District Courts," urged Black. "This Court cannot do it directly," maintained Frankfurter. Clark wanted local, variable responses based on local variations in the practice of segregation that would have to be dismantled. Jackson, in January 1954, suggested an approach, supported by Black and Clark, that was adopted by the Court: rearguments during the 1954 term of the Court to determine the implementation phase of the issue (ibid., pp. 91–93).
136. On May 21, 1954, four days after *Brown* was announced, Reed wrote to Frankfurter that while "there were many considerations that pointed to a dissent, . . . they did not add up to a balance against the Court's opinion . . . the factors looking toward a fair treatment for Negroes are more important than the weight of history" (Schwartz, *Unpublished Opinions,* p. 447).
137. Earl Warren, memorandum to the Court, n.d., EWP, Box 571.
138. *Brown* v. *Board of Education of Topeka,* 347 U.S. 482, 492–93 (1953).
139. Ibid., pp. 494–95. Schwartz indicates that this segment of the opinion, with its famous footnote 11 citing contemporary sociological and psychological experts, drew no complaints from any of the brethren. The law clerk who built the footnote, Earl Pollock, said that he added it to the opinion because "I was looking for a way to part company and to say that, whatever the situation was in the 1890s, we know a lot more about law in society than we did then" (Schwartz, *Unpublished Opinions,* p. 458).
140. *Brown* v. *Board of Education,* 347 U.S., at 493.
141. When he read the opinion in Court, the chief paused and added the word *unanimously* to the opinion (EWP, Box 571).
142. *Brown* v. *Board of Education,* 347 U.S., at 495.

143. Felix Frankfurter to Earl Warren, 14 May 1954, EWP, Box 571.
144. William O. Douglas to Earl Warren, 11 May 1954, EWP, Box 571.
145. Kluger, *Simple Justice,* p. 710.
146. Louis Lomax, *The Negro Revolt* (New York: Signet Books, 1963), p. 84.
147. Ibid., p. 708.
148. Felix Frankfurter to Earl Warren, 17 May 1954, EWP, Box 571.
149. Harold Burton to Earl Warren, 17 May 1954, EWP, Box 571.
150. *Brown* v. *Board of Education,* 347 U.S., at 495.
151. On Tuesday, May 18, 1954, the day after *Brown* was announced, Frankfurter sent a memorandum to the conference indicating that his law clerk, Alexander Bickel, had done exhaustive work in the Library of Congress on the legislative history of the Fourteenth Amendment and Frankfurter was taking the liberty of sending a second version of Bickel's report, revised by Frankfurter, to the brethren (EWP, Box 571).
152. Felix Frankfurter to Earl Warren, 5 July 1954, EWP, Box 574. Actually, in January 1954, months before the chief had begun to draft *Brown* I, Frankfurter had written another of his memoranda to his brethren. In the memo, he asserted that the Court could not change the pattern of Jim Crow "in a day" and "would [do] its duty if it decrees measures that reverse the direction of the unconstitutional policy so as to uproot it with all deliberate speed'" (Baker, *Brandeis and Frankfurter,* pp. 480–81).
153. The *Brown* II opinion, 349 U.S. 294 (1954), remanded the cases to the local federal courts "because of their proximity to local conditions and the possible need for further hearings" and because the local federal courts were best able to determine whether the local school board's action "constitutes good faith implementation of the governing constitutional principles." In developing the remedial decree, the federal courts were to be "guided by equitable principles, i.e., . . . a practical flexibility in shaping its remedies and by a facility for adjusting and reconciling public and private needs." The district courts had to "require that the defendants make a prompt and reasonable start toward full compliance with our May 17, 1954 ruling." The federal district courts had to issue orders and decrees "as are necessary and proper to admit to public schools on a racially nondiscriminatory basis with all deliberate speed the parties to these cases."
154. Conference notes, 16 April 1955, EWP, Box 574.
155. Felix Frankfurter to Earl Warren, 24 May 1955, EWP, Box 574. On May 27, 1955, Frankfurter once again implored the chief to make the substitution, writing, "I still strongly believe that 'with all deliberate speed' conveys more effectively the process of time for the effectuation of our decision" (EWP, Box 574). Black, however, did not like that phrase. According to his son, the phrase "disturbed" Black because "'it tells the enemies of the decision that for the present the status quo will do and gives them time to contrive devices to stall off segregation.' But he could not bring the Court to abandon unaminously the critical phrase. And Daddy was not about to do anything to fragment the Court in that landmark opinion" (Black, Jr., *My Father,* p. 209). A handwritten note Frankfurter sent to Black on May 4, 1955, testifies to Black's objections to "with all deliberate speed." Wrote Frankfurter, "I join the C.J.'s hope that you may be able to swallow this. I don't have to add that I welcome suggestions within the scope of the opinion" (HLBP, Box 323).
156. In the January 16, 1955, conference, Black had insisted that the Court not consider these cases as "class lawsuits." Given his fear about the violence and intimidation that would ensue after the implementation opinion was issued, he felt that "many Negroes would not like to be named in [any] judgment." Douglas, in that conference, had "doubts re Class Action, like Hugo" (EWP, Box 573).
157. *Cooper* v. *Aaron,* 358 U.S. 1, 10 (1958).
158. Quoted in Dunne, *Hugo Black and the Judicial Revolution,* p. 349.
159. Schwartz, *Super Chief,* p. 293.
160. Hugo Black to William J. Brennan, n.d. [September 1958], WJBP, Box 335.
161. Quoted in Schwartz, *Super Chief,* p. 300.
162. WODP, Box 1198.
163. Schwartz, *Super Chief,* p. 302.

164. Brennan interview.
165. William O. Douglas, memorandum for the file, n.d., WODP, Box 1198.
166. In mid-October 1958, Frankfurter wrote Black a note that had an attachment. It was a letter from the former president of the Arkansas Bar Association, A. F. House, who wrote, in part, that "in my humble opinion [your concurring opinion] will, more than any document or writing which has come out of the turmoil, recreate respect for the law" (HLBP, Box 335).
167. *Cooper* v. *Aaron,* 358 U.S., at 18.
168. See, for example, *Goss* v. *Board of Education,* 373 U.S. 683 (1963); *Griffin* v. *County School Board,* 377 U.S. 218 (1964); and *Green* v. *County School Board,* 391 U.S. 430 (1968).
169. "'All deliberate speed' was used to drag feet . . . [opponents] thought up ingenious as well as ingenuous plans to forestall [desegregation] programs" (Douglas, *Court Years,* p. 120).
170. *Green* v. *County School Board,* 391 U.S., at 438–39.
171. *Alexander* v. *Holmes County, Mississippi,* 396 U.S. 1218 (1969). Justice Black's opinion in chambers, 396 U.S. 19 (1969).
172. Black and Black, *Mr. Justice and Mrs. Black,* p. 230.
173. Conference notes, 9 October 1969, WODP, Box 1480.
174. Hugo L. Black, memorandum to the conference, 26 October 1969, HLBP, Box 428.
175. Hugo L. Black, draft dissent, 26 October 1969, HLBP, Box 428.
176. Ibid.
177. Black and Black, *Mr. Justice and Mrs. Black,* p. 233.
178. Ibid.
179. William O. Douglas, memorandum to the conference, 29 October 1969, WODP, Box 1480.
180. Quoted in Woodward and Armstrong, *The Brethren,* p. 96.
181. William O. Douglas, note for the file, 20 April 1971, WODP, Box 1453.
182. William O. Douglas to Warren E. Burger, 4 September 1970, WODP, Box 1514.
183. Woodward and Armstrong, *The Brethren,* p. 98.
184. William O. Douglas to Warren E. Burger, 10 December 1970, WODP, Box 1513.
185. Thurgood Marshall, memorandum to the conference, 12 January 1971, JMHP.
186. William O. Douglas to Potter Stewart, 19 February 1971, WODP, Box 1486.
187. See, for example, William O. Douglas to Warren E. Burger, 16 March 1971, WODP, Box 1486.
188. Conference notes, n.d., WODP, Box 1486.
189. Warren Burger, memorandum to the conference, 22 March 1971, WODP, Box 1486.
190. On April 9, 1971, however, Douglas wrote Burger a note asking the chief to "join me" in the opinion. "I think it is a good job" (WODP, Box 1486).
191. Hugo L. Black to Warren E. Burger, 25 March 1971, WODP, Box 1486.
192. Quoted in Woodward and Armstrong, *The Brethren,* p. 111.
193. *Swann* v. *Charlotte-Mecklenburg Board of Education,* 402 U.S. 1, 14 (1970).
194. William O. Douglas, note for the file, n.d., WODP, Box 1486.
195. See *Baker* v. *Carr,* 369 U.S. 186 (1962), and *Reynolds* v. *Sims,* 377 U.S. 533 (1964).
196. *United States* v. *Classic,* 313 U.S. 299 (1941); *Smith* v. *Allright,* 321 U.S. 649 (1944); *Terry* v. *Adams,* 345 U.S. 461 (1953).
197. *Gomillion* v. *Lightfoot,* 364 U.S. 339 (1960).
198. *Colegrove* v. *Green,* 328 U.S. 549 (1946).
199. In a letter to Black, on November 1, 1960, Frankfurter, acknowledging that they both wanted a unanimous opinion in the case, wrote, "So I am sending you my effort, with a view of avoiding what is avoidable [mention of *Colegrove*], before I circulate the opinion generally. No one else has seen it. I shall be grateful for your help" (Felix Frankfurter to Hugo Black, 1 November 1960, HLBP, Box 344).
200. *Gomillion* v. *Lightfoot,* 364 U.S., at 355.
201. *Baker* v. *Carr,* 369 U.S. 186 (1962).
202. See, for example, Charles Whalen and Barbara Whalen, *The Longest Debate: A Legislative History of the 1964 Civil Rights Act* (New York: New American Library, 1985), and Howard Ball, Dale Krane, and Thomas Lauth, *Compromised Compliance: Implementation of the 1965 Voting Rights Act* (Westport, Conn.: Greenwood Press, 1982).

203. *Jones* v. *Alfred Mayer*, 392 U.S. 409 (1967).
204. Schwartz, *Super Chief*, p. 702.
205. William O. Douglas, note for the file, 5 April 1968, WODP, Box 1423.
206. WODP, Box 1423.
207. *Heart of Atlanta Motel* v. *United States*, 379 U.S. 241 (1964); *Katzenbach* v. *McClung*, 379 U.S. 294 (1964).
208. Law clerk to William O. Douglas, note, n.d., WODP, Box 1347.
209. Conference notes, n.d., WODP, Box 1347.
210. Arthur Goldberg to William O. Douglas, 14 December 1964, WODP, Box 1347.
211. *Heart of Atlanta Motel* v. *United States*, 379 U.S., at 286.
212. Ibid., pp. 291–92.
213. Ibid., p. 279.
214. Baker, *Brandeis and Frankfurter*, p. 482.
215. For a classic view of the dilemmas that these federal district court judges faced, see Jack Peltason, *Fifty-Eight Lonely Men* (Urbana: University of Illinois Press, 1962).
216. HLBP, n.d., Box 335.
217. HLBP, n.d., Box 53.
218. Brennan interview.

Chapter 9

1. Elizabeth Black, interview with Tinsley Yarbrough, 6 July 1975. See also Black and Black, *Mr. Justice and Mrs. Black*, p. 234.
2. Black, *Constitutional Faith*, p. 32.
3. Ibid., p. 24.
4. Interview with Justice William J. Brennan, Jr., 29 October 1986, Washington, D.C.
5. Black, *Constitutional Faith*, p. 26.
6. Ibid., p. xvii.
7. Ibid., p. 11.
8. Interview with Chief Justice Warren Burger (retired), 21 December 1987.
9. Interview with Elizabeth Black, 28 August 1987.
10. Interview with Justice Arthur Goldberg (retired), 27 August 1987.
11. Brennan interview; see also Burton Atkins and Terry Sloope, "The 'New' Hugo Black and the Warren Court," *Polity* 18 (Summer 1986): 621–37.
12. See, for example, *Younger* v. *Harris*, 401 U.S. 37 (1971).
13. See *Day-Brite Lighting* v. *Missouri*, 342 U.S. 421 (1952), and *Olsen* v. *Nebraska*, 313 U.S. 236 (1941).
14. William O. Douglas, *An Almanac of Liberty* (Garden City, N.Y.: Doubleday, 1954), p. 5.
15. William O. Douglas, *We the Judges: Studies in American and Indian Constitutional Law* (Garden City, N.Y.: Doubleday, 1956).
16. William O. Douglas to William R. Johnson, 24 April 1960, in Urofsky, *Douglas Letters*, p. 158.
17. H. Frank Way analyzed the first ten years of Douglas's opinions for content as well as vote. Of the criminal cases he concluded, "In none of these cases did he ever make a statement which would excuse the illegal acts of the defendants by posturing some broad sociological explanation of criminal behavior nor did he ever question the substantive prohibitions of the particular criminal law" ("The Study of Judicial Attitudes: The Case of Mr. Justice Douglas," *Western Political Quarterly* [March 1971]: 18).
18. *Breithaupt* v. *Abram*, 352 U.S. 432, 442–43 (1957).
19. National Commission on Law Observance and Enforcement (Washington, D.C.: Government Printing Office, 1931).
20. William O. Douglas, "Vagrancy and Arrest on Suspicion," 70 *Yale Law Journal* 1 (1960).
21. See *Allee* v. *Medrano*, 416 U.S. 802 (1974).

22. Douglas, *Alamanac of Liberty,* p. 178. See also William O. Douglas, "On Misconception of the Judicial Function and the Responsibility of the Bar," 59 *Columbia Law Review* 227, 228 (1959).
23. Douglas, *We the Judges,* pp. 377–78.
24. See *Wyman* v. *James,* 400 U.S. 309, 334 (1971), Douglas, J., dissenting.
25. Interview with Cathleen Douglas-Stone, 14 November 1986, Boston.
26. Brennan interview.
27. For a full discussion, see chapter 2.
28. *Sniadach* v. *Family Finance,* 395 U.S. 337 (1969). Douglas prepared the majority, and Black dissented.
29. See *Katz* v. *United States,* 389 U.S. 347 (1967), Black, J., dissenting, and Douglas, J., concurring.
30. *Griswold* v. *Connecticut,* 381 U.S. 479 (1965), Black, J., dissenting.
31. Douglas, *We the Judges,* p. 263.
32. Ibid.
33. See Black's opinions in *Goldberg* v. *Kelly,* 397 U.S. 254 (1970), and *Rosado* v. *Wyman,* 397 U.S. 397 (1970), which were at odds with Douglas's position.
34. See *Wisconsin* v. *Yoder,* 406 U.S. 205 (1972), Douglas, J., dissenting. He joined the Court in school cases like *Tinker* v. *Des Moines School District,* 393 U.S. 503 (1969), and *Goss* v. *Lopez,* 419 U.S. 565 (1975). He joined the Court in its juvenile-justice cases, such as *In re Gault,* 387 U.S. 1 (1967).
35. See *In re Gault,* 387 U.S. 1 (1967), Black, J., dissenting.
36. *In re Gault; In re Winship,* 397 U.S. 358 (1970); *McKeiver* v. *Pennsylvania,* 403 U.S. 528 (1971), Douglas, J., dissenting.
37. Douglas, *Court Years,* p. 52.
38. *Barron* v. *Baltimore,* 32 U.S. (7 Pet.) 243, 247 (1833).
39. See *Hurtado* v. *California,* 110 U.S. 516 (1884), and *Maxwell* v. *Dow,* 176 U.S. 581 (1900).
40. *Twining* v. *New Jersey,* 211 U.S. 78 (1908).
41. Black, *Constitutional Faith,* p. 38.
42. Ibid., p. 38, quoting *Twining* v. *New Jersey,* 211 U.S., at 99.
43. *Palko* v. *Connecticut,* 302 U.S. 319 (1937).
44. *Chambers* v. *Florida,* 309 U.S. 227, 236 n. 8 (1940).
45. Hugo Black to Irving Dilliard, 25 July 1962, HLBP, Box 25.
46. *Betts* v. *Brady,* 316 U.S. 455 (1942).
47. Ibid., p. 474 n. 1, Black J., dissenting.
48. Howard, *Mr. Justice Murphy,* p. 429.
49. Felix Frankfurter to Hugo Black, 31 October 1939, quoted in ibid., p. 428.
50. Felix Frankfurter to Hugo Black, 13 November 1943, quoted in ibid., p. 431.
51. Hugo Black, memorandum to the conference, *Malinski* v. *New York,* 23 March 1945, HLBP, Box 118.
52. Ibid.
53. *Adamson* v. *California,* 332 U.S. 46 (1947), Black, J., dissenting.
54. Ibid., p. 50.
55. Ibid., p. 53.
56. Ibid., p. 69.
57. Ibid., pp. 71–72.
58. It was very similar to his counter-opinion in *Dennis* v. *United States,* 339 U.S. 162 (1950), and had the same target in mind.
59. *Adamson* v. *California,* 332 U.S., at 60.
60. Ibid., p. 62.
61. Draft, p. 7. Ibid., p. 65.
62. Hugo Black, dissent draft, HLBP, Box 284.
63. William O. Douglas to Hugo L. Black, 21 May 1947, HLBP, Box 284.
64. Douglas, *Court Years,* p. 54.

65. Ibid., pp. 54–55.
66. Charles Fairman, "Does the Fourteenth Amendment Incorporate the Bill of Rights: The Original Understanding," 2 *Stanford Law Review* 5 (1949).
67. Felix Frankfurter to Earl Warren, 19 November 1954, EWP, Box 353.
68. Charles Grove Haines to Hugo Black, 19 August 1947, HLBP, Box 284.
69. Douglas, *We the Judges*, p. 263.
70. *Everson* v. *Board of Education,* 330 U.S. 1 (1947); *Murdoch* v. *Pennsylvania,* 319 U.S. 105 (1943); *Cantwell* v. *Connecticut,* 310 U.S. 296 (1940); *West Virginia State Board of Education* v. *Barnette,* 319 U.S. 624 (1943).
71. *In re Oliver,* 330 U.S. 257 (1942); *Wolf* v. *Colorado,* 338 U.S. 25 (1949); *Louisiana ex rel. Francis* v. *Resweber,* 329 U.S. 459 (1947).
72. *Gideon* v. *Wainwright,* 372 U.S. 335 (1963); *Malloy* v. *Hogan,* 370 U.S. 1 (1964).
73. *Everson* v. *Board of Education,* 330 U.S. 1 (1947); *Murdoch* v. *Pennsylvania,* 319 U.S. 105 (1943); *In re Oliver,* 330 U.S. 257 (1942); *Gideon* v. *Wainwright,* 372 U.S. 335 (1963); *Pointer* v. *Texas,* 380 U.S. 400 (1965).
74. "There was no paradox for Frankfurter that judges should reject preferred freedoms as predilection and yet enforce natural justice notions of criminal procedure, no paradox that judges should retain due process supervision over substantive economic rights" (Howard, *Mr. Justice Murphy,* p. 429).
75. *Adamson* v. *California,* 332 U.S., at 66.
76. Ibid., pp. 67–68.
77. Alexander Meiklejohn, "What Does the First Amendment Mean?" 20 *University of Chicago Law Review* 461, 474–75 (1953).
78. *Pointer* v. *Texas,* 380 U.S., at 408–9, Harlan, J., concurring.
79. Harlan leaned on Clark during deliberation of the *Mapp* case with the threat that his decision would help Black and his colleagues who advocated incorporation: "P.S. If you don't mind my saying so, your opinion comes perilously close to accepting 'incorporation' for the Fourth A., and will doubtless encourage the 'incorporation enthusiasts'" (Schwartz, *Super Chief,* p. 396).
80. *Benton* v. *Maryland,* 395 U.S. 724 (1969), Harlan, J., dissenting.
81. *Duncan* v. *Louisiana,* 391 U.S. 145 (1968).
82. Ibid., p. 174.
83. See also *Benton* v. *Maryland,* 395 U.S., at 724.
84. *Duncan* v. *Louisiana,* 391 U.S., at 168.
85. Ibid., p. 169.
86. See, for example, *Griswold* v. *Connecticut,* 381 U.S., at 500, Harlan, J., concurring. See also Schwartz, *Super Chief,* p. 580.
87. *Adamson* v. *California,* draft, p. 1, Murphy, J., dissenting.
88. Frank Murphy to Hugo Black, n.d., HLBP, Box 287.
89. Howard, *Mr. Justice Murphy,* p. 433.
90. Ibid., p. 435.
91. Schwartz, *Super Chief,* p. 11.
92. Ibid., p. 137.
93. *Zap* v. *United States,* 328 U.S. 624, 630 (1946).
94. *United States* v. *White,* 401 U.S. 745, 756 (1971), Douglas, J., dissenting.
95. *Goldman* v. *United States,* 316 U.S. 129 (1942).
96. There is no small bit of irony in the fact that the search in question was authorized by the Justice Department headed by none other than Frank Murphy, then attorney general. Justice Jackson, who had succeeded Murphy, recused himself from the case, but threatened to explain the relationship between their two administrations if Murphy did not tone down some of his rhetoric in the dissent. See the exchange of memoranda in WODP, Box 63.
97. *Wolf* v. *Colorado,* 338 U.S. 25 (1949).
98. *Weeks* v. *United States,* 232 U.S. 383 (1914).
99. WODP, Box 179.

356 • *Notes*

100. *Mapp* v. *Ohio,* 367 U.S. 643 (1961). Douglas relied on Murphy again in *Stefanelli* v. *Minard,* 342 U.S. 117 (1951), Douglas, J., dissenting.
101. *Mapp* v. *Ohio,* 367 U.S. 643 (1961).
102. William O. Douglas, conference notes, *Mapp,* n.d., WODP, Box 1253.
103. Our assessment of the conference notes and memoranda is at variance with the analysis presented in Schwartz, *Super Chief,* pp. 392–96, and Dunne, *Hugo Black and the Judicial Revolution,* p. 364.
104. *Mapp* v. *Ohio,* 367 U.S., at 652.
105. Ibid., p. 656.
106. Tom Clark to Hugo Black, 6 June 1961, HLBP, Box 349.
107. *Mapp* v. *Ohio,* 367 U.S., at 655.
108. Hugo Black to Tom Clark, 15 June 1961, HLBP, Box 349.
109. Tom Clark to Hugo Black, 15 June 1961, HLBP, Box 349.
110. *Mapp* v. *Ohio,* 367 U.S., at 662.
111. Louis H. Pollak to Hugo Black, 26 June 1961, HLBP, Box 349.
112. Hugo Black to Louis Pollak, 29 June 1961, HLBP, Box 349.
113. *Olmstead* v. *United States,* 277 U.S. 438 (1928).
114. *On Lee* v. *United States,* 343 U.S. 747 (1952).
115. Ibid., pp. 762–63, Douglas J., dissenting.
116. *Irvine* v. *California,* 347 U.S. 128 (1954).
117. Ibid., p. 147.
118. Ibid., p. 149.
119. Ibid.
120. See, for example, Douglas, *Court Years,* pp. 386–87.
121. *Irvine* v. *California,* 347 U.S., at 149.
122. Ibid., p. 150.
123. Ibid., pp. 151–52.
124. William O. Douglas, *The Rights of the People* (Garden City, N.Y.: Doubleday, 1958), p. 151.
125. Douglas, *Almanac of Liberty,* p. 354.
126. *Osborn* v. *United States,* 385 U.S. 323, 353–54 (1966), Douglas, J., dissenting.
127. *Lopez* v. *United States,* 373 U.S. 427 (1963), Brennan, J., dissenting.
128. *Katz* v. *United States,* 389 U.S. 347 (1967). See also *Berger* v. *New York,* 388 U.S. 41 (1967).
129. *Katz* v. *United States,* 389 U.S., at 351.
130. Ibid., p. 353.
131. Ibid., p. 362.
132. William Brennan, memorandum for the file, *Alderman* v. *United States,* 394 U.S. 165 (1969), 17 March 1969; see also Urofsky, *Douglas Letters,* pp. 207–10, and Schwartz, *Super Chief,* pp. 750–52.
133. William O. Douglas file, 94-33476, Federal Bureau of Investigation Files, Washington, D.C.
134. See *United States* v. *United States District Court,* 407 U.S. 297 (1972).
135. *United States* v. *White,* 401 U.S. 745 (1971), Douglas, J., dissenting.
136. *Rochin* v. *California,* 342 U.S. 165 (1952).
137. Ibid., pp. 171–72.
138. Ibid.
139. Ibid., p. 173.
140. Ibid., p. 175.
141. Ibid., p. 177.
142. Ibid., p. 179, Douglas, J., concurring.
143. *Breithaupt* v. *Abram,* 352 U.S. 432 (1957).
144. *Schmerber* v. *California,* 384 U.S. 757 (1966).
145. *Breithaupt* v. *Abram,* 352 U.S., at 443, Douglas, J., dissenting.
146. WODP, Box 1178.
147. Ibid.
148. WODP, Box 1370.

149. *Chambers* v. *Florida,* 309 U.S. 227 (1940). See also *Ashcraft* v. *Tennessee,* 322 U.S. 143 (1944).
150. *Ashcroft* v. *Tennessee,* 322 U.S., at 155.
151. Harlan F. Stone to Hugo Black, 22 March 1944, HLBP, Box 271.
152. See, for example, *Mallory* v. *United States,* 354 U.S. 449 (1957).
153. William Brennan to William O. Douglas, 2 June 1964, WJBP, Box 113.
154. William O. Douglas to William Brennan, 3 June 1964, WODP, Box 1320.
155. Ibid.
156. Ibid.
157. *Gideon* v. *Wainwright,* 372 U.S. 335 (1963).
158. Schwartz, *Super Chief,* p. 458.
159. *Betts* v. *Brady,* 316 U.S. 455 (1942). Hugo Black had one more opportunity to add to the list of incorporated freedoms, this time the Sixth Amendment right to confrontation of witnesses against a criminal defendant (*Pointer* v. *Texas,* 380 U.S. 400 [1965]).
160. *Powell* v. *Alabama,* 287 U.S. 45 (1932).
161. *Betts* v. *Brody,* 316 U.S., at 476, Black, J., dissenting.
162. Douglas, *Court Years,* p. 187.
163. Ibid., p. 187.
164. See WJBP, Box 409.
165. *Argersinger* v. *Hamlin,* 407 U.S. 25 (1972).
166. *Crooker* v. *California,* 357 U.S. 433 (1958).
167. *Escobedo* v. *Illinois,* 378 U.S. 478 (1964); *Miranda* v. *Arizona,* 384 U.S. 436 (1966).
168. *Spano* v. *New York,* 360 U.S. 315 (1959).
169. *Escobedo* v. *Illinois,* 378 U.S., at 484–85.
170. Ibid., pp. 490–91.
171. Ibid., p. 493, Harlan, J., dissenting.
172. Ibid., p. 499, White, J., dissenting.
173. Ibid., p. 490.
174. Douglas, *Court Years,* p. 54.
175. *New York Times,* 11 March 1968, p. 1.
176. Murphy, *Fortas,* p. 426.
177. *United States* v. *Wade,* 388 U.S. 218 (1967).
178. *Coleman* v. *Alabama,* 399 U.S. 1 (1970).
179. WJBP, Box 416.
180. Warren Burger, memorandum to the conference, 9 January 1970, WODP, Box 1472.
181. Warren Burger, memorandum to the conference, n.d., WODP, Box 1472.
182. Douglas, *Court Years,* p. 231.
183. Burger interview.
184. *Avery* v. *Georgia,* 390 U.S. 474 (1968).
185. *Fay* v. *New York,* 332 U.S. 261 (1947).
186. *Williams* v. *Florida,* 399 U.S. 78 (1970). Black was gone from the Court when the question was raised concerning the acceptability of verdicts that were less than unanimous. Douglas argued vigorously against that idea on grounds that it simply shifted too much of the presumption of innocence from the defendant and the burden of proof beyond a reasonable doubt away from the prosecutor (*Apodaca* v. *Oregon,* 406 U.S. 404 [1972]). He was, however, a dissenter.
187. *Witherspoon* v. *Illinois,* 391 U.S. 510 (1968). Actually, Douglas issued a separate opinion that took issue with Stewart's majority opinion on a narrower aspect of the ruling.
188. *McGautha* v. *California,* 402 U.S. 183 (1971).
189. Ibid., p. 235, Douglas, J., dissenting.
190. Ibid., p. 225, Black, J., separate opinion.
191. *Irvin* v. *Dowd,* 366 U.S. 717, 727 (1961).
192. *Estes* v. *Texas,* 381 U.S. 532 (1965).
193. *Sheppard* v. *Maxwell,* 384 U.S. 333 (1966).

194. Conference notes, *Estes,* n.d., WJBP, Box 411.
195. William O. Douglas, "The Essence of Due Process" (Speech to the American Law Institute, 20 May 1953), reprinted in *Congressional Record,* 83rd Cong., 1st sess., 1953, 99:A2901-2. See also Douglas, "Communists Here and Abroad," *U.S. News & World Report,* 4 December 1953, pp. 110–12.

Chapter 10

1. Either Douglas or Black wrote the majority opinions in *Martin* v. *Struthers,* 319 U.S. 141 (1943); *Murdoch* v. *Pennsylvania,* 319 U.S. 105 (1943); *United States* v. *Ballard,* 322 U.S. 78 (1944); *Everson* v. *Board of Education,* 330 U.S. 1 (1947); *McCollum* v. *Board of Education,* 333 U.S. 203 (1948); *Zorach* v. *Clauson,* 343 U.S. 306 (1952); *Engel* v. *Vitale,* 370 U.S. 421 (1962); and *Torcaso* v. *Watkins,* 367 U.S. 488 (1961).
2. Elizabeth Black told of Hugo's love for a song or a session with his harmonica in *Mr. Justice and Mrs. Black.*
3. *Everson* v. *Board of Education,* 330 U.S. 1 (1947), cited in Black, *Constitutional Faith,* pp. 43–44.
4. Douglas, *Go East Young Man,* pp. 110–11.
5. Ibid., p. 110.
6. Ibid., p. 112.
7. *Gilette* v. *United States,* 401 U.S. 437, 465–66 (1971), Douglas, J., dissenting.
8. Mason, *Harlan Fiske Stone,* p. 598.
9. *Cantwell* v. *Connecticut,* 310 U.S. 296 (1940).
10. *Minersville School District* v. *Gobitis,* 310 U.S. 586 (1940).
11. Howard, *Mr. Justice Murphy,* p. 287.
12. Mason, *Harlan Fiske Stone,* p. 526.
13. Felix Frankfurter to Harlan Fiske Stone, 27 May 1940, HFSP. See also Mason, *Harlan Fiske Stone,* p. 526.
14. Douglas, *Court Years,* p. 46.
15. Mason, *Harlan Fiske Stone,* p. 533.
16. *Jones* v. *Opelika,* 316 U.S. 584 (1942).
17. *St. Louis Post-Dispatch,* 12 June 1942, WODP, Box 72; *Washington Post,* 10 June 1942, WODP, Box 72.
18. *Murdoch* v. *Pennsylvania,* 319 U.S. 105 (1943).
19. The reference to the cave was omitted from the published opinion, but the message remained the same. Jackson issued a dissent in *Murdoch,* but his real opposition statement came in a concurring opinion to the companion case of *Douglas* v. *Jeannette,* 319 U.S. 157 (1943). See Felix Frankfurter to Robert Jackson, n.d., RHJP, Box 127, and the bench notes from Owen Roberts to Jackson in the same file.
20. *Martin* v. *Struthers,* 319 U.S., at 141, 149.
21. Hugo Black, *Martin* v. *Struthers,* draft 1, p. 5, HLBP, Box 270.
22. See, for example, *Barenblatt* v. *United States,* 360 U.S. 109 (1959), Black, J., dissenting.
23. Black, *Martin* v. *Struthers,* draft 1, p. 6.
24. Hugo Black to Harlan Fiske Stone, 1 April 1943, HLBP, Box 270.
25. Douglas, *Court Years,* p. 44.
26. Ibid.
27. William O. Douglas, interview with Elizabeth Black, quoted in Black and Black, *Mr. Justice and Mrs. Black,* p. 72.
28. *West Virginia State Board of Education* v. *Barnette,* 319 U.S. 624 (1943). And see *Christian Science Monitor,* 15 June 1943.
29. *West Virginia State Board of Education* v. *Barnette,* 319 U.S., at 643, 644.
30. Wiley Rutledge to Hugo Black, 1 April 1943, HLBP, Box 270.
31. Harlan Fiske Stone to Hugo Black, 1 April 1943, HLBP, Box 270.
32. *Prince* v. *Massachusetts,* 321 U.S. 158 (1944).

33. Ibid., p. 166.
34. *Chaplinsky* v. *New Hampshire,* 315 U.S. 568 (1942).
35. *United States* v. *Ballard,* 322 U.S. 78 (1944).
36. *Sherbert* v. *Verner,* 374 U.S. 398, 411, 412 (1963).
37. *Wisconsin* v. *Yoder,* 406 U.S. 205 (1972).
38. *Planned Parenthood of Missouri* v. *Danforth,* 428 U.S. 52 (1976).
39. *Wisconsin* v. *Yoder,* 406 U.S., at 242, Douglas, J. dissenting.
40. *Everson* v. *Board of Education,* 330 U.S. 1 (1947).
41. Rutledge, draft dissent, *Everson,* p. 33 n. 59, 31 December 1946, HLBP, Box 285.
42. Quoted in Howard, *Mr. Justice Murphy,* p. 449.
43. Ibid., pp. 449–50.
44. Rutledge, draft dissent, p. 28.
45. Ibid., p. 19.
46. Hugo Black, draft dissent, *Everson,* p. 6, 6 December 1946, HLBP, Box 285.
47. Rutledge, second draft dissent, p. 26, 10 January 1947. Rutledge removed this important language while he was editing his January 16 version for what was to be a February 6 printing of the dissent. By then, of course, Black had made the critical change to his language about the scope of nonestablishment.
48. Thomas Reed Powell criticized the *Everson* majority opinion in "Public Rides to Private Schools," *Harvard Educational Review* 17 (Spring 1947): 73–84. Had he failed to make that distinction, Black would have been subject to considerably more critical comment.
49. *Everson* v. *Board of Education,* 330 U.S., at 19, Jackson, J., dissenting.
50. Irving Brant to Wiley Rutledge, 18 March 1947, WBRP, Box 143.
51. Max Lerner to Hugo Black, 19 February 1947, HLBP, Box 285.
52. See correspondence in HLBP, Box 285. See also Paul L. Murphy, *The Constitution in Crisis Times, 1918–1969* (New York: Harper & Row, 1972), p. 271.
53. *McCollum* v. *Board of Education,* 333 U.S. 203 (1948).
54. Ibid., p. 211.
55. Hugo Black, final slip opinion, pp. 7–8.
56. See Felix Frankfurter to Wiley Rutledge, 6 January 1948, WBRP, Box 166, and Felix Frankfurter to Robert Jackson, 6 January 1948, RHJP, Box 143.
57. Frank Murphy to J. F. T. O'Connor, 25 February 1947, quoted in Howard, *Mr. Justice Murphy,* p. 450.
58. Felix Frankfurter to Robert Jackson, n.d., RHJP, Box 143.
59. Harold H. Burton to Hugo Black, 4 January 1948, HLBP, Box 285.
60. Hugo Black to Harold H. Burton, 6 January 1948, HLBP, Box 295.
61. Hugo Black, memorandum to the conference, 11 February 1948, HLBP, Box 295.
62. Edward S. Corwin, "The Supreme Court as National School Board," *Thought* 23 (1948); 665–83.
63. *Zorach* v. *Clauson,* 343 U.S. 306 (1952).
64. Ibid., p. 312.
65. Ibid.
66. Ibid., pp. 313–14.
67. Robert Jackson to Felix Frankfurter, 30 April 1952, RHJP, Box 175.
68. *Zorach* v. *Clauson,* 343 U.S., at 325, Jackson, J., dissenting.
69. Robert Jackson to Felix Frankfurter, 30 April 1952, FFP, Box 70.
70. See *Washington Star,* 29 April 1952.
71. *Engel* v. *Vitale,* 370 U.S. 421 (1962).
72. Ibid., p. 430.
73. *Torcaso* v. *Watkins,* 367 U.S. 488 (1961).
74. Ibid., pp. 433–34.
75. Ibid., p. 436.
76. William O. Douglas to Hugo Black, 28 May 1962, HLBP, Box 354.
77. William O. Douglas to Hugo Black, 11 June 1962, HLBP, Box 354.
78. Ibid.

79. *Engel* v. *Vitale*, 370 U.S., at 443, Douglas, J., concurring.
80. *Walz* v. *Tax Commission*, 397 U.S. 664, 703 (1970), Douglas, J., dissenting.
81. *Abington School District* v. *Schempp*, 374 U.S. 203 (1963).
82. Ibid., p. 222.
83. James E. Clayton, "Dean Paints a Black Picture of Legal Absolutism," *Washington Post*, 10 March 1963, p. E3.
84. See, for example, *Chicago Sun Times*, 27 June 1962, editorial; *St. Louis Post-Dispatch*, weekly editorials, 2–8 July 1962, HLBP, Box 363.
85. *New York Times*, 26 June 1962, p. 1.
86. Black's papers contain a full file on "correspondence received prior to arguments and decision" (HLBP, Box 363).
87. Alexander Burnham, "Wide Controversy Stirred by Supreme Court Edict," *New York Times*, 27 June 1962, p. 1, HLBP, Box 363.
88. Edward T. Folliard, "President's Remedy for Court Ruling," *Washington Post*, 28 June 1962, HLBP, Box 363.
89. *New York Times*, 27 June 1962, HLBP, Box 363.
90. Ibid.
91. *Washington Post*, 28 June 1962, HLBP, Box 363.
92. Anthony Lewis, "Court Again Under Fire," *New York Times*, 1 July 1962, p. 10E.
93. Ibid.
94. Ibid.
95. See, for example, Kenneth M. Dolbeare and Phillip E. Hammond, *The School Prayer Decisions* (Chicago: University of Chicago Press, 1971); Charles A. Johnson and Bradley C. Canon, *Judicial Policies: Implementation and Impact* (Washington, D.C.: Congressional Quarterly, 1984); Stephen L. Wasby, *The Impact of the United States Supreme Court* (Homewood, Ill.: Dorsey, 1970); and Wasby, *The Supreme Court in the Federal Judicial System*, 3rd ed. (Chicago: Nelson-Hall, 1988).
96. *Alabama Journal*, 27 June 1962, p. 4-A.
97. Cornelia Edington to Hugo Black, n.d., HLBP, Box 363.
98. Hugo Black to Cornelia Edington, 26 July 1962, pp. 1–2, HLBP, Box 363.
99. William O. Douglas to Betty Whitesell, 20 June 1963, quoted in Urofsky, *Douglas Letters*, p. 151.
100. William O. Douglas to S. T. Leskosky, 29 December 1964, quoted in Urofsky, *Douglas Letters*, pp. 151–52.
101. *Epperson* v. *Arkansas*, 393 U.S. 97 (1968).
102. *Board of Education* v. *Allen*, 392 U.S. 236 (1968); *Walz* v. *Tax Commission*, 397 U.S. 664 (1970); *Lemon* v. *Kurtzman*, 403 U.S. 602 (1971); *Tilton* v. *Richardson*, 403 U.S. 672 (1971).
103. *Board of Education* v. *Allen*, 392 U.S., at 422, Douglas, J., dissenting.
104. *Lemon* v. *Kurtzman*, 403 U.S. 602 (1971), Douglas, J., concurring; *Tilton* v. *Richardson*, 403 U.S. 672 (1971), Douglas, J., dissenting.
105. *Lemon* v. *Kurtzman*, 403 U.S., at 630.
106. Arthur S. Link and William B. Catton, *American Epoch* (New York: Knopf, 1974), vol. 3, p. 84.

Chapter 11

1. See, for example, *Gibbons* v. *Ogden*, 22 U.S. 1 (1824); *Barron* v. *Baltimore*, 32 U.S. 243 (1833); and *Cooley* v. *Board of Wardens*, 53 U.S. 299 (1852). These questions that were, in the nineteenth century, very controversial were resolved in part by the Civil War.
2. Timothy O'Rourke and Abigail M. Thernstrom, "Justice Black: Local Control and Federalism," 38 *Alabama Law Review* 331, 335 (1985).
3. Madison, Hamilton, and Jay, *Federalist Papers*, No. 10, pp. 77–84; No. 51, pp. 320–25.
4. The Tenth Amendment, in its entirety, states, "The powers not delegated to the United States by the Constitution, nor prohibited by it to the States, are reserved to the States respectively,

or to the people." Article VI states, in part, "This Constitution, and the laws of the United States which shall be made in Pursuance thereof; and all Treaties made, or which shall be made, under the authority of the United States, shall be the supreme Law of the Land; and the Judges in every State shall be bound thereby, any Thing in the Constitution or Laws of any State to the Contrary notwithstanding."

5. Francis D. Wormuth and Edwin B. Firmage, *To Chain the Dogs of War: The War Power of Congress in History and Law* (Dallas: Southern Methodist University Press, 1986).
6. See, for example, *Carter* v. *Carter Coal Co.,* 298 U.S. 238 (1936); *Panama Refining Co.* v. *Ryan,* 293 U.S. 388 (1935); and *Schechter Poultry Co.* v. *United States,* 295 U.S. 495 (1935).
7. *Younger* v. *Harris,* 401 U.S. 37, 44 (1971).
8. Interview with Floyd Feeney, Hugo L. Black's law clerk, 1962 term.
9. *Southern Pacific Railroad* v. *Arizona,* 325 U.S. 761, 789 (1945), Black, J., dissenting.
10. Black, "Reminiscences," p. 10.
11. O'Rourke and Thernstrom, "Justice Black," pp. 334, 333.
12. Black, *Constitutional Faith,* pp. 11, 28. Holmes's dissent was *Tyson* v. *Banton,* 273 U.S. 418, 446 (1927). See also Holmes's opinion for the Court validating state sterilization statutes in *Buck* v. *Bell,* 274 U.S. 200 (1927).
13. Yarbrough, *Mr. Justice Black and His Critics,* p. 44.
14. O'Rourke and Thernstrom, "Justice Black," pp. 343, 341.
15. *Morgan* v. *Virginia,* 328 U.S. 373, 387 (1946).
16. Interview with Kenneth C. Bass, III, Hugo L. Black's law clerk, 1969 term.
17. O'Rourke and Thernstrom, "Justice Black," p. 344.
18. Interview with Justice William J. Brennan, Jr., 29 October 1986, Washington, D.C.
19. Reprinted, in part, in Black, *Constitutional Faith,* p. 24.
20. Douglas, in *Day-Brite Lighting* v. *Missouri,* 342 U.S. 421 (1952), voiced the New Deal vision of the role of the Court when he wrote that the Court did not sit "as a super-legislature to weigh the wisdom of legislation."
21. Yarbrough, *Mr. Justice Black and His Critics,* p. 36. See Douglas's dissenting opinion in *Younger* for an elaboration of this perception of federalism.
22. *Berman* v. *Parker,* 348 U.S. 26 (1954).
23. *Belle Terre* v. *Borass,* 416 U.S. 1 (1974).
24. *Maryland* v. *Wirtz,* 392 U.S. 183 (1968), Douglas, J., dissenting.
25. *Day-Brite Lighting* v. *Missouri,* 342 U.S. 421 (1952); *Williamson* v. *Lee Optical,* 348 U.S. 483 (1955).
26. Brennan interview. Brennan recalled that Black "used to get flaming mad about the [*South Carolina* v.] *Katzenbach* opinion."
27. *Allen* v. *State,* 398 U.S. 544, 596 (1969), Black, J., dissenting.
28. *South Carolina Highway Department* v. *Barnwell Brothers,* 303 U.S. 177 (1938). See, for example, Yarbrough, *Mr. Justice Black and His Critics,* p. 46.
29. *Massachusetts* v. *Laird,* 400 U.S. 886 (1970).
30. Schwartz, *Super Chief,* p. 755.
31. *Dombrowski* v. *Pfister,* 380 U.S. 479 (1965). According to Brennan's docket notes, Harlan would have vacated with directions to the lower federal court to abstain (WODP, Box 1350).
32. *Younger* v. *Harris,* 401 U.S. 37 (1971). *Younger* was the lead case; three other cases also raised this judicial federalism question: *Samuels* v. *Mackell,* 401 U.S. 66 (1971); *Boyle* v. *Landry,* 401 U.S. 77 (1971); and *Perez* v. *Ledesma,* 401 U.S. 82 (1971). Black wrote the majority opinions in all four cases.
33. Yarbrough, *Mr. Justice Black and His Critics,* p. 34.
34. *Wisconsin* v. *Constantineau,* 400 U.S. 433 (1971).
35. Quoted in Schwartz, *Super Chief,* p. 756.
36. William O. Douglas, conference notes, 1 May 1970, WODP, Box 1499.
37. Black and Black, *Mr. Justice and Mrs. Black,* p. 257. See his correspondence to the brethren in HLBP, Boxes 438 and 439.
38. *Younger* v. *Harris,* 401 U.S., at 44.
39. For example, see Black's dissenting opinion in *Griswold* v. *Connecticut,* 381 U.S. 479 (1965).

40. *Evans* v. *Newton,* 382 U.S. 296 (1966).
41. Under that doctrine, a "charitable bequest for 'public purposes' will be carried out as much as possible by a court of equity, even if the specific purpose is impossible of execution" (law clerk's memo to Douglas, n.d., WODP, Box 1471).
42. Ibid.
43. William O. Douglas, conference notes, n.d., WODP, Box 1471.
44. "We are the Supreme Court and we can do what we want," he said. Burger also wrote to Black, "This is a difficult case with a result I do not relish, but the question is one for the states (states, unlike federal agencies and this Court, are not infallible). Seeing it as a state question, I join your opinion" (Woodward and Armstrong, *The Brethren,* pp. 60–61).
45. *Evans* v. *Newton,* 382 U.S., at 442.
46. Ibid., p. 463, Douglas, J., dissenting.
47. *Palmer* v. *Thompson,* 403 U.S. 217 (1970).
48. Black and Black, *Mr. Justice and Mrs. Black,* p. 265.
49. Conference notes, n.d., WODP, Box 1510.
50. *Griffin* v. *Prince Edward County,* 377 U.S. 218 (1964).
51. Harry A. Blackmun to Hugo L. Black (and to the conference), 12 February 1971, WODP, Box 1510.
52. Hugo L. Black to Harry Blackmun, 16 February 1971, WODP, Box 1510. The case was *Bush* v. *Orleans Parish School Board,* 365 U.S. 569 (1961). In that case, Black joined the Court in affirming a lower court decision that had invalidated Louisiana legislation that gave the governor the power to close the public schools if they were ordered to integrate by the federal courts.
53. In a letter to Black dated May 13, 1971, Burger wrote that he had concluded, "we should affirm. It is a hard case . . ." (WODP, Box 1510).
54. *Palmer* v. *Thompson,* 403 U.S., at 220, 221, 227.
55. Ibid., pp. 234, 239, Douglas, J., dissenting. See his opinion for the Court in *Griswold* v. *Connecticut,* 381 U.S. 479 (1965), for his initial discussion of penumbral areas associated with privacy.
56. Brennan interview.
57. See *Bell* v. *Maryland,* 378 U.S. 226 (1963).
58. *United States* v. *Darby Lumber Company,* 312 U.S. 100 (1941); *Wickard* v. *Filburn,* 317 U.S. 111 (1942).
59. For an examination of *Hammer* and its overturn by the Court in *Darby,* see Howard Ball, *Judicial Craftsmanship or Fiat?* (Westport, Conn.: Greenwood Press, 1978), chap. 3.
60. *Hammer* v. *Dagenhart,* 247 U.S. 251 (1918).
61. *United States* v. *Darby,* 312 U.S., at 112.
62. Hugo Black to Harlan Fiske Stone, n.d., HFSP, Box 66.
63. Douglas, *Court Years,* p. 50.
64. Ibid.
65. *Wickard* v. *Filburn,* 317 U.S., at 129.
66. *Heart of Atlanta Motel* v. *United States,* 379 US. 241 (1964); *Daniel* v. *Paul,* 395 U.S. 298 (1969).
67. *Perez* v. *United States,* 402 U.S. 146 (1971).
68. *United States* v. *Bass,* 404 U.S. 336 (1971).
69. See the Court's overturn of Arizona legislation that burdened interstate commerce, *Southern Pacific Railroad* v. *Arizona,* 325 U.S. 761 (1945). Black dissented in this case because he felt that Congress alone should rectify these possible conflicts—not the federal courts.
70. See, generally, *Cooley* v. *Board of Wardens,* 53 U.S. 299 (1851).
71. William W. Bratton, Jr., "The Preemption Doctrine," 75 *Columbia Law Review* 263, 264 (1975).
72. *Hines* v. *Davidowitz,* 312 U.S. 52 (1941); *Pennsylvania* v. *Nelson,* 350 U.S. 497 (1956).
73. *Hines* v. *Davidowitz,* 312 U.S., at 61.
74. Quoted in Schwartz, *Super Chief,* p. 183. Clark and Harlan joined Warren's opinion. Reed, Minton, and Burton dissented.
75. Other examples of preemption rulings are Douglas's opinion in *City of Burbank* v. *Lockheed*

Air Terminal, 411 U.S. 624 (1973), involving federal control of aircraft noise that amounted to a federal occupancy of the field, and the Court's unanimous opinion in *Cooper* v. *Aaron* 358 U.S. 1 (1958), which was, in one sense, a preemption opinion.

76. William O. Douglas to A. N. Jayaram, 2 January 1968, quoted in its entirety in Urofsky, *Douglas Letters,* p. 156.

77. For cases before 1937, see, for example, *Crandall* v. *Nevada,* 6 Wall. 35 (1867), and *Paul* v. *Virginia,* 8 Wall. 168 (1869).

78. William O. Douglas, conference notes, n.d., WODP, Box 66.

79. Ibid.

80. James F. Byrnes, memorandum to the conference, n.d., WODP, Box 66.

81. Harlan F. Stone to James F. Byrnes, 1 November 1941, WODP, Box 66.

82. *Edwards* v. *California,* 314 U.S. 160, 163 (1941).

83. William O. Douglas to James Byrnes, 14 November 1941, WODP, Box 66.

84. *Edwards* v. *California,* 314 U.S., at 184. One of President Roosevelt's close advisers, Benjamin V. Cohen, wrote to Douglas to congratulate him on the concurring opinion. "It is good to be reminded that the Constitution was concerned with more than commerce and that the Court is not too timorous to say so" (Cohen to Douglas, 26 November 1941, WODP, Box 66).

85. See *Kent* v. *Dulles,* 357 U.S. 116 (1958); *Aptheker* v. *Secretary of State,* 378 U.S. 500 (1964); *Zemel* v. *Rusk,* 381 U.S. 1 (1965); and *United States* v. *Guest,* 383 U.S. 745 (1966).

86. Quoted in Brennan's opinion *Shapiro* v. *Thompson,* 394 U.S. 618, 623 (1968). In the District of Columbia case, the lower federal court ruled that the residency requirement violated the due process clause of the Fifth Amendment, while the lower federal court ruled the Pennsylvania statute unconstitutional in light of the equal protection clause (at 623–27).

87. Conference notes, n.d., WODP, Box 1441.

88. Earl Warren, draft opinion, *Shapiro,* n.d., WODP, Box 1442.

89. *Shapiro* v. *Thompson,* 394 U.S., at 631.

90. Memorandum, William J. Brennan to Potter Stewart, n.d., quoted in Schwartz, *Super Chief,* pp. 728–29.

91. Schwartz, *Super Chief,* p. 730.

92. *Shapiro* v. *Thompson,* 394 U.S., at 634. Stewart's concurring opinion noted that the right to travel, "like the right of association, is a virtually unconditional personal right, guaranteed by the Constitution to us all" (at 643).

93. Ibid., p. 641.

94. Ibid., pp. 647–48, 655.

95. Schwartz, *Unpublished Opinions,* p. 304.

96. Stone wrote, tersely, in *Darby* that the Tenth Amendment "states but a truism that all is retained which has not been surrendered."

97. *Maryland* v. *Wirtz,* 392 U.S. 183 (1968).

98. Ibid., p. 190.

99. Conference notes, n.d., WJBP, Box 414.

100. Ibid.

101. Otis Stephens and Gregory Rathjen, *The Supreme Court and the Allocation of Constitutional Power* (San Francisco: Freeman, 1980), p. 346.

102. As the Court noted in *Katzenbach* v. *McClung,* Harlan noted in *Maryland:* "87% of the $8 million spent for supplies and equipment by its public schools . . . represented direct interstate purchases."

103. *Maryland* v. *Wirtz,* 392 U.S., at 201.

104. Ibid., pp. 205, 207.

105. *National League of Cities* v. *Usery,* 426 U.S. 833 (1976).

106. *Garcia* v. *San Antonio Metropolitan Transit Authority,* 469 U.S. 528 (1985).

107. Ibid., p. 535.

108. Louise Bye Miller, "The Burger Court's View of Federalism" (Paper presented at the Annual Meeting of the American Political Science Association, September 1984, Washington, D.C.), p. 2.

109. *Turner* v. *United States,* 396 U.S. 398, 426 (1970).

110. William O. Douglas to Young Lawyers Section of the Washington State Bar Association, 10 September 1976, quoted in Urofsky, *Douglas Letters,* p. 162.

Chapter 12

1. General Statutes of Connecticut, section 53-32 (1858 rev.).
2. *Griswold* v. *Connecticut,* 381 U.S. 479 (1965).
3. William O. Douglas, "In Defense of Dissent," in *The Supreme Court: Views from the Inside,* ed. Alan F. Westin (Westport, Conn.: Greenwood Press, 1983), p. 55.
4. *Olmstead* v. *United States,* 277 U.S. 438, 478 (1928), Brandeis, J., dissenting.
5. William O. Douglas, in Eric Sevareid, *Conversations with Notable Americans* (Washington, D.C.: Public Affairs Press, 1976), p. 40.
6. Douglas, *Rights of the People,* p. 87.
7. Ibid., pp. 89–90.
8. Quoted in James MacGregor Burns, *Roosevelt: The Soldier of Freedom* (New York: Harcourt Brace Jovanovich, 1970), pp. 34–35.
9. Douglas, *Almanac of Liberty,* p. vi.
10. *Sampson* v. *Murray,* 415 U.S. 61, 95 (1974), Douglas, J., dissenting. See also *Arnett* v. *Kennedy,* 416 U.S. 134 (1974), Douglas, J., dissenting.
11. *Flast* v. *Cohen,* 392 U.S. 83, 110 (1968), Douglas, J., dissenting.
12. Douglas, *We the Judges,* p. 429.
13. Douglas, "In Defense of Dissent," p. 54.
14. Ibid.
15. William O. Douglas, "Stare Decisis," in Westin, *Supreme Court,* pp. 122, 124.
16. Ibid., p. 139.
17. Black, *Constitutional Faith,* pp. 3, 8.
18. Interview with Justice Harry Blackmun, 19 November 1986, Washington, D.C.
19. See *Gideon* v. *Wainwright,* 372 U.S. 335 (1963).
20. Blackmun interview.
21. *Olmstead* v. *United States,* 277 U.S., at 474.
22. *Goldman* v. *United States,* 316 U.S. 129, 136 (1942), Murphy, J., dissenting.
23. *Public Utilities Commission* v. *Pollak,* 343 U.S. 451, 467 (1952), Douglas, J., dissenting.
24. Ibid., p. 469.
25. Hugo Black to William O. Douglas, n.d., WODP, Box 171.
26. Groucho Marx to William O. Douglas, 2 July 1952, WODP, Box 207.
27. *Frank* v. *Maryland,* 359 U.S. 360 (1959), Douglas, J., dissenting.
28. *Pierce* v. *Society of Sisters,* 268 U.S. 510 (1925); *Meyer* v. *Nebraska,* 262 U.S. 390 (1923).
29. *Buck* v. *Bell,* 274 U.S. 200 (1927).
30. *Skinner* v. *Oklahoma,* 316 U.S. 535, 541 (1942).
31. Douglas, *Rights of the People,* p. 89.
32. Conference notes, *Poe* v. *Ullman,* 367 U.S. 497 (1961), n.d., WJBP, Box 407.
33. Conference notes, *Griswold,* n.d., WJBP, Box 411.
34. *NAACP* v. *Alabama,* 357 U.S. 449 (1958).
35. *Griswold* v. *Connecticut,* 381 U.S., at 484.
36. Ibid., p. 486.
37. Ibid., p. 510, Black, J., dissenting.
38. Ibid., p. 511.
39. Ibid., p. 511 n. 2, 518–19, 520.
40. *United States* v. *Vuitch,* 402 U.S. 62, 78 (1971), Douglas, J., dissenting in part.
41. Ibid., p. 80.
42. *Eisenstadt* v. *Baird,* 405 U.S. 438, 453 (1972). Douglas was still prepared to focus on the First Amendment for his justification. He claimed that when William Baird handed a woman a package of vaginal foam after his lecture on contraceptives at Boston University, he was clearly engaging in classic freedom of speech.

43. See, for example, *Boddie* v. *Connecticut,* 401 U.S. 371, 385 (1971). He joined Brennan's plurality in *Frontiero* v. *Richardson,* 411 U.S. 677 (1973), finding sex a suspect class, but no majority of the Court has ever been willing to agree on that point.
44. *Harper* v. *Virginia Board of Elections,* 383 U.S. 663 (1966).
45. Black, *Constitutional Faith,* p. 30.
46. *Harper* v. *Virginia Board of Elections,* 383 U.S., at 678, Black, J., dissenting.
47. *Boddie* v. *Connecticut,* 401 U.S. 371 (1971), Douglas, J., concurring.
48. Black, citing *Loving* v. *Virginia,* 388 U.S. 1 (1967), in *Boddie* v. *Connecticut,* 401 U.S., at 390, Black, J., dissenting.
49. *United States* v. *Kras,* 409 U.S. 434 (1973), Douglas, J., dissenting.
50. *Ortwein* v. *Schwab,* 410 U.S. 656 (1973), Douglas, J., dissenting.
51. *Levy* v. *Louisiana,* 391 U.S. 68 (1968); *Glona* v. *American Guarantee Co.,* 391 U.S. 72 (1968).
52. *Glona* v. *American Guarantee,* 391 U.S., at 75.
53. *Labine* v. *Vincent,* 401 U.S. 532 (1971).
54. Ibid., p. 539.
55. Ibid., p. 541, Brennan, J., dissenting.
56. The person generally credited with this phrase is Charles Reich, who coined it in "The New Property," 73 *Yale Law Journal* 733 (1964).
57. See, for example, *U.S. Department of Agriculture* v. *Murry,* 413 U.S. 508 (1973), and *Richardson* v. *Perales,* 402 U.S. 389 (1971), Douglas, J., dissenting.
58. On benefits and the right to travel, Douglas joined the Court in *Shapiro* v. *Thompson,* 394 U.S. 618 (1969); *Memorial Hospital* v. *Maricopa County,* 415 U.S. 250 (1974); and *Papachristou* v. *Jacksonville,* 405 U.S. 156 (1972).
59. *King* v. *Smith,* 392 U.S. 309 (1968), Douglas, J., concurring.
60. See *Rosado* v. *Wyman,* 397 U.S. 397 (1970), Douglas, J., concurring, and *Dandridge* v. *Williams,* 397 U.S. 471 (1970), Douglas, J., dissenting.
61. *Wyman* v. *James,* 400 U.S. 309, 326–27, 332–33 (1971), Douglas, J., dissenting.
62. *Thorpe* v. *Housing Authority of the City of Durham,* 393 U.S. 268 (1969), Douglas, J., concurring.
63. *Sniadach* v. *Family Finance,* 395 U.S. 337, 345 (1969).
64. Ibid., pp. 342–43, Harlan, J., concurring.
65. William Brennan to William O. Douglas, 17 October 1969, WODP, Box 1454.
66. Conference notes, n.d., WJBP, Box 208.
67. *New York Times* v. *Sullivan,* 376 U.S. 255 (1964).
68. Ibid., p. 293, Black, J., concurring.
69. See *Garrison* v. *Louisiana,* 379 U.S. 64, 79 (1964), Black, J., concurring; *Rosenblatt* v. *Baer,* 383 U.S. 75, 94 (1966), Black, J., dissenting; and *Time* v. *Hill,* 385 U.S. 374 (1967), Black, J., concurring.
70. *Curtis Publishing Co.* v. *Butts,* 388 U.S. 130, 172 (1967), Black, J., concurring.
71. *Branzburg* v. *Hayes,* 408 U.S. 665 (1972).
72. *Red Lion Broadcasting* v. *F.C.C.,* 395 U.S. 367, 387 (1969).
73. *Amalgamated Food Employees* v. *Logan Valley Plaza,* 391 U.S. 308 (1968).
74. *Lloyd* v. *Tanner,* 407 U.S. 551 (1972); *Hudgens* v. *NLRB,* 424 U.S. 507 (1976).

Chapter 13

1. Black and Black, *Mr. Justice and Mrs. Black,* pp. 274–75.
2. Harry S. Truman to William O. Douglas, 13 September 1951, HSTP, President's Secretary's Files.
3. William O. Douglas to Harry S. Truman, 25 September 1951, HSTP, President's Secretary's Files.
4. William O. Douglas to Robert Hutchins, 9 June 1966, WODP, Box 582.
5. William O. Douglas to Charles Percy, 9 May 1967, WODP, Box 582.

6. Harry S. Ashmore, *Report on Pacem in Terris II* (Santa Barbara, Calif.: Center for the Study of Democratic Institutions, 1967), WODP, Box 582.
7. William O. Douglas to Clark Clifford, 29 February 1968, WODP, Box 315.
8. Douglas, *Court Years*, pp. 329–30. This incident was confirmed in an interview with Cathleen Douglas-Stone.
9. Interview with Justice Arthur Goldberg, 27 August 1986, Washington, D.C.
10. Black and Black, *Mr. Justice and Mrs. Black*, pp. 233, 232.
11. It was the term in which *Goldberg* v. *Kelly*, 397 U.S. 254 (1970), was decided.
12. Black and Black, *Mr. Justice and Mrs. Black*, pp. 244, 248.
13. *Oregon* v. *Mitchell*, 400 U.S. 112 (1970).
14. *New York Times* v. *United States*, 403 U.S. 713, 715 (1971), Black, J., concurring.
15. Black and Black, *Mr. Justice and Mrs. Black*, p. 272.
16. Ibid., p. 277.
17. *Sniadach* v. *Family Finance*, 395 U.S. 337 (1969). See chapter 12.
18. Murphy, *Fortas*, pp. 217–24.
19. Ibid., p. 104.
20. Representative Andrews led a number of Douglas's opponents in a public chastisement of the judge (*Congressional Record*, 89th Cong., 2nd sess. 1966, 112: 15945–51, 16469); see also "House Urged to Investigate Douglas's Morality," *New York Times*, 19 July 1966, p. 43.
21. N. P. Callahan to the Director [J. Edgar Hoover], 19 July 1966, William O. Douglas file, 94-33476, Federal Bureau of Investigation Files, Washington, D.C.
22. *Saturday Review*, August 1966.
23. *Dennis* v. *United States*, 341 U.S. 494 (1951), Douglas, J., dissenting.
24. Most of the discussion concerning Douglas's activities with the Parvin Foundation and the Center for the Study of Democratic Institutions operated by the Fund for the Republic is taken from data found in U.S. Congress, House Committee on the Judiciary, *Final Report by the Special Subcommittee on H. Res. 920 of the Committee on the Judiciary, Associate Justice William O. Douglas*, 91st Cong., 2nd sess., 1970 (hereafter cited as *Final Report*).
25. *Final Report*, p. 74.
26. Ibid., pp. 175–76.
27. Ibid., p. 75.
28. Harry S. Ashmore to Carolyn Aggers, 4 November 1966, in *Final Report*, p. 91.
29. Harry S. Ashmore to Albert Parvin, 14 November 1966, in *Final Report*, p. 98; Albert Parvin to Harry S. Ashmore, 17 November 1966, in *Final Report*, pp. 101–2.
30. Harry S. Ashmore to William O. Douglas, 8 December 1966, in *Final Report*, pp. 104–5.
31. Memorandum, William O. Douglas to the chief justice, 31 October 1966, EWP, Box 352.
32. Robert M. Hutchins to William O. Douglas, 2 August 1967, in *Final Report*, pp. 107–9.
33. *New York Times*, 26 May 1969, p. 75.
34. See generally, Murphy, *Fortas*, and Robert Shogan, *A Question of Judgment: The Fortas Case and the Struggle for the Supreme Court* (Indianapolis: Bobbs-Merrill, 1972).
35. Shogan, *Question of Judgment*, p. 243.
36. See *Congressional Record*, 91st Cong., 1st sess., 1969, 115: 11260.
37. William O. Douglas to Albert Parvin, 12 May 1969, in *Final Report*, p. 110.
38. *Congressional Record*, 91st Cong., 1st sess., 1969, 115: 12949.
39. William O. Douglas to Clark Clifford, 23 October 1969, WODP, Box 315.
40. William O. Douglas to Clark Clifford, 17 November 1969, WODP, Box 315.
41. See, for example, *Johnson* v. *Powell*, 393 U.S. 920 (1968); *Scaggs* v. *Larsen*, 396 U.S. 1206 (1969); and *Jones* v. *Lemond*, 396 U.S. 1227 (1969).
42. F. Edward Hebert to Warren Burger, 9 August 1969; F. Edward Hebert to Erwin N. Griswold, 27 August 1969, in *Final Report*, pp. 61, 63.
43. See Milton Viorst, "Bill Douglas Has Never Stopped Fighting the Bullies of Yakima," *New York Times Magazine*, 14 July 1970, p. 8.
44. *Congressional Record*, 91st Cong., 2nd sess., 1970, 116: 11912. Looking back, Ford maintained that what he did "at the time may have been politically ill-advised, but it was not irresponsible" (*A Time to Heal* [New York: Harper & Row, 1979], p. 94).

45. *Final Report,* p. 349.
46. Interview with Cathleen Douglas-Stone, 14 November 1986, Boston.
47. William O. Douglas to Nancy Douglas, 5 December 1970, WODP, Box 1095.
48. Fred Rodell to Hugo Black, 6 May 1970, HLBP, Box 47.
49. Hugo Black to Fred Rodell, 13 May 1970, HLBP, Box 47.
50. Fred Rodell to Hugo Black, 1 June 1970; Hugo Black to Fred Rodell, 5 June 1970, HLBP, Box 47.
51. Douglas, *Court Years,* p. 377.
52. Ibid., p. 53.
53. Interview with Justice Harry Blackmun, 19 November 1986, Washington, D.C.
54. *Roe* v. *Wade,* 410 U.S. 113 (1973); *Doe* v. *Bolton,* 410 U.S. 179 (1973).
55. William O. Douglas to Warren Burger, 18 December 1971, WODP, Box 1523.
56. Warren Burger to William O. Douglas, 20 December 1971, WJBP, Box 281.
57. Harry A. Blackmun to Warren Burger, 18 January 1972, WODP, Box 1523; Blackmun, memorandum to the conference, 18 May 1972, WJBP, Box 282.
58. William O. Douglas to Warren Burger, 1 June 1972, WJBP, Box 281; Douglas, memorandum, 2 June 1972, WODP, Box 1588.
59. Douglas, memorandum, pp. 2, 3.
60. William O. Douglas to Warren Burger, 4 July 1972; Warren Burger to William Douglas, 27 July 1972; William O. Douglas to Warren Burger, 7 August 1972, WODP, Box 1588.
61. *Kleindienst* v. *Mandel,* 408 U.S. 753 (1972), Douglas, J., dissenting.
62. *Board of Regents* v. *Roth,* 408 U.S. 564 (1972), Douglas, J., dissenting.
63. *United Public Workers* v. *Mitchell,* 330 U.S. 75 (1947), Douglas, J., dissenting.
64. *Civil Service Commission* v. *National Association of Letter Carriers,* 413 U.S. 548 (1973), Douglas, J., dissenting; *Broadrick* v. *Oklahoma,* 413 U.S. 601 (1973), Douglas, J., dissenting.
65. *Broadrick* v. *Oklahoma,* 413 U.S., at 621, Douglas, J., dissenting.
66. *Branzburg* v. *Hayes,* 408 U.S. 665 (1972), Douglas, J., dissenting.
67. *Pell* v. *Procunier,* 417 U.S. 817 (1974), Douglas, J., dissenting; *Saxbe* v. *Washington Post,* 417 U.S. 843 (1974), Douglas, J., dissenting.
68. *Gertz* v. *Welch,* 418 U.S. 323 (1974), Douglas, J., dissenting.
69. *Columbia Broadcasting* v. *Democratic National Committee,* 412 U.S. 94, 148 (1973).
70. *Paris Adult Theatre* v. *Slaton,* 413 U.S. 49 (1973), Brennan, J., dissenting.
71. *Miller* v. *California,* 413 U.S. 15 (1973), Douglas, J., dissenting; *Paris Adult Theatre* v. *Slaton,* 413 U.S. 49 (1973), Douglas, J., dissenting.
72. *Stanley* v. *Georgia,* 394 U.S. 557 (1969).
73. *United States* v. *12 200-Foot Reels of Film,* 413 U.S. 137 (1973). See also *United States* v. *Orito,* 413 U.S. 146 (1973).
74. *Board of Education* v. *Allen,* 392 U.S. 236 (1968), Douglas, J., dissenting.
75. *Lemon* v. *Kurtzman,* 403 U.S. 602 (1971), Douglas, J., concurring; *Tilton* v. *Richardson,* 403 U.S. 672 (1971), Douglas, J. dissenting.
76. See, for example, *Hunt* v. *McNair,* 413 U.S. 734 (1973), Brennan, J., dissenting; and *Meek* v. *Pittenger,* 421 U.S. 349 (1975), Brennan, J., dissenting.
77. *Wisconsin* v. *Yoder,* 406 U.S. 205 (1972), Douglas, J., dissenting.
78. *Eisenstadt* v. *Baird,* 405 U.S. 438 (1972), Douglas, J., concurring.
79. *San Antonio Independent School District* v. *Rodriguez,* 411 U.S. 1 (1973).
80. *Brown* v. *Board of Education of Topeka, Kansas,* 347 U.S. 483, 493 (1954).
81. *Keyes* v. *School District No. 1,* 413 U.S. 189 (1973), Douglas, J., dissenting.
82. *Milliken* v. *Bradley,* 418 U.S. 717, 761–62 (1974), Douglas, J., dissenting.
83. See, for example, *United States* v. *Kras,* 409 U.S. 434 (1973), Douglas, J., dissenting; and *Ortwein* v. *Schwab,* 410 U.S. 656 (1973), Douglas, J., dissenting.
84. *Moose Lodge* v. *Irvis,* 407 U.S. 163 (1972), Douglas, J., dissenting.
85. *Kahn* v. *Shevin,* 416 U.S. 351 (1974).
86. *DeFunis* v. *Odegaard,* 416 U.S. 312 (1974), Douglas, J., dissenting.
87. *University of California Regents* v. *Bakke,* 438 U.S. 265 (1978).
88. *Flast* v. *Cohen,* 392 U.S. 83, 110 (1968), Douglas, J., concurring.

89. See, for example, *Association of Data Processing Service Organizations* v. *Camp,* 397 U.S. 150 (1970).
90. See, for example, *Warth* v. *Seldin,* 422 U.S. 490 (1975), and *O'Shea* v. *Littleton,* 414 U.S. 488 (1974).
91. See *National Railroad Passenger Corp.* v. *National Association of Railroad Passengers,* 414 U.S. 453 (1974), Douglas, J., dissenting; *O'Shea* v. *Littleton,* Douglas, J., dissenting; *United States* v. *Richardson,* 418 U.S. 208 (1974), Douglas, J., dissenting; *Schlesinger* v. *Reservists Against the War,* 418 U.S. 208 (1974), Douglas, J., dissenting; and *Warth* v. *Seldin.*
92. *Warth* v. *Seldin,* 422 U.S., at 519, Douglas, J., dissenting.
93. See, for example, *Eisen* v. *Carlisle & Jacquelin* (1974), Douglas, J., dissenting.
94. *SEC* v. *Medical Committee for Human Rights,* 404 U.S. 411 (1972).
95. Douglas, *Court Years,* p. 55.
96. Ibid. See also Douglas's opinions in *Massachusetts* v. *Laird,* 400 U.S. 886 (1970); *Mora* v. *McNamara,* 389 U.S. 934 (1967); and *Mitchell* v. *United States,* 386 U.S. 1206 (1967).
97. See, for example, *Gilette* v. *United States,* 401 U.S. 437 (1971), Douglas, J., dissenting; *Oestereich* v. *Selective Service Board No. 11,* 393 U.S. 233 (1968); and *Gutknecht* v. *United States,* 396 U.S. 295 (1970).
98. *United States* v. *United States District Court,* 407 U.S. 297 (1972), Douglas, J., concurring.
99. Ibid., pp. 329–33.
100. William O. Douglas file, 94-33476, FBI Files.
101. *Laird* v. *Tatum,* 408 U.S. 1 (1972), Douglas, J., dissenting.
102. *Gravel* v. *United States,* 408 U.S. 606, 638–39 (1972), Douglas, J., dissenting.
103. *United States* v. *Nixon,* 418 U.S. 683 (1974).
104. Douglas, *Court Years,* p. 376.
105. Cathleen Douglas-Stone interview; Black and Black, *Mr. Justice and Mrs. Black,* p. 239.
106. Warren Weaver, "Justice Douglas Suffers Stroke," *New York Times,* 2 January 1975, p. 31; Weaver, "Illnesses Cloud Court Operation," *New York Times,* 16 February 1975, p. 25; Weaver, "Douglas Not Planning to Retire," *New York Times,* 16 July 1975, p. 47.
107. Interview with Chief Justice Warren Burger, 21 December 1987, Washington, D.C.
108. Cathleen Douglas-Stone to the authors, 16 October 1989.
109. *Congressional Record,* 94th Cong., 1st sess., 1975, 121: 11453.
110. William O. Douglas to the brethren, 14 November 1975, WODP, Box 1759.

Chapter 14

1. Interview with Justice William J. Brennan, Jr., 29 October 1986, Washington, D.C.
2. Anthony Lewis, "Hugo Black: An Elemental Force," *New York Times,* 26 September 1971.
3. Yarbrough, *Mr. Justice Black and His Critics,* pp. 20, 50.
4. William O. Douglas to Edmond Cahn, 10 January 1962, WODP, Box 314.
5. *Bell* v. *Maryland,* 378 U.S. 226 (1964), quoted in Peter Irons, *The Courage of Their Convictions* (New York: Free Press, 1988), p. 147.
6. *Fortson* v. *Morris,* 385 U.S. 231 (1966), quoted in Black and Black, *Mr. Justice Black and Mrs. Black,* p. 157.
7. D. Grier Stephenson, Jr., "On Review," in *Supreme Court Historical Society Yearbook, 1984* (Washington, D.C.: Supreme Court Historical Society, 1984), pp. 132, 134.
8. James J. Magee, *Mr. Justice Black: Absolutism on the Court* (Charlottesville: University Press of Virginia, 1980), p. 194.
9. William O. Douglas to Young Lawyers Section of the Washington State Bar Association, 10 September 1976, quoted in Urofsky, *Douglas Letters,* p. 162.
10. Black and Black, *Mr. Justice and Mrs. Black,* p. 112.
11. Douglas, *Go East Young Man,* p. 450.
12. Schwartz, *Unpublished Opinions,* p. 10.
13. Ibid., p. 16.
14. Hugo Black, quoted in Jerome A. Cooper to Howard Ball, 8 May 1985.

Bibliography

Abraham, Henry J. *Justices and Presidents: A Political History of Appointments to the Supreme Court.* New York: Oxford University Press, 1974.

Alsop, Joseph, and Turner Catledge. *The 168 Days.* New York: Doubleday, Doran, 1938.

Ashmore, Harry S. *Report on Pacem in Terris II.* Santa Barbara, Calif.: Center for the Study of Democratic Institutions, 1967.

Atkins, Burton, and Terry Sloope. "The 'New' Hugo Black and the Warren Court." *Polity* 18 (Summer 1986): 621–37.

Baker, Leonard. *Brandeis and Frankfurter: A Dual Biography.* New York: New York University Press, 1986.

Ball, Howard. "Hugo L. Black: Twentieth-Century Jeffersonian." 9 *Southwestern University Law Review* 1049 (1977).

———. *Judicial Craftsmanship or Fiat?* Westport, Conn.: Greenwood Press, 1978.

Ball, Howard, Dale Krane, and Thomas Lauth. *Compromised Compliance: Implementation of the 1965 Voting Rights Act.* Westport, Conn.: Greenwood Press, 1982.

Berle, Adolf A., Jr. *Power Without Property.* New York: Harcourt, Brace & World, 1959.

———. *The Three Faces of Power.* New York: Harcourt, Brace & World, 1967.

Berle, Adolf A., Jr., and Gardiner C. Means. *The Modern Corporation and Private Property.* New York: Macmillan, 1932.

Berman, Daniel M. "Hugo Black and the Negro." 10 *American University Law Review* 35 (1961).

———. "Hugo L. Black: The Early Years," 8 *Catholic University Law Review* 103 (1959).

———. "The Racial Issue and Mr. Justice Black." 16 *American University Law Review* 386 (1967).

Black, Elizabeth. "Hugo Black: A Memorial Portrait." In *Supreme Court Historical Society Yearbook, 1980.* Washington, D.C.: Supreme Court Historical Society, 1980.

Black, Hugo, Jr. *My Father: A Remembrance.* New York: Random House, 1975.

Black, Hugo L. "The Bill of Rights." 35 *New York University Law Review* 865 (1960).

———. *A Constitutional Faith.* New York: Knopf, 1968.

———. "Inside a Senate Investigation." *Harper's,* February 1936, pp. 275–86.

———. "Reminiscences." 18 *Alabama Law Review* 1 (1965).

———. "There Is a South of Union and Freedom." 2 *Georgia Law Review* 1 (1967).

369

———. *The Utilities Lobby, Radio Address and Speech.* Washington, D.C.: Government Printing Office, 1935.

———. "William Orville Douglas." 73 *Yale Law Journal* 915 (1964).

Black, Hugo L., and Elizabeth Black. *Mr. Justice and Mrs. Black.* New York: Random House, 1986.

Blasi, Vincent, ed., *The Burger Court.* New Haven, Conn.: Yale University Press, 1982.

Branch, Taylor. *Parting the Waters: America in the King Years, 1954–63.* New York: Simon and Schuster, 1988.

Brandeis, Louis D. *Other People's Money.* New York: Harper & Row, 1967.

Bratton, William W., Jr. "The Preemption Doctrine." 75 *Columbia Law Review* 263 (1975).

Burns, James MacGregor. *Roosevelt: The Lion and the Fox.* New York: Harcourt, Brace & World, 1956.

———. *Roosevelt: The Soldier of Freedom.* New York: Harcourt Brace Jovanovich, 1970.

Cahn, Lenore, ed. *Confronting Injustice: The Edmond Cahn Reader.* Boston: Little, Brown, 1966.

Carson, Clayborne, et al., eds. *Eyes on the Prize: A Reader and Guide.* New York: Penguin, 1987.

Cohen, William. "Justice Douglas and the Rosenberg Case: Setting the Record Straight." 70 *Cornell Law Review* 211 (1985).

Corwin, Edward S. "The Supreme Court as National School Board." *Thought* 23 (1948): 665–83.

Countryman, Vern. *Douglas of the Supreme Court: A Selection of His Opinions.* Garden City, N.Y.: Doubleday, 1959.

———. *The Judicial Record of Justice William O. Douglas.* Cambridge, Mass.: Harvard University Press, 1974.

Dahlberg, Arthur. *Jobs, Machines, and Capitalism.* New York: Macmillan, 1932.

Danelski, David. *A Supreme Court Justice Is Appointed.* New York: Random House, 1964.

Daniels, Roger, Sandra Taylor, and Henry Kitano, eds. *Japanese Americans: From Relocation to Redress.* Salt Lake City: University of Utah Press, 1986.

DeBedts, Ralph. *The New Deal's SEC: The Formative Years.* New York: Columbia University Press, 1964.

Dolbeare, Kenneth M., and Phillip E. Hammond. *The School Prayer Decisions.* Chicago: University of Chicago Press, 1971.

Donovan, Robert J. *The Tumultuous Years.* New York: Norton, 1982.

Douglas, William O. *An Almanac of Liberty.* Garden City, N.Y.: Doubleday, 1954.

———. *America Challenged.* Princeton, N.J.: Princeton University Press, 1958.

———. *The Anatomy of Liberty.* New York: Trident Press, 1963.

———. *Beyond the High Himalayas.* Garden City, N.Y.: Doubleday, 1952.

———. "Communists Here and Abroad." *U.S. News & World Report,* 4 December 1953, pp. 110–12.

———. *The Court Years: 1939–1975.* New York: Random House, 1980.

———. *Democracy and Finance.* Port Washington, N.Y.: Kennikat Press, 1969.

———. *Democracy's Manifesto.* Garden City, N.Y.: Doubleday, 1962.

———. "Directors Who Do Not Direct." 47 *Harvard Law Review* 1305 (1934).

———. "The Dissenting Opinion." 8 *Lawyers Guild Review* 467 (1948).

———. *Freedom of the Mind.* Garden City, N.Y.: Doubleday, 1964.

———. "A Functional Approach to the Law of Business Associations." 23 *Illinois Law Review* 673 (1928).

———. *Go East Young Man: The Early Years.* New York: Random House, 1974.

———. "In Defense of Dissent." In *The Supreme Court: Views from the Inside,* edited by Alan F. Westin. Westport, Conn.: Greenwood Press, 1983.

———. "Jerome N. Frank." 10 *Journal of Legal Education* 1 (1957).

———. *My Wilderness.* Garden City, N.Y.: Doubleday, 1961.

———. *North from Maylaya.* Garden City, N.Y.: Doubleday, 1953.

———. *Of Men and Mountains.* New York: Harper, 1950.

———. "On Misconception of the Judicial Function and the Responsibility of the Bar." 59 *Columbia Law Review* 227 (1959).

———. *Points of Rebellion.* New York: Random House, 1970.

———. "Protecting the Investor." 23 *Yale Review* 521 (1934).

———. "Protective Committees in Railroad Reorganization." 47 *Harvard Law Review* 565 (1934).

———. *The Rights of the People.* Garden City, N.Y.: Doubleday, 1958.

———. *Russian Journey.* Garden City, N.Y.: Doubleday, 1956.

———. "Some Functional Aspects of Bankruptcy." 41 *Yale Law Journal* 329 (1932).

———. "Stare Decisis." In *The Supreme Court: Views from the Inside,* edited by Alan F. Westin. Westport, Conn.: Greenwood Press, 1983.

———. *Strange Lands and Friendly People.* New York: Harper, 1951.

———. *The Three Hundred Years' War: A Chronicle of Ecological Disaster.* New York: Random House, 1972.

———. *Towards a Global Federalism.* New York: New York University Press, 1968.

———. "Vagrancy and Arrest on Suspicion." 70 *Yale Law Journal* 1 (1960).

———. "Vicarious Liability and Administration of Risk: I & II." 38 *Yale Law Journal* 584 (1929).

———. "Wage Earner Bankruptcies—State vs. Federal Control." 49 *Yale Law Journal* 591 (1933).

———. *We the Judges: Studies in American and Indian Constitutional Law.* Garden City, N.Y.: Doubleday, 1956.

———. *West of the Indus.* Garden City, N.Y.: Doubleday, 1958.

Douglas, William O., and George E. Bates. "The Federal Securities Act of 1933." 43 *Yale Law Journal* 171 (1933).

———. "Secondary Distribution of Securities—Problems Suggested by Kinney v. Glenny." 41 *Yale Law Journal* 949 (1932).

———. "Some Effects of the Securities Act upon Investment Banking." 1 *University of Chicago Law Review* 283 (1933).

———. "Stock 'Brokers' as Agents and Dealers." 43 *Yale Law Journal* 46 (1933).

Douglas, William O., and Carrol M. Shanks. *Cases and Materials on the Law of Corporate Reorganization.* St. Paul, Minn.: West, 1931.

———. *Cases and Materials on the Law of Finance of Business.* Chicago: Callaghan, 1931.

———. *Cases on Business Units—Losses, Liabilities, and Assets.* Chicago: Callaghan, 1932.

———. *Cases on Business Units—Management.* Chicago: Callaghan, 1931.

———. "Insulation from Liability Through Subsidiary Corporations." 39 *Yale Law Journal* 193 (1929).

Douglas, William O., and Dorothy S. Thomas. "The Business Failures Project: A Problem in Methodology." 39 *Yale Law Journal* 1013 (1930).

———. "The Business Failures Project, II: An Analysis of Methods of Investigation." 40 *Yale Law Journal* 1034 (1931).

Douglas-Stone, Cathleen H. "William O. Douglas: The Man." In *Supreme Court Historical Society Yearbook, 1981.* Washington, D.C.: Supreme Court Historical Society, 1981.

Dunne, Gerald T. *Hugo Black and the Judicial Revolution.* New York: Simon and Schuster, 1977.

Durr, Clifford J. "Hugo Black: Southerner." 10 *American University Law Review* 27 (1967).

Easton, David. *The Political System.* New York: Knopf, 1953.

Elman, Philip. "The Solicitor General's Office, Justice Frankfurter and Civil Rights Litigation, 1946–1980: An Oral History." 100 *Harvard Law Review* 817 (1987).

Fairman, Charles. "Does the First Amendment Incorporate the Bill of Rights: The Original Understanding." 2 *Stanford Law Review* 5 (1949).

Ferrel, R., ed. *Off the Record: The Private Papers of Harry S. Truman.* New York: Harper & Row, 1980.

Ford, Gerald. *A Time to Heal.* New York: Harper & Row, 1979.

Fortas, Abe. "Mr. Justice Douglas." 73 *Yale Law Journal* 913 (1964).

Frank, Jerome. *Courts on Trial.* New York: Atheneum, 1971.

Fraser, Steve, and Gary Gustle, eds. *The Rise and Fall of the New Deal Order, 1930–1980.* Princeton, N.J.: Princeton University Press, 1989.

Fry, Amelia Roberts. "The Warren Tapes: Oral History and the Supreme Court." In *Supreme Court Historical Society Yearbook, 1982.* Washington, D.C.: Supreme Court Historical Society, 1982.

Galbraith, John Kenneth. *The Great Crash of 1929.* Boston: Houghton Mifflin, 1961.

Goldman, Eric F. *Rendezvous with Destiny.* New York: Vintage Books, 1955.

Greenberg, Jack. *Judicial Process and Social Change: Constitutional Litigation.* St. Paul, Minn.: West, 1977.

———. "The Supreme Court, Civil Rights and Civil Dissonance." 77 *Yale Law Journal* 1520 (1968).

Gregory, William A., and Rennard Strickland. "Hugo Black's Congressional Investigation of Public Utilities." 29 *Oklahoma Law Review* 543 (1976).

Hackney, Sheldon. "The Clay County Origins of Mr. Justice Black: The Populist as Insider." 36 *Alabama Law Review* 835 (1985).

Hamilton, Virginia Van der Veer. *Hugo Black: The Alabama Years.* University: University of Alabama Press, 1982.

———. "Lister Hill, Hugo Black, and the Albatross of Race." 36 *Alabama Law Review* 845 (1985).

Hofstadter, Richard. *The Age of Reform.* New York: Vintage Books, 1955.

Hopkirk, John W. "The Influence of Legal Realism on William O. Douglas." In *Essays on the American Constitution,* edited by Gottfried Dietze. Englewood Cliffs, N.J.: Prentice-Hall, 1964.

Howard, J. Woodford. "The Fluidity of Judicial Choice." *American Political Science Review* 62 (March 1968): 43–56.

———. *Mr. Justice Murphy.* Princeton, N.J.: Princeton University Press, 1968.

Hutchinson, Dennis J. "The Black–Jackson Feud." In *The Supreme Court Review, 1988,* edited by Philip Kurland and Gerhard Casper. Chicago: University of Chicago Press, 1989.

Irons, Peter. *The Courage of Their Convictions.* New York: Free Press, 1988.

———. *Justice at War.* New York: Oxford University Press, 1982.

Janeway, Eliot. "Bill Douglas, Fighter." *The Nation.* 11 January 1941, pp. 48–50.

Jennings, Richard W. "Mr. Justice Douglas: His Influence in Corporate and Securities Regulation." 73 *Yale Law Journal* 920 (1964).

Johnson, Charles A., and Bradley C. Canon. *Judicial Policies: Implementation and Impact.* Washington, D.C.: Congressional Quarterly, 1984.

Johnson, Nicholas. "Senator Black and the American Merchant Marine." 12 *University of Southern California Law Review* 399 (1967).

Kalman, Laura. *Legal Realism at Yale, 1927–1960.* Chapel Hill: University of North Carolina Press, 1986.

King, Mary. *Freedom Song: A Personal Story of the 1960s Civil Rights Movement.* New York: Morrow, 1987.

Kluger, Richard. *Simple Justice.* New York: Vintage Books, 1975.

Lash, Joseph P. *Dealers and Dreamers.* New York: Doubleday, 1988.

———, ed. *From the Diaries of Felix Frankfurter.* New York: Norton, 1974.

Lasswell, Harold. *Who Gets What, When, How.* New York: Meridian Books, 1958.

Leonard, Charles A. *A Search for a Judicial Philosophy: Mr. Justice Roberts and the Constitutional Revolution of 1937.* Port Washington, N.Y.: Kennikat Press, 1971.

Lerner, Max. "Wall Street's New Mentor." *The Nation,* 23 October 1937, p. 429.

Leuchtenburg, William E. *The Perils of Prosperity.* Chicago: University of Chicago Press, 1958.

Link, Arthur S., and William B. Catton. *American Epoch.* 3 vols. New York: Knopf, 1974.

Lockhart, William B., Yale Kamisar, and Jesse Choper. *The American Constitution.* 5th ed. St. Paul, Minn.: West, 1981.

Lofgren, Charles A. *The Plessy Case: A Legal-Historical Interpretation.* New York: Oxford University Press, 1987.

Lomax, Louis. *The Negro Revolt.* New York: Signet Books, 1963.

Louchheim, Katie, ed. *The Making of the New Deal: The Insiders Speak.* Cambridge, Mass.: Harvard University Press, 1983.

Lowenthal, Max. "Railroad Committees in Railroad Reorganizations." 47 *Harvard Law Review* 565 (1934).

———. "The Railroad Reorganization Act." 47 *Harvard Law Review* 18 (1933).

Madison, James, Alexander Hamilton, and John Jay. *The Federalist Papers.* New York: Mentor, 1961.

Magee, James J. *Mr. Justice Black: Absolutism on the Court.* Charlottesville: University Press of Virginia, 1980.

Mason, Alpheus Thomas. *Harlan Fiske Stone: Pillar of the Law.* New York: Viking Press, 1956.

Meador, Daniel J. "Mr. Justice Black: A Tribute." 57 *Virginia Law Review* 1109 (1971).

———. "Mr. Justice Black and His Law Clerks." 16 *Alabama Law Review* 57 (1963).

Meiklejohn, Alexander. "What Does the First Amendment Mean?" 20 *University of Chicago Law Review* 461 (1953).

Murphy, Bruce Allen. *The Brandeis/Frankfurter Connection.* New York: Oxford University Press, 1983.

———. *Fortas: The Rise and Ruin of a Supreme Court Justice.* New York: Morrow, 1988.

Murphy, Paul L. *The Constitution in Crisis Times, 1918–1969.* New York: Harper & Row, 1972.

Neuberger, Richard E. "Mr. Justice Douglas." *Harper's,* August 1942, pp. 314–21.

Note. "The National Security Interest and Civil Liberties." 85 *Harvard Law Review* 1130 (1972).

O'Brien, David M. *Storm Center.* New York: Norton, 1986.

O'Rourke, Timothy, and Abigail M. Thernstrom. "Justice Black: Local Control and Federalism." 38 *Alabama Law Review* 331 (1985).

Parrish, Michael E. "Justice Douglas and the Rosenberg Case: A Rejoinder." 70 *Cornell Law Review* 1048 (1985).

Peltason, Jack. *Fifty-Eight Lonely Men.* Urbana: University of Illinois Press, 1962.

Perkins, Frances. "The Principles of Social Security." In *New Deal Thought,* edited by Howard Zinn. Indianapolis: Bobbs-Merrill, 1966.

Powell, Thomas Reed. "Public Rides to Private Schools." *Harvard Educational Review* 17 (Spring 1947): 73–84.

Pusey, Merlo J. *Charles Evans Hughes.* 2 vols. New York: Macmillan, 1951.

Rehnquist, William H. *The Supreme Court: How It Was, How It Is.* New York: Morrow, 1987.

Reich, Robert. "Mr. Justice Black and the Living Constitution." 76 *Harvard Law Review* 673 (1963).

Rodell, Fred. "Bill Douglas, American." *American Mercury,* December 1945, pp. 656–65.

———. "Douglas over the Stock Exchange." *Fortune,* February 1938, pp. 16, 116–26.

Rumble, Wilfred E., Jr. *American Legal Realism.* Ithaca, N.Y.: Cornell University Press, 1968.

Schlesinger, Arthur M., Jr. *The Coming of the New Deal.* Boston: Houghton Mifflin, 1958.

———. *The Politics of Upheaval.* New York: Houghton Mifflin, 1960.

Schmidhauser, John R. *Judges and Justices.* Boston: Little, Brown, 1979.

Schwartz, Bernard. *Super Chief: Earl Warren and His Supreme Court.* New York: New York University Press, 1980.

———, ed. *The Unpublished Opinions of the Warren Court.* New York: Oxford University Press, 1985.

Schwarz, Gordon A. *Liberal: Adolph A. Berle and the Vision of an American Era.* New York: Free Press, 1987.

Sevareid, Eric. *Conversations with Notable Americans.* Washington, D.C.: Public Affairs Press, 1976.

Shannon, David A. "Hugo Lafayette Black as U.S. Senator." 36 *Alabama Law Review* 789 (1985).

Shogan, Robert. *A Question of Judgment: The Fortas Case and the Struggle for the Supreme Court.* Indianapolis: Bobbs-Merrill, 1972.

Silverstein, Mark. *Constitutional Faiths: Felix Frankfurter, Hugo Black and the Process of Judicial Decision Making.* Ithaca, N.Y.: Cornell University Press, 1984.

Simon, James F. *The Antagonists: Hugo Black, Felix Frankfurter, and Civil Liberties in Modern America.* New York: Simon and Schuster, 1989.

———. *Independent Journey: The Life of William O. Douglas.* New York: Harper & Row, 1980.

Stephens, Otis, and Gregory Rathjen. *The Supreme Court and the Allocation of Constitutional Power.* San Francisco: Freeman, 1980.

Stephenson, D. Grier, Jr. "On Review." In *Supreme Court Historical Society Yearbook, 1984.* Washington, D.C.: Supreme Court Historical Society, 1984.

Thornton, J. Mills, III. "Hugo Black and the Golden Age." 36 *Alabama Law Review* 899 (1985).

Tribe, Lawrence H. *American Constitutional Law.* 2nd ed. Mineola, N.Y.: Foundation Press, 1987.

Tushnet, Mark V. *The NAACP Legal Strategy Against Segregated Education, 1925–1950.* Chapel Hill: University of North Carolina Press, 1987.

Urofsky, Melvin I., ed. *The Douglas Letters.* Bethesda, Md.: Adler & Adler, 1987.

U.S. Congress. House. Committee on the Judiciary. *Final Report by the Special Subcommittee on H. Res. 920 of the Committee on the Judiciary, Associate Justice William O. Douglas.* 91st Cong., 2nd sess., 1970.

U.S. Congress. House. National Power Policy Committee. *A Report of the National Power Policy Committee with Respect to the Treatment of Holding Companies.* 74th Cong., 1st sess., 1935, H. Doc. 137.

Viorst, Milton. "Bill Douglas Has Never Stopped Fighting the Bullies of Yakima." *New York Times Magazine,* 14 July 1970, pp. 8, 33–42.

Wasby, Stephen L. *The Impact of the United States Supreme Court.* Homewood, Ill.: Dorsey, 1970.

———. *The Supreme Court in the Federal Judicial System.* 3rd ed. Chicago: Nelson-Hall, 1988.

Way, H. Frank. "The Study of Judicial Attitudes: The Case of Mr. Justice Douglas." *Western Political Quarterly* (March 1971): 12–23.

Whalen, Charles, and Barbara Whalen. *The Longest Debate: A Legislative History of the 1964 Civil Rights Act.* New York: New American Library, 1985.

White, G. Edward. "The Anti-Judge: William O. Douglas and the Ambiguities of Individuality." 74 *Virginia Law Review* 17 (1988).

———. *Earl Warren: A Public Life.* New York: Oxford University Press, 1982.

Williams, Juan. *Eyes on the Prize.* New York: Viking Press, 1987.

Williams, Richard L. "The Supreme Court of the United States: The Staff that Keeps It Operating." *Smithsonian,* February 1977.

Woodward, Bob, and Scott Armstrong. *The Brethren: Inside the Supreme Court.* New York: Simon and Schuster, 1979.

Woodward, C. Vann. *The Strange Career of Jim Crow.* New York: Oxford University Press, 1957.

Wormuth, Francis D., and Edwin B. Firmage. *To Chain the Dogs of War: The War Power of Congress in History and Law.* Dallas: Southern Methodist University Press, 1986.

Wyatt-Brown, Betram. "The Ethical Background of Hugo Black's Career." 36 *Alabama Law Review* 915 (1985).

Yarbrough, Tinsley E. "Justices Black and Douglas: The Judicial Function and the Scope of Constitutional Liberties." 1973 *Duke Law Journal* 441 (1973).

———. *Mr. Justice Black and His Critics.* Durham, N.C.: Duke University Press, 1988.

Index of Cases

Abington School District v. *Schempp*, 374 U.S. 203 (1963), 249–50

Abrams v. *United States*, 250 U.S. 616 (1920), 342 nn. 8, 19

Adamson v. *California*, 332 U.S. 46 (1947), 206–7, 209, 210

Adderley v. *Florida*, 385 U.S. 48 (1966), 165–66

Adler v. *Board of Education*, 342 U.S. 485 (1952), 345 n. 87

Albertson v. *S.A.C.B.*, 382 U.S. 70 (1965), 345 n. 95

Alexander v. *Holmes County, Mississippi*, 396 U.S. 1218 (1969), 183–85

Alexander v. *United States ex rel. Kulick*, 332 U.S. 174 (1947), 341 n. 142

Allee v. *Medrano*, 416 U.S. 802 (1974), 353 n. 21

Allen v. *State*, 398 U.S. 544 (1969), 259

Amalgamated Food Employees v. *Logan Valley Plaza*, 391 U.S. 308 (1968), 295

Apodaca v. *Oregon*, 406 U.S. 404 (1972), 357 n. 186

Aptheker v. *Secretary of State*, 378 U.S. 500 (1964), 345 n. 95, 363 n. 85

Argersinger v. *Hamlin*, 407 U.S. 25 (1972), 357 n. 165

Arnett v. *Kennedy*, 416 U.S. 134 (1974), 364 n. 10

Ashcraft v. *Tennessee*, 322 U.S. 143 (1944), 357 n. 149

Association of Data Processing Service Organizations v. *Camp*, 397 U.S. 150 (1970), 368 n. 89

Avery v. *Georgia*, 390 U.S. 474 (1968), 357 n. 184

Baker v. *Carr*, 369 U.S. 186 (1962), 188, 334 n. 57, 352 n. 195

Barenblatt v. *United States*, 360 U.S. 109 (1958), 155–56

Barron v. *Baltimore*, 32 U.S. (7 Pet.) 243 (1833), 202–3, 360 n. 1

Barsky v. *Board of Regents*, 374 U.S. 442 (1954), 345 n. 87, 346 n. 113

Bell v. *Maryland*, 378 U.S. 226 (1963), 167–68, 333 n. 33, 348 n. 72, 362 n. 57

Belle Terre v. *Borass*, 416 U.S. 1 (1974), 361 n. 23

Benton v. *Maryland*, 395 U.S. 784 (1969), 355 nn. 80, 83

Berger v. *New York*, 388 U.S. 41 (1967), 356 n. 129

Berman v. *Parker*, 348 U.S. 26 (1954), 361 n. 22

Betts v. *Brady*, 316 U.S. 455 (1942), 199, 204–5, 208, 222

Board of Education v. *Allen*, 392 U.S. 236 (1968), 360 nn. 102, 103, 367 n. 74

Board of Regents v. *Roth*, 408 U.S. 564 (1972), 367 n. 62

Boddie v. *Connecticut*, 401 U.S. 371 (1971), 365 n. 47

Boyle v. *Landry*, 401 U.S. 77 (1971), 361 n. 32

Brandenberg v. *Ohio*, 395 U.S. 444 (1969), 139

Branzburg v. *Hayes*, 408 U.S. 665 (1972), 365 n. 71, 367 n. 66

Breithaupt v. *Abram*, 352 U.S. 432 (1957), 219, 220, 353 n. 18

Broadrick v. *Oklahoma*, 413 U.S. 601 (1973), 367 n. 64

377

Brown v. Board of Education of Topeka, Kansas, 347 U.S. 483 (1954), 159, 172–79, 181, 182, 185, 191, 312, 350 n. 136

Brown v. Board of Education of Topeka, Kansas, 349 U.S. 294 (1955), 179–80, 351 n. 153

Brown v. Mississippi, 297 U.S. 278 (1936), 347 n. 21

Buck v. Bell, 274 U.S. 200 (1927), 364 n. 29

Bush v. Orleans Parish School Board, 365 U.S. 569 (1961), 362 n. 52

Cantwell v. Connecticut, 310 U.S. 296 (1940), 232–33, 237, 343 n. 35, 355 n. 70

Carter v. Carter Coal Co., 298 U.S. 238 (1936), 330 n. 12, 361 n. 6

Case v. Bowles, 327 U.S. 92 (1945), 341 n. 145

Chambers v. Florida, 309 U.S. 227 (1940), 30, 162, 163, 199, 204, 220, 334 n. 59, 347 n. 37

Chaplinsky v. New Hampshire, 315 U.S. 568 (1942), 359 n. 34

City of Burbank v. Lockheed Air Terminal, 411 U.S. 624 (1973), 363 n. 75

Civil Rights Cases, 109 U.S. 3 (1883), 159, 166

Civil Service Commission v. National Association of Letter Carriers, 413 U.S. 548 (1973), 367 n. 64

Cohen v. California, 403 U.S. 15 (1971), 343 n. 37

Colegrove v. Green, 328 U.S. 549 (1946), 188

Coleman v. Alabama, 399 U.S. 1 (1970), 357 n. 178

Columbia Broadcasting v. Democratic National Committee, 412 U.S. 94 (1973), 367 n. 69

Connecticut General Life Insurance Co. v. Johnson, 303 U.S. 77 (1937), 333 n. 18

Cooley v. Board of Wardens, 53 U.S. 299 (1852), 360 n. 1, 362 n. 70

Cooper v. Aaron, 358 U.S. 1 (1958), 181–82, 363 n. 75

Cox v. Louisiana, 379 U.S. 559 (1964), 165

Crandall v. Nevada, 6 Wall. 35 (1868), 363 n. 77

Crooker v. California, 357 U.S. 433 (1958), 357 n. 166

Dandridge v. Williams, 397 U.S. 471 (1970), 365 n. 60

Daniel v. Paul, 395 U.S. 298 (1969), 362 n. 66

Day-Brite Lighting v. Missouri, 342 U.S. 421 (1952), 353 n. 12, 361 nn. 20, 25

Debs v. United States, 249 U.S. 211 (1919), 342 n. 7

DeFunis v. Odegaard, 416 U.S. 312 (1974), 367 n. 86

Dennis v. United States, 341 U.S. 494 (1951), 139, 142–46, 302, 334 n. 58, 342 n. 1, 344 nn. 43, 58, 345 n. 68

Doe v. Bolton, 410 U.S. 179 (1973), 309

Dombrowski v. Pfister, 380 U.S. 479 (1965), 260, 261

Douglas v. Jeannette, 319 U.S. 157 (1943), 358 n. 19

Dred Scott v. Sandford, 19 Howard 393 (1857), 158

Duncan v. Kahanimoku, 327 U.S. 304 (1946), 109, 125–28, 341 n. 28

Duncan v. Louisiana, 391 U.S. 145 (1968), 209–10

Eagles v. United States ex rel. Samuels, 329 U.S. 304 (1946), 341 n. 42

Edwards v. California, 314 U.S. 160 (1941), 268, 269–70

Eisen v. Carlisle & Jacquelin, 417 U.S. 156 (1974), 368 n. 93

Eisenstadt v. Baird, 405 U.S. 438 (1972), 362 n. 42, 367 n. 78

Engel v. Vitale, 370 U.S. 421 (1962), 247–49, 250, 251, 358 n. 1

Epperson v. Arkansas, 393 U.S. 97 (1968), 360 n. 101

Escobedo v. Illinois, 378 U.S. 478 (1964), 223, 224

Estep v. United States, 327 U.S. 114 (1945), 129–30

Estes v. Texas, 381 U.S. 532 (1965), 226, 227

Evans v. Abney, 396 U.S. 435 (1970), 262–63

Evans v. Newton, 382 U.S. 296 (1966), 362 n. 40

Everson v. Board of Education, 330 U.S. 1 (1947), 235, 239–43, 244, 245, 246, 247, 248, 355 nn. 70, 73, 358 n. 1

Ex parte Endo, 323 U.S. 283 (1944), 115–16

Ex parte Milligan, 4 Wall. 2 (1865), 126, 341 n. 128

Ex parte Quirin, 317 U.S. 1 (1942), 117–19

Falbo v. United States, 320 U.S. 549 (1943), 128, 129, 130, 131

Fay v. New York, 332 U.S. 261 (1947), 357 n. 185

Feiner v. New York, 340 U.S. 315 (1951), 344 n. 52

Flast v. Cohen, 392 U.S. 110 (1968), 367 n. 88

Fleming v. Mohawk Wrecking and Lumber Co., 331 U.S. 111 (1946), 341 n. 145

Frank v. Maryland, 359 U.S. 360 (1959), 364 n. 27

Frontiero v. *Richardson*, 411 U.S. 677 (1973), 365 n. 43

Frowerk v. *United States*, 249 U.S. 204 (1919), 342 n. 7

Garcia v. *San Antonio Metropolitan Transit Authority*, 469 U.S. 528 (1985), 274

Garrison v. *Louisiana*, 379 U.S. 64 (1964), 365 n. 69

Gertz v. *Welch*, 418 U.S. 323 (1974), 367 n. 68

Gibbons v. *Ogden*, 22 U.S. 1 (1824), 360 n. 1

Gibson v. *Florida Legislative Investigating Committee*, 372 U.S. 539 (1963), 346 n. 120

Gideon v. *Wainwright*, 372 U.S. 335 (1963), 222–23, 225, 355 nn. 72, 73

Gilette v. *United States*, 401 U.S. 437 (1971), 368 n. 97

Gitlow v. *New York*, 268 U.S. 652 (1925), 342 n. 9, 344 n. 47

Glona v. *American Guarantee Co.*, 391 U.S. 72 (1968), 365 n. 51

Goldberg v. *Kelly*, 397 U.S. 254 (1970), 294, 354 n. 33

Goldman v. *United States*, 316 U.S. 129 (1942), 214, 216, 217, 284, 355 n. 95

Gomillion v. *Lightfoot*, 364 U.S. 339 (1960), 187–88

Goss v. *Board of Education*, 373 U.S. 683 (1963), 352 n. 168

Goss v. *Lopez*, 419 U.S. 565 (1975), 354 n. 34

Gravel v. *United States*, 408 U.S. 606 (1972), 368 n. 102

Green v. *County School Board*, 391 U.S. 430 (1968), 183, 352 n. 168

Gregory v. *Chicago*, 394 U.S. 111 (1968), 141, 343 n. 35

Griffin v. *County School Board*, 377 U.S. 218 (1964), 352 n. 168, 362 n. 50

Griswold v. *Connecticut*, 381 U.S. 479 (1965), 278, 283–84, 286–89, 291, 333 n. 33, 354 n. 30, 355 n. 86, 362 n. 55

Grovey v. *Townsend*, 295 U.S. 45 (1935), 160

Gutknecht v. *United States*, 396 U.S. 295 (1970), 368 n. 97

Hammer v. *Dagenhart*, 247 U.S. 251 (1918), 266

Harper v. *Virginia State Board of Elections*, 383 U.S. 663 (1966), 348 n. 51, 365 n. 44

Hearst v. *Black*, 87 F.2d 70 (D.C. Cir. 1938), 331 n. 40

Heart of Atlanta Motel v. *United States*, 379 U.S. 241 (1964), 190, 256, 259, 362 n. 66

Hines v. *Davidowitz*, 312 U.S. 52 (1941), 267–68

Hirabayashi v. *United States*, 320 U.S. 81 (1943), 110–13, 114

Hudgens v. *NLRB*, 424 U.S. 507 (1976), 365 n. 74

Hulbert v. *Twin Falls*, 327 U.S. 103 (1945), 341 n. 145

Hunt v. *McNair*, 413 U.S. 734 (1973), 367 n. 76

Hurtado v. *California*, 110 U.S. 516 (1884), 354 n. 39

Illinois ex rel. McCollum v. *Board of Education*, 333 U.S. 203 (1948), 243–45, 248, 358 n. 1

In re Anastaplo, 366 U.S. 82 (1961), 345 n. 87

In re Gault, 387 U.S. 1 (1967), 354 nn. 34, 35

In re Oliver, 330 U.S. 257 (1942), 355 nn. 71, 73

In re Winship, 397 U.S. 358 (1970), 354 n. 36

In re Yamashita, 327 U.S. 1 (1946), 99, 123–25, 135, 340 n. 115

Irvin v. *Dowd*, 366 U.S. 717 (1961), 357 n. 191

Irvine v. *California*, 347 U.S. 128 (1954), 214–15

Jewell Ridge Coal Corp. v. *Local 6167, UMW* 325 U.S. 161 (1945), 95–96

Johnson v. *Powell*, 393 U.S. 920 (1968), 366 n. 41

Joint Anti-Fascist Refugee Committee v. *McGrath*, 341 U.S. 123 (1950), 151–52

Jones v. *Alfred Mayer*, 392 U.S. 409 (1967), 189

Jones v. *Lemond*, 396 U.S. 1227 (1969), 366 n. 41

Jones v. *Opelika*, 316 U.S. 584 (1942), 234, 236, 237

Jurney v. *McCracken*, 294 U.S. 125 (1935), 331 n. 33

Kahn v. *Shevin*, 416 U.S. 351 (1974), 367 n. 85

Katz v. *United States*, 389 U.S. 347 (1967), 216–18, 354 n. 29

Katzenbach v. *McClung*, 379 U.S. 294 (1964), 190, 256, 259

Kent v. *Dulles*, 357 U.S. 116 (1958), 363 n. 85

Keyes v. *School District No. 1*, 413 U.S. 189 (1973), 367 n. 81

Kilbourn v. *Thompson*, 103 U.S. 168 (1881), 345 n. 98

King v. *Smith*, 392 U.S. 309 (1968), 365 n. 59

Kleindienst v. *Mandel*, 408 U.S. 753 (1972), 367 n. 61

Konigsberg v. *State Bar*, 366 U.S. 36 (1961), 345 n. 87

Korematsu v. *United States*, 323 U.S. 214 (1944), 113–15

Labine v. *Vincent,* 401 U.S. 532 (1971), 291–92

Laird v. *Tatum,* 408 U.S. 1 (1972), 368 n. 101

Lemon v. *Kurtzman,* 403 U.S. 602 (1971), 360 nn. 102, 104, 367 n. 75

Levy v. *Louisiana,* 391 U.S. 68 (1968), 365 n. 51

Lewis v. *Roberts,* 267 U.S. 467 (1925), 22

Lloyd Corporation v. *Tanner,* 407 U.S. 551 (1972), 105, 365 n. 74

Lopez v. *United States,* 373 U.S. 427 (1963), 216

Louisiana ex rel. Francis v. *Resweber,* 329 U.S. 459 (1947), 355 n. 71

McGautha v. *California,* 402 U.S. 183 (1971), 357 n. 188

McGrain v. *Daugherty,* 273 U.S. 135 (1927), 345 n. 98

McKeiver v. *Pennsylvania,* 403 U.S. 528 (1971), 354 n. 36

McLaurin v. *Oklahoma State Regents,* 339 U.S. 637 (1950), 170, 171, 172

Malinski v. *New York,* (1945), 205

Mallory v. *United States,* 354 U.S. 449 (1957), 357 n. 152

Malloy v. *Hogan,* 370 U.S. 1 (1964), 221, 355 n. 72

Mapp v. *Ohio,* 367 U.S. 643 (1961), 209, 212–13, 215, 355 n. 79

Martin v. *Struthers,* 319 U.S. 141 (1943), 235–36, 358 n. 1

Maryland v. *Wirtz,* 392 U.S. 183 (1968), 273–74, 361 n. 24

Massachusetts v. *Laird,* 400 U.S. 886 (1970), 361 n. 29, 368 n. 96

Maxwell v. *Dow,* 176 U.S. 581 (1900), 354 n. 39

Meek v. *Pittenger,* 421 U.S. 349 (1975), 367 n. 76

Memorial Hospital v. *Maricopa County,* 415 U.S. 250 (1974), 365 n. 58

Meyer v. *Nebraska,* 262 U.S. 390 (1923), 364 n. 28

Miller v. *California,* 413 U.S. 15 (1973), 311

Milliken v. *Bradley,* 418 U.S. 717 (1974), 312

Minersville School District v. *Gobitis,* 310 U.S. 586 (1940), 88, 91, 233–34, 236, 237

Miranda v. *Arizona,* 384 U.S. 436 (1966), 223–24, 225

Missouri ex rel. Gaines v. *Canada,* 305 U.S. 337 (1938), 162, 170

Mitchell v. *United States,* 386 U.S. 1206 (1967), 368 n. 96

Moose Lodge v. *Irvis,* 407 U.S. 163 (1972), 367 n. 84

Mora v. *McNamara,* 389 U.S. 934 (1967), 368 n. 96

Morgan v. *Virginia,* 328 U.S. 373 (1946), 258

Murdoch v. *Pennsylvania,* 319 U.S. 105 (1943), 234–35, 355 nn. 70, 73, 358 n. 1

NAACP v. *Alabama,* 357 U.S. 449 (1958), 282, 364 n. 34

National League of Cities v. *Usery,* 426 U.S. 833 (1976), 274

National Railroad Passenger Corp. v. *National Association of Railroad Passengers,* 414 U.S. 453 (1974), 368 n. 91

New York Times v. *Sullivan,* 376 U.S. 255 (1964), 79, 295, 310

New York Times v. *United States,* 403 U.S. 713 (1971), 366 n. 14

Oestereich v. *Selective Service Board No. 11,* 393 U.S. 233 (1968), 368 n. 97

Olmstead v. *United States,* 277 U.S. 438 (1928), 214, 216, 284

Olsen v. *Nebraska,* 313 U.S. 236 (1941), 353 n. 12

On Lee v. *United States,* 343 U.S. 747 (1952), 214

Oregon v. *Mitchell,* 400 U.S. 112 (1970), 300–301, 348 n. 51

Ortwein v. *Schwab,* 410 U.S. 656 (1973), 365 n. 50, 367 n. 83

Osborn v. *United States,* 385 U.S. 323 (1966), 356 n. 126

O'Shea v. *Littleton,* 414 U.S. 488 (1974), 368 nn. 90, 91

Palko v. *Connecticut,* 302 U.S. 319 (1937), 204, 206

Palmer v. *Thompson,* 403 U.S. 217 (1970), 262, 263–65, 275

Panama Refining Co. v. *Ryan,* 293 U.S. 388 (1935), 331 n. 52, 361 n. 6

Papachristou v. *Jacksonville,* 405 U.S. 156 (1972), 365 n. 58

Paris Adult Theatre v. *Slaton,* 413 U.S. 49 (1973), 367 n. 70

Paul v. *Virginia,* 8 Wall. 168 (1869), 363 n. 77

Pell v. *Procunier,* 417 U.S. 817 (1974), 367 n. 67

Pennsylvania v. *Nelson,* 350 U.S. 497 (1956), 267, 268

Perez v. *Ledesma,* 401 U.S. 82 (1971), 361 n. 32

Perez v. *United States,* 402 U.S. 146 (1971), 362 n. 67

Peterson v. *City of Greenville,* 373 U.S. 244 (1963), 348 n. 70

Pierce v. *Society of Sisters,* 268 U.S. 510 (1925), 239, 364 n. 28

Pierce v. *United States,* 252 U.S. 239 (1920), 342 n. 8

Pierre v. *Louisiana,* 306 U.S. 354 (1939), 162–63

Planned Parenthood of Missouri v. *Danforth,* 428 U.S. 52 (1976), 359 n. 38

Plessy v. *Ferguson,* 163 U.S. 537 (1896), 159–60, 162, 167, 169–70, 171, 172, 173, 174, 175, 176, 177–78, 179, 192

Poe v. *Ullman,* 367 U.S. 497 (1961), 283, 286

Pointer v. *Texas,* 380 U.S. 400 (1964), 209, 355 n. 73, 357 n. 159

Powell v. *Alabama,* 287 U.S. 45 (1932), 347 n. 20, 357 n. 160

Prince v. *Massachusetts,* 321 U.S. 158 (1944), 237

Public Utilities Commission v. *Pollak,* 343 U.S. 451 (1952), 364 n. 23

Red Lion Broadcasting v. *F.C.C.,* 395 U.S. 367 (1969), 295

Reynolds v. *Sims,* 377 U.S. 533 (1964), 352 n. 195

Richardson v. *Perales,* 402 U.S. 389 (1971), 365 n. 57

Rochin v. *California,* 342 U.S. 165 (1952), 200, 218–19, 220

Roe v. *Wade,* 410 U.S. 113 (1973), 309, 312

Rosado v. *Wyman,* 397 U.S. 397 (1970), 354 n. 33, 365 n. 60

Rosenberg ex ux. v. *United States,* 346 U.S. 273 (1953), 119–23, 157

Rosenblatt v. *Baer,* 383 U.S. 75 (1966), 365 n. 69

Rudolph v. *United States,* 370 U.S. 269 (1962), 328 n. 13

Sacher v. *United States,* 343 U.S. 1 (1951), 142, 344 n. 43

Salvatierra v. *Independent School District,* 284 U.S. 580 (1931), 160

Sampson v. *Murray,* 415 U.S. 61 (1974), 364 n. 10

Samuels v. *Mackell,* 401 U.S. 66 (1971), 261, 361 n. 32

San Antonio Independent School District v. *Rodriguez,* 411 U.S. 1 (1973), 367 n. 79

Saxbe v. *Washington Post,* 417 U.S. 843 (1974), 367 n. 67

Scaggs v. *Larsen,* 396 U.S. 1206 (1969), 366 n. 41

Scales v. *United States,* 367 U.S. 203 (1961), 150–51

Schechter Poultry Co. v. *United States,* 295 U.S. 495 (1935), 330 n. 12, 331 n. 53, 361 n. 6

Schenck v. *United States,* 249 U.S. 47 (1919), 342 nn. 7, 19

Schlesinger v. *Reservists Against the War,* 418 U.S. 208 (1974), 368 n. 91

Schmerber v. *California,* 384 U.S. 757 (1966), 219–20

Schneidermann v. *United States,* 320 U.S. 118 (1943), 344 n. 57

School District No. 7, Muskogee County v. *Hunnicut,* 283 U.S. 810 (1931), 160

Shapiro v. *Thompson,* 394 U.S. 618 (1969), 268, 270–72, 363 n. 86, 365 n. 58

Shelley v. *Kraemer,* 334 U.S. 1 (1948), 166

Sheppard v. *Maxwell,* 384 U.S. 333 (1966), 226–27

Sherbert v. *Verner,* 374 U.S. 398 (1963), 238

Sicurella v. *United States,* 348 U.S. 385 (1954), 341 n. 143

Sinclair v. *United States,* 279 U.S. 263 (1929), 345 n. 98

Sipuel v. *Oklahoma,* 332 U.S. 631 (1947), 170, 171

Skinner v. *Oklahoma,* 316 U.S. 535 (1942), 285

Slochower v. *Board of Education,* 350 U.S. 551 (1956), 345 n. 87

Smith v. *Allright,* 321 U.S. 649 (1944), 352 n. 196

Sniadach v. *Family Finance,* 395 U.S. 337 (1969), 301, 354 n. 28, 365 n. 63

South Carolina v. *Katzenbach,* 383 U.S. 301 (1966), 259, 348 n. 51

South Carolina Highway Department v. *Barnwell Brothers,* 303 U.S. 177 (1938), 361 n. 28

Southern Pacific Railroad v. *Arizona,* 325 U.S. 761 (1945), 257, 362 n. 69

Spano v. *New York,* 360 U.S. 315 (1959), 357 n. 168

Stanley v. *Georgia,* 394 U.S. 557 (1969), 367 n. 72

Stefanelli v. *Minard,* 342 U.S. 117 (1951), 356 n. 100

Street v. *New York,* 394 U.S. 576 (1969), 343 n. 37

Swann v. *Charlotte-Mecklenburg Board of Education,* 402 U.S. 1 (1970), 185–87

Sweatt v. *Painter,* 339 U.S. 629 (1950), 170–71, 172

Sweezy v. *New Hampshire,* 354 U.S. 234 (1956), 153, 154–55

Terry v. *Adams,* 345 U.S. 461 (1953), 352 n. 196

Testa v. *Katt,* 330 U.S. 386 (1946), 341 n. 145

Thornhill v. *Alabama,* 310 U.S. 88 (1940), 343 n. 31

Thorpe v. *Housing Authority of the City of Durham,* 393 U.S. 268 (1969), 365 n. 62

Tilton v. *Richardson,* 403 U.S. 672 (1971), 360 nn. 102, 104, 367 n. 75

Time v. *Hill,* 385 U.S. 374 (1967), 365 n. 69

Tinker v. *Des Moines School District,* 393 U.S. 503 (1969), 343 n. 37, 354 n. 34

Torcaso v. *Watkins,* 367 U.S. 488 (1961), 251, 358 n. 1, 359 n. 73

Twining v. *New Jersey,* 211 U.S. 78 (1908), 203, 206, 208, 212

United Public Workers v. *Mitchell,* 330 U.S. 75 (1947), 367 n. 63

United States v. *Ballard,* 322 U.S. 78 (1944), 358 n. 1, 359 n. 35

United States v. *Bass,* 404 U.S. 336 (1971), 362 n. 68

United States v. *Butler,* 297 U.S. 1 (1936), 330 n. 12

United States v. *Classic,* 313 U.S. 299 (1941), 352 n. 196

United States v. *Darby Lumber Company,* 312 U.S. 100 (1941), 266, 272, 273, 274

United States v. *Guest,* 383 U.S. 745 (1966), 363 n. 85

United States v. *Harris,* 106 U.S. 629 (1883), 158

United States v. *Kras,* 409 U.S. 434 (1973), 365 n. 49, 367 n. 83

United States v. *Nixon,* 418 U.S. 683 (1974), 315

United States v. *O'Brien,* 391 U.S. 367 (1967), 341 n. 144

United States v. *Orito,* 413 U.S. 146 (1973), 367 n. 73

United States v. *Richardson,* 418 U.S. 208 (1974), 368 n. 91

United States v. *Robel,* 389 U.S. 258 (1967), 345 n. 95

United States v. *Rumely,* 345 U.S. 41 (1953), 345 n. 98

United States v. *Seeger, et al.,* 380 U.S. 163 (1964), 341 n. 143

United States v. *12 200-Foot Reels of Film,* 413 U.S. 123 (1973), 367 n. 73

United States v. *United States District Court,* 407 U.S. 297 (1972), 105, 337 n. 179, 368 n. 98

United States v. *Wade,* 388 U.S. 218 (1967), 357 n. 177

United States v. *White,* 401 U.S. 745 (1971), 355 n. 94, 356 n. 135

University of California Regents v. *Bakke,* 438 U.S. 265 (1978), 313

Uphaus v. *Wyman,* 360 U.S. 72 (1958), 155, 156

U.S. Department of Agriculture v. *Murry,* 413 U.S. 508 (1973), 365 n. 57

Walz v. *Tax Commission,* 397 U.S. 664 (1970), 249, 360 n. 102

Warth v. *Seldin,* 422 U.S. 490 (1975), 368 nn. 90, 91

Watkins v. *United States,* 354 U.S. 178 (1956), 153–54

Weeks v. *United States,* 232 U.S. 383 (1914), 355 n. 98

Welsh v. *United States,* 398 U.S. 333 (1970), 341 n. 143

West Coast Hotel v. *Parrish,* 300 U.S. 379 (1937), 332 n. 73

West Virginia State Board of Education v. *Barnette,* 319 U.S. 624 (1943), 85–86, 91, 236–37, 334 n. 60, 355 n. 70

Wheeler v. *Montgomery,* 397 U.S. 280 (1970), 294

Whitney v. *California,* 274 U.S. 357 (1927), 342 n. 9, 344 n. 47

Wickard v. *Filburn,* 317 U.S. 111 (1942), 266, 267

Williams v. *Florida,* 399 U.S. 78 (1970), 357 n. 186

Williamson v. *Lee Optical,* 348 U.S. 483 (1955), 361 n. 25

Wisconsin v. *Constantineau,* 400 U.S. 433 (1971), 361 n. 34

Wisconsin v. *Yoder,* 406 U.S. 205 (1972), 238–39, 354 n. 34, 367 n. 77

Witherspoon v. *Illinois,* 391 U.S. 510 (1968), 357 n. 187

Wolf v. *Colorado,* 338 U.S. 25 (1949), 211–12, 213, 214, 215, 355 n. 71

Woods v. *Miller,* 333 U.S. 138 (1948), 341 n. 145

Wyman v. *James,* 400 U.S. 309 (1971), 293

Yates v. *United States,* 354 U.S. 298 (1957), 149–50

Younger v. *Harris,* 401 U.S. 37 (1971), 260–61, 275, 353 n. 12, 361 n. 21

Youngstown Sheet and Tube Co. v. *Sawyer,* 343 U.S. 579 (1952), 341 n. 150

Zap v. *United States,* 328 U.S. 624 (1946), 355 n. 93

Zemel v. *Rusk,* 381 U.S. 1 (1965), 363 n. 85

Zorach v. *Clauson,* 343 U.S. 306 (1952), 245–47, 368 n. 1

Index

Abortion rights, 311–12
Abraham, Henry, 77
Abstention concept, 260–62
Aggers, Carolyn, 303–5
Aid to Families with Dependent Children
  (AFDC) litigation, 292–93
Alien Registration Act (1940), 136, 142, 268.
  See also Smith Act
American Bar Association, 143
Anti-Saloon League, 21, 25
Arnold, Thurman, 198
Ashmore, Harry S., 303–4
Ashurst, Henry, 28

Banerjee, P. K., 299
Bates, George E., 43
Berle, Adolf A., Jr., 45
Berlin blockade, 136
Bethune, Mary McLeod, 163
Bickel, Alexander, 174
Biddle, Francis, 117
Bill of Rights, 202–3, 320. *See also*
  Constitution, U.S.: Fourteenth
  Amendment; Freedom of speech;
  Freedom of the press; Incorporation
  incorporation of, 202–10
Birth-control policy, 277, 283–84, 286–90,
  311
Black, Elizabeth Seay, 19–20, 30, 163, 183,
  196, 301, 302, 320
Black, Hugo L., 3, 4, 6, 7, 10, 13, 15, 30–31,
  77, 117–18, 165–69, 184–87, 191, 196,
  255–57, 262–64, 283, 294, 321–22
  and airmail contracts, 58
  Alabama background of, 12–15

allegation of resignation if Jackson named
  chief, 80–81
as antilynching-bill opponent, 66, 161
appointment of, to Court, 27–28, 88
Birmingham days of, 16–18
on birth control and free speech, 286
broadening of equal protection clause,
  opposition to, 291–92
campaigns of, for Senate (1926), 21–24
centrality of Bible to, 14–15
Chambers as best opinion, 162–63
clash with Jackson, 93–95
on Constitution as foundation of self-
  governance, 4
as county prosecutor, 18–19
and Court-packing plan, 27, 56–57, 73–74
critical of monopolies, 57–58
critical of NIRA program, 65
critique of brethren's global view of due
  process, 289–90, 291–93
critique of Vinson's *Dennis* opinion, 143–
  44
deference of, to military authority, 110–11
differences with Douglas, 6, 9–10
differentiates between speech and conduct,
  140–41
discusses resignation, 297
dissents in *Barenblatt* and *Uphaus,* 156–
  57
dissuades Douglas from leaving Court, 81–
  82
Douglas impeachment effort, reaction to,
  307–8
on due process, 79–81, 126–27, 194–97,
  203–4, 228

Black, Hugo L. (*continued*)
   durational residency requirement, view of,
      271–72
   early black fears about, 162
   elected as New Dealer, 54
   on federalism, 255–58, 261, 265, 275
   as First Amendment absolutist, 6, 7, 10,
      138, 141, 146, 204, 295
   First Amendment in a democracy, view of,
      138–39
   hard times, 296
   incorporation concept, view of, 204–8
   investigates marine shipping, 58
   involvement in Smith presidential
      campaign, 25–26
   Jeffersonian values of, 14, 57
   Jim Crowism and, 159–60
   judicial activist, labeled as, 283
   jurisprudence of, 79, 318–19
   jurisprudential clashes with Frankfurter,
      87–89
   and KKK, 16, 21–22, 24, 28–30, 162
   leaves the Court, 300–302
   and lobbying practices, 59–62
   and "Negro Propaganda" file, 161
   as New Deal supporter, 7, 26–28
   new press rights, view of, 295
   and new rights, 278, 281–82, 289
   new rights and constitutional changes, view
      of, 289
   on plenary power of Congress, 259–60,
      265–66
   Plessy, views of, 174–75
   as police court judge, 17–18
   and political role of Court, 6–7
   populism, influence of, 7, 13–14
   on preemption, 268
   and presidential powers, 6
   on property rights and protests, 167, 282
   proposes thirty-hour work-week bill, 64–65
   rejection of "balancing" test, 138–39
   rejection of "clear and present danger" test,
      138
   relationship with Douglas, 5–6, 9–10, 69–
      70, 79–81, 164–65, 260–62, 281–82,
      293–94, 301–2
   relationship with father, 14
   on right to counsel, 221–25
   on right to privacy, 7, 288–89
   on search and seizure, 200–201, 210
   Section 5 of Voting Rights Act, disapproval
      of, 259–60
   self-education of, 15–16, 24–25
   on self-incrimination, 217–19
   as Senate investigator, 58–61
   suffers stroke, 297
   surveillance of, by FBI, 146–47
   and trial by jury, 225–27
   and Vietnam War, 260
   and World War II, 107–8
Black, Hugo, Jr., 19, 78–79, 174–75, 301
Black, Josephine Foster, 19, 20
Black, Martha Josephine, 19
Black, Martha Toland, 13
Black, Orlando, 15
Black, Sterling Foster, 19
Black, William L., 13
Black codes, 159. *See also* Jim Crowism;
    "Separate but equal" doctrine
"Black Monday," 179
Blackmun, Harry A., 2, 3, 30, 261, 264–65,
   274, 309
   comments of, about Black, 78, 79, 321
Bolsheviks, 137
Bork, Robert, 283
Bosch, Juan, 306
Brandeis, Louis D., 45, 76, 77, 84, 87, 214,
   321
   on "clear and present danger," 138–39
   privacy, view of, 228, 278, 284
Brennan, William J., 30, 140, 156, 165, 216–
   17, 221, 261–62, 270–72, 287–90, 292,
   312, 314
   appointment of, to Court, 99–100
   Black and Douglas, views of, 78–79, 195,
      258, 318
   mediator role of, 308
Brown, Benjamin, 38
Brown, Henry B., 159
Brownell, Herbert, 121
Burger, Warren E., 77, 184–86, 225, 261, 264–
   65, 297, 306, 316
   and assignment clash, 309–10
   Black, Douglas, and, 104–6
Burton, Harold, 127
Butler, Nicholas Murray, 41–42
Butler, Pierce, 56, 76–77, 214. *See also* Four
   Horsemen
Buxton, C. Lee, 277
Byrnes, James, 57, 269–70

Cahn, Edmond, 280
Calhoun, John C., 3
Cardozo, Benjamin, 76, 77, 84, 204, 321
Celler, Emmanuel, 307
Center for the Study of Democratic
   Institutions, 303
Child labor, 265
Child Labor Act (1916), 265
Civil Rights Act (1866), 189–90
Civil Rights Act (1964), 168–69, 190, 259
Civil War, 259
Civil War Amendments, 203, 256, 265, 275.
    See also Constitution, U.S.: Fourteenth

Amendment, Thirteenth Amendment; Incorporation
Clark, Ramsey, 307
Clark, Tom C., 131–33, 168–69, 171–74, 209
Clifford, Clark, 306
Cohen, Benjamin, 54, 87
Cold war, 119
Coleman, William A., 175
Collier, Bernard, 305
Columbia University, and legal realist movement, 40–42
Commerce clause powers, 256, 265
Communism, 136–53
Communist party, 142, 268
Congress, U.S.
  investigative powers of, 153–54
  plenary power of, 189–91
Congress of Racial Equality (CORE), 188
Connecticut Planned Parenthood League, 277
Conscientious objectors, 128–31, 314
Constitution, U.S., 30–32
  Article IV, 268
  Article I, 258
  Eighth Amendment, 195
  federal tenets in, 256
  Fifth Amendment, 160, 194, 195, 206, 314
  First Amendment, 91–92, 137–57, 202–3, 310, 314
  Fourteenth Amendment, 158–59, 188, 194, 196, 203
  Fourth Amendment, 160, 195, 196, 212
  interpreted by Black and Douglas, 202
  Seventh Amendment, 195
  Sixth Amendment, 160, 195, 204–5
  "state action" concept in, 159
  Tenth Amendment, 272
  Thirteenth Amendment, 314
  Twenty-sixth Amendment, 301
Contraceptive information, 277, 283–84, 286–90
Cook, Walter Wheeler, 41
Corcoran, Tommy, 54, 81, 84
Crime, fear of, 193
Cull, James O., 34, 40
Cummings, Homer, 27, 72

David, David J., 17, 22
Davidson, Mercedes, 81
Davis, John W., 175
Davis, Sidney A., 307
Davis, William, 38
Dawes, Charles G., 25
DeWitt, J. L., 110
Dilliard, Irving, 65, 204
Donovan, Robert J., 131
Douglas, Arthur, 34
Douglas, Joan Martin, 302, 303

Douglas, Julia, 34–35
Douglas, Martha, 36
Douglas, Mildred, 42
Douglas, William O., vii, 8–11, 30, 33–34, 35–37, 38–40, 42–49, 80–81, 82–83, 84, 87, 105–6, 111–12, 118–23, 138, 144–45, 150–51, 156–57, 164, 167–68, 175–76, 185–87, 191, 198, 206–7, 213, 262–63, 266, 273, 274, 278, 286–87, 297–98, 307–12, 321–22
  appointment of, to Court, 3, 50–52, 54, 67–69, 77
  appointment of, to SEC, 44–46, 48–49, 70–72
  as bankruptcy scholar, 43–45
  birth control, view of, 278
  broadening of equal protection clause, support of, 290
  and Court-packing plan, 73–74
  critical of Warren, 103–4
  critique of Burger Court, 313
  declining health of, 298, 316–17
  and divorce, 36, 81
  on due process, 194–95, 197–200, 201–2, 203–4, 207, 227–28, 271–72, 292–93
  efforts to broker Vietnam peace, 299–300
  emnity toward Frankfurter, 90–93
  on federalism, 255–56, 258–59, 265, 275–76
  as First Amendment absolutist, 138–42, 146
  friendship with Fortas, 44–46. *See also* Fortas, Abe
  iconoclastic characteristics of, 7–8, 52–53
  impeachment efforts against, 302–4
  on independent judiciary, 280–81
  internationalism of, 8–9
  Jim Crowism and, 159
  judges as creators of new rights, view of, 277
  jurisprudence of, 318, 320–21
  liberty, view of, 10–11
  and Nixon, 314–15
  and Parvin Foundation, 302–3
  on precedent, 281
  presidential aspirations of, 81, 92
  on preventive detention, 116–17
  on privacy, 4, 284
  as professor at Columbia, 40–42
  as professor at Yale, 42–44
  as progressive 8, 259
  rejection of "clear and present danger" test, 139
  relationship with Black, 6, 33–34, 77–81, 97, 114, 161–62, 163–65, 196, 260–62, 296, 321–22
  retirement plans of, 315–16
  and rights, 221–25, 268–70, 286
  on search and seizure, 210

Douglas, William O. (*continued*)
  on standing to sue, 313–14
  on "state action," 168–69
  as student of Stone, 38
  surveillance of, by FBI, 146–47, 217, 315
  on trial by jury, 225–27
  and wiretapping cases, 214–16
  and World War II, 107–8, 115–16, 128–29,
    130
  Yakima background of, 34–35
Douglas, William O., Jr. (Bumble), 42
Douglas-Stone, Cathleen Heffernan, 81, 298,
    302, 316
  friendship with Elizabeth Black, 81
Dual federalism, 255. *See also* Federalism
Dual school system, 182–83
Due process of law, 193
  Black and Douglas disagreements over
    meaning of, 199–201
  as procedural fairness, 195
  seen as "fairness" by Douglas, 199
  seen as "shoot the works" clause by Black,
    194–95
Dunne, Gerald, 83, 94
Durr, Clifford, 20
Durr, Virginia Foster, 19, 20, 29, 147

Eisenhower, Dwight D., 81, 99, 103, 181
Elman, Philip, 91, 171, 173, 174, 175
Emerson, Thomas I., 171
Endo, Mitsuye, 115
"Equal but separate." *See* "Separate but
    equal" doctrine
Esdale, James, 20–21
Espionage Act (1917), 119, 121, 137

Fair Labor Standards Act (1938), 64, 265, 273,
    274
Fairman, Charles, 172, 207, 209
Farley, James, 28, 54
Farrow, Mia, 302
Federal Bureau of Investigation (FBI), 302,
    320. *See also* Hoover, J. Edgar
  appointment of Black and, 29
  surveillance of Black, 146–47
  surveillance of Douglas, 146–47, 315
  surveillance of justices, 217
Federal Communications Commission (FCC),
    62–63
Federalism, 255–76
Field, Stephen J., 3
Fleeson, Doris, 96
Ford, Gerald, 316
  Douglas attacked by, 306–7
  and impeachment of Douglas, 305–6
Fortas, Abe, 44–47, 91–92, 100, 164, 165,
    189, 261, 271, 305

drafts Douglas retirement letter, 316
  nomination of, as chief justice, 91–92, 169,
    224–25
  recruitment of, to Court, 83
  resignation of, 297, 298, 299
  views about Douglas, 164
  and Wolfson Foundation, 304–5
Fortas affair, 224–25
Four Horsemen, 72, 76–77. *See also* Butler,
    Pierce; McReynolds, James; Sutherland,
    George; Van Devanter, Willis
Framers, 256
Frank, Jerome, 44, 71
Frankfurter, Felix, 4, 22, 30, 68, 78, 80–82,
    84–86, 91, 108, 120–22, 127–28, 133,
    168, 182–83, 308
  appointment of, to Court, 77
  balancing and, 155–56
  Black and, 84–90, 143–45, 206–9, 321
  civil rights and, 160–61, 171
  deference of, to military authority, 111–12
  disdain for Murphy, 68, 109, 112–13
  Douglas and, 44, 84–86, 90–92, 111–12,
    129–30, 140
  on due process, 194
  Elman and, 172
  First Amendment and, 140, 205
  as grand strategist in *Brown,* 176–78
  Jackson and, 86–87
  NAACP and, 169–70
  as New Dealer, 54
  patriotism of, during war, 108
  on right to privacy, 285, 286
  on search and seizure, 210
  on self-incrimination, 217–19
  on sexual privacy, 283
  "spirit" of, in Court, 168
  Vinson and, 103
  on wiretapping, 215
Free speech and broadcasters' rights, 310–11
"Freedom of choice" plans, 182–83
Freedom of speech, 310
Freedom of the press, 310
Freeman, George, 13
Fund for the Republic, 303, 304

Gadsden, Philip, 62
Gaines, Lloyd, 162
Gay, Charles R., 47
Ginsburg, David, 307
Goebel, Julius, 41
Goheen, Robert F., 303
Goldberg, Arthur, 100, 223–24, 288
  changes in Black perceived by, 196
  federalism, view of, 259, 260–61
  on right of privacy, 287
  sit-ins and, 167, 168

Graves, Bibb, 24
Gray, John Chipman, 40–41
Great Depression, 4. *See also* New Deal;
    Roosevelt, Franklin D.
Griswold, Erwin N., 306
Griswold, Estelle, 277

Haines, Charles Grove, 97, 207
Halberstam, David, 54
Hand, Learned, 91
Harding, Warren, 76
Harlan, John M., 159, 207
Harlan, John M., Jr., 209–10, 273, 274, 301
    on "balancing of interests," 148, 283, 286
    First Amendment, view of, 140, 150–51
Harris, Crampton, 19, 20, 95, 96
Hatch Act litigation, 310
Haynesworth, Clement, 297
Hearst, William Randolph, 62, 63
Hebert, F. Edward, 306
Heflin, Thomas ("Tom-Tom"), 24, 25
Ho Chi Minh, 299, 303
Holding Company Act, 62
Holmes, Oliver Wendell, 40–41, 184, 214,
    265–66, 321
    and "clear and present danger" test, 138–39
    federalism, view of, 143, 148, 258
Hoover, Herbert, 57, 198
Hoover, J. Edgar, 29, 302. *See also* Federal
    Bureau of Investigation
    Ford and, 147
    and surveillance of Black and Douglas, 146–
        48, 217, 315
Hopson, Howard C., 62
House of Representatives, Un-American
    Activities Committee, 64
Howard, J. Woodford, 108
Hughes, Charles Evans, 30, 72, 77, 321
    assists Black in civil rights matters, 162
    Black and Douglas views of, 100–101
    and Court-packing plan, 72
    retirement of, 80
Humanitae Vitae (papal encyclical), 284
Humphrey, Hubert H., 224
Hutchins, Robert M., 41, 299, 303

Ickes, Harold, 27, 84
Incorporation, 202, 205–6, 208. *See also* Bill
    of Rights; Constitution, U.S.:
    Fourteenth Amendment; Due process of
    law
"Inherently suspect" categories, 290, 312–13
Internal Revenue Service (IRS), 303
Internal Security Act (1950), 152
Irons, Peter, 116

Jackson, Robert H.
    appointment of, to Court, 51, 85–87, 94

background of, 80–81, 97–98, 115, 120–23
    Black and, 94–98
    and *Brown,* 173
    clash with Black, 78, 93–98
    Douglas and, 97–98, 120–21
    federalism, view of, 267
    Frankfurter and, 84
    jurisprudence of, 85–87
    rejection of "clear and present danger" test,
        148
    as war-crimes prosecutor at Nuremberg, 85–
        86, 94–95
Janeway, Elliot, 8
Japanese-American exclusion cases, 109–17,
    119
Jefferson, Thomas, 14, 15
Jim Crowism, 158, 160, 161, 171, 191
    busing to end vestiges of, 185–86
    formal death of, in *Brown,* 179
Johnson, Lyndon B., 20, 168, 190
    break with Douglas, 298, 299, 300
    resignation of Warren and, 305
    and war on crime, 224
Judicial federalism, 260–62
Judicial restraint, 10

Kennedy, Joseph P., 44
    introduces Douglas to Roosevelt, 47
    supports Douglas for SEC, 74
Kennedy, Robert, 224
King, Martin Luther, Jr., 20, 224
Korean War, 131, 136
Korematsu, Fred, 113
Krock, Arthur, 51
Ku Klux Klan, vii, 16, 20–21, 25, 141

Lambert, William, 305
Landis, James A., 49
Lane, A. O., 17
Lattimore, Owen, 147
Legal realism, 41–43
Lerner, Max, 46
Lindbergh, Charles A., 60
Lippmann, Walter, 63
Literacy tests, 187
Little Rock school board, 180–81
Llewellyn, Karl, 41
"Lost Cause." *See* Ku Klux Klan
Lowenthal, Max, 68–69, 162
Loyalty oaths, 136
Loyalty-security programs, 20, 136–37, 151

McAdoo, William, 26
McCarthy, Joseph, 64
McCloy, John J., 115, 116
McCracken, William P., 60–62
McMillan, James B., 185

McPherson, Charles, 161
McReynolds, James, 56, 76–77. *See also* Four
    Horsemen
    anti-Semitism of, 76
Madison, James, 256, 275–76
Maloney, Francis, 69
Margold, Nathan, 169–70
Marshall, John, 203
Marshall, Thurgood, 100, 262, 264, 271
    abortion cases and, 312
    Brown argued by, 175–77
    busing, view of, 186
    as chief attorney for NAACP, 171
    gloomy after *Sipuel,* 172
Marx, Groucho, 285
Meiklejohn, Alexander, 138, 209
Meneely, A. Howard, 34, 42, 73
Middle America, 193
Miller, Charles A., 307
Minton, Sherman, 27
    dissents in *Youngstown,* 133
    resignation of, 99
Mississippi segregation, 263–64
Mollenhoff, Clark, 306
Moore, Underhill, 38, 41
Morgan, J. P., 50
Morton, Willie, 17
Multidistrict busing, 312
Murphy, Frank, 51, 84, 92
    appointment of, to Court, 98–99, 211, 215,
        216, 283
    civil rights and, 108–9, 111–12
    on right to privacy, 284

National Association for the Advancement of
    Colored People (NAACP), 160, 163, 188
    argues for overturn of *Plessy,* 169
    challenges "separate but equal" doctrine,
        172–79
    SNCC and, 167
National Industrial Recovery Act (NIRA), 55
National security policy litigation, 314
Natural law, 88–90
Nelson, Steve, 268
New Deal, as conservative movement, 4–5,
    47, 54–57, 64, 66–68, 76–78, 102
New due process, 278, 292–94
New equal protection, 290–92, 313. *See also*
    Constitution, U.S.: Fourteenth
    Amendment
New York Stock Exchange, 47, 49–50
Nixon, Richard M., 72, 132, 224, 315
    attacks Judiciary Committee, 306
    civil rights, view of, 187
    Court appointment battles of, 297
    crime and presidential campaign, 194
    impeachment of justices and, 305

names Burger as chief, 104
wiretapping policy, position of, 217
Nuremberg, war-crimes trials at, 85, 90, 285.
    See also Jackson, Robert H.

Oberdorfer, Louis, 301
Obscenity litigation, 311
O'Connor, John J., 62
Oklahoma Supreme Court, 170
Oliphant, Herman, 41
Omnibus Crime Control and Safe Streets Act
    (1964), 224
"Ordered liberty," 204. *See also* Black, Hugo
    L.; Douglas, William O.; Due process of
    law; Frankfurter, Felix; Incorporation
O'Rourke, Timothy, 258

Parvin, Albert, 303, 304, 305, 306
Pearl Harbor, 109
Pearson, Drew, 97
Pentagon Papers, 315
People's Republic of China, 302
Pepper, Claude, 30
Percy, Charles, 299
Perkins, Frances, 55, 65
Poll tax, 187, 291
Pollak, Louis H., 213
Populism, dark side of, 39
Populists, 39
Pound, Roscoe, 40–41
Powell, Lewis
    federalism, view of, 274
    and *Roe,* 309
    view of Burger, 105
Powell, Thomas Reed, 41
Power–right paradox, 10–11, 321–22. *See also*
    Black, Hugo L.; Douglas, William O.;
    Supreme Court, U.S.
Precedent, 281
Preemption doctrine, 267–68
Preferred position, 137–39
Public Utility Holding Company Act, 50

"Rational basis" test, 273
"Red Monday," 154
Red scare, 136–57
Reed, Stanley, 27, 77, 90, 99–100, 112, 133,
    174, 206
Rehnquist, William H.
    comments on *Rosenberg* case, 120
    early views of segregation, 172
    on Frankfurter–Jackson relationship, 86
    and *Roe,* 309
    and *Youngstown,* 134
Reich, Charles, 123
Richardson, Elliot, 87
Riddle, Mildred, 37, 42

Rifkind, Simon, 307
Right to counsel, 222
    extended to line-ups, 225
    extended to pretrial hearings, 225
Right to marital privacy, 277, 283–84, 286–90, 311
Right-to-privacy tensions, 283–90, 301–2
Right to travel, 268
Roberts, Owen, 30, 72, 77, 115–18, 162, 269
Robinson, Joseph, 73
Rodell, Fred, 121, 307
Roosevelt, Franklin D., 65, 91, 279
    attacks "economic royalism," 55–57
    Court-packing plan of, 56, 71–73
    federalism and New Deal policy of, 257
    first appointment to Court, 3, 12, 27
    nominates Stone, 80
    signs Executive Order 9066, 109–10
Rosenberg, Ethel, 119–21
Rosenberg, Julius, 119–21
Rutledge, Wiley B., 97, 99, 125
    appointment of, to Court, 98–99
    attitude about war, 108–9
    and civil rights, 171

School busing, 185–86
Schurz, Carl, 158
Schwartz, Bernard, 103, 261, 322
Schwellenbach, Lewis, 51
Search and seizure, 10, 200, 210–18. *See also*
        Constitution, U.S.: Fourth Amendment;
        Incorporation
Second New Deal, 70–72
Securities Act (1933), 43, 44
Securities and Exchange Act (1934), 44
Securities and Exchange Commission (SEC),
        43, 44, 45, 46, 47, 48, 49, 50, 67, 68, 198
Sedition Act (1918), 137
Selective Service Act (1940), 128, 130
Self-incrimination, 218–21
    and right to counsel, 221–25
Senate
    Internal Security Subcommittee, 20
    Judiciary Committee, 28
"Separate but equal" doctrine, 159–60
Shogun, Robert, 305
Silverstein, Mark, 13, 161
Simon, James, 41
Sinatra, Frank, 302
Sit-in cases, 221
Sit-ins, 166–68. *See also* "State action"
Smith, Alfred E., 25–27
Smith Act, 136, 146, 149
Social Security Act, 270
Southern Christian Leadership Conference
        (SCLC), 20, 180, 188

Soviet Union, 119–20, 136
Sprigle, Ray, 28
Stalin, Josef, 136
"State action," 159, 166, 167, 189–90, 263.
    See also Constitution, U.S.: Fourteenth
        Amendment.
State police powers, 262–65
Stephenson, D. Grier, 319
Stewart, Potter, 92, 186, 288, 314
    and *Bell,* 168
Stimson, Henry L., 110
Stone, Harlan F., 51, 77, 78, 80, 87, 124, 214,
        269, 321
    Black, Douglas, and, 22, 38, 101–2, 115–16,
        124
    on commerce clause, 266
    dissents in *Hirabayashi,* 111
    and *Endo,* 116
    martial law, view of, 127
Strict scrutiny, 137
Subversive Activities Control Board (SACB),
        136–37, 152–53
"Super chief." *See* Warren, Earl
Supreme Court, U.S., vii, 4, 9, 10, 11, 40, 54,
        65, 74, 76, 85, 101, 117–19, 158, 168,
        172
    and *Brown,* 172–80
    and *Dennis,* 40, 94–96
    development of new rights by, 277–96
    position of, on civil rights seesaw, 160
Sutherland, George, 56, 72, 76–77. *See also*
        Four Horsemen
Swaine, Robert, 49
Symbolic speech, 140–41

Taft, William H., 76, 214, 321
Taft-Hartley Act, 131
Taxing powers, 256
Teapot Dome scandal, 58, 59
Thernstrom, Abigail, 258
Thurmond, Strom, 224–25
Transfer plans, 182
Trial by jury, 225–27. *See also* Constitution,
        U.S.: Fourteenth Amendment, Sixth
        Amendment; Incorporation
Truman, Harry S., 102, 131, 151
    and Douglas, 132, 298–99
    and Jackson as possible running mate, 97–98
    and loyalty-security program, 20, 136–37,
        151
    names Vinson to Court, 94–95
    seizes steel mills, 131–32

Underwood, Oscar W., 22
University of Texas Law School, civil rights
        and, 171

Van Devanter, Willis, 56, 72, 76–77. *See also* Four Horsemen
Vanderbilt, Arthur T., 99
Veblen, Thorstein, 45
Vietnam War, 5, 193, 297, 299, 301, 306, 314
   and conscientious-objector litigation, 130–31
   federalism questions raised by, 257
Vinson, Fred M., 77, 81
   appointment of, to Court, 81, 94–95
   Black and Douglas views of, 102–3
   civil rights, view of, 172
   creates "gravity of evil" test, 143–48
   defends inherent power of president, 132–33
   and *Plessy,* 173–74
   and *Rosenberg,* 119–22
   on search and seizure, 217–18
Voting Rights Act (1965), 187

Wage Stabilization Board, 131
War powers, 256
War Relocation Authority, 114, 116
Warren, Earl, 77, 159, 261, 273, 304, 306
   appointment of, to Court, 99–100
   birth control and, 286
   and *Brown,* 177–79
   civil rights and, 149–50, 165, 177–81, 194, 210, 270–71, 272
   First Amendment jurisprudence of, 149
   on preemption, 268
   relationship with Douglas, 288
   resignation gambit of, 305
   resignation of, 224
   shifts Court away from *Dennis* jurisprudence, 148
   sit-ins and, 167–68
   writes *Miranda,* 224
   writes *Watkins,* 153–55
Watergate, 314
Wechsler, Herbert, 76
Whatley, Barney, 16
White, Walter, 161, 162
White primary, 187
Whittaker, Charles, 106
Williams, John, 305
Wilson, Woodrow, 76
Wiretapping, 214–18. *See also* Constitution, U.S.: Fourth Amendment, Sixth Amendment; Incorporation; Search and seizure
Wobblies, 36, 198
Wolfson, Louis E., 304, 305
Wollenberg, J. Roger, 307
Wyatt-Brown, Bertram, 20

Yale University, and legal realist movement, 42–43, 48
Yamashita, Tomoyuki, 123, 126
Yates, Yolanda, 149